CPM
McGRAW-HILL
JIM KELLY

P.J. BURNAM
PRECEDENCE DIAGRAMING
McGRAW-HILL (LONDON)

THE CONSTRUCTION LAW LIBRARY FROM WILEY LAW PUBLICATIONS

ALTERNATIVE CLAUSES TO STANDARD CONSTRUCTION CONTRACTS
James E. Stephenson, Editor

ALTERNATIVE DISPUTE RESOLUTION IN THE CONSTRUCTION INDUSTRY
Robert F. Cushman, G. Christian Hedemann, and Avram S. Tucker, Editors

ARBITRATION OF CONSTRUCTION DISPUTES
Michael T. Callahan, Barry B. Bramble, and Paul M. Lurie

ARCHITECT AND ENGINEER LIABILITY: CLAIMS AGAINST DESIGN PROFESSIONALS
Robert F. Cushman and Thomas G. Bottum, Editors

CONDOMINIUM AND HOMEOWNER ASSOCIATION LITIGATION
Wayne S. Hyatt and Philip S. Downer, Editors

CONSTRUCTION ACCIDENT PLEADING AND PRACTICE
Turner W. Branch, Editor

CONSTRUCTION BIDDING LAW
Robert F. Cushman and William J. Doyle, Editors

CONSTRUCTION CLAIMS AND LIABILITY
Michael S. Simon

CONSTRUCTION DEFAULTS: RIGHTS, DUTIES, AND LIABILITIES
Robert F. Cushman and Charles A. Meeker, Editors

CONSTRUCTION DELAY CLAIMS
Barry B. Bramble and Michael T. Callahan

CONSTRUCTION ENGINEERING EVIDENCE
Loren W. Peters

CONSTRUCTION FAILURES
Robert F. Cushman, Irvin E. Richter, and Lester E. Rivelis, Editors

CONSTRUCTION INDUSTRY CONTRACTS: LEGAL CITATOR AND CASE DIGEST
Wiley Law Publications Editorial Staff

CONSTRUCTION INDUSTRY FORMS (TWO VOLUMES)
Robert F. Cushman and George L. Blick, Editors

CONSTRUCTION LITIGATION FORMBOOK
David M. Buoncristiani, John D. Carter, and Robert F. Cushman

CONSTRUCTION LITIGATION: REPRESENTING THE CONTRACTOR
Robert F. Cushman, John D. Carter, and Alan Silverman, Editors

CONSTRUCTION LITIGATION: REPRESENTING THE OWNER (SECOND EDITION)
Robert F. Cushman, Kenneth M. Cushman, and Stephen B. Cook, Editors

CONSTRUCTION LITIGATION: STRATEGIES AND TECHNIQUES
Barry B. Bramble and Albert E. Phillips, Editors

CONSTRUCTION SCHEDULING: PREPARATION, LIABILITY, AND CLAIMS
Jon M. Wickwire, Thomas J. Driscoll, and Stephen B. Hurlbut

CONSTRUCTION SUBCONTRACTING: A LEGAL GUIDE FOR INDUSTRY PROFESSIONALS
Overton A. Currie, Neal J. Sweeney, and Randall F. Hafer, Editors

DRAFTING CONSTRUCTION CONTRACTS: STRATEGY AND FORMS FOR CONTRACTORS
Samuel F. Schoninger

HANDLING FIDELITY, SURETY, AND FINANCIAL RISK CLAIMS (SECOND EDITION)
Robert F. Cushman, George L. Blick, and Charles A. Meeker, Editors

HAZARDOUS WASTE DISPOSAL AND UNDERGROUND CONSTRUCTION LAW
Robert F. Cushman and Bruce W. Ficken, Editors

1990–1991 DIRECTORY OF CONSTRUCTION INDUSTRY CONSULTANTS
Wiley Law Publications, Editors

1991 WILEY CONSTRUCTION LAW UPDATE
Steven M. Goldblatt, Editor

PROVING AND PRICING CONSTRUCTION CLAIMS
Robert F. Cushman and David A. Carpenter, Editors

SWEET ON CONSTRUCTION INDUSTRY CONTRACTS
Justin Sweet

SUBSCRIPTION NOTICE

This Wiley product is updated on a periodic basis with supplements to reflect important changes in the subject matter. If you purchased this product directly from John Wiley & Sons, we have already recorded your subscription for this update service.

If, however, you purchased this product from a bookstore and wish to receive (1) the current update at no additional charge, and (2) future updates and revised or related volumes billed separately with a 30-day examination review, please send your name, company name (if applicable), address, and the title of the product to:

Supplement Department
John Wiley & Sons, Inc.
One Wiley Drive
Somerset, NJ 08875
1-800-225-5945

CONSTRUCTION SCHEDULING: PREPARATION, LIABILITY, AND CLAIMS

JON M. WICKWIRE

Wickwire Gavin, P.C.
Vienna, Virginia

THOMAS J. DRISCOLL

Hill International, Inc.
Willingboro, New Jersey

STEPHEN B. HURLBUT

Wickwire Gavin, P.C.
Vienna, Virginia

Wiley Law Publications
JOHN WILEY & SONS
New York • Chichester • Brisbane • Toronto • Singapore

Library of Congress Cataloging-in-Publication Data

Wickwire, Jon M.
    Construction scheduling : preparation, liability, and claims / Jon
M. Wickwire, Thomas J. Driscoll, Stephen B. Hurlbut.
        p.   cm. — (Construction law library)
    Includes index.
    ISBN 0-471-53223-1 (cloth) : $95.00 (est.)
    1. Construction contracts—United States.   2. Construction
industry—Law and legislation—United States.   3. Scheduling
(Management) I. Driscoll, Thomas J.   II. Hurlbut, Stephen Bingham.
III. Title. IV. Series.
KF902.W55   1991
343.73′078624—dc20
[347.30378624]   90-28396
                                                                 CIP

Printed in the United States of America

10 9 8 7 6 5 4 3 2 1

This book is dedicated to the pioneers of CPM network planning and scheduling at DuPont and Remington Rand/Univac led by John Mauchly, Jim Kelley, and Morgan Walker. Without physical changes to bricks and mortar, these individuals made one of the most significant contributions to the construction industry in the entire twentieth century.

PREFACE

Those familiar with today's construction industry can attest to the continued applicability of the old-fashioned notion, "Time is money." The timely, coordinated, and efficient execution of modern, sophisticated construction projects is more crucial than ever before. Owners, contractors, designers, construction managers, and sureties should be equipped to comprehend and address intelligently those schedule-related problems that inevitably arise in modern construction.

This book places special emphasis not only on planning and implementing the construction schedule as a management tool but also on the application of scheduling principles and procedures by the courts and boards of contract appeals. A thorough knowledge of these considerations and the ability to apply them to real performance problems are clearly prerequisites to successful performance of construction projects, given the current state of the industry. Whether we like it or not, construction scheduling is and will continue to be an important issue for construction lawyers, contractors, design engineers, consultants, and the other integral players on construction projects.

This book is intended to serve as a general guide to those who require a working knowledge of scheduling principles, their implementation under common, everyday circumstances, and the legal application of those principles. The authors have attempted to address the more salient issues that arise throughout the life of a project. These issues include:

Drafting scheduling specifications

Responsibility for developing a reasonable schedule and accurately updating it

Need to identify and analyze schedule-related problems as they occur

Identification of accepted and suggested techniques for CPM claims analysis

Theories of liability and pricing methods for time-related claims

Alternatives for resolution of claims and their attendant considerations

Role of the expert throughout the process.

Also addressed are recent pertinent trends and developments in construction law cases.

The authors bring to the table years of firsthand experience not only in the construction scheduling process but also in the utilization of scheduling principles and techniques when handling construction claims and litigation. Our practice and experience is national. Although we are familiar with federal contract law as well as the law of many states, construction law and practices can vary from state to state. Therefore, readers should be careful to consult local law for specific precedents before applying the scheduling principles and considerations touched upon in this book.

We wish to extend our gratitude to those persons whose assistance has made publication of the book a reality. Lance J. Lerman and Mark Berry of Wickwire Gavin of Vienna, Virginia, provided significant contributions in legal research and editing. Robert J. Smith of Wickwire Gavin of Madison, Wisconsin, provided assistance on risk allocation materials in chapter 1. Doug Coppi assisted in providing information and preparing a model for our use in the discussion of potential abuses of MICRO Computers. Judy L. Boggs offered invaluable assistance in the preparation of graphic materials. Finally, our special thanks are also extended to Linda Terrell James, Jacqueline M. Dingus, and Maryann E. Shaw, whose organizational skills and moral support enabled us to complete this work despite the demands of our professional and private lives.

January 1991   JON M. WICKWIRE
                                                  Vienna, Virginia

                                                  THOMAS J. DRISCOLL
                                                  Willingboro, New Jersey

                                                  STEPHEN B. HURLBUT
                                                  Vienna, Virginia

ABOUT THE AUTHORS

Jon M. Wickwire is a partner in the law firm of Wickwire Gavin, P.C., with offices in Vienna, Virginia; Washington, D.C.; and Madison, Wisconsin. He is a graduate of the University of Maryland and the Georgetown University Law Center. He has been actively involved in performance problems for the construction industry, as well as the preparation of major systems claims, and has acted as lead counsel on some of the largest construction claims and litigation in the United States in recent years. Mr. Wickwire is a member of the bars of the District of Columbia and Virginia. He has authored various books and articles on construction and public contract law, and he has lectured extensively throughout the country on these topics. He has also participated in seminars in assessing avoidance of litigation, risk analysis, and claims management. Mr. Wickwire is a founding fellow of the American College of Construction Lawyers, a member of the American Bar Association Sections of Litigation and Public Contract Law, a member of the Forum Committee on Construction, vice chairman of the Construction Committee and State and Local Contract Claims and Remedies Committee of the Public Contract Section of the American Bar Association, and a member of the National Contract Documents Committee of the Associated General Contractors. He also serves as a member of the National Panel of Arbitrators for the American Arbitration Association.

Thomas J. Driscoll is a principal in the engineering and construction management consulting firm of Hill International, Inc. He has more than 25 years of experience as an international consultant in project and construction management practice, and he is a recognized expert in the area of construction claims and delay analysis. Mr. Driscoll is a fellow member and past president of the Construction Management Association of America and served on its Board of Directors for six years. He received a B.S. in civil engineering from Widener University and is a Certified Management Consultant (CMC). He is a member of the Institute of Management Consultants, a member of the Panel of Construction Arbitrators for the American Arbitration Association, and is listed in the American Bar Association Register of Expert Witnesses in the Construction Industry (December 1983).

ABOUT THE AUTHORS

Stephen B. Hurlbut is a partner in the law firm of Wickwire Gavin, P.C., with offices in Vienna, Virginia; Washington, D.C.; and Madison, Wisconsin. He is a graduate of the University of Virginia and the Washington University Law School. He practices in the areas of construction and government contract litigation. He is a member of the bars of the District of Columbia and Virginia as well as the American Bar Association Litigation and Public Contract Law Section. Mr. Hurlbut was formerly a trial attorney with the United States Postal Service and has served as lead counsel for the government as well as private parties in a wide variety of construction related contract litigation. He has lectured frequently and authored a variety of articles on construction and government contract law issues.

SUMMARY CONTENTS

Short Reference List   xix

PART I   SCHEDULE PREPARATION AND
             IMPLEMENTATION

Chapter 1   Legal Significance of the Project Schedule   3
Chapter 2   Scheduling Methods Used Today   19
Chapter 3   Developing and Maintaining the Project Schedule   35
Chapter 4   Legal Aspects of Schedule Specifications   81
Chapter 5   Rights and Obligations in Scheduling   95
Chapter 6   Project Record-Keeping   131

PART II   CLAIM RECOGNITION, PREPARATION,
             AND PROOF

Chapter 7   Time-Related Clauses and Claims   153
Chapter 8   Time Impact Analysis Procedures   181
Chapter 9   Applying CPM Techniques to Contract Claims   201
Chapter 10   Calculating Contractor's Damages for Delay,
             Disruption, and Loss of Efficiency   285
Chapter 11   Calculating Owner's Damages for Delay   307
Chapter 12   Investigating, Preparing, Presenting, and
             Defending Claims   323
Chapter 13   Expert's Role in Preparing and Defending
             Schedule Claims   369
Chapter 14   Case Histories   401
Appendixes   433
Table of Cases   493
Index   513

DETAILED CONTENTS

Short Reference List

PART I   SCHEDULE PREPARATION AND IMPLEMENTATION

Chapter 1   Legal Significance of the Project Schedule

§ 1.1   Importance of Time in Construction Contracts
§ 1.2   Role of Scheduling and Project Management Today
§ 1.3   Project Players and Their Objectives
§ 1.4   —Owner
§ 1.5   —Architect/Engineer
§ 1.6   —General Contractor
§ 1.7   —Subcontractor and Supplier
§ 1.8   —Construction Manager
§ 1.9   —Scheduling Consultant
§ 1.10   Risks in Scheduling and Project Structure Alternatives
§ 1.11   —Conventional Construction Procurement
§ 1.12   —Multiple Prime Contractor Procurement
§ 1.13   —Construction Manager Procurement
§ 1.14   —Phased or Fast-Track Construction
§ 1.15   —Design-Build Technique
§ 1.16   Schedule Analysis as Legal Evidence

Chapter 2   Scheduling Methods Used Today

§ 2.1   Bar Charts
§ 2.2   —Bar Chart Fundamentals
§ 2.3   —Bar Chart Limitations
§ 2.4   Critical Path Method (CPM)
§ 2.5   —CPM Fundamentals
§ 2.6   —CPM Pitfalls
§ 2.7   Precedence Diagramming Method (PDM)
§ 2.8   —Precedence Fundamentals
§ 2.9   —Precedence Pitfalls

Chapter 3   Developing and Maintaining the Project Schedule

§ 3.1   Introduction
§ 3.2   Choosing the Right Scheduling Method

§ 3.3   Developing Schedule Specifications
§ 3.4   Responsibility for Schedule Preparation
§ 3.5   Role of General Contractor
§ 3.6   Role of Subcontractor
§ 3.7   Requirements for Successful Scheduling
§ 3.8   Planning Phase
§ 3.9   —Preparing the Activity List
§ 3.10   —Level of Detail
§ 3.11   Scheduling Phase
§ 3.12   —Activity Durations
§ 3.13   —Computation of Event Times
§ 3.14   Float Identification and Computation
§ 3.15   —Total Float
§ 3.16   —Free Float
§ 3.17   —Independent Float
§ 3.18   —Float Allocation Possibilities
§ 3.19   Computerization of Project Schedule
§ 3.20   —Popular Systems Used for Major Projects
§ 3.21   —Getting Started
§ 3.22   —Inputting Network Information
§ 3.23   —Guidelines for Data Takeoff
§ 3.24   —Computer Outputs
§ 3.25   Schedule Submittal and Approval
§ 3.26   —Schedule Review
§ 3.27   —Procedures for Schedule Review and Approval
§ 3.28   How to Update the Project Schedule
§ 3.29   —Need for Updating
§ 3.30   —Preparing to Update
§ 3.31   —Joint Update Meetings
§ 3.32   Management Reporting and Documentation
§ 3.33   —Problem-Identification Philosophy
§ 3.34   —Need for Good Project Records
§ 3.35   —Cash Flow Forecasting and Progress Payment Records
§ 3.36   —Use of Summary Networks
§ 3.37   Checklist for Effective Schedule Implementation
§ 3.38   —Pitfalls in Scheduling Systems

Chapter 4   **Legal Aspects of Schedule Specifications**

§ 4.1   Introduction
§ 4.2   Feasibility of Schedule
§ 4.3   Type of Diagram

§ 4.4 Number of Activities
§ 4.5 Approval
§ 4.6 Updating
§ 4.7 Cost Loading
§ 4.8 Float Use and Reporting
§ 4.9 Major Revisions and Time Extensions
§ 4.10 Examples of Schedule Specifications
§ 4.11 Factors Contributing to Poor Schedule Specifications

Chapter 5 Rights and Obligations in Scheduling

§ 5.1 Introduction
§ 5.2 Implied Obligations
§ 5.3 —Duty to Schedule and Coordinate
§ 5.4 —Duty to Not Delay, Hinder, or Interfere
§ 5.5 —Duty to Cooperate
§ 5.6 —Duty to Grant Reasonable Time Extensions
§ 5.7 Express Obligations
§ 5.8 Owner's Role in Scheduling
§ 5.9 —Owner-Issued Schedule
§ 5.10 —Progress Schedule Execution
§ 5.11 —Multiprime Contracting
§ 5.12 Prime Contractor's Role in Scheduling
§ 5.13 —Bid-Process Review of Scheduling
§ 5.14 —Preliminary Progress Schedule
§ 5.15 —Initial Approved Project Schedule
§ 5.16 —Project Schedule Updating
§ 5.17 —Coordinating Subcontractors
§ 5.18 Subcontractor's Role in Scheduling
§ 5.19 —Subcontractor Rights in Prime Contractor-Issued Schedule
§ 5.20 —Project Schedule Updating
§ 5.21 —Job-Coordination Meetings
§ 5.22 Project or Schedule Abandonment Due to Inadequate Scheduling
§ 5.23 —Effect of Schedule Abandonment
§ 5.24 Recognition of Contractor's Right to Finish Early and to Manage Schedule

Chapter 6 Project Record-Keeping

§ 6.1 Need for Good Records
§ 6.2 Job-Meeting Minutes
§ 6.3 Progress Charts and Reports

§ 6.4   Daily and Weekly Reports
§ 6.5   Weather
§ 6.6   Photographs
§ 6.7   Job Diary
§ 6.8   Procurement Records
§ 6.9   Test Reports and Test Records
§ 6.10   Change Orders
§ 6.11   Shop Drawings
§ 6.12   Correspondence
§ 6.13   Memoranda
§ 6.14   Cost Records
§ 6.15   Errors and Omissions Analyses
§ 6.16   Using Computers for Job Record-Keeping

PART II   CLAIM RECOGNITION, PREPARATION, AND PROOF

Chapter 7   Time-Related Clauses and Claims
§ 7.1   Excusable Delays
§ 7.2   Contract Provisions Pertaining to Delay
§ 7.3   Examples of Excusable Delay
§ 7.4   —Strikes and Labor Unrest
§ 7.5   —Unusually Severe Weather
§ 7.6   —Inability to Obtain Materials
§ 7.7   —Other Causes
§ 7.8   Compensable Delays
§ 7.9   —Examples of Compensable Delays
§ 7.10   Disruption
§ 7.11   —Assumptions Concerning Disruption
§ 7.12   —Ripple Effect
§ 7.13   —Examples of Disruption
§ 7.14   Suspension of Work
§ 7.15   —Suspension of Work Provisions
§ 7.16   —Recovery by Contractor
§ 7.17   —Concurrent Delay
§ 7.18   —Examples of Suspension of Work
§ 7.19   Disruption versus Delay
§ 7.20   —Impact of Disruption: Pure Delay versus Disruption
§ 7.21   No Damages for Delay Provisions
§ 7.22   —Interpreting No Damages for Delay Clauses
§ 7.23   Exceptions to Enforcement of No Damages Clauses
§ 7.24   —Delays Not Within Parties' Contemplation

§ 7.25 —Delays Amounting to Abandonment
§ 7.26 —Delays Caused by Bad Faith or Fraud
§ 7.27 —Delays Caused by Active Interference
§ 7.28 Acceleration
§ 7.29 —Actual Acceleration
§ 7.30 —Constructive Acceleration
§ 7.31 —Examples of Acceleration

Chapter 8 **Time Impact Analysis Procedures**

§ 8.1 Need for Recognizing and Incorporating Delays
§ 8.2 Understanding Float
§ 8.3 Understanding Concurrent Delay
§ 8.4 Preparing Time Impact Analyses
§ 8.5 Time Impact Analysis Model
§ 8.6 Advantages of Time Impact Analyses
§ 8.7 Guidelines for Negotiating Time Impacts

Chapter 9 **Applying CPM Techniques to Contract Claims**

§ 9.1 Court and Board Acceptance of CPM Techniques
§ 9.2 —Court and Board Sophistication in Addressing CPM Issues
§ 9.3 Court and Board Recognition of CPM's Dynamic Nature
§ 9.4 —Major Public Owners' Recognition of CPM's Dynamic Nature
§ 9.5 CPM Techniques Used for Time-Related Claims through the 1970s
§ 9.6 —Delay Claims
§ 9.7 —Acceleration Claim Analyses
§ 9.8 Issues from the 1970s about the Use of CPM
§ 9.9 —Float Time and Its Availability
§ 9.10 —Determining Credit for Innovative Sequence Changes and When to Measure Delay
§ 9.11 —Time Due Contractor for Change Orders Ordered after Current Contract Completion Date
§ 9.12 CPM Developments and Issues since 1974
§ 9.13 —CPM Acknowledged as Preferred Method for Proving Delays
§ 9.14 —Need to Establish Cause-and-Effect Relationship
§ 9.15 —Requirement for Contemporaneous Baseline in Measuring Quantum of Delay
§ 9.16 —Recognition of Float as Expiring Resource Available to All Parties
§ 9.17 —Demise of *Impacted As-Planned* Proof for Delays
§ 9.18 —Key Issues Involving Concurrent Delay and Extended Duration Claims

§ 9.19   —*But For* Test for Extended Duration Claims
§ 9.20   —Acceptance of Buy-Back Time and Sequence Changes
§ 9.21   —Denial of Automatic Time Extensions for Changes after Completion Date
§ 9.22   —Using CPM to Establish Early Completion Claims
§ 9.23   —Presumptions from CPM Approvals and Time Modifications
§ 9.24   —Limiting Recoverable Time in CPM Claims Presentations
§ 9.25   —Recognition of Risk Taking to Negate Effects of Delays to Critical Path
§ 9.26   —Need to Delineate Plan for Performance in Initial CPM Schedule
§ 9.27   —Fragnets, Windows, and Time Impact Analyses
§ 9.28   —Potential Abuses in Microcomputer Programs
§ 9.29   Specification of Time Impact Analysis
§ 9.30   Safeguards for Establishing Delay Quantum Baselines

Chapter 10   Calculating Contractor's Damages for Delay, Disruption, and Loss of Efficiency

§ 10.1   Introduction
§ 10.2   Credibility
§ 10.3   Disruption versus Delay Costs
§ 10.4   Reasonable and Actual Costs
§ 10.5   Total Cost Method
§ 10.6   Jury Verdict Method
§ 10.7   Forward Pricing
§ 10.8   Labor Costs
§ 10.9   Material Escalation
§ 10.10   Equipment Costs
§ 10.11   Extended Supervision
§ 10.12   Extended Jobsite Expense
§ 10.13   Extended Home Office Overhead
§ 10.14   Profit
§ 10.15   Loss of Efficiency
§ 10.16   Claim Preparation Cost
§ 10.17   Interest

Chapter 11   Calculating Owner's Damages for Delay

§ 11.1   Introduction
§ 11.2   Scope of Recoverable Damages
§ 11.3   Liquidated versus Actual Damages
§ 11.4   —Lack of Actual Damages

§ 11.5   —Prohibition Against Penalty
§ 11.6   —Concurrent Delay
§ 11.7   —Concurrent Delay as Bar
§ 11.8   —Apportionment of Liquidated Damages
§ 11.9   —Use of Critical Path Method Analysis
§ 11.10   —Substantial Completion and Beneficial Occupancy
§ 11.11   Actual Damages for Delay
§ 11.12   —Loss of Profits
§ 11.13   —Loss of Use
§ 11.14   —Increased Financing
§ 11.15   —Extended Maintenance and Operation Expenses
§ 11.16   —Special Damages
§ 11.17   —Attorneys' Fees
§ 11.18   —Interest
§ 11.19   Exemplary Damages

Chapter 12   **Investigating, Preparing, Presenting, and Defending Claims**

§ 12.1   Claim Monitoring: Three Warning Signs
§ 12.2   —Dollars
§ 12.3   —Sequence
§ 12.4   —Duration
§ 12.5   Claim Investigation
§ 12.6   —Data Sources
§ 12.7   —Physical Characteristics
§ 12.8   —Sequence of Work
§ 12.9   —Planned versus Actual Performance
§ 12.10   —Claims Costing
§ 12.11   —Bases of Claim
§ 12.12   —Contract Provisions
§ 12.13   —Change Orders
§ 12.14   Claim Preparation
§ 12.15   —Costing and Documentary Data Sources
§ 12.16   —Scheduling Documentation and Non-Network Exhibits
§ 12.17   —Final Claim Compilation
§ 12.18   Claim Presentation
§ 12.19   —Structure of Narrative
§ 12.20   —Supporting Exhibits
§ 12.21   Claim Defense
§ 12.22   —Actions upon Receipt of Claim
§ 12.23   —Audits
§ 12.24   —Alternatives to Confrontation and Litigation

§ 12.25 —Counterclaims
§ 12.26 —Assertion of Defenses
§ 12.27 —Choice of Forum and Value of Going First
§ 12.28 —Defensive Measures

Chapter 13 Expert's Role in Preparing and Defending Schedule Claims

§ 13.1 Introduction
§ 13.2 Familiarization Phase
§ 13.3 Investigation and Data-Gathering Phase
§ 13.4 Fact-Finding and Evaluation Phase
§ 13.5 Presentation Phase

Chapter 14 Case Histories

§ 14.1 Purpose
§ 14.2 Cedars-Sinai Litigation
§ 14.3 Durham Wastewater Treatment Plant Litigation
§ 14.4 Humana Litigation
§ 14.5 Edwards Air Force Base Test Support Facility
§ 14.6 Integrity and Credibility in Dispute Resolution

Appendixes

A. AIA Document A201-1987, Paragraph 3.10—Contractor's Construction Schedules
B. 1988 State of California Department of Transportation Scheduling Specifications
C. 1985 Corps of Engineers Edwards Air Force Base Test Support Facility Construction Specification, Section 17—Contractor Project Management System
D. Veterans Administration Master Specification, Section 01311—Network Analysis System
E. United States Postal Service Specification, Section 01030—Scheduling and Progress
F. Model Scheduling Specification
G. Excerpt from Veterans Administration VACPM Handbook Part VI—Contract Changes and Time Extensions

Table of Cases

Index

SHORT REFERENCE LIST

Short Reference	Full Reference
AGBCA	Department of Agriculture Board of Contract Appeals
AGC	Associated General Contractors
AIA	American Institute of Architects
ASBCA	Armed Services Board of Contract Appeals
BCA	Board of Contract Appeals Decisions (CCH)
CPM	critical path method
DOTCAB	Department of Transportation Contract Appeals Board
ENGBCA	Army Corps of Engineers Board of Contract Appeals
FAR	Federal Acquisition Regulations
GSBCA	General Services Board of Contract Appeals
HUDBCA	Housing and Urban Development Board of Contract Appeals
IBCA	Department of Interior Board of Contract Appeals
NASABCA	National Aeronautics and Space Administration Board of Contract Appeals
precedence	precedence diagramming method (also PDM)
PSBCA	Postal Service Board of Contract Appeals
RFI	request for information
VABCA	Veterans Administration Board of Contract Appeals
VACAB	Veterans Administration Contract Appeals Board

PART I

SCHEDULE PREPARATION AND IMPLEMENTATION

CHAPTER 1

LEGAL SIGNIFICANCE OF THE PROJECT SCHEDULE

§ 1.1   Importance of Time in Construction Contracts
§ 1.2   Role of Scheduling and Project Management Today
§ 1.3   Project Players and Their Objectives
§ 1.4   —Owner
§ 1.5   —Architect/Engineer
§ 1.6   —General Contractor
§ 1.7   —Subcontractor and Supplier
§ 1.8   —Construction Manager
§ 1.9   —Scheduling Consultant
§ 1.10   Risks in Scheduling and Project Structure Alternatives
§ 1.11   —Conventional Construction Procurement
§ 1.12   —Multiple Prime Contractor Procurement
§ 1.13   —Construction Manager Procurement
§ 1.14   —Phased or Fast-Track Construction
§ 1.15   —Design-Build Technique
§ 1.16   Schedule Analysis as Legal Evidence

§ 1.1   Importance of Time in Construction Contracts

Contracts for major commercial and construction projects contain a host of specific terms defining the duties and responsibilities of the parties to the agreement. On an elemental level, however, for a successful procurement each contract must identify and define the following three factors:

1. What is going to be provided
2. How much compensation is going to be paid for the thing or performance provided
3. When is the performance required.

3

These factors required of any agreement between parties can be described in three words: *scope, price,* and *time.*

This book's focus is the legal significance of the time for performance within the context of project schedules. In addition, it examines pragmatic factors that bear upon the different biases the various parties bring to the construction process in seeking to achieve their respective objectives.

To state it another way, the project schedule represents a point of reference by which the various parties measure their performance. In fact, the project schedule represents the hard data base, or a hard baseline, by which the parties measure each other's performance and assess their respective rights and obligations.

§ 1.2   Role of Scheduling and Project Management Today

In today's world of computers, advanced technology, rising inflation, and complex business relationships, the scheduling and management of construction projects has assumed greatly increased importance in the construction industry. More than ever before, contractors, owners, architects, and construction managers all recognize the importance of learning and implementing the most effective techniques in order to satisfactorily complete projects and maintain profitability.

To keep pace with these trends, the use of proper management techniques, including scheduling, is critical. The use of *network* techniques on major projects for planning and coordinating the work, already well accepted by the late 1970s, is an imperative for the 1980s and 1990s.

The importance of scheduling has increased for the following reasons:

Economics.   Volatile interest rates and continuing inflation have made it more important than ever for contractors and owners to bring in projects within the time estimated in the bid.

Scheduling efficiency.   Proper use of network planning techniques during construction provides to the executor of the project schedule the knowledge required to react (on a real-time project basis) to changing project needs and maintain the level of effort necessary to meet the completion dates.

Technology availability.   As a result of the increasing availability and decreasing costs of data control and the increasing capacity of minicomputers, parties are more likely than ever to avail themselves of sophisticated scheduling techniques, which afford increased visibility of status and progress during construction.

Legal application. Legal decisions utilizing network planning for project evaluations dictate that contracting parties are more likely to insist on use of appropriate scheduling techniques as a part of contractual performance.

Claim preparation. Increasingly sophisticated methods of claim preparation have made proper project scheduling integral to assessment of responsibility and to the recovery of cost overruns incurred on projects.

Unlike the situation just a few decades ago, sophisticated methods of scheduling, such as network techniques like the *critical path method* (CPM), are widely used and totally accepted today. Scheduling has become not only a tool for guiding performance during the life of the contract, but also a suitable method for gauging the accuracy and appropriateness of claims made as a result of the performance.

When properly used, the project schedule can be a critical tool for project management, analysis, control, and overall performance. It should be stressed that the schedule is not just a device for telling subcontractors where to move their work forces. Fully utilized, the project schedule is an important management tool that enables the contractor to use personnel wisely and to provide advance warning of situations that may threaten the profitability of a project.

The project schedule is also an analytical device for claim recognition, preparation, and proof. Proper use of the project schedule will warn the contractor when situations exist that may lead to cost overruns, claims, or other difficulties. In the event that a claim situation does occur, the project schedule is an important tool for comparing plan with actual performance to ascertain what went wrong and who was responsible. Courts and administrative boards of appeals have accepted proper scheduling techniques, particularly CPM, as a valid means of proving liability and damages.

§ 1.3 Project Players and Their Objectives

A variety of players must bring their skills and resources together to achieve the physical construction of a project. However, each of these players also is interested in achieving a successful procurement—one that allows the party to achieve its objectives.

The players on major construction projects can include the owner, the architect/engineer, the general contractor, subcontractors or trade contractors, suppliers, construction managers, multiple prime contractors, scheduling/claims consultants, and attorneys. Sometimes the parties to the construction project may have similar or identical objectives. At other times, objectives may diverge. A brief summary of these objectives is set forth in §§ **1.4** through **1.9**.

§ 1.4 —Owner

Owners dislike surprises on construction projects. Owners want quality projects delivered on time and within the bid or negotiated price for the particular project. On occasion, owners may put the importance of time of construction above all other constraints and demand that performance be completed within the original contract completion date in spite of major changes, delays, and other factors. On other occasions, owners may wish to delay the delivery of a project rather than be subjected to enormous impact or acceleration claims. Most of all, owners do not like contractors' claims.

§ 1.5 —Architect/Engineer

Architects and engineers like to see the successful completion of their design prior to commencement of performance. Thereafter, the architect and engineer like to see the project proceed with a minimum of effort on their parts in responding to design issues, shop drawings, and inspection of performance to support the construction operations.

Architects and engineers wish to avoid being sued by owners and, because of privity requirements, are frequently not sued by contractors. Architects and engineers are frequently required to act in a quasi-judicial capacity in evaluating questions of contract performance, as well as matters related to the time of performance (as that required by AIA Document A201-1987 ¶ 4.2.11). However, it is frequently difficult for the architect/engineer to maintain total independence without partiality because the architect/engineer is in privity of contract with the owner and is most concerned about satisfying the owner and avoiding claims from the owner for omissions or reimbursement of contractor claims.

§ 1.6 —General Contractor

General contractors today most typically are interested in goals similar to that of the owner. Specifically, general contractors want to achieve successful construction on time and within budget. When difficulties are encountered in achieving this objective, general contractors frequently are interested in avoiding liability to the subcontractor or trade contractor as well as the owner. When general contractors perform only the concrete work itself or are purely brokers on projects, they will typically have less risk associated with the project performance after the initial stages of the work since their only risk may be tied to project extensions involving jobsite overhead and corporate General and Administrative expenses. Through their use of exhaustion of the administrative remedies clauses, no damage for delay clauses, and pay-when-paid clauses and their ability to control payments to subcontractors, general contractors bring an entirely different set of biases (which may be adverse to that of subcontractors) to the table in dealing with the costs of major delays in project performance and the responsibility of individual parties to the process for those costs.

§ 1.7   —Subcontractor and Supplier

Subcontractors bear the burden of labor productivity risk on major construction projects because general contractors typically will perform a smaller percentage, if any, of construction on projects. As a result, the trade contractor bears the brunt of lost productivity associated with acceleration, lack of proper scheduling and coordination of projects, and wage escalation, plus other lost productivity from major delays in the completion of individual phases of the work as well as the overall project.

Suppliers, on the other hand, are interested in locking in both a time and a price for supplying individual components of the work. Where delays are experienced, suppliers may seek to renegotiate prices. In other cases, they may refuse to give firm prices substantially in advance of the time schedule for performance.

§ 1.8   —Construction Manager

Construction managers, whether under direct contract with the trade contractors or only under contract with the owner and serving as an agent of the owner, typically represent a viewpoint similar to that of the brokerage general contractor. Specifically, the construction manager is probably operating on some kind of fee basis and may be collecting funds monthly from the trade contractors for various services, such as hoisting. In addition, the construction manager may be paid on some sort of rate schedule basis for continuing to provide the services of a jobsite staff for extended project duration. Thus, the construction manager may be more interested in satisfying the owner's needs and objectives, whatever they may be on the particular project, and may be less interested in providing an environment by which the trade contractors can successfully achieve the labor productivity they need for a successful procurement.

§ 1.9   —Scheduling Consultant

The scheduling consultant who attacks the job properly seeks to develop a relationship of trust with the different participants in the process. The consultant must also seek information and input from the various players to develop a workable plan and project schedule. Such proper scheduling provides the best opportunity for a well-coordinated and well-sequenced project, one that delivers the project on time and within budget for all participants. Such an objective may not always be possible—and frequently is not. The scheduling consultant must therefore work hard with the executor of the project schedule, whether that be the general contractor, the construction manager, or even the owner, to make certain that the various participants in the construction process are working as a team toward agreed-upon objectives. Such objectives usually involve completion in the time allotted for performance in the manner and method reflected by the plan and the project schedule.

§ 1.10 Risks in Scheduling and Project Structure Alternatives

Every construction project faces a multitude of risks that can significantly jeopardize its success. Contracting parties must consider their respective risks and responsibilities as they relate to the project schedule.

A *risk matrix* (**Figure 1–1**) should be used with any procurement to properly identify the risks assumed by the various parties to the procurement. Each party should refer to the matrix and evaluate the extent of risk it is willing to undertake. Parties also should ascertain who is to bear the responsibility for other risks.

The selection of the procurement structure itself will have a strong influence on project risk allocation, as well as the duties assumed by the individual parties with respect to the schedule. The various procurement structures are discussed in §§ **1.11** through **1.15**.

§ 1.11 —Conventional Construction Procurement

In the majority of construction projects, the owner enters into a single contractual relationship with a general contractor, who is responsible for virtually all aspects of the construction work. The owner also contracts with an architect/engineer, who is responsible for the design of the project. See **Figure 1–2**.

Under this type of arrangement, the owner is responsible for providing to the contractor a reasonably accurate and complete project design, timely access to the site, and a site itself that generally conforms to the conditions or requirements set forth in the contract documents.[1] The

---

[1] *See, e.g.,* United States v. Spearin, 248 U.S. 132 (1918); Shintech, Inc. v. Group Constructors, Inc., 688 S.W.2d 144 (Tex. Ct. App. 1985); Peter Kiewit Sons' Co. v. United States, 151 F. Supp. 726, 138 Ct. Cl. 668 (1957).

Risk	Who Should Take?						How Managed?
	Owner	Contractor	Architect/ Engineer	Subcontractor	Construction Manager	Supplier	
Outside Influences							
Governmental acts							
Weather							
Acts of God							
Union strife, work rules							
Cost escalation							
Collapse of major project participants							
Resources and Prerequisites to Project							
Adequacy of project funding							
Adequacy of labor force							
Permits, licenses							
Site access							
Performance-related Elements							
Sufficiency of plans							
Underestimation of costs							
Owner-furnished material, equipment							
Contractor-furnished material, equipment							
Means, methods of construction							
Delay in presenting grievances							
Delay in addressing grievances							
Labor productivity							
Late approvals of submittals							
Subsurface conditions							
Delays							
Worker and site safety							
Catastrophic failures							
Failure of proprietary process essential to project							
Plan or design of schedule							
Use of excess time, float							
Failure to coordinate work							
Delayed resolution of errors, omissions							

Figure 1–1. Risk matrix showing risks and responsibilities that can affect project plans.

9

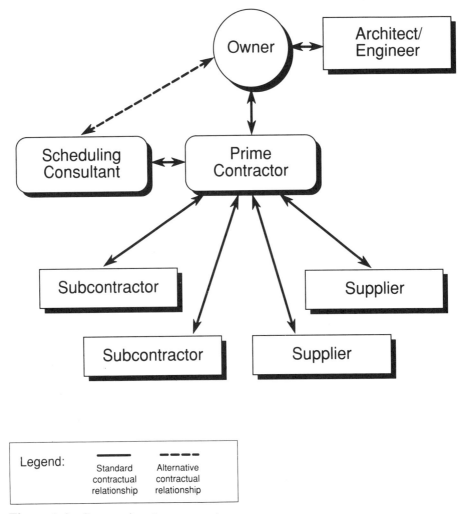

Figure 1–2. Conventional construction procurement.

general contractor is responsible for scheduling and coordinating the work.[2] Consequently, the general contractor either prepares the schedule documentation required by the contract in-house or retains a scheduling consultant to perform this work. In scheduling the overall project, the general contractor bears full responsibility to the owner for coordinating and resolving conflicts in the work schedules of the various subcontractors and suppliers on the project.

---

[2] *See* Able Elec. Co. v. Vacanti Randazzo Constr. Co., 212 Neb. 619, 324 N.W.2d 667 (1982); S. Leo Harmonay, Inc. v. Binks Mfg. Co., 597 F. Supp. 1014 (S.D.N.Y. 1984).

§ 1.12   —Multiple Prime Contractor Procurement

On occasion, owners will contract with a number of separate contractors on a single construction project (**Figure 1–3**). This format is known as *multiple prime contractor procurement.* This technique may be favored when the owner wishes to proceed prior to having a fully developed project design or feels it would be less costly to contract separately with various trade contractors.

Under this type of arrangement, the construction project is divided into work packages that generally fall along the lines of the various building trades. Responsibility for total project scheduling and coordination of construction most often falls upon the owner in a multiple prime contractor arrangement. Owners on multiple prime projects occasionally try to

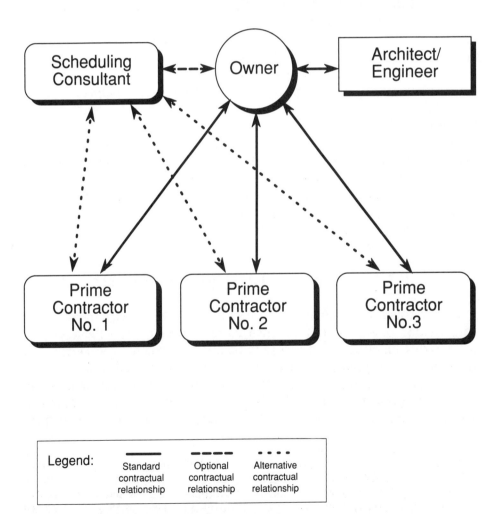

Figure 1–3. Multiple prime contractor procurement.

retain control of construction progress through financial means, yet attempt to limit their responsibility for coordination and scheduling of work by delegating this responsibility to a *general trade contractor.* Alternatively, owners on multiple prime contractor projects may retain scheduling consultants to prepare an overall project schedule as well as the schedule for each separate trade contractor.

The multiple prime contractor technique raises a number of difficult issues with respect to legal responsibility for the scheduling and coordination of work. The most important question raised is which party—the owner, the scheduling consultant, or the general trades contractor—has the ultimate right to control the schedule. Unless the contract documents provide otherwise, scheduling and coordination responsibility for multiple prime contractor projects rests with the owner.[3] Consequently, owners must carefully consider the risks attendant to the use of the multiple prime contractor format. All parties to construction contracts on projects utilizing the multiple prime contractor arrangement should endeavor to negotiate contractual terms that clearly and fairly delegate and allocate responsibility for coordination and scheduling.

Some owners on multiple prime contractor projects attempt to shift responsibility for scheduling and coordination to all of the contractors on the project. This is not a realistic approach. All contractors on the project should be required to participate and assist in the scheduling and coordination efforts. However, it is in the best interest of all parties to designate a single entity who is responsible for overall scheduling and coordination. Although this places additional risk on the party accepting this responsibility, the arrangement encourages resolution of scheduling and coordination problems prior to the development of a crisis.

§ 1.13   —Construction Manager Procurement

Owners frequently retain a *construction manager* to manage the design or construction of a project. The construction manager offers the advantage of construction or design expertise to the inexperienced owner. Generally, the construction manager procurement technique is used in conjunction with a separate contract between the owner and an architect/engineer who designs the project. Occasionally, however, the construction manager may also be responsible for design of the project. The construction manager

---

[3] Pierce Assocs., Inc., GSBCA No. 4163, 77-2 BCA ¶ 12,746 (1977), *on reconsideration,* 78-1 BCA ¶ 13,078, *aff'd,* 617 F.2d 223 (Ct. Cl. 1980); Shea-S&M Ball v. Massman-Kiewit-Early 606 F.2d 1245 (D.C. Cir. 1979); Hoffman v. United States, 340 F.2d 645, 166 Ct. Cl. 39 (1964); Hall Constr. Co. v. United States, 379 F.2d 559, 177 Ct. Cl. 870 (1966).

technique may also be used in conjunction with a single general contractor (**Figure 1–4**) or multiple prime contractors (**Figure 1–5**).

The contracting parties in a construction manager arrangement should give careful consideration to the extent of authority provided to the construction manager in dealings with the project contractors. On some projects, the construction manager is given complete control over the project contractors with respect to construction costs and scheduling. In this situation, the construction manager may also be responsible to the owner and bear the risk for the performance of the other project contractors. On other projects, the construction manager acts as the owner's agent and is delegated less control over the project contractors. In that type of arrangement, the construction manager has limited supervisory responsibility over the project contractors, but may have responsibility for

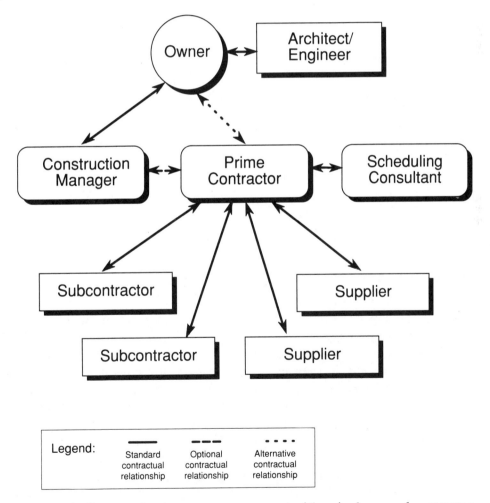

Figure 1–4. Construction manager procurement with a single general contractor.

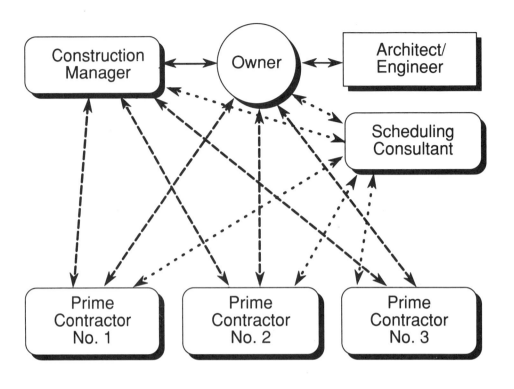

Figure 1–5. Construction manager procurement with multiple prime contractors.

providing detailed reports to the owner concerning the performance of the project contractors.

The contract documents for projects using construction managers should specify whether they have scheduling and coordination responsibility. When construction managers contract to complete a project within a guaranteed maximum price, they usually assume responsibility for scheduling and coordinating the work. However, construction managers may attempt to delegate this responsibility to general contractors or general trades contractors. On the other hand, when the construction manager is simply acting as an agent of the owner, the allocation of risk is less clear. If a single-general-contractor format is used, scheduling and coordination responsibilities should rest with the general contractor. However, where the multiple prime contractor technique is utilized, the parties should undertake to clearly specify which party has responsibility for scheduling and coordinating the work. Unless the contract provides otherwise the various prime contractors will have the right to look to the owner for scheduling and coordination of the work.[4]

§ 1.14   —Phased or Fast-Track Construction

The purpose of using the *phased* or *fast-track* construction technique is to begin construction as early as possible. Early phases of construction, such as site preparation and foundation work, typically will begin before the final design for the project is complete. Project design is completed concurrent with construction work on the early phases of the project.

When applied properly, phased construction can result in cost savings to the owner by minimizing the impact of inflation on construction costs. It also allows greater use of fixed-price contracts on very large projects. However, the owner typically will assume major responsibility and liability for scheduling and coordination of the work, particularly where multiple prime contractors are involved. The owner's risk is significant in phased construction and is especially heightened on fast-track projects. Owners on these types of projects should give careful consideration to interfacing the schedules of the various phases and the constraints on later phases created by the performance of precedent work in earlier phases of the project. The owner faces considerable risk in embarking on projects not fully designed, as later conditions may be unanticipated or different from earlier intentions.

Owners are potentially responsible for the extensive damages that can flow from flawed designs and from delays caused by performance problems on earlier phases.[5] In *Turner Construction Co.,*[6] the contractor, acting as a construction manager on a fast-track project, recovered delay costs incurred by the contractor and subcontractors in installing interstitial utilities at a large research facility. The government was responsible for design defects that were not revealed until construction and that required extensive redesign throughout the project. Although the contractor was responsible for coordination of the work, the government plans were so flawed that the major problems encountered could not be anticipated and the government/owner bore the full risk of the delays.

---

[4] Pierce Assocs., Inc., GSBCA No. 4163, 77-2 BCA ¶ 12,746, *on reconsideration,* 78-1 BCA ¶ 13,078, *aff'd,* 617 F.2d 223 (Ct. Cl. 1980).

[5] *Id.*

[6] ASBCA Nos. 25,447, 29,472, 29,591, 29,592, 29,593, 29,830, 29,851, 29,852, 90-2 BCA ¶ 22,649 (1990).

§ 1.15   —Design-Build Technique

On *design-build* projects, the owner provides the contractor with broad performance or program criteria. The contractor, typically a single entity with construction and design capabilities, provides both services for the project. Total responsibility, including all scheduling and coordination, lies with the single design-build contractor. Under this arrangement, owners or developers are able to contract away most of the risks associated with scheduling and coordination problems.

Design-build contracts typically impose scheduling requirements on both the design and the construction phases of the project.[7] Owners on such projects must guard against the tendency to assume the contractor will perform in accordance with contract milestones. This faulty assumption often leads owners to ignore the contractor's plan and schedule for performing the work, which can result in drastic consequences where the design-builder has performance problems or overbills the project on the basis of the percentage of work completed.[8] Although the owner's scheduling involvement may not be as great as on conventional projects, the owner must review the schedule logic, as well as periodic updates, to evaluate performance and determine whether intervention is appropriate under the circumstances.

§ 1.16   Schedule Analysis as Legal Evidence

In the 1960s boards of contract appeals and courts began recognizing network planning techniques as legal evidence in assessing the responsibility for and the quantum of delays associated with construction projects. A number of the cases addressing this issue concern circumstances where the network planning technique was actually used on the project to plan and schedule performance.[9] Others have refused to use network planning techniques as the gauge for performance where the network planning technique was not specified or actually used during performance to control the work.[10] However, boards have shown a willingness to accept the use of after-the-fact analyses of delays on the

---

[7] Loulakis & Love, *Exploring the Design-Build Contract,* Construction Briefings No. 86-13 at 10 (1986).

[8] *Id.*

[9] *Santa Fe, Inc.,* VABCA No. 2168, 87-3 BCA ¶ 20,104 (1987).

[10] *See, e.g.,* Chaney & James Constr. Co., FAACAP No. 67-18, 66-2 BCA ¶ 6066 (1967); Pathman Constr. Co., ASBCA No. 23,392, 85-2 BCA ¶ 18,096 (1985); Nello L. Teer Co., ENGBCA No. 4376, 86-3 BCA ¶ 19,326 (1986).

concerned project when the analyses reflect a reasonable reconstruction of the original plan and the effect of delays on the project.[11]

The recognition of CPM techniques in delay claim analysis has expanded greatly in recent years, becoming the preferred method of proof in the federal arena[12] and gaining wide acceptance in the state courts.[13]

The extent of the general understanding by the courts and boards of CPM's validity in evaluating contract performance and claims is demonstrated in a recent essay by a board of contract appeals on CPM scheduling. In *Utley-James, Inc.,*[14] the General Services Board of Contract Appeals describes fundamental network analysis concepts, recognizing sophisticated CPM techniques such as resource leveling, sequencing restraints, use of float and negative float, and buy-back time through acceleration. The instructive essay describes the usefulness of the tool in both project planning and claims analysis.

---

[11] Fletcher & Sons, Inc., VACAB No. 2502, 88-2 BCA ¶ 20,677 (1988); Fischbach & Moore Int'l, ASBCA No. 18,146, 77-1 BCA ¶ 12,300 (1976); Forsberg & Gregory, Inc., ASBCA No. 17,163, 76-2 BCA ¶ 12,037 (1976).

[12] *See, e.g.,* Fortec Constructors v. United States, 8 Cl. Ct. 490 (1985); Weaver-Bailey Contractors, Inc. v. United States, 19 Cl. Ct. 474, *reconsideration denied,* 20 Cl. Ct. 158 (1990); Williams Enters. v. Strait Mfg. & Welding, Inc., 728 F. Supp. 12 (D.D.C. 1990); Gulf Contracting, Inc., ASBCA Nos. 30,195, 32,839, 33,867, 89-2 BCA ¶ 21,812, *aff'd. on reconsideration,* 90-1 BCA ¶ 22,393 (1989).

[13] *See, e.g.,* Blake Constr. Co. v. C.J. Coakley Co., 431 A.2d 569 (D.C. 1981); Broadway Maintenance Corp. v. Rutgers State Univ., 90 N.J. 253, 447 A.2d 906 (1982); Walter Kidelie Contractors, Inc. v. State, 37 Conn. Supp. 50, 434 A.2d 962 (1981); Walter Toebe & Co. v. Yeager Bridge & Culvert Co., 150 Mich. App. 386, 389 N.W.2d 99 (1986).

[14] Utley-James, Inc., GSBCA No. 5370, 85-1 BCA ¶ 17,816 at 89,060–89,062 (1984).

CHAPTER 2

SCHEDULING METHODS USED TODAY

§ 2.1 **Bar Charts**

§ 2.2 **—Bar Chart Fundamentals**

§ 2.3 **—Bar Chart Limitations**

§ 2.4 **Critical Path Method (CPM)**

§ 2.5 **—CPM Fundamentals**

§ 2.6 **—CPM Pitfalls**

§ 2.7 **Precedence Diagramming Method (PDM)**

§ 2.8 **—Precedence Fundamentals**

§ 2.9 **—Precedence Pitfalls**

§ 2.1 Bar Charts

Prior to 1957, the most common and best-suited means of planning and scheduling a construction project was the bar chart. In fact, the architect, engineer, or contractor had little choice but the bar chart, because no other disciplined method was available.

Bar chart planning had its beginnings in the early 1900s, when Henry L. Gantt and Frederick W. Taylor presented the first scientific approach to the problems of work scheduling. The basis of their approach was the graphical presentation of work versus time via a bar chart.

§ 2.2 —Bar Chart Fundamentals

The bar chart generally comprises a horizontal scale that provides the time reference and a vertical list of the project components or work items to be performed (see **Figure 2-1**). Bars are drawn to graphically represent the span of time necessary to accomplish each work item. The plotting of the individual bars is left to the imagination and experience of the planner and those upon whom he relies for specific input about the development

19

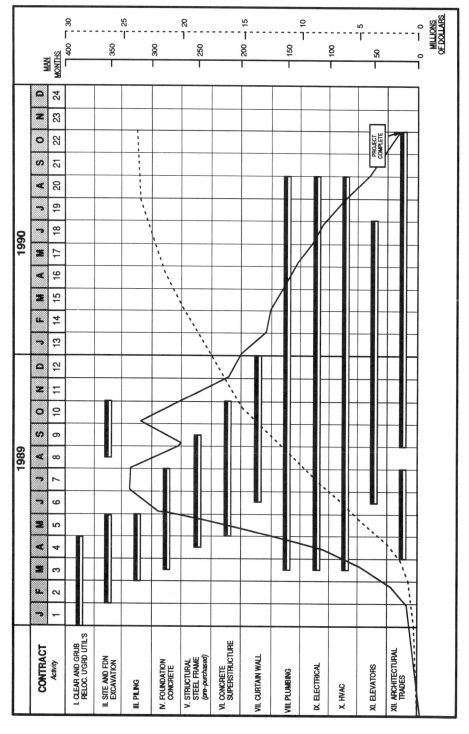

Figure 2–1. Bar chart schedule for construction of an office building.

20

of the schedule. This includes the start and finish of a bar and the implied successor or predecessor relationship of one bar to another.

The content of most bar charts is kept rather simple. However, some preparers take a more sophisticated approach and overlay cost and manpower forecast curves on the time grid and the bars that are plotted for each work item. Generally, an S curve is used to illustrate the cost projections and a bell curve is used to illustrate the schedule for manpower requirements. Each curve is generally supported by a matrix of weekly, monthly, or other units of time used in the time scale. The cumulative totals are sometimes shown directly under the time grid portion of the bar chart.

The physical progress of a job is generally shown by graphically plotting the amount of work completed or achieved for each bar as of a status report date. Physical effort is usually expressed as a percentage of the total time shown for each bar. Additional curves are usually plotted to show the cumulative actual costs expended and the manpower used as of the status report date. The actual cost and manpower expended for the respective report periods are generally recorded in the matrix below, facilitating a schedule-versus-actual comparison.

Of course, any changes in the original plans or sequence of activities are incorporated as part of the normal updating process to keep the bar chart current. Adjustments increasing or decreasing the cost and manpower curves also are included.

The project in **Figure 2–1** is a steel-frame office building. The bars are drawn to represent 12 major features of work. The black portion of each bar represents the planned schedule; the white portion is used to indicate progress as the chart is updated. The bell curve indicates the monthly manpower requirement; the S curve shows the estimated and cumulative cost. An index for each curve appears to the right of the chart.

§ 2.3   —Bar Chart Limitations

Considering the progress that has been made in construction industry methods, the bar chart is limited in its use and has a number of significant disadvantages. For example:

1. Size limits a bar chart in what it can graphically present
2. Bar charts do not show the interrelationships or interdependencies of one bar and another
3. Bar charts do not show available float or contingency time, nor can they show the delay impact of one bar on another
4. Bar charts are not capable of accurately distributing or controlling manpower and project costs

5. Adding more detail to the bar chart sometimes makes it harder to read, understand, and maintain.

Several of these limitations were recognized by the Armed Services Board of Contract Appeals in *Minmar Builders, Inc.*:[1] In considering the use of bar charts as proof of delay, the Board noted that:

> Although two of Appellant's construction schedules were introduced in evidence, one which had been approved by the Government and one which had not, neither was anything more than a bar chart showing the duration and projected calendar dates for the performance of the various contractual tasks. Since no interrelationship was shown as between the tasks[,] the charts cannot show what project activities were dependent on the prior performance of the plaster and ceiling work, much less whether overall project completion was thereby affected. In short, the schedules were not prepared by the Critical Path Method (CPM) and hence are not probative as to whether any particular activity or group of activities was on the critical path or constituted the pacing element for the project.

In conclusion, bar charts have limited value for scheduling and controlling large and complex construction projects. The proliferation of computers and the development of scheduling software have helped owners, architects/engineers, and contractors recognize the limitations of bar charts and minimize their use today. On large projects, bar charts can be effectively used as a visual report summary to present management with a total picture of the overall schedule and status of the project. Such a visual aid is most effective when the bar chart is accurately coordinated with, and summarized from, a detailed scheduling method such as CPM (see § 2.4).

§ 2.4 Critical Path Method (CPM)

The critical path method (CPM) of network scheduling, along with the lesser-used performance evaluation and review technique (PERT), originated in the mid-1950s. In 1956, the engineering control group of E.I. duPont de Nemours Company, under the direction of Morgan Walker, set out to improve their existing methods for controlling large chemical plant construction. Essentially, management was not satisfied with results of the methods then in use. Accordingly, an objective was established to develop a management tool that would centralize all the information essential for planning, scheduling, and controlling construction and facility maintenance.

---

[1] ASBCA No. 3430, 72-2 BCA ¶ 9599 at 44,857 (1972). *See also* H.W. Detwiler Co., ASBCA No. 35,327, 89-2 BCA ¶ 21,612 (1989).

In 1957, the Univac Applications Research Center, directed by Dr. John W. Mauchly, and Remington Rand, directed by James E. Kelley, joined the duPont effort. By the middle of 1957, the fundamentals of a new computer-oriented technique had been developed. Initial tests proved successful, and management decided to use this new technique to plan, schedule, and control a $10 million chemical plant in Louisville, Kentucky. The results of this project clearly demonstrated that CPM was a powerful tool.

CPM can be described as a graphic presentation of the planned sequence of activities that shows the interrelationships and interdependencies of the elements composing a project.[2]

The Corps of Engineers Board of Contract Appeals provided its own definition of CPM in *Continental Consolidated Corp.*[3] This definition is significant, not just for its recitation of basic network principles, but also for its recognition that CPM is a dynamic concept that changes during the life of the project and must be properly adjusted to reflect time due the contractor concurrent with events on the project:

> The CPM scheduling technique is one which requires a breakdown of the entire project into individual tasks and an analysis of the number of days required to perform each task. The analysis is then programmed into a computer which produces a chart showing the tasks and a line which controls the completion of the overall work. The line through the nodes, the junction points for completion of essential tasks, is known as the critical path. In addition, there are numerous side paths for subordinate tasks which normally can be performed without affecting the critical path. However, these subordinate tasks[,] if improperly scheduled or unduly delayed in performance, can on occasions become critical and thus change the critical path for the entire project.
>
> The critical path method of scheduling requires the logical analysis of all the individual tasks entering into the complete job and the periodic review and re-analysis of progress during the performance period. It is essential that any changes in the work and the time extensions due to the contractor be incorporated into the progress analysis concurrently with the performance of the changes or immediately after the delay and thus integrated into the periodic computer runs to reflect the effect on the critical path. Otherwise, the critical path chart produced by the computer will not reflect the current status of work performed or the actual progress being attained.[4]

---

[2] For a detailed textual treatment of network planning principles and the history of their development, see J. O'Brien, CPM in Construction Management (3d ed. 1984); Moder & Phillips, Project Management with CPM and PERT (2d ed. 1970); J. Fondahl, Handbook of Construction Management and Organization (1973).

[3] ENGBCA Nos. 2743, 67-2 BCA ¶ 6624 (1967).

[4] *Id.* at p. 30,715.

§ 2.5   —CPM Fundamentals

The foundation of the CPM technique is the arrow diagram or network of activities. The network graphically consists of arrows and circles that are used to describe the planned sequence and dependency relationships of work to be accomplished. The arrows represent work activities and each activity describes a specific task to be completed. Each work activity is assigned a time duration. One exception is the dummy activity (logic restraint) used to reflect proper logic sequencing and sometimes to keep a unique event numbering system for activities. The dummy activity is usually shown as a dotted line and has a zero time dimension.

The circles represent the start and finish for each activity or the junction point of two or more activities. The circles are called events and sometimes are referred to as nodes. Events or nodes are points in time. An activity start event (tail) is sometimes referred to as the "i" node and the activity finish event (head) is referred to as the "j" node. There is no particular significance to the use of the "i" or "j" reference. It was simply the choice of the original developers of the critical path method of scheduling for indicating the start and finish nodes of an activity.

The arrow diagram is prepared by arranging activities into a planned sequence based on preferential or absolute considerations for activity accomplishment. This is achieved by applying three basic rules of logic to each activity:

1. What activities must be completed before the activity in question can start?
2. What activities can be done concurrently?
3. What activities must follow the completion of the activity in question.

Activities may vary in length and be bent, but not broken, in order to graphically express the relationship of one activity to another, or for graphic convenience. **Figure 2–2** gives examples of possible relationships between activities in a CPM schedule.

Figure 2–3 is an example of a basic CPM schedule in summary form for construction of a 10-story office building. Also dealing with the office building project, **Table 2–1** provides a sample listing of detailed activity information contained in the CPM schedule. Activities are listed by ascending predecessor and successor event numbers. Similar computer sorts of activity information commonly used by the construction industry include sorts by early start, late start, late finish, and total float. The early and late dates for start and finish of each activity and total float are derived from network calculations based on the principles described in § 3.13.

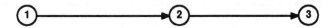

ACTIVITY 2–3 CANNOT START UNTIL
ACTIVITY 1–2 IS COMPLETE.

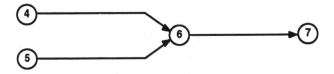

ACTIVITY 6–7 CANNOT START UNTIL
BOTH 4–6 AND 5–6 ARE COMPLETED.

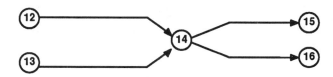

BOTH 12–14 AND 13–14 MUST BE
COMPLETED BEFORE EITHER 14–15 OR
14–16 CAN START.

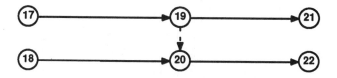

BOTH 17–19 AND 18–20 MUST BE COMPLETED
BEFORE 20–22 CAN START; 19–21 IS
CONSTRAINED BY 17–19 ONLY, NOT BY 18–20
*(19–20 IS A REAL CONSTRAINT ON ACTIVITY
20–22).*

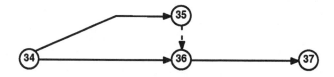

ACTIVITY 36–37 CANNOT START UNTIL BOTH
34–36 AND 34–35 ARE COMPLETED *(35–36 IS A
MECHANICAL DUMMY NECESSARY TO
PROVIDE A UNIQUE PAIR OF EVENT NUMBERS
FOR EACH ACTIVITY BETWEEN 34–36).*

Figure 2–2. Arrow diagrams representing activities and relationships between activities in a CPM schedule.

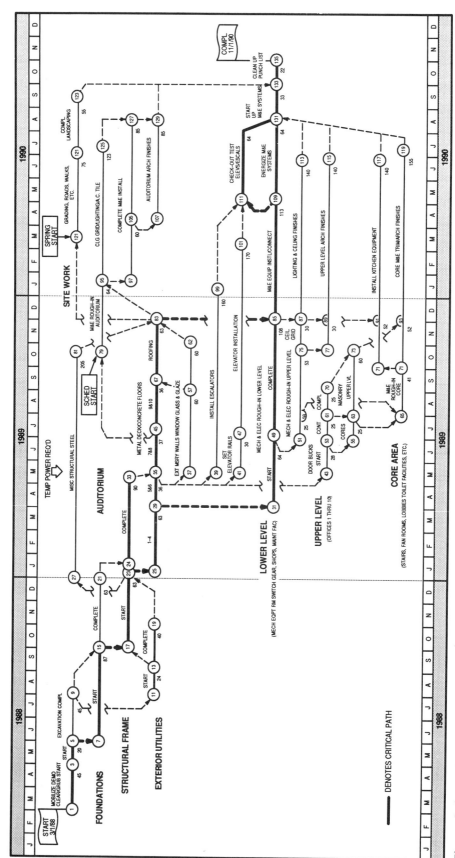

Figure 2–3. Basic CPM schedule for a 10-story office building.

Table 2-1

Computer Listing of Activity Data
I-J LISTING
(W/6 Holidays)

10 STORY OFFICE BUILDING
REPORT DATE: 03/27/90   RUN NO. 3

START DATE: 03/01/88
FINISH DATE: 11/01/90
DATA DATE: 03/01/88

Page No. 1

ACTIVITY PRED SUCC		ORIG DUR	REM DUR	PCT	ACTIVITY DESCRIPTION	EARLY START	EARLY FINISH	LATE START	LATE FINISH	TOTAL FLOAT
1	3	45	45	0	MOBILIZE/DEMOLITION/CLEAR/GRUB	01MAR88	02MAY88	01MAY88	02MAY88	0
3	5	20	20	0	START EXCAVATION	03MAY88	31MAY88	03MAY88	31MAY88	0
5	9	45	45	0	COMPLETE EXCAVATION	01JUN88	03AUG88	27JUN88	29AUG88	18
7	15	87	87	0	START FOUNDATIONS	01JUN88	03OCT88	01JUN88	03OCT88	11
11	13	24	24	0	START EXTERIOR UTILITIES	04AUG88	06SEP88	30AUG88	03OCT88	18
13	19	40	40	0	COMPLETE EXTERIOR UTILITIES	08SEP88	02NOV88	04NOV88	03JAN89	41
15	21	63	63	0	COMPLETE FOUNDATIONS	04OCT88	03JAN89	17OCT88	16JAN89	9
17	23	63	63	0	START STRUCTURAL FRAME	04OCT88	03JAN89	04OCT88	03JAN89	0
24	33	90	90	0	COMPLETE STRUCTURAL FRAME	04JAN89	09MAY89	17JAN89	22MAY89	9
25	29	63	63	0	METAL DECK/CONCRETE FLOORS 1-4	04JAN89	31MAR89	04JAN89	31MAR89	0
27	81	205	205	0	MISC. STRUCTURAL STEEL	04JAN89	20OCT89	15FEB89	04DEC89	30
29	35	36	36	0	METAL DECK/CONCRETE FLOORS 5,6,8	03APR89	22MAY89	03APR89	22MAY89	0
31	49	64	64	0	START MECH & ELEC R/I LOWER LEVEL	03APR89	20JUN89	03APR89	30JUN89	0
35	45	37	37	0	METAL DECK/CONCRETE FLOORS 7,8	23MAY89	14JUL89	23MAY89	14JUL89	0
37	57	60	60	0	EXT MSRY WALLS WINDOW GLASS & GLAZE	23MAY89	16AUG89	12JUN89	04SEP89	13
39	99	160	160	0	INSTALL ESCALATORS	23MAY89	09JAN90	28SEP89	14MAY90	89
41	47	30	30	0	SET ELEVATOR RAILS	23MAY89	05JUL89	07JUN89	19JUL89	10
43	53	28	28	0	START DOOR BUCKS	23MAY89	30JUN89	09JUN89	19JUL89	12
45	67	36	36	0	METAL DECK/CONCRETE FLOORS 8,9,10	17JUL89	04SEP89	17JUL89	04SEP89	0
47	101	170	170	0	ELEVATOR INSTALLATION	06JUL89	06MAR90	14SEP89	14MAY90	49
49	85	108	108	0	COMPL MECH & ELEC R/I LOWER LEVEL	03JUL89	04DEC89	03JUL89	04DEC89	0
51	59	25	25	0	BEG MECH & ELEC R/I UPPER LEVEL	03JUL89	07AUG89	20JUL89	23AUG89	12

§ 2.6 —CPM Pitfalls

The following pitfalls associated with CPM scheduling should be avoided or minimized:

Broad activity descriptions. The use of broad activity descriptions such as "start excavation," "continue excavation," and "complete excavation" should be kept to a minimum. Activity descriptions should be clear not only to the originator, but also to those who will use the network and computer tabulation and those who will be following the progress of the job.

Floating end dates. There are still a number of programs for computerized scheduling systems that allow floating end dates. This capability should be avoided. Because no contractual or fixed benchmark exists, performance is difficult to measure against floating end dates. Fixed end dates are, therefore, essential for best results.

Assuming unlimited resources. Planning a project under the assumption that unlimited resources are available should be avoided.

Omitting history. On large and complex projects, some CPM-users update the project schedule by simply zeroing out history prior to the status date and scheduling the balance of the project. Ignoring history by not taking the time to record actual dates and reflect an as-built schedule eliminates one of the primary benefits of network-based scheduling. The failure to maintain the integrity of the network logic in project updating can result in anomalies and incorrect results.[5]

Computer graphics limitations. Many CPM-users today try to avoid having to manually draw, periodically update, and maintain networks. Some users are led to believe that the network-based systems available

---

[5] For example, some monthly update menus allow the scheduler either to retain or to override the arrow diagram logic. If the logic is overridden, the computer program will break sequence restraints and reflect unrealistic prognostications of the remainder of the work for the project. Thus, when project restraints and logic are overridden, the update can continue to reflect large amounts of float although none exists or the project is negative.

In fact, proper scheduling practices absolutely require that actual start and finish dates be recorded in each monthly update and that logic ties not be broken or ignored unless the logic in the diagram is modified to reflect some new plan. Only with proper updating is it possible to provide the monthly visibility the executor of the project needs to react to events as they occur. Further, proper updating is imperative to the ability to perform "what if" calculations on a real-time basis dictated by recent decisions. *See, e.g.,* Santa Fe, Inc., VABCA No. 2168, 87-3 BCA ¶ 20,104 at 101,749, 101,760 (1987).

today can do almost anything when it comes to computer graphics. However, most are quite limited in terms of graphic output and the number of activities that can be plotted, particularly when time-scaled networks are desired. Graphic plotting can become complex because of the multiple predecessor and successor relationships of the activities.

Violating basic principles.   Essentially, all of the network-based systems available today are so sophisticated that they allow the CPM-user to violate the basic principles of planning and scheduling if the user so desires.

§ 2.7   Precedence Diagramming Method (PDM)

The *precedence diagramming method* was developed in 1964 by the H.B. Zachery Company in cooperation with IBM. Precedence is another networking technique and is basically a form of CPM. Use of the precedence method is very popular today because its techniques allow the user to avoid the use of dummy activities required in CPM networks to maintain logic relationships (see **Figure 2–2**). Its use for construction projects appears to be on the increase.

§ 2.8   —Precedence Fundamentals

Precedence activities consist of boxes or circular figures connected by zero-time lines, which provide a sense of direction flow. The phasing of activities is accomplished by the use of lead and lag times, sometimes called *logic connectors.* Dummy activities such as those used in CPM are not used in precedence diagramming. The calculation of event times and the reports that can be generated by precedence systems are essentially the same as those obtained from CPM.

Typical precedence relationships include start-to-start, end-to-end, end-to-start, delay start, delay finish, and the use of lead and lag connectors for establishing sequential relationships (see **Figure 2–4**). Note the use of both percentages and days as lead and lag times for phasing and sequencing activities. For example, the start of activity L is dependent on 25 percent completion of activity J. For activity O, 50 percent of its duration is based on the completion of activity M. The start of activity Q is dependent on five days of progress on activity P and 5 days of its remaining duration is dependent on the finish of activity P.

Figure 2–5 is an example of a simple precedence network. The lead and lag activities are expressed in either whole days or percentage of duration. Activity H represents an event time split; this activity has a start float of two days and a finish float of zero. Called *activity float splitting,* this

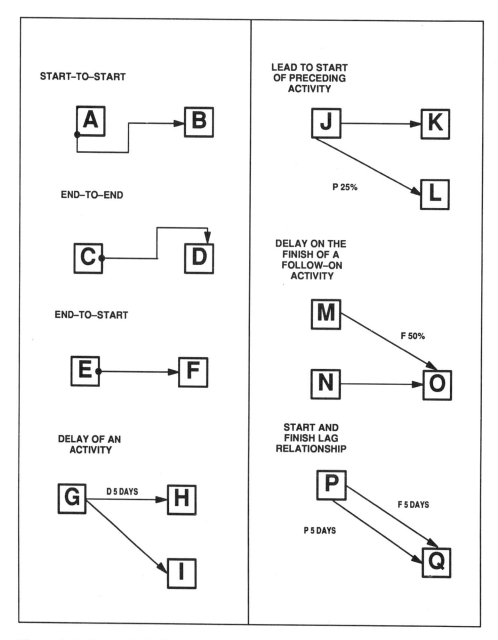

Figure 2-4. Typical relationships in precedence scheduling.

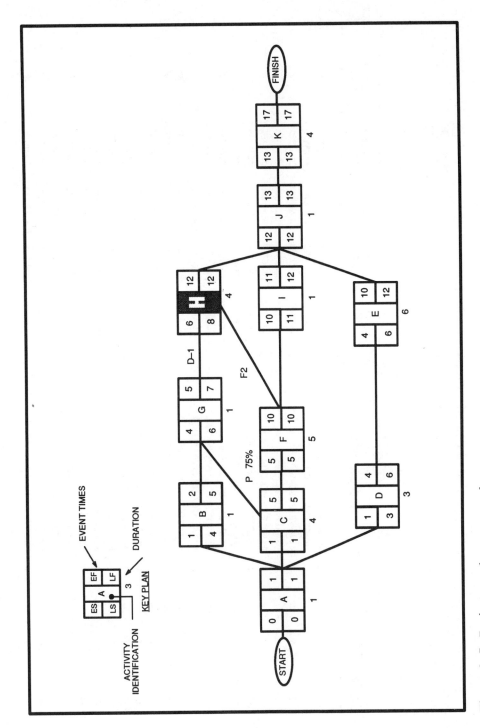

Figure 2–5. Basic precedence network.

31

Table 2-2

Activity Listing for Precedence Output

10 STORY OFFICE BUILDING
REPORT DATE: 03/27/90   RUN NO. 3

ACTIVITY LISTING
(W/6 Holidays)

START DATE: 03/01/88
FINISH DATE: 11/01/90
DATA DATE: 03/01/88

Page No. 1

ACTIVITY PRED SUCC	ORIG DUR	REM DUR	PCT	ACTIVITY DESCRIPTION	EARLY START	EARLY FINISH	LATE START	LATE FINISH	TOTAL FLOAT
1	45	45	0	MOBILIZE/DEMOLITION/CLEAR/GRUB	01MAR88	02MAY88	01MAR88	02MAY88	0
3	20	20	0	START EXCAVATION	03MAY88	31MAY88	03MAY88	31MAY88	0
5	45	45	0	COMPLETE EXCAVATION	01JUN88	03AUG88	27JUN88	29AUG88	18
7	87	87	0	START FOUNDATIONS	01JUN88	03OCT88	01JUN88	03OCT88	0
11	24	24	0	START EXTERIOR UTILITIES	04AUG88	06SEP88	30AUG88	03OCT88	18
13	40	40	0	COMPLETE EXTERIOR UTILITIES	08SEP88	02NOV88	04NOV88	03JAN89	41
15	63	63	0	COMPLETE FOUNDATIONS	04OCT88	03JAN89	17OCT88	16JAN89	9
17	63	63	0	START STRUCTURAL FRAME	04OCT88	03JAN89	04OCT88	03JAN89	0
24	90	90	0	COMPLETE STRUCTURAL FRAME	04JAN89	09MAY89	17JAN89	22MAY89	9
25	63	63	0	METAL DECK/CONCRETE FLOORS 1–4	04JAN89	31MAR89	04JAN89	31MAR89	0
27	205	205	0	MISC. STRUCTURAL STEEL	04JAN89	20OCT89	15FEB89	04DEC89	30
29	36	36	0	METAL DECK/CONCRETE FLOORS 5,6,8	03APR89	22MAY89	03APR89	22MAY89	0
31	64	64	0	START MECH & ELEC R/I LWR LVL	03APR89	20JUN89	03APR89	30JUN89	0
35	37	37	0	METAL DECK/CONCRETE FLOORS 7,8	23MAY89	14JUL89	23MAY89	14JUL89	0
37	60	60	0	BEG EXT MSRY WALLS WINDOW GLASS & GLAZE	23MAY89	16AUG89	12JUN89	04SEP89	13
39	160	160	0	INSTALL ESCALATORS	23MAY89	09JAN90	28SEP89	14MAY90	89
41	30	30	0	SET ELEVATOR RAILS	23MAY89	05JUL89	07JUN89	19JUL89	10
43	28	28	0	START DOOR BUCKS	23MAY89	30JUN89	09JUN89	19JUL89	12
45	36	36	0	METAL DECK/CONCRETE FLOORS 8,9,10	17JUL89	04SEP89	17JUL89	04SEP89	0
47	170	170	0	ELEVATOR INSTALLATION	06JUL89	06MAR90	14SEP89	14MAY90	49
49	108	108	0	COMPL MECH & ELEC R/I LWR LVL	03JUL89	04DEC89	03JUL89	04DEC89	0
51	25	25	0	BEG MECH & ELEC R/I UPPER LVL	03JUL89	07AUG89	20JUL89	23AUG89	12

occurs because the completion of activity H is dependent on the completion of activity F. A lag factor (F2) results in two days of activity H being dependent on the completion of activity F. Following the basic rules for calculating event times, the early start for activity H is project day six. Although the duration for activity H is only four days, activity H cannot finish until project day 12. The F2 lag factor controls the scheduled finish of activity H.

Table 2–2 is an example of an activity listing for precedence output. In comparing Table 2–2 with Table 2–1, the only differences are the activity references at the far left. Table 2–1 refers to start and finish nodes for each activity. Table 2–2 refers only to an activity number.

§ 2.9   —Precedence Pitfalls

Most of the pitfalls associated with CPM apply also to the precedence method. However, other complications can arise from the use of precedence methods. For example, activities that are not properly sequenced by lead or lag times may produce a confused situation. Thus, it is possible that a follow-on activity might be scheduled for earlier completion than its predecessor, which should logically be completed first (see Figure 2–6).

In addition, improper activity-splitting can cause the period between the start and finish dates of an activity to be greater than the activity duration assigned. This results in the calculation of erroneous float time. For an example of activity-splitting, see the calculations for activity H in Figure 2–5.

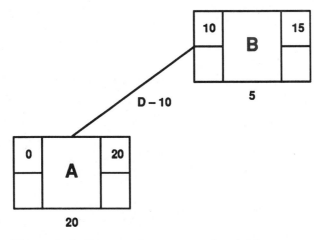

Figure 2–6. Improperly sequenced activities.

CHAPTER 3

DEVELOPING AND MAINTAINING THE PROJECT SCHEDULE

§ 3.1   Introduction
§ 3.2   Choosing the Right Scheduling Method
§ 3.3   Developing Schedule Specifications
§ 3.4   Responsibility for Schedule Preparation
§ 3.5   Role of General Contractor
§ 3.6   Role of Subcontractor
§ 3.7   Requirements for Successful Scheduling
§ 3.8   Planning Phase
§ 3.9   —Preparing the Activity List
§ 3.10   —Level of Detail
§ 3.11   Scheduling Phase
§ 3.12   —Activity Durations
§ 3.13   —Computation of Event Times
§ 3.14   Float Identification and Computation
§ 3.15   —Total Float
§ 3.16   —Free Float
§ 3.17   —Independent Float
§ 3.18   —Float Allocation Possibilities
§ 3.19   Computerization of Project Schedule
§ 3.20   —Popular Systems Used for Major Projects
§ 3.21   —Getting Started
§ 3.22   —Inputting Network Information
§ 3.23   —Guidelines for Data Takeoff
§ 3.24   —Computer Outputs
§ 3.25   Schedule Submittal and Approval
§ 3.26   —Schedule Review
§ 3.27   —Procedures for Schedule Review and Approval

§ 3.28   How to Update the Project Schedule

§ 3.29   —Need for Updating

§ 3.30   —Preparing to Update

§ 3.31   —Joint Update Meetings

§ 3.32   Management Reporting and Documentation

§ 3.33   —Problem-Identification Philosophy

§ 3.34   —Need for Good Project Records

§ 3.35   —Cash Flow Forecasting and Progress Payment Records

§ 3.36   —Use of Summary Networks

§ 3.37   Checklist for Effective Schedule Implementation

§ 3.38   —Pitfalls in Scheduling Systems

§ 3.1   Introduction

Prior to 1957, construction projects were traditionally scheduled by the bar chart method or on an ad hoc basis by those responsible for project completion. Since then, new and powerful techniques to plan, schedule, and control projects have grown from theory to widespread acceptance. Generally referred to as *networking techniques,* these new methods have been successfully applied to a wide variety of construction projects, both large and small. Today they are considered to be the most dynamic and effective management tools available to the construction industry.

§ 3.2   Choosing the Right Scheduling Method

One of the key decisions to be made before a project begins is which scheduling method is best-suited to the project. Frequently, the owner and designer decide on scheduling requirements as a part of the planning process for a project and the process of drafting specifications for bidding or negotiation. In making this decision, consideration should be given to:

1. The size and location of the project
2. Project phases and their timing
3. The number of parties to act as prime contractors
4. The need date for completion of certain milestones and the project as a whole
5. The experience of the owner, the architect/engineer, or the construction manager in the use of specific scheduling techniques
6. The capabilities and experience of the prime contractor(s) in preparing and implementing the project schedule required

7. The type and quality of data desired by the owner, architect/engineer, construction manager, or contractor to effectively plan, schedule, coordinate, monitor, appraise, and document the progress of the project

8. The amount of owner-furnished or third-party-furnished material and equipment involved.

Regardless of the scheduling system chosen, the owner or the owner's agent responsible for managing the project should have experience with the scheduling method selected. Next, a determination should be made regarding who will draft the specification and what it should include with respect to the responsibility for schedule preparation, approval, and implementation and to procedures for updating, reporting progress, and time extensions.

§ 3.3 Developing Schedule Specifications

After an owner or agent has chosen the proper scheduling technique, such as the critical path method (CPM), the precedence diagramming method (PDM), or the bar chart method, it is important to the success of the project that specifications outlining the scheduling requirements be carefully prepared and incorporated into the contract. Including such requirements will enable an owner to more effectively control and enforce the scheduling obligations of the parties involved.

Schedule specifications should be clear and concise, avoiding ambiguities and potential misunderstandings. Unfortunately, this is not often the case. Frequently, specifiers have little knowledge of the scheduling technique being specified and the responsibilities and liabilities they can incur (see **Chapter 4**).

Experience has shown that it is very difficult to establish standard schedule specifications for use by the construction industry today. For example, specifications may range from one paragraph to five or ten pages. The short ones are dangerous, and the long ones are expensive. However, experience also has shown that the more detail included in the specifications, the better chance there is to eliminate misunderstandings.

Good schedule specifications set forth the type of schedule that will be in effect for the project. Specifically, they address:

_____ 1. The scheduling method and techniques to be used
_____ 2. Which party has responsibility for preparing the schedule
_____ 3. Coordination of any multiple-contract situations that will exist on the project

_____ **4.** The amount or level of schedule detail required by the specification

_____ **5.** The need to incorporate all contractually specified milestones. This may include completion dates for critical components of work, deliveries of equipment, dates for promised information (such as owner-tenant layouts), dates for access to the project, and availability dates for key work areas (where renovation proceeds in existing facilities)

_____ **6.** The need for the contractor to identify dependencies that will restrain performance

_____ **7.** Processing procedures for shop drawings (preparation, submission, and approval)

_____ **8.** Processing procedures for submittals (initial and updates, plus frequency)

_____ **9.** Procedures for review and approval of the schedule

_____ **10.** Remedies for noncompliance (for initial schedule as well as updates)

_____ **11.** Updating procedures (specifying frequency, requirements for joint updating meetings between parties, the keeping of meeting minutes, data requirements, and methods for incorporating time-impact analyses and time extensions as part of the updating process)

_____ **12.** Progress reports

_____ **13.** Whether or not the schedule will be used for determining progress payments

_____ **14.** Procedures for justification of time extensions (using *time impact analysis*)

_____ **15.** Float utilization and availability to project and parties

_____ **16.** Involvement of subcontractors in the scheduling process.

§ 3.4 Responsibility for Schedule Preparation

Once the project delivery system and scheduling methods have been selected, the party responsible for preparing the project schedule must be designated. In the traditional approach, for example, an owner requires a general contractor to prepare the schedule. In addition, the owner has the option to require the general contractor to submit the schedule either for formal approval or for informational purposes only.

Under such circumstances, the general contractor also has options. For example, the general contractor may choose to prepare the schedule in-house or contract the services of a scheduling consultant to provide technical assistance if the required skills and experience are not available in the general contractor organization. On occasion, an owner may specify that the general contractor hire a scheduling consultant and sometimes the owner may even insist on approving the use of any consultant selected by the contractor.

Since many contracted parties lack the necessary skills required for successful scheduling, an owner may choose instead to provide to the contractor a scheduling consultant and may even pay for this service. This option also offers alternatives. For example, the scheduling consultant can work with the contracted party(s) and assist in developing a schedule for all work contracted; the resultant schedule can then be submitted by the contractor(s) to the owner for formal approval or informally agreed to by the owner. The scheduling specifications should include information on whether the schedule submittal requires a formal approval by the owner.

When an owner contracts the services of a construction manager as his agent, the construction manager is frequently responsible for overall scheduling and coordination when multiple-trade or multiple-prime contracts are used. As a result, the construction manager has several options for schedule development and implementation.

The construction manager may prepare an overall, detailed master schedule for the project. This type of schedule would usually be supported by milestone schedules and/or prebid integrated schedules for each of the key multiple prime or trade contracts that are anticipated to be let with this method of project delivery.

As trade contracts are let, the construction manager has the option to require each trade contractor to participate jointly in the development of the trade contract schedule. The objective is to reflect the trade contractors' plans and intentions to execute their work and to coordinate their dependencies with others.

The alternative to this procedure is to require trade contractors to prepare their own schedules, based on certain basic information provided by the construction manager, and submit them to the construction manager for approval.

After approval, the construction manager has the option to incorporate the trade contractors' schedules into the detailed master schedule or to maintain them separately. From the detailed information, a time-scaled *master summary control schedule* may be developed by the construction manager to provide management with overall project visibility and a management tool for use in periodic briefings and reports.

When design-build and guaranteed-maximum-price (GMP) construction manager project delivery systems are used, the scheduling options available to the design-build contractor and the GMP construction manager are basically the same as with the agency construction manager. **Figure 3–1** presents a summary of common methods and options that have been used by the construction industry to assign responsibility for schedule preparation, implementation, and control.

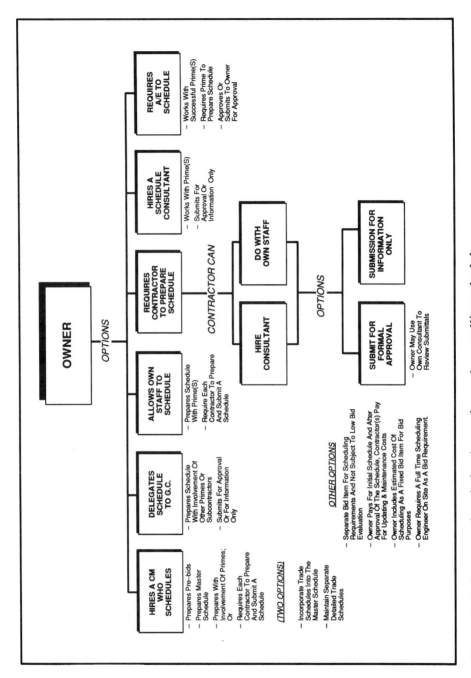

Figure 3-1. Owner options in implementing and controlling schedule.

40

§ 3.5 Role of General Contractor

Where the owner or construction manager specifies that a general contractor is responsible for preparing a project schedule, the contractor is obligated to develop, implement, and maintain the schedule in accordance with the schedule specifications included in the contract. In such cases, the contractor must commit to making the schedule work and to ensuring that staff members are equally committed and confident in their ability to respond to the scheduling requirements specified in the contract. If necessary, technical assistance, as well as formal or informal staff training, may be necessary and desirable.

If one of the network techniques is specified as the scheduling method to be used, it should immediately be determined whether the contractor has the technical capability and experience essential to schedule preparation and assuring contract compliance. If such capabilities are limited or do not exist, consideration should be given to hiring a scheduling consultant. The scheduling consultant can work with the contractor's staff and develop the plans and intentions of the contractor in the scheduling method specified by the contract. The consultant also can assist with the updates that follow and provide any necessary training.

The contractor should be committed to using the schedule to plan and execute the work specified by the contract. A commitment should also be made to using the schedule for monitoring progress, assessing alternative plans, documenting actual performance, periodically reporting, and preparing time impacts as supporting data for all time-extension requests.

The prime contractor is encouraged to involve major subcontractors and suppliers in the development and periodic updatings of the schedule. All major subcontractors should be required to furnish to the contractor the network logic and activity durations for their scope of work as input for overall schedule development. Particular attention should be paid to defining the dependency relationships between the contractor and subcontractor or other parties involved. In addition, it may be necessary for each subcontractor to provide information on estimated labor (by craft) and the estimated cost associated with each activity.

Once the initial schedule is developed by the contractor, it should be reviewed with each major subcontractor and supplier and then transmitted to each in writing with a request that any disagreements be submitted within a specified period of time. Agreement and commitment to the schedule is essential in developing and maintaining a good relationship between the contractor and his subcontractors and suppliers. Such agreements also will help avoid or minimize claims that the contractor's schedule was unrealistic or was forced upon the subcontractor.

The contractor also should involve his subcontractors and suppliers in the periodic updating process and in the preparation of time-extension analyses to ensure the overall schedule is properly maintained and reflects accurate projections.

§ 3.6   Role of Subcontractor

Most subcontracts include language that requires subcontractors to agree that they will not interfere with the work of others and that they will follow the progress of the work. Even if the contract lacks such express language, there is an implied obligation of the subcontractor to act reasonably to follow the work and begin when notified, as long as reasonable instructions are provided.[1] As a result, subcontractors should have a sincere interest in participating in the development and implementation of the prime contractor's schedule.

Unfortunately, many contractors fail to involve their subcontractors in the development and implementation of their schedules. Some contractors mistakenly believe that better control of the subcontractor is achieved this way. Some even believe that the subcontractor is prevented from taking advantage of the prime contractor or other subcontractors when he is not involved in the development and maintenance of the overall schedule. This view has not been shared by certain courts.[2]

If a subcontractor knows that the prime contractor is required by the owner to prepare a contract schedule, yet the prime contractor makes no effort to involve the subcontractor, the subcontractor is advised to request to be allowed to participate in developing the contractor's schedule. This participation should include, at a minimum, the work subcontracted. As an alternative, the subcontractor can prepare a plan and schedule for the work being subcontracted and send it to the prime contractor, preferably before the prime contractor is required to submit an overall schedule to the owner. The subcontractor's schedule should demonstrate the planned sequence of work anticipated, the estimated duration of each activity, the expected manpower, and the cost of each activity (if required) to be included in the schedule.

The schedule should identify the key dependencies between the subcontractor and the prime contractor or other subcontractors and suppliers involved with the subcontractor's work. If the prime contractor fails to involve the subcontractor in the development of the initial schedule, the subcontractor should go on record, by written notification to the prime contractor, confirming that the subcontractor requested to participate in

---

[1] Peter Kiewit & Sons Co. v. Iowa S. Utils. Co., 355 F. Supp. 376 (S.D. Iowa 1973); McCarty Corp. v. Pullman-Kellogg, 571 F. Supp. 1341 (M.D. La. 1983).

[2] *See* United States v. F.D. Rich Co., 439 F.2d 895 (8th Cir. 1971); Kroeger v. Franchise Equities, Inc., 190 Neb. 731, 212 N.W.2d 348 (1973).

the schedule preparation to develop reasonable dependency logic and durations. In addition, the notification from the subcontractor should establish the position that the resultant schedule may not reflect the planned sequence, assumed dependencies, and durations for specific activities anticipated by the subcontractor. The subcontractor also should insist on being involved in the periodic updates of the schedule and on receiving copies of all updates or revisions prepared and issued by the prime contractor.

The subcontractor should be cognizant of the prime contractor's responsibilities to subcontractors. For example, the prime contractor is obligated to prepare a schedule reflecting a normal and reasonable durations sequence.[3] The contractor is also obligated to perform so that the subcontractors are able to perform their tasks according to the established schedule, subject to reasonable revisions.[4] Further, the prime contractor is also obligated not to vary the schedule so that his subcontractors are adversely affected, even though the owner may consent to such variance.[5] However, the prime contractor does not guarantee that all activities will be performed exactly as planned. A prime contractor's performance need only be "within the bounds of reason" and in general accord with the project schedule.[6]

§ 3.7 Requirements for Successful Scheduling

There are advantages and disadvantages to each of the methods of schedule preparation and implementation identified in **Figure 3–1**. Although success has been achieved using all of these methods, each has had its own failures, due primarily to various user-oriented reasons.

Experience has shown that on fixed-price or lump-sum contracts, the best results have been achieved when the contractor is responsible for schedule preparation and maintenance, with the owner or the owner's agent reserving the right to approve the initial schedule.

This assignment of responsibility makes eminent sense considering the risks involved. On a fixed-price or lump-sum contract, the general contractor, in establishing its price, makes a number of assumptions based on the manner by which it can perform the required work at a lower cost

---

[3] *See* United States *ex rel.* Heller Elec. Co. v. William F. Klingensmith, Inc., 670 F.2d 1227 (D.C. Cir. 1982); Able Elec. Co. v. Vacanti & Randazzo Constr. Co., 212 Neb. 619, 324 N.W.2d 667 (1982).

[4] *See* Illinois Structural Steel Corp. v. Pathman Constr. Co., 23 Ill. App. 3d 1, 318 N.E.2d 232 (1974).

[5] Natkin & Co. v. George A. Fuller Co., 347 F. Supp. 17 (W.D. Mo. 1972).

[6] Southern Fireproofing Co. v. R.F. Ball Constr. Co., 334 F.2d 122 (8th Cir. 1964).

than the competition. Therefore, the general contractor is in the best position to plan and schedule its work and the work of the subcontractors and suppliers. If the general contractor lacks the technical capability to develop this information, there is always the option to hire a scheduling consultant to convert the plans and intentions to the scheduling technique specified in the contract.

When multiple prime contracts are involved in project delivery, the responsibility for overall schedule preparation is best left to the owner or the owner's agent. The owner is the only party with the authority and economic power to schedule and coordinate the multiple prime contractors involved. This does not, of course, preclude specifying and allowing the prime contractors to develop their own schedules for their own portions of the work and then monitoring them separately, or on an integrated basis, throughout the life of the project.

When a design-build contractor or a construction manager providing a GMP is involved, the contractor or construction manager should be directly responsible for scheduling and coordination of the work.

Regardless of the schedule preparation method chosen, the degree of success will depend on five key conditions:

1. All parties need to commit to making the schedule work.
2. A good scheduling specification must be prepared that properly communicates to all parties their contractually required responsibilities, methods, and procedures for scheduling.
3. Once the schedule is agreed upon, it must be implemented and periodically updated to reflect current status and how the remaining work is to be completed.
4. Timely and accurate submissions of delay analyses by all parties involved are a must to keep the schedule properly adjusted for excusable delay. Each party should strive to maintain a correct posture for the time of performance.
5. The owner, or the party having the responsibility for overall schedule and coordination and the economic power to enforce the schedule, must ensure schedule compliance by the various parties involved so as not to delay another party.

§ 3.8 Planning Phase

There is a basic rule to be followed in the development of schedules: The planning function should be separated from the scheduling function. Planning involves the development of an activity list and the arrangement of the activities in their logical sequence of execution.

§ 3.9   —Preparing the Activity List

A key step in the planning process is the development of an *activity list* of tasks to be performed. This is usually accomplished through meetings between the scheduling engineer and key project personnel. The purpose of these meetings is to obtain a comprehensive understanding of the overall project and its requirements and to review and analyze the various project documents as sources of activity and task information. One or more visits to the jobsite can be helpful in grasping the physical characteristics and noting any limitations of the site that must be considered as part of the planning process.

After the essential information is obtained and understood, the scheduling engineer establishes a work breakdown structure and organizes the overall project into major phases or subproject elements. For example, a work breakdown structure for a multistory building would include such subproject elements as site work, utilities, foundation, structural frame, roof, floor systems, exterior walls, electrical, mechanical, heating-ventilation-air conditioning (HVAC), elevators, interior finishes, life-safety systems, lobby, etc.

Once the subproject elements are identified, the scheduling engineer begins the development of a detailed activity list (breakdown of subtasks) for each subproject element. The objective is to establish appropriate levels of indenture (detail) for planning, scheduling, monitoring, controlling, and reporting on the overall project. The work breakdown structure and the levels of indenture established for the project should allow information to be accurately transferred from one level of indenture to another.

§ 3.10   —Level of Detail

The appropriate level of detail should be determined by including as many activities as seem necessary to effectively plan, schedule, and control the overall project. A specified minimum or maximum number of activities can be helpful, but it is not always the answer. Guidelines for determining the level of activity detail include:

1. The work breakdown structure established for the project (subproject areas, phases, functions, features of work, cost elements, and so forth)
2. The type of work to be performed and the labor trades involved
3. All purchase, manufacture, and delivery activities for major material and equipment
4. Deliveries of owner-furnished equipment or materials

5. All shop drawing preparation, submission, and approval activities
6. Approval required from third parties
7. Plans for all subcontract or trade contract work
8. Assignment of responsibility for performing activities
9. Access and availability to work areas
10. Identification of interfaces and dependencies with subcontractors and preceding or follow-on contractors
11. Contract milestones and completion dates
12. Tests and submission of test-results activities
13. Planning for phased or total takeover by the owner
14. Identification of any manpower or construction equipment restrictions.

After the activity lists are made, the scheduling engineer begins to rough out the logical sequence for each subproject element. This results in the development of a series of subnetworks. The next step is to tie the individual subnetworks into one overall, integrated, master-plan network for the project. The integrated plan is then reviewed in detail to ensure that all proper interfaces and dependencies between subnetworks and related activities have been incorporated. At this point, the integrated plan is then reviewed with key project personnel for validation of planned intentions. Upon acceptance, the initial planning phase is complete.

§ 3.11   Scheduling Phase

The scheduling phase follows the planning phase and involves the estimation of time durations for each activity in the network and the computation of start and finish dates for each activity.

§ 3.12   —Activity Durations

The next task in the schedule development process is to prepare a time estimate for each activity in the network.

Activity duration time estimates may be measured in working hours, days, weeks, or comparable units. The only suggested requirement is that the same unit of time be employed throughout the network. There are computer programs today that can handle variable-unit time estimates, but this capability is seldom used and is considered by many to be an exception rather than a rule.

The importance of accurate activity time estimates cannot be overemphasized, since all network calculations will be based upon them.

Consequently, the network time calculations will be only as valid as the initial estimates. Developing reliable estimates for each activity obviously can be a difficult task. Guidelines for estimating activity durations include the following:

1. Consider each activity independently.
2. Base all durations on a normal workday. Consider the desired crew size and equipment and material requirements and their availability. If overtime is required, indicate it on the specific activities in the network.
3. Take into consideration physical conditions, safety requirements, and any labor agreements that may be in effect.
4. Use standard time units.
5. Talk to the person or group responsible for activity execution. This most likely will be the most knowledgeable source of performance information available.
6. Check information sources such as the project cost estimate, project scope of work, equipment list, data from historical projects, labor productivity standards, suppliers, government agencies, unions, consultants, customs, and so forth.
7. Don't guess. Be analytical and systematic. Try using reliable construction reference manuals or similar sources of cost data.
8. Skip around the network when assigning duration estimates to specific activities. Don't follow a path of activities all the way through the network.
9. Obtain written duration estimates from each trade contractor or subcontractor involved in the project. When necessary, get schedules from trade contractors or subcontractors that show their plans and dependencies with the prime contractor or other involved parties. This is best achieved when it is a requirement of a contract scheduling specification. Unfortunately, many prime contractors keep subcontractors in the dark as to the project schedule.

§ 3.13   —Computation of Event Times

Once durations have been assigned to each activity, the next task is to schedule the project. This requires establishing the early start and finish dates and the late start and finish dates for each activity in the network, a process which is normally done with a computer. However, it can be performed manually for small networks without too much difficulty. A rule of thumb is to use a computer for a network of more than 250 activities. Regardless of whether it is done manually or by computer, the early dates are determined by a passing forward through the network and adding the durations of all activities along their respective paths. This process establishes the earliest possible starts and finishes for each activity, assuming that all preceding activities are accomplished by their early dates. The late dates are similarly determined, but by a backward pass through the network of activities. The late start and late finish dates are the latest allowable dates by which an activity can be performed without impacting a fixed milestone or completion date. The event times are usually computed by number of project days from the beginning of the project. Once computed, they can be converted to calendar dates.

There are five basic ground rules in computing event times and project duration by CPM:

1. The early start time for an activity is based on the highest lapse-time cumulative count for all activities of a path or paths of activities converging at the start of a successor activity (an event) on a forward pass.

2. The early finish time for an activity is the early start time plus the duration of the activity for which you want to determine the early finish.

3. The late finish time is based on the lowest lapse-time cumulative count for all the paths of activities converging at an event on a backward pass through the network.

4. The late start time for an activity is the late finish time minus the duration of the activity for which you want to determine the late start.

5. The project duration is the result of the longest path of activities through the network. This is the critical path.

Figure 3–2 illustrates the principles for computation of the early event times for a network. This is accomplished by following the various paths of activities forward through the network and adding the durations of the activities along the respective paths for which events are being computed. Where two or more paths intersect at an event, the highest cumulative count entering the event is continued forward along succeeding paths of activities. In **Figure 3–2**, for example, three paths intersect at event No. 14. The cumulative-days count along the path of activities 1-2, 2-3, 3-7, 7-9, and 9-14 is 43. The cumulative-days count along the path of activities 1-2, 2-3, 3-7, 7-11, and 11-14 is 28. And the cumulative-days count along the path of activities 1-2, 2-3, 3-8, 8-10, 10-13, and 13-14 is 35. Since 43 is the highest cumulative count coming forward into event 14, then the early start of activity 14-15 is project day 43. The controlling early count for each event is shown in the squares. The longest path through the network

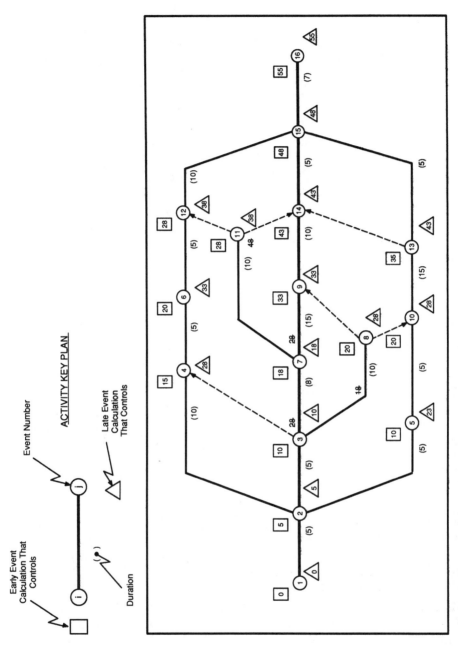

Figure 3–2. Network diagram showing early and late activity dates.

49

Table 3–1

Activity Listing in Project Days

I	J	Duration	Early Start	Early Finish	Late Start	Late Finish
* 1	2	5	0	5	0	5
* 2	3	5	5	10	5	10
2	4	10	5	15	18	28
2	5	5	5	10	18	23
3	4	0	10	10	28	28
* 3	7	8	10	18	10	18
3	8	10	10	20	18	28
4	6	5	15	20	28	33
5	10	5	10	15	23	28
6	12	5	20	25	33	38
* 7	9	15	18	33	18	33
7	11	10	18	28	28	38
8	9	0	20	20	33	33
8	10	0	20	20	28	28
* 9	14	10	33	43	33	43
10	13	15	20	35	28	43
11	12	0	28	28	38	38
11	14	0	28	28	43	43
12	15	10	28	38	38	48
13	14	0	35	35	43	43
13	15	5	35	40	43	48
*14	15	5	43	48	43	48
*15	16	7	48	55	48	55

* Critical path activity

is made up of activities 1-2, 2-3, 3-7, 7-9, 9-14, 14-15, and 15-16. The project duration is 55 days.

Figure 3–2 also illustrates the computation of late event times for a network. The process of computing late dates is essentially the same, except that the cumulative count is on a backward pass through the network of activities, totals are subtracted from the project duration (in this figure, 55 days), and the controlling factor is the lowest count coming back into an event.

In **Figure 3–2**, for example, two backward paths intersect at event 11. The backward cumulative-days count along the path of activities 15-16, 14-15, and 11-14 is 43. The backward cumulative days along the path of activities 15-16, 12-15, and 11-12 is 38. Since 38 is the lowest cumulative count coming into event 11, the latest finish for event 11 is project day 38. The controlling late finish count for each event is shown in the triangles.

Table 3–1 is an activity listing and tabulation of the early start and finish and late start and finish dates for each activity in the network.[7] Event times are shown in project days. For example, the earliest that activity 3-8 can start is project day 10. The latest it can start and not disrupt any succeeding activities is project day 18.

Table 3–2 is a project day conversion calendar. The calendar is a simple matrix of project days versus calendar days. A project calendar should be set up before any schedule calculations are made. Note that certain calendar days, such as weekends or holidays, are omitted when counting project days. Such a matrix may be set up for any project based on the dates that are to be used and omitted. Nonwork project days usually include weekends, holidays, and certain vacation days. Exceptions can normally be established when work must be performed on specified nonwork days. In addition, when scheduled holidays fall on a weekend, they normally are automatically moved to the next workday in the calendar year.

All network calculations are made in project days. Once these calculations are made, they are converted to calendar dates.

§ 3.14   Float Identification and Computation

Once the event times for a network of activities are computed, boundaries can be established for each activity. These boundaries are the early start (ES) and the late finish (LF) of the activity. The difference between the maximum time available to perform an activity and the duration of the activity is known as *total float* (see **Figure 3–3**). Float is the result of the interrelationships and interdependencies of the paths of activities that make up a network. It is the contingency time that is associated with a path or chain of activities. **Table 3–3** shows an activity listing like that in **Table 3–1**, but with a total float column added.

Three types of float can be measured in a basic network: *total float, free float,* and *independent float*. The difference between them is the manner in which they affect other activities in the network. Total float is the most commonly used. Free float and independent float do not lend themselves to common use, but an understanding of their computation is suggested.

---

[7] "I" and "J" refer to the start and finish events for an activity. They are identities used by the originators of the critical path method. There is nothing significant about the terms "I" and "J"; "A" and "B" could have been used. These are industry-accepted terms. Some software programmers use "I" and "J" (see **Fig. 3–2**); others may refer to "predecessor" and "successor."

Table 3–2
Project Day—Calendar Day Conversion Matrix

YEAR	MONDAY	TUESDAY	WEDNESDAY	THURSDAY	FRIDAY	SATURDAY	SUNDAY
1990	01-01OCT	02-02OCT	03-03OCT	04-04OCT	00-28SEP	NWD-29SEP	NWD-30SEP
1990	06-08OCT	07-09OCT	08-10OCT	09-11OCT	05-05OCT	NWD-06OCT	NWD-07OCT
1990	11-15OCT	12-16OCT	13-17OCT	14-18OCT	10-12OCT	NWD-13OCT	NWD-14OCT
1990	16-22OCT	17-23OCT	18-24OCT	19-25OCT	15-19OCT	NWD-20OCT	NWD-21OCT
1990	21-29OCT	22-30OCT	23-31OCT	24-01NOV	20-26OCT	NWD-27OCT	NWD-28OCT
1990	26-05NOV	27-06NOV	28-07NOV	29-08NOV	25-02NOV	NWD-03NOV	NWD-04NOV
1990	31-12NOV	32-13NOV	33-14NOV	34-15NOV	30-09NOV	NWD-10NOV	NWD-11NOV
1990	36-19NOV	37-20NOV	38-21NOV	HOL22NOV	35-16NOV	NWD-17NOV	NWD-18NOV
1990	40-26NOV	41-27NOV	42-28NOV	43-29NOV	39-23NOV	NWD-24NOV	NWD-25NOV
1990	45-03DEC	46-04DEC	47-05DEC	48-06DEC	44-30NOV	NWD-01DEC	NWD-02DEC
1990	50-10DEC	51-11DEC	52-12DEC	53-13DEC	49-07DEC	NWD-08DEC	NWD-09DEC
1990	55-17DEC	56-18DEC	57-19DEC	58-20DEC	54-14DEC	NWD-15DEC	NWD-16DEC
1990	HOL24DEC	HOL25DEC	60-26DEC	61-27DEC	59-21DEC	NWD-22DEC	NWD-23DEC
1990	HOL31DEC	HOL01JAN	63-02JAN	64-03JAN	62-28DEC	NWD-29DEC	NWD-30DEC
1991	66-07JAN	67-08JAN	68-09JAN	69-10JAN	65-04JAN	NWD-05JAN	NWD-06JAN
1991	71-14JAN	72-15JAN	73-16JAN	74-17JAN	70-11JAN	NWD-12JAN	NWD-13JAN
1991					75-18JAN	NWD-19JAN	NWD-20JAN

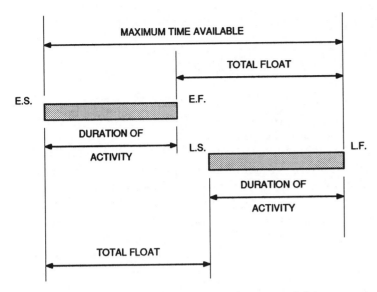

Figure 3–3. Determining total float for activities.

Table 3–3

Activity Listing Showing Total Float

I	J	Duration	Early Start	Early Finish	Late Start	Late Finish	Total Float
* 1	2	5	0	5	0	5	0
* 2	3	5	5	10	5	10	0
2	4	10	5	15	18	28	13
2	5	5	5	10	18	23	13
3	4	0	10	10	28	28	18
* 3	7	8	10	18	10	18	0
3	8	10	10	20	18	28	8
4	6	5	15	20	28	33	13
5	10	5	10	15	23	28	13
6	12	5	20	25	33	38	13
* 7	9	15	18	33	18	33	0
7	11	10	18	28	28	38	10
8	9	0	20	20	33	33	13
8	10	0	20	20	28	28	8
* 9	14	10	33	43	33	43	0
10	13	15	20	35	28	43	8
11	12	0	28	28	38	38	10
11	14	0	28	28	43	43	15
12	15	10	28	38	38	48	10
13	14	0	35	35	43	43	8
13	15	5	35	40	43	48	8
*14	15	5	43	48	43	48	0
*15	16	7	48	55	48	55	0

* Critical path activity

53

§ 3.15   —Total Float

Total float can be measured along a path of activities by comparing the difference between the early and late start dates or the early and late finish dates for an activity in a float path.

When the initial project schedule is computed, it is possible that the completion date determined will be later than the desired or scheduled completion date. This essentially means there is less time to implement the project than is required. As a result, a condition of *negative float* can exist.

When a project schedule is updated and actual start and finish dates for various activities are incorporated into the schedule, there may be situations where certain events are completed behind schedule. If the project completion date is not adjusted, the early event times for some of the remaining activities may be computed to be later than the late start and finish dates. This can also cause a condition of negative float.

In either case, time may be recouped by increasing resources, double-shifting, extending shifts, changing planned work sequences, or by similar managerial manipulations so that the original or current completion date can be achieved.

To demonstrate negative float, **Table 3–4** updates the schedule in **Table 3–3** with actual start and completion dates, as of report date 11/13/90 (project day 32). Note that three activities (7-9, 10-13, and 12-15) are still in progress as of the report date. The remaining durations are the estimates of time to complete activities reported to have started and remaining in progress as of the status date. Note also the use of remaining durations for these three activities and their projected completion influence on successor activity early start and early finish event times and float calculations.

§ 3.16   —Free Float

Free float can be used without affecting the early start time of all succeeding activities. For example, in a situation where two or more activities join, free float can be measured by subtracting the early finish date of the activity for which you want to determine the free float from the early start of the successor activity. See **Figure 3–4**. In other words, free float is the amount of time activity A can be delayed without delaying the earliest start of activity C.

§ 3.17   —Independent Float

Independent float, too, can be used without affecting the early start time of all succeeding activities; in this case, however, the previous job can be

Table 3–4
Activity Listing Showing Actual Dates, Negative Float, and Activity Variance

I	J	Scheduled/ Remaining Duration	Early Start	Early Finish	Late Start	Late Finish	Total Remaining Float
* 1	2	5	09/28/90A	10/05/90A			
* 2	3	5	10/05/90A	10/12/90A			
2	4	10	10/05/90A	10/19/90A			
2	5	5	10/05/90A	10/12/90A			
3	4	0	10/12/90A	10/12/90A			
* 3	7	8	10/12/90A	10/24/90A			
3	8	10	10/12/90A	10/26/90A			
4	6	8	10/19/90A	10/26/90A			
5	10	15	10/12/90A	10/19/90A			
6	12	5	10/26/90A	11/02/90A			
* 7	9	8	10/24/90A	**11/26/90		11/14/90	−7
7	11	3	10/24/90A	11/07/90A			
8	9	0	10/26/90A	10/26/90A			
8	10	0	10/26/90A	10/26/90A			
* 9	14	10	11/26/90	**12/10/90	11/14/90	11/29/90	−7
10	13	5	10/26/90A	11/20/90		11/29/90	+6
11	12	0	11/07/90A	11/07/90A			
11	14	0	11/07/90A	11/07/90A			
12	15	7	11/07/90A	11/23/90	11/29/90	12/06/90	+9
13	14	0	11/20/90	11/20/90	11/29/90	11/29/90	+6
13	15	5	11/20/90	11/28/90	11/29/90	12/06/90	+6
*14	15	5	12/10/90	**12/17/90		12/06/90	−7
*15	16	7	12/17/90	**12/28/90	12/06/90	12/17/90	−7

* Critical path activity
** Denotes dates later than late finish
A Denotes actual start or finish date

Update report period 11/13/90
(Project day 32)

55

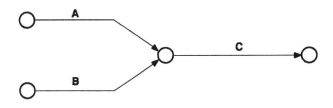

Free float activity "A" = ESc – EFA

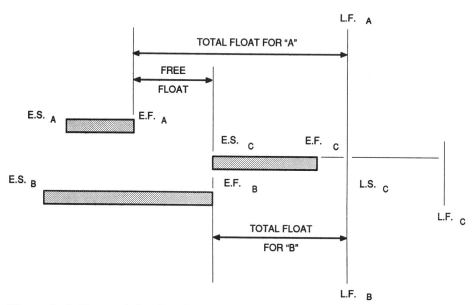

Figure 3–4. Determining free float.

completed at its *latest* time. In **Figure 3–5**, the early start of activity F minus the late completion of activity B becomes the minimum amount of time available to perform activity E. If this minimum time is greater than the duration of activity E, the excess is independent float. This type of float has a higher level of freedom than free float because any activity with independent float can be displaced backward or forward by that amount without disturbing any minimum time boundaries and without making any adjustments to the start and completion times of its neighboring activities. Independent float occurs infrequently in construction projects and, for this reason, it is seldom calculated.

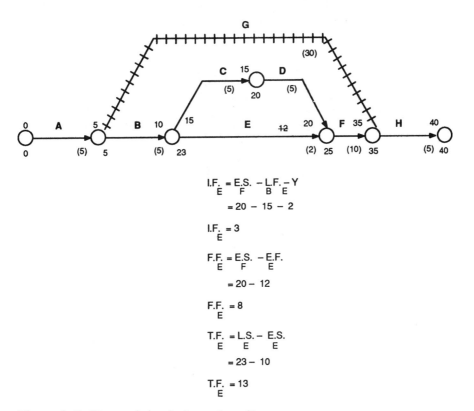

Figure 3–5. Determining independent float.

§ 3.18   —Float Allocation Possibilities

Several methods have been used to allocate and control float. One method simply allocates float to individual activities along a path of activities.

$$\frac{\text{Duration of activity}}{\text{Total duration of activity path}} \times \text{Total float on path}$$

The administration of this method can become horrendous, considering the dynamics of a schedule. It is, understandably, the least-utilized method of float allocation.

Another method uses *target* or *conditional* dates. Most, if not all, network-based project control systems have this capability. Essentially, the system allows specific dates to be entered that fix on, or override, the dates mathematically calculated by the computer. Such dates can be imposed on activity start or finish, or on event start or finish. Conditions that may be utilized include: not-earlier-than-start, must-start, not-later-

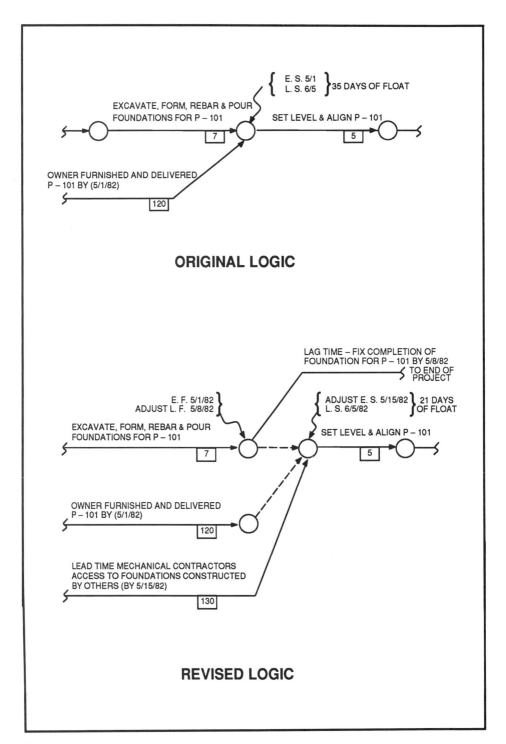

Figure 3-6. Lead time/lag time utilization.

than-finish, and must-finish. Target and conditional dates, if properly implemented and controlled, can be used to allocate project float to individual activities or phases of work for a single contract. Additionally, they can be used to allocate float to each contract when multiple prime contractors are involved. This technique can aid in minimizing the claimed delay of one contractor's performance on another.

The third—and most common—method is to use what are called *lead time* and *lag time* activities. These activities are logic restrictions that are inserted to influence certain activities and force specific dates to be computed and reflected in the output. These restraints are commonly used for phasing work, for equipment and manpower planning, and for fixing milestones (key events) and contractual dates. This method is simple, least expensive, easy to maintain, and provides better visibility for monitoring purposes. See **Figure 3–6**.

§ 3.19   Computerization of Project Schedule

As the use of computers and the application of networking techniques became broader and more varied in the construction industry, the ever-present problems of project implementation and control continued to increase. Although the use of computers and networking techniques has furnished management with tremendous quantities of important and meaningful project information, it has also presented a series of new problems.

Previously, decisions were often based upon sparse and limited information because management had limited access to many of the important facts about construction plans and actual performance. Today, the availability of computer power in a small, efficient, economical package has made it possible to establish better communication between the home office and the jobsite. Additionally, the use of microcomputers allows an effective data-processing link with the home office while at the same time providing the power of the stand-alone micro to the jobsite user. When linked to a mainframe, files and reports can be transferred, programs shared, and inquiries made.

§ 3.20   —Popular Systems Used for Major Projects

During the late 1970s, microcomputers came onto the computer market. These computers perform basically the same internal functions as the mainframes and minicomputers. Microcomputers are relatively inexpensive, and this factor makes it practical to have a dedicated computerized project-control system in the office or at the jobsite or, at least, separate from any central data-processing operation.

Today, a wide variety of project control systems are available, and particularly for microcomputers. The use of microcomputers is rapidly increasing because of turnaround time, ease of access, portability, cost, and the opportunity to learn by doing, which eliminates going through a systems group or organizational bureaucracy.

System access is also much easier today, whether the user employs a micro-, mini-, or mainframe-based software package. Modem hookups allow direct access via telephone lines to the project control software.

Among the vendors and systems available for use in large and complex projects are the following systems, all of which are considered to be highly competitive:

Name	Owner
ARTEMIS®	Metier Management Systems, Inc. P.O. Box 770020 Houston, TX 77215 (800) 777-7100
TRACKSTAR®	T&B Computing, Inc. 1100 Eisenhower Pl. Ann Arbor, MI 48108 (313) 973-1900
PROJECT/2®	Project Software & Development, Inc. 20 University Rd. Cambridge, MA 02138 (800) 366-7734
VISION®	Galaxy Applied Engineering 770 Airport Blvd. Burlingame, CA 94010 (415) 348-5625
MULTITRAK®	Multitrack Software Development 119 Beach St., 5th Fl. Boston, MA 02111 (617) 482-6677
PROMIS®	Strategic Software Planning Corp. 150 Cambridge Pkwy. Cambridge, MA 02142 (617) 354-1504
PLAN TRAC®	Computerline P.O. Box 1100 Auburn, MA 01501 (617) 294-1111

Name	Owner
OPEN PLAN®	Welcom Software Technology 15995 North Barkers Landing, Suite 275 Houston, TX 77079 (713) 558-0514
PRIMAVERA PROJECT PLANNER®	Primavera Systems, Inc. Two Bala Ave., Suite 224 Bala Cynwyd, PA 19004 (215) 667-8600
ALDERGRAF®	AlderGraf Systems, Inc. 10810 Old Katy Rd., Suite 102 Houston, TX 77043 (713) 467-8500

Although each system has proven to be more than capable, each has its advantages and disadvantages depending on the user's information needs, commitment, and application. The most serious limitation of any of these systems probably is the user's imagination.

It is not the intention of this discussion to review or quantify any of the systems in detail, but simply to state that they are available and are being used by owners, construction managers, architects, engineers, and contractors as tools for planning and controlling capital investment programs, individual projects, and separate contract.[8]

§ 3.21   —Getting Started

The best way to get started is to review and become familiar with the computer and the project control software for your project. All systems have a user manual that describes how to set up the project information on the computer's hard or floppy disk. Usually, a description of the system's capabilities is provided, along with detailed instructions on how to use the system's various features and capabilities. Some vendors of project-control systems conduct formal training and have user groups, which meet periodically to share experiences and introduce system enhancements.

---

[8] For a more comprehensive listing of available software packages, the Project Management Institute (PMI) has published a *Survey of Project Management Software Packages*. This information may be obtained from PMI's headquarters, at Project Management Institute, P.O. Box 43, Drexel Hill, PA 19026. PMI's telephone number is (215) 622-1796.

§ 3.22   —Inputting Network Information

For one of the systems described above to be used for processing basic networks, the network information must be converted to a form that can be entered into the computer—a procedure called *data takeoff.* In this procedure, data may be entered by batch input or by direct (*interactive*) input from the network.

The batch method is the more disciplined approach and may involve the use of a preprinted form, which requires transcribing basic network data into a prescribed input format before the data is entered into the computer system. **Figure 3–7** is an example of such a form for use in the critical path method. While some consider this to be an unnecessary step, preparing data-input sheets and then keying in the data is, in the long run, probably more accurate for large-scale networks than the direct approach.

Interactive input involves entering data into the system via a terminal connected to a central computer system or via a stand-alone workstation utilizing a registered copy of the project-control system software. In the interactive method, the user interacts with the computer in a request-response dialogue mode and directly enters (with immediate verification on a video screen) network activity information. Activities can be added, modified, or changed directly, without the intermediate step of data-file transfer.

This method is undoubtedly the most direct, but for large-scale networks (bulk data input), the potential for error greatly increases. Utilizing this method allows the elimination of the takeoff transcription process, because the required information is entered directly from the network diagram or printout. It is advisable to have the input listed separately for a final one-to-one checking prior to initial computer processing, because processing follows immediately upon command.

Either mode of entry allows activity information such as activity numbers, durations, and descriptions to be recorded in designated fields. Depending on the capability of the software used, data such as activity codes (responsibility, type, function, etc.), resources, and cost per activity may also be added. However, only the number, relationships, and duration of each activity are necessary for computing event times (early start and finish dates and late start and finish dates) and for making basic float calculations.

§ 3.23   —Guidelines for Data Takeoff

The chore of taking data off the network can be tedious, time-consuming, and even boring. However, the importance of this task, in light of the

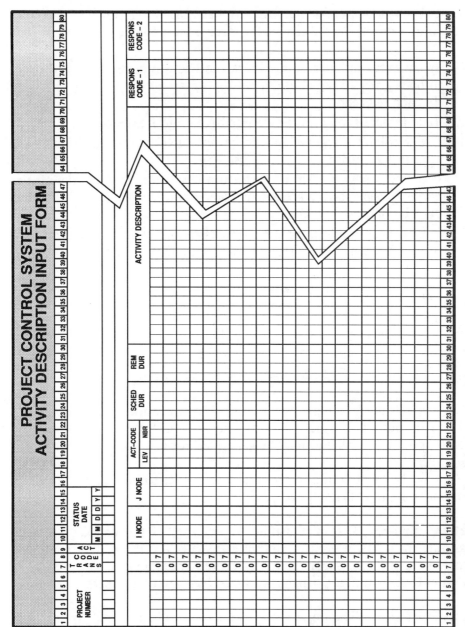

Figure 3–7. Reprinted form for batch-method input.

63

potential for errors, cannot be overemphasized. The following guidelines will aid in minimizing the chance for error on large-scale projects:

1. When event-numbering the initial network, number from low order to high order. Also, consider setting up an activity-coding structure for each reference.
2. Takeoff data should follow consecutive event numbers.
3. Use a color highlighter and strike out each activity in the network after it is recorded.
4. Use a two-person team to perform a large-volume data takeoff. Experience has shown a greater incidence of mistakes when this task is done by one.
5. Use strong graphic techniques and let the network information flow from left to right. Use arrowheads to show direction of flow.

When the network information has been transcribed to a computer-input document, the input forms are submitted to a data-entry operator for input.

§ 3.24   —Computer Outputs

After the computer completes processing the network events, the results can be outputted in various written forms. In addition, data may be stored on tape or disk and may be generated for a single project or multiple projects.

Among the most common outputs used for scheduling and controlling construction projects are the following:

Activity listing.   This is a listing, by activity, of the detailed working schedule for a single project. Activities usually are listed by ascending I event numbers and, secondarily, by J event numbers, or vice versa. In PDM output, a similar listing is produced by activity numbers.

Early-start sort.   This report lists network activities sorted by schedule early-start date and, secondarily, by activity number. An option usually exists to include only those activities scheduled to start in, for example, the next 30, 60, or 90 days (early look-ahead).

Late-start sort.   This report lists network activities that have not started and that are sorted by the schedule late-start date and, secondarily, by activity number. An option usually exists to include only those activities scheduled to start in, for example, the next 30, 60, or 90 days.

Total-float sort. This report lists network activities that have not started and that are sorted by the amount of total float for each activity and, secondarily, by activity number.

Activity-in-progress report. This report lists activities reported as started but not finished as of the last status report date. For each activity listed, the actual start date is usually shown, along with the latest allowable finish date and the projected finish date, based on the estimated remaining duration assigned to complete the activity in progress.

Responsibility-and-function sorts. This report lists schedule activities by responsibility and function and, secondarily, by activity number. The option also usually exists to list primarily by function and, secondarily, by responsibility. Additionally, these reports usually have an option to include only those activities scheduled during a look-ahead period, such as 30, 60, or 90 days. This listing may be by early or late start or finish date.

Project-statusing form. Some systems have the capability to generate computer source documents. The system automatically identifies activities that will require an update of status information and then formats transaction images for status inputs of those activities during the next updating process.

Computer graphics. A number of the systems discussed have graphics capabilities. Examples of computer graphics in such systems are network diagrams in CPM and PDM forms, time-scaled networks, bar charts, manpower and cost curves, and histograms.

§ 3.25 Schedule Submittal and Approval

For large projects, it is suggested that an owner allow a contractor at least 30 calendar days after notice to proceed for the preparation and initial submission of the project schedule. Requirements for schedule submissions should be clearly outlined in the contract's scheduling specification. For small projects ($2 million or less), a reasonable period for preparation of the initial scheduling requirements would be 14 to 21 days after notice to proceed. In addition, the owner is encouraged to specify in the contract scheduling specification the length of time needed for approval or comment on the contractor's submission(s).

If a contractor's schedule is disapproved or returned for corrections or revisions, the scheduling specification should be clear on when the contractor's schedule is to be resubmitted and the amount of time the owner will take to respond to that resubmittal.

§ 3.26   —Schedule Review

The contractor is encouraged to make every effort to comply with the submission requirements of the scheduling specification. A cover letter should accompany the timely submission. Upon receipt of the contractor's schedule, the owner should carefully review the schedule for technical requirements and compliance with the scheduling specification. If the owner disapproves, this should be done without delay and in writing, outlining the objections and the requirements for resubmission by the contractor.

If disagreements arise, the owner should encourage joint review meetings to resolve any major technical differences. For small or minority contractors having problems, the owner should consider providing limited technical assistance with the understanding that the resultant schedule is still the contractor's schedule.

It is suggested that the first schedule update be conducted within seven days after approval of a contractor's schedule. If an agreement on the initial schedule cannot be reached, the impasse should be well-documented. This includes keeping a record of correspondence, written comments on technical evaluation, copies of all submittals, and minutes of meetings.

§ 3.27   —Procedures for Schedule Review and Approval

To ensure timely approval of the schedule, it is recommended that the initial schedule be reviewed by both the contractor and the owner for reasonableness. The purpose of such review is to validate the schedule proposed and establish an early agreement between both parties on how the contractor plans to execute the work required. The following checklist is suggested for both the contractor and the owner in determining the initial schedule's reasonableness.

_____ 1. Perform a one-to-one data check to validate the consistency of the computer tabulation and the network.

_____ 2. Highlight the first five to seven paths of criticality (paths of least float) to review and understand the controlling logic and mathematics of the schedule. Determine if the critical path is proper and reasonable.

_____ 3. Review the proposed logic sequence and note any exceptions that might be taken. Validate absolute logic conditions and confirm key preferential logic conditions.

_____ 4. Check to ensure all owner-related functions outlined in the contract documents are properly incorporated. These include:

_____ **a.**   Access and availability dates for physical areas of the project

_____ **b.**   Intermediate completion dates established for follow-on contractors

_____ **c.**   Delivery of owner-furnished materials and equipment

_____ **d.**   Approval of shop drawings and samples

_____ **e.**   Joint occupancy dates

_____ **f.**   Beneficial occupancy dates.

_____ **5.**   Check the plan to see if all major-equipment restraints are properly reflected.

_____ **6.**   Review and spot-check activity durations for reasonableness.

_____ **7.**   Spot-check activity durations for quantities involved, crew-size requirements, and productivity factors. Challenge durations when appropriate.

_____ **8.**   Check the level of detail proposed. Is it consistent and balanced throughout the network or is it vague in certain areas? Is all of the work included? Is the level of detail adequate to plan, schedule, coordinate, monitor, control, and report on the progress of work?

_____ **9.**   Check the project milestones established and identify as contractual, absolute, or preferential.

_____ **10.**   Project past experience onto this project. Spot-check relationships or work phases and their timing—i.e., building enclosed to job completion, setting of switchgear to job completion, etc.

_____ **11.**   Check for involvement of subcontractors and suppliers and see if it is properly reflected. Are dependencies clearly defined? Any critical deliveries?

_____ **12.**   How is weather reflected? Are there any seasonal weather restrictions to consider?

_____ **13.**   Check for compliance with all contract specifications related to the schedule.

§ 3.28   How to Update the Project Schedule

Scheduling a construction project requires that a plan and strategy be developed and a determination made on the required resources (manpower, equipment, and materials, and their priorities). These are essential to achieving the goal of completion on time, within budget, and in accordance with the technical requirements. Schedules used to accomplish this goal have to be kept up-to-date to be useful in forecasting project completion.

They also become important tools in proving or disproving construction-delay, impact, inefficiency, and acceleration claims.

§ 3.29   —Need for Updating

A construction project by its very nature is dynamic. Plans and estimates, no matter how carefully thought out, are bound to change as a result of the unexpected. Strikes, unusually bad weather, sudden material shortages, unforeseen subsurface conditions, and change orders are a few of the many factors that may result in delays and a need to change the project plan and schedule. The project schedule must continually reflect these changes or it can become useless or misleading. To be successful, it must be revised on a regular basis.[9]

This periodic review of the project's plan, schedule, and progress is termed *updating*. The reasons for updating the network are to determine physical progress; to introduce project status and logical revisions; to provide a complete and accurate report of actual construction progress made versus the established schedule; and to determine how all parties intend to continue the work and meet the overall schedule objectives.

§ 3.30   —Preparing to Update

Initial updating should take place during the first week after the schedule is approved. Keep in mind that considerable time can pass between notice to proceed and final schedule approval.

Subsequent updates should take place on at least a monthly basis—and, in some cases, every two weeks—for the duration of the project. It is important that the frequency of updating be understood and specified in the scheduling specification.

Preparing to update requires that each party to the schedule gather status information on its share of the work. All such information should be reviewed, validated, and incorporated into the schedule-updating process at a joint meeting. Such meetings also provide the means to discover areas of time dispute at the earliest opportunity.

Each party compiling update data is encouraged to review and compare the diagram and the computer tabulation to identify all activities that were scheduled to start or be completed during the report period. The

---

[9] Fortec Constructors v. United States, 8 Cl. Ct. 490 (1985); Ballenger Corp., DOTBCA Nos. 74-32, 74-32A, 74-32H, 84-1 BCA ¶ 16,973 at 84,524 (1983).

status date should be marked throughout the arrow diagram by placing an inverted red triangle or similar marking over each activity for which early date count represents the status report date. This step will help quickly alert the parties to data that needs to be reported and will thereby facilitate the data-gathering process.

The next task is to determine the following:

1. Start and finish dates for all activities started and/or finished during the report period.

2. The current status of all activities reported as being in progress in the last update report. If they were completed during the current report period, the date of actual completion should be recorded. For those activities that remain in progress (including those started during the current update period), the remaining time duration should be estimated and recorded.

3. Activities that need to be resequenced, added, deleted, or modified to add clarification, to reflect a change in plan of operation, or to maintain required schedule detail for proper monitoring and control.

4. The fragnets that have to be incorporated into the schedule to reflect delays and/or change conditions that influence the schedule and progress of the project. (See **Chapter 8.**)

In addition to the above, if the project is legitimately behind schedule, the remaining schedule should be reviewed to determine areas of opportunity for recovery when deemed appropriate. Since many activities are planned and sequenced on a preferential, rather than absolute, basis, it is possible that some time can be recovered by resequencing certain activities. There may be some activities that can be reduced in duration by increasing manpower, employing multiple shifts, dovetailing tasks, and increasing the amount of support equipment. Every effort should be made to take advantage of time and prevent disaster in terms of ultimate cost and timely completion.

As the information is gathered, it is suggested that the current networks and computer tabulations be marked up in color when network changes and status information are recorded.

The party responsible for maintaining and controlling the schedule should establish a systematic approach for gathering and analyzing all project information and should coordinate and lead the update process by determining the time, date, and place for the meeting. Specific details about how to accomplish this should be included in the contract specifications for scheduling.

§ 3.31   —Joint Update Meetings

Joint update meetings are encouraged for maintaining proper communication and understanding regarding the project schedule. The party responsible for the schedule should chair such meetings. Attendees should include all contracted parties who are concerned with schedule and performance—especially major subcontractors. Although meetings should be informal, it is suggested that minutes be taken, printed, and issued to all parties attending. On a large, complex project involving many multiple primes, it may be necessary to have a series of schedule-update meetings.

Each contracted party should be required to come to the update meetings with the information outlined above. The purposes are to provide, as of the end of the updating period, a complete and accurate report of current design, procurement, and construction progress and to show how each project participant plans to continue work to meet all the contract completion dates. In addition, the update meetings will help enable participants to identify any problems or delays (and their causes), determine real or potential impact, consider alternatives, make decisions, and set responsibility and timing for responses.

§ 3.32   Management Reporting and Documentation

As part of the updating process, the party responsible for the schedule should prepare a narrative report after each update. The report should present the status of the overall project and highlight those areas or activities having problems and requiring owner and/or contractor management attention.

§ 3.33   —Problem-Identification Philosophy

The update narrative report should be geared to a problem-identification philosophy. Information should be based on an analysis of tasks in which current or potential problems exist; problems, for example, that concern such areas as schedule, cost, or technical performance, or a combination of these. Narrative descriptions of stated problems should include the following:

1.   The nature of the problem
2.   The reasons for cost and/or schedule variances
3.   The impact on the immediate task
4.   The impact on the total project.

After each problem is completely defined, a statement should be provided that details when and by whom the corrective action will be taken, along with the expected result of such action. The report should also discuss any changes in plans, change orders, delays, impacts, and time extensions that have been incorporated into the schedule during the reporting period. Further, the report should include an analysis of the project's critical path.

§ 3.34   —Need for Good Project Records

All parties involved in the construction process should be cognizant of the need for accurate and complete records to help maintain effective control of a construction project. Such records are the principal source of evidence for timely negotiation of change orders, resolution of disputes, and proof of time delays and damages.

When a party to a contract has to file a claim because of a breach or dispute with another party, the burden of proof is upon the claimant. Proof can be substantiated through the accurate and factual documentation of performance and the maintenance of project record-keeping systems covering transactions, correspondence, inspections, and various reports. Courts and boards require that disciplined standards of documentation and proof be followed.

Records should be preserved daily on every element of project administration, and actual performance should be recorded daily and to a standard that will enable a third party to reconstruct the project from the files, if necessary. Records useful in supporting or defending against time-extension requests and delay-damages claims include various cost estimates, schedules and updates, daily and weekly reports, general correspondence, memoranda for record, job diaries, progress photographs, test reports, purchase orders, delivery receipts, payroll records, labor wage agreements, job-cost reports, equipment-utilization records, and weather data. Also important are accurate records on change orders, shop drawings, and payment transactions. While relevant facts may be presented in oral testimony, job records are the principal source of evidence for resolving disputes and proving delay claims.

§ 3.35   —Cash Flow Forecasting and Progress
Payment Records

Network-based schedules have been used to develop progress payment requests, payment certifications, and cash flow projections. Such cost techniques require that the total project cost be broken down, distributed, and assigned to activities for which cost will be expended. An activity cost is assigned to each activity that has monetary value. The cost assigned is usually based on normal working and economic conditions and includes the cost of labor, fringes, material, and equipment. Cost items such as overhead, profit, and bonds and insurance are usually prorated on a weighted basis throughout all activities that have a monetary value.

Most, if not all, network-based systems have the capability to develop a schedule of anticipated earnings in the form of an envelope of cost curves representing earnings or percentage of contract value and can be based on early start, early finish, late start, and late finish of activities. A listing of partial-payment estimates by pay period and accumulation of cost-to-date can also be obtained. Such reports have been found to be useful by many users, particularly those in the public sector.

After the schedule is implemented and the periodic updates begin, a determination must be made on the cost value of work in place for each activity as of the status date. Adjustments that increase or decrease cost should be made for activities added or for those whose scope has changed. The update cost information is processed and the computer compiles the value of all work in place and determines the amount of progress payment due. Progress payment reports and updated cash flow forecast curves are usually part of the updating process when activity cost routines are used.

For owners with large programs (multiple projects or multiple prime contracts) composite curves can be generated by some of the network-based systems for any grouping of contracts or projects.

When network-based systems are used for progress payments and cash flow projections, there are several points of caution to remember:

1. Do not let progress payment and cash flow forecasting requirements be the main reason for using network-based scheduling techniques.
2. Do not allow payment for changed or extra work not yet included in the network by allowing progress to be reported against unrelated activities.
3. Do not, because of a cost dispute, prohibit assignment of network additions or revisions to an activity reflecting changed or extra work conditions. Simply make the logic changes, document the situation, and add the cost later when an agreement has been reached. Remember: The importance of the schedule is to control time, not money.

Table 3–5 is an example of a progress payment schedule report. The report shows the frequency, the scheduled or actual cost for each report period, and the cumulative cost. It also shows the projected cost values based on the reported status of the project.

Table 3-5

Progress Payment Schedule Report

Project: County Convention Center
Desc.: Philadelphia, Pennsylvania
Projected Completion Date 9/28/90

Project Number C104689
Start Date 7/1/88
Need Date 10/15/90
Status Date 10/31/89

DATE	DAYS	CURRENT SCHEDULE EARLY FINISH			WORK IN PLACE			CURRENT SCHEDULE LATE FINISH			PROJECTED SCHEDULE EARLY FINISH		
		Period Cost	Accum Cost	Percent of Cost	Period	Accum	Percent	Period Cost	Accum Cost	Percent of Cost	Period Cost	Accum Cost	Percent of Cost
08/31/88	0				172	172	.6%						
09/29/88	29				191	363	1.3%						
10/31/88	61				208	571	2.1%						
11/30/88	91				179	750	2.8%						
12/29/88	120				255	1005	3.7%						
01/31/89	153				1216	2221	8.3%						
03/30/89	211				1317	3538	13.3%						
04/30/89	242				1558	5096	19.2%						
05/31/89	273				1445	6541	24.6%						
06/29/89	302				1388	7929	29.8%						
07/31/89	334				1564	9493	35.7%						
08/31/89	365				1403	10896	41.0%						
09/28/89	394				1401	12297	46.3%						
10/31/89	427				1441	13738	51.7%						
12/31/89	458	2624	16362	61.6%				295	14033	52.8%	2627	16365	61.6%
01/31/90	489	219	18581	70.0%				2015	16048	0.4%	2219	18584	70.0%
02/28/90	517	1988	20569	77.5%				2012	18060	68.0%	1988	20572	77.5%
03/30/90	547	1617	22186	83.6%				1792	19852	74.8%	1614	22186	83.6%
04/30/90	578	1078	23264	86.6%				1533	21385	80.5%	1078	23264	87.6%
05/31/90	609	935	24199	91.1%				1304	22689	85.5%	935	24199	91.1%
06/29/90	638	878	25077	94.5%				1044	23733	89.4%	748	24947	94.0%
07/31/90	670	450	25527	96.1%				817	24550	92.5%	580	25527	96.1%
08/31/90	701	442	25969	97.8%				848	25398	95.7%	442	25969	97.8%
09/28/90	729	567	26536	100.0%				1138	26536	100.0%	567	26536	100.0%

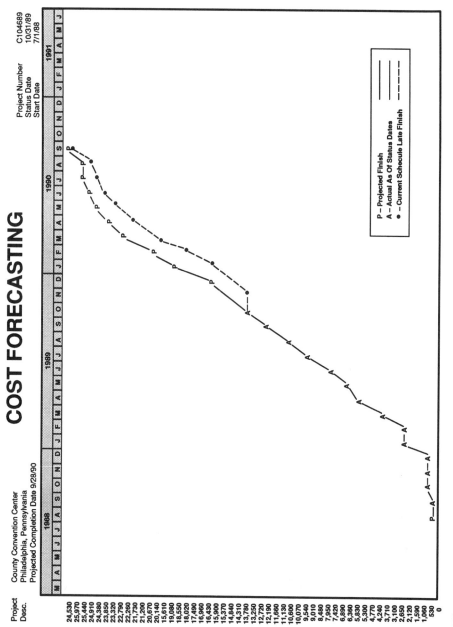

Figure 3–8. Cash flow projection record.

74

Figure 3–8 is an example of a cash flow projection report. This report shows the scheduled cost on a cumulative basis, the actual cost, and the projected schedule cost based on reported project status and cost expended to date.

§ 3.36 —Use of Summary Networks

After detailed networks are developed, it is suggested that a time-scaled *master summary control schedule* be prepared. This visual aid, which can vary in size, should accurately summarize the comprehensive detailed schedule and have common milestones (key events) for correlation and transfer of schedule and status information as it is reported on a detailed basis. The master summary control schedule can be used in periodic management briefings to present the overall status of the project. Color schemes may be added to highlight status and projection information. **Figure 3–9** is an example of how the master summary control schedule summarizes and correlates with a detailed schedule on a milestone basis. The establishment of milestones and key dates and the use of accurate levels of indenture allow full utilization of the transferability of information from one indenture level to another.

§ 3.37 Checklist for Effective Schedule Implementation

Making construction schedules work is vital to the success of the project. The following checklist can help owners, contractors, subcontractors, and consultants achieve their project goals and avoid being involved in complex delay and impact claims.

_____ Recognize the importance of scheduling

_____ Choose the proper scheduling method

_____ Become familiar with the scheduling requirements and project delivery system

_____ Understand the roles, responsibilities, and contractual relationships of the parties involved

_____ Retain a set of the original plans as bid and a clean set of the plans and specifications that became part of the construction contract documents

_____ Contractors should retain a complete set of construction estimate worksheets for each contract; owners should require contractors to furnish a breakdown of their bids

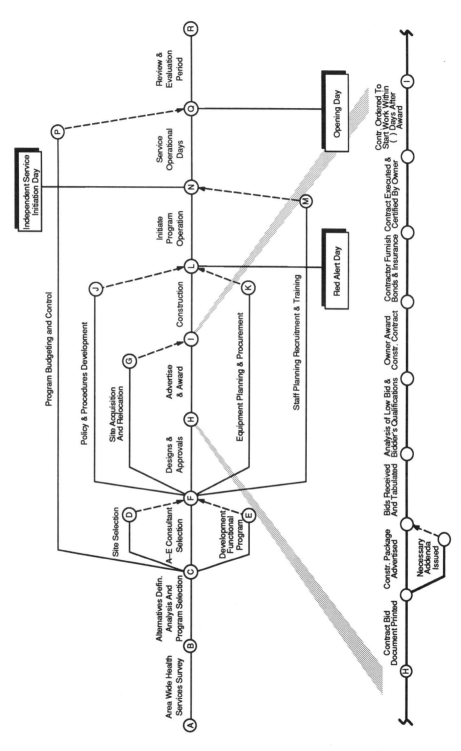

Figure 3-9. Master Summary Control schedule (detailed fragnet for advertisement and award on hospital project).

____ Train your staff in the proper use of scheduling techniques

____ Identify any contract provisions that may potentially generate disputes pertaining to schedule and delays

____ Prepare scheduling specifications that communicate clearly to the contractor; if any ambiguities exist, request a clarification in writing

____ Make a commitment to use the schedule so that all parties involved benefit and disputes can be avoided

____ Owners should require that prime contractors involve their subcontractors in the schedule development and updating process

____ Owners should review and approve contractor prepared schedules; contractors should insist on owner approval even when it is not required

____ Scheduling specifications should clarify when the contractor's proposed schedule is to be resubmitted and the amount of time the owner is allowed to respond

____ Owners should outline promptly in writing any objections to the contractor's schedule

____ Update at least monthly

____ Update jointly when possible and maintain accurate records of each update and report period; retain edited diagrams and computer tabulations; keep minutes of your update meetings

____ Evaluate your construction recordkeeping systems and ensure that all elements of the project, contract administration, and performance are being recorded

____ Require the field staff to record at least one or two weather observations each day and the effect those conditions had on job progress and cost

____ Keep daily equipment records showing the equipment at the site, hours operated, hours idled, work performed, and any repairs made

____ Keep a transaction register on all change orders from initiation to final settlement; include documentation to support time extension requests

____ Keep a transaction register for all shop drawings and material samples, showing scheduled and actual submission dates, time allowed and actual duration of approval, and any rejections or resubmissions

____ Prepare time impact analyses for all change orders and delays, including disruption, interference, actual suspension of work, and directed or constructive acceleration of work; keep a master ledger of time impacts reflecting the chronological influence of delays encountered

____ Maintain a ledger of all contract time extensions requested, approved, pending or denied

_____ When a delay occurs, initiate accounting procedures to identify, isolate, and record delay-generated costs

_____ When a directive to accelerate is issued or implied, contractors should establish that they were on or ahead of a properly adjusted schedule at that time; owners should make sure that the contractor is actually behind a properly adjusted schedule before directing him to accelerate at his own costs

_____ Keep all scheduling records for at least three years after the completion of the project

_____ When preparing change order proposals and time extension requests, contractors should include proper justification for excusable delay

§ 3.38   —Pitfalls in Scheduling Systems

Although the various scheduling techniques have great potential for success, there must be a commitment to make these systems work effectively for all parties involved. Some of the pitfalls and common reasons for failure include:

Lack of knowledge in the skillful application and use of scheduling systems by the owner, consultant(s), or contractors involved

Vesting the responsibility for specifying and implementing scheduling systems in the wrong group or individual

Using poor or vague specifications to specify scheduling system requirements in the contract document

Orienting scheduling systems to the computer rather than to the user

Requiring the contractor to use an owner-prepared schedule (it could be claimed that the owner is implying a warranty that the schedule is part of the specifications)

Reluctance by the owner, architect, or contractor to hire a schedule consultant when the need arises

Imposing an owner-selected, or hired, consultant on the contractor and taking advantage of that relationship

Competitive bidding of schedule consultants, which can result in a low bidder who provides only minimal service

The multiple prime contract system, which, when coupled with the lack of coordination and cooperation among contractors, makes the development and use of the schedule very difficult

Scheduling specifications that require the contractor to submit a preliminary schedule in advance of the final version; any schedule agreed upon should be based on the total planning of the project

Failure to spend the time and money to keep a schedule up to date through proper and periodic updatings

Failure to hold joint update meetings

Strict requirements imposed on the contractor regarding schedule maintenance and changes to the schedule (for example, allowing changes only after written request and subsequent approval is granted by the owner or his consultant)

Misunderstanding and abuse of float

Attempting to resolve the cost aspects of change orders before allowing schedule changes to reflect their impact

Failure to require contractors to provide time impact analyses to support time extension requests

Inadequate policy by the owner for granting timely extensions of time

Misunderstanding of concurrent and offsetting delay.

CHAPTER 4

LEGAL ASPECTS OF SCHEDULE SPECIFICATIONS

§ 4.1 Introduction

§ 4.2 Feasibility of Schedule

§ 4.3 Type of Diagram

§ 4.4 Number of Activities

§ 4.5 Approval

§ 4.6 Updating

§ 4.7 Cost Loading

§ 4.8 Float Use and Reporting

§ 4.9 Major Revisions and Time Extensions

§ 4.10 Examples of Schedule Specifications

§ 4.11 Factors Contributing to Poor Schedule Specifications

§ 4.1 Introduction

With increasing frequency, construction contracts contain detailed specifications sections that prescribe the form and detail of the project schedule and supporting data, the methods for adjusting and updating the schedule, and the use of the schedule for purposes of contract modifications, time extensions, and analysis of performance delays. These specifications and their interpretation must be carefully considered by contracting parties because they often result in important allocations of risk and responsibility. Major factors that must be considered in drafting schedule specifications include:

1. Feasibility of the schedule
2. Type of diagram used
3. Number of activities
4. Approval requirements
5. Updating procedures

81

6. Cost loading

7. Float use and reporting

8. Major revisions and time extensions.

A review of each of these factors is offered in this chapter, along with examples of schedule specifications and factors contributing to poor schedule specifications.

§ 4.2   Feasibility of Schedule

If the schedule specified for a project does not present a feasible or reasonable plan for the sequence and duration of the work and is not properly updated, it is worthless as a pragmatic tool to execute work in the field. Further, such a schedule is useless as a data base by which the parties or finders-of-fact can evaluate the actual performance of the work, the effect of delays on the project, and the responsibility of the parties for such delays.[1]

In a number of cases, courts and boards of contract appeals have refused to accept critical path method (CPM) schedules that were not properly prepared or that were not used to actually schedule the work in the field.[2]

Chaney & James Construction Co.,[3] decided in 1966, represented one of the first attempts to use a CPM schedule in claim presentation before a board of contract appeals. The contractor's network analysis was presented in a claim for delay and suspension of work.

In rejecting the conclusions found in the contractor's CPM study, the board held that

> these charts cannot be considered evidence of the facts they portray. While we accept the expert's testimony that the charts appear to be technically correct and logical, the work sequence shown was not demonstrated to be the only possible sequence in which the work could have been accomplished; nor was it demonstrated that the sequence presented in the charts was necessarily the best one. *The work sequence shown was not used in estimating and bidding the job since the original chart from which the two exhibits were derived was not in existence until late in 1962, near the end of the project.* Also, as the contractor's project manager admits, *the sequence shown on the critical path charts was not followed in performing the contract work.*

---

[1] Pathman Constr. Co., ASBCA No. 23392, 85-2 BCA ¶ 18,096 (1985); Nello L. Teer Co., ENGBCA No. 4376, 86-3 BCA ¶ 19,326 (1986).

[2] *See* Fortec Constructors v. United States, 8 Cl. Ct. 490 (1985); Chaney & James Constr. Co., FAACAP No. 67-18, 66-2 BCA ¶ 6066 (1967).

[3] FAACAP No. 67-18, 66-2 BCA ¶ 6066 (1967).

Under the circumstances the critical path charts cannot be accepted as establishing either the facts they portray or the reasonableness of the contract's assertions as to the influence of specific incidents on work progress.[4]

Chaney & James demonstrates that the CPM schedule should not only represent a feasible or reasonable plan for performance, but also should be utilized during construction to build the project.

In *Fortec Constructors v. United States,*[5] the contractor sought time extensions, extra costs, and remission of liquidated damages for modifications and government-caused delays experienced on a contract to build an aircraft fuel maintenance facility on an air force base. The government sought to use a CPM schedule analysis to show that the extra work was not on the critical path and, therefore, that the contractor was not entitled to time extensions.

The Claims Court rejected the government's CPM analysis, which it found was not properly updated. The court found that the CPM schedule was updated only once and did not reflect the actual critical path over the life and evolution of the project:

> The critical path changed from that depicted on the CPM diagram introduced into evidence. The Corps, however, refused to grant timely and adequate time extensions and to authorize revisions to the CPM to reflect the changed performance critical path. As a result, it is impossible to determine from the CPM diagram whether a particular activity was critical or noncritical, on schedule or behind schedule.[6]

§ 4.3   Type of Diagram

Schedule specifications need to detail clearly both the specific type of diagram and the network planning technique desired. Vague language may allow the contractor the opportunity to use bar charts, rather than CPM diagrams, as an appropriate schedule, even though it is intended that a CPM diagram be used on the project.

In *H.I. Homa Co.,*[7] for example, the contract contained the following provision: "The schedule shall show the order in which the contractor proposes to carry on the work, the dates on which he will start the several salient features (including procurement of materials, plant and equipment) and the contemplated days for completing same."[8] The specifications

---

[4] *Id.* at 28,076–77 (emphasis added).

[5] 8 Cl. Ct. 490 (1985).

[6] *Id.* at 505–06.

[7] ENGBCA No. PCC-41, 82-1 BCA ¶ 15,651 (1982).

[8] *Id.* at 77,301.

further provided that the schedule be of a type and size acceptable to the contracting officer. Under these circumstances, the board of contract appeals determined that a CPM network was not required by the contract since a bar chart would meet the specifications. Because the government had required a CPM schedule, the board determined that the contractor was entitled to additional compensation.[9]

§ 4.4 Number of Activities

Most schedule specifications require a network showing a minimum number of activities. Such a requirement is sometimes implemented by limiting the duration of individual activities to no more than a stated number of days.[10] It is very important to have a clear idea of the required level of detail for any network diagram. The appropriate number of activities is largely dependent upon the nature, size, and complexity of the project. If too many activities are required, the resulting diagram may not be an effective management tool for field construction. However, if too few activities are specified, the resulting activities may be so gross as to provide for a diagram that does not properly reflect the intricacies or interdependencies of various activities required to be completed on the project.

§ 4.5 Approval

Schedule specifications should establish whether formal approval of the schedule is required, as well as the party responsible for making the approval. Thus, the specifications should state whether the owner or architect/engineer or construction manager approves the CPM schedule. The specifications also should indicate the duration of the approval cycle.

Owners will occasionally refrain from approving or acting upon a contractor's proposed schedule because they fear that their response can later be used by the contractor as acceptance of the schedule and the owner's responsibility under the schedule. In many cases, this type of forbearance is unsuccessful. Courts have imposed implied obligations upon owners with regard to the schedule despite the owners' silence.[11] In one case, when an owner even orally disclaimed parts of the schedule but failed to

---

[9] *Id.*

[10] *See* AGC, The Use of CPM in Construction 131 (1976).

[11] Fullerton Constr. Co., ASBCA No. 12275, 69-2 BCA ¶ 7876 at 36,611-2 (1969). *See generally,* Wickwire, Hurlbut & Shapiro, *Rights and Obligations in Scheduling,* Constr. Briefings No. 88-13 (1988).

actually reject the contractor's initial proposed schedule, the owner was held to be bound to time durations contained in the submitted schedule.[12]

In addition, when a schedule is approved there is a rebuttable presumption of correctness or reasonableness of the schedule.[13]

§ 4.6   Updating

Most contracts require updating of the schedule during performance. Issues addressed by the specifications include the use of computers in updating, frequency of schedule updates, and what the updates must reflect about changes, delays, or modifications to the plan for the remainder of construction that may be contrary to the original network diagram. Many schedule specifications require owner approval prior to incorporating logic changes in schedule updates. An owner's refusal to permit such adjustments in the updates can render the schedule meaningless in terms of managing the project and analyzing subsequent schedule impact.[14]

§ 4.7   Cost Loading

Some owners require the schedule diagram of activities to be cost loaded for progress payment purposes. The level of detail required for such cost loading should be specified clearly. Owners often retain discretion to adjust the cost loading in order to make certain that they are not subjected to exaggerated front end loading in the cost loading of the diagrams.

§ 4.8   Float Use and Reporting

Schedule specifications should address a number of issues concerning float. First, the contract should state the desired requirements for reporting float. These provisions may require, for example, periodic reports of total or project float, free float, and activity-specific float. These reports can be a useful management tool. Second, the schedule specifications should address the availability of the use of float to the parties and the project. Without risk-allocating provisions, neither party will be entitled to priority in use of float time. In other words, if float is available along the channel of work involved, either party (as long as it is acting in good

---

[12] Fullerton Constr. Co., ASBCA No. 12275, 69-2 BCA ¶ 7876 (1969). *See also* G. Bliudzius Contractors, Inc., ASBCA No. 37707, 90-2 BCA ¶ 22,835 (1990).

[13] Santa Fe, Inc., VABCA No. 2168, 87-3 BCA ¶ 20,104 (1987).

[14] *See* Fortec Constructors v. United States, 8 Cl. Ct. 490 (1985). *See also* Corps of Engineers, Network Analysis Systems Guide, EP 415-1-4, at 8-1 (Aug. 1986).

faith) may, without being charged for a delay to the project, delay or extend work activities up to the point that the float is extinguished.[15]

§ 4.9   Major Revisions and Time Extensions

Schedule specifications should state whether the CPM or network diagrams are to be totally revised or significantly modified if there are major revisions in the project sequence. The contract should also indicate the party responsible for preparing such major revisions to the network diagram and describe the owner's rights to approval of any such major revisions. At a minimum, major changes and schedule impacts should be incorporated into the schedule as promptly as possible so that the CPM network accurately reflects current conditions.[16]

Contract drafters should also consider specifying the appropriate time for quantifying delays. For example, should the time-extension calculation for the delay be measured based on (1) a CPM update or diagram current as of the time of the delay, (2) the impact to the original CPM plan, or (3) a "20/20" hindsight look at the project? The reference point for measurement of the impact often will have a major effect on the length of the appropriate time extension.[17]

§ 4.10   Examples of Schedule Specifications

The appendixes include current examples of specifications used by the Corps of Engineers (see **Appendix C**), the Veterans Administration (see **Appendix D**), the Postal Service (see **Appendix D**), as well as the American Institute of Architects (AIA) (see **Appendix A**) specifications for requiring progress schedules on projects. **Appendix F** includes model specifications from a private-sector owner's viewpoint, which owners may consider for use.

---

[15] *See, e.g.,* Weaver-Bailey Contractors, Inc. v. United States, 19 Cl. Ct. 474, 481–82 (1990); Robglo Inc., VABCA Nos. 2879, 2884, 1990 VABCA LEXIS 27 (October 30, 1990).

[16] Corps of Engineers, Network Analysis Systems Guide, ER 1-1-11, at A-35 (Mar. 1973).

Failure to determine the time of a change ordered in the work is a mistake. If this action is postponed, the actual job status at the time the change was ordered may be extremely difficult to determine; consequently a reasonable evaluation at a later date may be impossible. In addition, control of the project is lost the minute a change is ordered without incorporating that change in the schedule. Experience indicates that procrastination in settlement of justifiable time extensions leads to an inordinate amount of claims and the possibility of constructive acceleration.

[17] Wickwire, Hurlbut & Lerman, *Use of Critical Path Method Techniques in Contract Claims: Issues and Developments, 1974 to 1988,* 18 Pub. Cont. L.J. 338, 367–75 (1989).

The examples that have been provided in these appendixes run the gamut from the most minimal kind of schedule requirement to that requiring the implementation of extremely detailed systems.

For example, the 1987 AIA A201 specifications requirement for a progress schedule runs only a few lines. The language in the AIA form calls for a progress schedule in only the most vague terms. This specifications requirement could be interpreted as calling for nothing more than some linear markings on the cardboard backing that comes back from the laundry with cleaned shirts.

The next level of detail in specifications might be that represented by the California Department of Transportation, which calls for a submission of the schedule by which the contractor proposes to carry out the work and for setting forth the dates on which the contractor will start the several salient features of the work and the contemplated dates of completion. This specifications provision is similar to that considered in the *H.I. Homa Co.* decision,[18] which was interpreted as clearly not requiring the submission of the CPM schedule or network analysis schedule.

From the AIA and California Department of Transportation specifications calling for only the most vague requirements, we move to an extreme level of detail represented by the Corps of Engineers network analysis system specifications for the Edwards Air Force Base test support facility, 1985 procurement. These specifications (excerpted in **Appendix B**) not only required a serious level of detail with respect to activities, but also cost loading; updating; and immediate action on changes. The specifications also contained specific provisions with respect to the utilization of float and the granting of time extensions.

In fact, the Edwards specifications clearly spell out the real-time interactive nature of the dynamic CPM process as work on the project moves forward and the contractor and owner interact about problems encountered on the site and variances in the sequence and durations of the activities. The specifications further recognize that the owner has extremely serious responsibilities, which he must satisfy, with respect to project changes and delays. The specifications state, in pertinent part, at page SC-18:

> Rapid resolution of change orders and the granting of other time extensions, where authorized by the Contracting Officer, is a critical part of the overall management system. Implementation of all justified activity and logic changes shall be made and reflected in the next weekly update after approval of the Contracting Officer.

The VA specifications, like the Corps of Engineers specifications, clearly recognize the dynamic nature of the CPM process, as well as the

---

[18] ENGBCA No. PCC-41, 82-1 BCA ¶ 15,651 (1982).

interactive nature of the relationship between the contractor and the owner. The specifications are unusual because they also give the VA control over the network computer data base and updating process.

The contractor, under the VA specifications, must request time on a timely basis, and the VA must grant time extensions on a timely basis. As detailed in the *Fortec Constructors v. United States* decision,[19] the owner cannot ignore obligations to act upon time extensions or updating requirements in a timely manner in the real-time environment.

The VA specifications are also of extreme interest because they include specific requirements about the conditions that must be satisfied to obtain time extensions and the point in time at which the time extensions are to be measured. The specifications state, in pertinent part, at § 1.13:

> The schedule must clearly display that the schedule has used, in full, all the float time available for the work involved in this request. The Contracting Officer's determination as to the total number of days of contract extension will be based upon the current computer-produced calendar-dated schedule for the time period in question and all other relevant information. Actual delays in activities which, according to the computer-produced calendar-dated schedule, do not affect the extended and predicted contract completion dates shown by the critical path in the network, will not be the basis for a change to the contract completion date.

The requirement in the VA specifications that the contractor establish the delay impact on the extended completion date (which would represent the current contract completion date as of the time of the update), as well as the predicted completion date, is clearly intended by the VA to deny the contractor time extensions when an individual delay represents a delay to an activity with negative float but does not represent the chain of activities in the most negative condition as of the date of the update. Thus, a delay to an activity with only −10 days' negative float will not qualify for a time extension on the project if there are activities at the same time in the then-current update with larger amounts (such as −300 days) of negative float.

The 1988 WMATA (available from the Washington Metropolitan Area Transit Authority) cost-loaded network analysis system, like the VA specifications, requires a fully detailed, time-scaled, graphic-arrow-diagram, cost-loaded CPM network. Of particular interest are the time-adjustment provisions that provide for: float as a resource for the project, the requirement that all float be exhausted before time adjustments are made, no adjustments to the milestone dates without an actual modification to the contract, and no delay as a basis for time extension unless it impacts

---

[19] 8 Cl. Ct. 490 (1985).

the critical path of the *currently* approved computer printout report. The specification states in pertinent part:

> Float time is not time for the exclusive use or benefit of either the Authority or the Contractor. *Extensions of time* for Contract performance as specified in the General Provisions *will be granted only to the extent that equitable time adjustments to the affected activity or activities exceed the total float time* along the affected paths of the approved computer printout report *in effect at the instant of one of the following:*
>
> a. NTP with a change.[20]
> b. Order of suspension or possession.
> c. Detection of a subsequently acknowledged differing site condition or excusable delay (emphasis added).

Through the requirement that the delay be demonstrated on the CPM schedule update current at the time of the delay, the WMATA specifications, like the VA and Corps of Engineers specifications, support the concept of contemporaneous pricing of delays to the project. This is also the manner of quantifying delays dictated by the principles enunciated in the *Fortec* decision by the claims court[21] and clearly implemented in the recent *Sante Fe, Inc.* decision of the VA Board of Contract Appeals.[22]

The August 1988 Postal Service network analysis specifications present requirements for a network system with a limited number of activities and with no requirement for time-scaling. While not in the same level of detail as other specifications, the Postal Service specifications also address the key issues of float (as being a resource of the schedule rather than of an individual party) and the baseline to be used for quantifying delays (which is identified as the effect of the change at the time the notice to proceed was issued). The specifications state in pertinent part:

> Float or slack is defined as the amount of time between the early start date and the late start date of any of the activities in the network analysis system schedule. Float or slack time is not time for the exclusive use of or benefit of either the Postal Service or the contractor. Extensions of time for performance required under the general contract clauses entitled *Changes, Differing Site Conditions, Termination for Default—Damages for Contractor Delay—Time Extensions, or Suspension of Work* will be granted only to the extent that equitable time adjustments for the activity or activities affected exceed the total float or slack along the channels involved at the time notice to proceed was issued for the change (emphasis added).

---

[20] NTP represents the Notice to Proceed authorizing work to proceed on a change.

[21] Fortec Constructors v. United States, 8 Cl. Ct. 490 (1985).

[22] VABCA No. 2168, 87-3 BCA ¶ 20,104 (1987).

Appendix F contains private-sector model specifications for use in requiring network analysis systems. These model specifications bear serious consideration for use due to the requirement that the parties participate in joint updating meetings monthly to verify: actual start dates, actual completion dates, cost values in place, any revised logic (as built or projected), effect of change orders, and so forth.

This joint updating process is extremely valuable since the parties are forced each month to address the issues of what the past month looked like in terms of completed activities and the logic by which the activities were completed. This procedure avoids the problem on many projects today where there may be three years of updates with no logic changes or recording of actual completion dates because of the failure of the parties to maintain the schedule. (Such manipulations can be accomplished through the use of logic overrides, without revising the logic in the diagram, on certain of the minicomputer programs.)

In addition, the private-sector model specifications are valuable because they clearly require the parties to demonstrate the necessity for time extensions, through the use of time-impact analyses and fragnets, on a timely basis—and they require the owner to respond on a timely basis to such requests.

§ 4.11 Factors Contributing to Poor Schedule Specifications

Clear and concise specifications outlining the responsibilities for scheduling and the requirements for preparation, approval, participation, use, maintenance, and reporting are essential for timely and successful completion of most projects. Unfortunately, poor scheduling specifications have contributed to the downfall of many projects. Some of the common problems associated with poor specifications include:

1. Not being specific about the method of scheduling required. In some contracts, for example, the scheduling specification has stated that "the contractor shall prepare a project schedule utilizing the Critical Path Method (CPM) of scheduling, or some other similar scheduling system." The words, "or some other similar scheduling system," can be interpreted that the requirement can be met by utilizing a bar-chart system. Obviously, a party bidding on a project may assume that he can prepare a bar chart that has a significantly lower cost for preparation and maintenance. A rule of thumb is that network-based scheduling techniques will cost approximately one-third to one-half of one percent of the construction value of the project. This means that the cost of network-based scheduling could be the difference

between winning or losing a competitively bid project—and the difference between the owner getting a good project schedule for performance or a poor project schedule resulting in chaos. Whatever the scheduling method chosen, it should be stated clearly and eliminate any options or ambiguities.

2.   Not requiring contractors to involve subcontractors in schedule development and implementation. This is compounded by the problem of prime contractors not including such requirements in their subcontracts. Owners are encouraged to include in the contract a requirement for prime contractors to involve major subcontractors in development and implementation of the project schedule.

3.   Specifying only a maximum number of activities required. The level of detail required should be based on specific criteria. Based on experience, a minimum number of activities should be specified to ensure a sufficient level of detail.

4.   Owners not approving or rejecting a contractor's schedule in a timely manner and not stating reasons for rejection when formal approval of a schedule is required. A number of specifications state that the owner will review and approve the schedule within a reasonable period of time. Others are silent. It is suggested that the owner state clearly in the specification how long he intends to take to review and approve the contractor's schedule or reject it as unreasonable or not feasible. Additionally, it should be understood how long the contractor has for each resubmittal and how long the owner has for review and approval of resubmittals.

5.   Stating that the schedule will be periodically updated, but not being specific about the frequency of such updates. The frequency of updating should be clearly stated, such as monthly or bi-weekly. If the specified frequency becomes unnecessary, the requirement can always be reduced to a lesser frequency either temporarily or permanently.

6.   Not requiring joint updates. Joint updates involving all key parties are encouraged to maximize communication about schedule, performance, problems, actions required, and intended plans for completion. The objective is to eliminate the surprises that can result when a single party independently prepares an update and distributes the updated version of the schedule to all other project participants.

7.   Not requiring that all physical access and availability restraints be incorporated into the project schedule. The party responsible for preparing the schedule should include this information in the schedule and define the relationship of each restraint to the sequence of work planned to accomplish the required scope of work within the time period specified.

8. Not specifying an explicit period for review and approval of shop drawings and other contractual submittals. Many contracts simply state that shop drawings will be submitted within a reasonable period of time. Define reasonable by stating specifically when submittals are to be made and the duration of their review and resubmittal periods.

9. Not requiring owner-furnished equipment to be incorporated into a contractor's schedule. This is essential for identifying proper dependency and time impact when delivery delays occur.

10. Not specifying, in the contract, all contractual dependencies with preceding, concurrent, and follow-on contractors in a multi prime contractor project. Additionally, not requiring prime contractors to define other key points of interface, particularly with the subcontractors and suppliers upon which they are dependent.

11. Allowing manpower and equipment restraints to create critical and near-critical paths. These situations may be the result of float abuses, which attempt to hide float that normally exists. Critical or near-critical paths are those with less than two weeks of contingency.

12. Not giving specific instructions for graphic techniques to be used for network or bar-chart construction. The failure to require readable, time-scaled diagrams for the original plan and updates can result in schedules that are useless and effectively unintelligible to the owner, subcontractors, architect/engineer, and contractor.

13. Not including in the specifications remedies for noncompliance of initial schedule submittal and subsequent update information.

14. Not including a narrative reporting requirement as part of the update process.

15. Not including a remedy for schedule-specification discrepancies. Most specifications include a reference to a standard of the industry. Unfortunately, many specifications fail to include a statement that, in the event of discrepancies, the specifications shall govern the development and utilization of the project schedule.

16. Stating a maximum duration requirement for activities. Keeping durations to a minimum, along with criteria for levels of indenture, is appropriate.

17. Not requiring time extensions to be justified by proper documentation (such as the use of time-impact analyses and fragnets) and not requiring that they be submitted to illustrate the impact of various types of delays.

18. Restricting network changes until the contractor submits details in writing and the owner formally approves. Such controls, if

misapplied by the owner as in *Fortec,*[23] can result in extensive, recoverable damages to the contractor because it was denied control over the schedule.

19. Preparing an integrated schedule for a project involving numerous prime contractors, subcontractors, and suppliers, and then not allowing their direct participation.

20. Completely restricting any schedule changes involving change orders and/or delays until an agreement on cost is reached.

---

[23] Fortec Constructors v. United States, 8 Cl. Ct. 490 (1985).

CHAPTER 5

RIGHTS AND OBLIGATIONS IN SCHEDULING

§ 5.1   Introduction

§ 5.2   Implied Obligations

§ 5.3   —Duty to Schedule and Coordinate

§ 5.4   —Duty to Not Delay, Hinder, or Interfere

§ 5.5   —Duty to Cooperate

§ 5.6   —Duty to Grant Reasonable Time Extensions

§ 5.7   Express Obligations

§ 5.8   Owner's Role in Scheduling

§ 5.9   —Owner-Issued Schedule

§ 5.10   —Progress Schedule Execution

§ 5.11   —Multiprime Contracting

§ 5.12   Prime Contractor's Role in Scheduling

§ 5.13   —Bid-Process Review of Scheduling

§ 5.14   —Preliminary Progress Schedule

§ 5.15   —Initial Approved Project Schedule

§ 5.16   —Project Schedule Updating

§ 5.17   —Coordinating Subcontractors

§ 5.18   Subcontractor's Role in Scheduling

§ 5.19   —Subcontractor Rights in Prime Contractor-Issued Schedule

§ 5.20   —Project Schedule Updating

§ 5.21   —Job-Coordination Meetings

§ 5.22   Project or Schedule Abandonment Due to Inadequate Scheduling

§ 5.23   —Effect of Schedule Abandonment

§ 5.24   Recognition of Contractor's Right to Finish Early and to Manage Schedule

§ 5.1   Introduction

Legal developments in the rights and obligations of the parties to the scheduling process have occurred primarily in two areas. First, developments have occurred because scheduling techniques are increasingly required by express contract provisions, and courts and government-agency boards of contract appeals review and enforce *express* scheduling obligations more frequently. Second, courts and boards of contract appeals have built upon the fundamental rights and obligations implied in every contract, including construction.

This chapter examines the issue of implied and express rights and obligations in the scheduling process from the viewpoint of the principal actors in construction: the owner, the prime contractor, and the subcontractor. This chapter provides an overview of the problems of each of these actors in construction scheduling and in development of their respective rights and obligations in the scheduling process.

§ 5.2   Implied Obligations

The parties to a construction contract, or, for that matter, any contract, generally are free to include any provision or language on which they agree in their contract.[1] Such provisions are referred to as *express* because they are enumerated between the parties.

Courts and government-agency boards of contract appeals also frequently read into contracts *implied obligations or warranties* that supplement the express obligations the parties have included. The key to understanding implied warranties is to apply a test of *fairness* to the relationship of the parties. Four such implied obligations relevant to scheduling are:

1. The duty to schedule and coordinate the work
2. The duty to not delay, hinder, or interfere with the work
3. The duty to cooperate
4. The duty to grant reasonable time extensions.

§ 5.3   —Duty to Schedule and Coordinate

Every construction contract imposes an implied obligation on the contractor (or on the owner in construction-management contracts) to schedule and execute the work of the various trades on the project in a normal and reasonable sequence of functions or activities. A prime contractor cannot

---

[1] Psaty & Furman v. Housing Auth., 76 R.I. 87, 68 A.2d 32 (1949).

schedule the work in a manner that favors the prime contractor's own performance and unreasonably interferes with the performance of the subcontractors. To do so would violate the implied obligation of the contractor to schedule the work of various trades in a reasonable manner.[2] A prime contractor's failure to coordinate and schedule the work of subcontractors may be fatal to the prime contractor's claim against the owner for delay costs.[3]

As part of the prime contractor's implicit obligation to not hamper a subcontractor's progress, prime contractors have been held responsible for their subcontractors' ascertainable delay costs, even in the absence of a contractually specified completion date.

For example, in *United States ex rel. Heller Electric Co. v. William F. Klingensmith, Inc.,*[4] a masonry subcontractor brought suit against the general contractor for delay to work done on a parking garage and building. The subcontract did not contain a specific completion date, but at the start of the project the subcontractor anticipated completing work in approximately 90 calendar days. The prime contractor delayed the subcontractor's performance on the parking garage such that it was not completed until 11 months after the work had begun. The general contractor contended it could not be found to have delayed the masonry subcontractor absent a completion date in the subcontract. The court (by implication found the subcontractor's anticipation of the work duration to be reasonable and) rejected the argument, stating:

> In a construction contract like the subcontract at issue here, the prime contractor implicitly promises to provide such working conditions as may be necessary to allow its subcontractor to carry out its obligations under the contract. If a contractor interferes with the work of its subcontractor, it has breached its obligation, and the subcontractor is entitled to recover for the resulting delays.[5]

The court determined the general contractor caused the delay, however, the amount of recovery was reduced because the subcontractor was found to have contributed to the delays on the building construction (adjacent to the parking garage).[6]

A contractor's preparation of a schedule for approval by the owner does not necessarily impose upon the contractor the obligation of ensuring that

---

[2] *See* E.C. Ernst, Inc. v. Manhattan Constr. Co., 387 F. Supp. 1001 (S.D. Ala. 1974), *aff'd in part, rev'd in part,* 551 F.2d 1026 (5th Cir. 1977).

[3] *See* Haas & Haynie Corp., GSBCA Nos. 5530, 6224, 6638, 6919, 6920, 84-2 BCA ¶ 17,446 (1984).

[4] 216 U.S. App. D.C. 408, 670 F.2d 1227 (D.C. Cir. 1982).

[5] *Id.* at 1230 (citing Burgess Constr. Co. v. Morrin & Son Co., 526 F.2d 108, 113 (10th Cir. 1975); George A. Fuller Co. v. United States, 69 F. Supp. 409 (Ct. Cl. 1947)).

[6] *Id.* at 1230.

all work will be completed according to schedule. Some courts view a schedule as a guideline, rather than an absolutely enforceable provision.[7] Thus, where there is no express contractual provision binding the parties to interim milestone duties in the schedule and the prime contractor has not otherwise hindered the subcontractors' performance, mere deviations from the construction schedule, by themselves, will not constitute a breach by the prime contractor.[8]

A subcontractor who cannot perform work as anticipated because of the prime contractor's failure or refusal to comply with the implied obligation to schedule and coordinate the work may have cause to abandon performance. In one case,[9] a prime contractor's failure to schedule and coordinate prevented the subcontractor from completing work within the time contemplated. The court found that this failure to schedule and coordinate work constituted a breach of contract that justified the subcontractor's abandonment of the project, as well as recovery of damages.

The recent trend of decisions shows the tendency of courts to recognize and impose upon prime contractors the obligation to schedule the work of the subcontractors.[10] However, courts in certain jurisdictions do not recognize breaches based upon a deviation from the schedule. In these jurisdictions, it is unlikely that a subcontractor will be justified in abandoning the project due to any failure by the prime contractor to schedule the work.[11] At any rate, abandonment should always be considered with extreme caution and, indeed, exercised only as a last resort under the most egregious circumstances.

§ 5.4 —Duty to Not Delay, Hinder, or Interfere

In executing a construction contract, all parties, including the owner, the prime contractor, and the subcontractors, impliedly warrant that they will

---

[7] *See* McCarty Corp. v. Pullman-Kellogg, 571 F. Supp. 1341 (M.D. La. 1983), *modified,* 751 F.2d 750 (5th Cir. 1985); Peter Kiewit Sons' Co. v. Iowa S. Utils. Co., 355 F. Supp. 376 (S.D. Iowa 1973).

[8] Peter Kiewit Sons' Co. v. Iowa S. Utils. Co., 355 F. Supp. 376 (S.D. Iowa 1973).

[9] Able Elec. v. Vacanti Randazzo Constr. Co., 212 Neb. 619, 324 N.W.2d 667 (1982).

[10] *See* United States *ex rel.* Heller Elec. Co. v. William F. Klingensmith, Inc., 216 U.S. App. D.C. 408, 670 F.2d 1227 (D.C. Cir. 1982); E.C. Ernst, Inc. v. Manhattan Constr. Co., 387 F. Supp. 1001 (S.D. Ala. 1974), *aff'd in part, rev'd in part,* 551 F.2d 1026 (5th Cir. 1977); L.L. Hall Constr. Co. v. United States, 177 Ct. Cl. 870, 379 F.2d 559 (1966); Pierce Assocs., Inc., GSBCA No. 4163, 77-2 BCA ¶ 12,746 (1977), *reconsideration denied,* 78-1 BCA ¶ 13,078, *aff'd and remanded,* 617 F.2d 223 (Ct. Cl. 1980); Blake Constr. Co. v. C.J. Coakley, 431 A.2d 569 (D.C. 1981); Able Elec. v. Vacanti Randazzo Constr. Co., 212 Neb. 619, 324 N.W.2d 667 (1982).

[11] *See* Drew Brown, Ltd. v. Joseph Rugo, Inc., 436 F.2d 632 (1st Cir. 1971).

not delay, hinder, or interfere with the performance of the other parties to the contract.[12]

To recover damages due to another party's interference with its work, an aggrieved party must prove the following elements:[13]

1. Its work was delayed or hindered.
2. It suffered damages because of the delay or hindrance.
3. The other party was responsible for the act or omission that caused the delay or hindrance.

Both action and inaction can constitute interference with a contractor's work. Where an owner has control over aspects of a contractor's performance, the failure to act in a timely manner may constitute interference with the contractor's work.[14]

The failure to act may have two consequences that courts find justify holding the interfering party liable for damages. First, if the contractor is delayed in beginning performance this results in overall delay in performance and increases costs due to the idle time of laborers and equipment and to performance under conditions different from those anticipated (for instance, performance during winter months instead of summer months).[15] Second, during the interim period when the contractor is unable to proceed with work, other contractors may have erected structures or performed other work that restricts the contractor's performance when finally able to proceed.[16]

---

[12] R.A. Weaver & Assocs., Inc. v. Haas & Haynie Corp., 663 F.2d 168 (D.C. Cir. 1980); Citizens Nat'l Bank v. Vitt, 367 F.2d 541 (5th Cir. 1966); Glassman Constr. v. Maryland City Plaza, Inc., 371 F. Supp. 1154 (D. Md. 1974), aff'd, 530 F.2d 968 (4th Cir. 1975); Lichter v. Mellon-Stuart Co., 193 F. Supp. 216 (W.D. Pa. 1961), aff'd, 305 F.2d 216 (3d Cir. 1962); Petrofsky v. United States, 222 Ct. Cl. 450, 616 F.2d 494, cert. denied, 450 U.S. 968 (1980); Della Ratta, Inc. v. American Better Community Developers, Inc., 38 Md. 119, 380 A.2d 627 (1977).

[13] Shintech, Inc. v. Group Constructors, Inc., 688 S.W.2d 144 (Tex. Ct. App. 1985); City of Houston v. R.F. Ball Constr. Co., 570 S.W.2d 75 (Tex. Civ. App. 1978).

[14] Havens Steel Co. v. Randolph Eng'g Co., 613 F. Supp. 514 (W.D. Mo. 1985), aff'd, 813 F.2d 186 (8th Cir. 1987); Kehm Corp. v. United States, 119 Ct. Cl. 454, 93 F. Supp. 620 (1950); Bates Lumber Co., AGBCA Nos. 81-242-1, 84-210-1, 88-2 BCA ¶ 20,707 (1988); Bryant & Bryant, ASBCA No. 27,910, 88-3 BCA ¶ 20,923 (1988); Carlon Davis Constr., Inc., ASBCA No. 32,578, 88-2 BCA ¶ 20,575 (1988); Tribble & Stevens Co. v. Consolidated Serv., Inc., 744 S.W.2d 945 (Tex. Ct. App. 1987).

[15] See Lichter v. Mellon-Stuart Co., 193 F. Supp. 216 (W.D. Pa. 1961), aff'd, 305 F.2d 216 (3d Cir. 1962).

[16] See Havens Steel Co. v. Randolph Eng'g Co., 613 F. Supp. 514 (W.D. Mo. 1985), aff'd, 813 F.2d 186 (8th Cir. 1987).

Other examples of interference—by an owner in the work of a prime contractor or by a prime contractor in the work of a subcontractor—include the following:

1. Issuance of a notice to proceed despite the known presence of delays[17]
2. Stopping payment on a check that is crucial to the liquidity of the contractor[18]
3. Changes to the contract that force the contractor to work out of sequence, on a piecemeal basis, or during a different time period[19]
4. Failure to keep the site in the condition specified in the contract[20]
5. Knowledge, and sometimes sanctioning, of other parties using the contractor's work site as a drainage area[21]
6. Failure to provide drawings, and changes to the drawings, that are necessary to the contractor's work[22]
7. Failure to disclose *superior knowledge* or information that is not readily available to the contractor and is crucial to performance.[23]

The owner's implied duty to the prime contractor, and the prime contractor's duty to the subcontractor, to not delay, interfere with, or hinder the other party's work, can be applied to any number of acts or omissions during the course of performance. Regardless of the act or omission involved, the implied duty to not delay, hinder, or interfere with the other party's work is a frequently encountered basis of recovery.

§ 5.5   —Duty to Cooperate

In every construction contract there is an implied duty on the party of all parties to cooperate with the other parties in rendering their

---

[17] United States Steel Corp. v. Missouri Pac. R.R., 668 F.2d 435 (8th Cir. 1982).

[18] Citizens Nat'l Bank v. Vitt, 367 F.2d 541 (5th Cir. 1966).

[19] B.J. Harland Elec. Co. v. Granger Bros., Inc., 24 Mass. App. Ct. 506, 510 N.E.2d 765 (1987).

[20] Coatesville Contractors & Eng'rs, Inc. v. Borough of Ridley Park, 509 Pa. 553, 506 A.2d 862 (1986).

[21] R.S. Noonan, Inc. v. Morrison-Knudsen Co., 522 F. Supp. 1186 (E.D. La. 1981).

[22] S. Leo Harmonay, Inc. v. Binks Mfg. Co., 597 F. Supp. 1014 (S.D.N.Y. 1984), *aff'd,* 762 F.2d 990 (2d Cir. 1985). *See also* Quaker Empire Constr. Co. v. D.A. Collins Constr. Co., 88 A.D.2d 1043, 452 N.Y.S.2d 692 (1982). *But see* McCarty Corp. v. Pullman-Kellogg, 571 F. Supp. 1341 (M.D. La. 1983), *modified,* 751 F.2d 750 (5th Cir. 1985).

[23] Helene Curtis v. United States, 160 Ct. Cl. 437, 312 F.2d 774 (1963). *But see* Commercial Contractors, Inc., ASBCA Nos. 30,675, 31,782, 88-3 BCA ¶ 20,877 (1988).

performance.[24] The duty to cooperate is, therefore, similar to the implied duty to not delay, hinder, or interfere with another party's work. Both duties address what the courts perceive as the fundamental relations between the parties necessary for performance of the contract.

As with the duty to not interfere, the duty to cooperate can be breached by a broad range of acts or omissions. A good example of the duty to cooperate, as it applies to the owner, is presented in *Housing Authority of City of Dallas v. J.T. Hubbell*.[25] In *Hubbell,* the Housing Authority for the City of Dallas issued a number of contracts for the development of a housing project. Separate contracts required demolition of existing buildings, grading and construction of foundations, construction of foundations, construction of dwelling units, installation of sewer facilities, underground utilities, electrical distribution, paving, sidewalks, and so on. A group of contractors brought an action seeking, among other things, to recover liquidated damages wrongfully withheld and damages for breach of contract for owner-caused interference, delays, and arbitrary conduct. The court found that the owner failed to cooperate when the owner: (1) failed to plan the development of the project as a whole so that the contractors would be able to complete their work within the time schedule for certain groups of buildings; (2) failed to furnish a master progress schedule, thus preventing the contractors from proceeding with their contracts in an orderly, efficient, and economical manner; (3) failed to coordinate the work of the various prime contractors, thus delaying completion of their work; (4) failed to proceed with underground utilities, thus delaying the contractors; (5) failed to proceed with the construction of sidewalks and clothes poles, thus delaying completion of the contractors' work; (6) failed to expedite the flow of information to the contractors so as to minimize delay in their performance; (7) failed to decide on a type of water heater within a reasonable time; (8) failed to deliver water heaters in such time that the contractors would not be delayed; (9) through the owner's architect, made arbitrary and capricious requirements as to the construction of the project.[26]

The court concluded that the owner caused the contractor's delay willfully, by unreasoning action, without due consideration, and in disregard of the rights of the other parties.

The above example is an extreme illustration of an owner's breach of the duty to cooperate. Courts generally do not require such a long list of failures by a contracting party in order to find a breach. A variety

---

[24] *See generally* Ginsburg & Eshelman, *Implied Duty of Cooperation,* Construction Briefings No. 87-12 (1987).

[25] 325 S.W.2d 880 (Tex. Civ. App. 1959).

[26] *Id.* at 891.

of acts and omissions will suffice.[27] For example, in *Department of Transportation v. Arapaho Construction, Inc.*,[28] the contractor (Arapaho) was to construct a bridge on a parkway for the department of transportation (DOT). However, the land where the parkway was to be constructed became the subject of a lawsuit. Ultimately, the Georgia Supreme Court upheld a permanent injunction against construction of the parkway.

Arapaho, unable to proceed with its work, then brought suit against DOT, contending that DOT breached its contract. DOT claimed that the termination provision of the contract, which precluded recovery for damages arising from court-ordered injunctions, barred Arapaho's claim.

However, the court held that the breach by DOT was not due to the issuance of the permanent injunction. Rather, the breach was one of a failure to cooperate, thereby totally and absolutely preventing Arapaho from performing its contract work. DOT failed to procure the requested right of way that would have allowed Arapaho to perform. As a consequence of the breach, the court found that Arapaho was entitled to not only its contract costs, but its unrealized profits as well.

The duty to cooperate also extends to requiring an owner (or an owner's architect) to promptly rectify errors and omissions in the contract drawings where those errors and omissions prove detrimental to the contractor's work. For example, one court found that the failure of the bid documents to disclose—and the owner's subsequent failure to disclose—that telephone service to the construction site could not be provided in the usual manner (through power lines), thereby requiring the contractor to construct an 11,000-foot trench, constituted a breach of duty to cooperate by the owner.[29]

As these examples illustrate, the duty to cooperate may take a variety of forms in any construction contract since the performance of any one party is likely to be dependent upon any number of acts to be performed by the other party. Without the cooperation of all parties to a construction contract, performance cannot occur or will be much more expensive than originally anticipated. All parties to the construction process should be familiar with the implied duty to cooperate as an important right within the package of rights every contract contains.

---

[27] *See* Hoel-Steffen Constr. Co. v. United States, 231 Ct. Cl. 128, 684 F.2d 843 (1982); S.A. Healy Co. v. United States, 576 F.2d 299 (Ct. Cl. 1978); Raytheon Serv. Co., GSBCA No. 5695, 81-1 BCA ¶ 15,002 (1981).

[28] 180 Ga. App. 341, 349 S.E.2d 196 (1986), *aff'd on appeal,* 257 Ga. 269, 357 S.E.2d 593 (1987).

[29] Richardson Elec. Co. v. Peter Francese & Son, Inc., 21 Mass. App. Ct. 47, 484 N.E.2d 108 (1985).

A final note of caution about the duty to cooperate: A contractor who is substantially behind schedule and is considered in default by the owner, albeit technically, should be careful to notify the owner of all reasons for his delay. Otherwise, a court may find that the owner did not breach its duty to cooperate since the contractor was afforded an opportunity to explain its own delay yet failed to provide any justification.[30]

§ 5.6   —Duty to Grant Reasonable Time Extensions

A construction contract often contains an express provision requiring the owner to grant the general contractor a time extension if certain delays are experienced on the project.[31] Such a provision may also be combined with a *No Damages for Delay* clause that limits the contractor to the remedy of a time extension in the event that certain contemplated delays are experienced.

Where a contract contains an express obligation on the owner's part to grant time extensions, the courts and government-agency boards of contract appeals have added to the express obligation an implied obligation requiring the owner to grant justifiable time extensions to the contractor *in a timely manner.*[32] This approach recognizes that a time extension is of no advantage to the contractor if it is not granted in a timely manner. Extensions must be timely to enable the contractor to incorporate the additional time into the progress schedule and coordinate the remainder of the work. Time extensions that are not granted until all the work is completed are of no use to the contractor in this process.[33]

Thus, when an owner demands that the contractor perform within the original or adjusted schedule, even though the contractor is entitled to a time extension, Courts have held that the contractor is "constructively accelerated."[34] Similarly, the failure of an owner to grant an adequate time extension in a timely manner may amount to an acceleration order.[35] Whether the extension has been granted in a "timely manner" will depend upon the facts of each case. An owner who waits until after the substantial completion date to grant a time extension will likely be faced with an

---

[30] *See* Spec, Inc., ASBCA No. 29,790, 88-2 BCA ¶ 20,756 (1988).

[31] *See, e.g.,* FAR 52.243-4, 52.249-14 (1987); AIA Document A201, General Conditions of the Contract for Construction, Art. 8.3 (1987 ed.).

[32] *See* Continental Consol. Corp. v. United States, 200 Ct. Cl. 737 (1972); M.S.I. Corp., GSBCA No. 2429, 68-2 BCA ¶ 7377 (1968).

[33] *See* Continental Consol. Corp. v. United States, 200 Ct. Cl. 737 (1972).

[34] *See* Norair Eng'g Corp. v. United States, 229 Ct. Cl. 160, 666 F.2d 546 (1981); American Mach. & Foundry Co., ASBCA No. 10,173, 67-2 BCA ¶ 6540 (1967).

[35] *See* M.S.I. Corp., GSBCA No. 2429, 68-2 BCA ¶ 7377 (1968).

acceleration claim.[36] When this occurs, the costs of acceleration, which arise from inefficiency, are compensable as a contract change. An owner simply cannot remedy failure to grant time extensions in a timely manner by belatedly addressing the contractor's entitlement to additional time well beyond the contract completion date. To grant the contractor additional time at this point is nothing more than an idle gesture, since the contractor would have already incurred acceleration expense to avoid claims for liquidated or delay damages.[37]

Granting a *timely* extension is especially crucial where a contractor is using the critical path method (CPM) to schedule the work. Unless a time extension is granted immediately upon determination of the extent of the delay, the CPM schedule cannot be revised to reflect the excusable delay. As a result, schedules for the periods covering the excusable delay would show the contractor to be behind schedule when, in fact, if the appropriate time extensions were incorporated into the computer runs, the contractor might be well ahead of schedule on the critical path.[38]

Consequently, owners who fail to grant the necessary time extension within a reasonable period, and thereby distort the CPM schedule, may find themselves liable to their contractors for acceleration costs.[39] Furthermore, if owners do wait until the end of the project to decide whether to grant a time extension, they may not rely on the CPM schedule to deny recovery, because the CPM schedule will not reflect changes in performance requirements.[40]

An illustrative example of the effect of failure to grant an extension in a timely manner is *Fortec Constructors v. United States.*[41] In *Fortec,* in a contract between the Army Corps of Engineers (Corps) and Fortec Constructors (Fortec) for the construction of an aircraft fuel and maintenance facility, Fortec claimed it was entitled to time extensions and increased costs due to several modifications that were issued unilaterally by the Corps. The Corps, relying on the CPM schedule, contended Fortec was entitled to neither a time extension nor any additional money. However, the court held that the Corps was not entitled to rely on the CPM schedule and its refusal to grant time extensions. The court found the Corps's

---

[36] *See* Continental Consol. Corp., ENGBCA Nos. 2743, 2776, 67-2 BCA ¶ 6624 (1967); M.S.I. Corp., GSBCA No. 2429, 68-2 BCA ¶ 7377 (1968); Contracting & Material Co. v. City of Chicago, 20 Ill. App. 3d 684, 314 N.E.2d 598 (1974), *rev'd,* 64 Ill. 2d 21, 349 N.E.2d 389 (1979).

[37] *Id.*

[38] *See* Continental Consol. Corp., ENGBCA Nos. 2743, 2776, 67-2 BCA ¶ 6624 (1967).

[39] Continental Consol. Corp. v. United States, 200 Ct. Cl. 737 (1972).

[40] *See* Fortec Constructors v. United States, 8 Cl. Ct. 490 (1985), *aff'd,* 804 F.2d 141 (Fed. Cir. 1986).

[41] 8 Cl. Ct. 490 (1985).

denial of Fortec's claim improper because it based its decision on an out-dated CPM schedule. As the court explained, the Corps's action served to benefit only itself:

> [T]he Corps failed to even consider several of Fortec's requests for additional compensation and time extensions until after the project was completed. Fortec could not update the CPM without receipt of modifications from the Corps adding the additional work, and then only with the concurrence of the Corps as to the time to be added . . . . Accordingly, Fortec was unable to update the CPM during construction.[42]

As a consequence of the Corps's refusal to grant modifications in a timely manner, the CPM schedule could not be modified and, thus, the CPM schedule did not reflect changes to the performance requirements. Thus, the Corps's reliance on the CPM schedule in deciding whether to grant Fortec's requests was an exercise in futility because it did not reflect the true schedule of the work. Consequently, the Corps's imposition of liquidated damages was not justified, and the court rescinded all of the liquidated damages imposed.[43]

The danger inherent in the owner's refusal to grant a time extension in a timely manner is discussed in the following excerpt:

> Failure to determine the time of a change ordered in the work is a mistake. If this action is postponed, the actual job status of the time the change was ordered may be extremely difficult to determine; consequently, a reasonable evaluation at a later date may be impossible. *In addition, control of the project is lost the minute a change is ordered without incorporating that change in the schedule.* Experience indicates that procrastination in settlement of justifiable time extensions lead to an inordinate amount of claims and the possibility of constructive acceleration.[44]

The above observation is amply supported by decisions in many cases in which the contractor was entitled to a time extension that was not granted in a timely manner.[45]

While there should be little doubt as to the owner's obligation to grant time extensions in a timely manner, owners frequently fail to do so. Decisions on requests for extensions are sometimes delayed or sidetracked for such reasons as:

---

[42] *Id.* at 504–06.

[43] *Id.* at 509.

[44] Army Corps of Engineers, Regulations, ER 1-1-11 App. A. ¶ 1-4e(2) (emphasis added).

[45] *See, e.g.,* M.S.I. Corp., GSBCA No. 2429, 68-2 BCA ¶ 7377 (1968).

1. A lack of expertise or experience on the part of the owner or architect (or their staffs) with respect to project scheduling. This can result in the fear or prejudicing the interests of the owner by mistakenly granting an extension of time when one may not be due—particularly during the early stages of the project when a time extension may not appear absolutely necessary.

2. A lack of confidence in the accuracy of the most recent schedule revision submitted by the contractor, which is often based upon a recognition by the owner or architect (or their staffs) that neither the owner nor the contractor are committed to, or rely upon, the progress schedule in the execution of the work.

3. The assertion of unreasonable and, perhaps, unjustified requests for time extensions by a contractor that is thought to "cry wolf" too often.

4. The existence of other pending claims or requests for a time extension that may be affected by the decision.

5. An agreement or verbal understanding (often subsequently forgotten or misinterpreted by one of the parties) that the contractor's request for a time extension will be deferred while other unresolved issues of greater significance between the parties are pending.

6. An unrealistic belief on the part of the owner or architect that the contractor will bring the project back on schedule because of the threat of liquidated damages.

Both owners and contractors should be cognizant of these conditions. The failure on projects to address time extensions in a timely and diligent fashion is a strong indication that scheduling disputes and litigation may arise.

§ 5.7 Express Obligations

Construction contracts often contain express provisions that bind the parties and affect their rights and obligations in the scheduling process. These express warranties may be boilerplate provisions that appear in standard form contracts or they may be the object of intense negotiation between the parties before they are included in the agreement. Any analysis of a construction contract and the rights of the parties thereunder should begin with a review of the contract's express provisions. However, it should be remembered that the critical implied obligations just reviewed will be read into the contract to amplify ambiguous express language. Further, express provisions that seek to limit liability are frequently unsuccessful because of the court's unwillingness to enforce any attempt to limit implied duties that promote basic fairness.

§ 5.8   Owner's Role in Scheduling

Traditionally, owners have taken a laissez-faire attitude towards the scheduling process during construction. Once construction contracts are executed, owners typically believe they have done everything necessary with respect to the schedule to ensure successful completion of their projects and that the rest is up to the contractors and architects. However, owners may find that they have assumed certain express obligations to contractors.

§ 5.9   —Owner-Issued Schedule

An owner who prepares and issues a schedule for construction may be assuming substantial risk. This risk may arise as a logical extension of a theory that has developed in decisions involving owner-issued specifications. Under this theory, first enunciated in the 1918 U.S. Supreme Court opinion *Spearin v. United States,*[46] where an owner issues design specifications, the contractor has the right to rely on the specifications as being accurate and correct. In *Spearin,* plans and specifications prepared by the government provided for reconstructing a sewer that intersected the project site for a dry dock. The contractor rebuilt the sewer as required under the contract documents and the sewer was accepted by the government. However, due to (1) a dam (unknown to either party) located in a connecting sewer within the Navy yard, but beyond the limits of the contractor's operations and (2) the general conditions of drainage (*known to the government* but not to the contractor), backwater burst the new sewer during a heavy rain and flooded the dry-dock excavation, causing extensive damage. The contractor declined to proceed with repairs unless the government paid for the damage and made the sewer system safe. In response, the government canceled the contract. The Supreme Court, in affirming a decision by the court of claims, held that when the government issues design specifications, it warrants the adequacy and accuracy of the specifications. The contractor has a right to rely on the specifications as being accurate and correct, such that increased costs incurred by

---

[46] 248 U.S. 132 (1918). *See* Richardson Elec. Co. v. Peter Francese & Son, Inc., 21 Mass. App. Ct. 47, 484 N.E.2d 108 (1985); Shintech, Inc. v. Group Constructors, Inc., 688 S.W.2d 144 (Tex. Ct. App. 1985); Newell v. Mosley, 469 S.W.2d 481 (Tex. Civ. App. 1971).

the contractor due to errors in specifications are recoverable. According to the court: "If the contractor is bound to build according to plans and specifications prepared by the owner, the contractor will not be responsible for the consequences of defects in the plans and specifications."

The responsibility of the owner in warranting the adequacy and accuracy of the specification is not overcome by the usual clauses requiring builders to visit the jobsite, to check the plans, and to inform themselves of the requirements of the work.

The Court's decision in *Spearin* is now a well-recognized principle in both state and federal construction contracts. In addition, where the owner submits a design specification and has superior knowledge of deficiencies in the specification, the owner may warrant that the contractor can perform its work according to specifications issued.[47] Where this proves not the case, and the contractor incurs increased costs, the owner may have breached the implied warranty attaching to such schedule or specification, enabling the contractor to recover.[48]

Courts have clearly imposed upon owners a duty to disclose *superior knowledge.* Such disclosure is required where an owner possesses vital information that the owner knows the contractor cannot obtain on its own.[49]

It is submitted that these theories may also be applicable in the area of owner-issued schedules. Thus, where an owner submits an owner-prepared schedule indicating a particular method of performance and has superior knowledge of deficiencies in the schedule, the owner may warrant that the contractor can perform the work according to the schedule issued. Where such deficiencies exist and the contractor incurs increased costs, the owner may have breached the implied warranty attaching to the schedule, enabling the contractor to recover.[50] Yet where the contractor does not intend to rely on the owner's CPM schedule, the contractor may not later complain of defects or errors in that schedule.

In *Utley-James, Inc. v. United States,* [51] the claims court held that the General Services Administration (GSA) preparation of a CPM schedule for the project could not be relied upon by the contractor because the

---

[47] *See* Helene Curtis v. United States, 160 Ct. Cl. 437, 312 F.2d 774 (1963).

[48] *See generally* J. Cibinic & R. Nash, Administration of Government Contracts 190–212 (1985); Patten, *The Implied Warranty That Attaches to Government Furnished Design Specifications,* 31 Fed. B.J. 291 (1972); 13 Am. Jur. 2d, *Building and Construction Contracts* § 28 (1969). *See also* W.F. Magann Corp. v. Diamond Mfg. Co., 775 F.2d 1202 (4th Cir. 1985).

[49] *See* Helene Curtis v. United States, 160 Ct. Cl. 437, 312 F.2d 774 (1963).

[50] *See* Able Elec. v. Vacanti Randazzo Constr. Co., 212 Neb. 619, 324 N.W.2d 667 (1982).

[51] 14 Cl. Ct. 804 (1988).

owner prepared the CPM for payment purposes and to monitor progress. The court further found that the contractor had maintained its own CPM schedule and paid no attention to the owner's (GSA) CPM. Similarly, in *Titan Pacific Construction Corp. v. United States,*[52] the court held that while the approved "as planned" CPM schedule was a useful administration tool for organizing the work and computing progress payments, it was not contractually binding for purposes of determining the impact of excusable delay or contract completion, especially where the contractor's actual performance deviated from the schedule.[53]

When the owner issues a schedule indicating the manner and method of performance, a contractor can be exposed to difficult problems arising out of its experience and knowledge. If the contractor is aware of a patent error in the sequence or durations of activities shown on the schedule and, nevertheless, undertakes to construct the project according to the schedule, the contractor's use of the owner schedule, regardless of this knowledge, appears to constitute assumption of the risk of meeting the schedule (much as is the case where there is patent error or ambiguity in the plans or specifications).[54]

§ 5.10   —Progress Schedule Execution

An owner is not relieved of responsibility with regard to the contractor's performance under the project schedule merely by taking a passive role in schedule preparation. Where a contractor is not working with an owner-issued schedule, the parties still should be aware of the owner's obligations regarding *execution* of the schedule during the course of performance.

The owner's obligations in execution of the project schedule have been recognized by the courts and government-agency boards of contract appeals in a number of decisions. These decisions generally refer to two important theories of contract law as the basis for owner obligations in execution of a schedule: (1) the implied obligation of every party to a contract to not do anything to hinder or to interfere with the other party's performance; and (2) the theory, discussed previously, that an owner will be responsible for increased costs incurred by the contractor where the contractor relies, to its detriment, upon information furnished by the owner, whether the information is in the form of drawings, specifications, or a progress schedule.

Relying on these two theories, courts have imposed numerous obligations on owners in execution of the progress schedule. For example, at the

---

[52] 17 Cl. Ct. 630 (1989).

[53] *Id.* at 632.

[54] *See* Hensel Phelps Constr. Co., ASBCA No. 35,767, 88-2 BCA ¶ 20,701 (1988), 12.

beginning of a project, an owner must issue a notice to proceed within a reasonable time after contract award to allow the contractor to begin work.[55] This obligation may tempt some owners to issue the notice to proceed immediately. However, issuing the notice to proceed when work cannot commence due to physical constraints may render the owner liable for the contractor's damages.[56]

A contractor's reliance on a notice to proceed that proves defective may also provide the basis for a contractor's recovery of additional costs incurred. For example, *United States Steel Corp. v. Missouri Pacific Railroad*[57] involved a claim for delay damage by a bridge builder, United States Steel (US Steel), against the owner, Missouri Pacific Railroad Company (MOPAC). US Steel argued that it was entitled to damages due to MOPAC's issuance of a notice to proceed when, in fact, US Steel could not begin its work. Upon MOPAC's issuance of the notice to proceed, US Steel immediately ordered the requisite materials, began its preparatory work, and set up its own construction schedule. However, the site was not ready until five and one-half months (175 days) later, due to the delays encountered by the substructure contractor.[58]

As a result of the delay, US Steel experienced "extra expenses for the attendant demurrage, equipment rental, and overhead." MOPAC countered that it was not responsible for US Steel expenses, because US Steel should have apprised itself of the other contractor's stage of progress.[59] However, the court rejected this argument, finding that US Steel's obligation to apprise itself of the construction progress was cut off by MOPAC's issuance of the notice to proceed and that once it was issued, US Steel was obligated to begin performance. Consequently, the court found MOPAC's issuance of the notice to proceed with the knowledge that the contractor could not begin work constituted active interference, which precluded enforcement of the no damages for delay clause and entitled US Steel to its costs associated therewith.

Accordingly, where the contract documents indicate certain site conditions, an owner has a duty to ensure such conditions are maintained. Consequently, the owner may be responsible for the contractor's increased costs associated with the owner's failure to maintain such conditions.[60]

---

[55] *See* Goudreau Corp., DOTBCA No. 1895, 88-1 BCA ¶ 20,479 (1988); Excavation Constr., Inc., ENGBCA No. 3858, 82-1 BCA ¶ 15,770 (1982). *But see* Mann Constr. Co., EBCA No. 362-6-86, 88-3 BCA ¶ 21,014 (1988).

[56] *See* United States Steel Corp. v. Missouri Pac. R.R., 668 F.2d 435 (8th Cir. 1982).

[57] *Id.*

[58] *Id.* at 437.

[59] *Id.* at 439.

[60] *See* Bagwell Coatings, Inc. v. Middle South Energy, Inc., 797 F.2d 1298 (5th Cir. 1986); Coatesville Contractors & Eng'rs, Inc. v. Borough of Ridley Park, 509 Pa. 553, 506 A.2d 862 (1986).

Similarly, an owner has a duty to provide owner-furnished equipment, materials, and information in a timely manner,[61] as well as to give timely approval of designs submitted by the contractor.[62] As these examples illustrate, careful attention to execution of the progress schedule should be of utmost concern to an owner in administration of a contract, even though the schedule may have been developed by others.

§ 5.11   —Multiprime Contracting

In *multiprime contracting,* a project is divided into various work packages, generally along the lines of the various building trades, and a separate prime contractor for each work package then contracts directly with the owner—or with the owner's representative, the construction manager. Under this system, there is no one general contractor responsible for completion of the entire project. Instead, there are multiple prime contractors, each responsible for executing a segment of the total work.

A variation of the multiprime mode of contracting is known as *phased construction.* This technique involves the overlapping of design and construction activities among several prime contractors, so that construction on the earlier phases of construction can proceed even though final design of the later phases of the project may not be entirely complete.

As a general rule, in multiprime contracting the owner becomes the executor of the project and assumes duties analogous to the normal prime contractor to schedule and coordinate the work. Accordingly, the owner will be held responsible for exercising due diligence in coordinating and supervising the work of all trades on the project. This was the decision in *Norman Co. v. County of Nassau,*[63] an action by a contractor against Nassau County for delay damages. The trial court granted judgment for the defendant and the contractor appealed. The supreme court held that the contractor was entitled to a trial on the allegation that the owner actively or willfully interfered with the contractor in the course of its work. The contract in *Norman* contained a no damages for delay clause which, the court noted, was not completely exculpatory; that is, if the contractor could demonstrate that the owner actively or willfully interfered with the contractor's performance, the no-damages-for-delay clause would not defeat recovery.

In fact, courts and boards of contract appeals have held that an owner, or an owner's construction manager if one is utilized, has an affirmative

---

[61] *See* Specialty Assembling & Packing Co. v. United States, 174 Ct. Cl. 153, 355 F.2d 554 (1966); C.N. Flagg & Co., ASBCA Nos. 26,444, 26,655, 84-1 BCA ¶ 17,120 (1983); Shintech, Inc. v. Group Constructors, Inc., 688 S.W.2d 144 (Tex. Ct. App. 1985).

[62] *See* Pathman Constr. Co., ASBCA No. 23,392, 85-2 BCA ¶ 18,096 (1985).

[63] 27 A.D.2d 936, 478 N.Y.S.2d 719 (1967).

duty to schedule and coordinate the work of the various multiple prime contractors.[64] An owner's responsibility includes taking steps to require timely completion of one contractor's work to prevent delay of or interference with another contractor, as well as scheduling work in a way that will allow contractors to be able to perform economically where their work physically interrelates with that of other contractors.

Pierce Associates, Inc.[65] is an illustrative example of the owner's duty to schedule and coordinate. In *Pierce,* multiple prime contracts were awarded and a schedule was set out for the progress. The government's schedule called for construction activities to begin with the work of the structural contractor followed by that of the mechanical contractor. As construction progressed, however, the structural contractor fell behind schedule, thereby delaying the mechanical contractor's work. The government and its construction manager, however, waited six months after the delay was apparent before demanding that the structural contractor expend extra effort to achieve the scheduled milestone dates.

The mechanical contractor sought an equitable adjustment of its contract price from the government for the delays and interruptions caused by the structural contractor's delay and the government's failure to resolutely and timely act to ensure completion of the structural work. Although the contract required the mechanical contractor to cooperate with other contractors on the project and, if required by the government, to make extra effort to maintain the schedule at no extra cost to the government, the contractor was entitled to the recovery sought. The board held:

> Under the terms of its contract, the government had the responsibility to make all reasonable efforts to keep its other contractors on schedule where the timely performance of one contractor was dependent on that of others. To allow the government to escape the responsibility imposed upon it by the terms of the contract and to deny Appellant the adjustment cognizable under a relief granting clause would remove much of the government's incentive to properly sequence the progress of a phased construction project.[66]

Similarly, in *Hall Construction Co. v. United States,*[67] plaintiff contracted with the government to repair and improve certain airstrips at a

---

[64] *See* Paccon, Inc. v. United States, 185 Ct. Cl. 24, 399 F.2d 162 (1968); Hall Constr. Co. v. United States, 177 Ct. Cl. 870, 379 F.2d 559 (1966); Hoffman v. United States, 166 Ct. Cl. 39, 340 F.2d 645 (1964); Stephenson Assocs., Inc., GSBCA Nos. 6573, 6815, 86-3 BCA ¶ 19,071 (1986); Pierce Assocs., Inc., GSBCA No. 4163, 77-2 BCA ¶ 12,746, *reconsideration denied,* 78-1 BCA ¶ 13,078, *aff'd and remanded,* 617 F.2d 223 (Ct. Cl. 1980).

[65] GSBCA No. 4163, 77-2 BCA ¶ 12,746, *reconsideration denied,* 78-1 BCA ¶ 13,078, *aff'd and remanded,* 617 F.2d 223 (Ct. Cl. 1980).

[66] *Id.,* 77-2 BCA at 63,682.

[67] 177 Ct. Cl. 870, 379 F.2d 559 (1966).

government installation. Plaintiff incurred increased performance costs when the government failed to make the necessary runways available for timely completion of plaintiff's work.

In connection with the project designed to improve the airfield, the government had let several simultaneous contracts. It then permitted an inefficient contractor who was behind schedule to proceed with work in preference to the plaintiff. The court held that this penalized the plaintiff, that the delay suffered by plaintiff was the fault of the government, and the increased costs were recoverable. In so holding, the court stated:

> It is plain that the government is obligated to prevent interference with orderly and reasonable progress of a contractor's work by other contractors over whom the government controls . . . nor will . . . failure of the defendant to discharge his obligations . . . be cured simply by waiving liquidated damages.[68]

The government may not avoid its duty to schedule, in the context of multiprime contracting, by placing responsibility for coordination on the various multiple prime contractors (as contrasted with charging one contractor with scheduling responsibility). In *Paccon, Inc. v. United States,*[69] the contractor (Paccon) sought to recover its increased costs of performance arising from the government's failure to make the jobsite available as specified in the government project schedule. The site was delayed by another contractor's failure to timely complete its work.

In remanding the case to the administrative board, the court held that Paccon would be entitled to recover for the delay if the government failed to enforce the project schedule it had imposed on the grading contractor. The court further held that where the government lets several contractors construct a project and provides in each contract that the contractor must cooperate and coordinate work with the work of other contractors in the project, the contracting officer has the right and the duty to see that the contractor lives up to the established project schedule.

Further, the presence of an exculpatory clause cannot relieve the government of its duty to schedule and coordinate multiple prime contractors. In *Stephenson Associates, Inc.,*[70] the board found that, although the contract contained a clause disclaiming owner liability for "[an]other contractor's failure to coordinate or his failure to comply with the directives of the construction manager or the contracting officer," such exculpatory language cannot relieve the government of its responsibility to coordinate the work of other prime contractors.[71]

---

[68] *Id.* at 879.

[69] 185 Ct. Cl. 24, 399 F.2d 162 (1968).

[70] GSBCA Nos. 6573, 6815, 86-3 BCA ¶ 19,071 (1986).

[71] *Id.* at 96,327.

This obligation to coordinate the prime contractors has been extended to require the owner to resolve disputes among the primes that interfere with job performance.[72] However, if the owner has delegated—in the contract—the duty to coordinate to one of the individual prime contractors, such as the general trades contractor, the owner may not necessarily be held liable where coordination is unsatisfactory.[73] Consequently, it is crucial to determine which party has responsibility for supervision and coordination. On multiprime projects where no party is designated, it has been held that the owner has impliedly assumed the responsibility to coordinate the work on the project.[74]

§ 5.12   Prime Contractor's Role in Scheduling

The obligations of prime contractors in the scheduling process raise various important considerations. These are reviewed below.

§ 5.13   —Bid-Process Review of Scheduling

In evaluating a project with a view towards preparing and submitting a bid, it is as important for contractors to evaluate whether they can comply with the contract performance period, since they are obligated to thoroughly review the plans and specifications and estimate quantities. In the inflationary environment in which all contractors operate, any delay to performance not only results in increased costs, but also drains the contractor's working capital, making it more difficult for the contractor to complete projects under construction and to bid future projects. Equally compelling inflationary pressures exert influence upon owners who, as a result, become more reluctant to grant time extensions and are more disposed to enforce liquidated damages provisions. Prime contractors bidding a job in this environment must make a decision whether they can meet the contract performance period. If the schedule is unrealistic, contractors should either include in their estimate some contingency for liquidated damages or not bid the job.

Of course, another alternative remains to contractors: to assume that the performance period can be met and, further, to assume that if delays are incurred, they will be excused by the owner and will be compensated

---

[72] General Ry. Signal Co., ENGBCA Nos. 4250, 4299, 4312, 4366, 4386, 4398, 4399, 4402, 4404, 4409, 4468, 85-2 BCA ¶ 17,959 (1985).

[73] *See* Broadway Maintenance Corp. v. Rutgers, 90 N.J. 253, 447 A.2d 906 (1982).

[74] *Id.*

for by time extensions. This course of action, however, is myopic and sure to result in disaster.

The better approach is for the prime contractor to examine the bid documents with a critical view. In this way, the contractor can determine whether the project can reasonably be completed within the contractually specified performance period.

§ 5.14   —Preliminary Progress Schedule

On larger construction projects, shortly after notice to proceed is issued, prime contractors frequently are required to prepare and issue a preliminary schedule revealing how they plan to execute the project in a timely manner. While the parties to the contract certainly should be thinking about the progress schedule at this early date (and, even earlier, during the bidding process), preliminary schedules are unlikely to be totally accurate. They are often prepared more with a view toward complying with a contract provision than toward actually illustrating how the contractor intends to schedule the work at this early stage. Therefore, the dates and logic shown on a preliminary schedule often are poorly thought out, based upon inaccurate or sketchy information, and otherwise unreliable. If this is the case, a contractor may submit the preliminary schedule only to find that it later is used to defeat his delay or acceleration claim.

Consequently, where a contractor is required to submit a preliminary schedule, the contractor should either make it clear to the owner that the schedule is preliminary and based only upon limited information known to the contractor at the time the schedule is submitted or be careful to ensure that the preliminary schedule submitted accurately reflects the contractor's plan for executing the work. If this is not done, the contractor may be bound to the preliminary schedule and precluded from asserting claims based on the final schedule (where it differs from the preliminary schedule).[75] In no event should the contractor merely submit the schedule to comply with a contract provision under the erroneous assumption that once having submitted the schedule, the contractor will not be bound by the information it details.

§ 5.15   —Initial Approved Project Schedule

The initial project schedule presents another problem to the contractor— the approval cycle. The contractor who submits the initial schedule often

---

[75] *See* Cimarron Constr. Co. & Williams Bros. Co., ENGBCA No. 2862, 69-2 BCA ¶ 8003 (1969).

receives no response from the owner because owners fear that any response will later be cited by the contractor as acceptance of the schedule and responsibility thereunder. Such an attitude on the part of the owner is illusory, since the courts will impose implied obligations on the owner with regard to the schedule regardless of the owner's silence.

The owner's failure to reject the contractor's schedule, despite oral disclaimers to parts of the schedule, may still bind the owner to the schedule.[76] An owner may not arbitrarily reject a project schedule on the basis that it lacks detail or is not in a specific format where the contract specifications do not contain such requirements.[77] In most cases, the initial progress schedule should be submitted to the owner for approval in a timely manner, and the delay or complete failure of the owner to act upon the schedule should be documented by the contractor. When the schedule is in fact approved, "there is a rebuttable presumption of correctness attached to [schedules] upon which the parties have previously mutually agreed."[78]

§ 5.16   —Project Schedule Updating

Because of deviations that inevitably defeat the contractor's best efforts to perform the project as scheduled, the contractor must properly update the project schedule. Without updating, the schedule is relegated to a document with no practical use other than a record of what the contractor wished to do, had it been able.

The consequence to an owner with respect to an out-of-date schedule is that it may not be used in evaluating contractor's claims for delay costs and time extensions where the schedule is out of date due to the owner's failure to approve changes to the schedule.[79] In *Ballenger Corp.,* the board indicated that the CPM schedule's "usefulness as a barometer for measuring time extensions and delay damages is necessarily circumscribed by the extent to which it is employed in an accurate and consistent manner to comport with the events actually occurring on the job."

If a prime contractor abandons his detailed progress schedule and adopts a more flexible, ad hoc schedule, the contractor may well end up in a dispute with subcontractors who planned work on the basis of the

---

[76] Fullerton Constr. Co., ASBCA No. 12,275, 69-2 BCA ¶ 7876 (1969).

[77] H.I. Homa Co., ENGBCA No. PCC-41, 82-1 BCA ¶ 15,651 (1982).

[78] Santa Fe, Inc., VABCA No. 2168, 87-3 BCA ¶ 20,104 (1987).

[79] Fortec Constructors v. United States, 8 Cl. Ct. 490 (1985), *aff'd,* 804 F.2d 141 (Fed. Cir. 1986); Ballenger Corp., DOTBCA Nos. 74-32, 74-32A, 74-32H, 84-1 BCA ¶ 16,973 (1983).

progress schedule and incurred increased costs as a result of the prime contractor's abandonment of that schedule.[80] For example, in *Natkin & Co. v. George A. Fuller Co.,*[81] the contract documents provided that CPM scheduling would be followed throughout the job. The defendants, Western Electric Company (owner) and the George A. Fuller Company (prime contractor), conceded, in argument, that the CPM schedule was not continually updated throughout the job. Western Electric met with Fuller to discuss review of the performance schedule to determine whether or not Fuller could shorten portions of the project the owner urgently needed complete.

One of the findings of fact adopted by the court in its opinion with regard to the CPM schedule was "the Critical Path Plan may become obsolete unless it is kept current." Other findings note that Natkin continued to ask that the CPM plan be updated and objected to the use of bar charts in lieu of CPM updates. Moreover, the CPM plan required updating during certain portions of the job.

The court concluded (1) that the defendants were not interested in establishing an accurate completion date in accordance with the method provided by the contract; (2) that no accurate or reasonable dates for overall completion of the job were in fact established in accordance with the contract procedures; and (3) that the various completion dates for particular portions of the work were dictated and established without Natkin's consent, regardless of what impact such dates might have had on the execution of the totality of the work covered by Natkin's subcontract. Natkin received a judgment against both the prime contractor and the owner. For a prime contractor, updating the project schedule is essential, not only to maintain the accuracy of this vital management tool, but also to ensure that the schedule does not become the basis for a claim alleging delay and failure to schedule the work.

§ 5.17   —Coordinating Subcontractors

Where a subcontractor has not been consulted concerning logic or durations utilized for the subcontractor's work on the project schedule and such logic or durations are not realistic, some courts have held that the schedule will not provide a basis for recovery against the subcontractor.[82]

---

[80] *See* E.C. Ernst, Inc. v. Manhattan Constr. Co., 387 F. Supp. 1001 (S.D. Ala. 1974), *aff'd in part, rev'd in part,* 551 F.2d 1026 (5th Cir. 1977); Natkin & Co. v. George A. Fuller Co., 347 F. Supp. 17 (W.D. Mo. 1972).

[81] 347 F. Supp. 17 (W.D. Mo. 1972).

[82] *E.g.,* United States v. F.D. Rich Co., 439 F.2d 895 (8th Cir. 1971).

For example, in *United States v. F.D. Rich Co.*,[83] a mechanical subcontractor brought a Miller Act suit for amounts due it under the subcontract. The prime contractor defended and counterclaimed on the basis that the subcontractor failed to perform timely in accordance with the performance durations set forth in computer printouts and, thereby, delayed completion of the project to the damage of the prime contractor.

The prime contractor, during the progress of the job, utilized a computer to program the various stages of construction and submitted these computer programs or printouts to each subcontractor as a guide for the particular subcontractor's production schedule. The program contained some built-in flexibility, but the late-start date supposedly represented an absolute deadline for the commencement of that particular activity. The court noted that the mechanical subcontractor failed to meet the prime contractor's computerized work schedules in many areas of construction during the two-year work period. The trial court rejected the prime contractor's contentions that the subcontractor had delayed the job. With regard to the time of performance specified in the computer printouts, the trial court concluded that "the evidence in this case clearly demonstrated that this electronic brain (located in Connecticut) received a great deal of bad information from the defendant's employees in Missouri."[84] The court characterized the computer work-completion dates, set without any consultation with the subcontractors, as "arbitrary."

Other courts have limited a subcontractor's right to rely on construction schedules, holding that the schedule represented a goal and that the subcontractors should anticipate delays.[85] This view was adopted by the court in *McCarty Corp. v. Pullman-Kellogg*.[86] In this case, the subcontractor was provided with a construction schedule. The subcontractor claimed damages due to the delays and the resulting deviation from the schedule. The court refused to award damages, finding that since the subcontractor was advised that the schedule was subject to an additional four-month extension, the schedule did not constitute an absolute guarantee. Rather, "it was more of a goal that all intended to work toward and any experienced subcontractor ought to anticipate some delays . . ."[87]

The best opportunity for a prime contractor to use project schedules to coordinate the performance of subcontractors occurs when a subcontractor expressly stipulates in its contract that it will be liable for actual

---

[83] *Id.*

[84] *Id.* at 900.

[85] *E.g.*, McCarty Corp. v. Pullman-Kellogg, 571 F. Supp. 1341 (M.D. La. 1983), *modified*, 751 F.2d 750 (5th Cir. 1985).

[86] *Id.*

[87] *Id.* at 1357.

damages resulting from delay and will strictly comply with the project schedule.[88]

An Illinois case suggests that the general contractor should use the project schedule in this manner. In *Illinois Structural Steel Corp. v. Pathman Construction Co.,*[89] the contract required the use of CPM scheduling. The prime contractor demonstrated that the subcontractor's delivery of steel was not in accordance with the schedule. In order to keep the work progressing, it was necessary to change the order of performance and begin masonry work sooner than provided for by the CPM schedule. To accommodate the changes, the contractor incurred increased costs of performance.

In affirming the lower court's decision in favor of the prime contractor, the appeal court noted that the subcontractor expressly stipulated in the contract that it would be liable for actual damages resulting from delay and that it would comply with the CPM schedule. Moreover, if the prime contractor did not finish the project within the contractually specified performance period, it was subject to liquidated damages under the contract with the owner. Therefore, the damages claimed by the prime contractor were foreseeable and recoverable.

The right of a prime contractor to control subcontractors through express contract stipulations concerning the project schedule is also confirmed by the very recent *Williams Enterprises, Inc. v. Strait Manufacturing & Welding, Inc.*[90] This case concerned the delay resulting from a structural steel collapse on the construction of a new gymnasium. Here, the court found the steel subcontractor responsible to the prime contractor (Smoot) for project delays where the subcontractors had been consulted concerning the logic and duration of the project schedule and had specifically agreed to be bound to the requirements of the project schedule. The decision stated:

> Data for this schedule were gathered by Smoot's manager, Arthur Durrah. He testified that in the process of schedule preparation, he consulted with subcontractors to verify the timing and duration of sub-elements of the work. This first project schedule, called for a computerized critical path method ('CPM') document, prepared on December 21, 1983, and approved in due course by the District.
>
> The subcontract between Smoot and Strait contained important provisions related to this present dispute. Section 1 of the subcontract incorporated by reference all terms of the prime contract between Smoot and the District, including the scheduling requirements. Section 2 required that

---

[88] *See* Illinois Structural Steel Corp. v. Pathman Constr. Co., 23 Ill. App. 3d 1, 318 N.E.2d 232 (1974).

[89] *Id.*

[90] 728 F. Supp. 12 (D.D.C. 1990).

Strait furnish all labor, materials, and equipment to erect structural steel, steel joist, and steel deck in strict accordance with specifications. Section 6 provided that Strait prosecute the work in a prompt and diligent manner whenever such work, or any part of it, became available, or at such other time the contractor may direct, so as to promote the general progress of the entire construction, and shall not, by delay or otherwise, interfere with or hinder the work of the contractor or any other subcontractor. Strait agreed to pay to Smoot such damages as Smoot might sustain by reason of any delays.

* * *

Section 6 of the subcontract specifically provides that the subcontractor will prosecute the work efficiently and promptly; further, that subcontractor agrees to pay to the Contractor such other or additional damages as the Contractor may sustain by reason of delay by the Subcontractor. This provision is an express statement of the generally recognized common law obligation of parties not to hinder or interfere with one another's performance. *Fuller Co. v. United States,* 69 F. Supp. 409, 411, 108 Ct. Cl. 70 (1947); *see also, United States ex rel. Heller Electric Co. v. Klingensmith, Inc.,* 216 U.S. App. D.C. 408, 670 F.2d 1227 (D.C. Cir. 1982); *Luria Brothers v. United States,* 369 F.2d 701, 708, 177 Ct. Cl. 676 (1966).

In an action between private parties, it suffices to show that a subcontractor caused a substantial delay in performance, that the contract terms forbade such a delay, and that the plaintiff was injured as a result. *United States ex rel. Gray-Bar Electric Co. v. J.H. Copeland & Sons,* 568 F.2d 1159, 1160 (5th Cir. 1978); *District Concrete Co. v. Bernstein Concrete,* 418 A.2d 1030, 1038 (D.C. 1980). Smoot has proved each of these elements.[91]

The prime contractors' successes in *Illinois Structural Steel* and *Williams Enterprises*[92] do not, however, justify the conclusion that the prime contractor may utilize a scheduling provision (which allows revisions in the CPM schedule to be made with respect to the subcontractor's activity durations) to make unreasonable changes in the durations and sequence of subcontractor performance. For example, in *Kroeger v. Franchise Equities, Inc.,*[93] the contractor filed suit for damages for breach of contract for carpentry work. The contract provided that plaintiff would begin and perform its work in accordance with a CPM schedule. The carpentry work was scheduled to be performed between December 3, 1970, and January 28, 1971. Plaintiff commenced work on November 20, 1970, but in December plaintiff received a telephone call from defendant's job superintendent stating he was "shutting the job down." The plaintiff heard

---

[91] *Id.* at 14, 22.

[92] *Id.*

[93] 190 Neb. 731, 212 N.W.2d 348 (1973).

nothing further from the defendant until April 1971, at which time plaintiff performed some additional work.

Among other things, defendant claimed that it had a right to reschedule work under the contract because of cold weather. The contract provided that, if the CPM schedule were revised, plaintiff would receive three days notice when the job would be ready and that all claims for damages for delay would be made promptly. The defendant contended that any delay to the job caused by the shutdown in the period December through April amounted to a revision in the CPM schedule within the meaning of the contract.

The appellate court found that insufficient evidence was adduced at trial on the issue of damages. Therefore, a new trial was ordered on the issue alone. However, as to the issue of liability, the court concluded that the contract provision allowing the prime contractor to revise the CPM schedule did not allow the prime contractor to reschedule the subcontractor's performance to the point that substantial delays were incurred by the subcontractor.

§ 5.18   Subcontractor's Role in Scheduling

Apathy is frequently the attitude of subcontractors toward the project schedule. Subcontractors often believe that since prime contractors manipulate project schedules to their benefit, there is no reason to become involved in the scheduling process. Therefore, subcontractors sometimes neglect their rights with regard to the project schedule and adopt a position of reacting to events, rather than attempting to control them.

Underlying this attitude is a failure on the part of subcontractors to recognize that they have specific rights, and that prime contractors have concomitant responsibilities, in the field of project scheduling. By asserting these rights, subcontractors can persuade prime contractors to recognize their positions with respect to a claim, or they can compel prime contractors to present subcontractors' claims to owners or otherwise derive positive benefits out of the project schedule.

§ 5.19   —Subcontractor Rights in Prime
Contractor-Issued Schedule

Subcontractors should be aware that a prime contractor has no right to simply abandon the project schedule or to fail to update the schedule in a timely fashion.[94] Similarly, a prime contractor may not unreasonably

---

[94] Natkin & Co. v. George A. Fuller Co., 347 F. Supp. 17 (W.D. Mo. 1972).

manipulate the schedule so as to delay subcontractors and impede their ability to effectively utilize the schedule.[95] Finally, a prime contractor cannot provide subcontractors with inaccurate schedule information or simply withhold material information regarding the schedule.[96] A prime contractor's obligations create rights the subcontractor should assert under appropriate circumstances.

As previously noted, virtually every construction contract creates implied warranties and obligations that subcontractors may invoke in the event some act or omission by the prime contractor damages them in their performance. These implied warranties have been applied to a wide variety of construction problems, including imposition upon the prime contractor of responsibilities in the issuance and execution of the project schedule.

§ 5.20   —Project Schedule Updating

This chapter has noted the effect on an owner of silence when the prime contractor issues the project schedule at the beginning of the project. The same principles may apply to subcontractor-prime contractor relations. Thus, subcontractors must address the question of their actions in response to the issuance of a project schedule by the prime contractor.

The alternatives available to a subcontractor are comparable to those available to an owner vis-à-vis a prime contractor. A subcontractor can review the schedule for the purpose of locating any errors—paying particular attention to that portion of the schedule which relates to the subcontractor's work—and notify the prime contractor of errors. Or, subcontractors can accept the schedule with silence in the hope that, by so reacting, they will not be held to the schedule. Subcontractors can also accept the schedule and note that they will attempt to comply with it to the extent that their performance is not delayed by downstream problems created by the prime contractor.

Ideally, however, subcontractors should not merely await action on the part of the prime contractor with regard to the project schedule and its updating, but should participate actively in the preparation of the initial schedule and in the updating process. Subcontractors should, on a periodic basis, provide updated information regarding the performance of their work, advise the prime contractor of the work of other trades that has an adverse impact on their work, and otherwise make known their

---

[95] Kroeger v. Franchise Equities, Inc., 190 Neb. 731, 212 N.W.2d 348 (1973).

[96] E.C. Ernst, Inc. v. Manhattan Constr. Co., 387 F. Supp. 1001 (S.D. Ala. 1974), *aff'd in part, rev'd in part,* 551 F.2d 1026 (5th Cir. 1977).

continually changing appraisal of the progress schedule. Only by taking such action can subcontractors preserve their rights and require the prime contractor to fulfill schedule obligations.

§ 5.21   —Job-Coordination Meetings

One way subcontractors can participate in the scheduling process on a direct project level is through job-coordination meetings. Meetings between prime contractors and subcontractors are one of the most effective means of resolving and avoiding disputes between contractors over schedule-related matters. A full airing of differences among the parties concerning such matters is a valuable management tool capable of producing innumerable rewards in terms of project efficiency.

Job-coordination meetings also serve another important function for subcontractors. Subcontractors may find that the prime contractor's interest in the project and the scheduling process declines as the prime contractor finishes its portion of the work. Having fulfilled the major part of its performance, the prime contractor may not take an effective, active role in scheduling the remainder of the work, in spite of the fact that the subcontractors' work has not yet begun. In such circumstances, subcontractors should conduct their own job-coordination meetings to schedule the remainder of the project and enable the various subcontractors to complete their performance in a timely and economical manner. Where a prime contractor has abdicated responsibility for project scheduling, the job-coordination meeting may be the only effective means available to subcontractors for completing performance without incurring increased costs.

§ 5.22   Project or Schedule Abandonment Due to Inadequate Scheduling

Abandonment of the project schedule or of the project itself, while fraught with potentially severe consequences, is a potential option available to contractors under particular circumstances. While it is true that the consequences of a hasty abandonment can be extremely severe, abandonment of the project schedule, or the project, should not be immediately dismissed by contractors as an unrealistic alternative. Instead contractors who are well-informed of the facts and circumstances giving rise to their position and who are aware of their rights and obligations, as well as the rights and obligations of the other parties, may be well-advised to consider abandonment as a rational course of action.

W.F. Magann Corp. v. Diamond Mfg. Co.[97] is an example of a subcontractor successfully abandoning the contract and recovering damages from the general contractor. Under this contract between Magann, the general contractor, and Diamond, the subcontractor, Diamond was to perform all the necessary dredging work. The subcontractor abandoned the contract for the following reasons:

1. Defective specifications
2. Differing site conditions that were not investigated by the owner once notice was given
3. Changed conditions for which Diamond was not compensated
4. Magann threatening Diamond that if it did not settle its claims with the owner, it would not be allowed to continue working on the contract.

The court found actions by Magann constituted breaches of the contract that justified Diamond's abandonment of the project.[98]

Not only was Magann precluded from recovering from Diamond for damages due to Diamond's abandonment, but Magann was liable to Diamond for the "reasonable value" of the work it had performed.[99] The court explained:

> Where, as here, there has been a breach of the subcontract by the general contractor who incorporated the specifications of the prime contract into the subcontract, and regardless of whether the breach was occasioned by the general contractor or the government or indeed, by both, the subcontractor can rescind the contract and seek restitution in *quantum meruit.*[100]

As *Magann* indicates, if a contractor finds that, because of the owner's or prime contractor's actions, the contractor's work has been altered or hampered drastically, abandonment may provide a way to recover the "reasonable value" of the contractor's work, with relief not limited to the contract price. Before abandonment is justified, there must be severe circumstances.

A contractor should be careful in choosing to abandon the contract. If the circumstances are later found to not justify abandonment, the contractor may be found in breach and held liable for damages. An alternative to such guesswork would be to obtain, prior to abandoning the contract, a declaration by a court that the other party is in breach.

---

[97] 580 F. Supp. 1299 (D.S.C. 1984).

[98] *Id.* at 1314.

[99] *Id.* at 1315.

[100] *Id.*

§ 5.23   —Effect of Schedule Abandonment

Both the owner and general contractor should be alert to the chance that they have abandoned the project schedule. The situation that frequently develops is that the construction project is delayed and the quantity of work remaining strongly suggests that the project will be even further delayed beyond the contractually specified completion date. For owners, this frequently means substantially increased costs, including increased financing expenses, temporary accommodations for employees, rental of manufacturing facilities until the factory can be completed, and so forth.

In such circumstances, the owner may be compelled—and, indeed, justified—in casting aside the project schedule and insisting upon a revised schedule that will provide occupancy and help reduce the owner's costs. Where the owner on the project has assumed the responsibility for coordination of numerous prime contractors, the temptation to assert control by abandoning the project schedule is even greater. The owner may believe that the position of coordinator of the various prime contractors confers the authority to so act. Due to the owner's desperate situation, the project schedule will be abandoned in an effort to expedite completion of the project on a work-available basis or some other informal scheduling method.

The danger to the owner inherent in such action is made clear by *Natkin & Co. v. George A. Fuller Co.* [101] Here, a mechanical subcontractor brought suit against the prime contractor, the George A. Fuller Co., and the owner, Western Electric Co., Inc. ("Western"). Natkin sought damages for additional costs due to delay and disruption of its work, as well as acceleration caused by the general contractor and Western. It appears that, for a variety of reasons, the project fell behind schedule and Western became anxious about achieving completion as soon as possible. Western decided to push particular portions of the job to completion and insisted upon direct negotiations with a number of important subcontractors, including Natkin, the project's mechanical subcontractor.

Concerned about contract completion, Western failed to schedule and control the project in accordance with the sequence established by the prime contractor's CPM schedule. Due to this interference, the prime contractor was unable to execute and schedule properly, to the detriment of Natkin. Fuller, the general contractor, failed and/or refused to update the schedule properly, which made it obsolete and of no use to Natkin, and Western was unwilling to accept completion dates later than those indicated on the updated network.

The court concluded that Western and the prime contractor abandoned the project schedule. As a result, both the owner and prime contractor lost

---

[101] 347 F. Supp. 17 (W.D. Mo. 1972).

control of the work; were unable to schedule the availability of men and materials to perform work upon which Natkin's work depended; allowed the work site to become congested; and, in general, gave up total control over the project. To make up for the delay to the project caused by their loss of control, the owner and the prime contractor threatened and co-erced Natkin to accelerate work, threats that were unwarranted given that delay to the project was the responsibility of the defendants.

An additional example of the inherent danger in abandoning the project schedule is found in *Haas & Haynie Corp.*[102] Here, the prime contractor and two of the subcontractors brought delay claims against the government. The contractors claimed that government-caused delays resulted in their performance beyond the completion date, thereby entitling them to extended performance costs.

The board, in examining the progress chart, found it was an inadequate gauge of whether performance had been extended due to government-caused delays because the contractor had failed to keep the chart current, thereby, in effect, abandoning the chart.[103] The prime contractor later attempted to revise the CPM chart and supplement it by meeting with the subcontractors. The board found this an inadequate solution and stated that the delays were due to the prime contractor's failure to coordinate the subcontractors, not due to changes by the government. Because the chart was not comprehensive, the contractors could not prove that the delays were caused by the government, thereby precluding recovery of their claims.[104]

The *Natkin* and *Haas & Haynie* cases make clear the substantial damages inherent in abandonment of the project schedule, particularly where all parties have agreed to rely upon the project schedule in planning their work. On a project, if the owner or general contractor concludes that the project schedule has become so hopelessly inadequate as to require abandonment, one way of proceeding may be by means of a change order executed by all parties to the contract. Such a change order might recognize that all parties agree that the schedule will be abandoned, that an alternative scheduling method will be adopted for the remainder of the work, and that no further claims shall be made by any party arising out of or resulting from the abandoned project schedule.

---

[102] GSBCA No. 5530, 84-2 BCA ¶ 17,446 (1984).

[103] *Id.* at 86,898.

[104] *Id.* at 86,900.

§ 5.24   Recognition of Contractor's Right to Finish Early and to Manage Schedule

Case law increasingly makes clear that not only federal courts and boards but also state courts now recognize that the contractor has both the right to finish early and the right to manage the schedule and deviate from the original plan to resequence, compress performance time, and react to changing conditions.

The typical right-to-finish-early case involves a situation where the contractor devises a schedule at the beginning of the project before the contractually specified completion date. In such cases where the owner causes the contractor's performance to extend beyond the contractor's planned completion date (in contrast to the contractually specified completion date), the contractor is entitled to recover the damages incurred for that late performance, even though the contractor may still complete the contract before the contractually specified completion date.[105]

The damage the contractor suffers in these cases is the loss of the benefit that would be gained by completing the project pursuant to the scheduled completion. This is measured by establishing the contractor's time-related costs per day and awarding the contractor these delay damages in the amount performance was extended beyond the early completion date.

Federal courts and administrative boards recognize that contractors have a right to finish early in order to minimize costs, perform work on other projects, and, most fundamentally, manage their own schedules.[106] These rights have been recognized to permit contractors to manage their own schedules, resequence, and effect trade-offs of resources to shorten or control projects.

As early as 1958, California courts recognized that in a delay situation a contractor's damages should be computed from the time the contractor reasonably planned to complete the project rather than the later contractually specified completion date. In *Maurice L. Bein, Inc. v. Housing Authority,*[107]

---

[105] Gardner Displays Co. v. United States, 346 F.2d 585 (Ct. Cl. 1965); C.W. Schmid v. United States, 173 Ct. Cl. 302 (1965); Barton & Sons Co., ASBCA Nos. 9477, 9764, 65-2 BCA ¶ 4874 (1965); Kemmons-Wilson, Inc. (Florida) & South Patton, Inc., A Joint Venture, ASBCA No. 16,167, 72-2 BCA ¶ 9689 (1972); Grow Constr. Co. v. State, 56 A.D.2d 95, 391 N.Y.S.2d 726 (1977); Sun Ship Building & Drydock v. United States Lines, Inc., 439 F. Supp. 671 (E.D. Pa. 1977); Lester N. Johnson Co. v. City of Spokane, 92 Wash. 2d 1005, 588 P.2d 1214 (1979); Maurice L. Bein, Inc. v. Housing Authority, 157 Cal. App. 2d 670, 321 P.2d 753, 764 (1958).

[106] Burrough Corp. v. United States, 634 F.2d 516 (Ct. Cl. 1981); Stagg Constr. Co., GSBCA No. 2664, 69-2 BCA ¶ 7914 (1969), *aff'd on reh'g,* 70-1 BCA ¶ 8241 (1970); Joseph E. Bennett, GSBCA No. 2362, 72-1 BCA ¶ 9364 (1972) at 43,467.

[107] 157 Cal. App. 2d 670, 321 P.2d 753, 764 (1958).

the owner's failure to provide access to a portion of work as promised delayed the contractor's completion of the project. In rejecting the owner's argument that the delay should be computed beginning with the completion date as required by the contract, the court found that the contractor, who had proved that it could have and would have completed the project at a much earlier date absent the delay, was entitled to delay damages from the earlier date.

Metropolitan Paving Co. v. United States[108] is generally recognized as the landmark federal decision on the right to finish early. *Metropolitan Paving* entered into a contract with the Air Force to pave an airfield. The contractor alleged that the government deliberately harassed him and engaged in dilatory tactics to delay performance. The court held against the contractor on the issue of whether the government actually delayed the project. However, in its opinion, the court stated:

> While it is true that there is not an "obligation" or "duty" of defendant to aid a contractor to complete prior to the completion date, from this it does not follow that defendant may hinder and prevent the contractor's *early completion* without incurring liability. It would seem to make little difference whether or not the parties contemplated an early completion, or even whether or not the contractor contemplated an early completion. Where defendant is guilty of "deliberate harassment and dilatory tactics" and a contractor suffers damages as a result of such action, we think that defendant is liable.[109]

Relying on this authority, the court of claims has allowed a contractor to recover delay damages despite its early completion of the contract.[110] Boards of contract appeals also have held that the government can be liable for delay even if the contract is completed early.[111] In *Barton & Sons, Co.,*[112] a paving repair contract was delayed due to a government drawing and its failure to provide usable material. The board permitted recovery for the delay even though the contractor did not give notice of his intention to complete early.

State courts have also moved to recognize the right to complete early. In *Grow Construction Co. v. State,*[113] the court rejected the argument that the

---

[108] 163 Ct. Cl. 420, 325 F.2d 241 (1963).

[109] 325 F.2d at 242 (emphasis added).

[110] *See, e.g.,* Gardner Displays Co. v. United States, 346 F.2d 585 (Ct. Cl. 1965); C.W. Schmid v. United States, 173 Ct. Cl. 302 (1965).

[111] *See, e.g.,* Barton & Sons Co., ASBCA Nos. 9477, 9764, 65-2 BCA ¶ 4874 (1965); Kemmons-Wilson, Inc. (Florida) & South Patton, Inc., A Joint Venture, ASBCA No. 16,167, 72-2 BCA ¶ 9689 (1972); Canon Constr. Corp., ASBCA No. 16,142, 72-1 BCA ¶ 9404 (1972); Sydney Constr. Co., ASBCA No. 21,377, 77-2 BCA ¶ 12,719 (1977).

[112] ASBCA Nos. 9477, 9764, 65-2 BCA ¶ 4874 (1965).

[113] 56 A.D.2d 95, 391 N.Y.S.2d 726 (1977).

contractor's timely completion of the contract prevented the contractor from recovering any damages due to delay. The court stated:[114]

> Claimant should rightfully expect to operate free from needless interference by the State, and, therefore, they are entitled to compensation whether or not they could have completed their work ahead of schedule and thereby saved substantial sums of money, absent the delays caused by the State.[115]

Washington courts have also recognized the right to early completion based on the duty not to hinder or delay the contractor.[116] Pennsylvania law was applied by a federal district court finding that ordered changes may also wrongfully interfere with a contractor's early completion. In *Sun Ship Building & Drydock v. United States Lines, Inc.,*[117] the district court found that United States Lines was liable for delay incurred by the contractor because it had issued a change order that precluded the contractor from completing the contract 15 days earlier than it could have.

The contractor's opportunity to complete early reflects the dynamic nature of the construction process. Schedules are dynamic and should reflect and adjust to the actual conditions encountered on the project. Thus, even when an activity has been completed before an early finish date, if the owner furnished defective specifications that delayed that activity, the contractor has been granted relief.[118]

---

[114] *Id.* (citing D'Angello v. State, 46 A.D.2d 983, 984, 362 N.Y.S.2d 233, 235, *aff'd,* 39 N.Y.2d 781, 350 N.E.2d 615, 385 N.Y.S.2d 284 (1976)).

[115] Grow v. State, 391 N.Y.S.2d at 329.

[116] Lester N. Johnson Co. v. City of Spokane, 92 Wash. 2d 1005, 588 P.2d 1214 (1979).

[117] 439 F. Supp. 671 (E.D. Pa. 1977).

[118] Stagg Constr. Co., GSBCA 2664, 69-2 BCA ¶ 7914 (1969), *aff'd on reh'g,* 70-1 BCA ¶ 8241 (1970).

CHAPTER 6

PROJECT RECORD-KEEPING

§ 6.1   Need for Good Records

§ 6.2   Job-Meeting Minutes

§ 6.3   Progress Charts and Reports

§ 6.4   Daily and Weekly Reports

§ 6.5   Weather

§ 6.6   Photographs

§ 6.7   Job Diary

§ 6.8   Procurement Records

§ 6.9   Test Reports and Test Records

§ 6.10   Change Orders

§ 6.11   Shop Drawings

§ 6.12   Correspondence

§ 6.13   Memoranda

§ 6.14   Cost Records

§ 6.15   Errors and Omissions Analyses

§ 6.16   Using Computers for Job Record-Keeping

§ 6.1   Need for Good Records

The contractor, owner, subcontractor, and construction manager all should be cognizant of the need for good, accurate, and complete records to assist in maintaining effective control of a construction project. Such records are the principal source of evidence for verifying that the work conformed with the contract documents. Proper record management permits timely negotiation of change orders, resolution of disputes, and proof of time delays and damages.

Courts and boards of contract appeals have clearly indicated to all parties the necessity to maintain proper project records to establish entitlement for claims and breaches of contract, as well as quantum of recovery. Such direction from the judiciary is well represented by the *J.M.T. Machine Co.*[1] and *Bechtel National, Inc.*[2] decisions.

In the 1985 *J.M.T. Machine Co.* decision, the board detailed its willingness to address a major contractor claim, which the government had objected to on the basis of "total cost," because the contractor had maintained accurate cost records of individual work elements of the project. In its decision, the board stated:

> Appellant objects vigorously to Government counsel's characterization of its equitable adjustment claim as a "sophisticated version of the total cost" approach.

> Appellant contends that it has identified each element of damages in great detail based on accurate cost records as supported by corroborating evidence. Its reply brief states (at 2):

>> Appellant has kept accurate costs records in this case, and appellant's testimony relates the actual observations of appellant as to the times required for individual tasks. The damages were caused by 74 changes in the piece parts, but the increase of performance time did not occur in discreet intervals separate from the other performance, rather it was a lengthening of the base performance required for many tasks, due to understated tolerances which required extreme tightening to meet stringent specifications. Thus, there could be no independent record of the extra time required separate and apart from the base time without the changes.

> We find it undisputed that appellant's claim of extra hours incurred on the subject contract because of defective TDP represents the difference between its estimated bid hours and the actual hours worked (findings 14,103).

> This is a typical 'total cost' approach which is not favored by the courts or the boards except in exceptional circumstances as pointed out by the Government. *WRB Corporation v. United States* [12 CCF ¶ 81,781], 183 Ct. Cl. 409 (1968); *S. W. Electronics & Manufacturing Corporation v. United States* [29 CCF ¶ 81,726], 228 Ct. Cl. 333, 655 F. 2d 1078 (1981).

> However, as appellant has emphasized, the availability of timecards and other cost information allows us to analyze and evaluate appellant's claim elements individually without regard to the total cost incurrence. We will proceed in this manner. *Cf. S. W. Electronics & Manufacturing Corporation v. United States,* 228 Ct. Cl. at 352.

> The *Bonacorso Construction Corp.,* GSBCA No. 2813, 70-1 BCA ¶ 8093 (1970) appeal, cited by the Government, has no bearing in this regard. There appellant submitted only a breakdown of its alleged costs in performing the changed work and introduced "no actual work reports, vouchers or wage records" and no testimony in support of the actual work. This

---

[1] ASBCA No. 23,928, 85-1 BCA ¶ 17,820, at 89,181 (1984).

[2] NASABCA No. 1186-7, 90-1 BCA ¶ 22,549, at 113,159 (1990).

is not the case here where we have available complete cost records and substantial testimony regarding the work performed.[3]

The *Bechtel* decision, on the other hand, illustrates the circumstance encountered by a contractor who attempted to prove up a $7 million claim without the necessary delay logs and diaries and contemporaneous meeting minutes to establish the effect of errors and omissions and requests for information (RFIs) on the project. The board decision stated:

> There is no significant discussion of the RFIs in the contemporaneous project records kept by the Contractor and the Government in the record of the appeal. Appellant did not establish the extent of the disruptive effects of the NASA RFIs that is claimed with documentary evidence. BNI project personnel did not keep notes or maintain any documentation of disruptive impact caused by the RFIs (Tr. I/571–72, 660, II/115, V/487, X/222, 228). There was no Contract requirement, and BNI did not have a company policy or requirement that project personnel maintain logs or diaries. Appellant did not have such logs or diaries to document job occurrences or use in the preparation of the claim (Tr. I/326–27, 562,63, IV/179, V/109, 220, 329, 474, 581, VIII/569–70, 626). The logs and diaries of BNI personnel that are in the record were submitted by Respondent to show that only one person maintained a daily record on the job that is available as evidence of what occurred (finding 81, *infra;* Ex. G-II.D., G-II.N., G-II.O., G-II.P.; Tr. I/362, 688–89, III/555, V/329–32, 473–75, 600–01, VIII/558–69, 594–95, 616, 625–26, 644, 932, 936–37, IX/601–06).
>
> Weekly status meetings were held involving representatives of Appellant, NASA and RS&H to discuss the work activities of the previous week, what was planned for the next week and problems that were presented, but there was no regular practice of reviewing the status of RFIs at these meetings . . . .[4]

* * *

We are not persuaded, however, that the extent of impact alleged resulted from the NASA RFIs. Appellant produced no contemporaneous documentation that substantiates the extent of the cumulative impact claimed. *Cf. H. W. Detwiler Company, Inc.,* ASBCA No. 35327, 89-2 BCA ¶ 21,612; *Argo Technology, Inc.,* ASBCA No. 30522, 88-1 BCA ¶ 20,381, at 103,060. The inability to ascertain the extent of cumulative impact and to obtain a reasonable estimate for a claim until contract completion is different than an inability to know, anticipate, or be aware of the facts of disruption and loss of productivity as they occur. Appellant asserted that it was impossible to observe loss of productivity, but such assertion does not excuse or satisfactorily explain the absence of contemporaneous recording of the extensive disruption claimed in this appeal. Appellant identified and

---

[3] J.M.T. Mach. Co., ASBCA No. 23,928, 85-1 BCA ¶ 17,820, at 89,181 (1984).

[4] Bechtel Nat'l, Inc., NASABCA No. 1186-7, 90-1 BCA ¶ 22,549, at 113,159 (1990).

reserved its cumulative impact claim early in December 1984, and it was not beyond the capabilities of this Contractor to record subsequent job occurrences that would have supported its claim.[5]

During the entire period of performance all parties should establish and maintain effective project record-keeping systems. These systems should:

1. Identify the type, quality, frequency, and distribution of the records to be handled
2. Utilize disciplined standards of documentation and proof
3. Preserve records daily on every element of project administration and performance to permit a third party to reconstruct the project from the files, if necessary.

Job records are the principal source of evidence for resolving disputes and minimizing the potential for claims. Records maintained on a project should include budget and cost estimates, general correspondence, schedules and updates, daily and weekly reports, memoranda for record, job diaries, progress photographs, test reports, purchase orders, delivery receipts, payroll records, labor wage agreements, job-cost reports, equipment-utilization records, and weather data. Accurate records of change orders, shop drawings, and payment transactions also are important.

Upon completion of the project, the owner may wish to require that all project records be turned over for permanent storage or other disposition.

§ 6.2 Job-Meeting Minutes

Copies of all job-meeting minutes and objections or exceptions taken by any of the parties involved should be retained. Minutes should be filed by date chronology or by job-meeting number, if assigned. The objective of the meeting minutes is to provide a complete and accurate record of the agenda and a summary of substantial discussions. Progress, problems, or issues discussed should be documented, identifying any actions to be taken, as well as when and by whom.

Job-meeting minutes should also present a record of those attending and absent from meetings. Send copies of minutes to all parties involved or needing to know about meetings or the particular topics discussed. Any party taking exception or objecting to any aspect of the contents of meeting minutes should be required to do so in writing by a certain time after each meeting.

---

[5] *Id.* at 113,178.

§ 6.3 Progress Charts and Reports

Progress charts and reports are invaluable tools for mapping project performance. Retain copies of all project schedules that are prepared and updated periodically throughout the life of the project. Bar charts, networks, manpower and cost projections, computer tabulations, and progress reports issued for record and information purposes are all essential in supporting claims. Additionally, copies of all contractor submittals, time extension analyses, and back-ups for major schedule revisions provide a useful history of project performance.

During the schedule updating process, information such as actual starts, actual completions, and percentage of completion for activities in progress *must* be recorded and retained. While this information is usually recorded as part of the scheduling records, incorporation in other project record-keeping systems is recommended.

§ 6.4 Daily and Weekly Reports

It is essential that field inspection and quality-assurance personnel maintain accurate daily and weekly reports. These reports should reflect office and field operations in a clear and understandable manner. All reports should be signed and reviewed for completeness and accuracy, then forwarded to the central office.

Daily reports should furnish a comprehensive summary of the day's activities. Identify dates of work initiation and completion, trades in use, equipment in use or idle, and causes and status of any delays incurred. Other performance-related activity must be noted as well. Controversies arising on site, weather and field conditions, site-safety conditions, corrective measures, and site visitors are all pertinent to any future claims.

Reports should be dated and consecutively numbered so they are easy to follow. Format continuity provides for clear and understandable reports. These basic guidelines enable both the contractor and owner to have accurate records in support or defense of any claims or disputes. **Figure 6-1** is an example of a daily report form for a project to document history and actual performance.

§ 6.5 Weather

Daily records should be kept on the actual weather conditions experienced at the project site. Record information on temperature, amount of rainfall or snow, and wind conditions, as experienced. Additionally, note

Project Daily Report

Date: _____

Report No.: _____

Day: _____

Weather: _____

Wind: _____

Temerature: 8:00 am _____ 2:00 pm _____

Hours: From _____ To _____

Work in Progress

1. Description of Work Performed:

2. Change Order Work Performed:

3. Verbal or Written Instruction Given:

Personnel on Site				Equipment Status			
Craft	Foreman	Journeyman	Apprentise	Description	# on Site	# Used	# Not Used
Total							

Prepared by:

Supervisor:

Figure 6–1. Project daily report.

Daily Construction Report

Date: _____

Report No.: _____

Commentary:

4. Open Issues Requiring Resolution:

5. Delays Encountered:

6. Visitors to Site:	**7. Safety:**

8. Equipment and Materials Delivered:	**9. Testing:**

10. General Comments:

Form No. 3
Page 2 of 2

Figure 6–1. *(continued)*

any physical conditions resulting from adverse weather, such as mud or flooding, that affect performance and cost.

Most contracts provide for time extensions when weather conditions exceed the normal climatic conditions expected for the jobsite area. Some contracts provide that time extensions for acts of God only apply if a specific part of the job is affected. Other contracts are silent on relief from severe weather conditions.

§ 6.6   Photographs

Photographic and videotaped records provide excellent visual proof of job condition and progress of work in dispute. Keep a camera (or videotape recorder) and necessary supplies for taking periodic progress photographs of the salient features of the project and record each phase of construction. Adequately identify each record, noting date, time of day, angle of the shot, work pictured, and so on. File all photographs chronologically, place them in a binder, and retain all negatives. Similarly, clearly label all videotapes and carefully store them to avoid accidental erasure.

When disputes or difficulties arise, photographs should be taken of the condition, both before and after remedial work is undertaken. Photographs should also be taken of any property damage or unusual technical difficulties and any use of new construction methods. Such photographic records prove invaluable in negotiating change orders, disputes, claims, or potential claims.

§ 6.7   Job Diary

The resident field manager and superintendent(s) should maintain a daily job diary that summarizes the day's events. All discussion, including telephone conversations and meetings, should be noted. Such notations should include pertinent comments or suggestions made by the parties involved and any decision made in response to such comments or suggestions.

All disputes or disagreements with the contracting parties should be fully detailed. Of particular importance are differences relating to method and scope of work, change orders, stop-work orders, defects or discrepancies in drawings and specifications, and payments. Keep references to personalities out of the job diary and, by all means, avoid negative personal comments.

In cases involving major disputes on detailed information that are likely to lead to a claim, a separate memorandum should be prepared to preserve all possible evidence.

The job diary should be a bound book and retained as a permanent record upon job completion. Contemporaneous entry into a coded data base is encouraged, because it facilitates later claim substantiation.

§ 6.8   Procurement Records

Keep records on all procurement transactions beginning in the early design stage and maintain them through construction completion. Although the owner, contractor, and/or construction manager will track procurement activities during all stages of project implementation, each trade contractor should maintain individual systems for control and surveillance during construction. Procurement records should be kept on all transactions involving preparation of drawings and/or specifications, inquiries, purchase orders, shop drawings, quotations, material-status reports, inspection and testing, deliveries, warehousing and storage, and receipt of technical information for operation and maintenance of equipment, where applicable. **Figure 6–2** and **Figure 6–3** are examples of reports for tracking, respectively, purchase orders and status of deliveries.

§ 6.9   Test Reports and Test Records

Fully document the testing of all materials and contractor-furnished equipment. Include in this record items to be tested and the specifications for testing. When testing occurs, record the date, parties conducting the tests, witnesses, and any failures or retests undertaken.

If material-testing laboratories are used, ensure the laboratory is qualified and approved to conduct the desired tests and understands the test procedures and requirements. Obtain records of all test findings and maintain them in a permanent file.

§ 6.10   Change Orders

Maintenance of accurate records and operational control over change orders is crucial, because change orders are frequently the subject of contract claims and disputes. Change discussions, regulations and approvals, change performance status, time and cost estimates, and the effect of change on the cost and time of the project should be documented.

It is suggested that the contractor maintain a contract change-order status report, a register for controlling change-order transactions. The purpose of this table is to provide a composite summary of vital status

PURCHASE ORDER LOG

CLIENT: _____

PROJECT DESCRIPTION: _____

PROJECT NO: _____

STATUS DATE: _____

| PURCHASE ORDER NO. | ISSUE DATE | VENDOR OR SUPPLIER | DESCRIPTION | ORIGINAL DOLLAR VALUE | DATE CHANGE ORDER NUMBER | | | | | CUMULATIVE DOLLAR VALUE | REMARKS |
					#1	#2	#3	#4	#5		

Figure 6–2. Purchase order report.

MATERIAL STATUS REPORT

CLIENT: _____

PROJECT DESCRIPTION: _____

PROJECT NO: _____

STATUS DATE: _____

PURCHASE ORDER		VENDOR OR SUPPLIER	DESCRIPTION	DATE				INSPECTION		DRAWING STATUS					REMARKS
NO.	DATE			REQ'D	SHIP SCHED	DEL SCHED	REC'D SITE	REQ'D	REPT NO.	APPR	AAN	CERT	CERT ANN	FINAL CERT	

Figure 6–3. Material-status report.

information of all changes and the change process throughout performance. Each change order should be recorded in this table, and its status should be noted and tracked with input under the following column headings: Change Order Number and/or Contractor Reference Number; Description and Date Initiated; Preliminary Estimate and Notice to Proceed; Change Control Board Estimate, Amount Approved, Date; Owner/Construction Manager Estimated Amount and Date Estimate Prepared; Contractor Proposal Cost and Date Proposal Received; Owner/Construction Manager Negotiated Amount and Date Negotiated; Status Time in Calendar Days, Requested/Recommended/Approved; Finance Department Approved Amount and Date; Type of Change; Who Initiated and Origin. To control costs and successfully negotiate change orders, early identification of changes and their impact on the project schedule is essential. By maintaining a single register, a project's change-order history can be readily produced. Simultaneous entry in a coded data base facilitates later retrieval of specific change orders.

In addition, it is suggested that the contractor maintain a file for each change that includes all relevant information about the time impact of the change on individual activities and events, as well as on the overall project. This information can be collected in a contemporaneous change order data impact record that should include an analysis of any impact on or disruption of base-contract work. **Figure 6–4** is an example of a change order data impact record, which can be maintained in each file for changes on the project.

In conjunction with the contemporaneous maintenance of change order data summary forms such as that in **Figure 6–4**, it may be helpful to maintain an overall summary chart of the time impact analyses of all change orders on the project. **Figure 6–5** provides an example of such a summary form.

It is suggested that such an individual file be maintained for each change on the project, as well as a separate file with copies of all impact analyses and summary reports for all changes (**Figures 6–4** and **6–5**) on the project.

§ 6.11   Shop Drawings

The development and implementation of disciplined procedures for processing shop drawings is essential. These procedures are necessary to ensure that required work is accomplished in strict accordance with the plans and specifications and within established completion dates. Because approval routings can take a considerable amount of time, efficient procedures keep shop drawings moving in accordance with the schedule,

Project:

No. _____   Owner/architect/engineer no. _____

Scope of changed work: _____

_____

Initiation date: _____   Initiation source (RFI, RFQ, Etc.): _____

Date proposal requested: _____

Original-proposal date & amount: _____

Original time requested: _____

Revised-proposal date & amount: _____

Revised time requested: _____

Notice-to-proceed date & amount: _____

Date formal change issued: _____ Change order no. _____

Time extension granted (calendar days): _____

Date field work commenced: _____

Date field work completed: _____

Floor & area affected: _____

Critical path method activity & event affected (Use IJ node nos. & description): _____

Impact on & disruption of base contract work (describe type of base contract work impacted, the crew size & effect; i.e., slowdowns, stop work, or having to move crews to other work areas): _____

Remarks:

_____

_____

Date: _____   Prepared by: _____

Figure 6–4. Change order data input record.

SUMMARY OF CHANGE ORDER IMPACT ANALYSES ON CPM SCHEDULE

PROJECT:

PREPARED BY _____
DATE _____

DESCRIPTION	C.O. #	C.O. #	C.O. #	C.O. #	C.O. #	C.O. #	C.O. #	C.O. #	C.O. #	C.O. #	C.O. #
LABOR DATA Trade											
Crew Size											
Crew Days											
Journeyman Hrs.											
CPM DATE I-J Networks Affected											
Activity Description											
Duration											
Float											
Adjusted Duration											
Adjusted Float											
Adjusted End Date											

Figure 6–5. Summary chart of change-order time impacts.

144

ensuring timely submittals and timely completion. The contractor is generally required to submit shop drawings for securing approval of materials or equipment used on the job, including catalog cuts, manufacturer's literature or data, drawings, lists, and other such materials as are required by the various technical sections of the contract specifications.

Timely approval of shop drawings is essential to the trade contractor completing on time. The trade contractor is generally required to submit a shop-drawing schedule, showing the anticipated time for commencement and completion of the required submittals, within a specified number of days after starting work. It is important that a reasonable, yet specific, period of time be established by the trade contractor and the reviewing authority for return of shop-drawing submittals. A reasonable period can be considered two or three weeks, depending on the complexity of the review. Established procedures minimize the chances for a claim or request for time extension, because unreasonable delay in approving shop drawings is avoided. If the contract does not specify a time period for the return of shop drawings, establish a date at the prework conference. Instruct all parties on procedures for submitting shop drawings and the amount of time anticipated for a response.

Maintain a transaction register of shop-drawing submittals that includes schedule submittal dates, actual submittal dates, approval and disapproval dates, and date of return to the owner or trade contractor. **Figure 6–6** is an example of a ledger and/or report format for shop-drawing transactions.

It may also be helpful to maintain a contemporaneous shop-drawing and material-approvals delay summary (**Figure 6–7**), detailing any wrongful rejections or unreasonable delays in approvals, as well as the impact of such delays on individual work activities and any attendant disruption of other associated work. As in the case of the change-order summary, it is suggested that a copy of this shop-drawing summary be maintained in the folder for each submittal, as well as in a separate folder including all such summary sheets.

§ 6.12 Correspondence

It is essential that records of all correspondence, including contract, corporate, financial, and confidential information, be handled timely and accurately. From a claims standpoint, particular attention should be given to the notice requirements of the contract.

In addition to the project record-keeping systems commonly used to control information, experience has shown that it is good practice to maintain separate auxiliary files for quick reference to certain contract or

SHOP DRAWING TRANSMITTAL LOG

DIV NO.	ID NO.	TRANS NO.	DRWG BLCK NO.	SHOP DRAWING DESCRIPTION	DATE REC'D FROM CONTRACTOR	DATE SENT TO ENGINEER	DATE RETURNED FROM ENGINEER	DATE RETURNED FROM CONTRACTOR	APPROVAL ACTION BY ENGINEER

APPROVAL STATUS CODES: A APPROVED   AAN APPROVED AS NOTED   D DISAPPROVED   P PARTIAL APPROVAL OR AAN/PARTIAL DISAPPROVAL

Figure 6–6. Record of shop-drawing transmittals.

146

Project:

Submittal no.: _____

Description of submittal: _____

_____

Date of original submittal: _____

Date of 1st rejection: _____

Reason for rejection: _____

Date of 1st resubmittal: _____

Date of 2nd rejection: _____

Reason for 2nd rejection: _____

(Use additional forms attached to record additional resubmittals and rejections.)

Date of final approval: _____

Number of calendar days between original submittal date and final approval
date: _____

Date that approval was required to meet original construction schedule:

_____

Calendar days delay to the field work per original schedule caused by late
approval: _____

Impact and disruption to base-contract work (describe in detail): _____

_____

_____

_____

_____

Prepared by: _____

Figure 6–7. Summary of shop-drawing and material approval delays.

project information. A numerical system with all memoranda, letters, field directives, and reports, each assigned a numerical control number and filed by contract in chronological order, is generally used. The file is normally broken down into two main parts: incoming and outgoing. These files may be expanded indefinitely. Similarly, coded entry of correspondence into computer data bases also provides instant retrieval of all relevant documents.

§ 6.13   Memoranda

Memoranda for record are suggested to record the facts on specific events, such as meetings, telephone conversations, accidents, traffic conditions, and so on, that are not normally reflected in documents. These memoranda should be signed and maintained in a separate file, with copies sent to appropriate parties. Additional copies should also be included in files maintained on specific problems or subjects.

§ 6.14   Cost Records

The contractor should maintain several categories of cost and financial records during the life of a project. These include original and updated project estimates, budget and job cost reports for all work activities, change-order estimates, contractor requests for payments, progress payments, purchase records, general-conditions costs, equipment-cost records, payroll records of the trade contractor and subcontractors, and wage agreements with the labor trades. These items are invaluable in substantiating claims and resolving disputes.

§ 6.15   Errors and Omissions Analyses

It is suggested that the contractor maintain an overall data base, as well as individual files, for all errors and omissions or other requests for clarification encountered during the life of the project. Typically, such matters are raised with the owners through the use of RFIs.

In any event, a separate file should be maintained on each request for information, as well as an errors and omissions data summary such as that contained in **Figure 6–8**. This summary form enables the recording of all relevant information on the effect of an error, particularly individual impact on work activities and disruption of work activities.

Project:

E & O No.: _____

Charter of E & O: _____

_____

Floor & area affected: _____

_____

Specification section references: _____

_____

Drawing references: _____

_____

Other documentation available (photos, special drawings, as-specified vs. as-built drawings, etc.): _____

_____

Date of notification of general contractor, architect/engineer, owner: _____

_____

Method & date of resolution (e.g., architect/engineer issues change request, clarification memo, etc.): _____

_____

Impact on & disruption of base-contract work (describe in detail, i.e., stopped work, moved to other work areas, lost hours, etc.): _____

_____

_____

_____

Prepared by: _____

Date: _____

Figure 6–8. Summary of error and omission impact.

§ 6.16   Using Computers for Job Record-Keeping

The contractor, as well as the owner, should evaluate the use of an overall computer data base to record, through individual computer data files, most, if not all, of the forms detailed in the preceding sections of this chapter. However, back-up copies of the computer information must be maintained. In addition, it is suggested that hard (paper) copies of the data also be maintained to ensure that there is no loss of critical project information because of a computer disk crash or other catastrophe.

PART II

CLAIM RECOGNITION, PREPARATION, AND PROOF

CHAPTER 7

TIME-RELATED CLAUSES AND CLAIMS

§ 7.1   Excusable Delays

§ 7.2   Contract Provisions Pertaining to Delay

§ 7.3   Examples of Excusable Delay

§ 7.4   —Strikes and Labor Unrest

§ 7.5   —Unusually Severe Weather

§ 7.6   —Inability to Obtain Materials

§ 7.7   —Other Causes

§ 7.8   Compensable Delays

§ 7.9   —Examples of Compensable Delays

§ 7.10 Disruption

§ 7.11 —Assumptions Concerning Disruption

§ 7.12 —Ripple Effect

§ 7.13 —Examples of Disruption

§ 7.14 Suspension of Work

§ 7.15 —Suspension of Work Provisions

§ 7.16 —Recovery by Contractor

§ 7.17 —Concurrent Delay

§ 7.18 —Examples of Suspension of Work

§ 7.19 Disruption versus Delay

§ 7.20 —Impact of Disruption: Pure Delay versus Disruption

§ 7.21 No Damages for Delay Provisions

§ 7.22 —Interpreting No Damages for Delay Clauses

§ 7.23 Exceptions to Enforcement of No Damages Clauses

§ 7.24 —Delays Not Within Parties' Contemplation

§ 7.25 —Delays Amounting to Abandonment

§ 7.26 —Delays Caused by Bad Faith or Fraud

§ 7.27 —Delays Caused by Active Interference

§ 7.28 Acceleration

§ 7.29 —Actual Acceleration
§ 7.30 —Constructive Acceleration
§ 7.31 —Examples of Acceleration

§ 7.1 Excusable Delays

Parties to a contract may include risk-allocation provisions that define those types of project delays that are excusable. In the event of a dispute, courts, arbitrators, or boards of contract appeals refer to the parties' contract as the embodiment of the agreement and will attempt to enforce such provisions in accordance with the parties' intent. Prior agreements about whether certain delays are the risk of the owner or the contractor will, to a large extent, determine whether a delay in performance of work is excusable or nonexcusable. Relief provisions relating to delay are a means of risk allocation between owners and contractors. Each party attempts to limit its own liability by allocating risk to the other party.

§ 7.2 Contract Provisions Pertaining to Delay

A number of well-known time-extension and delay provisions are widely in use in the industry today, including those in standard AIA contracts[1] and federal contracts. As an example, the standard excusable-delay provision for federal contracts states:

(a) Except for defaults of subcontractors at any tier, the Contractor shall not be in default because of any failure to perform this contract under its terms if the failure arises from causes beyond the control and without the fault or negligence of the Contractor. . . . Examples of these causes are (1) acts of God or of the public enemy, (2) acts of the Government in either its sovereign or contractual capacity, (3) fires, (4) floods, (5) epidemics, (6) quarantine restrictions, (7) strikes, (8) freight embargoes, and (9) unusually severe weather. In each instance, the failure to perform must be beyond the control and without the fault or negligence of the Contractor. "Default" includes failure to make progress in the work so as to endanger performance.

* * *

(c) Upon request of the Contractor, the Contracting Officer shall ascertain the facts and extent of the failure. If the Contracting Officer determines that any failure to perform results from one or more of the causes above, the [completion time] shall be revised, subject to the rights of the Government under the termination clause of this contract.[2]

---

[1] AIA A201-1987 ¶ 8.3.
[2] 48 C.F.R. § 52.249-14 (1989).

Under such provisions the contractor is entitled to an extension of time to complete work if the delay is *excusable*. No liquidated damages can be assessed during this extended performance period. The contractor is not necessarily entitled to additional compensation for expenses resulting from delay, even though excusable, provided the delay is not directly or indirectly the fault of the owner. This is referred to as a *noncompensable* delay because no monetary compensation is received for costs of delay.[3]

§ 7.3   Examples of Excusable Delay

As noted above, delays caused by acts of God usually are expressly excused in contractual time-extension provisions. *Act of God* typically refers to a natural occurrence caused directly and exclusively by natural forces without any human intervention, which could not have been reasonably foreseen or prevented by the contractor or any other party to the contract. This category includes earthquakes, landslides, tornadoes, hurricanes, lightning, and floods.[4]

In *Prather v. Latshaw*,[5] the contractor agreed to construct a drainage ditch and levee but failed to include in the contract a provision excusing delay due to acts of God. A large portion of the contracted work had already been performed when the site was inundated by a flood. The contractor claimed excusable delay, but the court denied the contractor's claim, finding that the contract had no provision excusing late completion due to acts of God. Accordingly, the contractor was held to the original completion date.

Some of the other frequently encountered causes of excusable delay are discussed in the following sections.

§ 7.4   —Strikes and Labor Unrest

Strikes are frequent causes of delay on construction projects. Generally, contract clauses listing strikes as an excusable delay also qualify that the cause for delay must have been unforeseen and beyond the control of the contractor. Any strikes foreseeable at time of contract signing are not considered excusable delay. For example, if a strike is in progress when the contractor prepares her bid and is still in effect when the bid is

---

[3] McNamara Constr. of Manitoba, Ltd. v. United States, 509 F.2d 1166, 1172 (Ct. Cl. 1975).

[4] New Pueblo Constr., Inc. v. State, 144 Ariz. 95, 696 P.2d 185 (1985); Tombigbee Constr. v. United States, 420 F.2d 1037 (Ct. Cl. 1970); LeFebvre v. Callaghan, 33 Ariz. 197, 263 P. 589 (1929); Maplewood Farm Co. v. City of Seattle, 88 Wash. 634, 153 P. 1061 (1915).

[5] 188 Ind. 204, 122 N.E. 721 (1919).

submitted and the contract is awarded, delay caused by the strike is clearly foreseeable.[6]

A contractor cannot be the cause of the strike. If the strike is within the contractor's control, the strike is then inexcusable and any resulting delay is noncompensable. Strikes within the contractor's control include those occurring after the contractor failed to pay employees,[7] and when the contractor discontinued paying travel time from the labor assembly point to the jobsite during performance of a contract.[8] Current commercial construction agreements state that only strikes at locations other than the project site or in violation of no-strike provisions in labor agreements are excusable.

§ 7.5   —Unusually Severe Weather

Unusually severe weather has long been listed as an excusable delay in government contracts,[9] and the concept also was added to the 1987 revision to the standard form AIA contract.[10]

It is important to note that courts must, on a case-by-case basis, consider such things as the geographic location of the jobsite, the nature of the work performed, the weather conditions reasonably anticipated by the contractor, and the previous experience that the contractor has in the area.

Weather delay is excusable *only* if the occurring conditions are unforeseeable and unusually severe for that particular place. Delay will not be excused if the conditions are normal for that area, no matter how severe the conditions.[11] The contractor must show more than the weather's interference with the work. Variations in the weather are always expected, and delays resulting from variations typical to the locale are not excusable.[12]

Various methods have been developed to measure unusual precipitation. One method is to compare the number of days of precipitation during the contract's progress with the average number of rain days during a prior, similar period in the area.[13] Another method is to compare the total

---

[6] Allied Contractors, Inc., IBCA No. 265, 1962 BCA ¶ 3501 (1962); Charles I. Cunningham, IBCA No. 242, 60-2 BCA ¶ 2816 (1970); Oliver-Elec. Mfg. Co. v. I.O. Teigen Constr. Co., 177 F. Supp. 572, 576 (D. Minn. 1959).

[7] Kobashigawa Shokai, ASBCA No. 13,741, 69-2 BCA ¶ 7973 (1969).

[8] Tri-State Constr. Co., IBCA No. 63, 57-1 BCA ¶ 1184 (1957).

[9] 48 C.F.R. ¶ 52.249-14 (1989).

[10] AIA A201-1987 ¶ 4.3.8.2.

[11] Broome Constr., Inc. v. United States, 492 F.2d 829, 835 (Ct. Cl. 1974); John E. Faucett, AGBCA No. 396, 76-2 BCA ¶ 11,946 (1976).

[12] Broome Constr., Inc. v. United States, 492 F.2d 829, 835 (Ct. Cl. 1974).

[13] Patt H. Dell, GSBCA No. 2811, 70-1 BCA ¶ 8152 (1970).

amount of precipitation during the period of contract construction with the average of the total precipitation in a comparable length of time during a prior period of years in the same area.[14]

When an unusually severe weather condition other than rain is alleged as the basis for an excusable delay claim, other means of measurement may be applied. Weather bureau records may be examined to determine the frequency with which a severe weather condition has occurred in the past for the geographic area in question.

An owner may insert provisions into the contract requiring that the contractor show the unusually severe weather conditions that caused the delay to the project before the contractor is permitted a time extension. For example, such a provision might read:

> Extensions of time, when recommended by the engineer, will be based upon the effect of delays to the project as a whole and will not be recommended for noncontrolling delays to minor included portions of the work, unless it can be shown that such delays did in fact delay the progress of the project as a whole.

This type of provision requires that the contractor, in order to obtain a time extension, demonstrate that the delay affected the critical path.

§ 7.6   —Inability to Obtain Materials

The standard excusable-delays provision on federal projects entitles the contractor to a time extension if the delay in completion of the work is attributable to "delays of subcontractors or suppliers arising from unforeseeable causes beyond the control and without the fault or negligence of both the contractor and such subcontractors or suppliers."[15] The contractor must show that delays caused by the inability to obtain materials were unforeseeable and beyond the control and without the fault or negligence of *both* the contractor and the supplier or subcontractor in question.

Rarely are a contractor's supplies or materials unobtainable from any source. More typically, the materials can be obtained, but only at a cost substantially in excess of what the contractor anticipated when she prepared the bid. When this happens, the contractor, in order to be relieved from contract performance, must demonstrate that the increased cost is so great that her performance would be commercially impracticable.

Courts and boards of contract appeals are generally reluctant to award relief to contractors on this basis and will do so only where the increase in price is extreme. The energy crisis of 1973–1974 produced many such

---

[14] Montgomery Constr. Corp., ASBCA No. 5000, 59-1 BCA ¶ 2211 (1959).

[15] *See* Excusable Delays provision, 48 C.F.R. § 52.249-14(b) (1989).

examples when petroleum-derived products in very short supply increased sharply in price. In most cases these products were obtainable, but only at a greater cost to the contractor. For example, in *Consolidated Molded Products, Inc.,*[16] the board rejected the contractor's claim that a 12 percent cost increase made the contract commercially impracticable. As a side note, the contracting officer earlier had allowed the contractor a time extension because the delay resulting from the unavailability of the petroleum-based product was excusable under the default clause.

§ 7.7   —Other Causes

General Condition ¶ 8.3.1 of AIA Document A-201 refers to "other causes beyond the contractor's control" that the architect may determine justify a time extension. This provision indicates that the parties who utilize the AIA contract do not intend to limit the bases for excusable delay to those items specifically enumerated in the clause.

The architect has the power to issue a time extension if she determines that the delay suffered by the contractor was caused by factors beyond the control of both parties. Therefore, if the contractor is impacted by some unforeseeable event and is not responsible, the architect may still provide relief upon proper notice from the contractor, even though the cause of the delay does not fit conveniently into the specific causes enumerated in General Condition ¶ 8.3.1.

§ 7.8   Compensable Delays

When (1) delay is caused by the owner or something or someone within the owner's control, (2) the delay results in additional costs to the contractor, and (3) the contractor has not assumed the risk of the delay, the owner's action (or inaction) entitles the contractor to increased costs due to the delay and a time extension. The contract need not state that the contractor is entitled to recover for owner-caused delays, because this is an implied warranty in every contract.[17] The contractor may, however, wish to include a specific clause relating to compensable delays (also referred to as owner-caused delays), thereby reinforcing her right to recover under an express warranty.

An example of the owner's implied obligation to not delay the contractor is found in *Northeast Clackamas Electric v. Continental Casualty*

---

[16] ASBCA No. 21,068, 76-2 BCA ¶ 12,177 (1976).

[17] See generally **Ch. 5**; Wickwire, Hurlbut, & Shapiro, *Rights & Obligations in Scheduling,* Construction Briefings 88-13 (1988).

Co.[18] A contractor performing a contract to construct 17 miles of power transmission lines began experiencing owner-caused delays when the contractor was about 30 percent finished. The delays included the owner's failure to timely and properly clear the right-of-way and to properly trim or fell trees ahead of the contractor's operations. The court found that the owner's duty to cooperate and to refrain from hindering the contractor in its work is implied by law:

> In every express contract for the erection of a building or for the performance of other constructive work, there is an implied term that the owner, or other persons for whom the work is contracted to be done, will not obstruct, hinder, or delay the contractor, but on the contrary, will and always facilitate the performance of the work to be done by him.
>
> * * *
>
> An implied, if not an express, covenant is contained in this contract, requiring defendant to furnish and deliver the site in a condition to permit the work to be done, and that a failure so to do is a wrongful breach of the contract for which the contractor may recover damages, is well settled by numerous cases.[19]

Accordingly, the contract need not contain an express provision making the owner liable for delays. Such liability is imposed on the owner for breach of the duty to cooperate.[20] As noted previously, owners occasionally seek to avoid this responsibility with a no damages for delay clause. However, without a "no damages" clause, delays may be compensable as violations of an express provision, such as the suspension of work clause, or as a breach of the implied obligation to not delay.

§ 7.9   —Examples of Compensable Delays

The many circumstances under which contracts are performed prohibit the compilation of an exhaustive listing of compensable delays. The contractor should be aware of the specific circumstances under which she performs and the provisions of her contract so that owner-caused delay can be identified when it occurs.

Failure of the owner to make timely progress payments may be the basis for a delay claim. If a contractor is delayed in the execution of her work by the owner's failure to make payments as required by the contract, the

---

[18] 221 F.2d 329 (9th Cir. 1955).

[19] *Id.* at 334.

[20] Ginsberg & Eshelman, *Implied Duty of Cooperation,* Construction Briefings 87-12 (1987).

contractor is entitled to recover damages from the owner.[21] Similarly, an owner's delay in investigating the contractor's request for a change or time extension may itself be a delay entitling the contractor to damages for owner-caused delay.[22]

In one case, the board found that a contractor was entitled to damages for owner-caused delay even though the contractor finished in advance of the contract completion date. The board noted that 89 days for review and approval of contractor-submitted shop drawings was unreasonable for a task that should have been accomplished in two weeks. In addition, because work that otherwise would have been performed between March and June had to be performed between June and August, the contractor suffered wage rate escalation because of higher wages in the later period and was entitled to recover the wage differential.[23]

Bureaucratic project delay incident to procedures imposed on the contracting officer by her superiors has been held to constitute a compensable failure to act within a reasonable time.[24] Government approval of another contractor's progress schedule with full knowledge that the schedule would result in interference with the work of the contractor-claimant also is a compensable delay.[25]

Other examples of compensable delays include:

1. The contracting officer's unreasonable delay in approving shop drawings, where the board held 15 days was a reasonable approval period under the circumstances but the government took 44 days[26]
2. Owner's unreasonable delay in making site available to contractor and then issuing a change adding a number of rooms, forcing contractor to perform in severe winter weather[27]
3. Owner's failure to inspect and accept technical manuals required under the contract[28]
4. Owner's refusal to respond to contractor's request for instructions after contractor had complained about delay incurred in construction of "flip-lip" at dam[29]

---

[21] Virginia Elecs. Co., ASBCA No. 18,778, 77-1 BCA ¶ 12,393 (1977) (improper rejection of an initial progress payment request caused a two-week delay in performance).

[22] J.C. Hester Co., IBCA No. 1114-7-76, 77-1 BCA ¶ 12,292 (1977).

[23] Sydney Constr. Co., ASBCA No. 21,377, 77-2 BCA ¶ 12,719 (1977); *see also* Kenworthy v. State, 236 Cal. App. 2d 378, 46 Cal. Rptr. 396 (1965).

[24] Merritt-Chapman & Scott Corp. v. United States, 192 Ct. Cl. 848, 429 F.2d 431 (1970).

[25] Warrior Constructors, Inc., ENGBCA No. 3134, 71-1 BCA ¶ 8915 (1971).

[26] Myers-Laine Corp., ASBCA No. 18,234, 74-1 BCA ¶ 10,467 (1974).

[27] S&E Contractors, Inc., ASBCA No. 97-12-72, 74-2 BCA ¶ 10,876 (1974).

[28] Orion Elecs. Corp., ASBCA No. 18,010, 75-1 BCA ¶ 11,006 (1974).

[29] Constructors-Pamco., ENGBCA No. 3468, 76-2 BCA ¶ 11,950 (1976).

5. Failure to provide owner-furnished materials, failure to make decisions within a reasonable time, and issuance of an addendum to the plans that misrepresented the rights-of-way required by other contractors.[30]

§ 7.10 Disruption

Disruption on a construction project can be defined as a material alteration of the performance conditions expected at the time of bidding such that the performance conditions actually encountered do not correspond to those contemplated, resulting in increased difficulty and cost of performance for the contractor. This is also referred to as *interference* or *hindrance.* When disruption occurs, the contractor cannot perform per the planned method she reasonably anticipated in preparing her bid and, as a result, incurs increased costs.

§ 7.11   —Assumptions Concerning Disruption

A contractor is entitled to schedule her work in such a manner that enables performance in a series of economical operations, each dependent upon a prior operation, and that, as a whole, represents the contractor's most efficient manner of performing. Disruption anywhere within the planned, sequential performance could have a very negative and disruptive impact on succeeding operations.

Neither party to a contract is permitted to act in a manner that will prevent the other party from rendering performance. As already noted in § 7.8 and reviewed in detail in **Chapter 5**, this is because there exists an implied duty to cooperate, an obligation that is the most fundamental of the implied obligations in contract law.[31]

Contractors should plan to perform their work in an efficient and economical sequence of operations. Owners or other parties to the contract implicitly obligate themselves to not interfere with this plan.[32]

Contractors should reasonably plan their method of performance. A contractor cannot assume that other parties will make unreasonable efforts to assist in performing. For example, it would be unreasonable for a contractor to disregard the fact that other trades may also be required to

---

[30] V.C. Edwards Contracting Co. v. Port of Tacoma, 83 Wash. 2d 7, 514 P.2d 1381 (1973).

[31] Nichols Dynamics, Inc., ASBCA No. 17,949, 75-2 BCA ¶ 11,556 (1975).

[32] *See* City of Seattle v. Dyad Constr., Inc., 17 Wash. App. 501, 565 P.2d 423 (1977) (contractor entitled to delay damages caused by (1) unnecessary corrective procedures ordered by the city and (2) inaccurate specifications).

work in common areas on the jobsite. A contractor simply cannot always expect sole access to a site. As such, a reasonable progress schedule must contemplate the interruptions that will normally be encountered on a project. A contractor's planned method of performance must be reasonable to recover the increased costs sustained as a result of disruption to the planned schedule.

§ 7.12   —Ripple Effect

Performance will usually involve a sequence of operations anticipated by the contractor. Once the sequence is disrupted anywhere within the proposed ordering of tasks, a ripple effect evolves and negatively affects performance on subsequent activities, creating additional delay even though these activities had not been directly affected by the initial disruption. For example, a change issued to a heating, ventilation, and air conditioning (HVAC) contractor requiring a change in the location of grilles in an air-distribution system is likely to have both direct and indirect effects upon the contractor's performance. The direct effects are likely to be the relocation of the grilles to other locations in the ceiling layout and the reordering of grilles if air distribution performance criteria have changed. The contractor is entitled to an equitable adjustment of the contract for the direct costs of the change, namely the cost of new and different grilles. However, such a change is also likely to result in indirect costs due to disruption of the contractor's other operations in the physical area of the change. Relocation of the grilles may disrupt other installations being performed by the HVAC contractor, who may have to revise or relocate ductwork running to the new grilles and move other equipment.

In another example of this ripple effect, a contractor was required, before proceeding with form work, to submit a scale model of a core support for approval by the engineer. The government specifications requiring this model stated that the model had to truly and accurately reproduce the configuration of the final work and had to serve as an aid in the design of the form work and as a visual aid for dependent construction procedures. The government's architect intended that the contractor produce a model with extremely close tolerances that could be used to verify the architectural design of the structure. However, the specification language in the contract requiring the model failed to convey this intent. Therefore, the contractor ultimately was able to establish that the model she submitted was adequate, even though its scale dimensions did not precisely comport with the figure dimensions on the contract drawings. Because of the contractor's compliance with the specifications, it was held that the government acted improperly in rejecting the contractor's model. The rejection had a ripple effect on the contractor's performance by delaying performance for an unreasonable period of time, during which a second model had to be constructed before the contractor could proceed with the design of the core form work.[33]

§ 7.13 —Examples of Disruption

The contractor who has a claim for disruption normally proceeds to recover under one or more provisions of her contract. In government contracts, recovery frequently occurs under the *changes* clause, the *suspension of work* clause, or the *differing site conditions* clause. The contractor must establish that one or more of these clauses affords a remedy for the disruption sustained.

The events that can give rise to a claim for disruption are varied as the types and requirements of construction contracts. The following examples of disruption are not meant to provide an exhaustive listing, but were chosen to show that a claim for disruption can arise in virtually every construction contract, regardless of the work involved.

1. Disruption in the planned work sequence due to misfabricated government-furnished steel.[34]

2. Delay in issuing a notice to proceed on a job that contractor planned to perform concurrently with another job (thereby obtaining cost savings) was a change in the contractor's manner of performance.[35]

3. Errors in surveying a proposed road, coupled with failure to designate feasible stockpile sites for temporary storage, resulted in a breach of duty to avoid unreasonably interfering with the contractor's performance.[36]

4. Failure to store government-furnished partitions and hardware in a readily identifiable fashion and, instead, mixing sizes and stock numbers in storage.[37]

5. Failure to maintain the condition of a road providing the contractor with sole access to the jobsite after the road was damaged by the operations of another contractor.[38]

6. Noise from a government power-check facility adjacent to the contractor's work site reduced the efficiency of the contractor's labor and was a change in the method or manner of performance.[39]

---

[33] Piracci Constr. Co., GSBCA No. 3477, 74-1 BCA ¶ 10,647 (1974).

[34] Power City & Equip., Inc., IBCA No. 490-4-65, 68-2 BCA ¶ 7126 (1968).

[35] Pan Arctic Corp., ASBCA No. 20,133, 77-1 BCA ¶ 12,514 (1977).

[36] Lewis-Nicholson, Inc. v. United States, 550 F.2d 26 (Ct. Cl. 1977).

[37] Ogburn & Assocs., Inc., GSBCA No. 4700, 77-1 BCA ¶ 12,473 (1977).

[38] Hensel-Phelps Constr. Co., ENGBCA No. 3368, 74-2 BCA ¶ 10,728 (1974).

[39] Nichols Dynamics, Inc., ASBCA No. 17,949, 75-2 BCA ¶ 11,556 (1975).

7.   Failure to provide the contractor with adequate access to the work site during a particular time period constituted a change in the manner of contract performance.[40]

8.   Accumulation of changed work required the contractor to perform a large portion of post office construction work out of sequence and in a manner that reduced normal efficiency (changes aggregated 10 percent of the estimated cost of the work).[41]

9.   Government delay in furnishing information forced the contractor to install dryer vent holes out of sequence and in a more costly manner.[42]

10.   Defective plans, failure to supply materials, misleading addenda, and the owner's failure to make prompt decisions caused the contractor to construct a railroad project piecemeal, rather than according to her proposed schedule, necessitating temporary shutdowns.[43]

11.   Delays in correcting inaccurate specifications protracted sewer line construction when work on the revised specifications could only proceed during low tides.[44]

§ 7.14   Suspension of Work

Under most construction contracts, the owner has the right to order the contractor to stop all or part of the work, either because of failure on the contractor's part to perform the work according to the contract documents or for the convenience of the owner.

§ 7.15   —Suspension of Work Provisions

The standard federal contract clause provides:

> (a)   The Contracting Officer may order the contractor, in writing, to suspend, delay, or interrupt all or any part of the work of this contract for the period of time that the Contracting Officer determines appropriate for the convenience of the Government.
>
> (b)   If the performance of all or any part of the work is, for an unreasonable period of time, suspended, delayed, or interrupted (1) by an act of the Contracting Officer in the administration of this contract, or (2) by the

---

[40] Reliance Enters., ASBCA No. 20,808, 76-1 BCA ¶ 11,831 (1976).

[41] Coley Properties Corp., PSBCA No. 291, 75-2 BCA ¶ 11,514 (1975).

[42] Fred A. Arnold, Inc., ASBCA No. 18,915, 75-2 BCA ¶ 11,496 (1975).

[43] V.C. Edwards Contracting Co. v. Port of Tacoma, 83 Wash. 2d 7, 514 P.2d 1381 (1973).

[44] City of Seattle v. Dyad Constr., Inc., 17 Wash. App. 501, 565 P.2d 423 (1977).

Contracting Officer's failure to act within the time specified in this contract (or within a reasonable time if not specified), an adjustment shall be made for any increase in the cost of performance of this contract (excluding profit) necessarily caused by the unreasonable suspension, delay, or interruption.[45]

Such provisions enable the owner or contracting officer to order the contractor, in writing, to suspend, delay, or interrupt all or any part of the work, for such period of time as may be determined to be appropriate, for the convenience of the owner or the government.

AIA Document A201 provides the owner and contractor with similar rights. Further, ¶ 14.3.2 provides that the contractor is entitled to an adjustment in the contract price, including profit, on the increased costs of performance, as long as the contractor was not responsible for the suspension or delay and an equitable adjustment has not been made or denied under another provision of the contract. Profit is not recoverable for pure delays under the federal suspension of work provision.[46]

§ 7.16   —Recovery by Contractor

A contractor on federal projects must show that her work was suspended, delayed, or interrupted for an *unreasonable* period of time by an act of the government in the administration of the contract. Under the federal suspension of work clause, the contractor must show that the period of delay was unreasonable, although all delays caused by defective specifications are considered unreasonable per se.[47] There is no such requirement in the AIA contract. Absent a suspension of work provision, it has been held that no equitable adjustment in money under the contract can be had for owner-caused delay; in such a situation, the contractor's remedy is an action for breach of contract.[48]

§ 7.17   —Concurrent Delay

Situations where both the contractor and owner have caused delays are known as concurrent delays. The general rule is that where both parties contribute to the delay neither party can recover damages absent a clear apportionment of the delay and expense attributable to each party.[49] If the

---

[45] 48 C.F.R. § 52.212-12 (1989).

[46] AIA A201-1987 ¶ 14.3.

[47] Chaney & James Constr. Co. v. United States, 421 F.2d 728 (Ct. Cl. 1970).

[48] Hoak Constr. Co., IBCA No. 353, 65-1 BCA ¶ 4665 (1965).

[49] Blinderman Constr. Co. v. United States, 695 F.2d 552, 559 (Fed. Cir. 1982).

delay caused by the government or owner can be separated or apportioned from the contractor-caused delay, the contractor may be able to recover a portion of her costs or at least avoid liquidated damages.[50] If, however, the contractor's own delay and that of the other party are so intertwined that they cannot be separated, the contractor is not entitled to recover for delay caused by the other party.[51] (See detailed discussion in **Chapter 9**.)

This underscores the need for all parties to document the record as events occur to substantiate a claim once it has been filed. Success or failure of a delay claim often hinges on which party keeps better records to buttress its position.

§ 7.18   —Examples of Suspension of Work

The following are some examples of various owner-caused acts or omissions that resulted in contract adjustments under the suspension of work provision:

1. Late issuance of notice to proceed[52]
2. Failure to respond to requests for deviation from contract requirements[53]
3. An eight-day delay in responding to a request for interpretation of a contract provision that was, under the circumstances, unreasonable[54]
4. The owner's failure to provide the required construction permit when the contractor was ready to begin work, thereby making the site unavailable[55]
5. Lack of funding that resulted in a five-month suspension and entitled the contractor to stand-by costs.[56]

Suspension of work may also result from the owner's failure to act upon the contractor's request for assistance or information critical to the contractor's performance.[57] In one case the owner's delay in granting an

---

[50] *See* William F. Klingensmith, Inc. v. United States, 731 F.2d 805 (Fed. Cir. 1984).

[51] William Passalacqua Builders, Inc., GSBCA No. 4205, 77-1 BCA ¶ 12,406 (1977).

[52] DeMatteo Constr. Co., PSBCA No. 187, 76-1 BCA ¶ 11,845 (1976).

[53] Hardie-Tynes Mfg. Co., ASBCA No. 20,582, 76-2 BCA ¶ 11,972 (1976).

[54] Royal Painting Co., ASBCA No. 20,034, 75-1 BCA ¶ 11,311 (1975); *see also* Hensler v. City of Los Angeles, 124 Cal. App. 2d 71, 268 P.2d 12 (1954).

[55] Rottau Elec. Co., ASBCA No. 20,283, 76-2 BCA ¶ 12,001 (1976).

[56] C.H. Leavell & Co. v. United States, 530 F.2d 878 (Ct. Cl. 1976).

[57] M.D. Funk, ASBCA No. 20,287, 76-2 BCA ¶ 12,120 (1976).

adjustment in price and time for completion was so severe it was held to constitute a constructive suspension.[58]

The actual suspension can come about in a variety of ways. In one case, the court held that issuance of a notice to proceed and commencement of construction on a canal project were improper when the government knew or should have known that local real estate owners were vigorously contesting the right of a state levee board to appropriate realty. The contractor recovered damages incurred when her work was constructively suspended by two gentlemen, armed with revolvers and shotguns, who essentially told the contractor to "get off their land."[59]

§ 7.19   Disruption versus Delay

As noted in § 7.10, disruption is any change in the method of performance or the planned work sequence contemplated by the contractor at the time the job was bid that prevents the contractor from actually performing in this manner. It is a material alteration of the performance conditions expected at the time of bid such that the performance conditions actually encountered do not correspond to those contemplated and, instead, increase the difficulty and cost of the contractor's performance. Because of the relationship between disruption and the contractor's anticipated or planned method of performance, disruption often is referred to as *interference* or *hindrance,* the idea being that, because of some act or omission on the part of the other party to the contract, the planned method of performance the contractor reasonably anticipated in preparing the bid cannot be followed and, as a result, the contractor incurs increased costs.

Disruption, therefore, involves several assumptions about construction contracts and the obligations of the parties who enter into them. First, it recognizes that, in bidding a construction contract, the contractor is entitled to schedule her work in such a manner that it can be performed in a series of economical operations. Each operation depends upon proper execution and completion of a prior operation. When taken together, these interdependent and successive operations represent the contractor's most efficient manner of performing. Hence, any disruption to one or more of these sequential operations has a disruptive impact upon succeeding operations.

Second, the parties to the contract must cooperate during the course of performance so that neither party acts or fails to act in a manner that

---

[58] Coleman Eng'g Co. v. North Am. Aviation, 65 Cal. 2d 396, 420 P.2d 713, 55 Cal. Rptr. 1 (1966).

[59] Delta Equip. & Constr. Co. v. United States, 113 F. Supp. 459 (Ct. Cl. 1953).

prevents the other party from rendering her performance. This is frequently referred to as the *implied duty to cooperate* and is one of the most elementary of implied obligations in contract law.[60] The concept of disruption as it relates to the implied duty to cooperate is that the contractor has planned to perform her work in an efficient and economical sequence of operations and the owner (or other party to the contract) impliedly obligates herself to not interfere with this plan.[61]

Finally, the contractor, in planning her method of performance, must act reasonably. She is not entitled to assume that other parties will make unreasonable efforts to allow her to render her performance. For example, a contractor who, in preparing her bid, contemplates that she will have sole access to and use of the jobsite to perform her work when she knows or should know from the contract documents or schedule that other trades will be required to be on-site during her operations, does not act reasonably when she prepares a progress schedule that shows her work proceeding without the normal interruptions that are ordinarily encountered on a project. For example, she cannot claim disruption if, in the course of her work, her operations were adversely affected by the presence of other trades when she should have anticipated that other trades would have to be on the job in order to perform the entire contract within the contractually specified performance period. Hence, the contractor's planned method of performance must be reasonable for her to recover the increased costs sustained as a result of disruption to that plan.

§ 7.20 —Impact of Disruption: Pure Delay versus Disruption

The impact of disruption on the contractor's operations usually is a loss in efficiency during the contract performance period; performance itself is not necessarily extended as a result of the disruption. Therein lies the difference between a claim for *pure delay* and a claim for disruption.

For example, if the contractor is required to complete her performance within 200 calendar days and during the performance of her work suffers disruption to one or more of her operations, she may suffer increased costs, but it does not necessarily follow that her performance will be extended beyond the 200 days allowed for completion. Thus, even though

---

[60] *See, e.g.,* Nichols Dynamics, Inc., ASBCA No. 17,949, 75-2 BCA ¶ 11,556 (1975).

[61] *See* City of Seattle v. Dyad Constr., Inc., 17 Wash. App. 501, 565 P.2d 423 (1977) (contractor entitled to delay damages caused by unnecessary corrective procedures ordered by the city and by inaccurate specifications); Fairbanks Builders, Inc. v. Morton DeLima, Inc., 483 P.2d 194 (Alaska 1971) (subcontractor compensated for delays caused by change in contractor's operating procedures).

the cost of performing the work that was disrupted is likely to be increased, the contractor still may be able to complete her performance within the contractually specified performance period.

An electrical contractor, for example, whose work crews are installing equipment in an interstitial electrical room and find their work hindered by the presence of other trades in the same room or by the presence of errors and omissions in the electrical drawings that must be corrected before the work can resume, is likely to be unable to complete her operations with the same degree of efficiency she anticipated in preparing her bid. To take another example, the HVAC contractor who is installing ductwork and who encounters a structural member, not shown on the contract drawings, that interferes with the duct layout is likely to suffer a loss of efficiency if her sheet metal crews must deactivate their operations until the error is corrected. By the same token, if, in order to maintain compliance with the overall schedule, the HVAC contractor must place additional workers on the job to work around such problems, her performance is apt to be disrupted without necessarily exceeding the overall performance period set forth in the contract.

Disruption thus may be distinguished from *pure delay*—the type of delay suffered by the contractor whose overall performance period is extended. The significance of this distinction is that the damages a contractor is entitled to recover for disruption are not the same type of damages the contractor is entitled to recover for pure delay. The damages associated with disruption are likely to be increased labor costs due to inefficiency, the increased manpower placed on a job to compensate for inefficiencies, increased labor costs due to the activation-deactivation of work, and additional equipment costs. Damages associated with pure delay, however, are those that result from an extended performance period, such as increased overhead and jobsite costs, equipment standby costs, wage escalation, and financing costs. It is important to keep in mind that in some cases these costs will overlap. It is also possible for a contractor to experience both delays and disruption. There is another significant point about the difference between disruption and pure delay that requires contractors to distinguish carefully between the two in documenting and prosecuting claims: the area of no damages for delay clauses. These clauses, which are discussed in greater detail in § 7.21 generally do not bar a contractor from recovering for disruption as opposed to pure delay unless the clause specifically references and disclaims liability for "hindrances, impact, or disruption." Thus, even though the contractor may have a no damages for delay clause in her contract, she still may be able to assert a claim for disruption.[62]

---

[62] *See, e.g.,* Buckley & Co. v. State, 140 N.J. Super. 289, 356 A.2d 56, 60–62 (Law Div. 1975).

§ 7.21   No Damages for Delay Provisions

Owners and contractors should be aware that the law places duties and obligations on all parties to the contract whether or not these duties and obligations are expressly set forth in the contract. The implied duties and obligations are discussed in greater detail in **Chapter 5.** Chief among these is the duty placed on all parties to *cooperate* in the performance of the contract. Furthermore, all parties are obligated to not hinder the others in the performance of their duties.

The duties to cooperate and to not hinder tend to shift greater liability onto the owner; as a result, owners frequently seek to include *no damage for delay* clauses in their contracts. These clauses take a variety of forms but in essence are contract provisions that attempt to deny the contractor the right to recover from the owner for damages due to delays. It is now common for owners to attempt to insert these clauses in their contracts. They may be worded similar to the following:

> In the event the contractor is delayed in the prosecution of its work by an act, omission, neglect, or default of the owner, the contractor agrees to make no claim for damages for delay in the performance of this contract and that any such claim shall be fully compensated for by an extension of time to complete performance.

In contrast, ¶ 8.3 of AIA Document A201 expressly reserves the right of either party to recover damages for delay, assuming other provisions of the contract, such as the notice requirements, are met. As previously noted, the federal suspension of work provision also provides an express remedy for recovery of delay damages.

§ 7.22   —Interpreting No Damages for Delay Clauses

Generally, no damages provisions, if they meet the ordinary rules governing the validity of contracts, are valid and enforceable to preclude an action by the contractor for damages for delay. No damage clauses are not void as against public policy and they have withstood challenges that such provisions amount to adhesion contracts.[63]

Courts have said that a contractor cannot render meaningless an express condition of her contract that she knowingly and freely accepted and that the contractee, who has very likely paid a contingency for exaction of

---

[63] Corinno Civetta Constr. v. City of New York, 67 N.Y.2d 297, 493 N.E.2d 905, 909, 502 N.Y.S.2d 681 (1986).

the no damages clause, cannot be deprived of the benefit of the no damage clause unless her conduct indicates bad faith or some other tortious intent.[64]

In *Wells Brothers Co. v. United States,*[65] the Supreme Court made the following observation:

> Men who take $1,000,000 contracts for government buildings are neither unsophisticated nor careless. Inexperience and inattention are more likely to be found in other parties to such contracts than the contractors, and the presumption is obvious and strong that the men signing such a contract as we have here protected themselves against such delays as are complained of by the higher price extended for the work.[66]

In effect, the Supreme Court recognized the no damages clause as a risk allocation device and that the owner may well have paid for the use of such a clause in the contract.

Because of the harsh results that flow from enforcement of no damages clauses, they are strictly construed against the drafter of the provision.[67] Further, broad language relating to delays due to "any other causes" may be subject to certain recognized judicial exceptions. Also, some courts have held that no damages for delay clauses will only apply in the instance of pure delay and the contractor may still be able to recover for the disruption caused by delays.[68]

§ 7.23   Exceptions to Enforcement of No Damages Clauses

Although courts have recognized the validity of no damages for delay clauses, these clauses are not enforced without limitations. No damages for delay clauses will not be enforced in the following situations:

1. Delays are not within the contemplation of the contract parties
2. Delays amount to an abandonment of the contract
3. Delays are caused by fraud or bad faith of the other contract party

---

[64] City of Houston v. R.F. Ball Constr. Co., 570 S.W.2d 75 (Tex. Civ. App. 1978).

[65] 254 U.S. 83 (1920).

[66] *Id.* at 87.

[67] United States Steel Corp. v. Missouri Pac. R.R., 668 F.2d 435, 438 (8th Cir. 1982).

[68] *See* John E. Green Plumbing & Heating v. Turner Constr. Co., 742 F.2d 965, 966–67 (6th Cir. 1984); Buckley & Co. v. State, 140 N.J. Super. 289, 356 A.2d 56, 60–62 (Law Div. 1975); Lichter v. Mellon-Stuart Co., 305 F.2d 216 (3d Cir. 1962).

4. Delays are caused by active interference of the other contract party.[69]

§ 7.24   —Delays Not Within Parties' Contemplation

Perhaps the most significant exception is that a no damages for delay clause will not protect an owner from liability for delays that are not within the contemplation of the parties. Essentially, whether a delay was within the contemplation of the parties is a question of fact. Courts vary in their approaches to this exception. In some jurisdictions, courts apply a foreseeability test that asks whether the delay could reasonably have been foreseen at the time the contract was made.[70] Thus, in these jurisdictions, a no damages for delay clause will not be enforced against delays that were not foreseen when the parties entered into the contract.

Courts in other jurisdictions have explicitly rejected the foreseeability test and have stated that it is the no damages for delay clause itself that governs whether a delay was within the contemplation of the parties.[71] In these jurisdictions, courts will examine a clause to determine what delays are covered, irrespective of whether the delays are foreseeable or unforeseeable, or reasonable or unreasonable. If a clause is found to cover all types of delays, regardless of their categorization, then the clause will be enforced and the delayed party may not recover for the delay.[72]

§ 7.25   —Delays Amounting to Abandonment

Under the exception for abandonment, courts look to the length of a delay in determining whether the no damages for delay clause is enforceable. However, other facts will be considered as well. Courts have stated that merely because a delay is long, it does not follow that the delay amounts to an abandonment of the contract.[73] The general standard enunciated for this exception has been that the length of the delay must be so great that

---

[69] Phoenix Contractors, Inc. v. General Motors Corp., 135 Mich. App. 787, 355 N.W.2d 673 (1984); Corinno Civetta Constr. v. City of New York, 67 N.Y.2d 297, 493 N.E.2d 905, 502 N.Y.S.2d 681 (1986). *See generally* Kovars & Shuham, *No Damage for Delay Clauses,* Construction Briefings 87-11 (1987).

[70] Grant Constr. Co. v. Burns, 92 Idaho 408, 443 P.2d 1005 (1968).

[71] City of Houston v. R.F. Ball Constr. Co., 570 S.W.2d 75 (Tex. Civ. App. 1978).

[72] Cunningham Bros. v. City of Waterloo, 254 Iowa 659, 117 N.W.2d 46 (1962); Western Eng'rs v. State Road Comm'n, 437 P.2d 216 (Utah 1968).

[73] *See, e.g.,* F.D. Rich Co. v. Wilmington Hous. Auth., 392 F.2d 841 (3d Cir. 1968).

the contractor is justified in treating the contract as ended—that is, the other party has abandoned its performance.[74] Consequently, this determination is a question of fact for the courts. Courts in one jurisdiction have placed another limitation upon the use of this exception. There, it must be shown that "the [delaying party] is responsible for delays which are so unreasonable that they connote a relinquishment of the contract . . . with the intention of never resuming it."[75]

§ 7.26   —Delays Caused by Bad Faith or Fraud

The most generally recognized exception to the enforcement of a no damages for delay clause is in the case of fraud or bad faith by the party seeking its enforcement. Courts have recognized that although a no damages clause is intended to protect a party from delay damages, it does not give a party a license to cause delays willfully by unreasonable actions.[76] This exception covers a variety of acts or omissions by an owner, but it may be a difficult exception to establish because it must be proven that the other party acted in bad faith or fraudulently. Simple negligence is insufficient.[77]

§ 7.27   —Delays Caused by Active Interference

Courts are generally in agreement that a broad no damages for delay clause will not be enforced when delay damages are caused by an owner's own interference with the work of the contractor. The *active interference* exception and the exception for delays not within the contemplation of the parties are similar concepts, and the courts use them interchangeably. Due to the implied duty of each contracting party to not hinder the performance of the other, active interference has been held to not be within the parties' contemplation of the application of a no damages for delay clause.[78]

---

[74] Wells & Newton Co. v. Craig, 232 N.Y. 125, 133 N.E. 419 (1921); American Bridge Co. v. State, 245 A.D. 535, 283 N.Y.S. 577 (1935); Brady & Co. v. Board of Educ., 222 A.D. 504, 226 N.Y.S. 707 (1928).

[75] Corinno Civetta Constr. v. City of New York, 67 N.Y.2d 297, 493 N.E.2d 905, 909, 502 N.Y.S.2d 681 (1986).

[76] Housing Auth. v. J.T. Hubbell, 325 S.W.2d 880 (Tex. Civ. App. 1959).

[77] Edwin J. Dobson, Jr., Inc. v. State, 218 N.J. Super. 123, 526 A.2d 1150 (App. Div. 1987).

[78] Peter Kiewit Sons' Co. v. Iowa S. Utils. Co., 355 F. Supp. 376 (S.D. Iowa 1973).

Various actions and omissions by owners have been found to constitute active interference, including (1) failure to maintain the work site in the condition specified in the contract's specifications, (2) issuance of a notice to proceed despite knowledge that the necessary prerequisite work was not completed, and (3) the knowledge (and sometimes sanctioning) of other contractors using the contractor's work site as a drainage area.[79]

However, as cautioned previously, not all jurisdictions will subject a no damages for delay clause to strict scrutiny; many will enforce a clause as long as it is broad enough to cover the delay encountered. Courts taking this approach have held that the active interference exception requires reprehensive behavior amounting to bad faith or evil-minded conduct.[80] One court enforced a no damages for delay clause even though the owner issued several hundred "change items" and more than 800 "clarifications" that varied the original plans and specifications a great deal.[81] An extreme example of a court's enforcement of a no damages for delay clause is a case in which a prime contractor maintained secret schedules and failed to inform the subcontractors of time extensions.[82] Despite these findings, it was held that these actions only amounted to a failure to coordinate the contract and that recovery was precluded by the presence of a no damages for delay clause.

§ 7.28 Acceleration

Acceleration occurs when an owner directs a contractor (or a prime contractor directs a subcontractor) to complete all or a certain portion of the work (1) prior to the date specified in the contract for completion or (2) prior to the completion date to which the contractor would be entitled if she received the appropriate time extensions. Ordinarily, the party directed to accelerate incurs increased costs resulting from extra manpower, overtime, increased equipment rental and inefficiencies associated with overtime, and the presence of additional work forces at the jobsite. There are two types of acceleration: *actual* and *constructive.*

---

[79] United States Steel Corp. v. Missouri Pac. R.R., 668 F.2d 435 (8th Cir. 1982); Coatesville Contractors & Eng'rs, Inc. v. Borough of Ridley Park, 509 Pa. 553, 506 A.2d 862 (1986); R.S. Noonan, Inc. v. Morrison-Knudsen Co., 522 F. Supp. 1186 (E.D. La. 1981).

[80] Edwin J. Dobson, Jr., Inc. v. State, 218 N.J. Super. 123, 526 A.2d 1150 (App. Div. 1987).

[81] City of Houston v. R.F. Ball Constr. Co., 570 S.W.2d 75 (Tex. Civ. App. 1978).

[82] Crawford Painting & Drywall Co. v. J.W. Bateson Co., 857 F.2d 981 (5th Cir. 1988).

§ 7.29   —Actual Acceleration

Actual acceleration occurs when the contractor receives a *specific directive* to complete work prior to the actual completion date set forth in the contract or as modified by the parties. Because one party has issued a directive to complete the work in a shorter period than the originally specified contract performance period, there should be no doubt that such a directive is an order to accelerate.

§ 7.30   —Constructive Acceleration

Constructive acceleration is usually not as obvious as an explicit directive from the owner or contracting officer to accelerate. It occurs when the contractor is forced by the owner to complete ahead of a properly adjusted progress schedule. This may mean that the contractor suffers an excusable delay but is not granted the time extension for the delay. If ordered to complete performance within the originally specified completion date, the contractor is forced to complete the work in a shorter period than she requires or to which she is entitled. Thus the contractor is forced to accelerate the work.

There are three situations where constructive acceleration occurs. The first is where an owner claims the contractor is behind schedule and issues a written or oral directive to the contractor to complete the work at a date ahead of a properly adjusted progress schedule. If the owner is wrong the contractor may recover her acceleration costs. If the owner is correct and the contractor is behind schedule, the contractor is responsible for making up the delay and, as such, the extra effort would not be compensable.

In the second situation, the contractor is entitled to a time extension and the owner threatens the imposition of liquidated damages or a default termination because the owner claims the contractor is behind schedule. In order for the contractor to recover, it must give the owner notice that it is being constructively accelerated.

Third, a contractor may ask for and be entitled to a time extension and the owner or its representative denies or fails to grant the extension in a timely manner. The contractor must give notice to the owner that it is being forced to accelerate due to the owner's failure to grant timely extensions.

It is important, especially when the contractor believes she is being accelerated but has not received a specific order to accelerate, that the contractor advise the owner or contracting officer that any efforts undertaken by the contractor to accelerate her performance are *not* being taken voluntarily. Because the contractor was not actually ordered to accelerate and, therefore, not entitled to compensation for the extra effort, this will be of great assistance in obtaining compensation.

§ 7.31   —Examples of Acceleration

In *M.S.I. Corp.,*[83] the General Services Board of Contract Appeals held that the contractor was entitled to an equitable price adjustment because it was directed by the government to accelerate the work. The opinion set forth the five elements normally required for a constructive acceleration claim. These include:

1. An excusable delay entitling a contractor to a time extension
2. A timely request for such an extension
3. Refusal of that request by the owner or contracting officer
4. A demand for completion within the original performance period
5. The incurrance of extra costs after acceleration.

In this case, the contracting officer did not grant the time extension until more than three years after substantial completion of the contract. The contractor, however, during this period of time, took inconsistent and varying positions as to the increased costs it was incurring. This proved to be the weakest link in the claim and the contractor's case was remanded to the contracting officer on the issue of damages.

In *Elte, Inc. v. S.S. Mullen, Inc.,*[84] a subcontractor contracted to quarry rock for a prime contractor. The prime contractor first directed the contractor to quarry in a location the owner had said suitable material was likely to be found. After quarrying in this spot for three months without finding suitable material, the subcontractor was directed to quarry in another spot. However, the prime contractor insisted that the subcontractor comply with the original progress schedule. Thus, the subcontractor was constructively accelerated. The court held that the subcontractor was entitled to her excess costs incurred due to the acceleration, because the accelerated effort had been required by the prime contractor's initial failure to supply a suitable source of rock and the prime contractor's failure to grant the subcontractor a time extension when it became necessary to find an alternative source.

Contracting & Material Co. v. City of Chicago[85] presents another example of constructive acceleration. A contractor erected a large public building

---

[83] GSBCA No. 2429, 68-2 BCA ¶ 7377 (1968).

[84] 469 F.2d 1127 (9th Cir. 1972).

[85] 20 Ill. App. 3d 684, 314 N.E.2d 598 (1974), *rev'd,* 64 Ill. 2d 21, 349 N.E.2d 389 (1976).

for the City of Chicago. During the course of performance, the city issued a written order suspending the work for a total of 46 days. Later, the contractor experienced a 58-day delay as the result of a strike and its request for a time extension was denied. Thereafter, the contractor presented a claim for acceleration costs. The trial court held that the contractor was entitled to recover these costs because the owner failed to grant a time extension, thereby constructively accelerating the contractor. On appeal, the Illinois Supreme Court reversed and denied the contractor's claim. The court determined that under the contract, strikes were not excusable delays. The court also held that the contract expressly prohibited time extensions for the owner-directed suspensions of work because the contractor had failed to provide the required two, eight-hour shifts per day. The court held that the owner had not breached the terms of the contract by refusing to grant the requested time extensions and, as a result, the owner had not accelerated the work.[86]

In *Siefford v. Housing Authority,*[87] the contractor sought acceleration costs because the owner repeatedly demanded that the project be finished on schedule, notwithstanding the fact that the contractor had suffered various delays—a classic example of constructive acceleration. The court, however, denied the claim for acceleration costs because the contract contained a no damage clause that stated "no damage or compensation of any kind shall be made to the contractor for damages because of hindrance or delay from any cause in the progress of the work, whether such hindrances or delays be avoidable or unavoidable." The court held that the language of this provision was so strict that even if the owner had caused the delay in question, the contractor would not be entitled to its delay damages and thus could not recover under an acceleration theory. The court's rationale in this case is questionable. The proper inquiry is not whether the contractor would have been entitled to delay damages. Rather, it appears the court ignored the issue of whether the contractor was improperly denied the right to additional performance time which, even in the face of the no damage clause, would constitute a breach of contract entitling the contractor to recover acceleration costs.[88]

In *Constructors-Pamco,*[89] the Corps of Engineers Board of Contract Appeals found the contractor had been constructively accelerated, noting that the government had made it "abundantly clear" that work had to be completed without any time extensions by:

---

[86] Contracting & Material Co. v. City of Chicago, 64 Ill. 2d 21, 349 N.E.2d 389 (1976).

[87] 192 Neb. 643, 223 N.W.2d 816 (1974).

[88] John E. Green Plumbing & Heating v. Turner Constr. Co., 742 F.2d 965, 966–67 (6th Cir. 1984); Buckley & Co. v. State, 140 N.J. Super. 289, 356 A.2d 56, 60–62 (Law Div. 1975); Lichter v. Mellon-Stuart Co., 305 F.2d 216 (3d Cir. 1962).

[89] ENGBCA No. 3468, 76-2 BCA ¶ 11,950 (1976).

1. Using contract language that stated that the contract date would be strictly enforced

2. Providing for the imposition of liquidated damages if the work was completed late

3. Refusing to grant a performance time extension for a blizzard, an obviously excusable delay

4. Refusing to respond to contractor's request for instructions on how to proceed after contractor had complained about delays and extra costs

5. Making it consistently clear in communications to contractor personnel on a daily basis that no time extensions would be permitted.[90]

In *Ashton Co.,*[91] the government failed to obtain weather data necessary to review a time extension request for unusually severe weather until after completion of the contract. The board admonished the government for this practice and noted that under appropriate circumstances the delay in obtaining such information could render the government liable for acceleration costs.[92]

Mere failure to grant a time extension does not, by itself, show that the government accelerated the contractor's work. Instead, the contractor must show that the government expressly or impliedly ordered the contractor to perform in a shorter period of time than that to which she was entitled. In *Pathman Construction Co.,*[93] the government impressed on the contractor that the building was urgently needed before winter of the following year and, by virtue of the contract's liquidated-damages provisions (which were read to the contractor in one instance), the government gave the contractor reason to believe that it intended to assess liquidated damages against the contractor if she did not complete earlier than was contractually required. It was held that the contractor was accelerated.

In *Continental Consolidated Corp.,*[94] the contractor was required to construct a missile launch complex and to schedule her performance with a CPM schedule. Although the contractor was responsible for some delay, she should have received an additional time extension. The board ruled that the government's directive to contractor to increase effort as to certain work items amounted to acceleration of the contractor's work and entitled the contractor to an equitable adjustment under the changes clause.[95]

---

[90] *Id.* at 57,277–78.

[91] VACAB No. 1195, 76-2 BCA ¶ 11,933 (1976).

[92] *Id.* at 57,199.

[93] ASBCA No. 14,285, 71-1 BCA ¶ 8905 (1971).

[94] ENGBCA No. 2743, 67-2 BCA ¶ 6624 (1967).

[95] *Id.* at 30,717.

A contractor need not request time extension and then have it denied in order to have claim for constructive acceleration when, under the circumstances, the contracting officer had unequivocally indicated that any such request would have been denied if made.[96] The contractor is not required to perform a useless act—in this case, making a request for a time extension that she knows will be denied. Moreover, if the contractor does formally request a time extension and it is denied, the contractor need not necessarily protest the denial when she knows that the contracting officer will not withdraw the denial. Nevertheless, prudence dictates that notice be provided in all possible instances of acceleration in order to minimize the scope of defenses available to the owner in the event of a dispute.

---

[96] Gibbs Shipyard, Inc., ASBCA No. 9809, 67-2 BCA ¶ 6499 (1967).

CHAPTER 8

TIME IMPACT ANALYSIS PROCEDURES

§ 8.1   Need for Recognizing and Incorporating Delays

§ 8.2   Understanding Float

§ 8.3   Understanding Concurrent Delay

§ 8.4   Preparing Time Impact Analyses

§ 8.5   Time Impact Analysis Model

§ 8.6   Advantages of Time Impact Analyses

§ 8.7   Guidelines for Negotiating Time Impacts

§ 8.1   Need for Recognizing and Incorporating Delays

Once a project has started, it becomes necessary to determine the amount of time impact that may be caused by the various types of delays encountered during the life of the project. A suggested method for calculating the extent of delay is the use of updated (as-built) critical path method (CPM) schedules in conjunction with a process called *time impact analysis*. This is a time-estimating procedure that utilizes networking techniques (*fragnets*) and an analysis of the facts associated with each delay to demonstrate the delay's effect on the project schedule. A fragnet is a sequence of new activities and/or activity revisions that are proposed to be added to the existing schedule to demonstrate the influence of delay and also the method for incorporating delays and impacts into the schedule. Its objective is to pinpoint, isolate, and quantify any time impact associated with a specific issue and determine its time relationship to past or current delays.

In recent decades, the techniques of time impact analysis have been used successfully on projects to justify or refute time delays. They have also been used in the after-the-fact evaluation of construction claims requiring the support of a schedule presentation. Such claims involved projects where a disciplined scheduling technique was used, abused, or not required at all. Time impact analysis procedures have been used since the

181

mid 1960s. One of the first known projects to have specified and used these techniques successfully as a contract requirement was the Apollo Space Program (Launch Complex 39) at Cape Kennedy, Florida.

The time impact analysis techniques are most effective when they are required by the contract and the procedures are outlined as part of the scheduling specification. Such specifications should require that a contractor prepare and submit fragnets and supporting documentation within a specified period of time after a delay occurs if he wishes to prove and demonstrate its influence or request an extension of time.[1]

Owners are encouraged to include time impact analysis procedures in contract documents. See model specification in **Appendix F**. The procedures should outline the method for preparation, suggest or give examples of format, specify the timing for submittals and approvals, and detail the procedures to be followed for incorporating the fragnets into the existing project schedule. Owners should not only require the contractors to follow such procedures, but also prepare independent time impact analyses themselves. These procedures will allow the key staff members of both parties to be prepared and in a position to timely evaluate any potential for delay and/or impact. The parties will also be able to more intelligently discuss, negotiate, and timely resolve the question of delay and/or impact at the earliest opportunity. In cases where disagreements arise, both parties will benefit from the exchange of time impact analysis information. They can also confirm a level of confidence in their respective positions. As a result, each party can consider its alternatives and take corrective or protective measures as may be required to protect its interests.

In the absence of time impact analysis requirements in the contract, contractors are encouraged to use such techniques to demonstrate delay and/or impact and to provide proof in support of all time extension requests. For example, time impact analyses can be submitted as part of the normal documentation expected for change order proposals. Time impact analyses can also be developed and discussed much earlier on an informal

---

[1] For guidance about how recognized agencies and authorities have used time impact analysis to determine the effect of delays, see J. O'Brien, CPM in Construction Management (3d ed. 1984); Army Corps of Engineers Modification Impact Evaluation Guide, EP 415-1-3 (July 1979) (available through Department of the Army, Office of the Chief of Engineers, Washington, D.C., 20314); and Veterans Administration's VACPM Handbook, H-08-11 (Mar. 1989) (available from Veterans Administration, Office of CPM, 811 Vermont Ave. N.W., Washington, D.C., 20420). The two agency manuals reflect similar procedures for analyzing the effect of delays on the project schedule through use of an updated schedule current or statused at the time the change or delay is encountered. See **Appendix G** for relevant examples from the VA manual. The two manuals do differ, however, in one significant respect. The Corps manual clearly requires as a part of the time impact analysis process that the reviewer take into account the effect or impact of individual changes on unchanged work as a separate step in the time impact analysis process (see EP 415-1-3, at 3 through 7).

basis, thereby initiating tentative agreements about impact long before the parties finally agree to the cost involved. At a minimum, the network logic describing the steps and actions associated with a change or delay could be presented and incorporated into the schedule, with all or some portion of the key activities having a zero duration, until an agreement on those activity durations in dispute or disagreement can be reached.

It is important to both parties to quickly identify which activities and paths of criticality are impacted by a change or delay. Waiting to resolve the final issues of cost and prohibiting schedule revisions prior to such agreements is a major contributing factor to schedule abuse and failure.

§ 8.2   Understanding Float

In preparing time impact analyses, it is imperative to understand *float*. Float is the contingency time associated with a path or chain of activities. It is the result of the interrelationships and interdependencies of the paths of activities that make up the schedule. Float is measured by comparing the start or finish of an activity on an early- and late-date basis. See **Chapter 3** for a detailed discussion of float.

Regardless of the content of contract provisions, there are a number of constants concerning float that apply to projects. For example:

1. Time cannot be stopped. It cannot be saved or stored. Activities are planned and scheduled to meet established goals within given time constraints. If the scheduled rate of progress is not achieved, any available float must be utilized or certain activities, milestones, or the overall project may fall behind schedule.
2. Activity duration changes and/or logic changes made as part of the updating process can increase or decrease available float.
3. Updating and incorporating actual finish dates to reflect history and as-built conditions can increase or decrease available float.
4. The incorporation of fragnets (additional or changed activities) into the CPM schedule during updates to reflect change orders, delays, and so on, can change float positions.
5. Extending contract milestones and completion dates based on approved time extensions can increase the remaining float.

§ 8.3   Understanding Concurrent Delay

It is also important, when performing time impact analysis, to understand concurrent delay and how it occurs. In general, concurrent delay can be described as a situation where two or more delays are occurring at the same time during all or a portion of the delay periods being considered. Whether such delays are excusable and compensable depends on the terms of the contract, the cause of the delays, the timing and duration of the delays, the party(s) responsibility for the delays, and the availability of float (*contingency time* in critical path analysis). See **Chapter 9** for a detailed discussion of these concepts.

There are several different situations in which concurrent delay occurs. First, is when, in two separate delays, both an owner and a contractor each simultaneously delay activities on separate critical paths and, thus, on the overall project. When these delays occur at the same time, are equal in duration for all or a portion of the delay periods being considered, and are related to activities on critical paths, the contractor is entitled to a time extension but not additional compensation. For the purposes of assessing liquidated damages, the general rule is that a contractor will not be charged for a controlling (critical path) delay for which he is responsible when his delay is concurrent with, or offset by, an owner-caused and controlling (critical path) delay of equal time. In order to recover any costs attributable to delay, a claimant must demonstrate that the contract performance was extended on the critical path solely as a result of compensable actions or omissions by the owner.

Thus, in this first example of concurrent delay (two concurrent delays of equal duration by the contractor and owner), if the owner and contractor delays occur on separate paths of activities and if one path is critical and the other has a positive float position (contingency) in excess of the amount of the delay period, the one party will be charged with responsibility for the delay even though the delays may be equal in duration.

The amount of the compensable time extension will depend on the extent of each delay and whether the owner or the contractor is responsible for the controlling delay.

A second type of concurrent delay occurs when one party is being delayed by another party by two separate circumstances affecting different paths of activities at the same time and when both delays simultaneously affect the overall completion of the project.

A third variation of concurrent delay may occur on projects involving multiple prime contractors, when three or more different parties (at least two contractors and the owner) cause delays at the same time with each delay having some impact on the overall combined project completion date.

§ 8.4 Preparing Time Impact Analyses

When change order delays or problems are encountered during performance, a time impact analysis should be prepared to document the facts and circumstances and to quantify the estimated delay and/or its impact on the project schedule. The impact analysis should be based on the current adjusted schedule, on excusable delays for which time extensions may still be pending, on job conditions encountered, and on the progress achieved up to the point in time when the present delay occurs. The analysis should also be based on the pertinent facts associated with the proofs required to support the delay issue: availability of manpower, crew size, productivity factors, equipment, and materials. In addition, each situation should be analyzed in light of pertinent contract clauses, contract drawings and specifications, job procedures, any written directives or verbal instructions received, and construction experience. Consideration should also be given to impact on unchanged work.

Upon completion of each impact analysis, an accurately written description of the facts and circumstances associated with a change or delay should be prepared. Factual references to contract clauses, schedule information, drawings, specifications, sketches, industry standards, and any written or oral communications should be properly identified to support positions and ultimate conclusions.

A step-by-step time impact analysis procedure for preparing and documenting time impacts as they occur should include the following key considerations. First, study the scope of the change (alleged or directed) or the extent of the delay encountered. For certain changes, attention may have to be given to identifying any performance that exceeds or does not meet contract requirements and to relating that performance to actions either caused or directed. Such changes usually involve quality, quantity, anticipated methods of work, or planned sequence of work.

Second, review all reference material such as appropriate contract clauses, construction drawings, sketches, specifications, vendor data, regulatory and third-party requirements, scheduling practices, field directives, daily progress reports, correspondence, pay records, and cost estimates. Prepare an accurate description of the directed or alleged changed condition or the delay encountered. Document the written, verbal, or constructive notice and be aware of the contractual notice and documentation support requirements for compliance.

Third, identify all contracting parties affected by the direct or indirect delay and request any participation or documentation assistance necessary.

Fourth, determine which activity or activities of the project schedule are potentially impacted by the added, delayed, or changed work. This may require that the existing schedule detail be amplified or further scrutinized for proper isolation, analysis, and qualification of any delay and/or impact. It is important in such analyses to maintain the integrity of various levels of network indenture and the transferability of information from one level of indenture to another.

Fifth, review the schedule and determine the scheduled start and finish dates for all affected activities. The use of the late start or late finish will depend on whether an impacted activity has started or not. In situations where an affected activity has not started, it may be necessary to accurately compute the remaining total float that exists. Take into consideration the current schedule, any pending adjustments to contract completion dates, activity in-progress status, the notice to proceed for a directed change, and dates of alleged or actual delay occurrence.

Sixth, from the project record-keeping systems and from contacts with key project staff, identify and document the facts associated with the change and/or delay issue. Also, determine the as-built and physical status of all activities in progress that are directly or indirectly impacted by the change and/or delay in question.

Seventh, prepare a fragnet analysis illustrating the sequence of delay and define its relationship to the current adjusted schedule. The fragnet should identify the first notice involved and the sequence of activities necessary to prepare for beginning the required work and should clearly demonstrate the alleged delay's effect or noneffect on the existing schedule and the remaining activities required to be performed. Particular attention should be paid to the method of incorporating the fragnet into the current or pending schedule. In preparing the analysis, give the benefit of doubt to the other party.

Eighth, prepare a written narrative of the overall schedule analysis and derive a time impact position to be taken for each delay. Weekends, holidays, and any recovery periods involved in the calculations should be noted as necessary. For change order work, consideration should be given to allowing reasonable time, where necessary, for the impacted party to evaluate and coordinate the scope of the changed conditions with subcontractors, vendors, and suppliers involved and to communicate proper direction to the field forces that will perform the work. A determination of the estimated late start date should be made to prevent any delay to the current adjusted or pending schedule. A comparison of this date with the date the contractor is able to begin work should be made. In addition, a determination of the net time impact (if any) associated with each delay should be quantified. Further, any relationship of the net delay to any other delays that were precedent or are on-going should be identified. Note any use or absorption of available float in the analysis.

§ 8.5   Time Impact Analysis Model

To demonstrate the time impact analysis approach, it may be helpful to apply the principles described above to a project model. Assume a general contractor was hired to construct a county office building on a lump-sum basis. The general contractor subcontracted a major portion of the work and there are liquidated damages for late completion of the project. As part of the contract requirements, the general contractor was required to prepare a CPM schedule and submit it to the owner for approval. The owner has approved the contractor's schedule. The contract states that time extensions are granted only to the extent that no float remains. Assume also that the current status of the project indicates the building structure, including floor slabs, is complete and the building is in the process of being enclosed. The September updated CPM schedule properly reflects all time extensions granted and pending to date. The general contractor's reported actual progress indicates that he and his subcontractors are performing according to the current adjusted schedule.

On October 20, the owner issues a stop work order for certain portions of drywall construction on the fifth floor of the building. At the time the stop work order is received by the contractor, the windows at the fifth-floor level are forecasted to be complete by October 26. Stud work for drywall construction on the same floor is projected to be complete by October 23. Placement of the drywall for each floor level is shown in the CPM schedule as being restrained by window installation and the rough-in of the electrical and mechanical required for completion of interior wall construction. Additional factors essential for conducting a delay analysis of this situation follow.

1. Drywall placement has not started.
2. The hold on drywall affects approximately 40 percent of the total drywall placement required for the fifth floor.
3. The design hold lasts 13 work days. A change order is issued to release the hold and also change the drywall specification to comply with the county fire code. Some minor, but additional, work is also involved.
4. The additional work is estimated to take approximately five work days (elapsed time), including some time required for local purchasing and delivery of new drywall materials. The additional work estimate also includes some minor changes to the electrical and mechanical rough-in. This added work is in addition to the remaining scope of drywall work on hold, which is estimated to be 40 percent, or two days.

Figure 8–1 provides an abstract from the September CPM schedule for work on the fifth floor and some additional information necessary for evaluating the effects of the stop work order and the changed work.

Figure 8–2 presents a suggested format for a time impact analysis that demonstrates the delay caused by the stop work order and the added work. Note the development of the logic sequence (fragnet) for the design hold and how it is proposed to be incorporated into the existing schedule. The

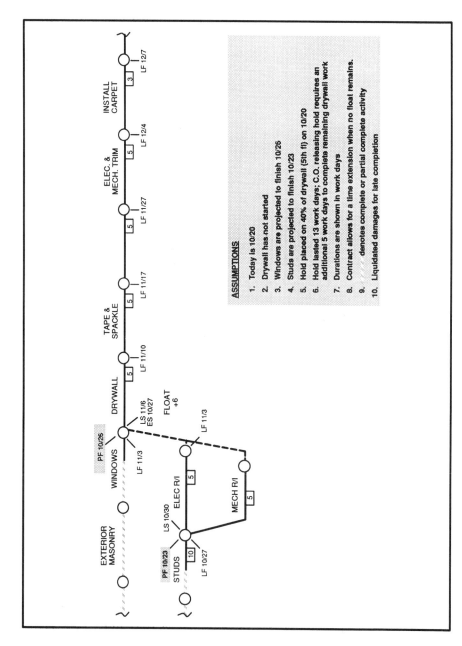

Figure 8-1. Portion of CPM schedule reflecting plan for fifth-floor work.

TITLE: John Doe County Office Building   Page: 1 of 1
             Change Order Number 29   Project No.: 14725
                                                       Date: 11/9/89
REFERENCES:Drawings Number A–190142, A–190157, A–190158,   By: TJD
             Letter Numbers 032,041; Field Directive Number 14;
             Change Order Number 9

DESCRIPTION OF CHANGE

A stop work order (Field Directive No. 14) was issued on October 20 for placing a hold on certain portions of drywall construction on the fifth floor. The stop work period lasted thirteen (13) work days. Change Order No. 9 was issued on November 8 to release the hold and also change some of the work yet to be performed.

EVALUATION

At the time the stop work order was received, the windows at the fifth floor level were forecasted to be complete by October 26 (late finish November 3). Stud work for drywall construction was projected to be complete by October 23 (late finish October 27). The CPM schedule shows that drywall placement (late start November 6) on the fifth floor is restrained by window installation and rough–in of electrical and mechanical within the interior wall systems.

Further evaluation results in a determination that the hold affects approximately 40% of drywall placement due to a specification change in material to comply with required fire rating. The changed work including procurement of local materials, will require approximately five (5) days of additional time versus adjusted plan to finish the remaining drywall work that was placed on hold. The following fragnet illustrates the influence of this change and suggests a proposed method for incorporating the resultant delay into the CPM schedule.

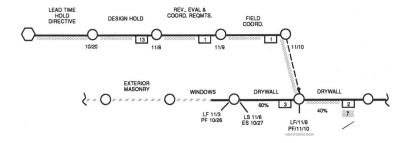

Note the split in the original drywall placement activity.

CONCLUSION

Total delay is estimated to be seven (7) work days, two (2) work days for the design hold and five (5) work days due to the changed work. Six (6) work days of available float mitigated part of the overall delay. A seven (7) work day time extension is requested.

Figure 8–2. Time impact analysis illustrating delay.

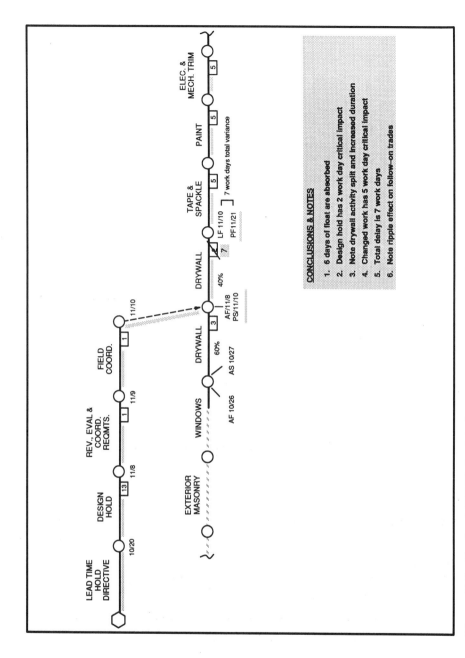

Figure 8-3. Revised CPM schedule incorporating fragnet.

190

sequence includes two activities for the contractor's internal coordination of the change. The purpose of these activities is to allow some time (two work days) for the contractor to coordinate with the subcontractor and vendors and to plan, schedule, and coordinate the field resources necessary to perform the work.

Note also how the existing drywall activity is split into two activities, in series, in order to accommodate the fragnet, demonstrate proper delay influence, and facilitate adding five days of additional time to complete the remaining work associated with the drywall change. As a result of the analysis, the total delay is determined to be seven work days (two work days due to the design hold and five work days to complete the remaining work). The analysis also shows that six work days of float that existed in the drywall activity sequence were absorbed, partially mitigating the design hold delay.

Absent any other considerations, the contractor is entitled to a seven work day extension of time, and the delay is considered to be compensable. **Figure 8–3** illustrates the revised portion of the CPM schedule with the fragnet incorporated as part of the updating process. Note the possible impact to the follow-on interior finish activities.

For a further illustration, the issue might be complicated now by taking it a step further: Suppose that the stud work did not finish as anticipated (10/23) and actually finished on 10/31, or two work days after the latest allowable finish date. The electrical and mechanical rough-in follows and completes within the planned five work days for each activity. How does this situation affect the previous determination? **Figure 8–4** presents the results of a combined schedule analysis and shows that the controlling delay remains seven work days (two work days for the design hold plus five work days for the placement of remaining drywall work). The analysis also shows that there is a two work day controlling delay associated with the late finish of stud work that is concurrent with a portion of the design hold period. The conclusion reached for this analysis is that the contractor is still entitled to a seven work day extension of time; however, only five work days are considered to be compensable because of the controlling amount of concurrent delay.

Now add one more consideration to further complicate the issue: Assume the electrical subcontractor does not finish his work in the five work days originally planned. For reasons of his own doing, he does not finish until 11/14 (an actual duration of 10 work days). How would this affect the combined analysis shown in **Figure 8–4**? The analyses and overall effect of all four conditions, the design hold, added work, and the late performance of the drywall and electrical subcontractors are demonstrated in **Figure 8–5**. The total delay is extended to 12 work days. Based on the combined analysis, the general contractor is responsible for 7 work days of

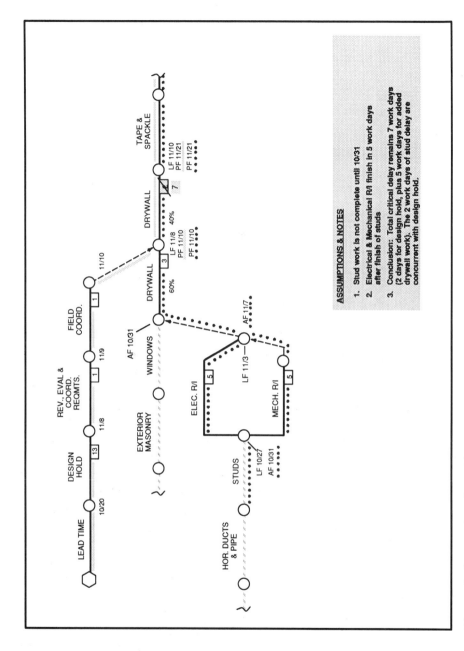

Figure 8–4. Results of combined schedule analysis illustrating concurrent delay.

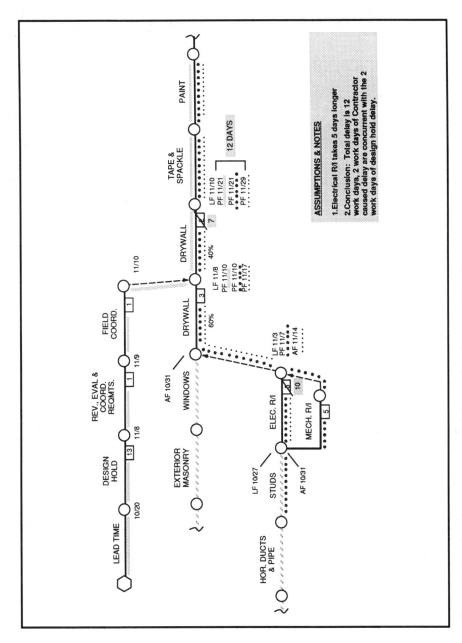

Figure 8–5. Time impact analysis illustrating further delay impact.

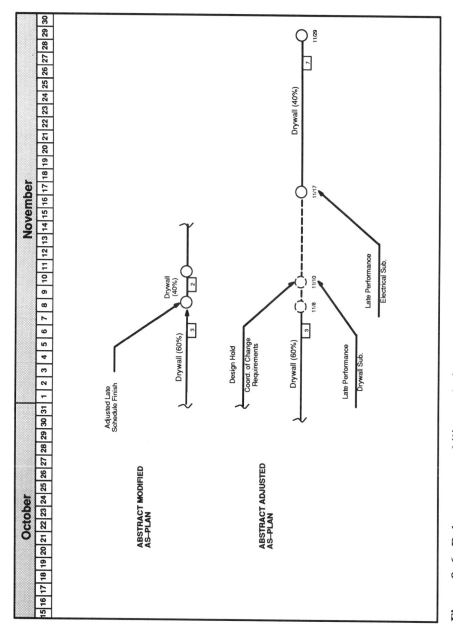

Figure 8-6. Delay compensability analysis.

delay. Two of these work days are concurrent with the 7 work days of delay associated with the design hold.

Figure 8–6 illustrates the key point, the start event of (*Drywall 40%*), for measuring and quantifying any delay, determining who is responsible for the delay, and deciding whether any delay is considered compensable. Note how the start of drywall is shifted to the right by the various issues.

Figure 8–7 presents an analysis of the concurrent delay issue and also the issue of compensability. The result of this analysis shows that the contractor is entitled to a seven work day time extension, including five work days of compensable delay. The concurrent and controlling delay caused by the drywall subcontractor mitigates the compensability of two work days of the delay caused by the owner. When the adjustments to the contract and the CPM schedule are made based on the results of the overall analysis, the contractor would be five work days behind schedule.

It is suggested that all time impact analyses be prepared and documented in a manner similar to **Figure 8–2**. Such analyses can be enclosed with change order proposals and written requests for time extensions. An alternative that can be less formal is simply redlining (editing) an abstract portion of the current issue of the CPM schedule (copy). Owners are encouraged to prepare similar analyses to support their time positions in all negotiations.

It is also suggested that a *master ledger of time impacts* be maintained. See **Figure 8–8** for an example. Each time impact analysis is listed chronologically (by date of occurrence) and shows the amount of delay associated with each delay issue. Having this type of information available for negotiations can be of great assistance in reaching fair and equitable settlements.

§ 8.6   Advantages of Time Impact Analyses

Networking techniques have great utility in evaluating delay and impact on a project. The logic of networking permits simultaneous proof of both the fact and cause of delay. Accordingly, time impact analysis can be an effective tool for determining whether or not certain work was delayed and had an impact on the overall project. Key advantages of networking techniques and the use of time impact analyses procedures include the following:

1. Networking techniques allow critical work items to be identified. The various paths of criticality and those impacted by delay can easily be recognized. The float, or contingency time, that exists and expires as job conditions change can also be identified. Such conditions provide a legitimate basis for using time impact analysis procedures.

2. The use of time impact analysis procedures provides a disciplined basis for two contractual parties to independently evaluate the

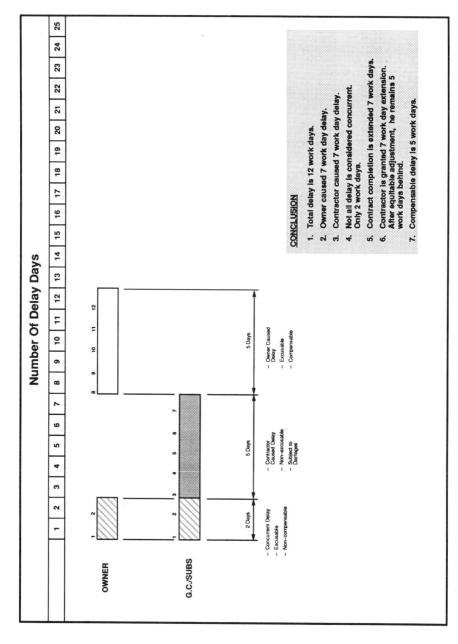

Figure 8–7. Analysis of concurrent delay and compensability.

"Work Days"

ITEM NO.	AREA OF DELAY	TOTAL DELAY BY ITEM	AMOUNT OF CONCURRENT DELAY WITH OTHER ITEMS	NET AMOUNT DELAY CLAIMED ON OVERALL PROJECT	COMMENTS
1	ERROR IN BUILDING LAYOUT	3	0	3	CHANGE ORDER NO. 1 FIELD DIRECTIVE NO. 3
2	FOUNDATION DIFFERING SITE CONDITION	2	0	2	CHANGE ORDER NO. 2
3	FLOOR SLAB PENETRATIONS	5	3	2	PARTIAL CONCURRENT DELAY WITH ITEM NO. 4
4	CARPENTER'S STRIKE	5	3	2	PARTIAL CONCURRENT DELAY WITH ITEM NO. 3
5	OSHA SUSPENSION	2	0	2	JOB SITE ACCIDENT
6	HURRICANE DORA	3	0	3	
7	DRYWALL DELAY–STUDS	2	2	0	CONCURRENT WITH ITEM NO. 9
8	ELEC. SUB DELAY	5	0	5	NON–EXCUSABLE DELAY
9	DESIGN HOLD–DRYWALL	7	2	7	FIELD DIRECTIVE NO. 14 CHANGE ORDER NO. 9
GRAND TOTALS			10	26	

Figure 8–8. Master ledger of time impacts.

impact of a suspected delay and reach a common basis to compare, analyze, and agree on the amount of delay and time impact involved. Time impact analysis techniques allow each party to demonstrate its understanding of a specific delay and offer proofs that specific acts or occurrences caused the delay.

3.   Time impact analysis provides the ability to determine the relationship of one delay to any other delays that may have occurred or may be occurring at the same time. Concurrent delay can be measured and quantified.

4.   Time impact analysis can be used to demonstrate the impact of delay on unchanged work. The combined results of a series of time impact analyses may even be helpful in demonstrating any cumulative impact.

5.   When delays and/or impacts occur, the use of time impact analysis techniques can aid in determining corrective actions for recovery. Analyses prepared and used in conjunction with the project schedule can aid in evaluating alternate plans and for establishing priorities, responsibilities, and time tables necessary to prevent, mitigate, or recover from delay.

6.   Disciplined and consistent application of time impact analysis procedures provides a means to realistically forecast the cumulative effect of impacts with respect to a certain milestone or the overall project completion date.

7.   Time impact analysis procedures can be useful in proving causation between a specific delay and its associated cost.

8.   Time impact analyses can be useful in asserting and proving a delay claim or in developing defenses against a delay claim. They can also be valuable in recognizing counterclaims.

9.   Time impact analyses are tools that can help keep a project schedule up-to-date and properly adjusted. As a result, it is possible to determine if a contractor is ahead or behind a properly adjusted schedule. This determination can be important to an owner who may consider directing a contractor to accelerate and recover any lost time. It can be equally important to the contractor.

10.   Time impact analyses aid in creating and preserving evidence of plans, delays, and actual performance.

The foundation for achieving most of the advantages cited above is specifying a requirement for time impact analysis to be part of change order proposals and all requests for time extensions. Time impact analysis procedures should be used by both owners and contractors. Experience has shown that such procedures usually force the key people who speak contractually for an organization to become involved with the schedule, the proofs of delay, and the quantification of related delay costs. In using time impact analysis, keep in mind that methodology does not constitute proof in and of itself, but is only a tool to be utilized when a delay claim or defense is to be proved.

§ 8.7   Guidelines for Negotiating Time Impacts

To assist in successfully negotiating time impact analyses, this section provides suggestions for contractors, owners, design professionals (acting as owner agents), and construction managers. Experience has shown that these guidelines can help an owner and the contractor maintain a properly adjusted CPM schedule. The parties will also have an effective management tool for monitoring, reporting, negotiating, and resolving delays and impacts as they occur during the balance of the project.

Document each change order and delay.   Determine and document on a chronological basis the time impact of each change order and delay encountered. Prepare a fragnet analysis for all delay situations. Even though a time extension for a particular delay may not be readily proven because of available and mitigating float, the mathematics of the schedule can be adjusted until delays accumulate to the point where a minor, apparently insignificant change results in a time extension. The parties are cautioned to not exaggerate the effects of a delay.

Fully support requests.   A request for a time extension or adjustment to the schedule should be made in writing in accordance with pertinent notice of delay requirements in the contract. Such requests should be supported by a time impact analysis similar to **Figure 8–2** and by all pertinent reference data.

Keep schedule current.   Keep the project schedule current and up-to-date. If the contract requires basic network revisions to be controlled administratively by the owner and subject to his approval before any changes to the schedule can be made, the contractor and the owner are advised to maintain as-built and as-adjusted versions of the schedule until proper schedule adjustments are made. Such contractual procedures can very quickly cause a good schedule to become ineffective. Properly adjusted schedules can be accomplished by duplicating the updated computer files and maintaining duel schedules and separate data bases.

Meet and decide on changes.   During periodic updates of the schedule, the owner and the contractor are encouraged to agree on how to incorporate each fragnet and/or network change into the schedule at the earliest opportunity in order to reflect delay, actual conditions, and plans for completion. Minutes of such meetings should be prepared and maintained in project files.

Quickly agree on delay impact.   Both parties should try to reach an early agreement on the degree of impact for each change order or delay, even though both parties may be miles apart on the issue of cost.

Fully prepare time impact analyses.   A party should know its strengths and weaknesses for each time impact analysis prior to any negotiating. In addition, it should know the relationships, if any, to all previous and pending delay issues. The party also should make sure that its time impacts analyses can be substantiated by proper facts and can be supported by the project records. Key facts should be simplified to make its position easily understood and persuasive.

Include impact costs in change order talks.   Impact costs should be part of the agenda in all negotiations of change orders.

Carefully define cost estimates.   Cost estimates for change orders should include costs for all related impacts, excusable and compensable delay, or schedule recovery when appropriate (unless reservation-of-rights procedures are in place). Each party should check to see if any impact costs are included in its estimate of cost. If using standard mark-ups, a party should determine what they include. Do they include costs associated with delay or the cost of any impact on unchanged work? Do they include cumulative impact? Impact costs should be isolated, separately identified, and correlated with the time impact analysis. Parties should make sure that the costs of both direct and indirect delaying factors are considered.

Check cost estimate for impact costs.   Owners, if no potential impact exists, should check the cost estimate to make sure it indicates it was considered and that the contractor had the opportunity (in fact was demanded or required) to present any impact costs. Separately identify and write zero as the amount estimated for impact costs.

Allocate scheduling costs.   Make sure an appropriate allowance for scheduling is included in the cost estimate for analyzing a change or delay and revising the project schedule as necessary. An owner should allow a reasonable cost for this activity.

Keep cost proposals current.   Check to make sure that each cost proposal uses current job status and the approved project schedule as the basis for justifying additional cost/time, both direct and impact.

CHAPTER 9

APPLYING CPM TECHNIQUES TO CONTRACT CLAIMS

§ 9.1   Court and Board Acceptance of CPM Techniques

§ 9.2   —Court and Board Sophistication in Addressing CPM Issues

§ 9.3   Court and Board Recognition of CPM's Dynamic Nature

§ 9.4   —Major Public Owners' Recognition of CPM's Dynamic Nature

§ 9.5   CPM Techniques Used for Time-Related Claims through the 1970s

§ 9.6   —Delay Claims

§ 9.7   —Acceleration Claim Analyses

§ 9.8   Issues from the 1970s about the Use of CPM

§ 9.9   —Float Time and Its Availability

§ 9.10   —Determining Credit for Innovative Sequence Changes and When to Measure Delay

§ 9.11   —Time Due Contractor for Change Orders Ordered after Current Contract Completion Date

§ 9.12   CPM Developments and Issues since 1974

§ 9.13   —CPM Acknowledged as Preferred Method for Proving Delays

§ 9.14   —Need to Establish Cause-and-Effect Relationship

§ 9.15   —Requirement for Contemporaneous Baseline in Measuring Quantum of Delay

§ 9.16   —Recognition of Float as Expiring Resource Available to All Parties

§ 9.17   —Demise of *Impacted As-Planned* Proof for Delays

§ 9.18   —Key Issues Involving Concurrent Delay and Extended Duration Claims

§ 9.19   —*But For* Test for Extended Duration Claims

§ 9.20   —Acceptance of Buy-Back Time and Sequence Changes

§ 9.21   —Denial of Automatic Time Extensions for Changes after Completion Date

§ 9.22   —Using CPM to Establish Early Completion Claims

§ 9.23   —Presumptions from CPM Approvals and Time Modifications

§ 9.24   —Limiting Recoverable Time in CPM Claims Presentations

§ 9.25   —Recognition of Risk Taking to Negate Effects of Delays to
          Critical Path

§ 9.26   —Need to Delineate Plan for Performance in Initial CPM
          Schedule

§ 9.27   —Fragnets, Windows, and Time Impact Analyses

§ 9.28   —Potential Abuses in Microcomputer Programs

§ 9.29   Specification of Time Impact Analysis

§ 9.30   Safeguards for Establishing Delay Quantum Baselines

§ 9.1   Court and Board Acceptance of CPM Techniques

Network analysis techniques were introduced into the construction field in the early 1960s. With government specification of the use of network analysis techniques for major projects and the perception by contractors (after a period of initial resistance) that network analysis techniques could be extremely important tools for project management, the use of the critical path method (CPM) to plan and schedule work has become the accepted standard in the construction industry.[1] Further, boards of contract appeals and the courts have shown their willingness to utilize network analysis techniques to identify delays and disruptions on projects, as well as the causes of delays and disruptions.

The basic technique used in evaluating contract claims with CPM is to compare the as-planned CPM schedule with the as-built CPM schedule. The technique can be summarized in the following five questions:

1. How was it planned that the project would be constructed?

2. How did construction actually occur?

3. What are the variances, or differences, between the plan for performance and the actual performance with respect to activities, sequences, durations, manpower, and other resources?

4. What are the causes of the differences or variances between the plan and the actual performance?

---

[1] *See, e.g.,* H.W. Detwiler Co., ASBCA No. 35,327, 89-2 BCA ¶ 21,612 (1989); Al Johnson Constr. Co. v. United States, 854 F.2d 467 (Fed. Cir. 1988); Umpqua Marine Ways, Inc., ASBCA Nos. 27,790, 29,532, 89-3 BCA ¶ 22,099 (1989); Williams Enters., Inc., v. Strait Mfg. & Welding, Inc., 728 F. Supp. 12 (D.D.C. 1990); Georgia Power Co. v. Georgia Public Serv. Comm'n, 196 Ga. App. 572, 396 S.E.2d 562 (1990).

5. What are the effects of the variances in sequence, duration, manpower, and so on as they relate to the costs experienced, both by the contractor and the owner for the project?

A recent United States Court of Claims decision[2] provides us with a good basic example of the court's acceptance of the process described above:

> The normal construction procedure as anticipated by Haney was to start the construction, then finish work from the bottom up in accordance with a 'critical path method' (CPM) of construction. The Government welcomed Haney's use of CPM as a planning and management tool. . . .
>
> Haney's original CPM schedule set completion of the basement and floors one through eight for July 10, 1974, and completion of all remaining work, including floors nine through eleven, by August 20, 1974. The base schedule was realistic and the work could have been performed in accordance with that schedule had it not been for the Government-caused delays.
>
> The CPM schedule reflected information furnished by the subcontractors which indicated how long the work should take. During the construction, the CPM was monitored by field reports submitted to the home office and by inspections of a field engineer. Computerized revisions of the CPM were made periodically to reflect the work progress and to administer and properly schedule the continuing activities. The CPM schedule was revised when the structural steel delay occurred. Thereafter, the CPM was used in scheduling further work, until the GSA change orders made this impractical.
>
> Haney's CPM technical staff and expert, who were familiar with the construction project during the time of the work and who had prepared or assisted in the preparation of the CPM schedule that was used for the project, prepared a technical analysis using the base CPM schedule. That analysis shows that the impact of the delaying events extended the time for performance of the job from August 20, 1974 to June 6, 1975.
>
> At trial, plaintiff presented expert testimony which established, by CPM analysis, the cumulative effect of each delay that occurred on the project. While the Government would not agree to the conclusions reached by plaintiff's expert (because it denied liability for various delaying events), the Government agreed during the trial that the CPM methodology used by plaintiff was correct and acceptable, and that the events described would cause a delay to the critical path of the project as demonstrated by Haney's CPM analysis.
>
> The CPM analysis of delay presented on behalf of plaintiff took into account, and gave appropriate credit for all of the delays which were alleged to have occurred, including the results of plaintiff's acceleration by expediting equipment and materials, working out-of-sequence, weather delays,

---

[2] Haney v. United States, 676 F.2d 584 (1982).

and the strike by the operating engineers. (Haney did not seek compensation for the latter event.)[3]

§ 9.2 —Court and Board Sophistication in Addressing CPM Issues

A few courts have not yet totally embraced CPM scheduling concepts and may not be completely comfortable with the use of such aids to assist the judge or fact finder.[4] More often than not, however, the courts and boards of contract appeals have shown an increasing level of knowledge and sophistication in using this tool in their decisions. This significant level of understanding is represented by the 1985 *Utley-James, Inc.*[5] and 1990 *Weaver-Bailey Contractors, Inc. v. United States*[6] decisions.

Utley-James, Inc.[7] provided an essay on CPM scheduling that includes consideration of such important concepts as the critical path, resource leveling, acceleration, and buy-back time:

11. In critical path scheduling, each task is related to those that logically must precede and follow it. For example, in a building constructed like the McNamara Building, the concrete for the third floor slab cannot be placed until the second floor slab has been poured and the necessary support structure has been completed. The second floor slab and the supports are said to be a 'restraint' on the third floor slab. The preparer of the CPM schedule must make sure to take into accounts all such restraints. . . .

12. In any CPM schedule there are what are called 'early start' and 'late start' dates. The connotations of these two terms are not the same, and the terms must be used carefully. The early start date is the earliest date by which a given activity logically can start, assuming all preceding activities are on schedule. The late start date is the latest date by which a given activity may start if the contractor is not to fall behind schedule. The terms 'early finish' and 'late finish' are parallel to 'early start' and 'late start,' but later in time by the number of days the activity is schedule to take. The number of days between early start and late start (or, what ought to be the same thing, between early finish and late finish) is called 'float.' If the schedule allows no more time to do the entire job than the entire job requires, there is no float in the job, and at any given place in the schedule there will be at least one job activity with no float. An activity with

---

[3] *Id.* at 595–6.

[4] *See, e.g.,* Indiana & Mich. Elec. Co. v. Terre Haute Indus., Inc., 507 N.E.2d 588 (Ind. App. 1987).

[5] GSBCA No. 5370, 85-1 BCA ¶ 17,816 (1984).

[6] 19 Cl. Ct. 474 (1990).

[7] GSBCA No. 5370, 85-1 BCA ¶ 17,816 (1984).

no float is said to be on the critical path. An accurate CPM schedule is a very powerful management tool for the contractor in its planning of the entire job.

13. Determining the critical path has an important effect on the Government's management of the contract as well. For example, a delay of fifty days on a job activity with more than fifty days' float should, in theory, have no effect on the completion of the job. The early start and early finish dates for that activity may move fifty days, but they should still be earlier than the late start and late finish dates. In contrast, a job activity on the critical path, for which there is no float, will have the same early start date and late start date (and the same date for both early finish and late finish). One day's delay to that job activity will cost one day in completion of the job unless it is somehow made up.

14. A job activity that is not originally on the critical path can get on the critical path as the result of a delay that uses up all of its float. If more than the original float is used up by a delay, the activity is not only on the critical path but behind it; unless the completion date for the entire job is extended, the float will become negative, i.e., the early start date will be later than the late start date. This will show that the job activity cannot be started until after its required completion date if the entire project is to adhere to the existing schedule. One of the ways to cure this problem is to change the schedule by extending the completion date for the entire project, thereby putting positive float at the end of the job that can then be distributed among the activities that have developed negative float.

15. The other cure for negative float is accelerating, i.e., performing activities on the critical path in less time than the schedule allows for. Almost every activity is a direct restraint on others, and the finish dates for a given activity is the start date for those it directly restrains. To give a simplified example, we will treat the placing of the concrete for each floor slab as a direct restraint on the placing of the next one. If each slab is scheduled for ten days but can be poured in eight, two days can be made up on each pour. If the floor slabs are on the critical path, a ten day delay can be made up by pouring five slabs in eight days each instead of ten (assuming that the acceleration of this activity does not put some other, unrestrained activity on the critical path in place of the slab).

16. Another concept of importance to CPM scheduling is resource leveling, also called resource loading. Consider, for example, the interior finish work in an office tower like the McNamara Building. The placing of each floor slab is logically restrained by the placing of the slab beneath it, but that is not necessarily true of interior finish work. There is no reason in theory why a carpeting contractor could not come in and carpet every floor of the building on the same day. But there are a variety of reasons why that is not done, and one of the principal reasons is that it makes no sense to supply that much material and that many workers to do all the floors at once when the work can be sequenced with all sorts of other work and handled over a convenient period of time with a suitably sized work

force. To give an accurate indication of the actual planned job schedule, a CPM schedule must take resource leveling into account.[8]

In *Weaver-Bailey Contractors, Inc. v. United States,*[9] the chief judge of the claims court provided a detailed exposition on float that implicitly recognizes float's availability to the parties to the project for use on a nondiscriminatory basis as an expiring resource. This landmark decision further confirmed the courts' increasing sophistication in working with CPM techniques.

§ 9.3   Court and Board Recognition of CPM's Dynamic Nature

The critical path through any CPM network is the longest chain or chains of connected activities through the project in terms of time. The great advantage to the critical path network planning technique is that it is not static. The plan reflected by the critical path network (and the critical path itself) will change as work is performed and events occur later or earlier than originally anticipated. The beauty of the CPM process is that it is dynamic and allows the executor of the schedule, at any given point in time, to react to events as they change. Resources (work forces, equipment, time) thus can be applied in a different fashion and still achieve the planned project completion or minimize the effect of delays.

If one takes away the ability of the executor of the project schedule to look forward and adjust her plan at any given point along the time line represented by the project, one takes away her control of the project, indeed, the life blood of her ability to control the project.

The boards and courts are fully aware of the dynamic nature of the CPM process. The United States Claims Court, in a recent landmark decision, *Fortec Constructors v. United States,*[10] recognized that control of a project, as well as the time extension process, is lost if the parties do not properly update the critical path diagram to properly reflect delays and time extensions. The decision stated, in pertinent part:

> If the CPM is to be used to evaluate delay on the project, it must be kept current and must reflect delays as they occur. In the instant case, the CPM was updated only once, in August of 1979. This update did not consider delays in work performed prior to the update, nor, obviously, in work that

---

[8] *Id.* at 89,060–62.

[9] 19 Cl. Ct. 474, 481–82 (1990).

[10] 8 Cl. Ct. 490, 504–08 (1985).

occurred after the update through the date of acceptance of the project by the Corps.

* * *

Despite the obvious failure of both parties to use the CPM for scheduling purposes during construction, the Government now claims that the additional work Fortec was required to perform does not justify any contract time extensions, since the CPM does not show that any of the additional work was on the project's critical path. In support of its position, the Government relies entirely upon the once revised CPM, which does not reflect the critical path actually followed during construction. It is interesting to note, however, that the Government, while arguing that it prepared CPM schedules to evaluate Fortec's claims for extension of contract time, introduced CPM schedules showing the "removal of telephone poles" to be on the critical path. As already discussed above, such telephone poles, since they never existed, could not have represented the critical path.

Mr. Cook testified that: (1) the CPM diagram introduced at trial did not depict the actual critical path, since it was not current as of the updated mathematical summaries offered into evidence; (2) the activities on the mathematical summaries would not show up after they were completed; and (3) the information set out on the mathematical summaries represented an estimate that was prepared prior to performance. Mr. Cook not only admitted that the CPM in evidence did not reflect actual performance, but he also admitted that the critical path can and does change during performance. Indeed, Mr. Cook acknowledged that delay encountered in completion of a noncritical item may make that item critical so that "every month, conceivably, the critical path would change," which is precisely what happened in the instant case. The critical path changed from that depicted on the CPM diagram introduced into evidence. The Corps, however, refused to grant timely and adequate time extensions and to authorize revisions to the CPM to reflect the changed performance critical path. As a result, it is impossible to determine from the CPM diagram whether a particular activity was critical or noncritical, on schedule or behind schedule. Further, the Corps failed to even consider several of Fortec's requests for additional compensation and time extensions until after the project was completed. Fortec could not update the CPM without receipt of modifications from the Corps adding the additional work, and then only with the concurrence of the Corps as to the time to be added. Contract § 1C-14(c)(2). Accordingly, Fortec was unable to update the CPM during construction. This inability, caused by the Corps' failure to act in a timely fashion, should not now be used as a sword against Fortec.

Reliance upon an incomplete and inaccurate CPM to substantiate denial of time extensions is clearly improper.

It is difficult, if not impossible, for this Court to comprehend how the Corps could have used the CPM to evaluate Fortec's time extension claims without modifying the CPM to reflect the additional work Fortec was directed to perform—the valve pit, the frame and grate, the hangar doors, and the roof ventilator. These items were all major components of the hangar project. If the Corps made such modifications to the CPM, this Court cannot understand why the Corps did not issue a formal modification (logic revision), which Fortec would have been required to include and use in its CPM analysis.

In *Continental Consolidated Corp.,*[11] . . . the Army Corps of Engineers Board of Contract Appeals held that if the CPM is used to evaluate requests for time extensions it must reflect actual project conditions. In *Continental,* the contractor sought extra costs incurred due to suspensions of work and due to subsequent acceleration. . . . The Government claimed that acceleration was justified, since the CPM revealed the project was behind schedule. The board rejected the Government's reliance on the CPM, stating that:

> It is essential that any changes in the work and time extensions due to the contractor be incorporated into the progress analysis *concurrently* with the performance of the changes or immediately after the delay and thus integrated into the periodic computer runs to reflect the effect on the critical path. Otherwise, the critical path chart produced by the computer will not reflect the current status of the work performed or the actual progress being attained.

. . . Since adequate time extensions were not granted immediately upon determining the extent of the delay, the board found that the CPM's completion schedule was distorted and unreliable as a basis for denying time extensions. *Id.*

In *J. A. Jones Constr. Co.,* ENGBCA Nos. 3035, 3222, 72-1 BCA ¶ 9261, the Army Corps of Engineers Board of Contract Appeals echoed its earlier concern that the CPM must reflect actual performance to be a reliable basis for evaluating requests for time extensions. . . . The board rejected the Government's reliance on the original, unadjusted CPM, stating that:

> The value and usefulness of the CPM . . . is dependent upon the Contracting Officer making prompt decisions when excusable delays are alleged by the contractor and upon the contractor promptly revising and updating the CPM chart to incorporate time extensions, whether they be tentative or finally determined, within a short time after occurrence of the delay.[12]

§ 9.4 —Major Public Owners' Recognition of CPM's Dynamic Nature

The standard operating manuals for the major government contracting agencies also recognize the dynamic nature of the CPM process, the necessity for updating schedules in a timely fashion, and the comparative

---

[11] ENGBCA Nos. 2743, 2766, 67-2 BCA ¶ 6624 (1967).

[12] 8 Cl. Ct. 490, 504–08 (1982).

process to be utilized in analyzing delays. For example, the 1985 Army Corps of Engineers regulation governing network analysis systems states:

> Changes to the work and occurrences which impact progress must be entered in the schedule logic in order to keep the schedule up-to-date and reflect actual job progress conditions.[13]

Further, the extremely detailed and valuable *Modification Impact Evaluation Guide* of the Corps of Engineers, EP 415-1-3, provides a detailed summary of the procedures to be utilized in determining time extensions based upon up-to-date information as the job progresses. The manual states in pertinent part:

> 3-4. *Summary.*
>
> a. Paragraph 3-3 defined procedures for developing the time requirements portion of a CPM schedule to reflect the changes necessary to accommodate the work as directly changed by a modification, and its effects on the unchanged work. These procedures are:
>
> (1) Define current job status. Compile data on actual progress, status of materials, manpower, equipment, and any other pertinent factors (para 3-1).
>
> (2) Analyze progress schedule. The process of accurately identifying and evaluating impact depends largely on an up-to-date CPM progress schedule. To effectively fulfill its contract administration responsibilities, the Corps of Engineers must exercise the authorities and options available to maintain progress schedule validity throughout the life of the project (para 3-2).
>
> (3) Procedures for developing a revised schedule (para 3-3).
>
> (a) Revise the schedule to show actual job status.
>
> (b) Insert the directly changed work.
>
> (c) Recalculate affected unchanged work (retaining presently assigned durations).
>
> (d) Reestablish critical path, and note time extension justified by direct changes.
>
> (e) Analyze schedule for impacted unchanged activities; assign new durations to these activities as appropriate.
>
> (f) Reestablish critical path, and note any slippage of final completion date indicated in (d), above. Difference is amount of time extension justified because of impact.[14]

---

[13] U.S. Army Corps of Engineers, Manual on Network Analysis Systems, ER 1-1-11, at 2 (Oct. 15, 1985).

[14] The U.S. Army Corps of Engineers Modification Impact Evaluation Guide, EP 415-1-3, at 3-7, 3-8 (1979). *See also* VACPM Handbook at 8-17 (March 1989).

§ 9.5   CPM Techniques Used for Time-Related Claims through the 1970s

By the early 1970s, the use of CPM techniques on construction projects had advanced to the point that a number of performance disputes considered the utility of this tool in assessing responsibility. Examples of construction disputes in which use of this tool was considered are disruption, delay, and acceleration claims.

§ 9.6   —Delay Claims

The basic technique utilized for delay claim presentations through the 1970s included establishing the following major elements:

1. Reasonable as-planned CPM schedule (see **Figures 9–1** and **9-2**)
2. As-built CPM schedule
3. As-built CPM schedule, including recognition and identification of all owner, Contractor, and excusable delays (see **Figure 9–3**)
4. Adjusted CPM schedule establishing completion absent owner delays (see **Figure 9–4**).

The basic concepts were discussed in a 1974 article, *The Use of Critical Path Method Techniques in Contract Claims:*[15]

> The value of a CPM claim presentation is the ability to visually segregate and identify those delays which are the direct responsibility of the government and to display the effect of these delays on project completion.
> In the recent case of *Canon Construction Corp.,* the Armed Services Board of Contract Appeals provided a clear and logical statement of the methods by which a CPM can be utilized to prove extended duration when the board stated:
>> A proper determination of this appeal required at the outset that the Board determine the date, as precisely as possible, upon which the appellant would have completed the contract work but for delays which might have been due either to Government fault or the performance of changed work. The next determination must be the actual date of the completion of the work. The difference between the two dates establishes the extended period of performance for which appellant would be entitled to be paid for extended fixed overhead costs.[16]

* * *

---

[15] Wickwire & Smith, 7 Pub. Cont. L.J. 1, 21–28 (1974).

[16] ASBCA No. 16,142, 72-1 BCA ¶ 9404 (1972) (footnotes deleted).

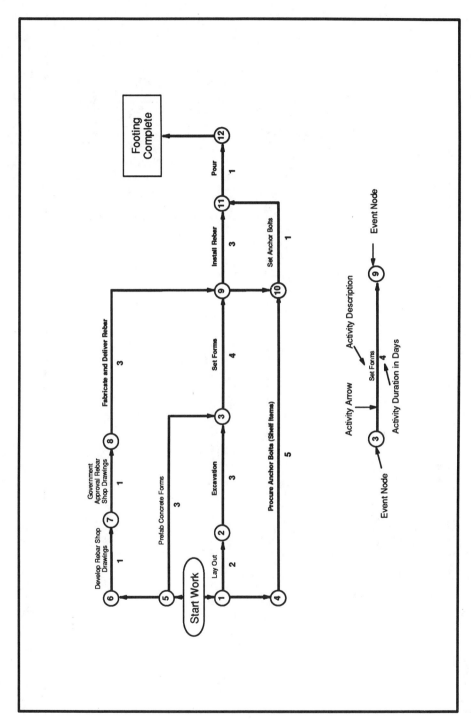

Figure 9–1. CPM schedule for a typical concrete footing.

211

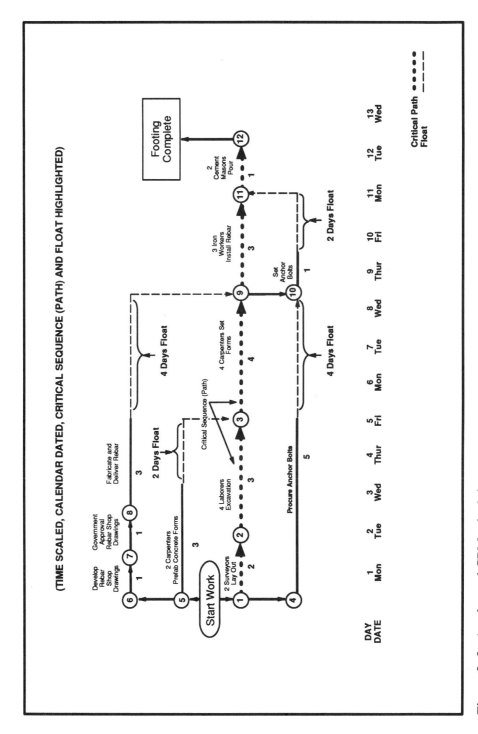

Figure 9–2. As-planned CPM schedule.

212

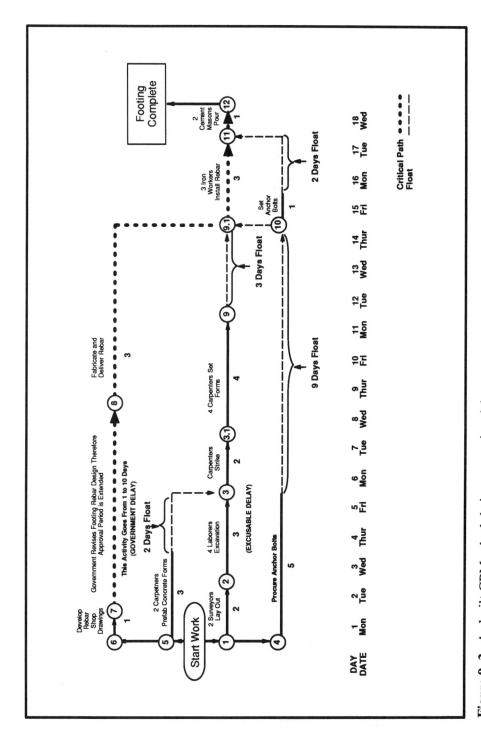

Figure 9–3. As-built CPM schedule incorporating delays.

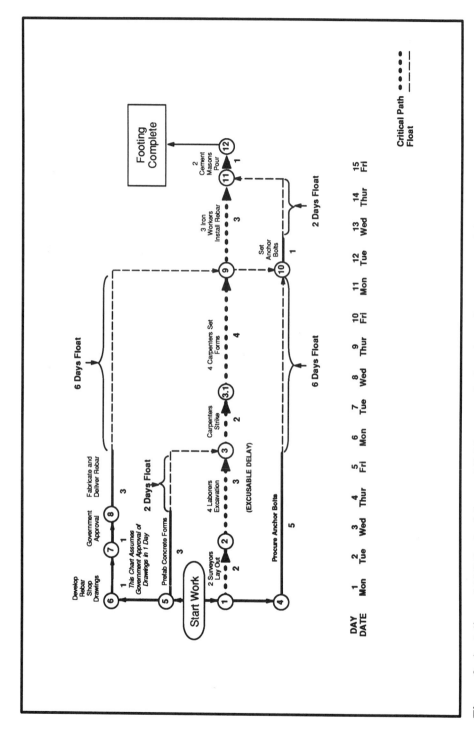

Figure 9–4. Adjusted CPM schedule establishing completion date absent owner delays.

One suggested approach to prove a delay claim would entail the preparation of the following four CPM schedules:

1.   A reasonable 'as-planned' CPM
2.   An 'as-built' CPM
3.   An 'as-built' CPM reflecting all delays—government, contractor and excusable
4.   An 'adjusted' CPM to establish completion of the project absent government delays

Each of these four CPM charts should be accompanied with an analysis of the project records which establishes the basis for the data reflected in each CPM as well as the basis for any estimates contained therein. The preparation of this support is required to lay the proper foundation for the CPM schedules' basis in the underlying project documents.

* * *

1. Reasonable 'as-planned' CPM

The purpose of this diagram and analysis is to establish the time the project would have been completed absent any delays. Additionally, this chart and analysis is important since it may serve as the starting point for the preparation of the fourth and final diagram, the 'adjusted' CPM which should establish the completion of the project absent government delays. In assembling the reasonable 'as-planned' CPM diagram and analysis, it is important to determine precisely the time schedule and sequence of construction the prime contractor and its subcontractors planned to utilize in constructing the project.

* * *

2. 'As-built' CPM

The preparation of this CPM, given the proper records, presents basically a problem of mechanics and little interpretation . . . Nonetheless, even where a CPM was utilized to schedule the project and updated during performance it would be advisable to check the updating against such project records as daily logs of construction, daily diaries, daily manpower reports, progress payment estimates, costs records detailing monthly installation of labor by codes and any available government records which verify the information contained in the updated chart.

* * *

3. 'As-built' CPM—Including All Delays—Government Contractor and Excusable

This diagram is basically an overlay of the delays encountered during the project on the 'as-built' CPM diagram previously discussed. The purpose of this portion of the presentation is to segregate precisely those delays which affected the project, to identify the activities affected by the delays and to display precisely the effect of the delays on the completion date of the project. To accomplish this, the report and CPM schedule must detail the reasons for the variations in the duration of activities and activity sequence changes which were identified in the 'as-built' CPM diagram and analysis.

* * *

4. 'Adjusted' CPM—Establishing Project Completion Date Absent Government Delays

There are basically two ways to approach the preparation of this chart and analysis. The first approach is to take the 'as-built' CPM, which has segregated all delays, into the categories of government, contractor and excusable and pull out of that diagram all government delays affecting the critical path. However, this method may well be unsatisfactory. Government delays may have so changed the sequence of construction that a realistic 'adjusted' CPM chart cannot be prepared merely by removing the government delays.

If the government delays were removed from the 'as-built' CPM and the actual durations adjusted back to the proper durations absent the government delays, the result could contain an inherent contradiction since the adjusted durations might be impossible considering the changed sequence. More specifically, delays may have required such drastic changes in sequences, such as the various trades jumping back and forth between floors a number of times, that it would be absurd to attempt to provide a realistic 'adjusted' CPM without also adjusting the actual sequence. As a result, it may be beneficial to pursue a second approach in preparing the 'adjusted' CPM by adjusting both activity durations and sequences to arrive at what would have been a realistic schedule absent government delays. However, if such a choice is made, the report must take into account any delays which were not the responsibility of the government.

Notwithstanding the approach taken, care must be taken to adjust activity durations which may appear to be contractor delays, but are really a direct result of the extended duration caused by the government. An example of this is the contractor's natural reluctance to 'hurry up and wait.' On a project which is severely delayed a contractor may frequently delay transmitting submittals or samples simply to avoid problems with changes in products or damage to material which may be delivered long before the installation can be made.

Of course, when the 'adjusted' CPM has been finalized, the amount of delay for which the government is liable is determined by the difference in time between the actual completion date shown on the 'as-built' CPM and the completion date shown on the 'adjusted' CPM.[17]

§ 9.7   —Acceleration Claim Analyses

The 1974 article *Use of Critical Path Method Techniques in Contract Claims*[18] also detailed the method of proof required for acceleration

---

[17] Wickwire & Smith, 7 Pub. Cont. L.J. 1 (1974).

[18] *Id.*

claims. This discussion included the addition of an as-built schedule detailing the effect of acceleration and an adjusted schedule detailing the time when the contractor was entitled to finish (see **Figures 9–5** and **9–6**):

Although there are many possible ways to establish entitlement to acceleration costs, use of the CPM diagrams and analyses detailed below is suggested since they should cover most of the factual situations encountered in an acceleration claim:

1. Reasonable "as-planned" CPM diagram and analysis
2. "As-built" diagram and analysis
3. "As-built" diagram and analysis reflecting all delays—government, contractor and excusable
4. "Adjusted" CPM diagram and analysis

To develop the first three charts, namely the reasonable "as-planned" CPM, the "as-built" CPM and the "as-built" CPM reflecting all delays, use of the same steps and careful preparation of the same charts as discussed in the delay section above should be undertaken. However, since the major focus of the court or board is necessarily upon the status of the project at the time of the acceleration order, this point in time should be highlighted on all three of the aforementioned diagrams and analyses. **Figures 9–2** and **9–5** set forth an example of a reasonable "as planned" CPM and "as-built" CPM diagram reflecting all delays. In addition, it is helpful for the analysis on each of the three diagrams to discuss precisely what the status of the project was at the time of the acceleration order.

The "adjusted" CPM will differ considerably from the "adjusted" CPM required under the delay claim, since the "adjusted" CPM used in an acceleration presentation must reflect not only those delays for which the government is responsible, but also all delays which entitled the contractor to a time extension, including strikes, unusually severe weather and other excusable delays. In this regard, it must be noted that the contractor may be entitled to a time extension even when a contractor delay is concurrent with a government or excusable delay.

Moreover, the basic purpose of the "adjusted" CPM for an acceleration claim is different from the "adjusted" CPM for the delay claim. In the delay claim the "adjusted" CPM is utilized to show when the project would have been completed absent the government caused delays. In the case of the "adjusted" CPM for the acceleration claim, the object is to demonstrate that the contractor was making adequate progress toward job completion when the acceleration order was given and was entitled to finish at a later date than actual completion.

In preparing the "adjusted" CPM for acceleration purposes it is therefore necessary to take actual durations of activities as recorded on the "as-built" and insert the time extensions upon the diagram which are appropriate. The process by which appropriate time extensions are determined is extremely important since the time extension due the contractor for a particular delay must take into account the disruption or loss of productivity

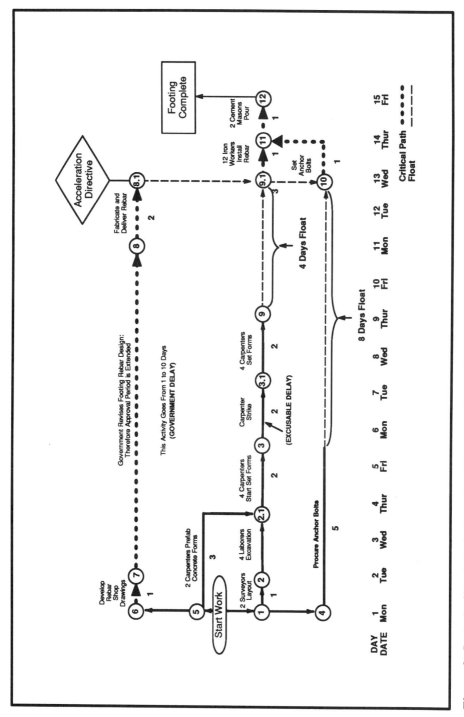

Figure 9-5. As-built schedule showing delays and the results of acceleration directive.

218

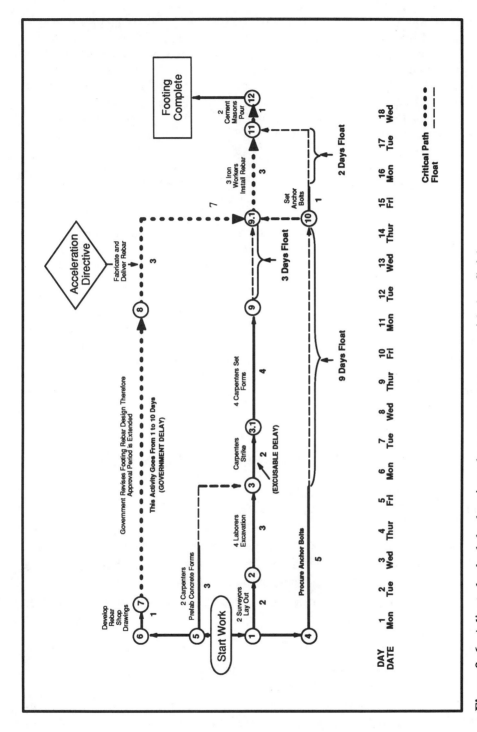

Figure 9–6. Adjusted schedule showing when contractor was entitled to finish.

type delay incurred if the contractor was unable to utilize the proper balance and spacing between the various activities for an economical scheduling of men, equipment, and material. Only if such disruption or loss of productivity is considered is it possible to determine the total amount of excusable delay affecting the critical path and to provide the contractor with all the delay to which it is entitled. By basing the time extensions due the contractor upon a reasonable balance and spacing between activities and upon reasonable resources of men, equipment and material the contractor should receive time extensions which covers all of the delay actually incurred on the project since the time extensions will take into account not only the delay to the operation immediately affected but also the disruption type delays to any subsequent operation in sequence.

Figure 9–6 illustrates an 'adjusted' CPM for an acceleration claim. As shown by the 'as-built' schedule (Figure 9–5) the contractor experienced two days delay due to a strike and nine days delay in approval of the shop drawings prior to the acceleration directive. Further, Figure 9–5 shows that the contractor completed three activities, the layout, the excavation and the setting of forms in a shorter time than originally planned (Figure 9–2). The 'adjusted' schedule (Figure 9–6) indicates that the contractor was one day ahead of a properly adjusted progress schedule at the time of the acceleration directive and that the contractor was entitled to complete the entire project at a later date than actual completion. This result is obtained in Figure 9–6 by utilizing the 'as-planned' time durations prior to and subsequent to the acceleration directive and by inserting the excusable or compensable delays.[19]

§ 9.8   Issues from the 1970s about the Use of CPM

A number of major questions about the use of CPM as a tool in resolving construction disputes arose in the 1970s, including:

1. Float time and its use and availability to the parties
2. Credit due the contractor for innovative sequence changes and the point in time when time extensions should be measured
3. Computation of any time due the contractor for changes issued after the current contract completion date.

§ 9.9   —Float Time and Its Availability

The basic problem with float relates to the right of the parties to the project to its use. In addition, the overall issue of float and its relationship to

---

[19] *Id.* at 31–34.

project delays involves the basic questions of causation and cause and effect. More specifically, **Figures 9–11** through **9–15 (§ 9–16)** detail circumstances where, absent any owner, contractor, or excusable delay, the project would not be delayed. Thus, each of these delays meets the *but for* test for purposes of causation. *But for* any of these delays, the project would not have been delayed. However, since the project, under critical path principles, will not be delayed until a delay occurs to the critical path, it must be decided whether each of these delays entitle the contractor to compensation in time extensions and extended duration expense. To state it another way, "When has any of these delays proximately caused a delay to the project?" The 1974 Wickwire and Smith article[20] highlighted this issue:

> A number of unresolved questions concern CPM float time. Float is the term used for the excess time contained on side path activities, those activities not on the critical path. The float is a very significant resource to a contractor since it allows flexibility in the schedule. A contractor can shift resources from an activity with float to apply pressure to another activity on the critical path which is behind schedule and delaying the project and still have enough time to come back and finish the side path activity by its scheduled completion.
>
> There is no dispute that government delays to a side path activity which expends all of its float time and restrains the critical path entitles the contractor to its increased costs for extended duration. The problem becomes quite difficult, however, when a number of different types of delay to the side path activity results in the expenditure of all of the float and finally in a delay to the entire project.[21]

§ 9.10   —Determining Credit for Innovative Sequence Changes and When to Measure Delay

Another major issue identified by the mid-1970s was the amount of credit a contractor should receive for time gained due to performing at a faster rate or through innovative sequence changes. See **Figure 9–7** for an illustration of this issue.

Another extremely important issue identified by the mid-1970s was the issue of the point in time when the delay should be measured. This issue arose from the potential conflict between the critical path concept that time extensions should be granted in a timely manner at the inception of delays and existing case law holding that a contractor should only receive

---

[20] Wickwire & Smith, 7 Pub. Cont. L.J. 1 (1974).

[21] *Id.* at 40–42.

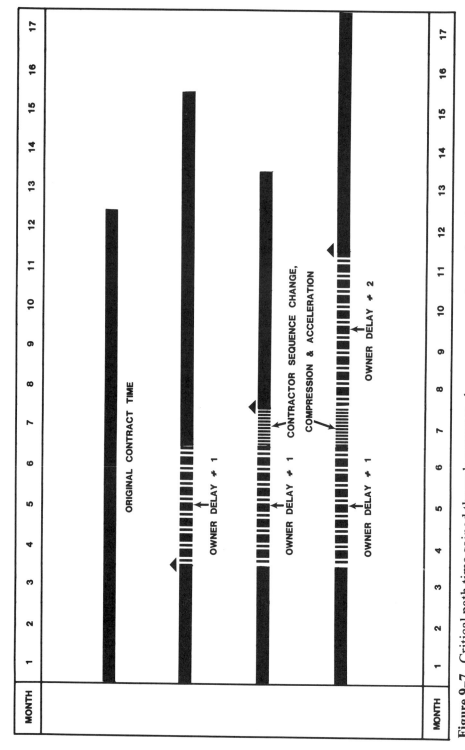

Figure 9-7. Critical path time gained through sequence changes, compression, and acceleration during performance. (▲ indicates update.)

222

time extensions to the extent a project is actually delayed. Both issues were identified by the 1974 Wickwire & Smith article:[22]

> The proper calculation of time extensions where a contractor performs innovative sequence changes is presently unresolved. This problem often must be resolved when analyzing the assessment of liquidated damages or evaluating acceleration claims.
>
> The longstanding rule with respect to the entitlement of a time extension is best stated in *Montgomery-Macri Company* and *Western Line Construction Co.*[23] where the board held:
>
>> "A contractor who seeks an extension of time on account of an excusable delay has the burden of proving . . . the extent to which the orderly progress or ultimate completion of the contract work as a whole was delayed thereby"; while another authority has commented that: "The contractor is entitled to only so much time extension as the Government's delay *actually* delayed the contractor in performing the contract."
>
> Thus, the more traditional view is that the contractor is only entitled to so much time extension as there was actual delay to the project. However, the question of the quantum of the time extension becomes more interesting when we add two additional questions: at what point in time should the delay to the project be measured, and at what point in time should the time extensions be granted.
>
> The importance of the point in time at which the delay is to be measured is illustrated by the following hypothetical: the owner directs a 120 day suspension in the studwork installation, a critical path activity, on an office building pending the issuance of a studwork change. Here obviously the contractor would be entitled to a 120-day time extension if the delay is measured at the time of the suspension order.
>
> The question becomes more difficult, though, when the contractor changes its sequence to avoid a portion of the delay to the entire project. . . .
>
> Nonetheless, the question with respect to the point at which the delay should be measured should also be considered in concert with the question as to when the time extension should be granted. The recent trend in this area is represented by *M.S.I. Corp.*[24] where the board stated:
>
>> [T]he Government not only must grant any justifiable time extension requested by a contractor for an appropriate number of days, but it must do so in a timely manner, without unreasonable delay.
>
> The above authority with respect to the proper point in time to grant a time extension provides strong support for the position that a time extension should be measured as soon as the entitlement is determined.[25]

---

[22] Wickwire & Smith, 7 Pub. Cont. L.J. 1 (1974).

[23] IBCA Nos. 59, 72, 1963 BCA ¶ 3819 (1963).

[24] GSBCA 2429, 68-2 BCA ¶ 7377 at 34,316–17 (1968).

[25] *See* Wickwire & Smith, *The Use of Critical Path Method Techniques in Contract Claims,* 7 Pub. Cont. L.J. 1, 43–45 (1974).

§ 9.11 —Time Due Contractor for Change Orders Ordered after Current Contract Completion Date

The ability of the critical path network principles to isolate the specific activities on the critical path at any given point in time, including periods after the contract performance time had expired, created another interesting situation in the mid-70s. This issue held great import in evaluating delays after the completion date of the contract. Specifically, even though a change might be ordered after the current completion date, it might not affect the longest chain of activities through the life of the project at that point (the critical path). This new capability not only flew in the face of the prior authority, allowing for per se time extensions for changes issued after the contract completion date, it raised a major new issue about whether there should be apportionment of concurrent delays for purposes of liquidated damages.

§ 9.12 CPM Developments and Issues since 1974

The period since 1974 has been marked by significant advancement in all phases of CPM analysis on contract disputes. The courts and boards have addressed a variety of questions and issues in that time. These decisions not only have evaluated the four major issues identified previously in the 1974 Wickwire and Smith article, but also have addressed and significantly advanced the state of the law concerning a number of additional critical questions.

Further, the period since 1974 has seen significant advancement in the use of microcomputers and microcomputer programs directly on the construction jobsite. This development has greatly advanced the utility of and access to CPM programs for smaller construction projects, but has also created certain problems concerning the dispute resolution process.

The material in §§ **9.13** through **9.28** reviews the key findings by the courts and boards with respect to these advancements since 1974 and also reviews certain of the potential abuses of the microcomputer programs.[26]

§ 9.13 —CPM Acknowledged as Preferred Method for Proving Delays

That CPM techniques have come to be acknowledged as the preferred method of proving and assessing delays is demonstrated by the increasing

---

[26] Substantial portions of further discussion in this chapter are based upon materials covered in Wickwire, Hurlbut, & Lerman, *Use of Critical Path Method Techniques and Contract Claims: Issues and Developments,* 18 Pub. Cont. L.J. 338, 359–88 (1989).

number of state court decisions in the past decade that reflect its use to assist the finder of fact.[27]

In addition, four recent decisions clearly spell out the preference of the judiciary that CPM proof for cause and effect on construction claims be provided. For example, in *Al Johnson Constr. Co. v. United States,*[28] the Court of Appeals for the Federal Circuit fully supported the board of contract appeals decision, which had criticized "the 'bar chart' appellant provided which lacked a 'critical path,' a favorite device with present day fact finders in contract disputes." Further, in *H.W. Detwiler Co.*[29] the board of contract appeals found that the selection by the contractor of a bar chart, rather than a CPM network, to schedule the work meant that the contractor was unable to satisfy the standard of proof the board was looking for in establishing delays to the project. In considering a specification that gave the contractor the option to use a CPM schedule (or a schedule with equal information), the board stated:

> Detwiler opted to schedule the work on a bar graph through which it reported both its scheduled and actual progress. Because Detwiler chose to use a bar graph to assess its progress, its proposed schedule was necessarily general and somewhat vague with respect to planning discrete construction activities (Gov't exh. E; R4, tab G).
>
> * * *
>
> As was held in *Wilner Construction Co.,* ASBCA No. 26621, 84-2 BCA ¶ 17,411: "It is well established that in order to recover for alleged compensable delay a contractor must demonstrate that delay was caused by the Government and, with a reasonable degree of accuracy, the extent of such compensable delay." *Accord: Celesco Industries, Inc.,* ASBCA No. 21928, 81-2 BCA ¶ 15,260 (1981).
>
> In our view, Detwiler has failed to meet this burden of proof. It provided very general, almost vague, evidence to the effect that the parties' failure to resolve the problem with the power lines delayed the masonry work.[30]

---

[27] *See, e.g.,* White & Steenmeyer v. King County, 57 Wash. App. 170, 787 P.2d 58 (1990); Attlin Constr., Inc. v. Muncie Community Schools, 413 N.E.2d 281 (Ind. Ct. App. 1980); Boston Edison Co. v. Department of Util., 393 Mass. 244, 471 N.E.2d 54 (1984); Walter Toebe & Co. v. Yeager Bridge & Culvert Co., 150 Mich. App. 386, 389 N.W.2d 99 (1986); Walter Toebe & Co. v. Dept. of State Highways, 144 Mich. App. 21, 373 N.W.2d 233 (1985); State v. Illinois Commerce Commission, 202 Ill. App. 3d 917, 561 N.E.2d 711 (1990); Indiana & Michigan Elec. Co., v. Terre Haute Indus., Inc., 507 N.E.2d 588 (Ind. App. 1987); McDevitt & Street Co. v. Marriott, 911 F.2d 723 (4th Cir. 1990); Georgia Power Co. v. Georgia Pub. Serv. Comm'n, 196 Ga. 572, 396 S.E.2d 562 (1990).

[28] 854 F.2d 467, 470 (Fed. Cir. 1988).

[29] ASBCA No. 35,327, 89-2 BCA ¶ 21,612 (1989).

[30] *Id.* at 108,792, 108,797.

In another ASBCA decision, *Umpqua Marine Ways, Inc.*[31] the board found that the contractor had not provided proper proof of Government delays alleged to be caused by engineering change proposals (ECPs):

> For some of the ECPs for which a precise period of delay impact has been alleged, the alleged period occurred well before the effective date of Modification P00005. For all other ECP's cited, Umpqua has failed to prove by critical path analysis or otherwise a cause-effect relationship between any matters related to the ECP and any item of work controlling the delivery of the boat.[32]

Finally, *Freeman-Darling, Inc.*[33] illustrates the effect on the parties of the unavailability of proper CPM proof. In this case, the contractor's presentation of an as-built CPM schedule contained numerous and serious inconsistencies and errors. As a result, the board determined that the CPM analysis did not provide the capability to apportion delays with respect to an analysis of liquidated damages. The board found that under circumstances where the concurrent delays could not be apportioned the contractor could not recover its increased cost for the period of the alleged delays and the government as well was denied the recovery of liquidated damages (because the contractor had to be credited with the time equal to the period of the unapportionable concurrent delay). Similarly, in *Industrial Constructors Corp.,*[34] the contractor introduced charts as showing the project critical path which did present proper CPM proof. Here the board found that the charts submitted were not, in fact, critical path charts. The charts were only bar charts. Like the *Freeman-Darling* decision, the board here refused to apportion responsibility for concurrent delays between the parties in the absence of proper CPM proof.

§ 9.14   —Need to Establish Cause-and-Effect Relationship

Recent board decisions *Preston-Brady Co.*[35] and *Titan Mountain States Construction Corp.*[36] confirm the basic concepts of proof detailed in the 1974 Wickwire and Smith article and the necessity to fully prove the specific cause-and-effect relationship between the plan for performance

---

[31] ASBCA Nos. 27,790, 29,532, 89-3 BCA ¶ 22,099 (1989).

[32] *Id.* at 111,124.

[33] GSBCA No. 7112, 89-2 BCA ¶ 21,882 (1989).

[34] AGBCA No. 84-248-1, 90-2 BCA ¶ 22,767 (1990).

[35] VABCA Nos. 1892, 1991, 2555, 87-1 BCA ¶ 19,649 (1987).

[36] ASBCA Nos. 22,617, 22,930, 23,095, 23,188, 85-1 BCA ¶ 17,931 (1985).

and the variances in performance during actual performance. In the *Titan Mountain States* decision, the board, in circumstances where the contractor's CPM expert did not personally examine any CPM print-outs, quality control reports, quality assurance reports, or payrolls and only cursorily reviewed project correspondence or other documents, held as follows:

> A contractor was not entitled to time extensions for delay and impact allegedly resulting from modifications, because his critical path method analysis did not establish a causal relationship between the modifications and the alleged delays attributable to them. The contractor alleged that various modifications justified time extensions for delay and impact; however, he presented no evidence from any of his subcontractors who had performed the work, and he did not establish the requisite causal relationship. Further, his CPM analysis was deficient because persons who prepared the analysis had no knowledge of how the work was performed or how it progressed. Moreover, the comparison of the CPM updates with the original CPM schedule disclosed only the differences between them and not the cause of the differences.[37]

Further, the *Preston-Brady* decision detailed the necessity that, in the post-*Fortec Constructors v. United States* environment, the CPM schedule, to demonstrate delay on the project, must be kept current and the comparative presentation of the plan versus as-built condition on the project must be grounded in the actual project records. The decision of the board stated:

> A CPM schedule, in order to properly demonstrate delay on a project, must be kept current to reflect those delays as they occur: *Fortec Constructors v. United States* [32 CCF ¶ 73,702], 8 Cl. Ct. 490, 505 (1985); *Ballenger Corp.*, DOTBCA Nos. 74-32, 74-32A, 74-32H, 84-1 BCA ¶ 16,973, at 84,524. Although *Preston-Brady* had initially prepared such a schedule, for its internal planning purposes only, it *never updated that schedule.* As we have already seen, there were several claimed delays throughout Phase I, yet the Progress Schedule remained unaltered.

* * *

> We do not endorse the COTR's method of calculating change order performance time, particularly since there is insufficient basis in the record for his assumption that a 5 man 'Change Order' crew was practical in such close quarters with other ongoing work. On the other hand, the Appellant has the burden of proving the extent of any delay which it claims as a result of this change order. (See cases cited in our Discussion of VABCA-1892 7 1991, Claim No. 1 *supra*). A general statement that disruption or impact occurred, absent any showing through use of updated CPM schedules, Logs or credible and specific data or testimony, will not suffice to meet

---

[37] *Id.* at 89,784.

that burden. This is particularly so where, as here, the Logs, when contrasted to the as-planned CPM schedule, show minimal delay to the very trades most directly involved in the change order at issue.[38]

In addition, recent state decisions also recognize the necessity for the contractor to explain not just the variances between the planned and actual CPM schedules, but also their cause (for example, owner, contractor, or excusable delays). Such a situation is represented by *Indiana & Michigan Electric Co. v. Terre Haute Industries, Inc.,*[39] in which the court, while accepting the critical path concept for establishing the extent of project delays, made clear the necessity for specific proof of the actual cause of project delays.

§ 9.15   —Requirement for Contemporaneous Baseline in Measuring Quantum of Delay

The particular reference point to be utilized to determine if the critical path has been affected by a delay and to determine the quantum of delay has represented the most significant issue related to the use of CPM techniques on contract claims since the mid-1970s. The questions involved are as follows:

1.   Do we value the delay at the inception of the delay? (In other words, do we forward-price the delay?)
2.   Do we price the delay as the delay is occurring or immediately after the delay? (We might describe this method as the real-time, or contemporaneous, delay determination and calculation.)
3.   Or, do we determine and value the delay after the fact, after the project is over? (In other words, do we utilize hindsight pricing of delays?)[40]

As detailed by *M.S.I. Corp.*[41] and the more recent *Fortec*[42] decision, the whole concept of CPM techniques is a dynamic one, in which the executor of the schedule analyzes the network planning techniques throughout the

---

[38] *See* Preston-Brady Co., VABCA Nos. 1892, 1991, 2555, 87-1 BCA ¶ 19,649, at 99,520 (1987).

[39] 507 N.E.2d 588 (Ind. App. 1987).

[40] The problem in question may not always arise, because the contemporaneous determination and pricing of delays may coincide with pure hindsight determination in valuation of delays to the critical path.

[41] GSBCA No. 2429, 68-2 BCA ¶ 7377 (1968).

[42] Fortec Constructors v. United States, 8 Cl. Ct. 490 (1985).

life of the project to identify and react to problems through the updating process and to apply appropriate resources to the critical path and other work activities to achieve the best timing for completion considering the goals of both cost and time. Thus, *Fortec*[43] tells us that without proper use of the updating process the utility of the CPM is lost.

On the other hand, the *Montgomery-Macri Co. & Western Line Construction Co.*[44] decision shows that the contractor receives time extensions only to the extent that the project is *actually* delayed by a particular delay.

The *Blackhawk Heating & Plumbing Co.* decision,[45] rendered in the mid-1970s, poses the problem[46] quite clearly:

> Appellant suggests that if the Contracting Officer had promptly acted upon appellant's time extension requests, as he ought to have, then they would have resulted in grants because of ductwork drawing delays which were then considered critical. Our review of this very complicated record does not persuade us that the Contracting Officer was bound to grant the delay requests on the evidence then before him. We do concede, however, that the amount of delay granted can well depend on the point in time at which the delay claim is analyzed and acted upon. (*See The Use of CPM Techniques in Contract Claims,* Wickwire and Smith, 7 Public Contract Law Journal 1, 43–45, Oct. 1974.) A contractor could be granted a time extension because of delay in an apparently critical activity when later evidence might show the activity noncritical and the time extension therefore unwarranted. The real point, as indicated in page 22 of our original opinion, is "that time extensions must be granted on the best evidence available." We had before us evidence as to how the project was actually built, evidence which did not exist at the time Appellant filed its claims. This evidence compelled us to find that the sixth floor ductwork delays were noncritical. Appellant has come forward with nothing to persuade us of any error in such finding.[47]

What, then, does the evolving body of contract clauses, manuals, regulations, and case authorities reveal about the critical issue of the point of reference for measuring delay?

---

[43] *Id.* at 504–08.

[44] IBCA Nos. 59, 72, 1963 BCA ¶ 3819 (1963).

[45] GSBCA No. 2432, 75-1 BCA ¶ 11,261 (1975).

[46] Fletcher & Sons, Inc., VABCA No. 2502, 88-2 BCA ¶ 20,677 (1988), provides a good example of the circumstances where a delay may appear to be critical on one update, but at a later date have moved off the critical path. *See* discussions at 104, 527–528. The question of the quantum reference point was rendered moot, however, in the Fletcher & Sons, Inc. decision because the government had already recognized its responsibility for the full delay across the span of the period in question for the second delay.

[47] Blackhawk Heating & Plumbing Co., GSBCA No. 2432, 75-1 BCA ¶ 11,261, at 55,578 (1975) (footnotes omitted).

The clear weight of authority[48] (case authority, contract clauses, and agency manuals)[49] since 1974 has been to give credence to the dynamic nature of the CPM process and require that the determination of delays affecting the critical path, as well as the quantum of such delays, should be developed contemporaneously as the project history unfolds, utilizing the updating process as the point of reference.

Contemporaneously evaluating delays requires starting the analysis with the beginning of the project and then stopping at various reference points monthly or quarterly during the life of the project to determine the location of the critical path, along with any delays or positive time gains to the project (by evaluating positive or negative float generated on the critical path during the period in question), until the completion of the project is reached.

Contemporaneous determination and pricing of delays on the critical path can also be developed after the fact by reviewing project records, starting from the beginning of the project. The occurrences and delay impacts are then reconstructed by moving through the various time reference points until the completion of the project is reached. Historical records are used in this manner to perform the contemporaneous analysis.

Examples of contract clauses that utilize such contemporaneous or current valuations of delays are found in Veterans Administration and Corps of Engineers specifications.[50] In addition, the same philosophy of contemporaneously addressing delays is represented in the major Corps of Engineers and Veterans Administration manuals.[51]

---

[48] Certain recent authority is not totally clear on the question. For example, the language at 729–30 of G.M. Shupe, Inc. v. United States, 5 Cl. Ct. 662 (1984), may be susceptible to the interpretation that a hindsight valuation of delays was utilized. However, other portions of the decision appear to indicate that the court looked to work schedule updates to determine the effect of delays. *See* discussions, generally, at 728–730.

[49] Commentators have also recognized the necessity to value time delays during performance on a contemporaneous basis. *See, e.g.,* Logcher, *Concurrent Delays In Construction Projects,* 115-2 J. Construction Engineering Mgmt. at 336 (June 1989), which noted:

The more difficult issues of determining new logic with out-of-sequence progress, determining when a party may have or should have taken some action, and the extent of impacts are all much more difficult than the analysis concepts presented here and in the paper.

The only real solution lies in a dynamic analysis process, where at the point of any delay action, a new forecast of project completion is generated to determine the impacts.

[50] *See, e.g.,* **Appendix D,** ¶ 1.13; **Appendix C,** ¶¶ (e)(3), (e)(4), (f)(5).

[51] The Corps of Engineers Modification Impact Evaluation Guide, EP 415-1-3 (1979), states at 3–5:

A major benefit of settling modifications before performance is that it encourages prompt revision of the progress schedule, thus maintaining accurate knowledge of the sequencing of the remaining work, the final contract price, and the final completion date. The schedule then remains a realistic tool for determining

Very significant recent case authority recognizes the necessity to use CPM schedules which evaluate delays contemporaneous with the events as they occur on the project to establish time extensions. This was clearly the

---

the impact of changes on the contractor's operations. An up-to-date CPM schedule is a prerequisite to forecasting the presence and extent of impact.

Further, as early as 1973, the Corps of Engineers Manual on Network Analysis Systems, ER 1-1-11, recognized, at 6:

d. Updating, or monitoring, for progress at specified intervals is necessary when network analysis system is used for planning and scheduling. In most instances monthly is adequate. The updating input information must be agreed upon by the contractor and the government prior to progress analysis and should include all conditions which would influence any data shown on the network diagram, such as (1) actual dates on which work was started or finished on activities during the period, (2) revised estimates of duration times or dollar values of activities due to contract modifications, more current information, delays, strikes, change of operations or procedures, (3) new activities for work previously overlooked or added by contract modification, (4) change of logic or restraints caused by changed operational procedures or contract modifications, and (5) deletion of activities inappropriately shown on the original diagram or deleted by changes to the contract. After entry of the actual data and/or revised estimates, the resulting mathematical analysis reveals project status in terms of float or slack, the value of work placed or earnings, and other management data. In addition to computer printouts or other analysis computations, narrative reports prepared from this data can be very useful to construction managers and the computations can serve as backup if additional detail is needed. In addition to progress data, narrative reports should indicate delays and plans for overcoming them.

e. The periodic updatings for progress will also serve as the basis for partial payments to the contractor when network analysis is specified for the contract schedule and control.

f. For modifications to the contract which could influence the order of work, restraints between various activities, or duration time estimates for any activities on the diagram, determination of the impact of such changes on the required contract completion date or dates will be made by network analysis system. This should be done during negotiations. When notice-to-proceed is issued to a contractor for a modification to the contract, the necessary logic changes will be made to the network diagram and analysis no later than the next updating after notice-to-proceed. This will normally be done by the contractor with prior approval of the logic changes by the government. When it is necessary to issue a notice-to-proceed with a change prior to completion of negotiations, the contracting officer may direct the logic changes necessary to the diagram to be used in subsequent updatings until negotiations are complete for the change. Whether or not negotiations have been completed, it is necessary that all modifications be included in the network analysis system at the time the change is ordered to evaluate the impact on the job and to avoid loss of control of the progress. Approval of input data for updating does not constitute approval of revised completion date which might result as output from the analysis. Approved time extensions must be entered as input data after contract modifications are signed by the Contracting Officer. *See also* VACPM Handbook, 8–13, 55–65, 73–84 (March 1989).

message provided by the landmark *Fortec Constructors v. United States*[52] decision quoted previously in regard to the dynamic nature of the CPM process.

However, even clearer case authority supporting the use of contemporaneous calculations of delay is reflected in a number of later decisions, from the mid-1980s. These include two *Santa Fe, Inc.*[53] decisions, in 1984 and 1987; the *Fred A. Arnold, Inc.*[54] decision in 1984; the *Titan Mountain States Construction Corp.*[55] decision in 1985; the 1990 decision in *Williams Enterprises, Inc. v. Strait Manufacturing & Welding Inc.;*[56] the 1990 decision in *Hull-Hazard, Inc.;*[57] and a 1989 board decision in *Gulf Contracting, Inc.*[58]

For example, in *Titan Mountain States Construction Corp.,*[59] the board, in denying a delay and acceleration claim, focused its attention on the failure of the contractor's CPM expert to explain the variances between the as-built CPM schedule and the updates of that schedule as the work progressed. In its headnote, the board found:

> Further, his CPM analysis was deficient because persons who prepared the analysis had no knowledge of how the work was performed or how it progressed. Moreover, the comparison of CPM updates with the original CPM schedule disclosed only the differences between them and not the cause of the differences.[60]

Again, in the *Fred A. Arnold, Inc.*[61] decision, the ASBCA calculated the effect of critical path delays to the project by comparing the various updates detailing the effect of changes at the time the events were occurring. The board stated:

> Appellant further complains that we 'consistently adopted the Government's position' without stating our reasons. Our reasons are clearly stated in our decision—namely, appellant's failure to carry its burden of proof.

---

[52] 8 Cl. Ct. 490 (1985), *aff'd*, 804 F.2d 141 (Fed. Cir. 1986).

[53] VABCA Nos. 1943–1946, 84-2 BCA ¶ 17,341 (1984); VABCA No. 2168, 87-3 BCA ¶ 20,104 (1987).

[54] ASBCA Nos. 27,151, 27,156, 27,170, 27,186, 27,191, 27,200, 84-3 BCA ¶ 17,517 (1984).

[55] ASBCA Nos. 22,617, 22,930, 23,095, 23,188, 85-1 BCA ¶ 17,931 (1985).

[56] 728 F. Supp. 12 (D.D.C. 1990).

[57] ASBCA No. 34,645, 90-3 BCA ¶ 23,173 (1990).

[58] ASBCA No. 30,195, 32,839, 33,867, 89-2 BCA ¶ 21,812, *on reconsideration*, 90-1 BCA ¶ 22,393 (1989).

[59] ASBCA Nos. 22,617, 22,930, 23,095, 23,188, 85-1 BCA ¶ 17,931 (1985).

[60] *Id.* at 89,784.

[61] ASBCA Nos. 27,151, 27,156, 27,170, 27,186, 27,191, 27,200, 84-3 BCA ¶ 17,517 (1984).

Appellant's evidence consisted for the most part of generalities, conclusions, and references to an early edition of a CPM analysis, which had been replaced by later editions at the time the changes at issue were ordered. . . .

On these issues, and against appellant's irrelevancies, generalities, and non-current CPM analysis, the Government presented a current CPM analysis showing the effect on contract completion of the six specific changes at the time the changes were ordered.[62]

In *Santa Fe, Inc.*[63] in 1984, the board considered the Veterans Administration clause that required delays to be evaluated in connection with the current CPM schedules to determine if the delays affected the "extended and predicted" completion dates for the contract. The contracting procedures in place for the 1984 decision were detailed as follows:

> NAS-4 provides that the VA shall "process monthly updated look-ahead reports and will generate computerized cost and schedule reports necessary for monitoring job progress." The Contractor is "responsible for the accurate and timely submittal of the updated Look-Ahead Report and the CPM data necessary to produce the computer reports . . ."
>
> At monthly job site meetings the contractor was also required to submit . . . "revised complete arrow diagram showing all completed and new activities, change orders and logic changes made on the subject update . . . ." (NAS-20).
>
> *   *   *
>
> Section NAS-13.A of the contract entitled, 'Adjustment of Contract Completion Time' provides that . . . the Contractor's "[s]ubmission of proof based on revised activity logic durations . . . must clearly display that the Contractor has used, in full, all the float time available for the work involved in this request." Paragraph A of NAS-13 further provides:
>
>> Actual delays in activities which, according to the computer-produced calendar-dated schedule, do not affect the extended and predicted contract completion dates shown by the critical path in the network will not be the basis for a change to the contract completion date.[64]

The fact that the owner (Veterans Administration) utilized current updates to evaluate the effect of delays for purposes of its presentation to the board is shown by the discussion contained in the board decision.[65] An example of the Veterans Administration's system in evaluating delays is set forth below:

> Utilizing the November 20, 1982 CPM printouts the Contracting Officer stated that "the durations of the change activities would reduce the TFL

---

[62] *Id.* at 87,231–32.

[63] VABCA Nos. 1943–1946, 84-2 BCA ¶ 17,341 (1984).

[64] *Id.* at 86,405.

[65] *Id.* at 86,406–407.

values of the work activities to 40 and 41 [days] respectively." Because the total float had "not been totally depleted by the durations of the change activities," he concluded that "the change did not impact the contractor's predicted completion date." (Clontz Affidavit at 5).[66]

The VA board confirmed its acceptance of the use of the current CPM updates to evaluate delays by the following language:

> At best, Appellant has shown only that the change orders "could have delayed" the contract completion work. The available CPM data and narrative reports which are based on information submitted by the Contractor not only fail to support Appellant's claim that the change orders extended its contract completion date, but demonstrate to the contrary because of available float time that they had no adverse impact on the Contractor's predicted contract completion date.[67]

Any doubt after the 1984 decision that the VA board was looking to CPM updates current at the time delays were occurring to evaluate the effect of such delays on the critical path was removed by the 1987 *Santa Fe, Inc.* decision. The relevant contract provisions in that case required use of current updates to evaluate delays.[68] The board's discussion of the use of current CPM updates to measure delays stated:

> Nor will we totally disregard the October CPM in favor of the November CPM, as the Government suggests, notwithstanding that significant revisions to the CPM were mutually effected by the parties in November 1981. We do not find that the November revisions were necessary to 'correct' the October CPM. Rather, the November CPM merely reflected a different plan for further prosecution of the work which differed from the previous plan. However, the adoption of an alternate method of performance in the later CPM does not, of itself, contradict the existence of a delay as shown in the preceding CPM. There is a rebuttable presumption of correctness attached to CPM's upon which the parties have previously mutually agreed. In the absence of probative evidence, not present in this appeal, that the delay shown was not in fact sustained we will rely on the October CPM for the period it was in effect, i.e., through the end of November 1981. For the subsequent period, we will rely on the November CPM. To put it another way, in the absence of compelling evidence of actual errors in the CPM's, we will let the parties 'live or die' by the CPM applicable to the relevant time frames. In that regard, the Government quotes from this Board's decision in *Santa Fe, Inc.,* VABCA Nos. 1943, 1944, 1945, and 1946, 84-2 BCA ¶ 17,341 at 86,411 as follows:

---

[66] *Id.* at 86,407.

[67] *Id.* at 86,411–412.

[68] VABCA No. 2168, 87-3 BCA ¶ 20,104, at 101,749 (1987).

. . . Indeed, it is the very existence of the contractually agreed upon CPM procedure which, when properly utilized, allows the Contracting Officer and subsequent review bodies to determine with greater exactitude whether, and to what extent, a particular change order affects the critical path and hence delays ultimate performance. See generally, *Hardeman-Monier-Hutcherson*, ASBCA No. 10444, 67-1 BCA ¶ 6158, *Canon Construction Corporation*, ASBCA No. 16142, 72-1 BCA ¶ 9404, Wickwire and Smith, *The Use of Critical Path Method Technique in Contract Claims*, 7 Pub. Cont. L.J. 1 (1974) and *Fischbach & Moore International Corp., supra*, ('critical path analysis offered . . . a ready and reasonable basis for segregating the delays' at 59,224).

Thus, we will apply the October CPM to the eleven-day period from the time the suspension commenced, November 19, 1981, until November 30, 1981, at which time the November CPM became effective. Under the earlier October CPM, the suspended AHU work was critical and we find that the first eleven days of the suspension entitles the Contractor to an eleven-day extension to the contract completion date. Under the November CPM, the balance of the suspension applied to non-critical work and no time extension is warranted.[69]

In the recent decision by the United States District Court for the District of Columbia in *Williams Enterprises, Inc. v. Strait Manufacturing & Welding, Inc.,*[70] the court considered the issue of the quantification of delays resulting from the collapse encountered during structural steel erection on the modernization and construction of a new gym at a high school. In this case, the court accepted methodology provided by the prime contractor's expert that compared the planned completion of steel erection with the actual erection of the steel, which was then checked against an analysis of the same period of delay by evaluating each period of delay chronologically in three phases.[71]

In *Hull-Hazard, Inc.,*[72] the board considered the proof presented by the contractor's expert, which was clearly based upon the chronological evaluation of the delays moving forward from the inception of the project through the various updates and evaluating the delays with each update. The court first noted the methodology propounded by the contractor's expert:

> Mr. Maurer, appellant's expert, testified about the critical delays to the project. His testimony was not challenged or rebutted by the Government. The analysis about the critical delays was based on appellant's original schedule, the schedule updates, the daily reports, project correspondence,

---

[69] *Id.* at 101,760.

[70] 728 F. Supp. 12 (D.D.C. 1990).

[71] *Id.* at 15–16.

[72] ASBCA No. 34,645, 90-3 BCA ¶ 12,173 (1990).

and the contract documents (tr. 2/55, 56). Mr. Maurer described his analysis as a step by step process, beginning with the original schedule and proceeding chronologically through the project, updating the sequence at intervals to see what happens as the project progressed (tr. 2/62). The delay analysis indicated that appellant's progress in performing the contract work was proceeding ahead of schedule through 30 September 1984. At that time the progress of the work, according to Mr. Maurer, would have resulted in the contract being completed on 24 October 1984. (Tr. 2/66; exh. A-73) The activities, testified by Mr. Maurer, which impacted and delayed the critical path were as follows: window submittal problem; telecommunications change order, the laundry room vent change order, the punchlists in the barracks buildings, and the dining hall completion. These were critical delays, in Mr. Maurer's analysis, to the project and the contract completion. (Tr. 2/66-71) The total project delay, testified Mr. Maurer, was ten months. The individual critical delays were found by Mr. Maurer to be as follows (exh. A-75; tr. 2/72-76):

Delay to Contract Completion

Cause	Time Period	Days
Windows	24 Oct 1984 to 24 Jan 1985	92
Telecommunication Change	24 Jan 1985 to 24 Mar 1985	59
Laundry Room Change	24 Mar 1985 to 30 May 1985	15
Punchlists	24 Mar 1985 to 30 May 1985	67
Dining Hall Completion	30 May to 26 Aug 1985	88

[*25]
The delay for the laundry room change is concurrent with the punchlist delay.

The ASBCA clearly accepted the quantification of the delays as established by the contractor's expert in considering various of the individual claims for which it found merit. This was reflected by the board's decision on the inspection (punchlist) claim and the dining hall completion claim.

The recent decision that details most clearly the acceptance by the judiciary of the contemporaneous method of quantifying or pricing the effective delays within time periods is *Gulf Contracting, Inc.,*[73] in which the board adopted the contemporaneous method to pricing delays as follows:

The Ockman Analysis

93. The Government engaged the services of Ockman & Borden Associates (Ockman) to analyze the delays encountered and to review Vinson's analysis. . . . [His] report formed the basis of the Government's defense.

---

[73] ASBCA Nos. 30,195, 32,839, 33,867, 89-2 BCA ¶ 21,812, at 109,755–756, *on reconsideration,* 90-1 BCA ¶ 22,393 (1989).

94. Ockman made some minor logic corrections to the approved CPM schedule and used it as a reasonable as-planned schedule (exh. G-39 at II-2). This as-planned schedule showed that the gymnasium had 64 calendar days of float, and Barracks 28430, the most critical barracks, had 138 calendar days of float (exh. G-39 at II-2). He then adjusted the approved CPM schedule by incorporating the impact of five activities he identified as affecting the critical path of the project. He summarized his approach as follows:

> The adjusted schedules were prepared by starting with the reasonable as-planned schedule and chronologically incorporating the time impacts, which occurred during the project, into this schedule. Once a time impact was identified, the original schedule dates were revised to create an adjusted schedule incorporating the time impact. The adjusted schedule was then revised to incorporate the next chronological time impact. In this way, each of the five controlling time impacts has been incorporated into the schedule as it occurred.

(Exh. G-39 at III-4).

* * *

101. Unlike Vinson's analysis which leaped from one unsupported conclusion to another, we find Ockman's analysis to be straight-forward and supported by the record that we have reviewed.

The decisions above emphasize the use of current updates of the CPM schedule at specific reference points during the life of the CPM project, to assess the location of the critical path as well as the pluses and minuses of slack on the critical path as it accumulates through the project. These decisions also provide support for the contractor's ability to collect on delay claims that represent more time than the period for which the project is actually delayed past the contract completion date (when the contractor has bought time back on the project). This principle appears to apply even where the original CPM only showed completing on the contract completion date. See **Figure 9–7** for an example of the compression's effect on project duration and delay quantification.

Consider as a hypothetical a project with an 18-month contract completion date and with an as-planned CPM schedule submitted by the contractor showing the full 18 months to complete the project. With 12 months of the construction expired, the update shows the contractor to be four months ahead on her critical path schedule with a new completion date at only 14 months, rather than 18 months. Starting with the next month, the project is delayed by a major owner modification by a further 10 months, pushing it out to a total of 24 months to completion. Obviously, under the use of the current CPM updates to evaluate delays to contractors, delay entitlement would be the total of the 24 months actual completion less the 14 months that it would have taken to complete the project, even though the original CPM schedule provided for an 18-month completion. Thus, the contractor would receive 10 months' compensable delay, even though the project completion date was extended by only six months and even though the original CPM schedule called for utilizing the full 18-month contract period.

A review of the as-planned CPM schedule in **Figure 9–2** in conjunction with **Figures 9–8, 9–9,** and **9–10** further illustrates the significance of the point of reference for measuring delays by showing the different results derived if hindsight evaluation, rather than contemporaneous evaluation, of delays is utilized. The as-planned CPM schedule in **Figure 9–2** shows a completion date for the construction of a concrete footing by day 13. The critical path on the plan is displayed in the center of the diagram and runs through the surveyor's layout, excavation, form setting, installation of rebar, and, finally, the pouring of concrete. In our model project, as detailed in **Figures 9–8, 9–9,** and **9–10**, the contractor experiences a number of delays. First, in the center of each diagram, a two-day delay is experienced after day two in activity 2–2.1 because of government layout changes. This government delay holds up the start of excavation and increases the float for procuring anchor bolts (**activity 4–10**) from four to six days.

With the additional two days of float, the contractor sits idle and waits to procure the anchor bolts until the full float is exhausted on day six. Thereafter, the contractor experiences a delay extending anchor bolt procurement from five to ten days because of a manufacturing difficulty (which is the contractor's responsibility in our model). With the introduction of these delays and all other durations remaining, the contractor completes the same project on day 20, seven days late.

Contrasting **Figure 9–2**, our as-planned CPM schedule, and **Figure 9–8**, a project update, reveals that at day six the contemporaneous pricing of delay (as prescribed by the recent *Fortec Constructors v. United States,*[74] *Santa Fe, Inc.,*[75] *Gulf Contracting, Inc.,*[76] and other decisions) requires a two-day time extension, which is also compensable as of day six of the project. By contrast, following the technique suggested by *Blackhawk Heating & Plumbing Co.*[77] and comparing the plan in **Figure 9–2** with a total hindsight evaluation of the project in **Figure 9–9** reveals that the critical path for the project, the longest chain of activities in terms of time, runs through the contractor delays for the project, bypassing the owner layout change. Under this analysis, the contractor could be liable for all seven days delay to the project.

---

[74] 8 Ct. Cl. 490 (1985), *aff'd,* 804 F.2d 141 (Fed. Cir. 1986).

[75] Santa Fe, Inc., VABCA Nos. 1943–1946, 84-2 BCA ¶ 17,341 (1984); Santa Fe, Inc., VABCA No. 2168, 87-3 BCA ¶ 20,104 (1987).

[76] Gulf Contracting, Inc., ASBCA Nos. 30,195, 32,839, 33,867, 89-2 BCA ¶ 21,812 (1989).

[77] GSBCA No. 2432, 76-1 BCA ¶ 11,649 (1975).

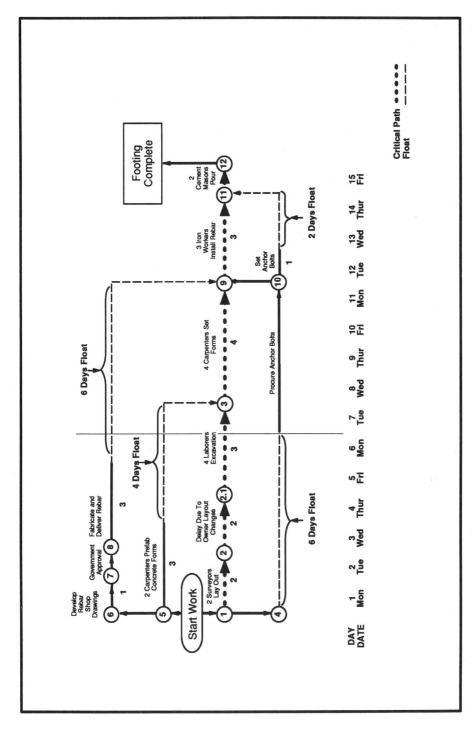

Figure 9–8. Contemporary evaluation of delays using update at day 6.

239

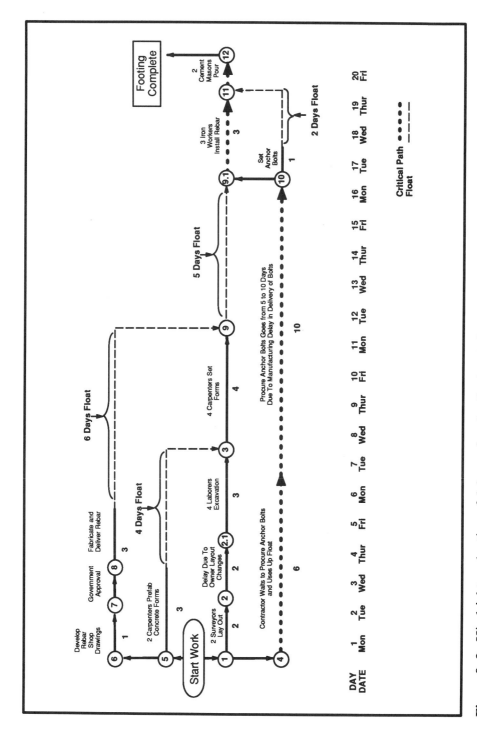

Figure 9–9. Hindsight evaluation of delays using the final as-built schedule.

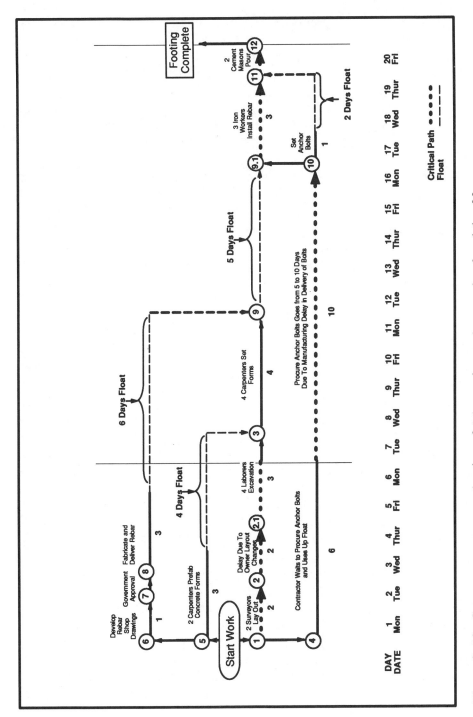

Figure 9–10. Contemporaneous evaluation of delays using updates at day 6 and day 20.

241

Finally, utilizing contemporaneous updates of the project on day six and day twenty, as detailed by comparison of **Figure 9–10** and **Figure 9–2**, would lead to the conclusion that the contractor is responsible for five days of delay, while the owner is responsible for two days.

§ 9.16 —Recognition of Float as Expiring Resource Available to All Parties

One of the most significant developments during the 1970s and 1980s has been the clear recognition that float is an expiring resource available to all parties working on the project.

Float, as described previously, is the excess time contained on side path activities (not on the critical path). Float is important because it allows a contractor to shift resources from an activity with float to apply pressure to an activity on the critical path that is behind schedule and delaying the project. The float time permits the contractor to subsequently return to the noncritical activity and complete it on time.

Government delays to a noncritical activity that expend all of the float time and impact the critical path entitle a contractor to increased costs for extended duration. The matter becomes more complex when different types of delay to noncritical activities expend all of the float and subsequently delay the entire project. For example, if an activity that has 20 days of float is delayed 30 days, the entire project will be delayed by 10 days. However, when the 30-day delay includes 10 days of contractor delay, 10 days of excusable delay, and 10 days of owner delay, it is unclear whether the contractor is entitled to recover for the 10-day delay to the project. When the contractor delay occurs first, excusable delay second, and the owner delay third, recovery for the 10 days delay is likely because the owner delay forced the noncritical activity onto the critical path. When the contractor delay occurs last and pushes the activity onto the critical path, the opposite result is likely. See **Figures 9–11** through **9–15** for examples of the various delay relationships.

The original 1974 Wickwire & Smith article,[78] in considering the rights of the various parties to benefits of float time, asserted that the contractor should be awarded her increased duration costs even where, as in the example above, the contractor delay occurred last. The article looked to *Joseph E. Bennett,*[79] in which the board noted that float provides the project manager with latitude in scheduling the noncritical activities to effect resource trade-offs, to decrease costs, or to shorten the length of the project.

---

[78] Wickwire & Smith, *The Use of Critical Path Method Techniques in Contract Claims,* 7 Pub. Cont. L.J. (1974).

[79] GSBCA No. 2362, 72-1 BCA ¶ 9364, at 43,467 (1972).

PLAN

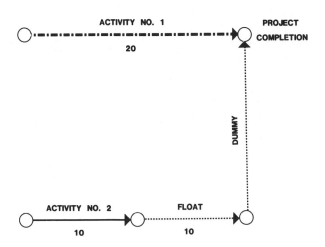

ACTUAL

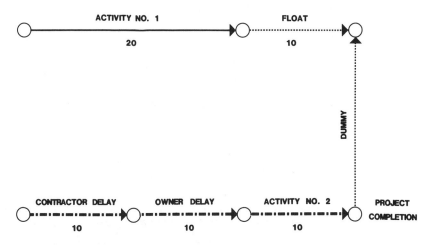

Figure 9–11. Effect of owner delay occurring last.

PLAN

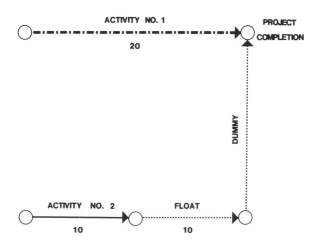

ACTUAL

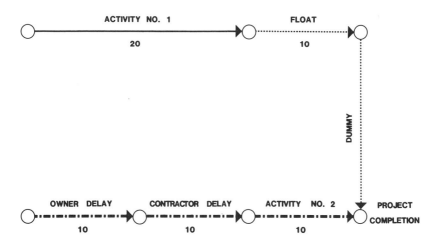

Figure 9–12. Effect of contractor delay occurring last.

PLAN

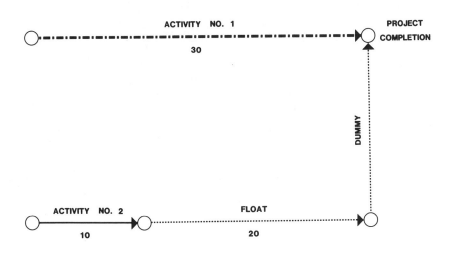

ACTUAL

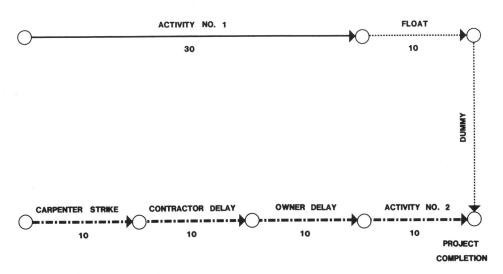

Figure 9–13. Effect of owner delay occurring last.

PLAN

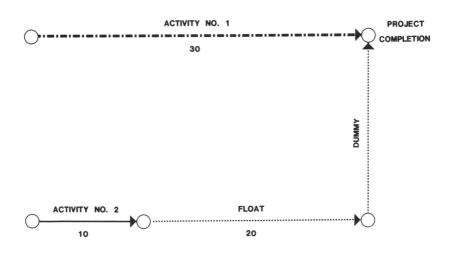

ACTUAL

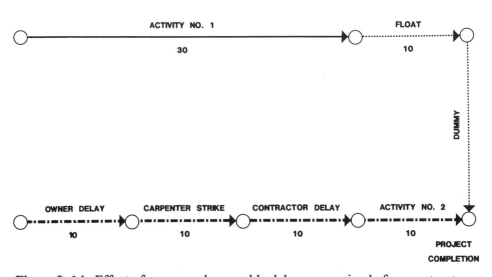

Figure 9–14. Effect of owner and excusable delays occurring before contractor delay.

PLAN

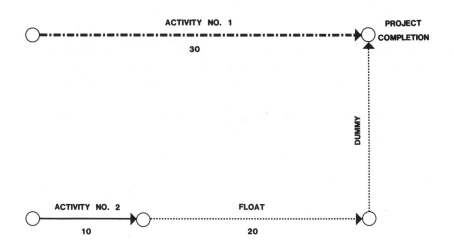

ACTUAL

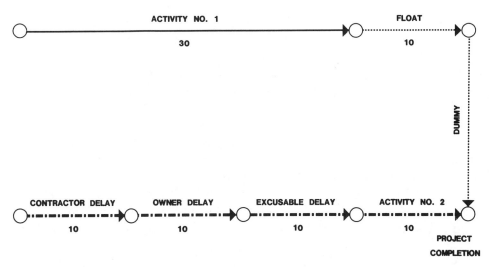

Figure 9–15. Effect of contractor and owner delays occurring before excusable delay.

Because this case authority recognized that the contractor is entitled to schedule the work and that float time is a resource used in scheduling the work, the article suggested that the contractor was entitled to benefit from the float.

Today, managers or executors of projects (usually the contractors) no longer have exclusive use of the float resource. Almost all significant public procurements include contract clauses providing that the float is not for the exclusive benefit of any one party to the project. Typically, no time extensions are allowed until the float is exhausted on the activity in question. These clauses permit the individual who "gets to" the float first to gain the benefit of the float. This also makes good sense when the causation principle of proximate cause is considered (*see, e.g., Ealahan Electric Co.*).[80]

Under this view of float, if the owner delays a particular activity while float is available until the point that only five days of float remain and, thereafter, the contractor delays that activity for 60 days, the contractor is responsible for 55 days of delay to the project. Of course, if the contractor uses the float first and the owner then delays the activity to the point that it impacts the critical path and the project is delayed, the owner becomes responsible for the delays to the project and for damages.

Since 1974, decisions by the courts and boards have confirmed that the party who gets to the float first receives the benefit of the float (until the float is actually used up and the project is delayed). These decisions have included a 1975 GSBCA decision, *Dawson Construction Co.;*[81] a 1987 ASBCA decision, *Titan Pacific Construction Corp.;*[82] a 1990 District of Columbia Federal District Court decision, *Williams Enterprises, Inc. v. Strait Manufacturing & Welding, Inc.;*[83] a 1990 Department of Transportation BCA decision in *Ealahan Electric Co.;*[84] and a 1990 claims court decision, *Weaver-Bailey Contractors, Inc. v. United States.*[85]

In *Dawson Construction Co.,*[86] the contractor was denied a time extension even when the government had caused delays to certain activities on a project for construction of a vehicle maintenance facility. The contractor claimed that a government delay in settling a dispute over who should pay for construction of a hydraulic lift pit had caused delay during the allowed slack time for that activity. The board denied appellant's claim

---

[80] DOTBCA No. 1959, 90-3 BCA ¶ 23,177 (1990).

[81] GSBCA No. 3998, 75-2 BCA ¶ 11,563 (1975).

[82] ASBCA Nos. 24,148, 24,616, 26,692, 87-1 BCA ¶ 19,626 (1987).

[83] 728 F. Supp. 12 (D.D.C. 1990).

[84] 1990 DOTBCA No. 1959, 90-3 ¶ 23,177 (1990).

[85] 19 Cl. Ct. 474 (1990). *See also* Robglo, Inc., VABCA Nos. 2879, 2884, 1990 VABCA LEXIS 27 (Pubcon Library, VABCA file) (Oct. 30, 1990)).

[86] GSBCA No. 3998, 75-2 BCA ¶ 11,563 (1987).

because there was no evidence that the critical path for the project was affected by the delay to lift pit construction (because that activity contained sufficient float to absorb the delay).

Similarly, *Titan Pacific Construction Corp.*[87] recognized that the issue is not who utilizes the float, but who is responsible for delay that impacts activities on the critical path or for delays to activities to the point they become critical and impact the critical path. The board in *Titan* found that change orders were a basis for time extensions, even though activities impacted by changes were not originally on the critical path to completion. The board reasoned that since the allotted float time was expended, activities not originally on the critical path became critical to timely contract completion. The board held that when the change orders were issued the activities affected by the change had become critical.

In the *Williams Enterprises*[88] decision, the district court considered the argument by the structural steel subcontractor responsible for the steel collapse on the project that a delay in approving structural steel shop drawings, which occurred in the very first month of the project, presented a delay concurrent with that caused by the collapse, which occurred much later in the life of the project. The court described this particular argument as the assertion of precollapse issues and found that the owner's delays in approving shop drawings had no impact on the critical structural steel activities because the steel erection commenced on August 13, 1984, the date established for the commencement of structural steel activities in the schedule. The court stated:

> (12) It is obvious that the critical path delay occurred from the date of the collapse until the steel was re-erected. Williams did not deny that this did not occur, but rather asserted that other events created a "concurrent delay." To avoid confusion, particular care is required in use of the word "concurrent." For example, Williams does not assert that it was delayed by Smoot or any other party in its work in erection of structural steel. Williams began work on August 13, 1984, and continued unimpeded until the day of the collapse. Further, no argument is made that any party interfered with the re-erection work; that process was completed on or about January 30, 1985. Thus, this delay was of Williams' making.
>
> (13) Stated otherwise, Williams' defense of 'concurrency' was that other events canceled out the delay resulting from the collapse and therefore absolved Williams of liability. Williams' arguments are best analyzed by dividing the project into three distinct periods: (1) pre-collapse issues; (2) the immediate impact period (September 25, 1984 to January 30, 1985); and (3) post-January 30 events. The Court concludes that the arguments are not meritorious.

---

[87] ASBCA Nos. 24,148, 24,616, 26,692, 87-1 BCA ¶ 19,626 (1987).

[88] 728 F. Supp 12 (D.D.C. 1990).

1.

(14) Williams pointed to delays in the approval of shop drawings for structural steel and shop drawings for precast fabrication which occurred in the first months of the Project. Both Williams and Strait argued strenuously that a delay in approval of structural steel shop drawings presented a concurrency with the delay caused by the collapse.

[1] The testimony and evidence, however, is to the contrary. Structural steel erection could not begin until shop drawings had been completed and the structural erection began in fact on August 13, 1984. Williams continued unimpeded until the September 25 day of the collapse. Similarly, it is clear that any delays in approval of precast shop drawings had no impact on the beginning or performance of structural steel erection in the period prior to the collapse. Any delays of other parties prior to August 13 could not be charged to defendants. The Court finds that there was no 'concurrent' delay in this period.[89]

Further, in the *Ealahan Electric Co.*[90] decision, the Department of Transportation Board of Contract Appeals considered an argument, also presented by the defendants in the *Williams Enterprises*[91] decision, to the effect that certain delays that occurred in an earlier time frame in the project were the basis for offsetting concurrencies for delays encountered in later time frames of the project. The board found this attempt to move delays from one time frame to another to be invalid, stating in pertinent part:

> Certain of the delays caused by Ealahan occurred in an earlier time frame than the change orders issued by the Coast Guard. Such delays are not concurrent. Though Ealahan may have delayed completion by its actions early in the project, we find that these delays are independent of delays caused by the Coast Guard in a later time period. A contractor is entitled to a time extension for government-caused delays although it also has delayed performance, where such delays have occurred in a different time period than the government-caused delays, assuming the actions delayed the job completion.

Most significantly, the *Weaver-Bailey Contractors, Inc. v. United States*[92] decision in 1990 by the chief judge of the claims court removes any doubt that may have existed about the availability of float, as an expiring resource, to the parties to the project as long as they act in a reasonable manner. The court in this case totally rejected the government's argument that

---

[89] *Id.* at 16.

[90] 1990 DOTBCA No. 1959, 90-3 BCA ¶ 23,177 (1990).

[91] 728 F. Supp. 12 (D.D.C. 1990).

[92] 19 Cl. Ct. 474 (1990).

the contractor's failure to prosecute work during earlier time frames when float was available excused the government from its responsibilities for changes resulting from increases in excavation required later in the project, after the float had expired. The court provides us an insightful essay on the meaning of float:

> [A]s winter was approaching, plaintiff suddenly learned that the total amount of unclassified excavation it was required to perform was not 132,000 cy, but rather 186,695 cy.
>
> Plaintiff's planned work schedule was disrupted by the re-evaluation that the earthwork portion of the project had increased dramatically. Plaintiff was forced to concentrate its efforts on completing the earthwork, instead of grading and finishing the slopes and placing rip-rap. . . . [p]laintiff's project superintendent, gave uncontroverted testimony emphasizing that Weaver-Bailey could have completed the finishing operations in about a month, had the extra earthwork not been required. Once the winter weather set in, it was too late to do the final grading . . . .
>
> * * *
>
> [t]he conclusions . . . [the Government claims expert] draws from his critical path analyses reflect a misunderstanding of the concept of float time.
>
> To reiterate, a critical path activity is one which, if allowed to grow in duration at all, will cause the overall time required to complete the project to increase. By contrast, an activity with float time may grow in duration up to a certain point, without an adverse impact on the time required to complete the project. Consider the example of a contractor who committed himself to building a house, beginning on January 1, 1989. The contractor has determined that he will need one year to complete the job. Pouring the foundation is a critical path activity because any increase in the amount of time required to complete the foundation will cause an increase in the amount of time needed to complete the house; work on the walls, floors, roof, and utilities cannot begin until the foundation is complete.
>
> Suppose that as part of the job, the contractor promised to build a fence along two edges of the property, and that building the fence will take 20 days. No other work depends on the completion of the fence, so delaying work on the fence until December 11, 1989 will not put the contractor in danger of late completion. In other words, building the fence is an activity with a lot of float time. However, float time is never unlimited. If on December 20 the contractor has yet to begin the fence, or if there is more than 11 days' worth of fencing work to be done as of December 20, then the contractor will not finish the job on time. From the foregoing, one can make the following generalization: regardless of whether an activity is on the critical path of a project, if the time required to complete the activity is greater than the time remaining to complete the project, then project completion will be delayed.

Consider now the effect on our hypothetical contractor if on December 1, before fencing work had begun, the buyer of the house told the contractor that he would like all four sides of the property to be fenced, thereby doubling the fencing work. Clearly the contractor could not complete the entire project by the end of the year, but through no fault of his own. The time required for the fencing portion of the job is now 40 days, and the contractor has only 31 days left. Weaver-Bailey was in much the same position as our hypothetical contractor when it discovered in October that the unclassified excavation portion of the project had increased. It was progressing toward a late November or early December completion, until the work was increased by 41%.

* * *

The court does not see how Weaver-Bailey can be faulted for the way it handled the unclassified excavation. . . . Once the Corps' underestimate was revealed, Weaver-Bailey acted reasonably under the newly-imposed time constraints. Weaver-Bailey does not have unlimited resources, and it concentrated its manpower in the areas which it thought needed the earliest attention.[93]

In fact, what all the decisions above are telling us is that in CPM analyses for delays, fact finders must take the project as they find it at the time that the delay is occurring. Thus, if a delay occurs when the project still has significant float available on the activities delayed, no delay to the entire project is encountered and the party responsible for the delay is not going to be charged for extending the project duration. If, however, the delay pushes the activity onto the critical path and the entire project is extended, the party responsible for that particular delay will be held to have proximately caused delays to the project.

§ 9.17   —Demise of *Impacted As-Planned* Proof for Delays

A favorite device CPM experts presented throughout the 1960s, 70s, and 80s for asserting delay claims against owners was to take the as-planned or an adjusted as-planned CPM schedule for the project and impact that diagram or network solely by the acts and claims asserted to be the owner's responsibility. The "great lie" in such an analysis is that it fails to require the contractor to accept responsibility for her own delays and to give the owner credit for delays that might not be the responsibility of either the contractor or the owner, such as weather or strikes.

Recent landmark decisions, however, make it clear that such CPM analyses will not be acceptable in the 1990s. The three decisions that best

---

[93] *Id.* at 475, 481–82.

exemplify these principles are *Gulf Contracting, Inc.,*[94] *Titan Pacific Construction Corp. v. United States,*[95] and *Ealahan Electric Co.*[96]

The Armed Services Board of Contract Appeals first considered the *Gulf Contracting, Inc.*[97] in 1989. The dispute in question concerned the construction of a barracks complex for Fort Gordon, Georgia. The contractor's CPM expert provided a CPM presentation for the project that compared a reconstructed as-planned schedule with an as-built schedule and then, in an adjusted CPM schedule, reduced the durations of the actual time taken for concrete and masonry work to those of the fastest concrete and masonry durations experienced in construction. In analyzing the impact of the owner changes to the project, the contractor's expert excluded all contractor disruptions from the project analysis. The analysis by the contractor's expert contrasted with the analysis by the government expert, which utilized a chronological approach starting with the reasonable as-planned schedule and moving forward through the project chronologically incorporating the time impacts that occurred. In the government expert's CPM analysis, once a time impact was identified the original schedule dates were revised to create an adjusted schedule incorporating the time impact. The adjusted schedule was then revised to incorporate the next chronological time impact. Thereafter, the project schedule was periodically updated to incorporate the new time impacts.

In making its 1989 decision in *Gulf Contracting, Inc.*[98] the board accepted the presentation of the government expert and totally rejected the impacted analysis performed by the contractor's expert. The board stated:

> In support of its claim, Gulf relied on the analysis of its expert, Vinson. Vinson claimed to have performed an in-depth review of all correspondence and data pertinent to the progress of the project (finding 81). If this was indeed the case, we do not believe that Vinson could have missed the well documented performance problems that existed between Gulf and Hughes. Vinson said that he was instructed to 'exclude other disruptions from the claim' (finding 92). We have found that Vinson's analysis systematically excluded all delays and disruptions except those allegedly caused by the Government (finding 92). We conclude that his analysis was inherently biased, and could lead to but one predictable outcome. For our

---

[94] ASBCA Nos. 30,195, 32,839, 33,867, 89-2 BCA ¶ 21,812 (1989).

[95] 17 Cl. Ct. 630 (1989).

[96] 1990 DOTBCA No. 1959, 90-3 BCA ¶ 23,177 (1990). The only decision in recent times that recognizes any possibility of using an impacted as-planned schedule for delay assessment is Turner Constr. Co., ASBCA No. 25,447, 90-2 BCA ¶ 22,649, at 113, 737–742. However, this 217-page decision is not clear about whether the board accepted an impacted as-planned schedule or the delay analysis based on actual historical durations.

[97] ASBCA Nos. 30,195, 32,839, 33,867, 89-2 BCA ¶ 22,812 (1989).

[98] *Id.*

purposes therefore, we deem Vinson's analysis to be totally unreliable. To be credible, a contractor's CPM analysis ought to take into account, and give appropriate credit for all of the delays which were alleged to have occurred. *Haney v. United States* [30 CCF ¶ 70,189], 676 F.2d 584 (Ct. Cl. 1982); *Pathman Construction Co.,* ASBCA No. 23392, 85-2 BCA ¶ 18,096 (CPM analysis with 'built-in bias' rejected).[99]

Further, on reconsideration in *Gulf Contracting, Inc.,*[100] the ASBCA again reaffirmed its rejection of the contractor's analysis and noted that the contractor must take full responsibility for all its faults during performance. The board stated:

> We believe Vinson was fully capable of analyzing the well documented delays and disruptions caused by Gulf and Hughes, and to compare them, toe to toe, with the delays and disruptions said to have been caused by the Quad-T welding sequence change. Vinson, however, chose to avoid scrutiny of the contractor's acknowledged problems by hiding behind what he called the 'model barracks' approach. For purposes of computer analysis, this approach reduced the actual durations of the concrete and masonry work to those of the fastest actual concrete and masonry durations experienced in constructing the 'A' and 'B' barracks (see finding 87).
>
> Gulf argued that the model barracks approach assessed "to the contractor the maximum amount of cost and time that could be associated with those other problems." That might well be the case. But it did not eliminate the possibility that even in using the fastest actual construction time, appropriate credit had not been given to all contractor-caused delays and disruptions. More plausible would have been for Vinson to assess against Gulf the longest masonry and concrete durations for each barracks. It was easy to gloss over Gulf's and Hughes' problems by shifting the focus to the contractor's best performance model, but we must be persuaded that Gulf has taken full responsibility for its faults, and that the Government was only being asked to pay for what was its responsibility.[101]

In contrast to the board position on the *Vinson* analysis was the specific willingness of the board of contract appeals in *Gulf* to accept proper CPM methodology as provided by the government expert in evaluating the delays to the project as they occurred chronologically, commencing with the as-planned schedule and then moving forward to evaluate each delay through the various project updates as they were occurring.

The *Titan Pacific Construction Corp. v. United States*[102] claims court decision concerned a Naval contract for the relocation of ordinance facilities

---

[99] *Id.* at 109, 758–759.

[100] ASBCA Nos. 30,195, 32,839, 33,867, 90-1 BCA ¶ 22,393 (1989).

[101] *Id.* 90-1 BCA ¶ 22,393, at 112,521.

[102] 17. Cl. Ct. 630 (1989).

in Washington state. The work involved the construction of several new buildings and a reservoir and extensive roadwork and earthwork. The work was to be performed in three phases. The contractor, at the inception of performance, provided the owner with an as-planned CPM, which was then corrected and approved. The contractor, in its presentation to the board of contract appeals, attempted to avoid the effect of liquidated damages that had been assessed against its performance. In its presentation, the contractor sought to substantially revise the as-planned schedule for wet- and dry-season restraints to provide a much later projected completion date. In addition, in providing the analysis of the impact of delays upon the approved as-planned schedule, or the adjusted as-planned schedule, for what the expert described as "like-time" analysis, the contractor's expert totally failed to take into account the actual activities occurring on the project and the contractor's responsibility for the durations of the activities. The claims court decision stated the following:

> Plaintiff's 'like-time' argument assumes that the final approved as-planned CPM network delineates procedures that are fixed and contractually binding without regard to actual operations on the project. The approved CPM network diagram is an administrative tool that is useful in organizing and directing work, reporting progress, and for requesting progress payments for work accomplished. Analyses made after project completion, however, that make adjustments to attain new and revised projected scheduling depend on theoretical contingencies. They are of limited value.

> Plaintiff's delay/impact claims expert did not present a comparison of either the October 17, 1977, as-planned schedule, or his as-planned schedule adjusted for wet and dry season restraints, with actual activities on the project—the as-built schedule. The Board had before it the records that reflect actual field operations and was in a position to relate the as-built schedule to the expert's theoretically adjusted as-planned schedule.

> * * *

> Plaintiff's calculations in application of its 'like-time' theory disregard the facts found by the Board as to the sequence of work, the quality of work, and the effects of weather on the Phase III work in the years 1977, 1978 and 1979. The calculations reflect a theoretical application to a CPM as-planned schedule that was not intended to be followed. The calculations disregard the facts that actually existed in the on-site operations.[103]

Finally, in the recent *Ealahan Electric Co.*[104] decision, the Department of Transportation Board of Contract Appeals rejected the CPM analyses of both the government CPM expert and the contractor. This particular project concerned a contract to renovate an existing facility at the Coast

---

[103] *Id.* at 637–38.
[104] 1990 DOTBCA No. 1959, 90-3 BCA ¶ 23,177 (1990).

Guard Montauk Station. In this case, the contractor's expert did not consider *Ealahan's* actual performance in the development of its analysis. As stated by the board:

> Rather, he solely considered the impact of various change orders on Ealahan's completion schedule, without regard to the actual performance of appellant of the original contract work. (Tr. 195) In other words, this witness took the critical activities from Ealahan's progress schedule and added the time it actually took Ealahan to perform the Coast Guard change, beginning with the date of each request for proposal. (Tr. 133) According to appellant, by using this method the appellant would retain the benefit of any float built into the original schedule. This method did not take into account Ealahan's own delays during performance.

The board also rejected the analysis of the government expert because of similar deficiencies. Like the contractor, the owner failed to consider the impact of the client's delays to the project. The board stated:

> We reject the analysis of both appellant's and respondent's experts. Mr. Stoker, for appellant, failed to consider the impact of Ealahan's own delays on the completion date. This must be considered as Ealahan is not entitled to a time extension if it delayed performance during the same period of time that Coast Guard actions delayed work. Mr. Beach's analysis is rejected because his analysis failed to consider the impact of the Coast Guard changes on actual performance.

The trend in the law to disregard impacted as planned CPM analysis as a basis for measuring delays is logical and well founded, specifically in connection with impacted as-planned CPM analyses used to answer the question (at least on each monthly update) "When would the contractor have finished absent (*but for*) the owner delays?" As detailed later, the *but for* standard is alive and well.

§ 9.18   —Key Issues Involving Concurrent Delay and Extended Duration Claims

Two basic questions are of great significance to the whole issue of concurrent delays:

First: Must the contractor satisfy the same standard to establish the right to time extensions (thereby avoiding liquidated damages) as that required to prove an extended duration claim? (*Extended duration claim* here refers to a contractor's affirmative claim for delay costs.)

Second, concerning the evaluation of concurrent delays: What developments have occurred with respect to the willingness of courts and boards to apportion concurrent delays between the parties utilizing CPM principles?

Four recent decisions address the differences in proof between time extension and extended duration claims. These decisions indicate there is a difference in the proof required.

In *Cline Construction Co.,*[105] the board, in discussing the effect of concurrent delays, noted:

> Concurrent delay does not bar extensions of time, but it does bar monetary compensation for daily fixed overhead costs of the type claimed by Cline because such costs would be incurred on account of the concurrent delay even if the Government-responsible delay had not occurred. *Commerce International Co. v. United States* [9 CCF ¶ 72,781], 167 Ct. Cl. 529, 338 F.2d 81 (1964). . . . Cline has presented no evidence that those segments of the work which were delayed by the Government-responsible causes cost more to perform in a later period than they would have cost if performed at the time originally schedule. . . .[106]

In *Titan Pacific Construction Corp.,*[107] the board, in evaluating the record regarding various delays, stated:

> Although our findings establish that appellant incurred many delays through its own fault and that of its subcontractors which prevented it from completing Phase II until 30 October 1978 . . . they also establish that the Government contributed to the delays by issuing change orders, modifying Phase II requirements, as late as 20 July 1978, . . . 31 August, 1978, . . . 20 September 1978, . . . and 19 October 1978. . . .
>
> Under those circumstances, the delays are not compensable so as to entitled appellant to delay damages therefore, but the Government's actions relieve appellant from liability for liquidated damages. *Myers-Laine Corporation,* ASBCA No. 18234, 74-1 BCA ¶ 10,467. Consequently, the Government's assessment of liquidated damages amounting to $8,787 for Phase II was improper and must be set aside.[108]

Similarly, in *Utley-James, Inc.,*[109] the board noted:

> A delay for which the Government is responsible is excusable by definition, and it may also be compensable. The rule is that for a delay to be compensable under either the Changes clause or the Suspension of Work clause, it

---

[105] ASBCA No. 28,600, 84-3 BCA ¶ 17,594 (1984).

[106] *Id.* at 106.

[107] ASBCA Nos. 24,148, 24,616, 26,692, 87-1 BCA ¶ 19,626 (1987).

[108] *Id.* at 99,353.

[109] GSBCA No. 5370, 85-1 BCA ¶ 17,816 (1984), *aff'd,* Utley-James, Inc. v. United States, 14 Cl. Ct. 804 (1988).

must result solely from the Government's action. . . . If a period of delay can be attributed simultaneously to the actions of both the Government and the contractor, there are said to be concurrent delays, and the result is an excusable but not a compensable delay. . . .[110]

Consequently, for purposes of establishing entitlement to a time extension, a contractor need only demonstrate that concurrent causes of delay resulted in a specific amount of delays to project completion. The contractor need not demonstrate that project completion would have occurred earlier than actual completion but for the government's actions.

The distinction in the differences in proof required for time extensions and for extended duration claims was again confirmed in 1989 by the decision of the General Services Board of Contract Appeals in *Freeman-Darling, Inc.*[111] This case, which concerned a remodeling contract for a United States Customs Service Facility, addressed the issues of an extended duration claim on the part of the contractor and the assessment of liquidated damages on the part of the owner. In finding that the contractor was not entitled to recovery for extended duration expense, but was still entitled to remission of liquidated damages, the board stated:

> That delay was concurrent with delays due to changes and strikes. The law is well settled that where both parties contribute to the delay neither can recover damages, unless there is clear evidence by which we can apportion the delay and the expense attributable to each party. *Blinderman Construction Co. v. United States,* [30 CCF ¶ 70,619], 695 F.2d 552, 559 (Fed. Cir. 1982); *Active Fire Sprinkler Corp.,* GSBCA No. 5461, 85-1 BCA ¶ 17,868, at 89,484 (1984). Since no method is apparent for apportioning the delays, appellant may not recover increased costs for the period of June 25 to August 2, 1982. Correspondingly, for purposes of liquidated damages, appellant must be credited with an extension equal to the delay that occurred during that period.[112]

A number of cases provide guidance on how courts and boards treat the use of CPM techniques to prove apportionment or nonapportionment of concurrent delays. *John Murphy Construction Co.*[113] reflects the traditional unwillingness of the courts and boards to apportion concurrent delays. However, this decision involved a project where CPM was not specified. Further, the issue presented to the board was whether the contractor would be entitled to recovery from the government. In denying recovery, the board refused to apportion concurrent delays where the

---

[110] Utley-James, Inc., GSBCA No. 5370, 85-1 BCA ¶ 17,816, at 89,109 (1984) (citations omitted).

[111] GSBCA No. 7112, 89-2 BCA ¶ 21,882 (1989).

[112] *Id.* at 110, 100.

[113] AGBCA No. 418, 79-1 BCA ¶ 13,836 (1979).

contractor was responsible for concurrent delays affecting work in the orderly sequence of events necessary to timely completion of the contract.[114] In another 1990 decision, *Industrial Constructors Corp.,*[115] the board made it clear that the lack of proper CPM evidence caused its inability to apportion delays.

In addition, a number of examples exist where CPM network analysis systems have been used in analyzing concurrent delays. In *Santa Fe, Inc.,*[116] the board advises that to excuse the contractor from the assessment of liquidated damages she must clearly establish that the concurrent owner delay affected the critical path. After noting that the contractor accepted responsibility for a major portion of the delay in completion, the board questioned whether the government contributed to the contractor's delayed performance by using change orders, thereby forfeiting all or part of its right to assess liquidated damages. The board upheld the assessment when it concluded that the contractor had failed to prove any impact on the contract completion date because the CPM presentation showed that there was sufficient float time available to absorb the delays.[117] In doing so, the board relied primarily on the following quote from the decision in *Blackhawk Heating & Plumbing Co.,*[118] where the board upheld an assessment of liquidated damages after concluding that the late contract completion was attributable to contractor delays:

> The rule has been applied by this Board in situations where it was difficult to apportion responsibilities for delay as between the parties; and, too, the record did not disclose whether or not the delays were critical to project completion. Since liquidated damages are only imposed for delays in project completion, it is manifest that only those delays should be considered which actually affect project completion. By their nature the delayed activities involved must necessarily lie on the critical path as it was actually completed. In terms of the concurrent delay rule then, the concurrent delay must pertain to activities whose completion was critical to completion of the project itself. Appellant cannot successfully urge, as it apparently seeks to do, that because critical contractor-caused delays . . . were concurrent with noncritical Government delays . . . the imposition of liquidated damages may be avoided. Relief from the imposition of liquidated damages must depend upon showing concurrent delay in respect to activities on the critical path.[119]

---

[114] *Id.* at 67,874.

[115] AGBCA No. 84-248-1, 90-2 BCA ¶ 22,767 (1990).

[116] VABCA Nos. 1943–1946, 84-2 BCA ¶ 17,341 (1984).

[117] *Id.* at 86,411.

[118] GSBCA No. 2432, 76-1 BCA ¶ 11,649 (1975), *on reconsideration,* 75-1 BCA ¶ 11,261 (1975).

[119] *Id.* at 55,579 (citations omitted).

In *Williams Enterprises, Inc. v. Strait Manufacturing & Welding, Inc.,*[120] the court considered strenuous claims by the structural steel subcontractor, who had been responsible for a collapse in the steel erection process, that a concurrent delay had been presented by the delay in the approval of shop drawings for the structural steel and precast fabrication. Here the district court, in a clear decision apportioning the delay responsibility between the parties, found that the delays in the approval of the shop drawings for the structural steel had occurred in the first few months of the project and that these delays had not affected the project critical path during the later period when the critical path was actually delayed by the steel collapse.

In *H&S Corp.,*[121] the Armed Services Board of Contract Appeals apportioned alleged concurrent delays between the parties arising out of the construction of a Naval Container Operation Facility. Like the decision in *Williams Enterprises,*[122] the board found that one party's allegation of concurrent delay was no defense to a claim by the other party, since the alleged concurrent delay did not indeed affect the critical path of the project. In the case of the *H&S*[123] decision, the government was the party asserting the concurrent delay as a defense. In denying this defense, the board stated:

> Turning first to the concurrent delay issue, we agree with the Government that a contractor-caused delay affecting the construction of the footings would have a significant effect on this contract's critical path. The overwhelming flaw in the Government's concurrent delay argument, however, resides in the premise that appellant's failure to gain approval of the building system caused the delay.
>
> * * *
>
> The Government cannot, from these facts, construct a scenario in which the very real delay caused by the unsuitable soil and additional earth work is nullified by the time it took to resolve the building load error. This failure proves fatal to the Government's defense. "The defense of concurrent delay is valid only when applied to an actually established delay, not merely an alleged delay." *Essential Construction Company, Inc. and Himount Constructors, Ltd., A Joint Venture,* ASBCA No. 18706, 82-2 BCA ¶ 16,906 at 84,114.[124]

---

[120] 728 F. Supp. 12 (D.D.C. 1990).

[121] ASBCA No. 29,688, 89-3 BCA ¶ 22,209 (1989).

[122] 728 F. Supp. 12 (D.D.C. 1990).

[123] ASBCA No. 29,688, 89-3 BCA ¶ 22,209 (1989).

[124] *Id.* at 111,720–721.

The 1990 *Sierra Blanca, Inc.*[125] decision also provides a clear example of apportionment between contractor and owner of concurrent delays using critical path principles:

> The issue before us is whether or not appellant is entitled to the day-for-day delay of the 184 days it contends it experienced or to some lesser amount as a result of concurrent delays attributable to other non-Government responsible causes.
>
> * * *
>
> Since appellant began work on the critical metal deck forty eight days late, any extension of the contract completion date must take this into account.[126]

In *Utley-James, Inc.,*[127] the board demonstrated a willingness to apportion or discriminate between concurrent delays to determine the actual delays to the critical path. The board specified the finder of fact should not assess the contractor with responsibility for delays that would not have affected the critical path, because such delays fall within the category of "Why hurry up and wait?" Consider the following passage:

> [S]trictly speaking, there can be but a single delay over a given period of time, and when that delay has multiple, indivisible causes, it is attributable not to either party but to both. Hence it would probably be more accurate to speak not of concurrent delays but of a single delay with concurrent causes. We note this even though, for convenience, we will use the standard terminology for the most part.
>
> When venturing into this area, we must be wary of deciding too readily that there was a concurrent delay. We considered this issue in *Warwick Construction, . . .* and concluded that, at the very least, we would not require a contractor claiming a compensable delay to prove that in the absence of the Government's delaying actions, it would have completed the job on schedule. However, we also adverted to *Warwick, id.,* to the basic principle of *Wunderlich Contracting Co. . . .* which requires that a contractor seeking compensation establish "the fundamental facts of liability, causation, and resulting injury." That, we said, "has always been the law," and we adhere to it in this appeal as we have in the past.
>
> The lesson of *Warwick* is that certain kinds of second-guessing are proscribed. To take an easy example, if the job schedule was originally such that the contractor needed certain widgets on hand by January 1, but because of a six-month delay attributable to the Government, the contractor rescheduled the delivery for July 1, the Government cannot be heard to say

---

[125] ASBCA 32,161, 33,333, 33,336–337, 33,555, 90-2 BCA ¶ 22,846 (1990).

[126] *Id.* at 114,728–729.

[127] GSBCA No. 5370, 85-1 BCA ¶ 17,816 (1984).

the delays were concurrent because the contractor would have had to wait six months for the widgets anyway. In such a situation there is no reason to doubt that the contractor could have had the widgets on January 1 and proceeded on schedule absent the Government-caused delay. Such a simplistic example poses no problem at all. The problem lies not in reaching the right conclusion, given such an example, but in determining whether a given fact situation is an example of such an occurrence or is instead an example of a true concurrent delay.[128]

Based on *Utley-James,*[129] when the owner causes delays to the critical path, it is permissible for the contractor to relax its performance of non-critical work to the extent that it does not impact project completion (and still avoid the defense of concurrent delay). This concept is the same basic principle as that represented in *Weaver-Bailey Contractors, Inc. v. United States,*[130] the landmark claims court decision on float in which the court found that the contractor had the right to plan its work in accordance with its own plans or reasonable resource usage (regardless of the fact that this utilized float).

§ 9.19   —*But For* Test for Extended Duration Claims

Canon Construction Corp.[131] provides a clear and logical exposition of the methods used to prove an extended duration claim. The board in *Canon* required a determination of the actual date of work completion. The board then compared this date with the date the contractor would have completed the contract work, *but for* the delays that were the responsibility of the owner. The difference, of course, represented the compensable period.

Since the *Canon*[132] decision, other authority indicates that a concurrent delay will not foreclose the contractor from recovering delay damages when the concurrent contractor delay does not affect the critical path. In *Fischbach & Moore International Corp.,*[133] the board stated:

> We take no issue with the application of the *Commerce* rule to the facts of this case insofar as the concurrent delays for which appellant is responsible affected work in the critical path to timely completion of the contract.

---

[128] *Id.* at 89,109 (footnotes omitted).

[129] GSBCA No. 5370, 85-1 BCA ¶ 17,816 (1984).

[130] 19 Cl. Ct. 474 (1990).

[131] ASBCA No. 16,142, 72-1 BCA ¶ 9404 (1972).

[132] *Id.*

[133] ASBCA No. 18,146, 77-1 BCA ¶ 12,300 (1976).

If the concurrent delays affected only work that was not in the critical path, however, they are not delays within the meaning of the rule since timely completion of the contract was not thereby prevented.

With regard to the alleged intertwining of Government-caused and concurrent delays in this case, we have found, in the critical path analysis offered by appellant, a ready and reasonable basis for segregating the delays. If the delays can be segregated, responsibility therefor may be allocated to the parties. . . . And if there is no basis in the record on which to make a precise allocation of the responsibility, an estimated allocation may be made in the nature of a jury verdict. . . . The seemingly contrary result in *Commerce* is explained by the fact that the Court was unable, on the record in that case, to separate delays for which the Government was not responsible from those for which it was. . . . As will be seen in the discussion that follows, we have no such difficulty in the present case.[134]

Courts and boards have consistently held that only delays to the critical path should be considered. This raises a question about whether a contractor must give credit back for contractor delays that would have delayed the project but for owner actions. The board in *Fischbach & Moore*[135] applied the same reasoning used in *Canon*[136] and reiterated the proposition that the contractor cannot recover unless it proves that such costs would not have been incurred *but for* the government action: "It is axiomatic that a contractor asserting a claim against the Government must prove not only that it incurred the additional costs making up its claim but also that such costs would not have been incurred *but for* Government action."[137]

Recent authority supports the proposition that it is the contractor's responsibility to return credit for any claim of compensable time for noncompensable delays, such as strikes or weather, that would have otherwise delayed the project.[138] The *but for* principle recognized by *Canon*[139] and *Fischbach & Moore*[140] was again reaffirmed in *John Murphy Construction Co.,*[141] in which the board stated:

Conversely, it does not appear from the record that but for the Government caused delays Appellant could have completed the work by December 13. It is concluded, therefore, that despite the delays caused by the Government the record establishes that from the time scheduled for commencement of the

---

[134] *Id.* at 59,224 (citations omitted).

[135] ASBCA No. 18,146, 77-1 BCA ¶ 12,300 (1976).

[136] ASBCA No. 16,142, 72-1 BCA ¶ 9404 (1972).

[137] *Id.* at 59,224.

[138] *See, e.g.,* Haney v. United States, 230 Ct. Cl. 148, 167–68, 676 F.2d 584, 595–96 (1982).

[139] ASBCA No. 16,142, 72-1 BCA ¶ 9404 (1972).

[140] ASBCA No. 18,146, 77-1 BCA ¶ 12,300 (1976).

[141] AGBCA No. 418, 79-1 BCA ¶ 13,836 (1979).

project, Appellant was at least concurrently responsible for the delay in the process of the work. Appellant must bear the responsibility for the consequences of his search for a less costly source of water and the manner in which he chose to sequence and perform the work. . . .

In this case, the concurrent delays for which Appellant was responsible affected the work in the orderly sequence of events necessary to timely completion of the contract. Although no critical path method of scheduling was called out in the contract, decisions involving such critical path scheduling would appear to be analogous and therefore applicable. *Fischbach & Moore International Corp.,* ASBCA No. 18146, 77-1 BCA ¶ 12,300. The Board there said:

> It is axiomatic that a contractor asserting a claim against the Government must prove not only that it incurred the additional costs making up its claim but also that such costs would not have been incurred but for Government action.[142]

§ 9.20 —Acceptance of Buy-Back Time and Sequence Changes

The courts and boards recognize that a contractor experiencing delay to the critical path may overcome that delay or totally obviate it by additional manloading of equipment, by overtime, or by performing sequence changes. In other words, the contractor can *buy back* the lost time through acceleration of work or by achieving better efficiency than anticipated and completing subsequent activities on the critical path in shorter durations than those originally planned.[143]

In addition, many of the specifications in use today, such as the Veterans Administration's master network analysis specification (**Appendix D**) and the Corps of Engineers specifications,[144] require contractors to calculate on monthly updates time lost or gained on the critical path. Accordingly, contractors will normally receive the benefit of time they gain on the critical path to overcome the effect of prior delays to the critical path or to allow completion of the project earlier than detailed on the original critical path for the project. The right of the contractor to complete early (in accordance with CPM analyses) and receive compensation when such early completion is foreclosed is detailed in § **9.22**. The monthly evaluation of gains and losses as events occur on the critical path and the responsibility for such delays were also acknowledged by a 1984 article.[145]

---

[142] *Id.* at 67,874.

[143] *See* Utley-James, Inc., GSBCA No. 5370, 85-1 BCA ¶ 17,816, at 89,060–062 (1984).

[144] *See, e.g.,* Corps of Engineers *Contractor Prepared Network Analysis System* clause, ER 1-1-11, app. A, ¶ (e) (1985).

[145] *See* Nielsen & Galloway, *Proof Development for Construction Litigation,* 7 Am. J. Trial Advoc. 433, 444–45 (1984).

Board authority that has recognized the concept of buy-back time includes *Dawson Construction Co.,*[146] in which the board implicitly recognized the contractor's ability to buy back time and receive time extensions for delay even when the contractor modifies the sequence to avoid impact on the critical path.[147]

§ 9.21   —Denial of Automatic Time Extensions for Changes after Completion Date

The objective of CPM analysis is to segregate delays that delay the critical path and, therefore, the entire project. As of 1974, however, cases concerning time extensions for change orders issued subsequent to the contract completion date appeared to conflict with this reasoning.[148] Those decisions held that change orders issued after the original completion date automatically entitle the contractor to a time extension for the entire contract to the date when the additional work was completed or reasonably should have been completed. The extensions on these cases were granted without any regard to the cause of the delay in the original contract work. Current authority applying CPM analyses to discriminate between delays that affect the critical path and those that do not indicates that those decisions are no longer valid.[149]

The argument typically asserted by the contractor in addressing the issue of delays to chains of activities extending after the completion date is that any activities showing negative float are critical, because by definition they will delay the project past the contract completion date. This view of negative float activities, however, fails to acknowledge that there is still a critical path represented by the negative slack activities with the highest numerical designation (for example, −180 days versus −50 days). The activity chain representing the highest negative slack (for example, the −180 days) represents the longest chain of activities through the project in terms of time. This view is consistent with some of the earliest network analysis materials. For example, in the 1962 *NASA PERT & Companion Cost Guide,*[150] the critical path was defined as "[t]he particular sequence of activities in a network that comprise the most rigorous time constraint in the accomplishment of the end event. The path with the smallest amount of positive slack or largest amount of negative slack."

---

[146] GSBCA No. 3998, 75-2 BCA ¶ 11,563 (1975).

[147] *Id.* at 55,200, 55,202.

[148] Wickwire & Smith, *The Use of Critical Path Method Techniques in Contract Claims,* 7 Pub. Cont. L.J. 1, 42–43 (1974) (citing Jan R. Smith, Contractor, FAACAP 66-21, 65-2 BCA ¶ 5306 (1966) and cases cited therein).

[149] *See* Santa Fe, Inc., VABCA Nos. 1943–1946, 84-2 BCA ¶ 17,341 (1984).

[150] At A-1 (Oct. 30, 1962).

The issue of delays to activities with negative float was considered in the 1984 *Santa Fe, Inc.*[151] decision, where the contractor asserted that any work sequence or CPM path of activities that runs past the contractually required completion date is critical and delays on these work sequences due to changes are on the critical path.

The contractor argued that the impact of changes or unchanged work cannot be demonstrated by regular CPM rules because "all uncompleted work becomes negative and therefore critical once the scheduled completion date has been reached."[152]

In rejecting the contractor's assertion that changes issued after the scheduled completion date automatically entitled it to a time extension, the board noted that delays that do not affect the extended and predicted contract completion dates, shown by the critical path in the network, should not be the basis for a change to the contract completion date. The board stated:

> . . . a close examination of . . . cases cited by Appellant reveals that the important issue is not when the change order was issued, but the impact that change had on the completion of the project.
>
> In this connection see *Electronic & Missile Facilities, Inc.*, GSBCA No. 2787, 71-1 BCA ¶ 8785 where the Board said at 40,809–810:
>
> > It is our view that where a change is ordered the extension of time for completion is measured by the amount of delay attributable to the change, whether the change is ordered before or after the original contract completion date. *M.S.I. Corporation*, VACAB 626, 68-1 BCA ¶ 6773. . . .[153]

Santa Fe, Inc.[154] may not apply to all cases because of the peculiar language in the *Santa Fe* contract requiring that the delay analyses show that the "predicted" completion date was delayed. This naturally would represent the chain of activities with the highest negative slack. However, *Santa Fe*[155] appears to represent a logical extension of the use of network analysis systems to isolate delays affecting the critical path for the project. That a project extends beyond the contract completion date does not mean that the longest chain of activities through the network in terms of time and the delays that affect that chain cannot be determined.

---

[151] VABCA Nos. 1943–1946, 84-2 BCA ¶ 17,341 (1984).

[152] *Id.* at 86,408.

[153] *Id.* at 86,411.

[154] VABCA Nos. 1943–1946, 84-2 BCA ¶ 17,341 (1984).

[155] *Id.*

§ 9.22   —Using CPM to Establish
Early Completion Claims

When an owner prevents early completion, a contractor can use a CPM presentation to seek and recover additional compensation. A number of recent cases illustrate the trend of authority in this area.

In *Montgomery-Ross-Fisher, Inc.,*[156] the fact that a contractor completed the project within the contract period did not invalidate its delay claim. The contractor argued that it could have completed the project early, but for government delays. The Postal Service board held in favor of the contractor, finding that changes had impacted on the contractor's right to complete early. The board noted that the contractor's CPM expert was more credible than the government's and that the government expert had relied upon erroneous data.

In *Green Builders, Inc.,*[157] the contract required completion within one year. The contractor, in developing the CPM schedule, anticipated completion within seven months and based its bid on the early completion schedule. Redesign delayed completion of the project until three months after the contractor's projected completion date—two months before the contractual completion date. The contracting officer denied the claim because the project was completed before the contract completion date. The board found that the contractor had a right to recover delay costs based on the scheduled early completion date because the contractor showed its performance plan was reasonable.

Three decisions in 1990 provide extensive further guidance in the area of using CPM to establish early completion claims. One of these decisions, *Williams Enterprises, Inc. v. Strait Manufacturing & Welding, Inc.*[158] breaks new ground because it holds that the prime contractor can recover from a subcontractor when the subcontractor denies the prime contractor the ability to complete at a date earlier than the date specified in the contract with the owner. This holding was, however, made in circumstances in which the prime contractor had specifically consulted the subcontractors to verify the timing and duration of the subelements of their work and in which the subcontractor had agreed to be specifically bound to the CPM scheduling requirements. Pertinent sections of the court's decision stated:

(3) Section 6 of the subcontract specifically provides that the subcontractor will prosecute the work efficiently and promptly; further, that subcontractor agrees to pay to the Contractor such other or additional damages as the

---

[156] PSBCA Nos. 1033, 1096, 84-2 BCA ¶ 17,492 (1984).

[157] ASBCA No. 35,518, 88-2 BCA ¶ 20,734 (1988).

[158] 728 F. Supp. 12 (D.D.C. 1990).

Contractor may sustain by reason of delay by the Subcontractor. This provision is an express statement of the generally recognized common law obligation of parties not to hinder or interfere with one another's performance. *Fuller Co. v. United States,* 69 F. Supp. 409, 411, 108 Ct. Cl. 70 (1947); *see also, United States ex rel. Heller Electric Co. v. William Klingensmith, Inc.,* 670 F.2d 1227 (D.C. Cir. 1982); *Luria Brothers v. United States,* 369 F.2d 701, 608, 177 Ct. Cl. 676 (1966).

(4) In an action between private parties, it suffices to show that a subcontractor caused a substantial delay in performance, that the contract terms forbade such a delay, and that the plaintiff was injured as a result. *United States ex rel. Gray-Bar Electric Co. v. J.H. Copeland & Sons,* 568 F.2d 1159, 1160 (5th Cir. 1978); *District Concrete Co. v. Bernstein Concrete,* 418 A.2d 1030, 1038 (D.C. 1980). Smoot has proved each of these elements.

(5) The steel erection activity was an activity on the critical path of the Project. By definition, a delay to the critical path activity will result in a delay to the entire project resulting in compensable costs. Stephen M. Siegfried, *Introduction to Construction Law,* Chapter 12, page 243 (ALI-ABA, 1987); Bramble and Callahan, *Construction Delay Claims* (John Wiley & Sons 1987), pp. 9–10, p. 145.

(6) Smoot may properly commit its resources and those of its subcontractors to its projected CPM completion date—even if that date is earlier than the final date required by the contract with the owner—and may recover damages from a subcontractor which causes delay. *District Concrete Co. v. Bernstein,* 418 A.2d 1030, 1038 (D.C. 1980); *Grow Construction Co. v. State,* 56 A.D.2d 95, 391 N.Y.S.2d 726, 728 (1977); *Canon Construction Co.,* ASBCA 16142, 72-1 BCA ¶ 9404 (1972).[159]

The second 1990 decision, *Sierra Blanca, Inc.,* concerned delay claims associated with the construction of a range operations/instrumentation laboratory for the Naval Facilities Engineering Command. In considering the contractor's claim for compensation, the board stated the following about its right to finish early:

Appellant's plan to finish early was reasonable and to the extent that the Government's failure to timely approve the masonry block contributed to delay in that early schedule, appellant, as we have concluded is entitled to be compensated. *Owen L. Schwamm Construction Co.,* ASBCA 22407, 79-2 BCA ¶ 13,919 (1979). We have found that the delay in the installation of the masonry block was on the critical path from the time it could have commenced on 12 July 1984, and as such, had an effect upon the overall completion of the contract work.[160]

---

[159] *Id.* at 22–23.

[160] ASBCA No. 32,161, 33,333, 33,336–337, 33,555, 90-2 BCA ¶ 22,846 (1990).

The final 1990 decision, *VEC, Inc.,*[161] also from the Armed Services Board of Contract Appeals, is a reminder that the contractor's claims for damages arising from denial of its ability to complete work early on a project, while a viable cause of action, must have strong bona fides. In fact, absent the contractor establishing clear factual bases of its actual intent to finish early, the contractor's claims will be denied. The board stated:

> We must first address the issue of whether or not appellant is entitled to compensable delays for the performance period exceeding appellant's alleged estimated or desired performance period of 120 days. We have held that for time extension and liquidated damages purposes and for recovery under a SUSPENSION OF WORK clause, a contractor is entitled to the benefit of "cushion" of extra time that would result from planned early completion of the work. *G & S Construction, Inc.,* ASBCA No. 28677, 86-1 BCA ¶ 18,740; *Sydney Construction Co., Inc.,* ASBCA No. 21377, 77-2 BCA ¶ 12,719. However, the factual bases underlying these holdings were that the contractors had established their intent to perform the contract on an accelerated schedule in advance of the contractually mandated completion date and that this intent was supported by the course of the contractors' actions and performance activities during the contract performance that would have led to such an early completion absent Government caused delays.

§ 9.23   —Presumptions from CPM Approvals and Time Modifications

A number of presumptions arise as a result of government's adoption of CPM techniques, approval of CPMs, and agreement on time modifications to the contract schedule and the CPM schedule. If the parties agree the CPM schedule is a reasonable plan for performing the work, the schedule is presumed correct. A contractor or the government must overcome this presumption in arguing that the original plan did not reflect necessary modifications or was overly pessimistic regarding the time scheduled for performance.

For example, in *Santa Fe, Inc.,*[162] the board noted that "[t]here is a rebuttable presumption of correctness attached to CPMs upon which the parties have previously mutually agreed."[163] Thus, an owner may be

---

[161] ASBCA No. 35,988, 90-3 BCA ¶ 23,204 (1990). *See also* Robglo, Inc., VABCA Nos. 2879, 2884, 1990 VABCA LEXIS 27 (Pubcon Library, VABCA file) (Oct. 30, 1990).

[162] VABCA No. 2168, 87-3 BCA ¶ 20,104 (1987).

[163] *Id.* at 101,760.

responsible for the time allotted in a CPM schedule for owner approvals when the owner approves the schedule.[164]

Most recently, in a 1990 decision of the Armed Services Board of Contract Appeals, *G. Bliudzius Contractors, Inc.,*[165] the board considered the contractor's entitlement to compensation for delays alleged in the construction of temporary lodging facilities at a naval training center arising from the timing of the approval of its contractor quality control plan (CQC). In finding that the government was late in providing the necessary approval, the board looked to the exact time for approvals detailed in the contractor's CPM plan. The board stated:

> We have found that a period of ten working days for approval of the CQC plan was allowed in appellant's revised CPM network diagram. We conclude that conditional approval of the CQC plan should have been given within that period so that—as we have found—the construction would have started on 20 August.[166]

Contractual modifications to the performance schedule may also create presumptions. An agreement by the government to extend the time of performance for changes to the work creates a rebuttal presumption that the government was responsible for the delay and that the time granted is compensable.[167] In the 1987 *Elrich Construction Co.* decision,[168] the Armed Services Board considered whether appellant was entitled to an equitable adjustment in the contract price to cover indirect costs arising out of government-ordered changes. The government argued that appellant could not rely on the 201 days in time extensions granted in modifications for changes as proper proof of compensable delay to the project. The board rejected the government's argument:

> Government's joinder in contract amendments numbered P00013, P00014, P00035, P00039, and P00045 amounts to a recognition that the overall project performance was delayed in excess of 201 days above and beyond the original contract completion date. Agreeing to extend the time for performance of the contract gives rise to a presumption, subject

---

[164] Fullerton Constr. Co., ASBCA No. 12,275, 69-2 BCA ¶ 7876 (1969).

[165] ASBCA No. 37,707, 90-2 BCA ¶ 22,835 (1990), 1990 ASBCA LEXIS 134.

[166] *Id.* at 11,661.

[167] *See* Schuster Engineering, Inc., ASBCA Nos. 28,760, 29,306, 30,683, 87-3 BCA ¶ 20,105, at 101,802 (1987); Elrich Constr. Co., ASBCA No. 29,547, 87-1 BCA ¶ 19,600, at 99,149 (1987); Robert McMullan & Son, Inc., ASBCA No. 19,023, 76-1 BCA ¶ 11,728, at 55,903 (1976); Singleton Sheet Metal Works, Inc., ASBCA No. 12,402, 69-1 BCA ¶ 7444, at 34,543 (1968).

[168] ASBCA No. 29,547, 87-1 BCA ¶ 19,600 (1987).

to rebuttal, that Government was responsible for the delay. *Robert Mc-Mullan & Son, Inc.*[169]

§ 9.24 —Limiting Recoverable Time in CPM Claims Presentations

If multiple owner delays affect independent sequences of work during the same period, the contractor may only recover for the actual delay to the critical path. Accordingly, a contractor may not "double dip" by aggregating delays to independent activity chains so that the cumulative delay exceeds the period of time in question (absent evidence of compression or acceleration to show extra time gained during the period). Thus, compensable delay is limited to the ultimate delay as reflected by the critical path. It is also limited to the total amount of time in the period under consideration.

These principles are fully recognized in two recent decisions, *Ealahan Electric Co.*[170] and *Fletcher & Sons, Inc.*[171] In the *Ealahan* decision, the board was faced with the issue of certain aspects of the contractor's claim, concerning overlapping delays to the critical path, which it found to have merit. In finding that the contractor's recovery for critical path delays was limited to the time period in question, absent evidence of acceleration, the board stated:

> This leaves us with a consideration of the amount of time actually spent by appellant on the performance of the ten change orders. Ealahan has presented detailed evidence that critical path areas including carpentry, sheetrocking, painting, framing, and other work, were affected by each change order. The evidence is sufficient that the critical path was affected by these changes. Though appellant introduced evidence as to the actual amount of days spent on each change, since there is an overlap in the periods of time during which the changes were performed, we cannot simply add up the time taken for each change in determining the amount of delay attributable to these changes.
>
> Since the work on many changes was performed at the same time, Ealahan is entitled to a time extension only from the date the first change impacted its performance, to the day the final change was completed. In other words where two or more changes are performed during the same time, a contractor is only entitled to a contract extension for the calendar time taken in performing the changes, absent evidence of acceleration.

---

[169] ASBCA No. 19,023, 76-1 BCA ¶ 11,728, at 99,149 (1976).

[170] DOTBCA No. 1959, 90-3 BCA ¶ 23,117 (1990).

[171] VABCA No. 2502, 88-2 BCA ¶ 20,677 (1988).

A similar result was reached in *Fletcher & Sons, Inc.*[172] There, the Veterans Administration board considered a claim of multiple delays to independent sequences of work during the same time frames. Time extensions had been granted previously for certain of the delays during the concerned period.

In rejecting a claim for any further delays to critical path work for the period in question, the board concluded that the contractor's recovery for delay was limited to the total number of days in the period under consideration:

> Appellant has been fully compensated for the additional time it had to be on the project. As a result of the ductwork and partition walls, Phase I of the project was extended from January 11 to February 25. The fact that multiple delays may have been occurring during that time period does not justify compensation for a greater period than that time span.[173]

§ 9.25 —Recognition of Risk Taking to Negate Effects of Delays to Critical Path

The dynamic nature of the CPM process, described in §§ **9.3** and **9.4**, provides significant opportunities to the parties in addressing project delays as they occur during performance. The contractor and the owner are able to react to changing events to modify logic in attempting to bring the project in on time and on budget. In fact, the parties can remove restraints by waiving various contractually specified approvals and allowing construction to proceed in their absence.

Most significantly, the opportunity is present for either the contractor or the owner, under the right circumstances, to run certain risks that can negate the effect of any delay that might otherwise be the specific party's responsibility. Such a circumstance was recently confronted by the Armed Services Board of Contract Appeals in *H&S Corp.*[174] In the *H&S* decision,[175] the contractor and the owner negotiated direct costs for a change order directed by the owner to certain earthwork, but were unable to agree on the overhead costs of a 118-day delay associated with the earthwork change. The owner defended the case on the basis that the delay caused by the change was nullified by the time the contractor took to resolve a contractor building-load error that related to the footings and foundation.

---

[172] *Id.*

[173] *Id.* at 104,528.

[174] ASBCA No. 29,688, 89-3 BCA ¶ 22,209 (1989).

[175] *Id.*

However, the board found that the contractor proceeded with the footing construction regardless of the problem with the building-load error and that no work was actually delayed on the project. The board stated as follows:

> Turning first to the concurrent delay issue, we agree with the Government that a contractor-caused delay affecting the construction of the footings would have a significant effect on this contract's critical path. The overwhelming flaw in the Government's concurrent delay argument, however, resides in the premise that appellant's failure to gain approval of the building system caused the delay.
>
> The Government initially chose to return submittal 62 rather than review it (finding 20). When the Government later returned the submittal package, including submittal 80, the Government directed appellant to redesign the foundation to accommodate the apparently heavier building loads (finding 23). However, appellant's earthwork subcontractor performed earthwork throughout the duration of the alleged concurrent delay and completed the earthwork on 30 August (findings 11–13), appellant did not wait for the 7 October approval before proceeding with the footings but started footing work on 9 September (findings 12, 17), and the footings were finally poured in the manner and size appellant proposed in the submittal (finding 25). Further, the building load mistake resulted only in confusion—no work was delayed or changed (finding 27). Finally, nothing in the contract required Government approval of the building system before pouring the footings.
>
> The Government cannot, from these facts, construct a scenario in which the very real delay caused by the unsuitable soil and additional earth work is nullified by the time it took to resolve the building load error. This failure proves fatal to the Government's defense. "The defense of concurrent delay is valid only when applied to an actually established delay, not merely an alleged delay." *Essential Construction Company, Inc. and Himount Constructors, Ltd., A Joint Venture*, ASBCA No. 18706, 83-2 BCA ¶ 16,906 at 84,114.[176]

The significance of the *H&S*[177] decision is as a reminder that the contractor or the owner can frequently negate the effect of delays to the project or delays that would otherwise be charged to that party's responsibility. This can be done by being willing to take the risk of performing certain work or taking certain actions prior to formal approval so that no delay is actually incurred on the project. Of course, in taking such steps, the contractor or owner risks further damage in that, if the unapproved installation proves wanting and has to be torn out (or the risk-taking step

---

[176] *Id.* at 111,720–721.

[177] ASBCA No. 29,688, 89-3 BCA ¶ 22,209 (1989).

withdrawn), more delay will be charged to that party and charged to the project than would have otherwise been encountered.

§ 9.26   —Need to Delineate Plan for Performance in Initial CPM Schedule

Three recent decisions confirm the proposition that the contractor must, at the inception of the project, make every effort to delineate all significant features of its plan for performance concerning resources, durations, and logic. Further, the contractor's intent should be communicated clearly to the owner and its agents. The three recent decisions on this subject are *Volpe-Head,*[178] *VEC, Inc.,*[179] and *LaDuke Construction & Krumdieck, Inc.*[180]

In the *Volpe-Head*[181] decision, the Corps of Engineers Board of Contract Appeals confronted a claim by a contractor asserting that it had planned to construct a station entrance, passageway, and center service area for a Washington Metropolitan Area Transportation Authority subway station concurrently with the construction of the main station itself. The owner defended on the basis that the contractor failed to establish that its original plan had provided for concurrent construction and that the delays encountered on the project did not in any way impact the contractor since the contractor had always planned to perform the construction in consecutive stages. In holding for the owner, the board decision recognized both the burden of proof on the part of the contractor to clearly establish its plan, as well as the failure of the CPM plan itself to provide for the concurrent construction staging. The decision stated:

> Respondent maintains that Appellant has failed in its burden of proof. Respondent also put on a case that shows the planning and contemporaneous documentation by Appellant was in part consistent with either concurrent or consecutive excavation and, in other respects, was more consistent with a plan to do the project in consecutive stages. Respondent also offered evidence that Appellant caused a concurrent delay in the CSA&P.
>
> *   *   *
>
> Appellant supports its argument for concurrent construction planning by contentions that the CPM schedule, support of excavation shop drawings, evidence respecting material deliveries and the minutes of progress meetings all support its case. Analysis of Appellant's contentions, the

---

[178] ENGBCA No. 4726, 89-3 BCA ¶ 22,105 (1989).

[179] ASBCA No. 35,988, 90-3 BCA ¶ 23,204 (1990).

[180] AGBCA No. 83-177-1, 90-1 BCA ¶ 22,302 (1989).

[181] ENGBCA No. 4726, 89-3 BCA ¶ 22,105 (1989).

supporting citations to the record and the record as a whole does not convince us that a plan for concurrent construction has been proved. Appellant has not carried its burden. Rather, the preponderance of the evidence is more consistent with a plan for consecutive execution of the project. (Findings 37, 45–46).[182]

The *Vec, Inc.*[183] decision concerned the construction of a covered storage addition to an existing storage facility. In this case, the contractor asserted that it had planned to finish well in advance of the contract-specified performance time and supported its testimony with a CPM chart prepared the day before the hearing. The board, in rejecting the contractor's position, clearly noted its rejection of the hypothetical, after-the-fact CPM, which was not even consistent with the schedule of progress payments submitted to the owner during construction. The board decision stated:

> We have held that for time extension and liquidated damages purposes and for recovery under a SUSPENSION OF WORK clause, a contractor is entitled to the benefit or "cushion" of extra time that would result from planned early completion of the work. *G & S Construction, Inc.,* ASBCA No. 28677, 86-1 BCA ¶ 18,740; *C. N. Flagg & Co., Inc.,* ASBCA Nos. 2644, 26655, 84-1 BCA ¶ 17,120; *Sydney Construction Co., Inc.,* ASBCA No. 21377, 77-2 BCA ¶ 12,719. However, the factual bases underlying these holdings were that the contractors had established their intent to perform the contract on an accelerated schedule in advance of the contractually mandated completion date and that this intent was supported by the course of the contractors' actions and performance activities during the contract performance that would have led to such an early completion absent Government caused delays.
>
> We are not persuaded that appellant did establish such an intent here and that its actual course of actions and performance supported such an intent. Except for the critical path chart appellant prepared the day before the hearing and appellant's president's testimony, there was no persuasive evidence that appellant, at the time of award, had a firm commitment or intent to complete the project within 120 days or that it communicated that intent to the Government. There were no charts or workpapers which may have been prepared prior to or immediately after award that would indicate the planning of an early completion but for Government caused or adverse weather delays. Rather, the testimony of appellant's president and the critical path chart he prepared the day before the hearing, in our opinion, represent after-the-fact projections and hypotheticals only. Moreover, its proposed schedule submitted to the Government for progress payment purposes, its schedule of material submittals, and its course of performance are all consistent with a performance schedule of 180 days.

---

[182] *Id.* at 111,170.

[183] ASBCA No. 35,988, 1990 ASBCA LEXIS 323 (July 31, 1990).

The *LaDuke Construction & Krumdieck, Inc.*[184] decision not only confirmed the necessity that the contractor must clearly display its plan for performance, but also that the logic sequences shown in the CPM schedule, and particularly on the critical path, represent a good plan for performance. Specifically, the board found that the contractor had to show that the plan represented a logical prosecution of the work. The board decision stated:

> It is not enough for Appellant's principals or their equipment operator to say that the "critical path" ran through the drain field and comfort station. Appellant must additionally show that a logical prosecution of the work required that the drain field and comfort station be completed before any other part of the project could advance. *See, Franklin L. Haney v. United States,* [30 CCF ¶ 70,189], 230 Ct. Cl. 148, 167–168; 676 F.2d 584 (1982).[185]

§ 9.27 —Fragnets, Windows, and Time Impact Analyses

Fragnets, windows, and time impact analyses are techniques for looking at individual segments of CPM networks. Fragnets are subnetworks, used to break one or more activity shown on a CPM diagram into a finer level of detail to develop the individual subactivities necessary for completion of the activity shown on the critical path. For example, the description of an activity on a critical path network for mechanical rough-in or structural steel erection may be made up of a number of different activities.

Fragnets also show added activities (necessary as a result of additional work) or logic revisions (required by delays or a determination that the original plan for performance is not workable). Since the 1960s, fragnets have been recognized as worthwhile analytical devices to compare portions of CPM schedules as planned with the actual events in the field as they are impacted by changes, delays, contractor inefficiencies, or other causes.[186] Fragnets prove useful for claim presentations and time impact analyses because they present a visual picture of the effect of individual delays on isolated activities. These presentations first show the isolated impact, then use other visual symbols to show places on the as-planned and as-built schedules where the entire network has been impacted by the delays reflected in the fragnet. The 1979 *Corps of Engineers Modification Impact Evaluation Guide,* the 1989 *VACPM Handbook,* and the 1984 text

---

[184] AGBCA No. 83-177-1, 90-1 BCA ¶ 22,302 (1989).

[185] *Id.* at 112,002.

[186] *See, e.g.,* NASA PERT and Companion Cost Guide (Oct. 30, 1962).

CPM in Construction Management[187] provide excellent examples of time impact analyses utilizing fragnet presentations.

Window analyses operate in the same manner as the schedule update procedures required by the Corps of Engineers and Veterans Administration (VA) scheduling specifications. Like the VA and Corps procedures, window presentations focus on the effects of delays on specific periods by looking at the gains or losses to the critical path as they occur within each update period.[188]

§ 9.28   —Potential Abuses in Microcomputer Programs

The explosion in the use of microcomputers on project sites along with powerful microcomputer programming, such as Primavera® or Alder-Graf®, have presented great benefits for the construction community. However, such programs present the potential for significant abuses because of the opportunity to (1) not properly update the project, (2) record the actual completion dates, (3) override the project logic, and (4) remove delays to the critical paths on monthly updates without modifying the actual logic of the diagram.

The Primavera model (**Figures 9–16** through **9–21**) details a simple project for the excavation of certain footings, for forming the footings along with installation of the rebar and placement of the concrete in the

```
---------------------------------------------------------------------------------------------
HURLBUT/COPPI                    PRIMAVERA PROJECT PLANNER        EXAMPLE OF PROGRESS OVERRIDE

REPORT DATE 15OCT90  RUN NO.   4     PROJECT SCHEDULE            START DATE  1JAN91  FIN DATE 28JAN91
            19:38
SCHEDULE REPORT - SORT BY ACTIVITY NOS                          DATA DATE   1JAN91  PAGE NO.   1


----- -----  ---- ---- - ---  -------------------------------  -------- -------- -------- -------- -----
ACTIVITY    ORIG REM                     ACTIVITY DESCRIPTION   EARLY    EARLY    LATE     LATE     TOTAL
   ID       DUR  DUR CAL  %   CODE                              START    FINISH   START    FINISH   FLOAT
----- -----  ---- ---- - ---  -------------------------------  -------- -------- -------- -------- -----
      10      5    5 1   0    EXCAVATE FOOTINGS                 1JAN91   7JAN91   1JAN91   7JAN91    0
      30     10   10 1   0    FORM, REBAR AND POUR FOOTINGS     8JAN91   21JAN91  8JAN91   21JAN91   0
      40      5    5 1   0    SET STEEL                         22JAN91  28JAN91  22JAN91  28JAN91   0
```

Figure 9–16. Activity description for simple footings project.

---

[187] U.S. Army Corps of Engineers, Modification Impact Evaluation Guide, EP 415-1-3, 3-8 through 3-19 (1979) (available from Corps of Engineers Publications Dept., 2083 52nd Ave., Hyattsville, Md., 20781-1102); Veterans Administration, VACPM Handbook 8-17, 73-84 (March 1989); J. O'Brien, CPM in Construction Management 367–90 (1984).

[188] *See* Nielsen & Galloway, *Proof Development for Construction Litigation,* 7 Am. J. Trial Advoc., 433, 444–48 (1984).

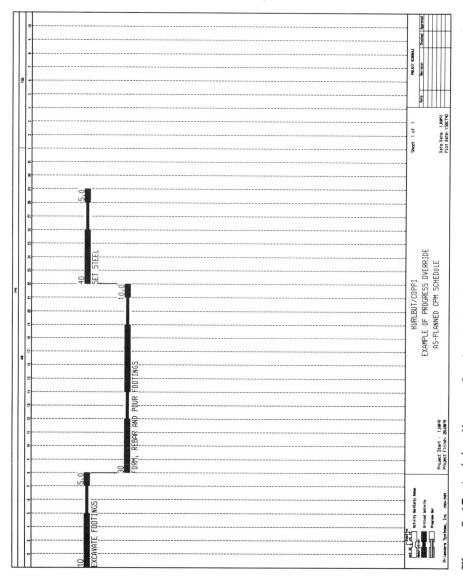

Figure 9-17. Activity diagram for simple footings project.

footings, and finally for setting steel on top of the footings. As detailed in the plan for performance on the activity description and activity diagram (**Figures 9–16** and **9–17**) the project is to be performed in a sequential manner with the excavation of footings as the first activity, forming, rebarring, and pouring footings as the second activity, and setting the steel as the final activity. The duration of the first activity is five days; the duration of the second, 10 days; and the duration of the final activity, five days. The project is to take from January 1 until January 28 with consideration for weekends.

However, with the first update (**Figures 9–18** and **9–19**), it can be seen that the project, as is frequently the case, does not proceed per the plan. The update, on January 4, just three days after the commencement of the activity, reflects a minor sequence change, with an early start for forming certain of the footings. It is discovered after two days of excavation that not all of the excavation would have to be completed prior to starting certain of the smaller footings on the western third of the project site. The update, therefore, reflects a change in the logic with an early start to forming the footing. This, in turn, would normally reflect an early completion in construction, prior to the January 28 date anticipated on the original plan. However, on the third day of the project, on the date of the update, a delay is encountered on the project caused by redesign for the larger footings on the eastern two thirds of the project site. The updated chart, therefore, shows an extended duration of four work days, to February 1, resulting from the seven-work-day delay occasioned by the footing redesign.

Most interesting, however, is the third chart project update (**Figures 9–20** and **9–21**), also on 4 January, at the inception of the delay caused by the footing redesign. This update, however, does not reflect a delay to the project completion. The reason for the failure to disclose the interdiction of forming the footings over the eastern two thirds of the site is that the logic of the diagram has been overridden. The owner's expert in this case

```
-------------------------------------------------------------------------------------------------------------
HURLBUT/COPPI                          PRIMAVERA PROJECT PLANNER          EXAMPLE OF PROGRESS OVERRIDE

REPORT DATE 15OCT90  RUN NO.   5       PROJECT SCHEDULE                   START DATE  1JAN91  FIN DATE 28JAN91*
            19:39
SCHEDULE REPORT - SORT BY ACTIVITY NOS                                   DATA DATE   4JAN91  PAGE NO.   1


----- -----  ---- ---- - ---  ----------  --------------------------------  -------- -------- -------- -------- -----
ACTIVITY  ORIG REM                        ACTIVITY DESCRIPTION              EARLY    EARLY    LATE     LATE     TOTAL
   ID     DUR  DUR CAL %  CODE                                              START    FINISH   START    FINISH   FLOAT
----- -----  ---- ---- - ---  ----------  --------------------------------  -------- -------- -------- -------- -----
     10    5    2 1 60         EXCAVATE FOOTINGS                            1JAN91A  7JAN91            8JAN91      1
     20    7    7 1  0  DLAY    DELAY CAUSED BY FOOTING REDESIGN            4JAN91   14JAN91  31DEC90  8JAN91     -4
     30   10    9 1 10         FORM, REBAR AND POUR FOOTINGS                3JAN91A  25JAN91           21JAN91    -4
     40    5    5 1  0         SET STEEL                                    28JAN91  1FEB91   22JAN91  28JAN91    -4
```

Figure 9–18. Updated activity description reflecting delay.

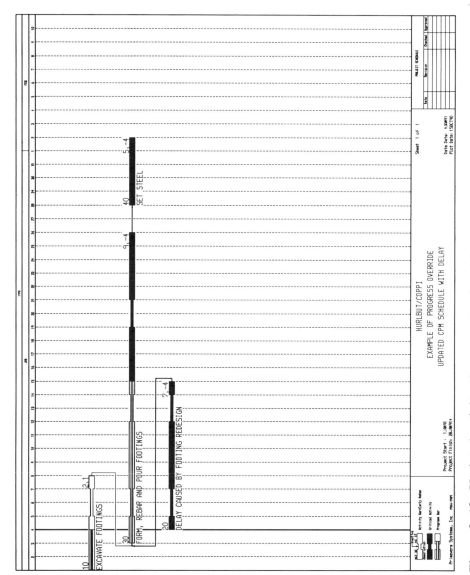

Figure 9–19. Updated activity diagram reflecting delay.

```
------------------------------------------------------------------------------------------------------------
HURLBUT/COPPI                        PRIMAVERA PROJECT PLANNER           EXAMPLE OF PROGRESS OVERRIDE

REPORT DATE 15OCT90  RUN NO.   3        PROJECT SCHEDULE                   START DATE  1JAN91  FIN DATE 28JAN91*
            19:40
SCHEDULE REPORT - SORT BY ACTIVITY NOS                                    DATA DATE   4JAN91  PAGE NO.   1
```

ACTIVITY ID	ORIG DUR	REM DUR	CAL	%	CODE	ACTIVITY DESCRIPTION	EARLY START	EARLY FINISH	LATE START	LATE FINISH	TOTAL FLOAT
10	5	2	1	60		EXCAVATE FOOTINGS	1JAN91A	7JAN91		28JAN91	15
20	7	7	1	0	DLAY	DELAY CAUSED BY FOOTING REDESIGN	4JAN91	14JAN91	18JAN91	28JAN91	10
30	10	9	1	10		FORM, REBAR AND POUR FOOTINGS	3JAN91A	16JAN91		21JAN91	3
40	5	5	1	0		SET STEEL	17JAN91	23JAN91	22JAN91A	28JAN91	3

Figure 9–20. Updated activity description reflecting logic violation.

has chosen to assert, without modification to the logic in the network, that excavation was no longer a restraint to the remaining footings and forming the footings could take place at the same time as the excavation. This, of course, represents a physical impossibility, because the excavation was a condition precedent.

The purpose of this example is to detail exactly how careful parties must be in the use of the extremely valuable CPM tool. In the third activity report and diagram, the material appears to be very professional and appropriate. Unless the parties and the professionals assisting them are vigilant, no one may pick up the fact that a progress override has been utilized on updates to avoid the effect of delays. For this reason, the parties must always check the basic precepts upon which CPM plans, updates, and analyses are prepared.

§ 9.29   Specification of Time Impact Analysis

The *time impact analysis* technique is most effective when required by the contract as part of the schedule specifications. Schedule specifications should require the contractor to prepare and submit fragnets within a specified time to demonstrate the influence of delays or support requests for extensions of contract time as events occur on the project. Typically, this should be done as part of the updating process. As discussed in § 9.27, a fragnet may detail a sequence of new activities or network revisions that are proposed for addition to the existing network schedule to illustrate, graphically and mathematically, the method for incorporating delays and changed conditions.

Contract schedule specifications should also include a detailed procedure for time impact analysis. The procedure should cover preparation, format, submittals, the approval process, and the incorporation of fragnets into the existing project schedule. The owner should also consider

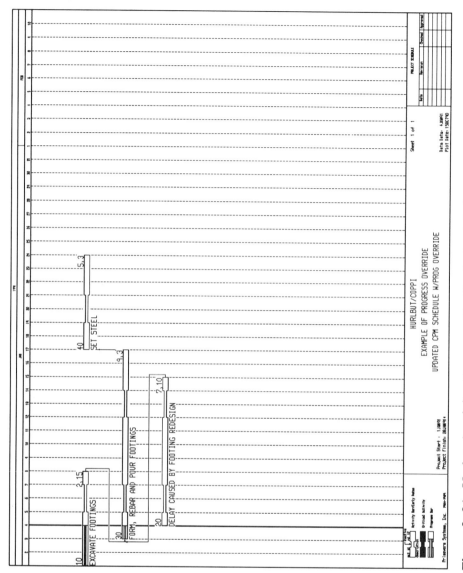

Figure 9–21. Updated activity diagram reflecting logic violation.

preparing its own independent estimate of time impact analyses so that key owner staff are prepared to discuss, negotiate, and resolve the question of impact at the earliest opportunity. When disputes arise, both parties benefit from the exchange of information, and it enables each to take protective measures should a formal claim become necessary.

In the absence of time impact analysis requirements in the contract, contractors should still consider use of the fragnet technique to demonstrate and support their time extension requests and change order proposals. Preparation of individual narrative impact analyses for each delay or change should become part of the contractor's justification process. In this manner, the specific facts underlying each problem will be recorded and available for negotiations during performance or for future reference in overall delay claim presentations.

Each time impact analysis should identify the individual problem, such as a suspension, differing site condition, change order, or delayed approval. In addition, the analysis must reference appropriate documentation, such as specifications references, contract drawings, or sketches. Finally, the time impact analysis must detail the activities affected in the network in light of the approved or current CPM schedule, taking into account existing job conditions; availability of manpower, equipment and materials; any new activities made necessary by the change; and any impact on unchanged work. **Chapter 8** provides a detailed discussion of suggested procedures for time impact analyses.

§ 9.30   Safeguards for Establishing Delay Quantum Baselines

The substantial case authority detailed in this chapter, the extensive federal procurement specifications requiring network analysis systems, the updating requirements and prerequisites for time extensions, and the principles outlined in the 1974 Wickwire and Smith article all indicate that the establishment of delay quantum baselines to determine time extensions or compensable delays is a serious task that requires substantial thought to ensure that the appropriate tests can be met.

One of the more significant issues concerning CPM time evaluations is hindsight pricing of delays as opposed to current or contemporaneous pricing of delays. The need to satisfy the *but for* test must also be factored into the evaluation. For this reason, it may be helpful to consider the following steps in preparing a delay quantum presentation or evaluation.

First, make certain a reasonable as-planned CPM schedule is available. Then prepare the as-built CPM or check the completed as-built CPM for accuracy. Develop the variations (along with appropriate fragnets) that exist between the as-planned and as-built CPM schedules and the causes of such variations in the critical path that have caused the extensions of the project completion date. Develop from this analysis the amount of time that can be claimed and defended.

Second, prepare an analysis of delays to the critical path using a current time analysis such as those detailed by the Veterans Administration and Corps of Engineers updating procedures. This, of course, is the same procedure as the window method. Determine the positive and negative changes for each update or period of reference and the causes for delays in that period. Compute the periods of delay, as developed over the various updates, that are the responsibility of the government or the contractor or are excusable.

Third, compare the two analyses set forth above to see if differences exist between the hindsight evaluation and the contemporaneous evaluation of delays on the project. Then, compare both evaluations to the *but for* analysis and the adjusted schedule indicating when the project should have been completed absent the government delays, to make certain that the government receives appropriate credit for delays that would have extended the critical path for the project regardless of the government delays (delays such as strikes and unusually severe weather, for which credit was given in, for example, *Haney v. United States*).[189] These comparison tests resemble the steps used in the preparation of the critical path method diagram to determine the longest chain of activities through the project in terms of time (namely, the critical path). More specifically, the comparison steps set forth above are similar to the mathematical calculations of a forward pass through the I-J CPM diagram, and then a backward pass through the I-J CPM diagram, to determine the longest chain of activities through the project in terms of time.[190]

If the answers derived from this contemporaneous versus hindsight evaluation of delays cannot be reconciled, analyze the relevant contract provisions to determine whether the contract specifies a particular baseline for use in delay quantification. If the contract provisions fail to provide such guidance, consider the presentation in light of recent decisions, such as *Fortec Constructors v. United States*,[191] which dictate the use of contemporaneous delay valuation.

---

[189] 230 Ct. Cl. 148, 676 F.2d 584 (1982).

[190] *See* Corps of Engineers, Manual on Network Analysis Systems, ER 1-1-11, Glossary of Terms (Mar. 1, 1973).

[191] 8 Cl. Ct. 490 (1985), *aff'd,* 804 F.2d 141 (Fed. Cir. 1986).

CHAPTER 10

CALCULATING CONTRACTOR'S DAMAGES FOR DELAY, DISRUPTION, AND LOSS OF EFFICIENCY

§ 10.1 Introduction

§ 10.2 Credibility

§ 10.3 Disruption versus Delay Costs

§ 10.4 Reasonable and Actual Costs

§ 10.5 Total Cost Method

§ 10.6 Jury Verdict Method

§ 10.7 Forward Pricing

§ 10.8 Labor Costs

§ 10.9 Material Escalation

§ 10.10 Equipment Costs

§ 10.11 Extended Supervision

§ 10.12 Extended Jobsite Expense

§ 10.13 Extended Home Office Overhead

§ 10.14 Profit

§ 10.15 Loss of Efficiency

§ 10.16 Claim Preparation Cost

§ 10.17 Interest

§ 10.1 Introduction

Early recognition of facts that support construction claims is critically important. Once recognized, compilation of appropriate documentation, including cost accounting, can be promptly commenced if the cost, duration, and sequence reviews described in earlier chapters have been carefully maintained. Failure to maintain requisite controls may result in potential claims going unrecognized until long after damages have been incurred. Timely recognition and documentation of a claim ensures accurate quantification and maximum credibility.

Regardless of when the basis for a claim is discovered, identification of all associated costs is necessary to utilize these costs in negotiation, claim presentation, and arbitration or trial. Costs incurred must be demonstrated accurately and conclusively in order to maximize recovery. The techniques of preparing a cost presentation and its substance are discussed in this chapter.

§ 10.2   Credibility

Typically, the recipient of a claim is initially most concerned with the amount of the claim, not the basis for entitlement. Accordingly, the costing or calculation portion of a presentation often is reviewed first. The costing presentation section, therefore, should be clearly organized and divided into sections consistent with the respective categories of claims. Pricing methodology should be explained so the recipient is aware that there is substance to the claim and that "puffing" has been minimized. A straightforward cost presentation with reasonable detail will bolster the credibility of both the pricing and the entitlement components of a claim.

Although the appearance of a pricing presentation is important, a realistic calculation of all costs claimed is equally crucial. Patently defective and even marginal "nickel and dime" claims may diminish the believability of otherwise clearly supportable items. Mathematical errors, claims for items clearly within the scope of the contract, incorrect wage rates, overstated worker hours, and inflated claims are readily detected and should be removed. Obviously, claimants should seek all monies for which there is a legitimate basis, even if the facts are in dispute, but grossly inflated figures tend to weaken the settlement prospect for other valid items.

Large claims (usually in excess of $100,000), particularly on federal projects, will usually trigger an audit of the claimant's records. Such audits are intended to prevent frivolous claims and to verify claim items with merit. Frivolous and unsubstantiated claims may lead to civil fraud liability and, possibly, criminal penalties.

Government contractors may be subject to the False Claims Act,[1] which provides that anyone who presents a claim to the United States for approval while knowing that the claim is false or fraudulent or who supports a claim with a false invoice, bill, or voucher is liable for a minimum $5,000 penalty and *triple* the amount of damages sustained by the government

---

[1] 31 U.S.C. §§ 3729–3733 (1983 & Supp. VI, 1990).

and costs of suit.[2] For claims subject to the Contract Disputes Act,[3] contractors may be liable to the government for an amount equal to any unsupported portion of a claim (and the government's costs to review that portion of the claim) to the extent the inability to support the claim is due to factual misrepresentation or fraud by the contractor.[4] In recent years the federal government has been devoting increasing resources to enforcement of these statutes, and ongoing developments at the General Services Administration suggest increased future emphasis.

Realistic pricing and an appropriate presentation are indispensable to a successful claim presentation and invaluable tools for litigation. Various methods and types of pricing are reviewed in the following sections.

§ 10.3 Disruption versus Delay Costs

Disruption results from changes in the method of performance or planned work sequence and causes the contractor to incur additional costs over and above those contemplated at the time of bidding. These costs are categorized as additional work, inefficiencies, increased manpower and equipment to overcome inefficiency, and increased labor and equipment costs to demobilize and remobilize forces. The time of project performance is not necessarily extended. Disruption costs are typically incurred during the original performance period.

Pure delays result primarily in extension of the overall project performance period. Damages associated with pure delays include extended overhead and jobsite costs, equipment standby costs, wage escalation, financing costs, and extended supervision. These costs are incurred during the delay period.

§ 10.4 Reasonable and Actual Costs

The term *equitable adjustment* as used in government contracts as well as private construction contracts refers to the additional compensation to which a contractor is entitled under various situations. Many contracts do not include standards for measurement of the appropriate amount of additional compensation due. Courts and boards have, therefore, been called upon to define the term *equitable adjustment*. The Supreme Court has held that an equitable adjustment means a "fair allowance" and requires

---

[2] *See* Gravitt v. General Elec. Co., 680 F. Supp. 1162 (S.D. Ohio 1988).

[3] 41 U.S.C. §§ 601–613 (1987).

[4] 41 U.S.C. § 604 (1987).

"the ascertainment of the cost . . . and the addition to that cost of a reasonable and customary allowance for profit."[5]

There are different theories regarding the proper basis for calculating an equitable adjustment. Some writers favor an objective theory;[6] others have argued for a subjective approach.[7]

The subjective theory dictates that the proper measure of compensation is the actual cost to the contractor, irrespective of its reasonableness in the marketplace.[8] The objective theory looks to the "reasonable value" of the change or work in question. In *S.N. Nielsen Co. v. United States*,[9] for example, a portion of the contractor's scope of work was reduced by the government. The contractor had allocated only $22,000 for the work in his bid, but his actual cost after the change was $19,000. The government established that it would have actually cost the contractor $60,000 to perform the work as originally contracted. The Court of Claims upheld the Corps of Engineers Board of Contract Appeals in finding that the government was entitled to a credit of $41,000, instead of the $3,000 proposed by the contractor.

In *Bruce Construction Co. v. United States*,[10] the Court of Claims clarified the proper method for calculating equitable adjustments. In *Bruce Construction* the government directed the contractor to use more expensive building blocks than originally specified in the contract. The contractor claimed he was entitled to additional compensation because the change would add value to the project. However, the contractor actually paid no more to his supplier for the "more expensive" block because the supplier was a friend. In finding that the contractor was not entitled to additional compensation, the Court of Claims observed:

> Equitable adjustments in this context are simply corrective measures utilized to keep a contractor whole when the Government modifies a contract. Since the purpose underlying such adjustments is to safeguard the contractor against increased costs engendered by the modification, it appears patent that the measure of damages cannot be the value received by the Government, but must be more closely related to and contingent upon

---

[5] United States v. Callahan-Walker Constr. Co., 317 U.S. 56 (1942).

[6] Spector, *Confusion in the Concept of Equitable Adjustments in Government Contracts,* 22 Fed. B.J. 5, 6 (1962).

[7] McBride, *Confusion in the Concept of Equitable Adjustments: A Reply,* 22 Fed. B.J. 235, 240 (1962).

[8] North Slope Technical, Ltd. v. United States, 14 Cl. Ct. 242 (1988); Shank-Artukovich v. United States, 13 Cl. Ct. 346, 361 (1987); Ensign-Bickford Co., ASBCA No. 6214, 60-2 BCA ¶ 2817 (1960); Lofstrand Co., ASBCA No. 4336, 58-2 BCA ¶ 1962 (1958).

[9] 141 Ct. Cl. 793 (1958).

[10] 324 F.2d 516 (Ct. Cl. 1963).

the altered position in which the contractor finds himself by reason of the modification.[11]

The court further explained that the appropriate focus should be upon reasonable and actual costs and that there is a rebuttable presumption that actual costs paid are reasonable.[12] Subsequent decisions have relied upon *Bruce Construction* in finding that a contractor's actual costs are, prima facie, reasonable costs with respect to determining the appropriate equitable adjustment.[13]

A contractor's demonstration of his actual costs by introduction of his business cost records and the presumption that these records are reasonable may be subject to attack on the basis that they are unsubstantiated or unreliable. In *Art Metal U.S.A., Inc.,*[14] the General Services Administration board found that, because a contractor's cost control records were unreliable and unsupported by the record, they could not support the equitable adjustment claim. The board stated:

> We have also observed that the presumption of reasonableness of costs calculated from business data compilations may be attacked by a showing that there was no basis for it to be drawn, and we have found that the additional productive direct labor hours appellant is claiming here were calculated from data that are neither trustworthy nor reliable. If it has been demonstrated that the source data are not reliable or trustworthy, are costs calculated from such data still presumed reasonable in the absence of affirmative evidence of objective unreasonability? We think not. The presumption is no more pervasive than the business records exception to the rule against hearsay.[15]

A recent revision to the Federal Acquisition Regulations attempts to limit the effect of *Bruce Construction* and its progeny. That regulation provides:

> A cost is reasonable if, in its nature and amount, it does not exceed that which would be incurred by a prudent person in the conduct of competitive business. Reasonableness of specific costs must be examined with particular care in connection with firms or their separate division that may not be subject to effective competitive restraints. No presumption of reasonableness shall be attached to the incurrence of costs by a contractor. If an initial review of the facts results in a challenge of a specific cost by the contracting

---

[11] *Id.* at 518.

[12] *Id.* at 520.

[13] *See, e.g.,* Allied Repair Serv., Inc., IBCA 1381-6-80, 83-1 BCA ¶ 16,204 (1982); Canon Constr. Corp., ASBCA No. 15,208, 71-1 BCA ¶ 8780 (1971); Hayes Int'l Corp., ASBCA No. 9750, 65-1 BCA ¶ 4767 (1965).

[14] GSBCA No. 5898 (5245)-REIN, 83-2 BCA ¶ 16,881 (1983).

[15] *Id.* at 83,986.

officer or the contracting officer's representative, the burden of proof shall be upon the contractor to establish that such cost is reasonable.[16]

Contractors on federal projects should, therefore, solicit outside quotations and other independent data for submission with their claim to substantiate the reasonableness of actual costs. Furthermore, notwithstanding the foregoing regulation, contractors should argue that *Bruce Construction* is still good law and that a contracting officer cannot arbitrarily "challenge" a claimed cost. The contracting officer's challenge should be based on reasonably specific and adequate factual evidence. At any rate, the question of the continuing viability of the *Bruce Construction* rationale in the federal arena remains for future cases to decide.

§ 10.5   Total Cost Method

Although the appropriate amount of an equitable adjustment should be based on the actual and reasonable added cost of the affected or impacted work, circumstances occasionally make it difficult to designate or allocate specific costs to specific portions of work. Under these circumstances contractors frequently utilize the *total cost* method to price the adjustment. The total cost method is least favored by courts and boards.[17]

Under the total cost approach the estimated total cost of a project is subtracted from the actual total cost. Critics of this method assert that it results in equitable adjustments that have little or no relationship to the change or problem in question. The total costs incurred, they argue, may well result from problems attributable to the contractor, not the owner or the change. In addition, the bid estimate may be based upon an unreasonably low assessment of project cost.

The total cost method will not be used if there is another, more reliable method available to establish the cost.[18] While not favored, the use of the total cost approach is not prohibited per se.[19] Courts and boards permit recovery under the total cost method where proper safeguards exist, there is no better method of proving costs, and there is some basis for reaching a

---

[16] 48 C.F.R. § 31.201-3(a) (1988).

[17] Meva Corp. v. United States, 206 Ct. Cl. 203, 220, 511 F.2d 548, 558 (1975); WRB Corp. v. United States, 183 Ct. Cl. 409, 426 (1968); Steve Beylund, AGBCA No. 87-215-3, 87-3 BCA ¶ 19,975 (1987); Schuster Eng'g, ASBCA No. 28,760, 87-3 BCA ¶ 20,105 (1987).

[18] Wunderlich Contracting Co. v. United States, 173 Ct. Cl. 180, 351 F.2d 956 (1965).

[19] Boyajian v. United States, 191 Ct. Cl. 233, 423 F.2d 1231 (1970); United States Indus., Inc. v. Blake Constr. Co., 671 F.2d 539 (D.C. Cir. 1982); Timber Investors, Inc. v. United States, 218 Ct. Cl. 408, 587 F.2d 472, 484 (1978).

determination of a reasonable amount related to the entitlement found.[20] The acceptability of the total cost method hinges on proof that (1) the nature of the particular losses makes it impossible or highly impracticable to determine them with a reasonable degree of accuracy, (2) the contractor's bid or estimate was realistic, (3) his actual costs were reasonable, and (4) he was not responsible for the added expenses.[21]

Where no other basis for pricing a claim exists, the Court of Claims has attempted to eliminate the objectionable aspects of the total cost approach by closely scrutinizing the costs incurred, disallowing those that are the contractor's responsibility, and either averaging estimates of other bidders or using the government's estimate to minimize the possibility of an unreasonably low bid.[22]

To minimize the potential for problems that most frequently generate criticism of the total cost approach, courts and boards have frequently embraced a "modified" total cost approach. Under this approach, questionable portions of estimated or actual costs are excluded from the calculation so that the result is not distorted. For example, in *Hewitt Contracting Co.,*[23] the government generally acknowledged and the board accepted the reasonableness and accuracy of the contractor's claimed total costs for road reconstruction except for those associated with one aspect of performance relating to thickening the road base. The board allowed an appropriate credit against the claimed total cost to reflect Hewitt's responsibility for thickening the road base. The decision noted the reasonableness of Hewitt's bid—only four percent lower than the second-lowest bidder. Also, the contractor's work was made more difficult and costly by deficient government design, harassment, overinspection, acceleration demands, suspensions of work, and improper termination. The combination of these factors made it impossible for the board to compute or even segregate the individual claims except for the road base claim. Consequently, it found no alternative to the use of the modified total cost method for establishing the adjustment. With increasing frequency, however, boards of

---

[20] Glasgow, Inc. v. Department of Transp., 108 Pa. Cmmw. 48, 529 A.2d 576 (1987); United States *ex rel.* United States Steel Corp. v. Construction Aggregates Corp., 559 F. Supp. 414 (E.D. Mich. 1983); Moorehead Constr. Co. v. City of Grand Forks, 508 F.2d 1008 (8th Cir. 1975); WRB Corp. v. United States, 183 Ct. Cl. 409 (1968).

[21] J.D. Hedin Constr. Co. v. United States, 171 Ct. Cl. 86, 347 F.2d 235, 246 (1965); Hewitt Contracting Co., ENGBCA Nos. 4596, 4597, 83-2 BCA ¶ 16,816, at 83,643 (1983); Claude C. Wood Co., AGBCA No. 83-106-3, 83-1 BCA ¶ 16,543, at 82,259–260.

[22] Teledyne McCormick-Selph v. United States, 588 F.2d 808 (Ct. Cl. 1978). *See* Boyajian v. United States, 191 Ct. Cl. 233, 423 F.2d 1231 (1970) (thorough discussion of total cost method cases).

[23] ENGBCA Nos. 4596–4597, 83-2 BCA ¶ 16,816 (1983).

contract appeals have been rejecting the total cost method in favor of the *jury verdict,* which is discussed in the following section.[24]

§ 10.6   Jury Verdict Method

Courts and boards have increasingly utilized a *jury verdict* approach to quantify equitable adjustments.[25] After consideration of all the evidence in the record, expert and otherwise, the board or court then determines on a somewhat subjective basis, much like a jury does, how much should be paid. Use of this exercise, known as the *jury verdict* method, was described by the board in *Air-A-Plane Corp.*:[26]

> The jury verdict will generally be used only: . . . where each side presents convincing but conflicting evidence as to what the amount the equitable adjustment should be . . . , neither side is considered entirely correct . . . , some allowance by the Board is proper, and where evidence is sufficient to permit the Board to make some reasonable decision as to the proper allowance . . . .

In one case, the Armed Services board refused to apply the jury verdict method because the contractor failed to comply with an additional requirement that there be "convincing proof of the nature and kinds of increased costs incurred."[27] The Court of Claims uses the jury verdict method where precise measurement of cost is not available.[28] The court attempts to make a reasonable approximation of costs resulting from causes for which the government is responsible.

The jury verdict is employed only when there is sufficient evidence to reasonably approximate damages. Compelling evidence of quantum is typically required:

> [The jury verdict] method is followed by the Courts and this and other Contract Appeals Boards as a last resort when there is clear entitlement to

---

[24] *See, e.g.,* Warren Painting Co., Inc., ASBCA 18,456, 74-2 BCA ¶ 10,834 (1974); J.W. Bateson Co., VABCA No. 1042, 73-2 BCA ¶ 10,340 (1973); Road-Roc Inc., AGBCA 263, 73-1 BCA ¶ 9938 (1973); Webber Constructors, IBCA 721-6-68, 69-2 BCA ¶ 7895 (1969).

[25] *See, e.g.,* S.W. Elecs. & Mfg. Corp. v. United States, 228 Ct. Cl. 333, 351, 655 F.2d 1078 (1981); Specialty Assembling & Packing Co. v. United States, 174 Ct. Cl. 153, 355 F.2d 554, 572 (1966); Assurance Co. v. United States, 813 F.2d 1202, 1205 (Fed. Cir. 1987); Schuster Eng'g, ASBCA No. 28,760, 87-3 BCA ¶ 20,105 (1987).

[26] ASBCA No. 3842, 60-1 BCA ¶ 2547 (1960).

[27] Planetronics, Inc., ASBCA Nos. 7202, 7535, 1962 BCA ¶ 3356 (1962).

[28] *See* J.G. Watts Constr. Co. v. United States, 174 Ct. Cl. 1 (1966).

costs which cannot be established precisely, and where there is substantial and reasonable evidence which can be the foundation of a sound, unspeculative approximation which is fair to both parties.[29]

In one case a number of unknown factors, including apportionment of responsibility for delay, made it impossible to determine the amount of entitlement with any precision. The jury verdict was utilized as the appropriate method of calculating damages.[30] In another case, the contractor offered no documentation or testimony to support his quantum claim. However, the board concluded that the record supported a larger equitable adjustment than the amount offered by the government. The board resorted to a jury verdict to arrive at a reasonable approximation of the amount owed by the government.[31]

§ 10.7   Forward Pricing

The preceding sections examine pricing methods for quantifying claims after the work has been performed, based upon actual historical costs. This is also known as *hindsight pricing.* Under some circumstances, parties may desire to *forward price* the adjustment. The term *forward pricing* refers to the practice of reaching agreement on the price of an equitable adjustment prior to proceeding with the work in question. Forward pricing of changes is consistent, particularly from the owner's or government's viewpoint, with the whole philosophy behind firm-fixed-price contracts. Use of forward pricing should be a goal of all owners and government agencies.[32] Of course, such equitable adjustments may include a contingency to compensate contractors for the extra risk they bear in these situations.

Forward pricing maximizes the likelihood that (1) the contractor has more incentive to accomplish work in the most efficient manner, (2) the original allocation of risk is unaltered, and (3) the burden of proving that price is reasonable remains with the contractor.[33] From the contractor's point of view, it may be less advantageous to forward price contract modifications. By utilizing hindsight pricing the contractor can be less cost conscious, the contractor will have actual cost data to present to the

---

[29] International Equip. Servs., Inc., ASBCA Nos. 21,104, 23,170, 83-2 BCA ¶ 16,675, at 82,925 (1983).

[30] William P. Bergan, Inc., IBCA No. 1130-11-76, 79-1 BCA ¶ 13,671 (1979). *See also* Tutor-Saliba-Parini, PSBCA No. 1201, 87-2 BCA ¶ 19,775 (1987).

[31] Harold Benson, AGBCA No. 384, 77-1 BCA ¶ 12,490 (1977).

[32] *See, e.g.,* U.S. Army Corps of Engineers, Modification Impact Evaluation Guide, EP 415-1-3, at 3–4 (July 2, 1979).

[33] *Id.*

government, and some risks contractually assigned to the contractor are shifted to the owner or the government.[34]

Forward pricing should only be utilized where adequate known and estimated data is available. However, circumstances often dictate that the equitable adjustment cannot be determined until after all pertinent material and labor costs are actually incurred. Nevertheless, major benefits of forward pricing, particularly with respect to time extensions, are that it encourages prompt revision of the progress schedule and maintains accurate current knowledge of the sequencing of remaining work, the contract price, and the final completion data. Only under these conditions can the schedule continue to be an effective tool for managing a project and for determining the impact of changes on contractor operations. An accurate, updated critical path method (CPM) schedule is necessary to forecast the existence and extent of impact.

§ 10.8   Labor Costs

With respect to disruption or additional work, contractors are entitled to recover added labor costs, including basic wages to workers and working foremen who perform field work. In addition, contractors may generally claim *labor burden* or *fringe benefits* such as employment taxes under the Federal Insurance Contributions Act (FICA) or the Federal Unemployment Tax Act (FUTA), holiday pay, and sick leave costs.

With respect to delay claims, contractors are more likely to incur wage escalation costs. Most contracts are predicated upon a calculation of hourly labor rates, taking into account existing rates at the time of the bid as well as foreseeable increases. They also take into account the number of hours expected to be billed in a given period. An original plan for wage rates and labor hours might look like the following:

Period No.	1	2	3
Wage rate	$ 3.75	$ 4.00	$4.25
Estimated hours	10	10	0
Estimated wages	$37.50	$40.00	$ 0

The actual situation at the conclusion of the project, extended due to compensable delays, might look like the following:

Period No.	1	2	3	4
Wage rate	$3.75	$4.00	$ 4.25	$ 4.50
Hours worked	0	0	10	10
Total wages	$ 0	$ 0	$42.50	$45.00

---

[34] *Id.*

In this example, the planned expenditure was $77.50, but the actual expenditure was $87.50. Hence, the contractor would be entitled to claim $10 in wage escalation costs if all of the delay is compensable.[35]

During periods of delay it may also be necessary to retain workers or supervisors when it is not feasible or economical under the circumstances to dismiss them. In such cases, contractors have been permitted to recover these idle-labor costs.[36]

§ 10.9   Material Escalation

Delay in necessary actions, such as completion of drawings, approval of samples and submittals, and review of shop drawings, often results in an inability to order material during the early portion of the performance term. The contractor faced with such circumstances may be unable to take advantage of the prices on which he based his bid and may be required to purchase the material at a higher price. The difference between the contemplated price and the actual expense constitutes a legitimate and compensable claim item.[37]

§ 10.10   Equipment Costs

On occasion it is necessary for a contractor to use additional equipment over and above the equipment spreads reasonably contemplated at the time of contracting in order to comply with an owner's acceleration order. The costs of this additional equipment may be recovered by the contractor. Where equipment is owned, the *Associated General Contractors of America (AGC) Schedule* is commonly used to calculate the contractor's ownership expense. This equipment rate guide reflects the experience of equipment owners and average working conditions. The AGC schedule has been used and accepted by courts and boards in determining equitable adjustments.[38]

---

[35] *See* Keco Indus., Inc., ASBCA Nos. 15,184, 15,547, 72-2 BCA ¶ 9576 (1972). *See also* Sovereign Constr., Ltd., ASBCA No. 17,793, 75-1 BCA ¶ 11,251 (1975).

[36] Laburnum Constr. Corp. v. United States, 325 F.2d 451, 163 Ct. Cl. 339 (1963); Barnet Bremer, ASBCA No. 6194, 1962 BCA ¶ 3381 (1962). *See also* Hardeman-Monier-Hutcherson, ASBCA No. 11,785, 67-1 BCA ¶ 6210 (1967) (remote location of construction site in Australia made it impossible for workers to be employed elsewhere).

[37] Paccon, Inc., ASBCA No. 7890, 65-2 BCA ¶ 4996, at 23,578–79 (1965); Layne-Minn., Inc. v. Singer Co., 574 F.2d 429 (8th Cir. 1978).

[38] Mid-West Constr. Co. v. United States, 461 F.2d 794, 198 Ct. Cl. 572 (1972); Nolan Bros. v. United States, 437 F.2d 1371, 194 Ct. Cl. 1 (1971); Basic Constr. Co., ASBCA No. 22,931, 79-2 BCA ¶ 13,947 (1979).

The current Federal Acquisition Regulations (FAR) provision indicates that actual cost data from the contractor's accounting records should be used to calculate equipment costs.[39] When these costs cannot be determined through this method, the cost may be determined by use of a schedule designated by the contracting agency. The provision specifically refers to the "Construction Equipment Ownership and Operating and Expense Schedule" published by the Army Corps of Engineers as an example of such a schedule. The cost of equipment rented from independent firms not affiliated with the contractor must be based on actual and reasonable rental payments.[40]

In cases of suspensions or delays, contractors are entitled to recover idle equipment as stand-by costs when it is impractical to transport and use the equipment elsewhere. Because this idle equipment does not suffer wear and tear, the courts frequently allow only 50 percent of the AGC rate.[41] Of course, if the equipment is rented the contractor may recover actual costs. However, the contractor has an obligation to mitigate damages, and rented equipment should be returned if it is feasible and economical under the circumstances.[42]

§ 10.11 Extended Supervision

The cost of the additional time that a contractor's project management personnel, such as the project manager and superintendent, are involved with the project is also compensable.[43] Basic labor escalation is usually recovered through wage rate differentials, because workers in the respective trades are rarely on site until work is available. However, supervisory staff usually stay with the project from inception to conclusion. Thus, a delay will result in additional supervisory payments for the extended time of performance. These compensable costs are calculated from the original completion date to the actual completion date. Where the period of delay is partially compensable and partially noncompensable, an allocation must be made between the compensable and noncompensable periods.

It is sometimes difficult to determine which employees should be claimed. A problem frequently arises in determining whether middle management personnel are treated as supervisors or as part of the overall

---

[39] FAR § 31.105(d)(2)(i)(A), 48 C.F.R. § 31.105(d)(2)(i)(A) (1990).

[40] FAR § 31.105(d)(2)(ii), 48 C.F.R. § 31.105(d)(2)(ii) (1990).

[41] *See, e.g.,* L.L. Hall Constr. Co. v. United States, 177 Ct. Cl. 870, 881–884, 379 F.2d 559 (1966) and cases cited therein.

[42] Tutor-Saliba-Parini, PSBCA No. 1201, 87-2 BCA ¶ 19,775 (1987); Folk Constr. Co. v. United States, 2 Cl. Ct. 681 (1983).

[43] T.C. Bateson Constr. Co., ASBCA No. 6028, 1963 BCA ¶ 3692 (1963).

labor force. An appropriate rule of thumb is that if the employees are not "production" employees, their wage-related costs should be claimed. Stated differently, if the employee's presence is required on site after the original completion date, irrespective of what type of work is underway, that cost should be claimed as extended site supervision.

Contractors should be careful to read general provisions in their contracts relating to equitable adjustments and overhead mark-up limitations. Some of these provisions state that supervision is included in overhead and that overhead is limited to a percentage of the direct cost of additional or changed work. Therefore, to the extent that project duration is extended due to changes, additional supervision costs are subsumed within the allowable overhead mark-up on the direct costs and cannot be claimed independently.[44]

§ 10.12   Extended Jobsite Expense

When a delay in completion occurs, a contractor may incur added expenses for jobsite equipment, tools, utilities, trailers, and other items that must remain on the jobsite for longer periods of time than originally planned. If the delay is otherwise compensable, these costs may be recovered. One method of evaluating these costs, as discussed previously, involves recourse to the monthly cost, AGC schedule rate, or rental value of machinery on the jobsite. However, one note of caution is in order. As discussed in the previous section, some contracts stipulate that these costs are included in the overhead mark-up upon direct costs, which is limited to a specified percentage of the additional direct cost. This prohibits claiming such extended jobsite costs as separate items.

§ 10.13   Extended Home Office Overhead

Every construction project must carry a portion of the contractor's home office overhead. General and administrative (G&A) overhead is not billed as a direct expense to specific projects, yet it fulfills a management function for all projects. G&A constitutes a portion of the cost of doing business for each project and also a cost of doing business for the company as a whole.

Home office or G&A expenses include items such as salaries and rent. Contractors must remember to consult all relevant regulations in determining total overhead cost. For example, the FAR prohibits inclusion of the following in the total G&A pool: bad debts, contributions and

---

[44] Jack Picoult Constr. v. United States, 207 Ct. Cl. 1052 (1975).

donations, entertainment, interest, organization costs, and various other items.[45]

Where construction operations are halted or project completion is delayed, the direct costs of the project to which overhead is charged are reduced, resulting in some amount of overhead being "unabsorbed." Where the delay or extended performance is compensable, the unabsorbed or extended overhead may be recovered by the contractor.[46]

The formula most widely used to calculate daily extended overhead costs is known as the Eichleay formula.[47] The Eichleay formula is now widely accepted by courts and boards.[48] The formula is expressed as follows:

$$\frac{\text{Contract Billings}}{\substack{\text{Total billings for} \\ \text{actual contract period}}} \times \substack{\text{Total overhead} \\ \text{incurred during contract}} = \substack{\text{Overhead allocable} \\ \text{to the contract}}$$

$$\frac{\text{Allocable Overhead}}{\substack{\text{Actual days of} \\ \text{contract performance}}} = \substack{\text{Overhead allocable} \\ \text{to contract per day}}$$

$$\text{Daily overhead} \times \text{Number of days of delay} = \substack{\text{Extended or} \\ \text{unabsorbed overhead}}$$

In a 1984 case, the U.S. Court of Appeals for the Federal Circuit approved use of the Eichleay formula and, at the same time, simplified the contractor's proof requirements. In *Capital Electric Co. v. United States*,[49] the court noted that the contractor is required only to show that it was not prudent or practical to shift forces from the delayed project to new work during the delay. This requirement can be met in a number of ways. First, contractors can demonstrate that performance was simply stretched out and that work forces were not truly "freed-up." Second, the contractor can show that his limited bonding capacity or working capital prevented him from undertaking additional work. Finally, the requirement can be met based upon the uncertainty or length of the delay period. Short delays simply do not permit a contractor to shift forces. Where the length of the

---

[45] FAR § 31.205, 48 C.F.R. § 31.205 (1989).

[46] Eichleay Corp., ASBCA No. 5183, 60-2 BCA ¶ 2688 (1960), *aff'd on reconsideration*, 61-1 BCA ¶ 2894 (1961).

[47] *Id.*

[48] *See, e.g.,* George Hyman Constr. Co. v. Washington Metro. Area Transit Auth., 816 F.2d 753 (D.C. Cir. 1987); Cieszko Constr. Co., ASBCA No. 34,199, 88-2 BCA ¶ 20,653 (1988); Shirley Contracting Corp., ASBCA No. 29,848, 87-2 BCA ¶ 19,759 (1987).

[49] 729 F.2d 743 (Fed. Cir. 1984).

delay is uncertain, it would be foolish for the contractor to shift forces to another project.

Entitlement to extended home office overhead can result from pure delays, suspensions of work, differing site conditions, and/or changes in the scope of work.[50] Where the extended performance results from differing site conditions or changes, the contractor is entitled to an equitable adjustment for the increased direct cost of the work. This equitable adjustment normally includes a percentage mark-up on direct costs for overhead. This can lead to duplication of costs in the event of an extended overhead claim. The contractor should address the duplication problem by giving the owner a credit for that portion of the overhead mark-up that was *intended* to cover home office overhead.[51]

Contractors sometimes cannot determine the extent of extended overhead costs when negotiating a direct cost equitable adjustment. Contractors should therefore reserve the right to submit a claim for impact and delay costs—including extended overhead—in the direct cost proposal and any contract modification for those direct costs. Failure to do so can result in the owner's avoidance of responsibility for extended overhead costs by raising the defense of accord and satisfaction.[52]

Contractors should also pay special attention to the language in the general provisions providing for an equitable adjustment. For example, the Veterans Administration has used a changes clause that limits overhead allowances to 10 percent of the direct cost of changed work and provides that the overhead mark-up is considered "general home office expenses."

The Court of Appeals for the Federal Circuit has held the changes clause enforceable and limits the contractor's recovery of extended home office overhead costs resulting from changes to 10 percent of the direct cost of the changed work.[53]

---

[50] Savoy Constr. Co. v. United States, 2 Fed. Procurement Dec. (Fed. Publications, Inc.) ¶ 210 (Fed. Cir. 1984); Chantilly Constr. Corp., ASBCA No. 24,138, 81-1 BCA ¶ 14,863 (1980).

[51] *See* J.D. Hedin Constr. Co. v. United States, 347 F.2d 235, 259 (Ct. Cl. 1965); Cieszko Constr. Co., ASBCA No. 34,199, 88-1 BCA ¶ 20,223 (1987); Excavation-Constr., Inc., ENGBCA No. 3837, 86-1 BCA ¶ 18,638, at 93,669 (1985); Canon Constr. Corp., ASBCA No. 16,142, 72-1 BCA ¶ 9404, at 43,667 (1972) (board found that 10% markups for overhead and profit did not duplicate extended overhead costs).

[52] *See, e.g.,* Schuster Eng'g, Inc., ASBCA Nos. 28,760, 29,306, 30,683, 87-3 BCA ¶ 20,105, at 101,802 (1987).

[53] Santa Fe Eng'rs, Inc. v. United States, 801 F.2d 379 (Fed. Cir. 1986).

§ 10.14   Profit

Contractors recover profit on additional costs incurred because of changed performance as part of an equitable adjustment.[54] The more important issue is the amount of profit to which the contractor is entitled. In the absence of limiting statutory or contractual provisions, contractors have normally been permitted to recover a "reasonable" profit, which is not necessarily the same rate of profit incorporated in the bid.[55]

Consideration should be given to the amount of risk involved and the difficulty of the work in determining the appropriate level of profit.[56] When the cost of a change is already known, it has been held that a lower risk exists, which entitles the contractor to a lower rate of profit.[57] A rate of 10 percent profit, however, has generally received routine acceptance by the boards.[58]

It is important to keep in mind that profit is not allowed on price adjustments under the standard federal suspension-of-work clause, which specifically excludes profit.[59] When changes are intermingled with suspensions, it is common to allocate the claimed amount between the two clauses, in which case profit is allowed on those costs allocated to the changes-clause claim.[60] If a contractor's extended overhead claim is based on the differing site conditions or changes clause, the contractor is also entitled to a percentage recovery of profit on the extended overhead costs.[61] Many private contracts do not exclude profit from price adjustments for delays.[62]

Some agencies attempt to limit the amount of profit by regulation or standard contractual provisions.[63] The General Accounting Office (GAO)

---

[54] United States v. Callahan-Walker Constr. Co., 317 U.S. 56, 61 (1942); General Builders Supply Co. v. United States, 409 F.2d 246, 187 Ct. Cl. 477 (1969); R.C. Hedreen Co., ASBCA No. 20,004, 76-2 BCA ¶ 12,202 (1976).

[55] See Itek Corp., ASBCA No. 13,528, 71-1 BCA ¶ 8906 (1971) (10% profit allowed although original contract based upon 15% profit).

[56] Id. See also American Pipe & Steel Corp., ASBCA No. 7899, 1964 BCA ¶ 4058 (1964).

[57] Aerojet Gen. Corp., ASBCA No. 17,171, 74-2 BCA ¶ 10,863 (1974).

[58] See Carvel Walker, ENGBCA No. 3744, 78-1 BCA ¶ 13,005 (1977); J&T Constr. Co., DOTBCA No. 73-4, 75-2 BCA ¶ 11,398 (1975); Lanco-Indus. Painting Corp., ASBCA No. 14,647, 73-2 BCA ¶ 10,073 (1973).

[59] Dravo Corp., ENGBCA No. 3915, 79-1 BCA ¶ 13,603 (1978).

[60] Gunther & Shirley Co., ENGBCA No. 3691, 78-2 BCA ¶ 13,454 (1978).

[61] Federal Contracting, Inc., ASBCA No. 28,957, 84-2 BCA ¶ 17,482, at 87,097 (1984) (allowing 10% profit on extended overhead for differing site condition delays and no profit on extended overhead for suspension of work).

[62] See, e.g., AIA A201-1987, Art. 8.

[63] See GSA Form 1139, cl. 23; P.S. (Postal Service) Form 7391, cl. 8 (1987) (both limiting profit on equitable adjustments to 10%).

recently ruled that such profit limitations in fixed-price construction contracts violate FAR § 15.901(c), which prohibits administrative profit ceilings that are less than any applicable statutory ceilings.[64] However, a recent board decision enforced such a profit limitation provision, noting that the contractor had not protested prior to award of the contract.[65] Contractors who see such a provision when reviewing a federal bid package should immediately lodge an objection with the agency. It is also advisable to consult counsel to determine whether a protest is in order.

§ 10.15 Loss of Efficiency

It is generally very difficult to formulate a comprehensive pricing format for costs incurred as a result of disruption, lost efficiency, and the requirement that work be performed out of sequence because such costs are often not specifically identified in project cost records. Nevertheless, contractors must develop a method for pricing these costs because the potential loss can be enormous.

Proof that lost productivity has occurred requires a showing that a given unit of production actually required more labor than would have been required but for some action of the government or owner. Although courts and boards have permitted contractors some leeway in proving the amount of damages, they have held the same contractors to higher standards in terms of proving the cause of the damage or inefficiency.[66]

A number of methods can be used to prove the amount of lost efficiency. The least-favored technique, discussed earlier in this chapter, is the total cost approach. Because a contractor must prove that he is not responsible for increased costs, a successful total cost presentation is a difficult task. Utilization of the total cost approach also permits the owner to introduce evidence of damaging mistakes, errors, and inefficiencies attributable to the contractor. This can severely weaken the contractor's overall presentation.

Despite such problems the total cost approach often is both appropriate and permissible, especially if the breach by the owner is clear, but damages cannot easily be calculated. For example, if a contractor is performing remodeling work and the owner, in violation of the contract, refuses to give the contractor access to certain job areas because the owner wants to continue using them, denial of access causes a major disruption of

---

[64] Lecher Constr. Co., Comp. Gen. B-224,357, 86-2 Comptroller General's Procurement Dec. (Fed. Publications, Inc.) ¶ 369 (1986).

[65] Bruce Anderson, Co., ASBCA No. 35,791, 89-2 BCA 21,871 (1989).

[66] Zinger Constr. Co., ASBCA No. 23,853, 84-1 BCA ¶ 16,993 (1983); Piracci Corp., GSBCA No. 6007, 82-2 BCA ¶ 16,047 (1982).

the work. Although it may be virtually impossible to calculate precisely the loss of efficiency, the disruption, and the additional cost caused by denial of access on a large project, the contractor is still entitled to recover his costs. Contractors may also employ a *modified total cost* approach that focuses on the portion of work affected by the disrupting event.

The most-favored techniques for pricing lost efficiency consider the additional effort required as a result of a delay or disruption in order to produce the same level of output—the cause-and-effect approach. Methods used to price inefficiency in this fashion include the following.

Perhaps the most widely accepted technique, known as the *measured mile* approach, is to compare a contractor's rates of production for periods both prior to and during the "impacted" period.[67] This technique will be most effective when the comparison periods are close in time, involve very similar types of work, and occur on the same contract. A good example is comparison of productivity levels during the periods in which successive floors of a multistory office building are constructed. To the extent there is no "unimpacted" period for comparison, the contractor can utilize his productivity rates for similar work over a longer period that would reflect more normal production rates.[68] When using production rates for work on other projects, contractors should ensure that (1) the work on the other project is substantially similar to the impacted work, (2) weather conditions were similar, and (3) the average skill of the craftsmen involved on the two projects is similar (for example, do not compare union and nonunion or rural and urban projects).[69]

A number of studies published by construction industry organizations have calculated average rates for loss of efficiency due to overtime work, using industry statistical data. It is almost universally accepted that scheduling overtime on a sustained basis will have an adverse impact on labor productivity.[70] Although the additional hours worked will yield additional production, the additional output will be at a regressive rate. As an employee works more overtime hours, the rate of production will decrease and unit labor costs will increase. Industrywide studies have calculated the average lost productivity rates for given levels and periods of scheduled overtime.[71] The AGC has concluded that after several weeks

---

[67] United States Indus., Inc. v. Blake Constr. Co., 671 F.2d 539, 547 (D.C. Cir. 1982); Abbett Elec. Corp. v. United States, 142 Ct. Cl. 609 (1958).

[68] *See, e.g.,* Maryland Sanitary Mfg. Co. v. United States, 119 Ct. Cl. 100 (1951).

[69] Clarke-Baridon, Inc. v. Merritt-Chapman & Scott Corp., 311 F.2d 389, 395 (4th Cir. 1962).

[70] *See Scheduled Overtime Effect on Construction Projects,* Business Roundtable (1980); *Overtime, Construction and Productivity,* Associated General Contractors of America, National Joint Guideline No. 8 (1979); *Overtime v. Productivity,* 35 Electrical Contractor, 1 (1970).

[71] *See, e.g.,* Scheduled Overtime Effect on Construction Projects.

of overtime, working five 10-hour days, the productive value of a labor dollar drops to less than 74 percent of a normal work week labor dollar. If six 10-hour days are worked, the productive value is less than 62 percent of a normal work week, and when seven 12-hour days are worked, the productive value of a labor dollar is less than 40 percent of a normal work week labor dollar.[72] These industry studies are useful in substantiating lost-efficiency claims. However, additional evidence pertaining to the loss of efficiency on the project must be introduced to corroborate the industry data.[73]

Once the loss-of-efficiency factor is determined, that factor should be applied to all labor costs incurred in performing affected work during the impact period. In making this calculation, contractors should include all indirect labor burden that is typically incurred on the type of project in question. These indirect costs (other than overhead) should be calculated on a daily, as opposed to percentage, basis.

§ 10.16   Claim Preparation Cost

The cost of legal, accounting, and consulting services incurred in preparing and prosecuting a claim is not an allowable expense under the Federal Acquisition Regulations.[74] The underlying rationale for this principle is that such costs were not incurred in the performance of the work and, therefore, do not fall within the scope of costs covered by an equitable adjustment.[75]

The one exception to the FAR rule apparently exists when (1) the costs are incurred in preparing an equitable adjustment proposal during performance, (2) the request is meritorious on its face, and (3) the matter was never disputed by the parties to the extent it became a claim.[76] However, this appears to be the minority view.

Additionally, under the Equal Access to Justice Act, contractors who prevail on a claim before a board or court may be entitled to recover

---

[72] Overtime, Construction and Productivity, Associated General Contractors of America, National Guideline No. 8 (1979).

[73] Capital Elec. Co., GSBCA No. 5316, 83-2 BCA ¶ 16,548 (1983), *rev'd on other grounds,* Capital Elec. Co. v. United States, 729 F.2d 743 (Fed. Cir. 1984).

[74] FAR § 31.205-33, 48 C.F.R. § 31.205–233 (1990).

[75] G&T Dev. Co., DOTCAB No. 75-4, 77-1 BCA ¶ 12,494 (1977); N.P.D. Contractors Inc., ASBCA No. 14,798, 71-1 BCA ¶ 8862 (1971). *But see* Aerospace Corp. v. United States, 579 F.2d 586 (Ct. Cl. 1978) (attorney's fees incurred in Freedom of Information Act (FOIA) action to obtain information that might be helpful to a separate contractor "claim" held to be an allowable cost under cost-reimbursement contract).

[76] Singer Co. v. United States, 568 F.2d 695 (Ct. Cl. 1977); Allied Materials & Equip. Co., ASBCA No. 17,318, 75-1 BCA ¶ 11,150 (1975).

attorney and professional or expert fees incurred if the contractor is a small business and the government's position was not substantially justified.[77]

§ 10.17   Interest

Interest on claims against the federal government is recoverable only if expressly authorized by contract or statute.[78] An example of such express authorization is found in the Contract Disputes Act (CDA) of 1978.[79] The CDA provides that interest shall be paid on amounts found due to contractors from the date the contracting officer receives the claim until it is paid. The Prompt Payment Act[80] requires the government to pay an interest penalty on late payments to contractors. Once paid by the government, the obligation for timely payment is imposed upon the prime contractor, who has seven days to make payment to his subcontractors before incurring interest penalties at the same rate imposed on the government.[81]

An issue that sometimes arises is whether contractors may claim and recover interest on borrowings or equity capital used to finance the project. The cost principle found at FAR § 31.205-20 provides:

> Interest and other financial costs.
>
> Interest on borrowings (however represented), bond discounts, costs of financing and refinancing capital (net worth plus long-term liabilities), legal and professional fees paid in connection with preparing prospectuses, costs of preparing and issuing stock rights, and directly associated costs are unallowable except for interest assessed by State or local taxing authorities under conditions specified in 31.205-41 (but see 31.205-28).

Before implementation of this cost principle, contractors could recover interest costs incurred to finance changes.[82] With the promulgation of the new regulation, courts and boards are now less likely to allow recovery of

---

[77] *See* 5 U.S.C. § 504 (1977 & Supp. VI, 1990) and 28 U.S.C. § 2412(d) (1978 & Supp. VI, 1990).

[78] *See, e.g.,* Grenite-Groves v. Washington Metro. Area Transit Auth., 845 F.2d 330 (D.C. Cir. 1988).

[79] 41 U.S.C. § 611 (1987).

[80] 31 U.S.C. §§ 3901–06 (1983 & Supp. VI, 1990).

[81] *Id.* at § 3905(b), (c); FAR 52.232-27.

[82] Bell v. United States, 404 F.2d 975 (Ct. Cl. 1968) (contractor allowed to recover monies expended to pay interest on borrowings directly attributable to the contract as an equitable adjustment).

interest costs.[83] However, in *Automation Fabricators & Engineering Co.,*[84] a claim for interest incurred solely to finance government-caused delays and changes was sustained, despite the government's contention that federal statutory law denies payment of interest when a contract or regulation prohibits such payment. The board recognized a contractor's right to be reimbursed for financing interest expenses incurred during government-caused delay and found the interest prohibition of the pricing-of-adjustments clause nonbinding, because the clause, by its own terms, was merely a guideline to be used in negotiating equitable adjustments.

A more difficult issue is whether the limitation on recovery of interest is inapplicable in a breach of contract action because the relief sought is extracontractual. FAR § 31.102 provides:

> Fixed-price contracts.
>
> The applicable subparts of Part 31 [the cost principles] shall be used in the pricing of fixed-price contracts, subcontracts, and modifications to contracts and subcontracts whenever (a) costs analysis is performed, or (b) a fixed-price contract clause requires the determination or negotiation of costs . . . .

A breach of contract action for damages is distinct from the pricing of fixed-price contracts for which the cost principles are intended. Theoretically, the cost principles should not apply to limit breach of contract damages.[85] Under this approach a contractor who proceeds on a breach of contract or rescission theory may consider claiming actual financing costs or the costs of equity capital that are reasonably attributable to the government's actions. However, the General Services Administration board

---

[83] Framlau Corp. v. United States, 568 F.2d 687 (Ct. Cl. 1977) (court will not permit recovery of interest regardless of whether debt or equity capital was used); Dravo Corp. v. United States, 594 F.2d 842 (Ct. Cl. 1979) (no recovery for use of capital in lieu of interest costs on borrowing); Creative Elec., Inc., ASBCA No. 26,368, 83-1 BCA ¶ 16,363 (1983) ("The cost principle states clearly that interest on borrowings 'however represented' is unallowable. Accordingly, when a claim is made for 'interest,' calling it an element of profit does not change the result."); *Compare* Ingalls Shipbuilding Div., Litton Sys., Inc., ASBCA No. 17,579, 78-1 BCA ¶ 13,038 (1978) (permitting a contractor to recover compensation for use of his capital as an element of profit, reasoning that it is not prohibited because contractor was not recovering this cost as an element of interest). *See also* Automation Fabricators & Eng'g Co., PSBCA No. 2701, 90-3 BCA ¶ 22,943 (1990).

[84] PSBCA No. 2701, 90-3 BCA ¶ 22,943 (1990).

[85] *See* J. Cibinic & C. Nash, Administration of Government Contracts, 473 (2d ed. 1985) (citing Meva Corp. v. United States, 206 Ct. Cl. 203, 511 F.2d 548 (1975), where the overhead portion of a damages claim was computed using the jury verdict method rather than the cost principles).

has held that a contractor may not avoid the prohibition against recovery of interest costs by characterizing the claim as one for breach of contract damages.[86]

Of course, on private or nonfederal projects these FAR limitations do not apply, and a contractor must determine whether interest or financing costs are recoverable in his jurisdiction. In some jurisdictions such costs are viewed as consequential damages and are, therefore, not recoverable unless they were contemplated by the parties at the time of the agreement.[87]

---

[86] Robert J. DiDomenico, GSBCA No. 5539, 82-2 BCA ¶ 16,093 (1982).

[87] Morris v. Mosby, 227 Va. 517, 317 S.E.2d 493 (1984).

CHAPTER 11

CALCULATING OWNER'S DAMAGES FOR DELAY

§ 11.1   Introduction

§ 11.2   Scope of Recoverable Damages

§ 11.3   Liquidated versus Actual Damages

§ 11.4   —Lack of Actual Damages

§ 11.5   —Prohibition Against Penalty

§ 11.6   —Concurrent Delay

§ 11.7   —Concurrent Delay as Bar

§ 11.8   —Apportionment of Liquidated Damages

§ 11.9   —Use of Critical Path Method Analysis

§ 11.10   —Substantial Completion and Beneficial Occupancy

§ 11.11   Actual Damages for Delay

§ 11.12   —Loss of Profits

§ 11.13   —Loss of Use

§ 11.14   —Increased Financing

§ 11.15   —Extended Maintenance and Operation Expenses

§ 11.16   —Special Damages

§ 11.17   —Attorneys' Fees

§ 11.18   —Interest

§ 11.19   Exemplary Damages

§ 11.1   Introduction

Courts permit recovery by owners for a variety of damages resulting from contract violations by contractors, architects, engineers, construction managers, and sureties. Damages may be recoverable by owners who have suffered injury from the failure of professionals such as architects and engineers to meet standards of care. Types of damages available to an owner include delay damages (actual and liquidated), damages for

307

defective performance, damages for termination and abandonment, interest, attorneys' fees, and exemplary (punitive) damages.

Contract damages are intended to give the injured party the benefit of the bargain by awarding the party a sum of money that will, to the extent possible, put her in as good a position as she would have been had the contract been performed. This chapter provides an overview of methods that may be used in calculating owner delay damages, which typically are a major component of construction damages.

§ 11.2   Scope of Recoverable Damages

In evaluating the types and measure of contract damages, it is important to understand the distinction between general or direct damages and special or consequential damages. A good explanation of the distinction appears in *Roanoke Hospital Association v. Doyle & Russell, Inc.,*[1] in which the court states:

> there are two broad categories of damages *ex contractu:* direct (or general) damages and consequential (or special) damages. Direct damages are those which arise 'naturally' or 'ordinarily' from a breach of contract; they are damages which, in the ordinary course of human experience, can be expected to result from a breach. Consequential damages are those which arise from the intervention of 'special circumstances' not ordinarily predictable. If damages are determined to be direct, they are compensable. If damages are determined to be consequential, they are compensable only if it is determined that the special circumstances were within the 'contemplation' of both contracting parties. Whether damages are direct or consequential is a question of law. Whether special circumstances were within the contemplation of the parties is a question of fact.[2]

Contemplation of the contracting parties includes both what was actually foreseen and what was reasonably foreseeable.[3] Generally, contemplation must exist at the time the contract is executed.[4] However, this rule is not absolute. When the breach alleged is an unexcused delay in completion and if the completion date has been altered by mutual consent of the parties, contemplation is to be determined as of the date of amendment.[5]

Damages in tort, or negligence, are not limited by the direct/consequential distinction of contract damages. In tort, damages are allowed that will place the plaintiff in the position she would have been absent the tort

---

[1] 215 Va. 796, 214 S.E.2d 155 (1975).

[2] 214 S.E.2d at 160 (citations omitted).

[3] *Id.* at n.4.

[4] S.C. Corbin, Contracts § 1012(89) (1964); Restatement (Second) of Contracts § 351 (1979).

[5] Roanoke Hosp. Ass'n v. Doyle & Russell, Inc., 215 Va. 796, 214 S.E.2d 155 (1975).

committed by the defendant. This measure of recovery is distinct from that allowed in a contract action. In tort, the court does not look to the damages anticipated by the parties at the time of the contract's inception, but, rather, what damages flowed proximately from the tortious conduct. Hence, damages in tort need not have been within the contemplation of the parties to permit recovery and may be larger than those recoverable in a contract action.

The damages cited above are based upon common law remedies for breaches of contract or tort. A contract may, by design, careful drafting, or inadvertence, contain specific clauses that allow or deny the recovery of specific categories of damages, such as attorneys' fees, interest at the prime rate, loss of grant funding, or special termination damages. The use of AIA and government contract forms is so standard that the effect of special clauses contained in those forms is included in this chapter.

§ 11.3   Liquidated versus Actual Damages

Many construction contracts contain a provision that fixes a specific amount of damages the owner is entitled to in the event the contractor fails to complete the project by the contract completion date. Such a provision is generally referred to as a *liquidated damages clause,* because the clause *liquidates,* that is, makes certain the amount of, damages the owner will recover in the event of delay.

A significant question for any owner is whether to include a liquidated damage provision in her construction contract. Although liquidated damages may help provide some certainty as to damages that will be recovered, they also may fall far short of actual damages. Thus, if the potential for actual damages is very large, an owner may wish to forgo including a contractual provision that limits recovery for delay damages to a liquidated amount and seek recovery of actual losses for delay items such as interest payments on a construction loan or loss of rental income.

Liquidated damages clauses are included in contracts usually because it is difficult to ascertain the exact amount of damages caused by delay. It is wise, therefore, to specify a fixed amount of damages recoverable by the owner to put the contractor on notice as to her liability if she fails to complete on time. Courts uphold liquidated damages provisions as long as there is a finding that it would be difficult to ascertain the exact amount of delay damages and the specified amount is reasonable under the circumstances.[6] However, when the liquidated damages provision can fairly

---

[6] *See, e.g.,* Monsen Eng'g Co. v. Tami-Githens, Inc., 219 N.J. Super. 241, 530 A.2d 313 (1983); Southwest Eng'g Co. v. United States, 341 F.2d 998 (8th Cir.), *cert. denied,* 382 U.S. 819 (1965); Better Food Mkts. v. American Dist. Tel. Co., 40 Cal. 179, 253 P.2d 10 (1953).

be described as a penalty, liquidated damages will not be imposed.[7] Further, an owner's contribution to the cause of delay may affect her ability to recover otherwise lawful liquidated damages.

§ 11.4 —Lack of Actual Damages

A provision imposing liquidated damages will not be ignored merely because the parties have stipulated that actual damages were not sustained by the owner.[8] In *Southwest Engineering Co. v. United States,*[9] the government sought to impose on the contractor liquidated damages of $8,300. The contractor was late in completing four separate facilities. In attempting to avoid liquidated damages, the contractor argued that the government had not suffered actual damages, to which the government agreed. Nonetheless, liquidated damages were imposed. The court noted that two requirements are considered to determine whether a provision for liquidated damages will be enforced. First, the amount of liquidated damages fixed must be a reasonable forecast of just compensation for the harm that is caused by the breach of contract. Second, the harm that is caused by the breach must be impossible (or very difficult) to accurately estimate.[10]

Once those requirements have been met, the court will not look with disfavor upon a liquidated damages provision.[11] Moreover, those requirements are adjudged as of the time the contract was executed, rather than when the contract was breached.[12] Therefore, whether actual damages were incurred is incidental to application of a liquidated damages clause.

§ 11.5 —Prohibition Against Penalty

If the contractor can show that the liquidated damages clause constitutes a penalty, the clause will be invalidated.[13] Two factors combine in

---

[7] Priebe & Sons, Inc. v. United States, 322 U.S. 407 (1947). *See also* § 8.5.

[8] Berger v. McBride & Sons Builders, 447 S.W.2d 18 (Mo. Ct. App. 1967).

[9] 341 F.2d 998 (8th Cir. 1965).

[10] *Id.* at 1001.

[11] *See* Loggin Constr. Co. v. Stephen F. Austin Univ. Bd. of Regents, 543 S.W.2d 682 (Tex. Civ. App. 1976); Annotation, *Contractual Provision for Per Diem Payments for Delays in Performance as One for Liquidated Damages for Penalty,* 12 A.L.R. 4th 891 (1982).

[12] Priebe & Sons, Inc. v. United States, 332 U.S. 407 (1947); Bethlehem Steel Corp. v. City of Chicago, 350 F.2d 649 (7th Cir. 1965); Equitable Lumber Corp. v. IPA Land Dev. Corp., 38 N.Y.2d 516, 344 N.E.2d 391, 381 N.Y.S.2d 459 (1976); S.L. Rowland Constr. Co. v. Beall Pipe & Tank Corp., 14 Wash. App. 297, 540 P.2d 912 (1975).

[13] Restatement (Second) of Contracts § 356(1) (1979); Priebe & Sons, Inc. v. United States, 332 U.S. 407 (1947).

determining whether an amount of money fixed as damages is so unreasonably large as to be a penalty.

First, the liquidated amount must either reasonably reflect the actual amount of loss resulting from the delay or reasonably approximate the loss anticipated at the time of entering the contract. Second, the actual harm or loss must be difficult to ascertain with sufficient certainty. The greater the degree to which the fixed amounts fail to meet this standard, the greater the likelihood a penalty will be found.[14] Such penalties are disfavored because they are mainly intended to compel performance of contract by threat.[15]

Accordingly, liquidated damage clauses have been invalidated when fixed minimum damage bore no relationship to potential losses[16] or did not compensate for various levels of loss.[17] In *Brecher v. Laikin,*[18] the court held that a liquidated damage clause that does not differentiate between serious or trivial breaches of contract is necessarily a penalty.

The contractor should be alert to the specific liquidated damages provision in her contract. If the contract provides for the same penalty whether the contractor is one day late or 1,000, it is likely that it will be construed as a penalty and the liquidated damages clause will be unenforceable. Most liquidated damages provisions in construction contracts are based upon a fixed amount per day, which obviates the possibility of the provision being cast aside as a penalty on the above basis. If the liquidated damages clause is deemed an unenforceable penalty, the owner may still seek recovery of her actual damages for delay.[19]

§ 11.6   —Concurrent Delay

Enforcement of liquidated damages may be affected by concurrent delay. This concern arises when the party seeking to impose liquidated damages contributes to the project delay. If an owner is partly responsible for a delay for which she seeks compensation, imposition or enforcement of liquidated damages may be prevented.

Jurisdictions vary widely in their approach to concurrent delay and its effect on liquidated damages clauses. Some courts find entitlement to liquidated damages is completely extinguished if the plaintiff is shown to

---

[14] Restatement (Second) of Contracts § 356 comment 6 (1979).

[15] Marathon Battery Co., ASBCA No. 9464, 1964 BCA ¶ 4337 (1969).

[16] *See, e.g.,* Clermont v. Secured Inv. Co., 25 Cal. App. 3d 766, 102 Cal. Rptr. 340 (1970).

[17] *See, e.g.,* Standard Coil Prods., Inc., ASBCA No. 4878, 59-1 BCA ¶ 2105 (1959).

[18] 430 F. Supp. 103 (S.D.N.Y. 1977).

[19] *See, e.g.,* Aetna Casualty & Ins. Co. v. Board of Trustees, 223 Cal. App. 2d 337, 35 Cal. Rptr. 765 (1963).

have contributed to the delay, regardless of the degree of contribution.[20] Other courts are willing to apportion delays or utilize the concept of proportional fault to enforce some measure of liquidated damages in concurrent delay situations.[21]

§ 11.7   —Concurrent Delay as Bar

When an owner is responsible for a concurrent cause of delay in a contractor's performance, some courts refuse to assess liquidated damages against the contractor.[22] In *Acme Process Equipment Co. v. United States,*[23] the court held that when delays are caused by both parties to the contract, the court will not attempt to apportion the delay, but will simply hold that provisions of the contract concerning liquidated damages are null and the owner is allowed to seek her actual damages.[24]

This all-or-nothing approach to entitlement to liquidated damages has been interpreted in the past to apply regardless of the extent of owner-caused delay.[25] Thus, even a minimal contribution to overall delay may bar recovery of all liquidated damages, as some courts are reluctant to apportion fixed damages not intended to compensate concurrent delays.[26]

However, an early Supreme Court case suggests that the degree of owner-contributed delay must be material. In *United States v. United Engineering-Contracting Co.,*[27] the Court, relying on trial court findings, held that the contractor could have completed the job in a timely manner had the government not interfered with the performance. The Supreme Court later characterized the decision as requiring a *but for* analysis,

---

[20] *See, e.g., In re* Construction Diversification, Inc., 36 Bankr. 434 (E.D. Mich. 1983); San Ore-Gardner v. Missouri Pac. R.R., 496 F. Supp. 1337 (E.D. Ark. 1980); Turzillo Contracting Co. v. Messer & Sons, Inc., 234 Ohio App. 2d 179, 261 N.E.2d 675 (1969); State v. Parson Constr., 93 Idaho 118, 456 P.2d 762 (1969); Shintech, Inc. v. Group Constructors, Inc., 688 S.W.2d 144 (Tex. Ct. App. 1985).

[21] *See, e.g.,* Nomelli Constr. Co. v. Department of Water Resources, 19 Cal. App. 3d 240, 96 Cal. Rptr. 682 (1971); E.C. Ernst v. Manhattan Constr. Co. of Tex., 551 F.2d 1026 (5th Cir. 1977); Southwest Eng'g Co. v. United States, 341 F.2d 998 (8th Cir. 1965); Buckley & Co. v. State, 140 N.J. Super. 289, 356 A.2d 56 (Law Div. 1975).

[22] Glassman Constr. Co. v. Maryland City Plaza, Inc., 371 F. Supp. 1154 (D. Md. 1974); Fruin-Colnon Int'l, S.A. v. Concreto, S.A., 231 F. Supp. 14 (D.C.Z. 1964); General Ins. Co. of Am. v. Commerce Hyatt House, 5 Cal. App. 3d 460, 85 Cal. Rptr. 317 (1970).

[23] 177 Ct. Cl. 324 (1965).

[24] *See also,* Intertherm Inc. v. Structural Sys., Inc., 504 S.W.2d 64 (Mo. 1974).

[25] *See In re* Construction Diversification, Inc., 36 Bankr. 434 (E.D. Mich. 1983).

[26] *See, e.g.,* Babylon Assocs. v. County of Suffolk, 475 N.Y.S.2d 869, 101 A.D.2d 207 (1984).

[27] 234 U.S. 236, 34 S. Ct. 843 (1914).

prohibiting award of liquidated damages if the contractor could have completed on time *but for* the government-caused delay.[28] This early rule disfavoring apportionment has been criticized, however, as its "underlying policies do not remain in full force."[29]

§ 11.8   —Apportionment of Liquidated Damages

The developing trend in judicial opinions favors apportionment of fault when an owner claiming liquidated damages partially contributes to delay.[30] However, availability of this remedy requires the ability to apportion delays, and when apportionment would prove too speculative, recovery of liquidated damages may be barred.[31]

Nonetheless, mere difficulty in proving apportionment may not act as a total bar. In *E.C. Ernst, Inc. v. Manhattan Construction Co. of Texas,*[32] the court noted:

> Today, given the increasing complexity of contractual relationships, liquidated damages provisions have obtained firm judicial and legislative support. . . . As long as the owners delay is not incurred in bad faith, it is not unjust to allow proportional fault to govern recovery. . . . We do not disagree with the difficulty of the task [of apportioning damages], but recovery should not be barred in every case by a rule of law that precludes examination of the evidence.[33]

If an owner's actual damages exceed liquidated damages, the owner cannot attempt to vitiate the clause by arguing she was a concurrent cause of delay.[34] To allow such a recovery would permit the owner to profit from her own wrong.[35]

---

[28] Robinson v. United States, 261 U.S. 486, 489, 32 S. Ct. 420 (1923).

[29] E.C. Ernst v. Manhattan Constr. Co. of Tex., 551 F.2d 1026, 1038–39 (5th Cir. 1977), *cert. denied sub nom.* Providence Hosp. v. Manhattan Constr. Co. of Tex., 434 U.S. 1067, 98 S. Ct. 1246 (1978).

[30] Calumet Constr. Corp. v. Metropolitan Sanitary Dist., _____ Ill. App. _____, 533 N.E.2d 453 (1988); Concrete Materials, Inc. v. Smith & Plaster Co., 127 Ga. 813, 195 S.E.2d 219 (1973); Buckley & Co. v. State, 140 N.J. Super. 289, 356 A.2d 56 (Law Div. 1975).

[31] San Ore-Gardner v. Missouri Pac. R.R., 496 F. Supp. 1337 (E.D. Ark. 1980).

[32] 551 F.2d 1026 (5th Cir. 1977).

[33] *Id.* at 1038–39.

[34] *See* X.L.O. Concrete Corp. v. John T. Brady & Co., 482 N.Y.S.2d 476, 104 A.D.2d 181, *aff'd,* 66 N.Y.2d 970, 489 N.E.2d 768, 498 N.Y.S.2d 799 (1984); Mars & Assocs. v. Facilities Dev. Corp., 124 A.D.2d 291, 508 N.Y.S.2d 87 (1986).

[35] Mars & Assocs. v. Facilities Dev. Corp., 124 A.D.2d 291, 508 N.Y.S.2d 87 (1986).

§ 11.9 —Use of Critical Path Method Analysis

An interesting development concerning the relationship between concurrent delays and liquidated damages is the use of critical path method (CPM) analysis to distinguish between delays that are unimportant and those that actually affect the critical path for the project.[36] In *Sante Fe, Inc.*, the board held that a change order issued after the completion date for the project could not be used as an excuse to avoid liquidated damages because the change order did not affect the critical path (due to float time).[37]

In government construction contracts, delay need not be compensable to the contractor to avoid the imposition of liquidated damages. However, where government action results in delay, this delay must occur on the critical path to bar imposition of liquidated damages. As stated in *Utley-James, Inc.*:[38]

> A delay for which the government is responsible is excusable by definition, and it may also be compensable. The rule is that for a delay to be compensable under either the Changes clause or the Suspension of Work Clause, it must result solely from the government's action. If a period of delay can be attributed simultaneously to the actions of both the government and the contractor, they are said to be concurrent delays, and the result is an excusable but not a compensable delay. Frequently in the decisions such phrases as "government delay" or "government-responsible delay" or "contractor responsible delay" are used, and we have used them ourselves. But they are not always precisely correct; strictly speaking there can be but a single delay over a given period of time, and when that delay has multiple, indivisible causes, it is attributable not to either party but to both. Hence it would probably be more accurate to speak not of concurrent delays but of a single delay with concurrent causes. . . .
>
> When venturing into this area, we must be wary of deciding too readily that there was a concurrent delay. We considered this issue in *Warwick Construction, Inc.*[39] and concluded that, at the very least, we would not require a contractor claiming a compensable delay to prove that in the absence of the government's delaying actions it would have completed the job on schedule. However, we also adverted in *Warwick* to the basic principles of *Wunderlich Contracting Co. v. United States*,[40] which requires that a contractor seeking compensation establish the fundamental facts of liability, causation, and resulting injury.

---

[36] *See* Blinderman Constr. Co. v. United States, 695 F.2d 552 (Fed. Cir. 1982).

[37] VABCA Nos. 1943, 1944, 1945, 1946, 84-2 BCA ¶ 17,341 (1984).

[38] GSBCA No. 5370, 85-1 BCA ¶ 17,816, at 89,109 (1984), *aff'd*, Utley-James, Inc. v. United States, 14 Cl. Ct. 804 (1988).

[39] GSBCA Nos. 5070, 5387-88, 5457, 5543, 82-2 BCA ¶ 16,091, at 79,854–55 (1982).

[40] 173 Ct. Cl. 180, 199, 351 F.2d 956, 968–69 (1965).

The board then provided the following example to demonstrate that delay must occur on the critical path:

> If the job schedule was originally such that the contractor needed certain widgets on hand by January 1, but because of a six month delay attributable to the government, the contractor rescheduled delivery for July 1, the government cannot be heard to say the delays were concurrent because the contractor would have had to wait six months for the widgets anyway. In such a situation there is no reason to doubt that the contractor could have had the widgets on January 1 and proceeded on schedule absent the government caused delay.[41]

The trend of modern authority is a willingness on the part of the courts and boards to use critical path method techniques to apportion concurrent delays between the parties and to allow the imposition of liquidated damages where the contractors' delays affect the critical path for the project. As noted in *Utley-James,* where a single delay to the critical path or paths of the project is caused by concurrent causes, liquidated damages will not be enforced.

§ 11.10   —Substantial Completion and Beneficial Occupancy

Liquidated damages clauses entitle the owner to compensation from the contractor when the contractor fails to complete the job by the contract completion date. Therefore, when the project is completed or substantially completed, it may be inequitable to require the contractor to pay liquidated damages. Clearly, then, liquidated damages cease to apply at the time of completion. Moreover, when the owner takes early beneficial occupancy, the contractor may also be excused from liquidated damages.[42] The court in *Aetna Casualty & Surety Co. v. Butte-Meade Sanitary Water District*[43] provided the following definition:

> There is substantial performance of such a contract where all the essentials necessary to the full accomplishment of the purposes for which the thing contracted for has been constructed are performed with such an approximation to complete performance that the owner obtains substantially what is called for by the contract.[44]

---

[41] GSBCA No. 5370, 85-1 BCA ¶ 17,816, at 89,109 (1984).

[42] Gary Constr. Co., ASBCA 19,306, 77-1 BCA ¶ 12,461 (1977); J&A Pollin Constr. Co., GSBCA No. 2780, 70-2 BCA ¶ 8562 (1970).

[43] 500 F. Supp. 193 (D.S.D. 1980).

[44] *Id.* at 198 (quoting 13 Am. Jur. 2d, *Building and Construction Contracts* § 43, at 46 (1964)).

The courts have long recognized that completion does not occur overnight or at one time, but occurs in phases. Beginning with early cases that held it would be unjust for a contractor to be deprived of the benefit of her performance when 99 percent of the project is completed and only 1 percent remains,[45] the courts have gradually fashioned the doctrine of *substantial completion*. According to the doctrine, the contractor is not denied all remedies merely because she fails to complete the project fully. Furthermore, liquidated damages will not be assessed because if the project is deemed substantially completed, liquidated damages would be a penalty.[46] Instead, the contractor is entitled to the value of her performance less some amount fixed as damages sustained by the owner.[47]

The doctrine of substantial completion has been applied to offset the harsh impact of liquidated damages. According to this doctrine, liquidated damages cannot be assessed against the contractor when the contractor substantially completes the job. Therefore, what is of significance to the contractor is not necessarily the date of final completion or the date of completion of punch list work or the date of acceptance by the owner, but, rather, the agreed-upon date of substantial completion, for this halts application of the liquidated damages provision.[48]

In *Ray Martin Co.,*[49] the board defined substantial completion as the date on which the government "was first afforded the opportunity to possess and engage the substance, but not necessarily every aspect, of the benefit for which it contracted." Therefore, substantial completion may well occur before final inspection of the work. Whether or not the owner actually takes possession of and occupies the building is not determinative of whether completion has occurred.[50]

In one case, a contractor sought to hold a subcontractor liable for liquidated damages it had incurred when the Army Corps of Engineers found the project was not "functionally operational" for 136 days beyond the contract completion date. The court, however, found that the project could have been rendered "functionally operational" without completion by the subcontractor and, thus, delay by the subcontractor did not cause assessment of liquidated damages. In addition, the court found that the subcontractor had not done anything that prevented the contractor or

---

[45] Continental Ill. Nat'l Bank v. United States, 121 Ct. Cl. 203 (1952) (assessment of liquidated damages when job was 99.6% complete would constitute a penalty).

[46] Hungerford Constr. Co. v. Florida Citrus Exposition, Inc., 410 F.2d 1229 (5th Cir. 1969).

[47] *Id.*

[48] *See, e.g.,* Urban Plumbing & Heating Co., IBCA No. 43, 56-2 BCA ¶ 1102 (1956); Continental Ill. Nat'l Bank v. United States, 121 Ct. Cl. 203 (1952).

[49] VACAB No. 333, slip op. (Nov. 3, 1961).

[50] United States *ex rel.* Control Sys., Inc. v. Arundel Corp., 814 F.2d 193 (5th Cir. 1987).

other subcontractors from rendering the project functionally operational. The subcontractor was therefore not liable to the prime contractor for the liquidated damages she incurred.[51]

§ 11.11   Actual Damages for Delay

When a partial or total breach of contract by the contractor, construction manager, or architect/engineer causes a delay in the completion of a project and no liquidated damage provision liquidates and limits recovery, the owner may seek a variety of damages to compensate her for delay. As a general rule, damages must either arise naturally from the breach or must have been within the contemplation of the parties in the event of a breach.[52] Thus, courts apply either an objective standard (what the reasonable person would foresee as the result of a breach—or, damages *arising naturally*) or a subjective standard (the expectations of the contracting parties).

The type of damages an owner may recover for delay are many and varied, including lost profits/rents/business; loss of use/rents; interruption; interest and increased financing; extended administration; extended maintenance and operation; and special damages.

§ 11.12   —Loss of Profits

The delay of use of a facility could, and usually does, involve loss of profits. Generally, a party is entitled to recover lost profits in a breach of contract action when the profits are (1) within the contemplation of the parties at the time the contract was made, (2) the proximate result of defendant's breach and (3) proven with reasonable certainty.[53] Proving certainty of lost profits often presents the greatest obstacle in recovery of lost profits. As stated in *Alpine Industries, Inc. v. Gohl:*

> [T]he doctrine respecting the matter of certainty, properly applied, is concerned more with the fact of damage than with the extent or amount of

---

[51] *Id.*

[52] T.D.S. Inc. v. Shelby Mutual Ins. Co., 760 F.2d 1520 (11th Cir. 1985). *See also* Mendoyoma v. County of Mendocino, 8 Cal. App. 3d 873, 87 Cal. Rptr. 740 (1970).

[53] Alpine Indus., Inc. v. Gohl, 30 Wash. App. 750, 637 P.2d 998 (1981) (quoting Larsen v. Walton Plywood Co., 65 Wash. 2d 1, 390 P.2d 677 (1964). *See also* Fields Eng'g & Equip. v. Cargill, Inc., 651 F.2d 589, 593 (8th Cir. 1981) (recovery of profits allowable where: (1) there is proof that loss occurred, (2) such loss flowed directly from the breach and was foreseeable, and (3) there is proof of a rational basis from which the amount can be inferred or approximated).

damage. . . . Since the basic foundation of the rule of certainty is to assure that one will not recover where it is highly doubtful that he has been damaged in the first instance (as where he claims loss of profits in a business which is not shown to have any established record of earnings), the jury does not commit forbidden speculation when, once the fact of damage is established, it is permitted to make reasonable inferences based upon reasonably convincing evidence indicating the amount of damage.[54]

Accordingly, where the delayed owner intends to undertake a new business venture with no prior record of profitability, recovery may be denied per se as too speculative.[55] However, other jurisdictions permit recovery for new business ventures if anticipated profits may be demonstrated with "reasonable certainty."[56] This view has been adopted by the *Restatement (Second) of Contracts,* which states that "damages are not recoverable for loss beyond an amount that the evidence permits to be established with reasonable certainty."[57] Loss of rental income is often a direct consequence of delay and is recoverable with sufficient proof of rental value.[58]

To prove lost profits of a business venture, expert testimony is clearly admissible.[59] Quantum may be demonstrated through record of prior profitability[60] or, for new ventures, subsequent profitability.[61]

§ 11.13 —Loss of Use

The rental or usable value of a property is often used to determine the appropriate measure of damages when it is not possible to prove lost profits with any precision or certainty.[62]

---

[54] 30 Wash. App. 750, 637 P.2d 998, 1001 (1981) (quoting Gaasland Co. v. Hyak Lumber & Millwork, Inc., 42 Wash. 2d 705, 712–13, 257 P.2d 784 (1953)).

[55] *See* A&P Bakery & Supply Co. v. Hawateh, 388 So. 2d 1071 (Fla. Dist. Ct. App. 1980).

[56] *See* Malley-Duff & Assoc. v. Crown Life Ins. Co., 734 F.2d 133 (3rd Cir. 1984); Reeder v. Old Oak Town Center, 124 Ill. App. 3d 1045, 464 N.E.2d 113 (1984); J'Aire Corp. v. Gregory, 24 Cal. 3d 799, 598 P.2d 60, 157 Cal. Rptr. 407 (1979); Oliver B. Cannon & Son v. Dorr-Oliver, Inc., 394 A.2d 1160 (Del. Super. Ct. 1978).

[57] § 352 (1979).

[58] Marshall v. Charles F. Schultz, Inc., 438 So. 2d 533 (Fla. Dist. Ct. App. 1983); J. Clutter Custom Digging v. English, 393 N.E.2d 230 (Ind. App. 1979).

[59] Alpine Indus. v. Gohl, 30 Wash. App. 750, 637 P.2d 998, 1001 (1981); Cates v. Morgan Portable Bldg. Corp., 591 F.2d 17, 22 (7th Cir. 1979); Natco, Inc. v. Williams Bros. Eng'g Co., 489 F.2d 639 (5th Cir. 1974).

[60] *See* Poultry Health Serv. of Ga., Inc. v. Moxley, 538 F. Supp. 276 (S.D. Ga. 1982); Lewis v. Mobil Oil Corp., 438 F.2d 500 (8th Cir. 1971).

[61] *See* Multivision Northwest, Inc. v. Jerrold Elecs. Corp., 356 F. Supp. 207, 216–17 n.4 (N.D. Ga. 1972); Pace Corp. v. Jackson, 284 S.W.2d 340, 348 (Tex. 1964).

[62] Restatement (Second) Contracts § 348(1) (1979); Bird v. American Sur. Co., 175 Cal. 625, 166 P. 1009 (1917).

Usable or rental value is also generally used as the basis for calculating the owner's measure of delay damages. When an adequate substitute space is available, it is incumbent on the owner to find and use such space and thereby mitigate her damages, assuming that to do so is not unreasonably burdensome. Some courts calculate the usable value based on the rental value of the contract property,[63] while others focus on the cost of substitute space.[64]

The usable or rental value as a measure of damages is also helpful when the owner is not involved in a commercial enterprise. Such was the case in *Ambrose v. Biggs,*[65] in which the owner had contracted for the construction of a home. When the construction was delayed, the court found rental value was the proper measure of damages to compensate the family for its loss of use of the property and house.

§ 11.14   —Increased Financing

An owner is entitled to recover financing cost incurred as a result of extending the construction loan through the period of delay.[66] For example, according to the court in *Roanoke Hospital Association v. Doyle & Russell, Inc.,* when a construction project is delayed, "the interest cost incurred and the interest revenue loss during such an extended term are predictable results of the delay and are, therefore, compensable direct damages."[67] However, the incremental increase in rate of interest for a permanent loan that was delayed from a period of lower rates has been held to be unrecoverable, consequential damages.

An approved measure of an owner's damage attributable to interest costs is to calculate the interest paid during the period from the original contract completion date through the actual completion date.[68]

---

[63] *See* Crain v. Sumida, 59 Cal. App. 590, 211 P. 479 (1922); J.A. Tobin Constr. Co. v. Holtzman, 207 Kan. 525, 485 P.2d 1276 (1971).

[64] Sommerville v. Delbsa, 133 W. Va. 435, 56 S.E.2d 756 (1949); National Dairy Corp. v. Jumper, 241 Miss. 339, 130 So. 2d 922 (1961).

[65] 156 Ill. App. 3d 515, 509 N.E.2d 614 (1987).

[66] *See* United Telecommunications, Inc. v. American Television & Communications Corp., 536 F.2d 1310 (19th Cir. 1976); Hemenway Co. v. Bartex, Inc. of Tex., 373 So. 2d 1356 (La. Ct. App. 1979), *cert. denied,* 376 So. 2d 1272 (La. 1979); Dean W. Knight & Sons, Inc. v. First W. Bank, 84 Cal. App. 3d 560, 148 Cal. Rptr. 767 (1978); Roanoke Hosp. Ass'n v. Doyle & Russell, Inc., 215 Va. 796, 214 S.E.2d 155 (1975); Certain-Teed Prods. Corp. v. Goslee Roofing & Sheetmetal, Inc., 26 Md. App. 452, 339 A.2d 302 (1975).

[67] 215 Va. 796, 214 S.E.2d 155, 160–161 (1975).

[68] Midwest Concrete Prods. Co. v. LaSalle Nat'l Bank, 94 Ill. App. 3d 394, 418 N.E.2d 988, 990 (1981).

§ 11.15   —Extended Maintenance and Operation Expenses

Recovery of extended maintenance and operation expenses is important when the owner is required to maintain an old facility while construction of a new facility is delayed past the completion date. In such circumstances, these additional expenses are recoverable.[69] A common example of this type of expense is the additional rent often incurred by an owner who is kept out of a new facility. It may be necessary for the owner to enter a new lease or pay an inflated monthly rental at the existing facility while awaiting completion of the new project.

Although these expenses may be recovered, it is important to subtract any benefit the owner may realize when calculating the amount of damages suffered. For example, if the owner would have utilized the space regardless of her ability to move into the new facility, recovery would not be available. Additionally, courts generally will not force the delaying contractor to shoulder both the rental or usage value of the new facility and the cost of the old or substitute space. To hold otherwise would permit the owner to seek double recovery.

§ 11.16   —Special Damages

An owner is entitled to special damages arising from a contractor's breach if the recovery of such damages was within the contemplation of both parties at the time of execution of the contract.[70]

The decision in *Roanoke Hospital Association v. Doyle & Russell, Inc.*[71] illustrates this principle. The owner, in addition to seeking extended financing costs, sought the incremental interest expense incurred as a result of obtaining the financing for delayed construction during a period of higher interest rates. Additionally, the owner wanted the incremental increase of interest rate for the permanent building loan, which, because of delay, had to be obtained during a later period of high interest rates. The court, noting that these additional costs were caused by external market conditions, not construction delay, concluded that the expenses were consequential damages. Since neither party had intended to include these expenses as an element of damages at the time of contracting, relief for these items was denied.[72]

---

[69] Fruehauf Corp., PSBCA No. 478, 74-1 BCA ¶ 10,399 (1974).

[70] Washington & Old Dominion R.R. v. Westinghouse Co., 120 Va. 633, 91 S.E. 646 (1917).

[71] 215 Va. 796, 214 S.E.2d 155 (1975).

[72] 214 S.E.2d at 161.

An owner can obviate problems related to recovery of special or consequential damages by specific contract provisions that address the special damages the owner desires to recover. For example, in *Subcontractor Trade Association, Inc. v. Carroll*,[73] the court upheld the inclusion of a clause stating that the contractor would be liable for all damages flowing from the contractor's breach, including loss of federal grant fund caused by such breach, even when such damages exceeded the contract price.

§ 11.17   —Attorneys' Fees

The majority rule enforced by courts does not allow the recovery of attorneys' fees without a statute or contract provision authorizing their recovery.[74] The court in *St. Joseph Hospital v. Corbetta Construction Co.*[75] stated that:

> Attorneys' fees and the ordinary expenses and burdens of litigation are not allowable to the successful party in the absence of some agreement or stipulation specially authorizing the allowance thereof, and this rule applies equally in courts of law and in courts of equity.

Thus, an owner should always include a provision in her contract that allows the recovery of such fees.

Attorneys' fees may be recoverable if the conduct involved is something more than a mere breach of contract. If fraud or tortious behavior is present, recovery of such expenses may be allowed.[76]

§ 11.18   —Interest

In addition to recovery of financing costs, an owner may be entitled to pre- and post-judgment interest on the amount of damage due and owing. An owner must rely either on specific contract provisions or on the applicable statute for the recovery of interest.[77] The important consideration for owners in the recovery of interest is to include a clause in the contract

---

[73] 92 Misc. 2d 917, 401 N.Y.S.2d 962 (1978).

[74] Austin v. Parker, 672 F.2d 508, 518–19 (5th Cir. 1982).

[75] 21 Ill. App. 3d 925, 316 N.E.2d 57, 76 (1974).

[76] Waldinger v. Ashbrook-Simon-Hartley, Inc., 564 F. Supp. 970 (C.D. Ill. 1983) (intentional interference with a contractual relationship gave rise to an award of damages that included attorneys' fees).

[77] Newbert v. Foxworthy, 71 Ill. App. 3d 438, 389 N.E.2d 898 (1979); Plant Planners, Inc. v. Pollock, 91 A.D.2d 1017, 457 N.Y.S.2d 890 (1980), *aff'd,* 60 N.Y.2d 779, 457 N.E.2d 781, 469 N.Y.S.2d 675 (1983).

that will allow not only recovery at the desired rate, but also recovery of any fluctuations.

§ 11.19 Exemplary Damages

As a general rule, exemplary (or punitive) damages are not recoverable for a mere breach of contract, regardless of the motives surrounding the breach. The nonbreaching party is considered adequately compensated for the breach by the award of compensatory damages of the type and measure discussed herein.

In order to recover exemplary damages in breach of contract situations, the conduct giving rise to the breach must also constitute a maliciously committed, intentional tort or other illegal or wrongful act, such as fraud.[78]

Situations in which exemplary damages have been recovered by owners include a contractor's intentional failure to disclose latent deviations from design plans[79] and a contractor's use of hazardous wiring that varied from contract specifications.[80] Proof of fraud or other maliciously committed intentional tort is difficult. Hence, only in rare circumstances have exemplary damages been recovered by owners in construction contract cases.

---

[78] Harper v. Goodin, 400 N.E.2d 1129 (Ind. Ct. App. 1980); Lucariells v. Clayton D. Masonry Contracting, Inc., 115 A.D.2d 319, 495 N.Y.S.2d 873 (1985).

[79] F.D. Borkholder Co. v. Sandock, 274 Ind. 612, 413 N.E.2d 567 (1980).

[80] Smith v. Johnston, 591 P.2d 1260 (Okla. 1979).

CHAPTER 12

INVESTIGATING, PREPARING, PRESENTING, AND DEFENDING CLAIMS

§ 12.1   Claim Monitoring: Three Warning Signs

§ 12.2   —Dollars

§ 12.3   —Sequence

§ 12.4   —Duration

§ 12.5   Claim Investigation

§ 12.6   —Data Sources

§ 12.7   —Physical Characteristics

§ 12.8   —Sequence of Work

§ 12.9   —Planned versus Actual Performance

§ 12.10 —Claims Costing

§ 12.11 —Bases of Claim

§ 12.12 —Contract Provisions

§ 12.13 —Change Orders

§ 12.14 Claim Preparation

§ 12.15 —Costing and Documentary Data Sources

§ 12.16 —Scheduling Documentation and Non-Network Exhibits

§ 12.17 —Final Claim Compilation

§ 12.18 Claim Presentation

§ 12.19 —Structure of Narrative

§ 12.20 —Supporting Exhibits

§ 12.21 Claim Defense

§ 12.22 —Actions upon Receipt of Claim

§ 12.23 —Audits

§ 12.24 —Alternatives to Confrontation and Litigation

§ 12.25 —Counterclaims

§ 12.26   —Assertion of Defenses

§ 12.27   —Choice of Forum and Value of Going First

§ 12.28   —Defensive Measures

§ 12.1   Claim Monitoring: Three Warning Signs

Among the most difficult challenges confronting construction management are determining when a claim exists and properly investigating and pursuing it. The same problem exists for an owner who determines that a claim is likely and that appropriate action must be evaluated and undertaken.

Perspective for both contractors and owners is often hindered by the fact that construction management must focus on day-to-day events. Because of this focus, management does not take the opportunity to review and analyze the entire project picture to determine if there is a basis for pursuing a claim. Yet, by using proper monitoring procedures it is possible, in most cases, to determine if a claim should be investigated. These procedures can be accomplished through at least monthly review meetings. In fact, it may even be possible to isolate increased costs in such reviews before the increase has occurred.

In undertaking the monitoring procedures to determine if a claim investigation should even be initiated, there are three major guidelines or warning signs that should be constantly evaluated: dollars, sequence, and duration.

§ 12.2   —Dollars

The first and most important warning sign for the construction manager is the amount of *dollars* being expended on a project. By the use of monthly cost reporting and monthly review meetings, the construction manager can determine if labor and/or material dollars are being expended at a greater rate than that anticipated in the estimate (as adjusted by any change orders). When such an overrun condition exists, it is imperative that the manager investigate whether the overrun is caused by claimable items or nonclaimable items such as changes in the work, overinspection, or labor inefficiency not arising from claim items (for example, a material error in the estimate). Examples of reports that can assist the manager in evaluating dollars on a periodic basis are detailed in **Figure 12–1**, the monthly total cost and man-hour reports, and **Figure 12–2**, the project summary cost analysis. It might also be helpful to include a bid recap by area or structure (**Figure 12–3**) in the project coding system.

DEPT -   OPER. ACTIVE TO DATE - INCLUDING COMPLETED OPER.

OPERATION	PCT CMP	WORK QUANTITY CURRENT	WORK QUANTITY TO DATE	CURRENT BUDGET	CURRENT COST	CURRENT SAVING	BUDGET	TO DATE COST	TO DATE SAVING	TOTAL BUDGET	PROJECTED COST	PROJECTED SAVING
YY094 Metals Fabrication												
01 Metals Fabrication												
Plan Matl.												
100.00 LB												
YY094 total Item							66513	66513	66513	7950	7950	
P-Quality Assurance								71840	71840	7950	7950	
TOTAL ACTIVE OPERATIONS												
TOTAL DORMANT OPERATIONS								71840	71840	7950	7950	
TOTAL UNSTARTED OPERATIONS												
TOTAL COMPLETED OPERATIONS												
SERVICE SUMMARY												
Job Matl.								71840	71840	7950	7950	
Perm Matl.								71840	71840	7950	7950	

DEPT   OPER. ACTIVE TO DATE - INCLUDING COMPLETED OPER.

DEPT	PCT CMP	WQ CURRENT	WQ TO DATE	BUDGET	TO DATE COST	TO DATE SAVING	TOTAL BUDGET	PROJECTED COST	PROJECTED SAVING
Project									
Indirects	100	2284	2284	1089922	2007423	1717501	1091111	2784547	1693437
Manhours	100			35580	117865	82305	35580	118144	82588
Labor	100			397116	1212065	814948	397110	1181009	783455
Equipment	100	2921	2921	302200	504863	202065	202200	504407	202767
Job Matl.	100	637	637	345007	1012364	666758	348795	1020209	673414
Perm Matl.	100				58957	58957		59128	59128
Subcontract	100			45000	19174	25824	45000	19194	25826
Site Work	100			1753618	2080796	355178	1734086	2080932	354644
Manhours	100			50986	62836	11450	51026	82882	11816
Labor	100			501043	726545	164702	562363	726732	164358
Equipment	100				24680	24680		24860	24860
Job Matl.	100			23000	134540	111590	23000	134590	111590
Perm Matl.	100			101700	216895	115195	101700	216695	115195
Subcontract	100			1047025	986036	60989	1047625	980036	70989

Figure 12-1. Monthly total cost and man-hour reports.

325

OPERATION	PCT CMP	WORK QUANTITY CURRENT	WORK QUANTITY TO DATE	CURRENT BUDGET	CURRENT COST	CURRENT SAVING	TO DATE BUDGET	TO DATE COST	TO DATE SAVING	TOTAL BUDGET	PROJECTED COST	PROJECTED SAVING
Concrete Work	100	/	/	/	141	141	//4172590	/4211621	///39231	/4172540	/4211821	////39231
Manhours	100						6650	11887	5237	6650	11867	5237
Labor	100						79800	140422	60022	79800	140422	60622
Equipment								2940	2940		2940	2940
Job Matl.	100						4000	5640	1640	4000	5640	1640
Perm Matl.	100	/		/	141	141	153500	3422369	3268865	153500	3422389	3268884
Subcontract	100						3935290	640430	3294860	3935290	640430	3294660
Masonry Work	100						80420	100985	26565	80420	108985	26565
Manhours	100							3	3		3	3
Labor	100							36	36		36	36
Perm Matl.	100						65037	65037	65037	65037	65037	65037
Subcontract	100						60420	41912	36500	60420	41912	36508
Metals	100						587785	584059	3724	507763	584059	3724
Manhours	100						14880	6497	6384	14880	8497	6344
Job Matl.	100						12901	963	11938	12901	963	11930
Perm Matl.	100						77672	415541	337869	77672	415541	337869
Subcontract	100						310216	59798	258418	318216	59798	258418
Wood & Plastics	100						162821	314675	151654	162621	314675	151854
Manhours	100						5580	12082	6502	5580	12082	6502
Labor	100						59981	136934	76953	59981	136934	96953
Job Matl.	100						1500	5264	3734	1500	5264	5784
Perm Matl.	100						101340	163457	62117	101340	163457	62117
Subcontract	100							9000	9000		9000	9000
Thermal & Moisture Pkd	100						12672	126566	1864	12672	126566	1854
Manhours	100						351	1054	703	351	1054	703
Labor	100						4903	12496	7593	4903	12496	7593
Job Matl.								253	253		253	253
Perm Matl.	100						15000	57571	42571	15000	57571	42571
Subcontract	100						106621	56270	46551	106021	50270	48551

Figure 12-1. *(continued)*

326

OPERATION	PCT CMP	WORK QUANTITY CURRENT	WORK QUANTITY TO DATE	CURRENT BUDGET	CURRENT COST	CURRENT SAVING	TO DATE BUDGET	TO DATE COST	TO DATE SAVING	TOTAL BUDGET	PROJECTED COST	PROJECTED SAVING
Doors & Windows	100						214716	232975	18254	214716	232975	16259
Manhours	100						3100	3093	7	3100	3043	7
Labor	100						33325	35958	2631	33325	35956	2631
Job Matl.	100						1000	372	628	1000	672	672
Perm Matl.	100						22065	62692	40627	22065	62042	40627
Subcontract	100						158326	133954	24372	158326	133954	24372
Finishes	100						592309	540710	51599	592309	542309	51599
Manhours	100							22	22		22	22
Labor	100							251	251		251	251
Equipment	100							8	8		8	8
Job Matl.	100							329	329		329	329
Perm Matl.	100						74106	74106	74106	74106	74106	74106
Subcontract	100						592304	466015	126294	592309	466015	126294
Specialties	100				420	420	16963	20180	3217	16963	20180	3217
Manhours	100						149	121	28	149	121	28
Labor	100						1602	2012	410	1002	2012	410
Perm Matl.	100				420	420	600	7746	7146	600	7746	7146
Subcontract	100						10461	10422	4334	14761	10422	4339
Equipment	100						26457	22148	4309	26457	22148	4309
Manhours	100						88	122	24	88	112	24
Labor	100						966	1164	198	900	1164	196
Perm Matl.	100						7000	2493	4507	7000	2493	4507
Subcontract	100						18491	18491		18491	18491	
Furnishings	100						2240	1909	339	2248	1909	339
Perm Matl.	100							460	460		460	460
Subcontract	100						2248	2369	121	2248	2309	121
Conveying Systems	100						51699	43489	6410	51899	43489	6410
Manhours	100						400	193	207	400	193	207
Labor	100						4400	2063	2337	4400	2063	2337
Equipment	100							9682	4682		4682	4982
Job Matl.	100						500	500	500	500	500	500
Perm Matl.	100						17152	7539	9613	17152	7539	9613
Subcontract	100						29847	24205	5642	29047	24205	5642

Figure 12-1. *(continued)*

327

OPERATION	PCT CMP	WORK QUANTITY CURRENT	WORK QUANTITY TO DATE	CURRENT BUDGET	CURRENT COST	CURRENT SAVING	TO DATE BUDGET	TO DATE COST	TO DATE SAVING	TOTAL BUDGET	PROJECTED COST	PROJECTED SAVING
Mechanical	100						1159918	1430972	271054	1159918	1430972	27105
Manhours	100						15456	26133	10677	15456	26133	10677
Labor	100						183888	351425	168037	163806	351423	100037
Job Matl.	100						6950	39642	32692	6950	39642	32692
Perm Matl.	100						307653	660030	352377	307653	660030	352377
Subcontract	100						661427	379375	282052	661427	379375	282052
Electrical	100						1943000	1931496	11504	1943000	1931496	11504
Manhours								1103	1103		1103	1103
Labor								14808	14808		14808	14808
Job Matl.								3	3		3	3
Perm Matl.								1062532	1062532		1062532	1062532
Subcontract	100						1943000	654153	1088847	1943000	654153	1088847
Process Pipe & Equipment	86				6273	6273	7382062	2441110	8560481	8560401	9241472	681072
Manhours	100						54256	121466	67232	54326	113919	59593
Labor	100						640200	1564502	924102	641027	1474035	633007
Equipment					6273	6273		1752	1752		1627	1627
Job Matl.	25						2708	17946	15158	11300	20686	9337
Perm Matl.	79						3840144	6351149	2511005	4849144	5697160	847459
Subcontract	95						2698430	1600022	1016468	3058930	2048022	1010904
Extra Work								583472	583472		554841	554841
Manhours								11772	11772		17092	17092
Labor								243265	243265		234417	234417
Equipment								30410	30410		30417	30417
Job Matl.								24450	24450		25777	25777
Perm Matl.								148616	148616		139385	139385
Subcontract								137130	137130		125845	125845
Change Orders	65						158380	17602	140778	243360	94974	148366
Manhours	93						1686	325	1361	1816	455	1361
Labor	32						34610	3588	31022	10645	74839	32006
Equipment	100						2167		2167	2167		2167
Job Matl.								1473	1473		1473	1473
Perm Matl.	95						18322	425	17897	19897	1297	17097
Subcontract	90						103282	12116	91165	115154	17365	97789

Figure 12-1. *(continued)*

328

OPERATION	PCT CMP	WORK QUANTITY CURRENT	WORK QUANTITY TO DATE	CURRENT BUDGET	CURRENT COST	CURRENT SAVING	TO DATE BUDGET	TO DATE COST	TO DATE SAVING	TOTAL BUDGET	PROJECTED COST	PROJECTED SAVING
Service Summary												
Job Matl.								71840		7950	7950	
Perm Matl.									71840	7950	7950	
TOTAL ACTIVE OPERATIONS					8560	8560	90892	599043	500151	99960	604338	504378
TOTAL DORMANT OPERATIONS							807342	4698088	3290241	1994721	5395433	1400712
TOTAL UNSTARTED OPERATIONS										96049	77372	
TOTAL COMPLETED OPERATIONS					558	558	18564027	20265560	1681553	18564027	20265580	1681553
PROJECT TOTALS	94				9118	9118	19501630	24962712	5460481	20774757	24342723	3567965
MANHOURS	100						189162	384603	195441	189402	370753	167351
LABOR	97						2101677	4555736	2379961	2255209	4496413	2241704
EQUIPMENT	100			2921	2921		304367	574337	269916	304367	574367	264954
JOB MATL.	96			5636	5636		398246	1243309	845063	415063	1262172	846276
PERM MATL.	82			141	141		4662148	12648555	8180407	5472020	12114480	6442460
SUBCONTRACT	99			420	420		11955393	5740873	6214520	12127265	5894836	6232424

Figure 12–1. (*continued*)

	Work in Progress 5-31-88 Budget	3.584% Mark-up	Budget & Mark-up	Work in Progress Actual	Difference
Labor	2,951,746	105,790	3,527,802	6,527,802	[3,470,266]
Material	6,245,259	223,830	6,469,089	7,341,795	[872,706]
Job expense	179,571	6,435	186,006	594,438	[408,432]
Non-prod. labor	397,320	14,238	411,558	721,761	[310,203]
Prime cost	9,773,896	-0-	-0-	-0-	-0-
Mark-up	350,293	-0-		-0-	-0-
Total	10,124,189		10,124,189	15,185,796	[5,061,607]

Figure 12–2. Project summary cost analysis.

	SITE	MULTI-PURPOSE BUILDING	HANGAR	TOTAL (PHASE 1)	ENTRY BLDG.	E.R. DOCK	BLDGS. 181, 182 204, 205	SITE 2	TOTAL (PHASE 2)	GRAND TOTAL (PHASE 1&2)
ELECTRICIAN & MANHOURS										
MATERIALS										
SUB-CONTRACTS										
SALES TAX										
LABOR-PRODUCTIVE										
SUPERVISION										
NON-PRODUCTIVE LABOR										
INSURANCE & PAYROLL TAXES										
JOB EXPENSES										
FRINGES										
PRIME COSTS										
OVERHEAD & PROFIT										
PER ESTIMATE TOTALS										
BID TO										

Figure 12-3. Bid recap by area and structure.

331

§ 12.3   —Sequence

Another very important warning sign is the *sequence* of the installation. This is an extremely effective management tool because the manager can use periodic reviews to determine if the sequence of installation by the concerned trade or trades is going to be different, or has been different, from that originally planned.

By using monthly reviews or other periodic reviews to determine if the work is going as planned on general and specific bases, the manager can spot trouble areas ahead of time, either to resolve the matter by consulting with the other contracting parties or to commence preparation of claim and proper claim notice. These sequence reviews should not be restricted to the general sequence of the installation. Frequently, major increased costs will be incurred as a result of what appears to be a minor change in the sequence of installation of different trades or within the sequence of installation of a particular trade.

§ 12.4   —Duration

The last warning sign that may indicate increased costs occurs when the periodic reviews by the manager determine that the *duration* for the specific trade or trades will be extended. This review is also extremely important because it may give rise to a claim for extended duration expenses, for wage escalation, or for lost efficiency due to extended duration.

Contract clauses used by owners today frequently seek forfeiture of otherwise valid claims for extended duration expense through the use of extremely strict notice provisions.[1] Vigilance toward the possibility or fact of extended duration, coupled with appropriate notice (or actual knowledge by the owner), can mean the difference for a contractor between success and financial disaster.[2]

---

[1] An example of such clauses is detailed by the following language:

> The Contractor shall not be entitled to any extension of time for delays resulting from any conditions or other causes unless it shall have given written notice to the owner, within 20 calendar days following the commencement of each such condition or cause, describing the occurrence, the activities impacted, and the probable duration of the delay. The contractor's complete claim submittal for a time extension shall be submitted no later than 20 calendar days after the inception of the delay or request of the owner or Architect/Engineer.

[2] Courts and boards have recognized exceptions to strict notice provisions: Big Chief Drilling Co. v. United States, 15 Cl. Ct. 295 (1985); H.H.O. Co. v. United States, 12 Cl. Ct. 147 (1987); Hoel-Steffen Constr. Co. v. United States, 197 Ct. Cl. 561, 456 F.2d 760 (1972); Pat Wagren, IBCA No. 1612-8-82, 85-2 BCA ¶ 18,103 (1985); Smith & Pittman Constr. Co., AGBCA No. 76-131, 77-1 BCA ¶ 12,381 (1977) (if government/owner not prejudiced by lack of written notice, no bar to recovery); Glassman Constr. Co. v.

The duration warning sign also is extremely important if the extended duration is caused by activities involving the contractor's own trade or trades, when the contractor might be accused of delaying the project. In such cases, it is important to assess corrective actions, as well as the proper defensive posture. The contractor will need to consider filing proper defensive notices and requesting time extensions to avoid liquidated damages or claims from the other contracting parties for increased costs.

§ 12.5 Claim Investigation

Once it has been determined from such warning signs that there is a basis for investigating a claim, it is important to pursue an investigation that will fully retrieve the necessary information. Such investigations have been successfully performed in many different ways by many different individuals. The approach detailed here is just one means of effectively investigating the basis for a claim to determine the action required. Review and analysis of the following project factors is suggested as part of the claim investigation: data sources; the project's physical characteristics; the sequence of work; planned versus actual performance; claims costing; bases of claim; contract provisions; and change orders.

By pursuing these steps, which constitute the *initial review* process, the manager should be able to develop all he needs to know about whether any claim process should be considered. This process can, in most cases, be accomplished in less than a week, and a determination of appropriate action can then be made.

§ 12.6 —Data Sources

The first step in claim investigation is to review the available data sources for information relating to the claim. This activity is extremely important because a claim must rest on solid documentation to allow proper proof at

---

Maryland City Plaza, Inc., 371 F. Supp 1154 (D. Md. 1974), *aff'd,* 530 F.2d 968 (4th Cir. 1975); Buckley & Co. v. State, 140 N.J. Super. 289, 356 A.2d 56 (1975) (cannot rely on failure of written notice if owner caused delay itself); United States v. John Kerns Constr., 140 F.2d 792 (8th Cir. 1944); G.M. Shupe, Inc. v. United States, 5 Cl. Ct. 662 (1984) (owner under actual notice of claim). However, courts and boards have denied recovery where no notice at all was given: Mingis Constructors, Inc. v. United States, 10 Cl. Ct. 173, *aff'd,* 812 F.2d 1387 (Fed. Cir. 1987); Emlyn T. Linkous, GSBCA No. 3832, 74-1 BCA ¶ 10,473 (1974); Ardelt-Horn Constr. Co., ASBCA No. 14,550, 73-1 BCA ¶ 9901 (1973), *aff'd,* 207 Ct. Cl. 995 (1975). And in one case the court denied recovery although oral notice was given: Progressive Builders, Inc. v. District of Columbia, 258 F.2d 431 (D.C. Cir. 1958), *cert. denied,* 358 U.S. 881 (1958).

a hearing or trial. The data sources can be broken down into two major categories: documentary data sources and cost data sources.

Documentary sources include daily logs, weekly progress meeting minutes or jobsite meeting minutes, diaries, photographs, correspondence, interoffice memoranda, requests for information (RFIs), progress schedules, equipment rental reports, the contract, change orders and proposed change orders, shop drawings and shop drawing logs, equipment submittals and equipment submittal logs, weather reports, and computerized data base. Each of these sources can be extremely important to the investigation and preparation of a claim. Further, by utilizing proper data retrieval techniques, it is frequently possible to use such records to determine when changes in sequence have occurred; when verbal directions have occurred; when certain jobsite visits have taken place; when written directives have been provided; when claim notices have been transmitted; the substance of errors, omissions, delays, and/or approvals; and other such factors.

Further, it is possible to use such sources to actually reconstruct cost information in a coherent fashion for proper claim support when normal cost records are inadequate. On a major claim such as the construction of a large office building, for example, a contractor's cost records may be inadequate to determine which man-hours had been expended in specific work areas and on specific types of installations. To reconstruct the actual spread of the labor to the work areas and work items, the contractor should utilize the weekly progress meeting minutes, equipment rental reports, and project photographs to ascertain, within approximate time frames, when the specific trade had been working on certain floors. This information should be evaluated in conjunction with input from the individuals who had actually managed the project to develop strong information supporting the increased costs incurred as a direct result of the actions of other contractors and the owner. This reconstituted information presents the contractor's best estimate of the actual costs incurred absent normal cost data.[3]

The second category of data sources, *cost data sources,* is also of primary importance. Proper maintenance of cost information allows the retrieval of data showing exactly where money was lost and, in many cases, for what reason.

Proper cost data sources allow the manager to determine the labor codes, the project locations where the money was lost, and the specific period of time when the loss was experienced. Cost data sources typically include such items as monthly labor reports; monthly material reports; overall-dollar computer printouts for the project, including expenses and

---

[3] *See* Louis M. McMaster, Inc., AGBCA No. 80-159-4, 86-3 BCA ¶ 19,067 (1986).

overhead; payroll records; overall company general and administrative (G&A) reports; and the original bid estimate. These records, if properly maintained and established, allow the manager to retrieve many types of information. For example, monthly labor reports, such as the examples in **Figure 12–4**, should be established on vertical and horizontal bases to detail not just man-hours alone, but also man-hours by trade, classification within trade, work area, and type of work item. Then when these vertical and horizontal summaries are tracked with the original bid estimate or the original bid estimate is broken down to conform with the format of the monthly labor reports, it is possible to determine precise physical and temporal information on lost labor.

In this regard, it should be noted that labor dollars are not always the same as labor man-hours. For example, because of a mistake in a contractor's favor in the bid estimate on wage rates, the contractor's actual performance may be within his original budget for labor dollars but may miss his estimate for labor man-hours. The actual expenditure of labor for the project thus would actually include more man-hours than estimated under the original bid. In this example, even though labor dollars are within the budget, a claim may exist. Of course, similar principles may tip the scales in favor of the owner. The simple fact that the contractor has overrun its labor dollars and manhour estimate will not justify recovery to the contractor without a specific demonstration that the owner's action caused the increased dollars.[4]

In analyzing cost data sources, it is extremely important to know how the cost records are set up on an overall company basis. Significant questions include:

1. In what account are the fringes carried?
2. Where on the books is the foreman carried?
3. Where is the project engineer carried?
4. Where are the small tools carried?
5. How is the company's overall overhead computed?
6. Where is equipment rental carried?
7. Which charges are direct job charges versus items contained in the general overhead pool?
8. How do overruns in the labor and material accounts compare and is there any correlation between the two?

---

[4] This is the reason why total cost is disfavored. *See, e.g.,* Schuster Engineering, ASBCA No. 28,760, 87-3 BCA ¶ 20,105 (1987); Steve Beylund, AGBCA No. 87-215-3, 87-3 BCA ¶ 19,975 (1987); Meva Corp. v. United States, 206 Ct. Cl. 203, 220, 511 F.2d 548, 598 (1975); WRB Corp. v. United States, 183 Ct. Cl. 409, 426 (1968).

	DESCRIPTION	% COMP.	Budget Manhours Thru CO	Earned Manhours	Recorded Manhours	Variance From EST Thru This Month	Variance From EST Thru Last Month	Variance Change Since Last Month	Hours To Complete	REMARKS
01	Conduit-Slab-Br.Ckt.- Bsmt.&P.Bsmt.	100	2,000	2,000	2,535	(535)	(535)	-0-	-0-	
02	Conduit-Slab-Br.Ckt.- 1st Floor	100	1,975	1,975	2,869	(893)	(893)	-0-	-0-	
03	Conduit-Slab-Br.Ckt.- 2nd Floor	100	1,320	1,320	1,681	(361)	(361)	-0-	-0-	
04	Conduit-Slab-Br.Ckt.- 3rd Floor	100	1,475	1,475	1,507	(32)	(32)	-0-	-0-	
05	Conduit-Slab-Br.Ckt.- 4th Floor	100	777	777	1,070	(293)	(293)	-0-	-0-	
06	Conduit-Slab-Br.Ckt.- 5th Floor	100	789	789	869	(80)	(80)	-0-	-0-	
07	Conduit-Slab-Br.Ckt.- 6th Floor	100	776	776	773	3	3	-0-	-0-	
08	Conduit-Slab-Br.Ckt.- Penthouse	100	126	126	207	(81)	(81)	-0-	-0-	
09										
10	Conduit-Exp.-Conceal- Bmt. & P.Bmt.	100	2,530	2,530	4,817	(2,287)	(2,182)	(105)	-0-	
11	Conduit-Exp.-Conceal- 1st Floor	100	3,060	3,060	4,662	(1,602)	(1,602)	-0-	-0-	
12	Conduit-Exp.-Conceal- 2nd Floor	100	2,030	2,030	3,263	(1,233)	(1,233)	-0-	-0-	
13	Conduit-Exp.-Conceal- 3rd Floor	100	2,275	2,275	3,463	(1,188)	(1,188)	-0-	-0-	
14	Conduit-Exp.-Conceal- 4th Floor	100	1,075	1,075	2,079	(1,004)	(1,004)	-0-	-0-	
15	Conduit-Exp.-Conceal- 5th Floor	100	1,150	1,150	1,954	(804)	(804)	-0-	-0-	
16	Conduit-Exp.-Conceal- 6th Floor	100	1,200	1,200	1,822	(622)	(622)	-0-	-0-	
17	Conduit-Exp.-Penthouse	100	260	260	308	(48)	(48)	(4)	-0-	
18	Conduit Underground (See 710)									
19	Conduit-Duct Banks & Manholes	100	1,300	1,300	455	845	853	(8)	-0-	
20	Underfloor Systems (Duct)	100	595	595	684	(89)	(89)	-0-	-0-	
21	Feeder/Conduit	100	3,305	3,305	3,091	214	214	-0-	-0-	
22	Telephone Service & Riser Conduit	100	840	840	769	71	75	(4)	-0-	
			28,858	28,858	38,077	(10,019)	(9,898)	(121)		

Figure 12-4. Detailed monthly labor report.

336

DESCRIPTION	% COMP.	Budget Manhours Thru CO	Earned Manhours	Recorded Manhours	Variance From EST Thru This Month	Variance From EST Thru Last Month	Variance Change Since Last Month	Hours To Complete	REMARKS
Wire, 600V Br.Ckt.-Pipe Basement	100	130	130	300	(170)	(190)	20	-0-	
Wire, 600V Br.Ckt.-Basement	100	525	525	906	(381)	(381)	(2)	-0-	
Wire, 600V Br.Ckt.-1st Floor	100	590	590	1,055	(476)	(476)	-0-	-0-	
Wire, 600V Br.Ckt.-2nd Floor	100	360	360	683	(223)	(223)	-0-	-0-	
Wire, 600V Br.Ckt.-3rd Floor	100	340	340	713	(373)	(373)	-0-	-0-	
Wire, 600V Br.Ckt.-4th Floor	100	235	288	(53)	(53)	(53)	-0-	-0-	
Wire, 600V Br.Ckt.-5th Floor	100	225	225	326	(101)	(101)	-0-	-0-	
Wire, 600V Br.Ckt.-6th Floor	100	240	240	312	(72)	(72)	-0-	-0-	
Wire, 600V Br.Ckt.-Penthouse	100	110	110	134	(24)	(24)	-0-	-0-	
H.V. Cable-15 KV	100	115	115	110	5	5	-0-	-0-	
H.V. Term.	100	230	230	194	36	36	-0-	-0-	
Feeder Conductors	100	2,290	2,290	1,464	826	826	-0-	-0-	
Indoor Substation-(3-1500 KVA)	100	240	240	246	(6)	(6)	-0-	-0-	
Switchgear-Secondary -Indoor	100	450	487	(37)	(33)	(4)	-0-	-0-	
Busways	100	400	400	396	4	8	(4)	-0-	
Panelboards-Basement	100	626	626	723	(92)	(83)	(14)	-0-	
Panelboards-1st Flr	100	393	393	326	67	67	-0-	-0-	
Panelboards-2nd Flr	100	271	271	303	(32)	(32)	-0-	-0-	
Panelboards-3rd Flr	100	214	214	203	11	11	-0-	-0-	
Panelboards-4th Flr	100	105	105	119	(14)	(14)	-0-	-0-	
Panelboards-5th Flr	100	81	81	102	(21)	(21)	-0-	-0-	
Panelboards-6th Flr	100	111	111	129	(18)	(18)	-0-	-0-	
Transformers-Indoor	100	280	280	303	(23)	(23)	-0-	-0-	
Emergency Generator	100	990	990	525	465	473	(8)	-0-	
Motor Control Centers	100	330	330	476	(146)	(134)	(12)	-0-	
Isolating Transformers & Panels	100	110	110	102	8	14	(6)	-0-	
		9,991	9,991	10,536	(845)	(315)	(30)	-0-	

Figure 12-4. (continued)

DESCRIPTION	% COMP.	Budget Manhours Thru CO	Earned Manhours	Recorded Manhours	Variance From EST Thru This Month	Variance From EST Thru Last Month	Variance Change Since Last Month	Hours To Complete	REMARKS
Lighting Fixtures—Pipe Basement	100	70	70	131	(61)	(61)	(61)	-0-	
Lighting Fixtures—Basement	100	1,685	1,685	1,868	(183)	(103)	(80)	-0-	
Lighting Fixtures—1st Floor	100	1,922	1,922	1,888	34	37	(3)	-0-	
Lighting Fixtures—2nd Floor	100	918	918	1,121	(203)	(203)	-0-	-0-	
Lighting Fixtures—3rd Floor	100	1,142	1,142	1,401	(259)	(259)	-0-	-0-	
Lighting Fixtures—4th Floor	100	442	442	553	(111)	(111)	-0-	-0-	
Lighting Fixtures—5th Floor	100	457	457	455	2	2	-0-	-0-	
Lighting Fixtures—6th Floor	100	422	422	494	(72)	(72)	-0-	-0-	
Lighting Fixtures—Penthouse	100	60	60	101	(41)	(73)	(4)	-0-	
Lighting Fixtures—Operating Rooms	100	50	50	129	(79)	(55)	(24)	-0-	
Change Orders	100	664	664	441	223	223	-0-	-0-	
Page 3		7,832	7,832	8,582	(750)	(639)	(111)	-0-	
Page 1		28,858	28,858	38,877	(10,019)	(9,898)	(121)	-0-	
Page 2		9,991	9,991	10,836	(845)	(815)	(30)	-0-	
TOTALS: PAGES 1,2,3		46,681	46,681	58,295	(11,614)	(11,352)	(262)	-0-	

Figure 12–4. (continued)

338

DESCRIPTION	% COMP.	Budget Manhours Thru OO	Earned Manhours	Recorded Manhours	Variance From EST Thru This Month	Variance From EST Thru Last Month	Variance Change Since Last Month	Hours To Complete	REMARKS
Alarm Systems Connections	100	660	660	1,106	(446)	(356)	(90)	-0-	
& Control Dev.	100	1,627	1,627	2,537	(910)	(890)	(20)	-0-	
Parking Lot Lighting (Outdoor)	100	1,210	1,210	740	470	470	-0-	-0-	
13.8 HV Walk-in Switchgear	100	640	640	254	386	396	(10)	-0-	
Lighting Protection System	100	485	485	465	20	20	-0-	-0-	
Startup & Cleanup	100	4,000	4,000	3,742	258	165	93	-0-	
, Devices & Plates-Basement	100	465	465	413	52	46	6	-0-	
, Devices & Plates-1st Floor	100	647	647	724	(77)	(74)	(3)	-0-	
, Devices & Plates-2nd Floor	100	286	286	231	55	55	-0-	-0-	
, Devices & Plates-3rd Floor	100	301	301	226	75	75	-0-	-0-	
, Devices & Plates-4th Floor	100	205	205	284	(79)	(79)	-0-	-0-	
, Devices & Plates-5th Floor	100	185	185	199	(14)	(14)	-0-	-0-	
, Devices & Plates-6th Floor	100	213	213	260	(47)	(47)	-0-	-0-	
TOTALS: PAGES 1,2,3		46,681	46,681	58,295	(11,614)	(11,352)	(262)	-0-	
LABOR – PRODUCTIVE TOTALS		57,605	57,605	69,476	(11,871)	(11,585)	(286)	-0-	
General Foreman & Foreman	100	5,300	5,300	12,077	(6,777)	(6,667)	(110)	-0-	
Field Admin. - Project Engineer	100	6,000	6,000	8,144	(2,144)	(2,144)	-0-	-0-	
Field Engr. & Drftg., Field Clerk	100	4,000	4,000	7,426	(3,426)	(3,168)	-0-	-0-	
TOTALS FOR PROJECT General Foreman & Start Up & Clean Up TOTAL FOR PROJECT		72,905	72,905	97,123	(24,218)	(23,822)	(390)	-0-	
To deduct for hours transferred from		(400)	(400)	-0-	400	-0-	(400)	400	
TOTALS _ COMPLETION		72,505	72,505	97,123	(24,618)	(23,822)	(796)	400	

Figure 12-4. (continued)

339

The importance of properly maintaining costing information is reflected in a major claim settled with the Corps of Engineers on a turbine installation contract on dams on the Snake River a number of years ago. In this particular case, the contractor felt that all of his increased costs, which amounted to more than $1,000,000, resulted directly from actions of the government. The contractor looked to actions that occurred over the second half of the project, but when a cost analysis was performed, it was determined that during the second half of the project the contractor had expended only about $500,000 more than he had anticipated after taking into consideration the original estimate and a large change order for acceleration. Once this fact was determined, it was necessary to return to the first half of the project to review the appropriate cost records. In this review it was determined that substantial increased costs had been incurred on other portions of the work at an earlier time and, also, from a reconstruction with job records, that the increased costs were incurred as a direct result of government actions (special requirements for the use of torque wrenches). The contractor, although he had overlooked these costs, was entitled to compensation for them. Without properly maintained records, it would have been impossible to claim the full amount that was due the contractor and to obtain an equitable adjustment to the contract above the $500,000 mark.

Once a working knowledge has been obtained about the data sources and cost information sources available on a specific project, it is possible to move to the next step in the claim investigation. Without establishing the existence of such data sources, however, it will be almost impossible to back up or check the statements of project personnel about responsibility for increased costs.

§ 12.7 —Physical Characteristics

The next area of investigation concerns the project's overall physical characteristics. Prior to commencing this review, however, the manager should make sure he does not have an overly discreet problem that would necessarily limit the investigation. Although he may be confronted with a claim that involves a simple set of facts and a clear-cut legal issue that does not require exhaustive analyses, more typically on major construction project claims the investigation will require analyses of complicated facts and a full understanding of the project's physical characteristics. In such situations, to gain an understanding of the project and the nature of any problems encountered during construction, the manager should first identify the major physical installation of the concerned trade (or trades) and, also, the major installations of the other interactive trades on the project. Next, the manager should determine the location of major systems (such as major mechanical systems or switchgear) throughout the structure or project and their characteristics and installation requirements as they relate to the activities of the concerned and interactive trades.

Finally, the manager should identify any physical peculiarities or other peculiarities of the project affecting the installation of the concerned trade and all other relevant trades. This could include anything from the type of site (such as inaccessible or inadequate storage areas) to such items as weather and/or unusual structural design (such as large post-tensioned beams that are to be penetrated by large ductwork throughout the structure). Each project is a little different—and, frequently, a great deal different—from the next; unless the manager isolates and identifies the physical characteristics and peculiarities of the project, it will be impossible for him to have a proper understanding of the problems encountered during actual construction.

§ 12.8 —Sequence of Work

Upon determining the physical characteristics and peculiarities of the specific project, the manager's next step is to analyze the major installations of the various trades and of the specific trade with which the manager is concerned to determine how the work fits together.

In all construction there are physical constraints that require one item of work to be done before another. In this step in the manager's review, he should first determine the physical constraints in the sequence of the various installations. Next, he should determine the sequence of installation in accordance with proper construction practices. For example, it may be possible to install electrical bus duct above HVAC ductwork after it has been installed, but it would be extremely foolish and stupid to do so and not in accordance with good construction practices.

Other examples of physical constraints on the sequence of work are:

Always commencing construction projects from their low point, so that one works or constructs upward and exposes as little excavation as possible.

And always constructing from large-dimensioned installations (such as pipe or duct) and working towards the smaller installations. Completing the smaller installation last allows any corrective make-up adjustments to be made at the smallest and least costly point.

§ 12.9 —Planned versus Actual Performance

Once the investigating manager has determined the proper sequence of work for the concerned trade and related trades in accordance with good construction practices, he can evaluate any scheduling information that was provided by the general contractor (or prepared by the general contractor if the manager is the general contractor) to determine, both as to sequence and duration, how the work was to fit together and how it actually was put in place. This does not, of course, mean that the original scheduling information provided was correct or in accordance with good construction practices. The original plan must always be evaluated for major logic errors in sequence, durations, or resources.

Such a problem was encountered on a claim involving a structure for a federal project in which the prime contractor's original schedule showed the drywall installation commencing well before the roof was to be placed upon the structure in an area where rains were not infrequent. In this particular case, it was therefore necessary in the claim evaluation to modify the original schedule to reflect good construction practices by correcting this logic error, which would have been picked up in normal construction performance.[5]

The importance of determining the physical characteristics and peculiarities of the project and the sequence and duration of the work cannot be overemphasized. In any proper claim investigation and presentation, it is necessary to be able to understand and communicate the planned or normal performance of the work as a bench mark against the actual problems encountered in performance.

§ 12.10   —Claims Costing

Typically, the manager will—or should—perform the claim investigation review during actual construction performance. For this reason, the validity of any initial review of claims costing will depend in great part upon the existence and accuracy of a cost-to-complete report or a work-in-place report that enables reasonable projections of cost, both for the project as a whole and for individual components of the work.

Without such a cost-to-complete report, maintained on a monthly or other reasonably periodic basis, it is extremely difficult for the manager to determine—or have any idea about—the final cost figures on a project.

A good example of this information's importance is reflected in a claim presentation involving a sheet metal contractor. In this case, the claim investigation and preparation were undertaken about midway through performance. At that time, the sheet metal contractor was asked what the final cost figures on the project were going to look like. The sheet metal contractor replied that he had spent about $400,000 out of a $600,000 budget and thought he was about 50 percent complete. However, the

---

[5] This claim involved the construction of a large federal office building in Louisville, Ky.

contractor had no accurate work-in-place report that would enable accurate projection of the increased costs through to completion and no cost-to-complete report that would enable determination of the final cost figures. From the sheet metal contractor's figures of $400,000 spent on a $600,000 budget for 50 percent completion, one would believe that the final overrun would be about $200,000. However, the decision was made, at that time, to require an on-the-job review of the project to determine more accurately the actual percentage of work in place.[6] This jobsite review, which took nearly a week, determined that the contractor was substantially below 50 percent complete and, utilizing engineering estimates based on the historical production rate to project the increased costs, a much higher claim amount was submitted. However, it was later determined that even this amount was inadequate and the amount of the claim had to be raised at a later date.

Such adjustments should be avoided, if possible, because the contractor's negotiating posture and credibility may be affected if he continually has to raise his estimates of the claimed amount. In addition, problems can be encountered with respect to notice requirements and the amount claimed.

The initial review of claims costing and the later preparation of actual costing on claims are extremely important exercises. Such a review is almost never performed properly if accurate historical data of incurred costs and work completed is not available. In other words, for a manager to know where he is going, he has to know where he has been.

Further, definition of the work *cost* itself presents enormous problems. A contractor might say that he lost $500,000 on a project, but what precisely does he mean by that statement? Is this not an actual out-of-pocket loss, taking into account only direct job charges without looking at general and administrative expense and profit or does his statement represent only net profit?

It is extremely important for management to know precisely what kind of a dollar or cost loss, if any, is being incurred on a project. Managers might take the following approach to solving this problem.

First, he should determine the actual out-of-pocket loss on the entire project. For example, the contract amount might be $2,000,000 and actual direct charges to the project might amount to $2,300,000 for an actual out-of-pocket loss of $300,000. Another way of looking at actual out-of-pocket loss is to look at just the labor or material and determine the actual dollar loss by calculating the overrun of labor expenditures above the bid estimate, as adjusted by change orders, and by overhead and profit included in the bid.

---

[6] This claim involved the construction of a 480-bed Veterans Administration Hospital in Columbia, Mo.

The manager should also evaluate individual overruns and underruns by individual labor and material codes for explanations and evaluation of the precise cause and effect of the loss on the project and for evaluation of whether the claimable loss on direct job charges should be more or less than the amount reflected by the gross direct job charge overrun.

Yet, this approach does not really reflect what the contractor's *real* loss on the project has been. If the project had run properly, the contractor would have recovered not only his actual direct charges to the project, but also his overhead and profit on the job, plus financing expense. A number of other steps are required to evaluate where a contractor is actually situated on a project.

To determine the true total loss on a project that has not been extended, distorting overall company G&A expense or overhead expense, the contractor might utilize the *total cost* approach:

$$\text{Actual Cost} + \text{Overhead and Profit}$$
$$-(\text{Contract Price} + \text{Change Orders})$$
$$= \text{Total-Cost Loss Computation}$$

The manager can also prepare a cost curve to develop the shortfall on cash flow throughout the life of the project. This can be utilized in conjunction with specific borrowings, United States Treasury rates, or prime rate calculations to determine the financing cost of lost revenues.

Another way of looking at excess costs relates to increased costs incurred as a result of extended duration. This can occur both in the expense category, if one is carried on the books for people such as the project manager, for equipment, for site trailer, for utilities, and so on, and also in the company overall G&A account. In both cases, the expenditure of cost is a function of time, and if a project is extended beyond the planned completion date or beyond the planned duration, expense-type items and general overhead costs and resources will have to be expanded for the project. For this step, the manager can take a quick look at the monthly expenses and multiply them by the extended number of months. Also, he can calculate a monthly rate for G&A expense (using the gross sales method, gross expenditures method, or bid estimate method) to develop the increased costs incurred as a result of extended duration. See **Chapter 10** for details on extended duration costs.

Thus, when the initial review of the claims costing is completed, the manager should have some idea of his out-of-pocket loss without overhead and profit, from a total cost standpoint, and including any increase in costs incurred as a result of extended duration. Although it is true that there may be an area of overlap between extended duration expenses, such as G&A and mark-up for overhead, claimed on a total-cost-type presentation, by making appropriate adjustment it is possible to assert both types of costs in an attempt to maintain the maximum dollar recovery. Further, the manager should take a look at these different approaches, not only to see how badly he has been hurt, but also to get an idea about how the cost can be presented to maximize his recovery in any claim presentation.

Once he has an idea of the overall project loss, he should examine specific components of labor and material and expense budgets to determine major areas of overrun.

§ 12.11   —Bases of Claim

By this stage it might be assumed that the project presents a complex fact situation, that the manager has developed in his initial review an idea of the data sources, the project's physical characteristics, and the sequence of the work, and that he has initially reviewed the cost status of the project. His next step is to evaluate the bases for a claim.

Basically, the manager should debrief key project personnel as to major problems on the project. Then, he should track the actual sequence and duration of work activities against the planned sequences and durations, along with cost records, to ascertain whether the major problems cited in his interviews present a viable foundation for making a claim. Assume, for example, that site work on a hypothetical project was supposed to begin in August of 1988 but could not because of delay in site access caused by the owner. As a result, excavation did not start until late fall and concrete operations had to be suspended for the winter. In the original plan, the concrete work could have been performed in the winter because the working platform would have been gotten out of the ground. In this example, the manager should compare the planned and actual sequence durations and cost codes. Also, he must not make the mistake of thinking he is looking at merely a simple extended duration claim of a few months for G&A and extended jobsite facilities costs. This major delay at the inception of the project has the potential to cause major problems for his entire project, as becomes evident when the potential impact of this initial suspension is projected for all trades involved in the project.

Once the manager has an idea of the divergence between the planned and actual performance of the work, he must take a long hard look at the cost increase figures he developed (in looking at the cost records) and determine whether they have any relationship to the actual problems encountered during performance that are the responsibility of the other side. It is of no help to the manager of a mechanical contractor if the cost increases were incurred on underground yard piping for sanitary and storm lines when the *actual* problems, which are the owner's responsibility, occurred later in the project, when 90 or 95 percent of the mechanical work was accomplished and after all the overrun was experienced.

It is necessary to tie the problems that are the responsibility of the opposing party to the specific cost increases experienced on the project. If increased costs cannot be tied to any compensable activities or event, the claim should be abandoned.

This does not mean that claims should not be presented on labor codes or projects that turn out to be profitable. Just because the labor code or project underran the budget does not mean that a cost increase was not experienced.

When a contractor claims his total-cost loss on the project, the response by the owner or by the prime contractor frequently is that many of the problems were the responsibility of the contractor and that the contractor would never have met his budget. Contractors do frequently meet and exceed individual budgets; the contractor is entitled to all of the profit he would have made if the project had been completed without the interference or wrongful actions of the other party. Thus, it is possible to show, through actual cost records that compare normal or undisrupted production and disrupted production, that the contractor would have beaten his original estimate by, say, 40 percent rather than the five percent actually achieved when the work activity was disrupted by changes. However, claims must be reasonably grounded in the facts and cannot represent absurd views of profit that bear no relationship to past profits on similar projects.

Assuming that the review of the bases of claim and the review of the cost situation, as it relates to the problems, were the responsibility of the other party and that the data sources appear to be adequate to support the maintenance of a claim, the manager might feel ready to decide at this time whether to pursue a claim. But there are further steps that must be undertaken prior to making that decision, including reviews of the contract and change orders and satisfaction of notification requirements.

§ 12.12   —Contract Provisions

The review of the contract provisions and satisfaction of notice provisions are areas that illustrate the importance of the manager consulting his house counsel or his lawyer to ensure that there is no legal bar or other substantial defense to a claim he may wish to submit.

For example, a complete review should be made of contract provisions to determine whether the contract contains no-damage-for-delay clauses, grandfather clauses, boilerplate clauses on errors and omissions and on coordination of work, strict notice provisions, or specific contract provisions relating to specific claim items that present substantial defenses. This is not to say, however, that the fact that such clauses are contained in the contract will always bar recovery. The law has provided for exceptions to such clauses when it would be unfair and unequitable to enforce punitive provisions.[7] However, it is necessary to obtain sound legal advice to be certain of the risks involved in major claim and prosecution and to weigh this against the amount of money that might ultimately be recovered.

§ 12.13   —Change Orders

Change orders must be reviewed to make certain that there are no problems with release and settlement or accord and satisfaction. A contractor may have an extremely well-grounded claim for disruption or acceleration of unchanged activities, but if he has already executed change orders, supplemental agreements, or other instruments that include language of complete accord and satisfaction for all claims arising under any theory, serious consideration must be given to abandonment of the claim effort.

Finally, the record of correspondence should be reviewed and key personnel interviewed to make sure that appropriate notice has been given, ideally in writing, to protest the actions of the other party that gave rise to the increased costs and to provide notice of the increased costs incurred as a result. Once again, when written notice has not been provided, sound legal advice is necessary to evaluate the exceptions to contractual notice requirements recognized in the appropriate jurisdiction. Possible exceptions include verbal notice, actual knowledge of the other party, and an absence of prejudice to the other party.[8] Here, also, the manager needs to make a judgment based upon good information.

Having completed all prescribed reviews, the manager can make a decision about the advisability of prosecuting a claim. If he decides to proceed, his next task is claim preparation.

§ 12.14   Claim Preparation

Immediately upon deciding to prosecute a claim the manager should review the record to ensure that no further claim notices are required and, if

---

[7] *See, e.g.,* Peter Kiewit Sons' Co. v. Iowa S. Util. Co., 355 F. Supp. 376 (S.D. Iowa 1973) (no damage for delay clause unenforceable); J.W. Bateson Company, Inc., VACAB No. 1148, 79-1 BCA ¶ 13,573 (1978) (contractor reasonably relied on defective mechanical drawings, despite government allegation that drawings were merely diagrammatic); PT&L Constr. Co. v. Department of Transp., 108 N.J. 539, 531 A.2d 1330 (1987) (owner's disclaimer of liability for changed site conditions did not bar contractor recovery where critical information concerning soil conditions was not provided to contractor.)

[8] *See, e.g.,* Big Chief Drilling Co. v. United States, 15 Cl. Ct. 295 (1985); Hoel-Steffen Constr. Co. v. United States, 197 Ct. Cl. 561, 456 F.2d 760 (1972); Smith & Pittman Constr. Co., AGBCA 76-131, 77-1 BCA ¶ 12,381 (1977).

they are, to transmit those immediately. Next, the manager should review the record-keeping to determine if any further records might be required to enhance and buttress the claim presentation.

Finally, the manager should determine the form and manner in which the claim is going to be presented and prepare a schedule for the claim preparation. Once again, sound legal advice is extremely important in deciding among the potential forums for resolution. For example, the manager may wish to process his claim as: a request for an adjustment; a request for a change order; an administrative remedy per special contract procedure; an arbitration, in accordance with contract provisions in certain contracts; specially agreed upon procedures for alternative dispute resolution; or a suit in state or federal court.

Although the format of the material prepared for a suit is somewhat different from that in a claim presentation, for purposes of the following material it will be assumed that a claim presentation is the method selected.

The work involved in preparing a major claim often is mind-boggling, but for the person given this job the steps can be fairly systematic if a good plan of attack is followed. Frequently, the preparer is confronted with a file cabinet full of documents and with project personnel who want to talk about specific problem items or more specific incidents on the project without any consideration of the overall picture that gave rise to the present state of affairs.

For this reason it is critical for the individual performing the claim preparation to approach the material in an organized fashion, so that the relevant information about claims and defense can be retrieved in a usable fashion.

§ 12.15   —Costing and Documentary Data Sources

Having performed the initial investigation and having determined that there is a basis for prosecuting a claim, it is necessary next to extract the relevant information from the data sources available:

Preparation of summaries of correspondence, memorandums, logs, diaries, and weekly meetings.   Handling a mass of documentation requires that a large group of papers and records be reduced to a few pages. To perform this task, summaries should be prepared of the critical correspondence, memorandums, logs, and so on. That is not to suggest that all correspondence be summarized, but only those items that appear to relate to claim areas or that suggest further possible claim areas. The format of such summaries with respect to project correspondence is extremely important.

For example, the summary should reflect not only the date of the correspondence, but also the companies between which it was transmitted, the individuals transmitting and receiving it, and its substance. In addition, a further designation should be added at the time the summary is made— a column to be utilized for coding the various summaries to claim areas. **Figure 12–5** offers an example of the type of summary that would be utilized for both correspondence and interoffice memorandums. Of course, the availability of database computer programs, such as dBASE® and Legal/Base, are of great assistance today in sorting and maintaining information like that contained in **Figure 12–5**.

Summaries that are prepared for diaries and logs and weekly meetings need not, of course, reflect all of the columnar types of information detailed in the correspondence and interoffice memorandum summary. However, these other summaries should condense and properly identify (or quote) the substance of critical entries on the other records.

Preparation of claim listings for change orders, bulletins, RFIs, photographs, and shop drawing submittals and logs. Documentation of change orders and the like must also be placed into a database that allows relevant information to be retrieved for claim purposes. This should not require an extensive amount of work if the company has maintained proper logs on its change orders and shop drawing submittals. What is required is a summary of the substance of the change orders—for example, identifying the change order by date submitted, date acted upon, amount, subject, and specific activities impacted by the change and then assigning the document to a claim or defense area. This same type of exercise would also apply to bulletins and requests for information. **Figures 12–5** through **12–8** offer examples of documents and graphics summarizing schedule changes.

Coding of claim summaries and claim listings to delay issue files, claim areas, and areas of possible defense. After entering the summaries for correspondence, interoffice memorandums, and diaries into a data base and preparing the claim listings for change orders and bulletins, the individual preparing the claim should have a good idea what information is available and some concept of what actually occurred on the project. At this point (if it was not possible earlier) he should review his summaries and claim listings and make up a list of codes for the delay issue files, claim areas (such as temporary heat claim), possible claim areas, and possible areas of defense. Codes can then be applied to the columns that have been set up on the claim listings and summaries. The preparer may wish to establish a protocol of more important and less important areas in establishing the coding system (such as the "A," "B," "C" system discussed in **Chapter 13**).

Of course, in some cases, one document may relate to more than one claim or defense area. Once the coding has been accomplished, the documents can be reproduced and placed into claim files coinciding with the

DOC NO	DATE	SERIAL NO	ADDRESSEE	AUTHOR	COPY	REFERENCE	CODE MV	SUMMARY
203242	02/24/81		Brown, N/XYZ Co.	Smith, O/Luck Electric Co.	Hurlbut, O/ Systnet		1.1	Agreement extending a date in the teaming agreement from 03/31/81 to 07/28/82.
203257-	/ /					Brown, N	1.1	Teaming Agreement.
203599	/ /						1.1	Joint Venture diagram.
203611-203612	03/28/82	000029	Jones, G/ Luck Electric Co.	Groves, D/Luck Electric Co.			16 13.7 1.1	Memo: establishment of new Data Link Profit Center in Maryland with Smith in charge, incentives to keep him there.
203651-203652	09/20/81		Motley, J/Motley & Squires	Groves, D/Luck Electric Co.	Smith, O Hurlbut, O		1.1 1.2 1.3	Letter - re: documents for consideration (1) teaming agreement; (2) Joint Venture Agreement; and (3) Letter of Intent.
203653-203655	09/19/81	000045	Smith, M/Luck Electric Co.	Groves, D/ Luck Electric Co.	McGowan,J Hurt, K		1.1 1.2 1.3 16	Letter details proposed structure and organization of Maryland Data Link entity.
204200-204201	12/28/84		Boggs, J/Luck Electric Co.	James, J/Luck Electric Co.	Toomey, D	Daly, J	14.2 8.1 1.1 16	Memo re: the licensing issue. Faircorp has been authorized to develop certain software, thus avoiding the need to provide any of XYZ Co.'s software to Faircorp.
204204-204210	09/27/81				Groves, D Brown, M Hurlbut, O		1.1	Teaming agreement signed by Luck Electric Co., XYZ Co., and Systnet.
204211	12/30/84		Boggs, J/Luck Electric Co.	James, J/Luck Electric Co.	Toomey, D	Vita, J Caskey, B Brown, N Smith, M	14.2 1.1 16	Memo on the licensing issue. Demand has been made on XYZ Co., who is citing the teaming agreement as notice of their intent to preserve their copyright and license rights.

Figure 12–5. Summary of correspondence and memorandums.

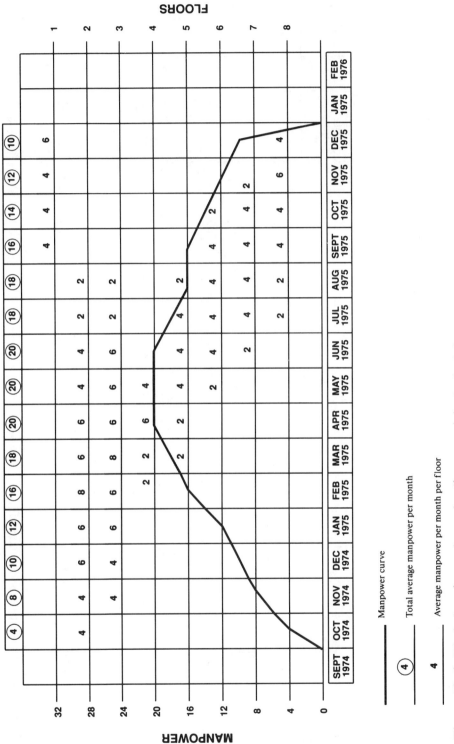

Figure 12–6. Work duration and man-loading per original schedule.

351

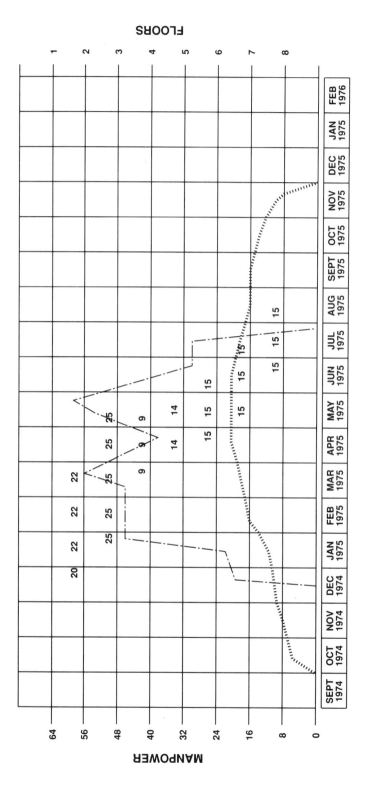

Figure 12–7. Work duration and man-loading as required under accelerated November 15, 1974, schedule.

352

FLOOR 7

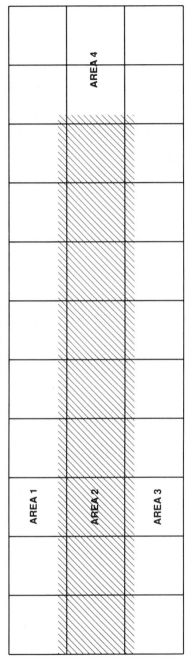

AREA	ACTUAL RELEASED DATE	NOV 74 SCHEDULE	APR 75 SCHEDULE
1	Framing Feb 14, 1973	Early 21 Days	No Date Shown
	S/R May 22, 1975	Late 36 Days	Late 15 Days
2	Framing June 9, 1975	Late 34 Days	Late Date Shown
	S/R Pending	* Late 73 Days	* Late 52 Days
3	Framing Feb 14, 1975	Early 21 Days	No Date Shown
	S/R May 22, 1975	Late 36 Days	Late 15 Days
4	Framing Pending	* Late 99 Days	No Date Shown
	S/R Pending	* Late 64 Days	No Date Shown
FLOOR 7			

* Days indicated are until
June 28, 1975. Area has
not yet been released.

Figure 12–8. Schedule change effect, by area.

coding. These files will help the preparer in composing narratives on each of the claim items.

Preparation of cost analyses. Preparing cost analyses can present a major undertaking if the information is not available from current project records. The data required is a cost history of all relevant phases of the work, specifically: (1) a planned man-loading analysis by week, hour, trade, classification within trade, labor code, work area, and dollars and (2) an actual man-loading analysis broken down by the same categories.

As detailed previously, when cost information is not maintained in a fashion that such information is retrievable, it is sometimes necessary to resort to other devices to obtain the data. For example, a rough but reasonable approximation of the area in which a number of workers were performing their installation at any given point in time can be obtained if good daily logs, weekly meeting minutes, or diaries were maintained.

Of course, if the cost records simply do not allow the retrieval of this information or if other records do not allow approximation of the information, at the very least, total hours and dollars might be retrieved from payroll records. In such a circumstance, it may be necessary to go to a total-cost type of presentation or a modified total-cost presentation after appropriate consideration of and adjustment for any contractor inefficiencies or contractor bid errors.

In any event, if the information detailed in steps (1) and (2) or an approximation of this information can be obtained, it should be analyzed with reference to the claim areas and defenses that have been developed and copies of the appropriate costing information should also be placed in the coded claim preparation files.

Material cost analysis. The same type of cost analysis that was performed with respect to labor should also be performed with respect to material. What is required is a cost breakdown of both the planned and actual material cost expenditures by bid item, work area, labor code, and so on.

Once these analyses have been completed, they should be placed in the coded claim or delay issue files, where relevant. The importance of material costing analyses is often underestimated. For example, when there is dearth of labor information, but the preparer is certain that substantial increased labor costs were incurred on a specific item of work because of a problem for which the other contracting party is responsible, it is sometimes possible to utilize material analyses to retrieve the appropriate information.

A good illustration of this situation is presented by the mechanical contractor who knows that substantial errors and omissions in the plans have caused him to incur substantially increased costs. In such a case, he may know that the errors and omissions have caused him to install many more fittings in major mechanical piping than were originally estimated and that most of the labor in such an installation is in the fittings and not in the straight runs of pipe. Here, the mechanical contractor could make an analysis of the number of fittings from the original estimate sheet and then could specify the actual number of fittings purchased not only to determine the material overrun, but also to provide a basis for utilizing standard estimating procedures to factor out the increased costs of labor or the errors and omissions.

Analysis of equipment expenditures. In analysing equipment expenditures the manager should determine what equipment it was planned would be used on the project and what expenditures were actually incurred for which specific equipment. There is no set format for this particular type of analysis, but cost records should be available that allow the necessary information to be retrieved and then segregated into claim areas for placement in the coded claim files.

Analysis of jobsite expense and G&A. Analysing jobsite and G&A expense involves an expansion of the work previously detailed. With respect to jobsite expense, the analysis should basically separate and segregate those items of jobsite expense that are a direct result of some claim item that has been previously segregated or that is a direct result of extended duration for which the other contracting party is responsible. Once the information has been determined it can also be placed in the coded claim files.

G&A expense analysis involves collecting the necessary information from the records of the corporation for the original G&A expense on which the project was bid; actual audited G&A figures; information relating to the gross receipts on the particular project, as contrasted to the gross receipts for all projects, for the company during the period of time concerned; and, finally, the gross expenditures for the particular project and for the entire company for the period of time concerned.

§ 12.16   —Scheduling Documentation and Non-Network Exhibits

In preparing a claim, the manager should review all contract provisions related to preparation and maintenance of the schedule, as well as cognizable time adjustment provisions. He should evaluate carefully any contract provisions establishing the baseline by which delays are to be measured. And he should evaluate the pragmatic and legal effect of the original project schedule: Was it approved? Does it contain serious or fatal flaws? Do adjustments need to be made in the as-planned schedule?

The manager should work with his outside or in-house scheduling expert to develop an analyses of performance that illustrates the variances between the planned and actual construction, as well as the causes of the variances. They also should prepare time impact analyses, moving from the beginning to the end of the project, as detailed in **Chapter 13**.[9]

The manager and his experts also should consider the use of non-network charts to augment or highlight the specific effect of delays on individual activities. See **Figures 12–6** through **12–9** for examples of the use of plan views and graphs to illustrate individual delays and acceleration.

§ 12.17   —Final Claim Compilation

The most difficult problem in preparing a claim is putting it all together into one coordinated presentation. The presentation should provide a basic word picture of cause and effect; specifically, it should provide a factual and accurate narrative as to how the project should have been

---

[9] In preparing the time impact analyses and quantifying the effect of changes or delays on the critical path, the manager should pay careful attention to the contemporaneous procedures detailed in Ch. 3 of the Corps of Engineers Modification Impact Evaluation Guide, EP 415-1-3 (1979), in the app.:

3-4.   Summary

a.   Paragraph 3-3 defined procedures for developing the time requirements portion of a CPM schedule to reflect the changes necessary to accommodate the work as directly changed by a modification, and its effects on the unchanged work. These procedures are:

(1) *Define current job status.* Compile data on actual progress, status of materials, manpower, equipment, and any other pertinent factors (para. 3-1).

(2) *Analyze progress schedule.* The process of accurately identifying and evaluating impact depends largely on an up-to-date CPM progress schedule. To effectively fulfill its contract administration responsibilities, the Corps of Engineers must exercise the authorities and options available to maintain progress schedule validity throughout the life of the project (para. 3-2).

(3) *Procedures for developing a revised schedule (para. 3-3).*

(a)   Revise the schedule to show actual job status.

(b)   Insert the directly changed work.

(c)   Recalculate affected unchanged work (retaining presently assigned durations).

(d)   Reestablish critical path, and note time extension justified by direct changes.

(e)   Analyze schedule for impacted unchanged activities; assign new durations to these activities as appropriate.

(f)   Reestablish critical path, and note any slippage of final completion date indicated in (d), above. Difference is amount of time extension justified because of impact.

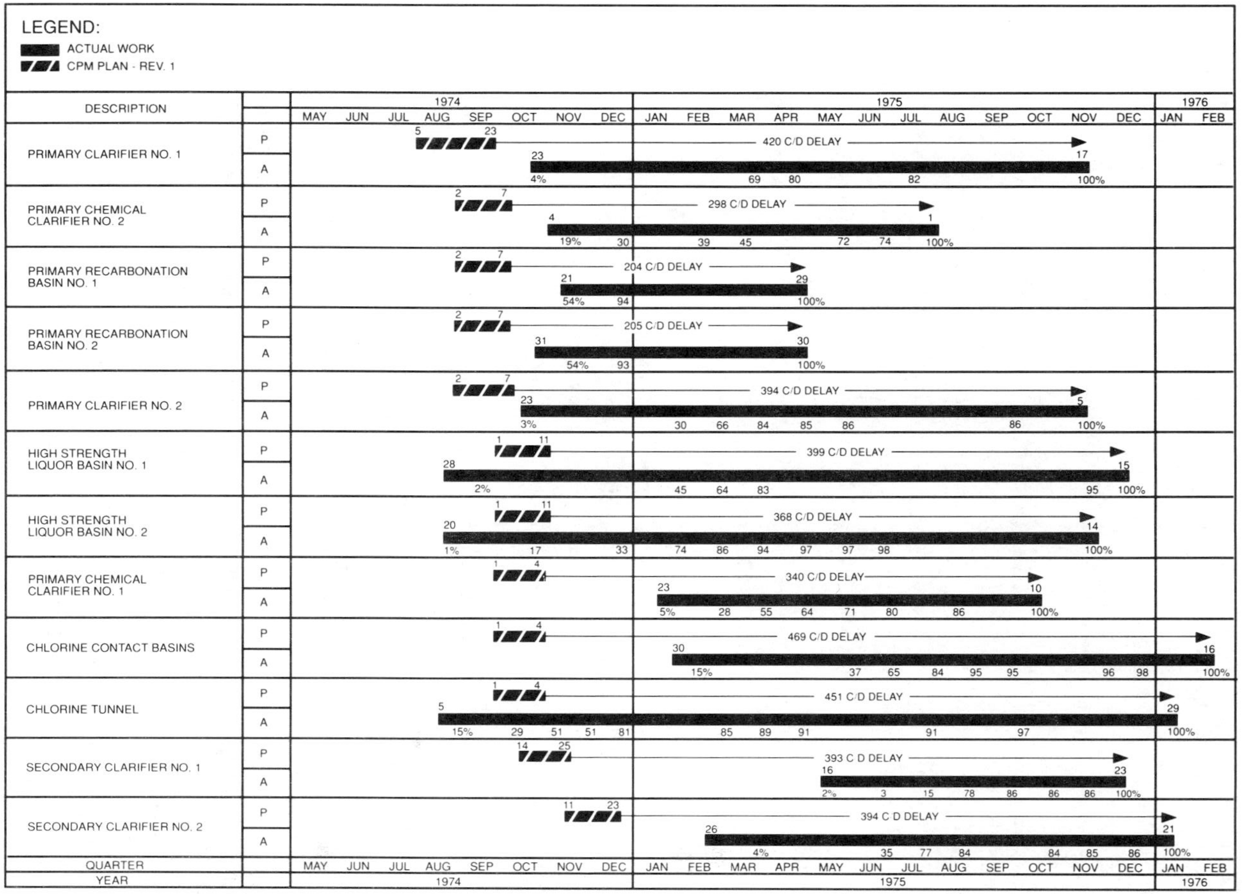

Figure 12–9. Treatment-structures plan versus actual form, rebar, and concrete-pour operations for wastewater treatment plant project.

357

executed versus how it was actually executed and the causal relationship of the other party's actions upon the manager's work efforts.

§ 12.18   Claim Presentation

The means by which the claim is presented has a great deal to do with its ultimate success—and also the amount at which it is settled. Basically, there are two criteria in maximizing claim posture. First, the claim presentation should reflect a cogent and intelligible explanation of the factors for which the other party is responsible that gave rise to the increased costs. Second, the document itself must look, and actually be, impressive.

The individuals who make the final decision about the settlement or nonsettlement of the claim frequently have little knowledge of the project's actual history. Although claims are not always settled by the presentation's sheer weight, executives are sometimes swayed by the appearance of a comprehensive presentation. Of course, if the executive evaluating the document sees that the presentation is not only impressive but also a cogent explanation of the increased costs, grounded in the facts and job records, he may think twice about the extensive work he will have to perform to rebut the effort you have put forth.[10]

There is always a substantial risk in making a detailed claim presentation. By taking such a step the manager invariably presents a significant amount of information that will be subject to attack. Nonetheless, it has been suggested that the most progress can be made in resolving disputes by laying all of the cards on the table and challenging the other party to disprove the critical facts the manager has identified as central to the dispute. The alternative to the detailed claim presentation is a much shorter document that generally alleges the facts giving rise to the increased costs, followed by litigation. This approach has the advantage of holding back the "good stuff" until closer to trial time, but it also greatly decreases the chances of settlement.

If the decision is made to utilize a detailed claim presentation, a few rules can be of substantial aid in preparing the submission:

1.   The submission should present a complete package, with all necessary supporting data, so that it can be utilized at trial as the basis for proving the claim with little extra work.

---

[10] To make sure that the evaluating executive understands the basic theory and essence of the allegations, the presenter should prepare an executive summary to go with his major presentation (or arrange for a face-to-face verbal explanation).

2. The presentation should offer a complete, accurate, and truthful narrative about the conditions encountered on the project.

3. The presentation should admit and take into account problems that are the manager's own responsibility and that had a significant effect on the project. (The alternative to this can be a disaster when the manager's credibility is shattered at a hearing or trial.)

4. Finally, the submission should reflect pricing that is not grounded in the "twilight zone."

Certainly, it should shed the best light on the facts, but it should be based on actual cost records that can survive an audit. One sure way of closing the door to settlement is to present absurd claim amounts that the other party knows have no relationship to the actual cost records.

The following sections discuss assembly of a claim presentation with these rules in mind.

§ 12.19   —Structure of Narrative

Formation of contractual relationship.   One of the first questions an outsider faces in reviewing a claim presentation is the role of the different players in the dispute. To assist the outsider—the arbiter or judge, who has never reviewed the project before—an introductory section of the claim presentation should detail the formation of the contractual relationship between the parties, the critical contract provisions relating to the claim, and the scope of work and schedule required by the contract or subcontract. The contractor may also wish to provide a brief history of his company and his experience on similar projects.

Description of project and of major installations of various trades.   One of the major problems the fact finder confronts in evaluating a claim is the effect of the claim items upon performance. The manager must therefore lay some sort of framework for the individual evaluating the claim about the effect of the other contracting party's actions on his performance. To facilitate this, a second introductory section of the claim presentation should provide a description of the project's size, its physical characteristics, and the major installations of other trades.

Key physical characteristics and keys to successful construction.   A section of the presentation should focus on the key physical aspects of construction that represented difficult stages in the work and that must be executed properly to achieve a successful project. In addition, the contractor may wish to discuss here any key sequencing in the project activities or any external considerations that significantly bear on the project's success (such as achieving a working platform with the placement of structural concrete prior to winter or building close-in prior to winter to allow interior trades to proceed with work).

Overview of plan versus actual performance and claim items causing increased costs. The cardinal purpose of the claim presentation is to provide a complete narrative detailing the full effect of the actions of the other party upon the contractor's performance. Obviously, the heart of the presentation is the detailed analyses of claim items. However, if the individual evaluating the claim has no background knowledge or has no knowledge of the planned performance, he will have little understanding of the effect of a change in sequence or a change in equipment characteristics on the contractor's performance.

Upon completing the description of the contractual relationship and the description of the project and major installations of the various trades, the contractor should next address in narrative detail his plan for performance, in conjunction with his original CPM; the actual sequence of performance resulting in increased costs, in conjunction with his as-built CPM; and the claim items causing the actual sequence of performance and associated cost increases. The review of the planned versus the actual performance can be presented through a number of approaches, such as a strict chronological review, a review by area of project, or a review by system.

Detailed analyses of major substantive claim items. The heart of the claim presentation is the detailed analyses or narratives of individual claim items, and these narratives can be presented in a number of different ways. However, the purpose will be best served if the narrative or analysis presents a complete statement of the facts, including specific cost categories, that details the full effect of the action of the other contracting party on the contractor's performance. The importance of this effort and the need for accuracy in this portion of the presentation cannot be overemphasized.

Conclusion and amount requested. Once the contractor has described the contractual relationship, the characteristics of the project, the major installations, and the plan for performance, has briefly covered the actual sequence and claim items, and has made a detailed analysis of the individual claim items, his conclusion should set forth the amount requested and the bases for arriving at the amount requested. He should set forth the theory upon which the pricing was determined and explain the pricing for exhibits and all appropriate back-up. To complete the narrative, he should recount, in no more than a page or two, the plan for performance and the specific wrongful acts impacting the actual performance.

§ 12.20 —Supporting Exhibits

Pricing. If at all possible, the pricing set forth in the claim should represent the final amount requested, broken down and supported in such a fashion that it can be utilized in any trial or hearing as the proof of the increased costs. If this cannot be done, the amounts detailed should be clearly denoted as not being final amounts and as being subject to revision at a later time. In addition, the pricing attachment or exhibit should include all appropriate back-up information so that it is clear that the costs claimed are actually from the books of the corporation. For example, union books can be utilized to show the actual wage rates paid, annual reports can be utilized to show the annual G&A expenses, and so forth. The manager should give serious consideration to the use of production analyses comparing undisrupted periods and the disrupted period (or undisrupted project productivity and disrupted productivity). He should also give serious consideration to using the curves and pricing methodology detailed in § 4 of Appendix B of the Corps of Engineers' *Modification Impact Evaluation Guide,* EP 415-1-3 (1979).[11]

Photographs and videotape. All photographs that support the information contained in the complaint and that are not contained directly in the claim narrative should be used as an exhibit to the claim presentation and referenced at the appropriate place in the claim narrative. Consider also the use of a video presentation to visually review the key components of the project, the plan for performance, and specific physical effects on performance.

Correspondence. All relevant correspondence should be included as an exhibit to the presentation so that the individual evaluating the claim can review the actual letters referenced or quoted in the claim narrative. The contractor may wish to include all correspondence in one exhibit on a chronological basis.

Errors and omissions studies. Any errors and omissions studies or other studies that provide substantial support for the claim but that are not, for some reason, properly included in the claim narrative, should be utilized

---

[11] Other pricing resources include studies distributed by the National Electrical Contractors Association and the Mechanical Contractors Association. *See also* **Ch. 10** of this book and Ch. 6, *Current Practices For Handling and Evaluating Work—Face Activities and Cases,* and Ch. 9, *Factors Affecting Humans As Workers In Construction,* C. Oglesby, H. Parker, & G. Howell, Productivity Improvement in Construction (1989).

in an exhibit to the claim so that full utility can be gained for the work effort.

Audits.   Any audits of the actual claim itself should be set forth as an exhibit to the claim. An audit from a recognized CPA is always of assistance in establishing to the other side that the contractor is serious about the costs claimed and that the amount of the claim is proper.

Scheduling analyses.   All scheduling documents, as well as after-the-fact CPM analyses, bar charts, histograms, or S curves, that are not directly incorporated into the claim narrative, should be set forth as an exhibit to the claim along with an appropriate explanation of the relevance of the documents.

Points and authorities.   Legal authorities are of frequent assistance in supporting both the general concept of the claim and specific items that may present particular problems.

§ 12.21   Claim Defense

Different companies and different individuals approach the defense of claims with many different philosophies. Some companies never admit claims and always make the other side go all the way through litigation and appeals. Others are ready to settle claims as soon as they are received without checking any of the facts or back-up data. Obviously, neither of these two extremes present the best course of action. The first type of company could frequently end up with legal fees equalling the amount of the original payment and with a much greater loss than would otherwise have been sustained. The second type of company could end up with a much higher payment than could otherwise have been negotiated or litigated because of its failure to perform proper analyses.

In any event, it is necessary, upon receiving a claim, to evaluate the claim properly and obtain sound legal advice about the company's rights and obligations. The actions in reviewing a claim or in preparing a defense are similar to the steps in preparing a claim.

§ 12.22   —Actions upon Receipt of Claim

One of the first steps to undertake upon receiving a claim is to transmit a letter acknowledging receipt and requesting additional time to review the claim or providing a general total denial of the claim. An immediate general denial of the claim could well trigger an immediate demand for arbitration or immediate litigation.

Regardless of whether the claim recipient chooses to merely acknowledge the claim or to deny the claim immediately, he should utilize a rational decision-making process as well as the investigative process detailed previously. That process should include the following steps:

1. A review of the claim document to determine the basic factual allegations that form the linchpin for the alleged damages.
2. A review of the claim's pricing. In this review, the issue is whether the opposing contractor's alleged damages match up with the wrongs claimed committed by the recipient's organization from a causal standpoint.
3. An analysis of the legal and contractual setting that bears upon the opposing contractor's ability to recover an equitable adjustment or damages. For example, what kinds of clauses are present in the contract that address issues such as entitlement to time extensions, no damages for delay, requirements to contemporaneously price impact costs with direct costs, ownership of float, notice provisions, and so forth. In addition, the recipient should look at the contractual status of the project as it relates to the contractor's claims. Has the contractor released such claims by execution of contract modifications or waived claims by his conduct as a volunteer or through laches? Next, the recipient should evaluate the contractual setting of the jurisdiction or jurisdictions in question.
4. Just as in the case of the contractor's task in the claim preparation process, the claim recipient must undertake an investigation to determine:

    The major physical characteristics of the project

    Key installations and sequencing required for a successful project construction

    Reasonableness in the duration and sequencing of the contractor's original plan for performance

    How the planned conditions for performance compare with the actual conditions for performance

    Other potential excusable or contractor delays that may have affected the performance and cost claimed by the contractor.
5. The claim recipient should review cost and data records to develop summaries and coding that establish a data base to evaluate the key factual allegations of the contractor's claims. Such summaries would include important correspondence, RFIs, change orders, shop drawing reviews, photographs, and so on.

6. The recipient should evaluate retention of experienced legal counsel and scheduling experts.

§ 12.23   —Audits

If the claim recipient has requested time to evaluate the claim rather than providing a general denial and if he wishes to have additional time to prepare his own exhibits and analyses as well as evaluating the other party's claim, one step he could well take is to demand or request that an audit of the relevant costs in the claimant's records be performed by the recipient's CPA prior to commencing any negotiations.

Owners and prime contractors who are defending claims rarely realize that they are in a strong negotiating posture to demand an audit prior to any negotiations. If the opposing contractor thinks he is really due some money, he should be willing to show he truly lost it. In fact, if the claimant is unwilling to submit to the audit, the recipient's equitable posture is quite good. For example, he receives a claim, requests time to evaluate the claim, and requests that, prior to negotiations, he be allowed to examine the other party's books. If the other party refuses to allow him to examine the books, he can properly take the position that he has always been willing to compensate the claimant for valid costs but the claimant has been totally unreasonable in refusing to allow him to evaluate the real facts and costs relevant to the claim. Of course, if the claimant does file suit, one of the first steps the recipient should take on discovery is to demand the audit that was previously denied.

§ 12.24   —Alternatives to
Confrontation and Litigation

Owners should assemble a critical analysis or crisis analysis group to undertake a detailed review of the risks and costs associated with major complex construction confrontation, when litigation can cost in the hundreds of thousands of dollars or even more. The decision-making group should utilize the following procedures in the evaluation process:

First, the group should get an idea of the significant considerations related to the contractor's claim. For example, was the owner late with schedules or approvals? Was the owner late in furnishing equipment? Was the contractor damaged by change orders on the project? Was he even more damaged by terrible inefficiencies from travelling workers who had to be utilized due to a scarcity of labor in the particular marketplace?

Next, the group should identify the major legal factors that bear on the claim and the likelihood of legal problems affecting the decision of the court or board or arbitrators evaluating the contractor's claims.

The crisis analysis group should identify the owner's goals and objectives as they relate to the project as well as the claim. Is the owner more interested in the strict monetary bottom line of defending against the contractor's claim or is he more interested in a continuing relationship with the contractor? Perhaps the owner is most interested in timely completion of the project without a great deal of adverse publicity.

Once the group has identified the owner's major goals and objectives, it should prepare a list of the options available to the owner to achieve them. For example, the owner may know that terminating the contractor will allow the owner to bring in a much stronger team to complete the project in a timely fashion. However, does this option run the risk of enormous potential damages to the contractor, not only for this project, but for other lost profits due to loss of bonding capacity?

Of course, the group should evaluate options in terms of those that represent low risk and high risk, as well as those that present the greatest chance for potential benefit.

In the course of evaluating the owner's options, the group should consider likely responses that its selection of options will create on the other side. The group should carefully consider the option of settlement or even the use of alternative dispute resolution procedures or mediation. A mediocre settlement is almost always better than a good lawsuit. Embarking on major complex construction litigation ties up a huge amount of time of key company personnel, who may lose profits on other projects while they spend time in prosecuting or defending the big claim.

Alternative dispute resolution (ADR) procedures or mediation may also provide a vehicle for gaining a perspective about the merits of each side's position from a third party each respects. Such ADR procedures can frequently knock sense into the parties and enable them to reach a resolution of their dispute.

§ 12.25   —Counterclaims

Owners and contractors who are defendants frequently fail to maximize their position when they fail to consider the value of asserting counterclaims. As in the case of an affirmative claim, no counterclaim should be presented that is not based upon the facts and that decreases the presenter's credibility by its assertion. On the other hand, if reasonable facts and legal theory exist to support a counterclaim, it should, in all probability, be asserted.

Any counterclaim that has a reasonable chance for success or presents a reasonable posture grounded in the facts, along with a high dollar amount, may create doubt in the mind of the opposing party. This may cause the contractor to settle the case at some point in time or decrease his ultimate award from litigation.

Another situation when a counterclaim can clearly be of value is the opportunity to assert one of the opposing side's claims as your own counterclaim. If the claimant has a strong claim item but his opponent has a reasonable legal theory or some other basis and facts for turning that claim around and using it against the claimant, the opponent may wish to assert a counterclaim to create doubt not only in the claimant's mind, but also possibly in the mind of the finder of fact.

A final note about counterclaims relates to their negotiating value. Positions that have a reasonable basis in fact and law and that can be reasonably asserted as a counterclaim will be of use. However, counterclaims that are not reasonably grounded in facts or legal theory can increase a claimant's recovery because of erosion in his opponent's credibility with the finder of fact.

§ 12.26   —Assertion of Defenses

A host of defenses, such as statute of frauds, laches, waiver, lack of notice, and so forth, are available to the recipient of a claim. The question is whether they apply to his fact situation. Because of the difficulty in identifying applicable defenses, sound legal advice should be sought even before a suit is filed. For example, if a manager or owner receives a claim during construction, or after construction, and responds to the claim, his response may waive certain defenses or may fail to assert certain defenses to effectively preserve his rights. In addition, care must be taken not to assert defenses that will decrease his credibility with the court or finder of fact. This can happen when, for example, he asserts 15 defenses and only one of the defenses applies to his particular fact situation.

§ 12.27   —Choice of Forum and
Value of Going First

The strategy involved in dealing with a claim or a possible or actual lawsuit is one of the most interesting yet difficult aspects of construction claims. Further, strategy can play a significant role in the recipient's ultimate success in dealing with the claim situation.

In this regard, the party who is receiving the claim should consider his opportunities with respect to choosing the forum and the value of suing first. Frequently, the parties have a choice of different forums: federal court if jurisdictional requirements are met, state court, and arbitration or administrative hearings. If the one party sues first, the other may have an opportunity, because of binding arbitration clauses, to force the first party to arbitration. However, this is not always the case, and other forums may be more advantageous—for example, a federal court with a docket of one year or a state court with a docket of four years. Further, requiring arbitration may be more advantageous than a court suit, even though there may be a shorter time span prior to hearing, because of the limited discovery available under arbitration proceedings.

One of the other significant factors that should be considered is the value of suing first. There is a significant advantage, in certain cases, of presenting proof first, because the jury or judge or finder of fact are fresh to the fact situation and the other side must then rebut. Thus, while it means a greater burden to carry in terms of proof, suing first means "telling your side of the story" first, which can be a very great advantage.

§ 12.28 —Defensive Measures

The first steps after being sued are to secure counsel and file the appropriate answers. Thereafter, working with counsel, the defendant should utilize his summaries coded to the various areas, prepare other exhibits necessary for trial, and prepare the witnesses for trial.

Something defendants often overlook is the value of discovery devices in applying pressure to the other side. It is possible to impose significant burdens upon the opposing party through the use of detailed interrogatories, such as contention interrogatories requesting that the other party detail each and every fact that formed a basis for a specific statement in the complaint, the witnesses who have personal knowledge of the facts, all correspondence relied upon by the opposing party with respect to that allegation, and so on. In addition, if the defendant is properly prepared, depositions of corporate representatives can be of great value in applying pressure to the other side through requests that it back up the facts of the allegations contained in its complaint with specific dates and correspondence. In this regard, consider noticing the deposition of the corporate representative as to significant aspects of the contractor's case.

One of the most important factors in defending is to take the offensive away from the other side. In defending against a complex claim where the claimant has provided limited factual back-up, the defendant has significant opportunities to occupy the other party's time and efforts until the time of trial and to make him work double time to get ready for trial by lodging entirely proper discovery requests.

CHAPTER 13

EXPERT'S ROLE IN PREPARING AND DEFENDING SCHEDULE CLAIMS

§ 13.1 Introduction

§ 13.2 Familiarization Phase

§ 13.3 Investigation and Data-Gathering Phase

§ 13.4 Fact-Finding and Evaluation Phase

§ 13.5 Presentation Phase

§ 13.1 Introduction

An expert's specific tasks in preparing or defending against a delay damage claim are dependent upon the charter established by counsel and the client as to the expert's exact role. In this regard, it must be clearly noted that any reports or conclusions developed by the expert must be fair to all sides, firmly grounded in the facts of the project, and derived from complete and proper reviews of appropriate project data. Thus, for expert testimony to be of value, it must reflect a fair and complete review (prepared by the expert or by someone whose credentials are properly established) of the project data and it must reflect analyses that take into account major and controlling delays of all parties on the project.

The collapse of expert testimony that was not properly grounded in the facts of projects and that did not appropriately consider delays of all parties is clearly demonstrated in three recent cases: *Weaver-Bailey Contractors, Inc. v. United States,*[1] *Titan Pacific Construction Corp. v. United States,*[2] and *Gulf Contracting, Inc.*[3]

---

[1] 19 Cl. Ct. 474 (1990).

[2] 17 Cl. Ct. 630 (1989).

[3] ASBCA Nos. 30,195, 32,839, 33,867, 89-2 BCA ¶ 21,812 (1989).

In the *Weaver-Bailey* decision, the claims court considered the testimony of a government claims analyst put forward to present the proposition that government changes to increase the quantity of unclassified excavation on the project had not delayed the critical path to the project. In rejecting the testimony and the expert, the court found serious deficiencies in the factual data that formed the bases for the critical path analyses and a lack of connection of the analyst to the project:

> At trial, the government presented the testimony of David Berkey, a claims analyst with the United States Army Corps of Engineers, Tulsa, Oklahoma District. Mr. Berkey testified as to his analysis of Weaver-Bailey's claim. Mr. Berkey had nothing to do with the Weaver-Bailey contract until after the contract had been completed. Mr. Berkey has no experience in earthwork, nor as an engineer. In essence, Mr. Berkey testified as an expert, giving his view of the validity of plaintiff's claim, based solely on documents obtained from the Corps and from plaintiff, and his training in claims analysis.

> Defendant introduced into evidence several worksheets prepared by Mr. Berkey, purporting to show the start and finish dates of various tasks on the project. The evidentiary value of these exhibits is dubious, considering that they were prepared by someone with no personal knowledge of the project, and were summaries of other documents not in evidence. Plaintiff cast serious doubt on the conclusions reached by Mr. Berkey, by pointing out that Mr. Berkey had misinterpreted much of the data upon which he relied.

* * *

> Mr. Berkey used a computer to perform two critical path analyses of the Weaver-Bailey contract. One is called "planned schedule," the other, "actual durations/sequences." The court heard foundational testimony on the power of Mr. Berkey's computer and the program he used in performing his critical path analyses. While the court appreciates the value of computers in making complex tasks simpler, it must be remembered that a computer-generated analysis is no better than the data which is entered into the computer.

* * *

> As the discussion above indicates, the court has serious doubts as to the validity of the data Mr. Berkey used to create exhibit 30. Many of Mr. Berkey's assumptions are based upon rehashings and interpretations of a collection of documents not even in evidence; indeed, plaintiff demonstrated persuasively that at least some of Mr. Berkey's data were either unverified or simply wrong.[4]

---

[4] 19 Cl. Ct. 474, 479–81 (1990).

In the *Titan Pacific* decision, the claims court considered the testimony of the contractor expert put forward to support an adjusted planned CPM, which was impacted by certain alleged owner deficiencies, but which did not take into account any comparison of the as-planned schedule with the actual activities as they occurred on the project. The expert testimony was clearly rejected:

> Analyses made after project completion, however, that make adjustments to attain new and revised projected scheduling depend on theoretical contingencies. They are of limited value.
>
> Plaintiff's delay/impact claims expert did not present a comparison of either the October 17, 1977, as-planned schedule, or his as-planned schedule adjusted for wet and dry season restraints, with actual activities on the project—the as-built schedule. The Board had before it the records that reflect actual field operations and was in a position to relate the as-built schedule to the expert's theoretically adjusted as-planned schedule.
>
> Plaintiff's 'like-time' analysis to attain a revised completion date, matches excusable delay to the as-planned work schedule and the time period in which the affected activity was delayed. Plaintiff points out that there were excusable delays in 1977, 1978 and 1979, and argues that all time extensions should be matched to the period during which the delays occurred and the particular earthwork activities affected.
>
> Plaintiff's calculations in application of its 'like-time' theory disregard the facts found by the Board as to the sequence of work, the quality of work, and the effects of weather on the Phase III work in the years 1977, 1978 and 1979. The calculations reflect a theoretical application to a CPM as-planned schedule that was not intended to be followed. The calculations disregard the facts that actually existed in on-site operations.[5]

Finally, in the *Gulf Contracting* decision, the Armed Services Board of Contract Appeals rejected the testimony of the contractor's critical path method (CPM) expert, who had excluded owner disruptions from his analyses of the project:

> In support of its claim, Gulf relied on the analysis of its expert, Vinson. Vinson claimed to have performed an in-depth review of all correspondence and data pertinent to the progress of the project (finding 81). If this was indeed the case, we do not believe that Vinson could have missed the well documented performance problems that existed between Gulf and Hughes. Vinson said that he was instructed to 'exclude other disruptions from the claim' (finding 92). We have found that Vinson's analysis systematically excluded all delays and disruptions except those allegedly caused by the Government (finding 92). We conclude that his analysis

---

[5] 17 Cl. Ct. 630, 635–38 (1989).

was inherently biased, and could lead to but one predictable outcome. For our purposes therefore, we deem Vinson's analysis to be totally unreliable. To be credible, a contractor's CPM analysis ought to take into account, and give appropriate credit for all of the delays which were alleged to have occurred. *Haney v. United States* [30 CCF ¶ 70,189], 676 F.2d 584 (Ct. Cl. 1982); *Pathman Construction Co.,* ASBCA No. 23,392, 85-2 BCA ¶ 18,096 (CPM analysis with "built-in bias" rejected).[6]

The watchwords for the expert role in preparing scheduling analyses must include fair and complete reviews of all relevant project data. The expert should not accept any engagement that requires her to ignore or exclude the sins of her client.

Once the charter and role of the expert have been properly established, the process by which the expert prepares her report is typically organized into four broad phases:

1. Familiarization
2. Investigation and data gathering
3. Fact finding and evaluation
4. Presentation of report and conclusions.

Throughout all phases, it is important that the expert participate in periodic reviews with legal counsel. Additionally, it should be recognized that although these phases and tasks are presented in a chronological sequence, they do, in fact, overlap. Feedback and recycling are frequently required, particularly between the investigation and fact-finding phases.

§ 13.2 Familiarization Phase

The familiarization phase is essential to effective interpretation and participation in a claim. In addition to providing the necessary overview of the project and an understanding of the claim theories and issues involved, it provides a sound basis for planning, organizing, and conducting the remaining phases with maximum efficiency. The familiarization phase includes the following tasks:

Review of the project requirements. An initial understanding of the project is accomplished by thoroughly reviewing all contract documents, including the plans and specifications.

---

[6] ASBCA Nos. 30,195, 32,839, 33,867, 89-2 BCA ¶ 21,812, at 109,758–59 (1989).

Review of overall submission with legal counsel. In situations where a defendant receives a delay and/or cost impact claim, it is additionally suggested that an independent and detailed review of the overall claim submission be made in consultation with legal counsel. Attention should be directed to:

1. Identification of the issues offered to support the claimed theories of recovery

2. Factual presentations offered for each claim issue

3. Elements of proof required to support each claim issue

4. The methodology used in presenting any comparisons of planned and as-built or as-adjusted schedule analyses, and the specific procedures and techniques used by the claimant to isolate and quantify specific delays and delay to the overall project

5. Any delays accepted by the claimant as her responsibility and how her delay is treated with regard to the alleged compensable delays

6. The position taken on the availability of float

7. Identification and treatment of concurrent and offsetting delay situations

8. Time extensions requested, granted, pending, and denied (in total or partial)

9. Compliance with notice and claim documentation requirements of the contract

10. Identification of individuals who are most knowledgeable about the claimant's performance and the alleged problems that were encountered

11. Timeliness of change orders and contract modifications (issuance and responses) and, consequently, the potential delay to and impact on job progress

12. Methods to prove or refute alleged inefficiency and related costs

13. The type of delay damages being sought and the proofs offered

14. The use of reservation of rights to impact and/or acceleration costs

15. Identification of potential contractual and performance defenses that could be relied upon.

Meetings with key project personnel for further background information. Meetings with key project personnel should be held to identify and review the types of claim issues involved, identify major and potential controlling delays, discuss other related problems encountered on the project, and identify documents necessary to resolve each claim issue. Progress photographs should be reviewed to gain a thorough understanding of any special or unique conditions that existed during construction.

Visits to the actual construction site.   Site visits are suggested in order to become familiar with the physical aspects of the project and to achieve a better understanding of specific claim issues. If construction is still in progress, the expert should determine existing field conditions, the status of construction, and the plans by all parties involved to complete the balance of the project.

Review of project's record systems.   The expert should review the quality and type of project record systems that were, or are, being kept to determine if an effective program was, or is, in place for monitoring and documenting actual performance on the project. If the project is still in progress, the expert should determine the need for and recommend any additional methods and procedures considered essential for creating and preserving evidence of planned and actual performance.

Assessment of overall claim.   The expert should establish an effective method of inquiry for preparing a timely assessment of the overall claim. She should also establish priorities, plans, responsibilities, and timetables for executing the specific tasks that will follow.

§ 13.3   Investigation and Data-Gathering Phase

The investigation and data-gathering phase is oriented toward identifying and collecting the specific data required to document original plans and actual performance and to identify and confirm the problems and delays encountered. This phase generally requires considerable time in the field offices of the project. The material gathered through the following tasks provides the base for the fact-finding and evaluation phase, which follows:

Review of project records.   The expert should review existing project records to identify all key documents pertaining to the project schedule, actual performance, problems, and delays that were encountered. Such records include, but are not limited to, the contract drawings and specifications, general correspondence, memorandums, requests for information (RFIs), change order files, minutes of job progress meetings, diaries, cost estimates, cost accounting and payment records, job cost systems, wage agreements, photographs, daily logs, contract files, progress reports and project schedules (including any updates), purchase and material status reports, material delivery receipts, test reports, and consultant reports. Copies should be made of all documents that will be needed for further analysis and/or factual documentation of problems, delays, and disputes.

Chronological listing of claim issues. As part of the review described above, the expert should work with counsel to develop a chronological listing of major claim issues, problems, and delays. The listing should be prepared and organized according to the date of initial occurrence as recorded in the project records. Such listing of claim issues, problems, and delays should be coordinated with and incorporated into the coded data base described in **Chapter 12**.

The listing of items can be categorized as owner-caused, contractor-caused, caused by third parties, or beyond the control of the parties. In addition, items may be categorized by type of issue or by project area. The expert should keep in mind that it may not be possible to identify all of the key claim issues on the initial attempt. The list of issues can be updated and refined as the investigation process continues and other issues are discovered.

As part of the initial issue- or problem-identification process, the expert should list as part of each problem or delay identified any status comments included in the records that show when a specific problem or delay started, continued, or ended. Also, she should list as recorded any action or recommended actions taken, or not taken, to resolve each problem.

Prioritizing fact-finding and analysis requirements. Once the initial issues are identified, it may be cost beneficial to develop criteria for prioritizing the fact-finding and analysis requirements for each delay issue. The objective is to select those issues that have the highest return on investment and the greatest potential for demonstrating the elements of proof required for recovery or defense. Criteria may be based on area of the project, type or nature of the delay, estimated dollar value, number of days of suspected delay, potential for legal merit, ease of documentation, time frame when the delay issue begins, and whether a counterclaim issue exists. The use of an A,B,C technique and the establishment of initial criteria for within each category priorities each category and is oftentimes helpful. For example, an A is assigned to each of the strongest issues, B to the next, and C to all remaining. After the initial ranking of issues is complete, a review of all three listings should be made for possible criteria changes and reranking. Once these listings are established, additional priorities within each grouping can be established.

Development of delay issue files. After the foregoing information has been extracted, file folders should be established for each delay issue. Copies of all reference materials, including instructions, status, actions, and performance data, should be assembled in chronological order and coded with respect to each delay. For quick reference, an index of all material should eventually be included in each delay issue file.

Review of contract. Depending upon the particular situation and to the extent necessary, a review of the contract and its scheduling requirements should be made to determine the following:

1. Responsibility for schedule preparation and approval (noting any conflicts among responsible parties)
2. The quality of response expected
3. The involvement of subcontractors in preparation of the schedule
4. The approval status of the schedule (Does an approved schedule exist?)
5. The existence of owner protective clauses in the contract (Does a no damage for delay clause exist? Does a notice clause exist?)
6. Quality of schedule maintenance (Does the schedule reflect how the project was constructed? Do actual start and finish dates exist for each activity? Are there any broken logic sequences?)
7. Frequency of schedule updates and how they were conducted (Were they conducted jointly? Did subcontractors participate?)
8. The contract procedure for incorporating network changes (What does the contract say about changes and float?)
9. Whether requests for time extensions were made (If any were granted, on what basis? Were any time extension requests denied? Are any pending?)
10. Reasons for abandoning the schedule (if an issue).

Assistance in discovery process. The expert should consider assisting counsel on scheduling issues in the discovery process. This may include questions to be asked in requests for admissions, interrogatories, and during the depositions of key adversary personnel. For example, questions may be directed toward the following issues:

1. Establishing the facts relating to preproject planning, preparation, and approval of the schedule; periodic updatings; actual performance; documentation; specific delays and corresponding costs; and time extension analysis
2. Identification of specific records the opposition will use to support or defend the facts and their position for both time and cost impact
3. Determining the thrust of expert testimony to be used in the areas of schedule impact and delay-related costs
4. Identification of evidentiary tools (such as scheduling and delay analysis exhibits) to be used by the opposition during the dispute resolution process (including those already prepared and those that are anticipated for the trial or hearing).

Assistance in depositions.   The scheduling consultant should attend the depositions of key adversary personnel. In this capacity, the consultant can listen and assist counsel in pursuing pertinent details of technical questions to be asked on schedule, delay, cost, actual performance, and related matters.

§ 13.4   Fact-Finding and Evaluation Phase

The tasks associated with the fact-finding and evaluation phase are oriented toward providing a clear understanding of the delays and issues identified and organizing them into a comprehensive position. Effective coordination with legal counsel is particularly important during this phase to ensure that all findings are correlated with the legal plan and strategy. Key tasks during this phase are:

Establishment of an as-planned schedule.   The *as-planned schedule* can be the initially approved schedule required by the owner or an amplified version of it. In certain situations, it may be necessary to amplify the level of detail that will be required or to modify the approved schedule to reflect errors in logic that are absolute. When no CPM schedule was required or when it was required but not submitted or submitted but not formally approved, it may be necessary to develop a revised or prototype schedule using the best and most credible information available to reflect the original plan and intentions. Possible sources for a reconstructed schedule may include the master schedule prepared by the owner or his agent, prebid analyses, and schedules included in the bidding documents. Regardless of the source, the purpose of the as-planned schedule is to illustrate the original work plan for organizing, sequencing, and executing the scope of work in accordance with the specified period of time. In addition, it becomes the baseline against which actual performance and the impact of delays can be measured.

Figure 13–1 is an example of a summary as-planned schedule that accurately summarizes a detailed plan for a fossil fuel power plant project. Emphasis was given to the areas of the project impacted so that the influence of the controlling delays encountered could be demonstrated. Emphasis was also placed on key milestones, major dependencies, and contractual interfaces among the project participants involved in the project. Once the as-planned schedule is established, its reasonableness should be questioned by addressing four basic considerations:[7] (1) Is the work sequence shown in the schedule the only possible sequence in which the work could be accomplished? (2) Is the sequence presented in the schedule

---

[7] Chaney & James Constr. Co., FAACAP No. 67-18, 66-2 BCA ¶ 6066 (1967).

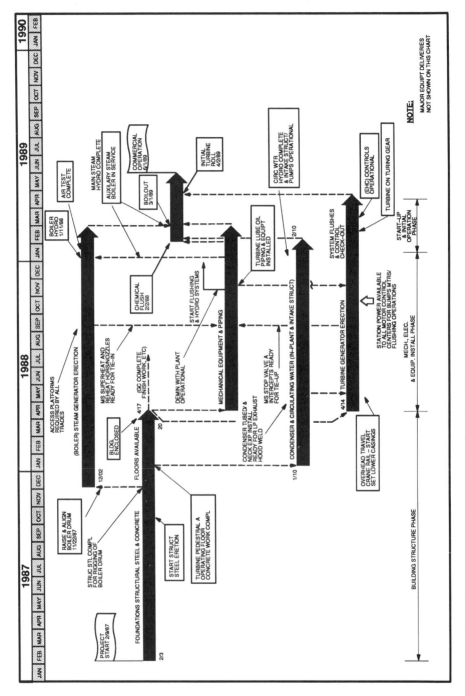

Figure 13-1. Summary as-planned schedule for 300-megawatt power plant.

the best? (3) Is the sequence of work reflected in the estimating and bidding of the work? (4) Is the sequence shown in the schedule the same sequence followed and used in managing the project?

Although network-based schedules do not have to be perfect or exacting in all details, they should reasonably demonstrate the original intentions for planning, monitoring, controlling, and reporting for the overall project.

Detailed analysis of project records.   With the base schedule established, a more detailed analysis of the project records begins, with attention directed toward the issues, problems, and delays that are identified. Starting with the first day of the project, the records are reviewed and analyzed on a day-by-day or month-by-month basis, moving forward from the beginning to the end of the project. The activities in the as-planned schedule and the problem priority listing that was developed earlier can be used as a guide. Key objectives are to establish and confirm the chronological sequence of delays as they were encountered, to determine if a relationship exists between a specific delay and any other delays, and to identify delays affecting the project's critical path.

Identification of data comparing actual and planned performance.   The scheduling expert next should focus on identification of documents and key facts regarding actual versus planned performance. Actual start and finish dates should be extracted from the project records and noted for key activities in the detailed and summary as-planned schedules. Any logic changes or additions that are necessary to reflect any variance or change in the planned versus the actual sequence of work also should be recorded as part of the investigation of delay and actual performance. In addition, other key facts and circumstances necessary to demonstrate the influence of problems and delays should be noted. The objective of this task is to develop an *as-built schedule.* The purpose of the as-built schedule is to demonstrate the actual performance and work sequence versus that which was planned and to highlight the major and controlling delays encountered in constructing the project.

Because of the dynamic nature of the CPM process and the necessity to evaluate delays at the time they occurred on the project, in accord with recent decisions,[8] the as-built analyses should include the ability to evaluate delays.

In performing the as-built schedule task, attention should be directed to any variances between how a particular activity, phase, or operation was planned to have progressed and how it actually progressed and to

---

[8] *See, e.g.,* Santa Fe, Inc., VABCA No. 2168, 87-3 BCA ¶ 20,104 (1987); Fortec Constructors v. United States, 8 Cl. Ct. 490 (1985).

identifying the points at which any delay occurs. This schedule is essentially based on, and supported by, the detailed facts included in the project records.

Figure 13–2 is an example of a summary as-built schedule, which highlights and summarizes a more detailed analysis. On large-scale projects, it may be necessary to involve certain members of the project staff (field inspection, purchasing, contract administrators, and so on) in the gathering of as-built data. This can be very cost effective if administered properly. To aid in such situations, a standard format and procedure for gathering as-built data can be developed, explaining the kinds of information desired for documenting a problem or task being researched (**Figure 13–3**). Information to gather as part of the as-built fact-finding may include:

1. Activity actual start
2. Activity actual finish
3. Delays encountered and caused by other parties and records of start and finish dates of each such delay
4. Delays encountered and caused by the party responsible for documentation
5. Specific actions or directions given to resolve problems or delays
6. Correction or noncorrection of improper or defective work
7. Nonproductive time
8. Lack of materials or lack of labor
9. Lack of a manufacturer's representative
10. Changes in management or reorganization of phases
11. Inefficient work periods
12. Efficient work periods
13. Testing (finish) or rework
14. Modifications (work performed and resources required)
15. Crew size (classification and number of workers)
16. Equipment required, actually used, or idled
17. Weather conditions and acts of God
18. Strikes or other job actions
19. Unforeseeable site conditions
20. Suspensions of work
21. Periods of waiting for instructions for continuation of work efforts to mitigate delays encountered
22. Activities upon which a delayed activity is dependent
23. Activities that are dependent on a delayed activity's completion
24. Changes in logic sequencing.

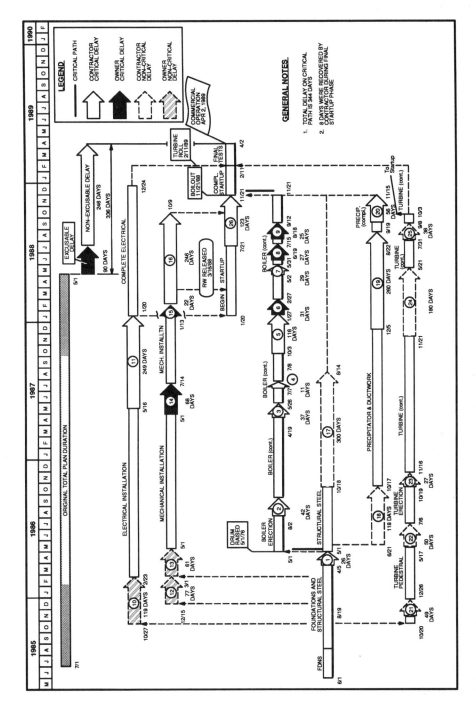

Figure 13-2. Summary as-built schedule for 650-megawatt power plant.

381

Columns header: DESCRIPTION | 1989 [AUG | SEP | OCT | NOV | DEC] | 1990 [JAN | FEB | MAR]

CONDENSER TEST & FLUSH

7 START CLEANING CONDENSER (C-1)

18 FOUND LOCUSTS IN CONDENSER TUBE (C-2) — 15 FOUND BENT TUBES (C-2)

31 CONDENSER BEING CHECKED FOR WTR. TEST (C-3)

5 CONDENSER CLEAN-UP WORK COMPLETED (C-4) — 7 CONDENSER FLUSH STARTED (C-5)
8 CONDENSER FLUSH COMPL. START FILLING (C-6)
9 ABC CONTRACTING FILLED CONDENSER WITH WTR. & — 11 ALL THEY FOUND WERE LEAKS (C-7)
18 XYZ CONSULTANTS STILL HOLDING ON DECISION (C-8) — 14 IF FILLED NEED DIRECTION (C-8)
EXHAUST PIPE WILL WEIGH 79 TONS — STARTED & STOPPED FILL AGAIN. B.F.P.

2 XYZ CONSULTANTS APPROVES SKETCH DESIGN — 2 FOR PIPE STAND (C-10)

12 6" VACUUM PIPE LEAKING (C-12)

19 BUTTERFLY VALVES IN B.F.P. TURBINE EXHAUSTERS (C-14) — 18 BUTTERFLY VALVES LEAKING (C-13)
PUT IN SOME TYPE OF SILICONE TO HELP CLOSE — 20 'CANT FILL CONDENSER FAST ENOUGH'
(C-15)
26 BUTTERFLY VALVE LEAKING. SILICONE SEALANT ADDED. (C-17) — 23 (1.) REPORT ON CONDENSER PROBLEM
TO B. JONES FROM C. SMITH (C-16)

1 WATER BOXES LEAKING LIKE A SIEVE (C-18) — 3 REDOING WATER BOX BOLTING UNDER
MFG. DIRECTION (C-19)
13 COMPL. TORQUING OF WATER BOXES UNDER M.F.G. — 8 CONT. FILLING CONDENSER. LEAKING
DIRECTION (C-20) — RETORQUING PROCEDURE
16 WATER BOX TEST IS AGAIN A FAILURE (C-21) — 17 FROM SAME PLACES AS BEFORE.
22 MANUFACTURER MAN ON SITE DIRECTING INSTL. OF ZERK — 24 REPAIRS TO THE CONDENSER ARE COMPL.
FITTINGS AND PERMATEX. LEAKS IN TUBE SHT. & CONDENSER — FILLING WITH WATER FOR TEST (C-24)
WALL (C-23)
29 LEAKS CONTINUE (C-25)
1 LAST MENTION OF CONDENSER WORK IN LOGS UNTIL — 4 MTG HELD AND M.F.G. DECIDES TO TEST
3/1/90 (C-26) — ONLY AT NORMAL OPER. COND. (C-27)
7 ABC CONTRACTOR FILLS CONDENSER AGAIN (C-28) — 11 CONDENSER LEAKS TESTS STOPPED
BECAUSE OF AFFECT ON FINAL
ALIGNMENT OF TURBINE (C-29)

28 NO MANUFACTURER REPRESENTATIVE ON — SITE - WILL AIR TEST (C-31)

FOUND 3 LEAKS WITNESSED — 4 BY OWNER (C-32)
PUMPING IN SEALING COMPOUND (C-33) — MANUFACTURER BOUGHT — 10 CONDENSER (C-34)

Figure 13-3. Format for gathering data for as-built schedule (condenser test and flush activity).

382

The end product should be a historical record of what actually happened during the life of the project and during the activities being investigated. Each person responsible for gathering as-built information should also prepare a detailed and complete written narrative description of the facts and their findings. If the initial CPM schedule is carefully developed and properly maintained throughout the project, it can, in effect, become the as-built schedule, because it should reflect precisely how the job was executed. Achieving this objective requires more than just recording start and finish dates to reflect actual happenings. It also requires that the logic be changed to reflect the as-built sequence and the problems and delays that are encountered.[9]

Researching claim issues. During the detailed review described above, each claim issue, problem, or delay also should be thoroughly researched. If necessary, further discussions should be held with the key staff. The ultimate objective is to identify and demonstrate the impact of each delay situation at the time it occurred as accurately as possible. This includes both excusable and nonexcusable delay. In addition, information should be obtained concerning time extensions granted and pending, the job conditions that existed at the time of delay, the causes of delay, who is responsible for the delay, when the delay started and ended, and what progress had been made on various activities impacted. Further, determine if any other events were delaying the project concurrently and identify the party responsible for such delay. Finally, determine if steps were taken or should have been taken to mitigate the effects of any delay and the extent to which such efforts were useful.

For each problem or delay, a *time impact analysis* should be prepared and a conclusion on time impact reached. This written narrative should describe the circumstances and events of delay; present the facts, analysis, and findings; and justify the conclusions reached. Conclusions should include a determination of responsibility for delay, the quantification of the net time impact associated with each delay, and identification of its relationship to any other delays that occurred previously or are occurring concurrently. Appropriate references to factual documents should be made and attached as necessary.

Fragnets or network changes that are needed to illustrate each time impact should be prepared. In addition, the method to be used to incorporate the delay into the overall schedule and delay analysis on a chronological basis should be identified. The objective is to reflect what a properly

---

[9] As detailed previously, one of the more significant problems encountered today occurs when jobsite personnel fail to record actual start and finish dates and, rather than modifying logic to reflect some new plan, override network logic to eliminate delays (which the computer program identifies) to the critical path of the network.

adjusted schedule should be, based on the recognition of excusable and controlling delays. This results in what is called an *as-adjusted schedule.*

It is possible that the as-adjusted schedule could be the same as the as-built schedule. It is also possible that a post facto time extension analysis will show that a properly adjusted completion date is earlier than, or later than, the actual completion date. The latter situation may prove whether a decision to direct a contractor to accelerate was proper or improper. It may also be the basis for proving or disproving constructive acceleration. **Figure 13–4** offers an example of a summary comparison of various schedule analyses.

Evaluation of labor efficiency. The schedule expert should investigate and determine specific periods of labor inefficiency that may have been experienced because of overtime, overmanning, change in planned sequence, or demobilization and remobilization. She should consider the value of a comparative analysis of these periods with those in which productivity was considered to be normal. The expert is reminded that inefficiency or loss of productivity is difficult to prove.

As detailed in **Chapter 10**, several methods have been used to demonstrate the effect of inefficiency or loss of labor productivity, including:

1. Comparison of historical normal activity data with inefficient activity data, all within the same project
2. Comparison of historical activity data from other projects with inefficient activity data from the troubled project
3. Comparison of estimated labor with actual labor expended
4. *S* curve schedule versus actual (theory that the difference between two curves on the horizontal correlates with actual delay and cost for period)
5. Revenue per manhour (comparison of expected revenue for each expected manhour with the actual revenue from the actual manhours expended)
6. Use of the measured mile[10] (comparison of the unit productivity costs in an unimpeded time period or physical area to that achieved in the claimed disrupted time period or areas.

Quantification of extended equipment costs. The expert should identify periods of time when owned or rented equipment was planned to be on the jobsite, was actually used, or remained idle because of delays. Coordinate this information with those responsible for calculating damage cost. The objective of this task is to quantify the extended cost of equipment for

---

[10] *See, e.g.,* Zink, *The Measured Mile,* 28-4 Cost Engineering J. (1986).

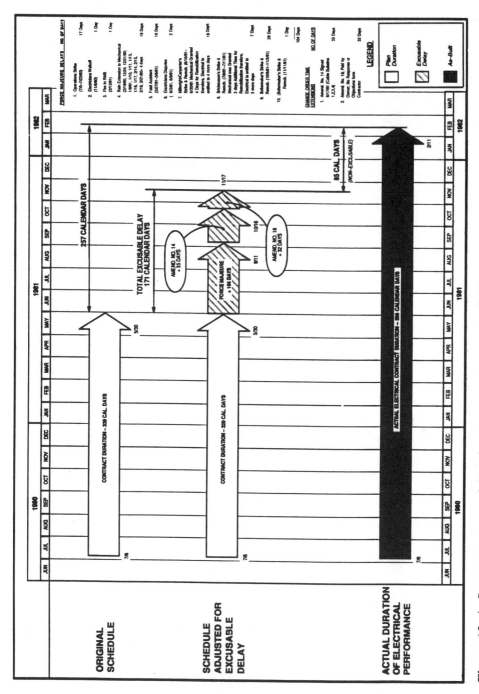

Figure 13–4. Summary comparison of various schedule analyses.

ITEM NO	AREA OF DELAY	TOTAL DELAY BY ITEM	AMOUNT OF CONCURRENT DELAY WITH OTHER ITEMS	NET AMOUNT OF DELAY CLAIMED ON OVERALL PROJECT	COMMENTS
1	SCHEDULE OMISSIONS	75	0	75	
2	LATE BOILER DRUM	54	49	5	
3	SUSPENSION WINTER 1974–75	126	0	126	
4	OSHA SUSPENSION	23	0	23	NO TIME IMPACT INCLUDED FOR REMOBILIZATION
5	FRONT STANDARD INTERFERENCE	100	23	77	PARTIALLY CONCURRENT WITH DELAY NO. 4
6	H.P. SHELL T-OFF / T-ON WIRE	20	0	20	
7	L.P. FINAL ASSEMBLY	71	61	10	CONCURRENT DELAY WITH ITEM NO. 8
8	LACK OF HEAT WINTER 1975–76	122	0	122	WORK CONTINUED DURING THIS PERIOD
9	MAIN & REHEAT PIPING TO H.P.	103	0	103	
10	HIGH PRESSURE FINAL	23	0	23	
11	INSTALL BFPT, BFP & BOOSTER	73	68	5	CONCURRENT WITH DELAY NO. 6, 7, 8 & 9
12	CONDENSER TEST / LEAK	137	0	137	CONDENSER ACCEPTED ON 3/10/77 PENDING VACUUM TEST
13	BFPT FLUSH	69	69	0	
14	LUBE OIL FLUSH	22	0	22	DELAY DEPENDS ON BOILER NOT BEING CONTROLLING FACTOR
15	EHC FLUSH	119	119	51	CONCURRENT WITH DELAY 12, 13 & 14
	GRAND TOTALS		425	763	

Figure 13–5. Summary analysis of time delays (in days).

the period of utilization beyond the planned duration for each equipment item and the project as a whole.

Summary analysis of time delays.   Upon completion of the as-built and/or as-adjusted schedule(s), it is suggested that a *summary analysis of time delays* be prepared. This exhibit lists all major time delays and shows the total time delay caused by each problem, the amount of delay that is concurrent with other problems, and the net amount of delay to be claimed for each problem on the overall project. This exhibit, when properly prepared, will also serve as a check to ensure all time loss on a project is taken into account. **Figure 13–5** is an example of a summary analysis of time delays.

Computation of final delay damages.   Upon completion of the overall project delay analysis, the computation of final delay damages can be prepared based on the net amount of excusable delay considered to be compensable. The calculation of any delay damages should be done with care and supported by factual evidence included in the project records.

§ 13.5   Presentation Phase

The presentation phase activities will vary from project to project and will ultimately depend on the expert's findings, conclusions, order of presentation, and procedures to be followed. Careful evaluation of the audience to whom the previously developed information must be effectively communicated is required to establish the most suitable presentation techniques. Here again close coordination with legal counsel is necessary to ensure that the presentation is supportive. The expert should keep in mind that the effective presentation of a claim is an exercise in salesmanship, communications, and tactics. Key tasks during this phase include the following:

Preparation of an overall time and cost impact report.   The schedule expert should prepare a report on time and cost impacts that presents an understanding of the project and the claim issues; the approach and methodology used, including review of all relevant job records; an analysis of the schedule; the major delays and problems encountered during the project; the assignment of delay responsibility; the calculation of delay damages; and the findings, opinions, and conclusions reached.

Preparation of summary as-planned, as-built, and as-adjusted schedules.   The expert should prepare summary time-scaled networks of the as-planned, as-built, and as-adjusted schedules. These are considered necessary for accurately summarizing the detailed schedule and the actual performance and for presenting the analysis of delays and the findings. The objective of these exhibits is to enable a clear presentation of the facts during any negotiations, arbitration, or litigation processes. Emphasis in such time-scaled summaries is generally placed on identifying major activities or phases of work, key project milestones, and major interfaces and on highlighting the effect of major delays encountered during project execution. The use of summary time-scaled networks in claims presentations is encouraged; experience has shown that detailed networks or schedule presentations, while important, do not usually achieve the proper attention level of those who will be making the decisions.

Evaluation of special graphics.   The expert should review and determine the need for, and value of, including special graphics such as the following:

1. A series of charts presenting the details of major and controlling delays on an individual basis. These charts would be coordinated with the detailed and summary schedule presentations. **Figures 13–6** and **13–7** offer network examples and **Figure 13–8** offers a bar chart example.

2. A chart plotting and analyzing change orders (**Figure 13–9**). A similar presentation of requests for information (RFI's) and responses can also be helpful.

3. A manpower chart showing a comparison of planned versus actual resources expended, including overtime and multiple shift hours (**Figure 13–10**). The expert also should attempt to show causation between planned and actual manhours (**Figure 13–11**).

4. A chart showing a comparison of the promised and actual delivery dates for equipment and materials.

5. A chart comparing concurrent delay existing on a series of paths and noting excusable and nonexcusable delay and compensable and noncompensable delay periods (**Figure 13–12**).

6. A chart showing correlation between problems encountered and operating results (**Figure 13–13**).

7. A chart showing the effect of work performed out of sequence and its delay, impact, and disruption (**Figures 13–14** and **13–15**).

8. A model which can prove to be a highly persuasive means for demonstrating the facts of a case.

Finally, the expert is reminded in **Figure 13–16** that bar charts can fail to demonstrate causation and delay and often ineffectively support a claim position. If bar charts are used in a claim presentation, care must be taken to correct or compensate for these insufficiencies.

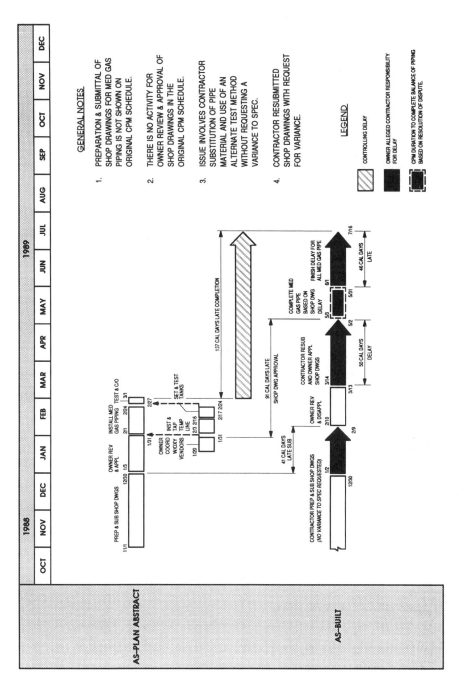

Figure 13-6. Network time impact analysis for delay in completion of medical gas piping.

389

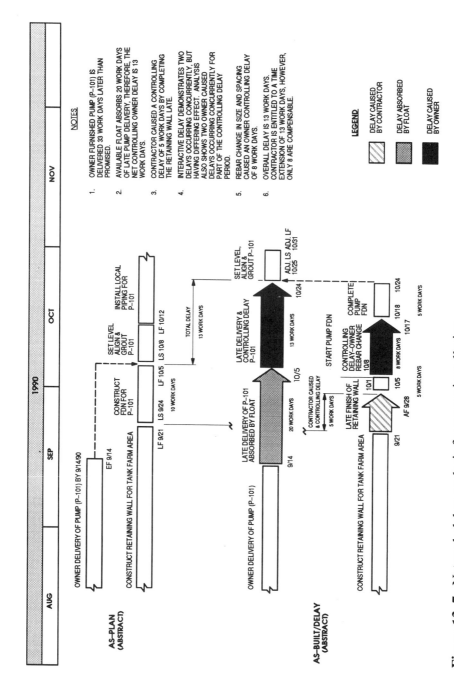

Figure 13–7. Network delay analysis for pump installation.

390

ACTIVITY DESCRIPTION

	1975			1976					
	NOV	DEC	JAN	FEB	MAR	APR	MAY	JUN	JUL

NO BUILDING HEAT – DURING WINTER 1975–1976

INSTALL & ALIGN L P DIAPHRAMS

INSTALL LP ROTOR–WHEEL & DIAPHRAMS CLEAR

LP ROTOR NOT INSTALLED DUE TO BAD BEARING

REMOVE LP ROTOR & DIAPHRAMS & CLEAN

REASSEMBLE LP COMPLETE

105 DAY DELAY

LEGEND

☐ Planned Schedule

▨ Work in Progress

|||| Rust Condition—Causing Inefficiency

Delay being encountered, however, Work is progressing

█ Delay being encountered–Delay has an impact on Work item and/or Overall Project Completion Date

---- Logical Restraint

COMMENTS

DATE	DESCRIPTION	DOCUMENT NO.
11/28/75	Water in L.P.	LP-1
12/2/75	Rigged L.P. outer cover for removing	LP-2
12/5/75	Chips and slag and shot in L.P.	LP-3
12/15/75	Drilling 24 each 2" holes	LP-4
1/6/76	Completed drilling 24 holes	LP-5
1/14/76	Cleaning bearings	LP-6
1/22/76	Reset L.P. wire, changed one diaphragm, sold wire	LP-7
1/23/76	Removed all the L.P. diaphragms for final cleaning before L.P. assembly	LP-8
1/29/76	Turbine manufacturer was satisfied that the unit was clean	LP-9
1/30/76	Started final L.P. reassembly	LP-10
2/5/76	Turbine manufacturer wants the no. 4 bearing back in the factory for repairs and would not let contractor block up the L.P. spindle and continue reassembly	LP-11
3/1/76	Cleaned up L.P. no. 4 bearing which was returned on 2/27/76	LP-12
3/16/76	Awaiting Turbine manufacturer clearance on wheel checks	LP-13
3/30/76	L.P. inspected for final assembly by contractor, consultant, owner and turbine manufacturer, approval granted. Started L.P. assembly	LP-14

Figure 13–8. Bar chart time analysis for delay in low-pressure (L.P.) section final assembly.

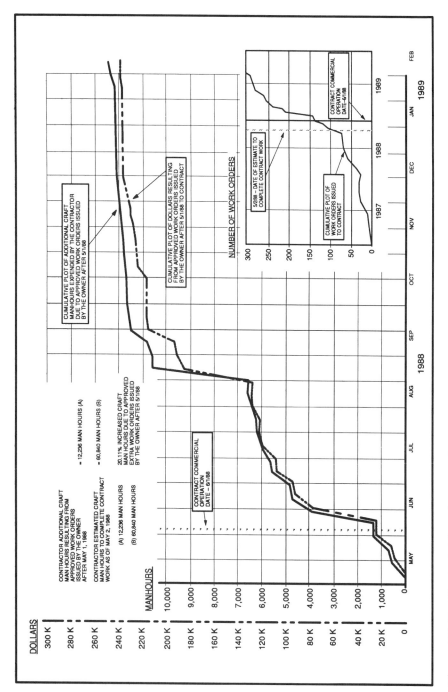

Figure 13–9. Chart plotting change orders.

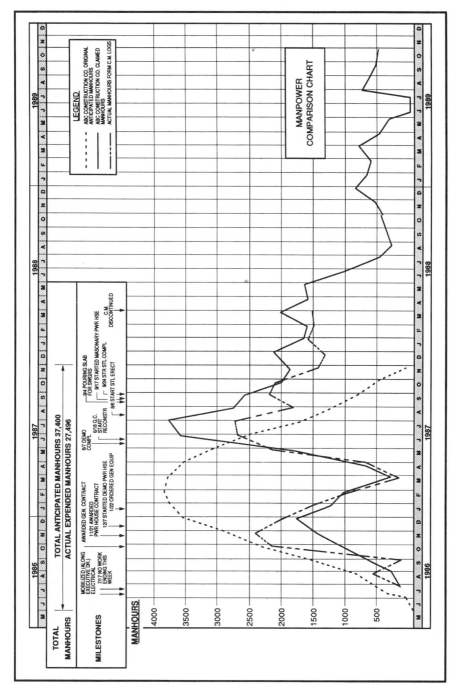

Figure 13–10. Manpower chart comparing planned and actual resources.

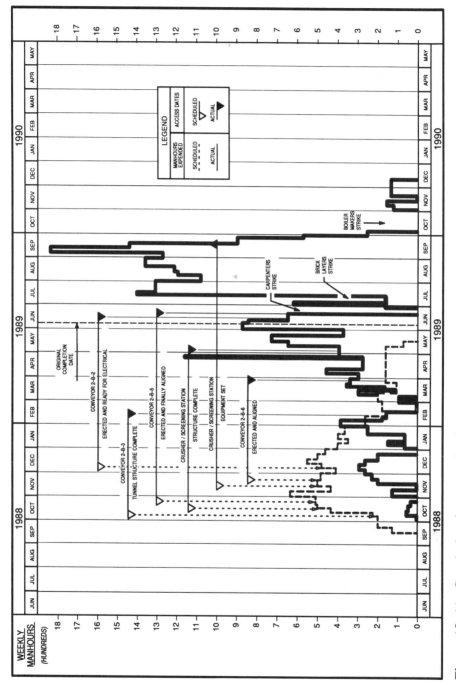

Figure 13–11. Graph showing causation between planned and actual manhours.

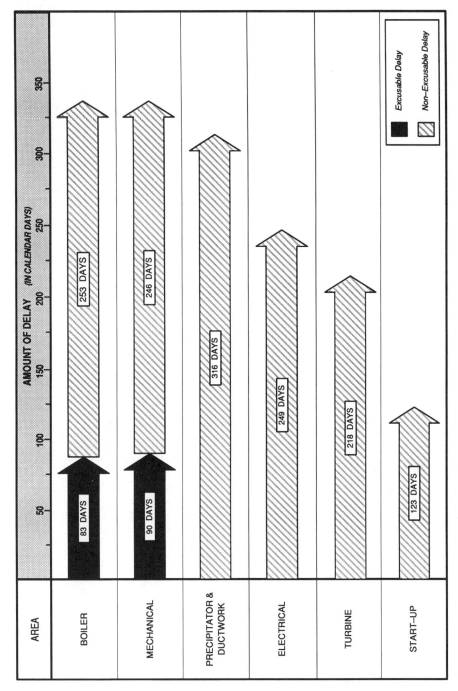

Figure 13–12. Summary analysis of concurrent delay on power plant project.

395

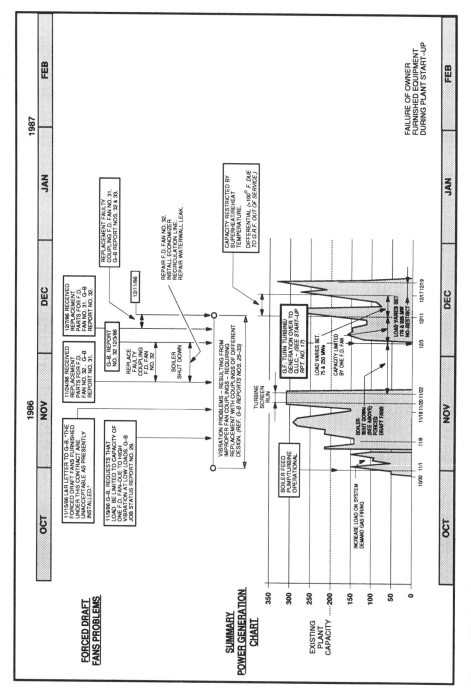

Figure 13–13. Correlation of problems encountered and operating results.

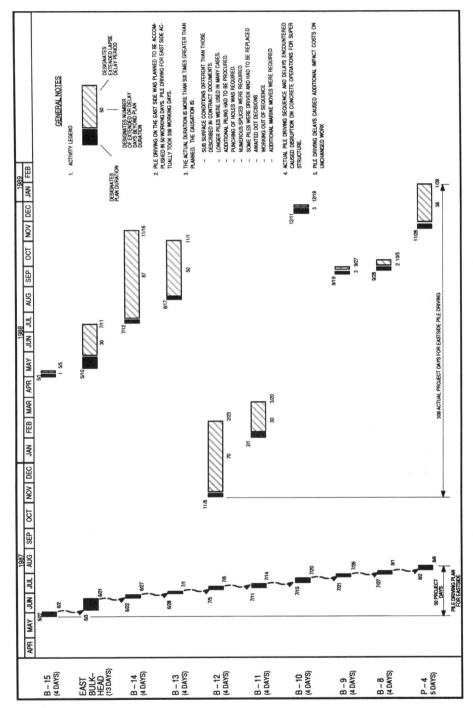

Figure 13-14. Chart showing effect of pile-driving work performed out of sequence.

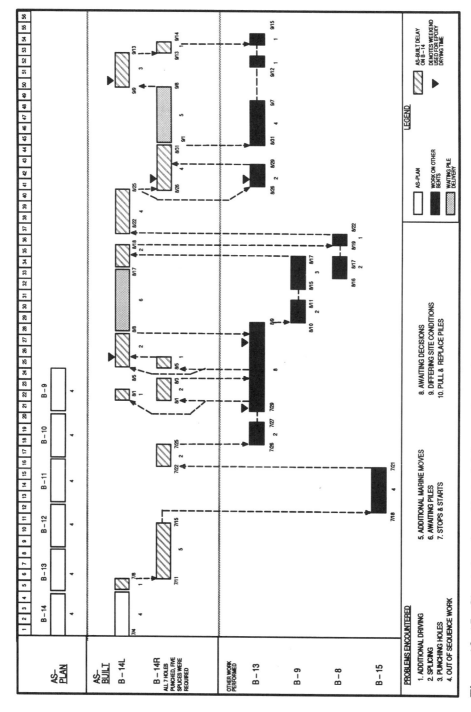

Figure 13–15. Chart showing effect of delays and out-of-sequence pile-driving work.

398

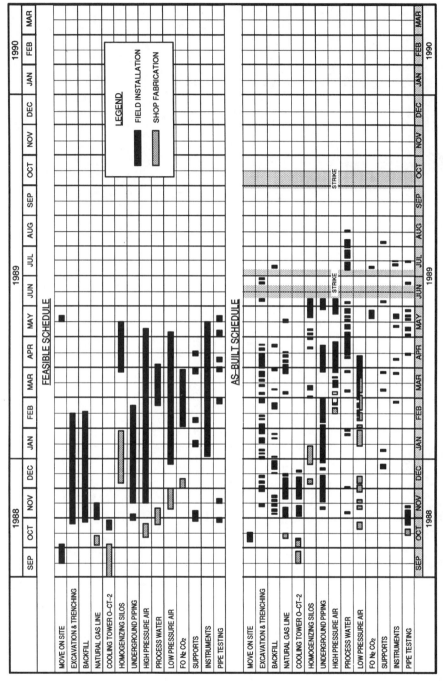

Figure 13–16. Bar chart comparison of as-planned and as-built schedules that fails to demonstrate causation and delay.

399

CHAPTER 14

CASE HISTORIES

§ 14.1 Purpose

§ 14.2 Cedars-Sinai Litigation

§ 14.3 Durham Wastewater Treatment Plant Litigation

§ 14.4 Humana Litigation

§ 14.5 Edwards Air Force Base Test Support Facility

§ 14.6 Integrity and Credibility in Dispute Resolution

§ 14.1 Purpose

The purpose of presenting the case histories in this chapter is twofold. The first purpose is to provide summaries of four construction projects in which critical path method (CPM) principles were central to resolution of the disputes. The four projects are Cedars-Sinai Hospital in Los Angeles; the Humana Audobon Hospital in Louisville, Kentucky; the Durham Advanced Wastewater Treatment Plant in Portland, Oregon; and the Edwards Air Force Base Test Support Facility, in Edwards, California. Three of these projects involved disputes in which litigation was well advanced prior to settlement. This chapter will review in detail the role played by key witnesses in the application of CPM principles and the claimant's right to recovery in these cases.

The chapter's second purpose is to provide real-world examples of issues central to the ability of parties to the construction process to resolve their disputes. These issues are integrity and credibility and their relationship to project management and dispute resolution. We will examine these concepts with a special emphasis on the effects of failure to adhere properly to principles of acceptable behavior.

§ 14.2 Cedars-Sinai Litigation

The Cedars-Sinai litigation in Los Angeles in the late 1970s involved a dispute, with very large dollar amounts claimed, between the owner, architect/engineer, and contractor. For purposes of this discussion, the strategy pursued by the owner with its CPM expert and construction manager in asserting delay claims against the contractor was the most significant aspect. This strategy was based upon abuses of CPM principles.

This review addresses the manner in which the owner's CPM analysis was prepared; the means by which the CPM presentation's bankrupt foundations were discovered; and the examination of the witnesses who exposed those bankrupt foundations.

During the late 1960s and early 1970s, Cedars-Sinai wished to construct a major health care facility in Los Angeles. At that time there was a concern about the number of hospital beds in California. Legislation was being considered for a statewide planning body to require certificates of need as a prerequisite to licensing of hospital beds.

Cedars apparently obtained relief from the licensing requirement in the legislation adopted by the state. Basically, the relief provided that Cedars would not have to obtain a certificate of need for the new $70 million facility to be constructed as long as construction was started and completed by certain times. Typical of the correspondence on this issue was a May 11, 1972, letter from the hospital director to the architect/engineer for the project, which stated:

> Any extension of the construction period beyond that indicated in your "Schedule of Work" of November 23, 1971 is unacceptable, both by reason of state legislation that requires 100% completion of our project by January 1, 1975, and by reason of the impact of higher costs due to escalation during a longer period of construction.[1]

Cedars retained the services of an architectural joint venture to design a state-of-the-art facility with *interstitial floors* to allow for modification of the hospital in the future and for the installation of many sophisticated systems (such as a fully automated material handling system). Interstitial designs are major undertakings requiring extreme care in the coordination of the design of the various installations, plus truss members, to be included in the interstitial spaces.[2] The Cedars interstitial spaces involved additional complications because they included 42 electrical rooms and crossovers for the mechanized materials handling system.

The facility designed by the architect/engineer provided for a U-shaped configuration, with the base of the U spanning a street. The total design was for more than 1.5 million square feet, with 1,120 beds. Included in the design were two bases, a professional tower (at the base of

---

[1] The date for completion required by the state statute was later extended by one year.

[2] *See, e.g.,* J.W. Bateson Co., VACAB No. 1148, 79-1 BCA ¶ 13,573 (1978).

the U spanning the street), and patient wings (sitting on top of the bases—the legs of the U).

With the need to meet the requirements of the grandfather clause in the statewide health enabling legislation, the architect/engineer came under intense pressure to complete the design. Budget problems were encountered that caused the architect/engineer to forgo significant coordination checking of the design. Questions were also raised about paying the architect/engineer for accelerated design expense. (These questions were raised after the architect/engineer advised the owner of the significant risks of going forward with unchecked and uncoordinated plans).

The construction contract was awarded in late 1972 for approximately $70 million. The contract included the standard AIA conditions at the time, which called for the architect/engineer to act in a quasijudicial capacity in reviewing the contractor's changes, time requests, and claims in the first instance. The specified performance period was 1,120 days from the notice to proceed in November 1972, which provided for completion at the end of 1975.

Upon commencing construction, the contractor and its subcontractors almost immediately experienced major delays, disruptions, and increased costs associated with:

1. Extensive defects and discrepancies in plans and specifications. (These errors were associated with the lack of design coordination. Additional major revisions in the plans were required after award of the construction contract to satisfy the required city plan check, which had not been completed prior to bidding.)
2. Site availability, foundation (piling) changes, and weather constraints.
3. Changes in project scope.
4. Delayed approvals.

In addition, the owner hired a construction manager to act in contravention of the quasijudicial role required of the architect/engineer by the construction contract's AIA 201 general conditions concerning changes, time extensions, and so forth.

The delays and changes continued throughout performance, with the contractor and its subcontractors incurring massive overruns and with certain of the subcontractors in financial jeopardy.

The potential existed that the required completion date for licensing the 1,120-bed facility would not be met. Whether for this reason or others, Cedars and its construction manager refused to grant any significant time extensions during performance. This was in spite of the contractor encountering conditions specified in the contract as requiring

time extensions. Significant acceleration expense was the inevitable result of this conduct by the owner.

The contractor advised the owner throughout performance of the problems and the need for time extensions. The parties were unable to resolve
the extensive claims for increased costs at the completion of the work.

On the same day that the contractor sued for approximately $30 mil-
lion in increased costs, the owner also sued, for approximately $30 mil-
lion in delay damages. The owner added the architect/engineer as a party
to the suit.

With litigation underway, the contractor was faced with establishing
factual bases for its request for increased costs. The contractor and its subcontractors prepared a multivolume presentation of the specific facts
about the owner's actions and their impact (including plans detailing the
physical modifications required throughout the project due to errors and
utilizing color-coded charts displaying changes in routing, sizing, eleva-
tion, and so on).

A second goal for the contractor was to determine the bases for the
owner's claim for delay damages, given the fact that the contractor finished very close to the contract completion dates after extensive acceleration efforts by the work forces on the project.

This review will focus on the contractor's second·goal. The initial step
undertaken was to ask through interrogatories the bases upon which delay
claims were being asserted and the manner by which the dollar amounts
were computed. The interrogatories revealed that the owner was asserting
a novel and specious theory of recovery. Specifically, the owner indicated
that it was entitled to delay damages for the contractor's failure to complete early under the owner's reading of the time of completion clause in
the contract's AIA general conditions. General Condition 8.2.2 stated:

> The Contractor shall begin the Work on the date of commencement as de-
> fined in Subparagraph 8.1.2. He shall carry the Work forward expedi-
> tiously with adequate forces and shall complete within the Contract Time.

Further, the owner's answer to Interrogatory No. 2 revealed the owner's
theory that the contractor should have finished in June of 1975, six
months in advance of the contract completion date.

In its answer to this interrogatory, the owner essentially redefined the
completion date as the *default date* and looked to a CPM firm for justification in espousing the position that such an early completion was reasonable from an assessment of the project halfway through performance,
when many events had occurred that required the contractor to be provided with time extensions into 1976 and beyond. Interrogatory No. 2 and
the response stated:

Interrogatory No. 2. Please state the date which [the owner] contends is the authorized contract completion date.

Answer to Interrogatory No. 2. Pursuant to the contract for the construction of the Cedars-Sinai Medical Center Hospital, defendant [John Doe,] Inc. (hereinafter [Doe]) was required to diligently and expeditiously perform the obligations of the general contractor so that the construction of the Medical Center would be completed in a timely fashion. Under the terms of the said construction contract, the failure by [Doe] to complete the project within 1,120 days from the date of notice to proceed constituted an automatic default by [Doe] under the construction contract. While [Doe] could apply for reasonable extensions of such default deadline, the existence of such default date did not absolve [Doe] of the obligation to proceed expeditiously with the construction of the project and to complete the project in a reasonable time.

As the result of [Doe's] failure to provide plaintiff with a construction schedule conforming to the contract requirements, plaintiff was required to retain the services of Logistics Analysis Associates in order to determine the date on which plaintiff could anticipate the completion of the Medical Center. *After analyzing every facet of the construction project based on the status of the project as of July 1974, Logistics Analysis Associates concluded that the reasonable and expeditious construction of the Medical Center in conformance with the contract would result in completion by no later than May or June of 1975.*[3]

After receiving the owner's response to Interrogatory No. 2, the contractor deposed the director of the hospital early in the litigation concerning the bases for asserting the owner's claim for delay damages due to the contractor's failure to complete early. This deposition confirmed the total reliance the owner was placing on the Log/An firm for the basis of its $30 million suit. Key points established by this testimony included:

1. The owner relied solely upon Log/An for the June 1, 1975 project completion date.
2. Log/An prepared a totally independent analysis of the project and an independent schedule.
3. Log/An analyzed every facet of the contract in preparing its schedule for completion.

---

[3] This excerpt from the interrogatory answer and subsequent references in this chapter to specific documents, interrogatories, and depositions have been taken directly from the actual court records and discovery documents in the litigation. In certain instances in these discussions, names have been changed or deleted in the interest of the privacy of individuals.

4. Log/An's analysis reflected the status of the work at the time that the schedule was prepared in August of 1974, including all prior delays.

5. Log/An's schedule for a June 1, 1975, completion provided that [Doe] should complete the work six months ahead of the original completion date for the project.

With all attention now focused on the CPM expert as the total authority for the Cedars suit, the contractor moved to depose the Log/An representative who had worked on the project for Cedars. The examination of this individual was revealing because it highlighted one of the key points of scheduling projects by network planning principles: The CPM network schedule is only as good as the information upon which it is based.

In this case, the impression left by the answer to Interrogatory No. 2 was that the technically capable and experienced Log/An firm had exercised independent expertise and judgment, looking at all facets of the project halfway through construction, and concluded that the contractor should have finished six months early. Nothing could have been further from the truth.

Although the individual assigned to the project had some knowledge of computers and network planning principles, he had merely acted as a computer programmer on behalf of the construction manager for the project. In his deposition the Log/An representative stated:

1. He had no opinion on the total times for performance of construction.

2. Log/An developed a plan and not a schedule, and the work Log/An did was never to be referred to as a schedule.

3. Log/An did not develop a plan that took into account the status of the work as of June, July, or August of 1974. Log/An rather prepared a plan that was totally hypothetical, going back, at the very least, to the beginning of 1974 and then projecting forward from that time, on a hypothetical basis, activity durations prepared by others.

4. The construction manager's project manager and staff were the primary and basic source for logic, information, and duration estimates. Log/An did not have any significant construction experience and did not provide any of the logic or activity duration estimates.

In addition, the Log/An representative provided his diary in response to a subpoena for his deposition. This diary revealed further facts about the CPM firm's *lack* of independence, rather than its earlier image as an independent engineering firm making reasonable judgments as to the progress of the work during construction. The diary also revealed that the CPM firm had been working with the construction manager's representative and the attorneys for the hospital to plan the hospital's lawsuit as early as mid-1974. Excerpts from these notes stated:

5/16/74 Meeting

Primary requirement to protect owner:

(1) Document what contractor plan supposed to be and if he misses, protect owner against law suit for extension payment

(2) Document impact of owner caused delays to measure real cost to contractor or, better yet what extra cost to get back on schedule

There will be litigation: —How does [the contractor] get compensated for future time

Need coverage on future years expert witness needs

6/3/74 Cedars Sinai Meeting

General

Agreed that owner in box—18 months gone in project with some owner caused changes that are not documented. Best we can hope for is plan that covers rest of work and gives basis for arguing with contractor on delay impact of future owner caused delays.

7/12/74

. . . [CM Project Manager]

1) Staff, A & D [Architectural and Design Committee of Board of Directors of Hospital] encouraged that [Doe] schedule can be shortened

2) Time estimates on new nets

   a) A & D wants to hold off on going to [Doe] until attorneys consider implications for law suit. Meetings of [the Log/An representative] with [hospital counsel] to see if going to affect legal position against [Doe].

The testimony and exhibits provided by the Log/An representatives destroyed the capability of that firm as a witness competent to testify that the contractor should have completed early. After this testimony, Log/An was no longer the "august" expert, but rather the computer programmer preparing for a lawsuit. The depositions had identified the individual providing the plan of performance (including all logic and durations) to Log/An as the project manager for the owner's construction management firm.

Prior to proceeding with the deposition of the construction manager, it was necessary to find out how the owner, Log/An, and the construction manager had taken a terribly complex project severely impacted by changes, plan errors, site restraints, and other owner delays halfway through the project and arrived at the conclusion that it was not only reasonable for the contractor to finish on time, but that it should finish early. This task was accomplished by analyzing documentation obtained through discovery from Log/An and Cedars about the August 1974 computer run setting the early completion date.[4] Key points identified by this analysis were the following:

1. There was no overall network prepared by the construction manager or Log/An for the project.

2. There was no critical path that could be identified for the project because each floor was a separate network.

3. The Log/An computer run had higher floors finishing before lower floors and lower areas of the building.

4. The Log/An schedule did not take the project as it found it in the summer of 1974 (as claimed in the response to Interrogatory No. 2) but rather hypothesized what progress should have been made from January 1974 to the summer of 1974.

5. The Log/An schedule did not have proper restraints between trades on individual floors. This reflected the "meet-at-the-middle school of scheduling." By this school, the electrician starts in one corner, the HVAC trades start in another corner, the studworkers start in the third corner, and the drywall forces start in the fourth corner and all trades meet at the middle.

6. There were absolutely no restraints between floors.

7. The schedule also reflected the concepts of *Total Project Acceleration* (that with unlimited amounts of resources and manpower, any project can be built in a day, even the Great Wall of China). There was no stair-step sequence reflecting line-of-balance principles, with a crew of workers of a particular trade moving up through the building from floor to floor. In addition, there was no recognition of the relationship of the different trades staging their stair-step sequences before or after one another (in accordance with the physical constraints of the different installations).

Figure 14-1 provides an example of the extreme procedures to which the construction manager had resorted to assert the early completion claim. The figure shows a manloading philosophy (performing work on all floors at the same time) totally contrary to the principles of manload leveling (recognized in the industry and the *Utley-James, Inc.*[5] decision). This example is for the electrical trades for just one month (as derived from the August 1974 Log/An computer run). It is further important to remember in viewing this example that the other trades, with no restraints

---

[4] This task was greatly assisted by Philip Lanterman & Assocs., who identified and explained the errors and anomalies present in the Log/An material.

[5] GSBCA No. 5370, 85-1 BCA ¶ 17,816 (1984), *aff'd.*, Utley-James, Inc. v. United States, 14 Cl. Ct. 804 (1988).

	T 1	W 2	T 3	F 4	M 7	T 8	W 9	T 10	F 11	M 14	T 15	W 16	T 17	F 18	M 21	T 22	W 23	T 24	F 25	M 28	T 29	W 30	T 31
Pro tower plaza																							
3rd floor	18	18	8	8	10	8	6	6	6	6	6	6	12	6	6	6	6	18	16	16	18	18	16
4th floor	2	2	18	18	18	18	18	18	18	20	20	22	22	16	12	18	18				8	8	10
5th floor	5	3	2	3	4	3	3	2	2	2	2	2	4	5	3	3	3	4	3	3	2		
6th floor	16	16	14	14	12	16	10	10	10	10	10	4	4	14	12	16	10	10	10	10	2	2	2
7th floor	24	18	16	12	18	18	16	16	16	18	16	16	14	14	12	16	10	10	10	10	10	4	4
8th floor	18	18	18	18	18	20	24	18	18	18	18	18	18	18	18	18	20	22	24	18	16	12	18
Sub-total	83	75	79	73	80	83	77	70	70	74	72	68	70	59	51	61	57	54	53	47	54	44	50
S. Patient tower plaza																							
3rd floor	12	12	12	12	12	12		6	6	6	6	6	6	4	4	6	6	6	6	6	6		
4th floor	6	6	6	6	6	6	6	6	6	6	6	6	6	6	6	6	6	6	6	6	6	6	6
5th floor	6	6	6	6	6	6	6	6	6	6	6	6	6	6	6	6	12	12	12	12	12	12	12
6th floor	6	6	6	6	6	6	6	6	6	6	6	6	6	6	6	6	6	6	6	6	6	18	12
7th floor	6	6	6	6	6	6	6	6	6	6	6	6	6	6	6	6	6	6	6	6	6	6	6
8th floor	6	6	6	6	6	6	6	6	6	6	6	6	6	6	6	6	6	6	6	6	6	6	6
Sub-total	42	42	42	42	42	42	30	36	36	36	36	36	36	36	34	36	36	36	36	36	36	48	42
N. Patient tower plaza																							
3rd floor	12	12	12	12	12	12		6	6	6	6	6	6	6	4	4	6	6	6	6	6		
4th floor	6	6	6	6	6	6	6	6	6	6	6	6	6	6	6	6	6	6	6	6	6	6	6
5th floor	6	6	6	6	6	6	6	6	6	6	6	6	6	6	6	6	12	12	12	12	12	12	12
6th floor	6	6	6	6	6	6	6	6	6	6	6	6	6	6	6	6	6	6	6	6	6	18	12
7th floor	6	6	6	6	6	6	6	6	6	6	6	6	6	6	6	6	6	6	6	6	6	6	6
8th floor	6	6	6	6	6	6	6	6	6	6	6	6	6	6	6	6	6	6	6	6	6	6	6
Sub-total	42	42	42	42	42	42	30	36	36	36	36	36	36	36	34	34	36	36	36	36	36	48	42
Grand total	167	159	163	157	164	167	137	142	142	146	144	140	142	131	119	131	129	126	125	119	126	140	134

Figure 14–1. Electrical manloading, October 1974, Cedars-Sinai hospital project.

between floors or within the sequence on each floor, contained similar manloading for occupying all areas of the building at the same time.

With the proper homework accomplished, the contractor proceeded with the deposition of the construction manager's project manager. This examination confirmed the following:

1. That no limits had been placed on total manpower in the Log/An schedule

2. That the Log/An schedule was not current at the time it was prepared, but seven months out of date

3. That the unconnected, individual Log/An networks had higher floors finishing before lower floors (for example, eighth-floor electrical rough-in to be completed in May 1974 and third-floor electrical rough-in not to be completed until August 1974

4. That the schedule showed the elevator hoist being rigged eight separate times, with higher floors being rigged before lower floors (rather than once when the entire hoistway was available from top to bottom)

5. That the network for each floor failed to include restraints between activities of different trades, which were a condition precedent to follow-on work on individual floors

6. That there was no critical path for the entire project or even an overall network

7. That the Log/An schedule reflected 24 separate unconnected projects for each individual floor

8. That there were no restraints between floors in the Log/An schedule

9. That manloading in the Log/An schedule was excessive (such as 490,000 manhours for electrical work)

10. That the durations for activities were unrealistic (such as 10 days for electrical rough-in of one entire floor of the professional tower)

11. That the contractor was never advised that it should finish the contract six months early.[6]

With the results developed from the depositions of the hospital director, the Log/An representative, and the construction manager's project manager, the contractor moved for summary judgment on the claim by the hospital that the contractor should have completed the project early. Summary

---

[6] Further facts, apart from the Log/An schedule, undermined the testimony of the construction manager's project manager. Specifically, the proposal to Cedars for construction management services had listed this individual as a civil engineer with 15 years' experience. While this individual had extensive valuable experience in the construction field, he had not graduated from college and could not recall any engineering courses taken in school.

judgment was granted to the contractor with respect to this issue of claims for delays in advance of the contract completion date.

Thereafter, the parties in this case proceeded with an extremely valuable procedure, which was instrumental in settlement. Specifically, the parties agreed to a two- to three-day minitrial before a special settlement judge, in which all the parties presented their respective positions, with principals of the litigants present. While the minitrial did not immediately result in a settlement, it was clearly instrumental in the confidential settlement reached a few months later.

§ 14.3   Durham Wastewater Treatment Plant Litigation

The Durham Wastewater Treatment Plant litigation in Portland, Oregon, in the early 1980s was an exciting experience in the application of CPM concepts and principles.

The claim presentation and litigation involved an attempt by the contractor to apply the type of principle (hindsight analysis of the critical path) seen in *Blackhawk Plumbing & Heating Co.*[7] to assert that a supervening delay wiped out all prior delays to the critical path. The contractor claimed that the application of the supervening-delay principles entitled it to compensation for the entire extended period of contract performance.[8]

The owner's defense involved the application of two significant principles, namely that delays should be contemporaneously valued based on the conditions in existence during the life of the project (as in the Ockman analysis in *Gulf Contracting, Inc.*),[9] and that the contractor had to take into account when he would have finished absent alleged owner delays to the project (which is represented by the concept of the adjusted CPM *but for* analysis enunciated in *Canon Construction Corp.*).[10]

The project concerned the construction of advanced wastewater treatment facilities at the Durham plant for the Unified Sewerage Agency of Washington County, Oregon. This project was awarded in the mid-1970s for $22 million and was to take two years. Construction overran by a year. The contractor submitted claims to the owner complaining of various project delays. When the owner was unconvinced by the claim presentations, the contractor sued for $6 million. Most of the dollar amount demanded in the suit was for delay damages.

---

[7] GSBCA No. 2432, 75-1 BCA ¶ 11,261, *on reconsideration,* 76-1 BCA ¶ 11,649 (1975).

[8] 76-1 BCA ¶ 11,649, at 55,578 (1975) (argument of the contractor at Durham was tailored to the language in Blackhawk Plumbing & Heating Co.).

[9] ASBCA Nos. 30,195, 32,839, 33,867, 89-2 BCA ¶ 21,812 (1989).

[10] ASBCA No. 16,142, 72-1 BCA ¶ 9404 (1972).

The major facilities constructed on the project were the incinerator, treatment structures, and pump station. In executing the actual work on the project, the contractor submitted and received approval of its CPM schedule. This schedule, which was somewhat aggressive on concrete durations, indicated a typical critical path for such projects. Thus, the critical path would start out in excavation, then move to concrete placement activities, then to structural steel, next to equipment setting for major equipment, and finally into testing and finish activities at the close of the project.

The major delays the contractor asserted as the bases for its $6 million request were associated with the instrumentation installation (Robertshaw instrumentation equipment, for which approvals had been delayed due to design or subcontractor problems) and with 30 Pratt valves and associated operators to be installed in certain process piping (for which approval and installation were allegedly delayed due to an *or equal* manufacturer dispute).[11]

The problems complained of by the contractor did not surface until later in the project, when construction was well advanced and other contractor delays had impacted the critical path. Included in these contractor delays were late performance throughout all areas of the concrete and electrical work; late delivery and installation of major equipment (such as centrifuges, barminutors, and switchgear) from various major manufacturers; and contamination of plant process lines with tar introduced into the system by the contractor.

The most significant of these delays was the complete and total failure of the contractor to execute the critical concrete pouring operations per its plan. The time taken for most concrete operations on most structures on the project totalled one to two years longer than the original schedule. Regardless of any question of the merits of the instrumentation and valve delays, there was no doubt that the concrete activities came before the valve and instrumentation installations and that the concrete work was a condition precedent to these installations. (Without the concrete structures there was no place to install the instrumentation and pipe valves).

---

[11] This dispute related to the implementation of typical procurement statutes and contract provisions that represent to bidders that any time a particular brand name is specified the contractor is free to use other brands of equipment for the installation as long as it is equal in performance and functional characteristics (and as long as the specification does not indicate that the equipment is to be procured on a sole-source basis). The contractor also asserted two other delays of less significance: motor control centers (MCCs) and the power substation. These allegations were of little utility to the contractor, however, because the contractor's in-house expert was forced to acknowledge these items were associated with contractor problems. For example, substation delays were caused by the failure of the electrical subcontractor to provide fuses.

In seeking to overcome the fatal deficiencies to any delay claim caused by its performance, the contractor claimed that the instrumentation delay was a supervening delay that overcame all prior delays. Its in-house CPM expert stated: "We made an overall analysis, and all of this was negated by all these delays, were superseded by the instrumentation delay overall, by the delivery of the panels."

In its claim presentation, the contractor sought to obscure the fact that the concrete work was a condition precedent to other work by developing a summary critical path chart with very gross activity designations. This chart was flawed because it neglected to show the completion of the concrete activities that were a condition precedent to the installation of equipment, piping, valves, and instrumentation, and so on.

On the contractor's claim chart (**Figure 14–2**), the concrete work was shown by just two activities for the treatment structures and incinerator: (1) *excavation & begin concrete* and (2) *balance of concrete.*

To avoid the effects of the contractor's critical concrete delays (upon which all the equipment, piping, and instrumentation work depended) and blame the owner for all delays to the project, the contractor's chart presentation led the viewer to believe that the follow-on piping and equipment installations could have started after the completion of the undefined *excavation & begin concrete* activity.

Once suit had been filed, the owner had to determine how to most economically establish the suspect nature of the contractor's position that the whole project had somehow been delayed by the instrumentation and valve installations late in the project.

The decision was made to impeach the contractor with its own people. The owner would depose the contractor's in-house CPM expert, who had prepared the original CPM schedule and who had later developed the contractor claim presentation with the assistance of outside experts. The outline of points to establish through this adverse witness included the following major lines of attack:

1. Confirm that the contractor identified the instrumentation approval question and Pratt valves approval as the major delays forming the basis for the critical path delay claim

2. Directly impeach the contractor's position on the merits of these two delays, as well as their effect on the project, with the contractor's own records and letters from its project manager

3. Attack the whole premise or theory of supervening delays as a basis to avoid the earlier contractor delays that had impacted the critical path. First, establish the validity of the original CPM and the sequence of work and restraints shown in the contractor's plan for performance. This examination was to establish that certain concrete

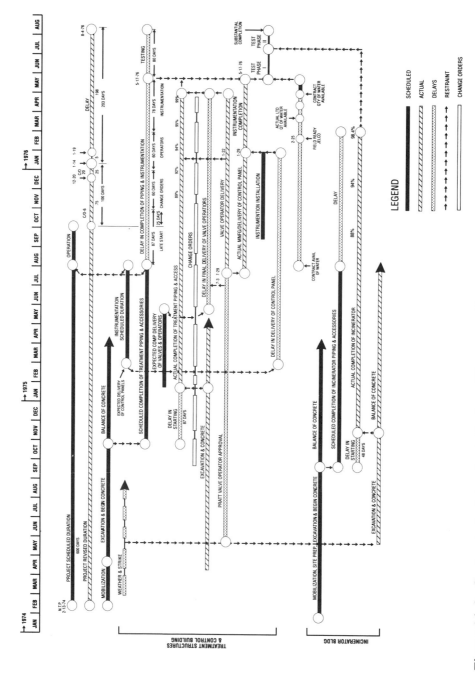

Figure 14–2. Contractor's claim chart, Durham Wastewater Treatment Plant project.

414

activities were a physical constraint on the installation of the piping, equipment, wiring, and instrumentation. Second, establish contractor responsibility for various delays throughout the life of the project and march through the project chronologically using the schedule updates (per the approach in *Fortec Constructors v. United States,*[12] *Sante Fe, Inc.,*[13] and *Gulf Contracting, Inc.*[14]) to show that the earlier delays had impacted and delayed the critical path first and that these earlier delayed activities were a condition precedent to the later activities alleged to be supervening. Also seek confirmation of contractor delays that were concurrent with the instrumentation delays and Pratt valve delays in the second half of the project.

4. Next, the intent was to present the in-house CPM expert with the *but for* issue about what the project would have looked like without the two alleged owner delays, but taking into account the actions that were the contractor's clear responsibility, per *Canon Construction Corp.*[15]

5. Next, the intent was to examine the contractor on misrepresentations made during claim presentations that the owner had been given the benefit of all contractor delays in calculating the request for all time and dollar overruns on the project. The further intent was to question the integrity of the claims that had been created.

6. Next, the owner intended to attack the contractor on the bases of its own theory of the supervening delays. The idea was to ask the expert whether contractor delays that had shown up during the latter stages of the project and continued on for a longer period than the alleged instrumentation and Pratt valve delays would not constitute a supervening delay, wiping out any right of the contractor to recovery.

7. Finally, the intent was to see whether the in-house CPM expert, after being confronted with all the contractor problems, still felt that the contractor claim presentation and suit were fair to the owner.

The testimony by the contractor's in-house expert in response to the major lines of attack identified by the owner developed the following points:

With respect to the issue of major delays forming the basis for the contractor's critical path delay claim, the expert confirmed that the valve and instrumentation delays were the two major delays assessed as the owner's responsibility.

---

[12] 8 Cl. Ct. 490 (1985).

[13] VABCA No. 2168, 87-3 BCA ¶ 20,104 (1987).

[14] ASBCA Nos. 30,195, 32,839, 33,867, 89-2 BCA ¶ 21,812 (1989).

[15] ASBCA No. 16,142, 72-1 BCA ¶ 9404 (1972).

With respect to the direct impeachment of the contractor's position on the two major delays alleged by the contractor, mainly the Pratt valves and Pratt valve operators, as well as the instrumentation panels, the contractor's in-house expert was forced to make significant admissions. First, he admitted that the lack of the Pratt valves and valve operators did not actually stop the pipe installation or overall progress on the project. In the absence of the 30 Pratt valves, the contractor left blanks in the pipe where the valves were to be installed and came back at a later date to install the valves and associated wiring. Apart from the cost of the comeback operation, the delay of the Pratt valves was more of an aggravation than actual damage to the project (per the admission of the contractor's own project manager).

With respect to the issue of the instrumentation the contractor had identified as the major delay during the last third of the project, the contractor's in-house expert acknowledged the judgment of the contractor's project manager that the delays in the instrumentation installation resulted from the failure of the electrical contractor to man the project.

The third area of inquiry was to attack the entire theory of supervening delays as a basis to avoid the contractor delays to the critical path encountered earlier in the project. The first item established was the validity of the original CPM schedule and sequence of work. On this point, the contractor's expert readily acknowledged that the contractor, as well as the concrete subcontractor, were satisfied with the logic and activity durations in the original schedule.

In addition, the witness acknowledged that the critical path for the project was located mainly in the incinerator building, because this was the largest structure from an equipment standpoint, where work would start. As to this work, the witness acknowledged that the critical path ran through the excavation, then into the concrete, and then into structural steel, equipment setting, and piping.

The witness also acknowledged that the three key structures on the project were the incinerator building, the treatment structures, and the pump station.

With respect to the contractor's responsibilities for delays to the critical path during the first half of the project, which were a condition precedent to the installation of any pipes, valves, or instrumentation, the contractor's expert was forced to make a number of significant admissions, including acknowledgment that the owner had no responsibility for the late concrete and structural steel installations in the incinerator and treatment structures.[16] Further admissions included the following:

---

[16] The contractor's expert was also forced to admit during the deposition that the concrete work on the various structures throughout the project had been delayed anywhere from 300 to 600 days.

Q. What was the cause of the concrete being late? I'll phrase it to you that way.

A. Just slow. I don't think they had enough means to do it properly.

Q. Would it be a fair statement to say that the concrete forces on the project were inadequate to complete the work in the time that you had shown on the schedule?

A. Well, in my judgment, yes.

Q. To your knowledge, did the valve operators and the instrumentation delay the excavation and back fill of the treatment structures?

A. I don't think so.

Q. Did the valve operators and the instrumentation delay the rebar on the treatment structures?

A. No.

Q. Did the valve operators and the instrumentation delay the forms and concrete on the treatment structures?

A. No.

Q. Did the valve operators and the instrumentation delay any equipment installations on the treatment structures?

A. No.

With respect to the critical issue of why the project was delayed on an overall basis, the witness acknowledged that the poor performance by the concrete work forces on the project had pushed all the follow-on work downstream and, in itself, delayed the project by a year.

Q. Why do you think the project took so long?

A. Various circumstances, delays.

Q. What circumstances and delays?

A. Well, various delays. I have no—haven't made any determination, you know, how much each delay caused it, like the weather, strikes, holds, engineering, change orders. That's a broad description.

Q. Well, if we get down to major aspects of the work like the treatment structures and the incinerator, that's where the guts of this project is, isn't that right?

A. Yes.

Q. And the concrete sub didn't get out there and perform the concrete, did he?

A. He didn't do a satisfactory job. He was—his speed was slow. He was slow.

Q. Well, he delayed the whole project, didn't he?

A. That I can't say.

Q. Well, he didn't get the concrete done on time, did he?

A. Well, he was sure late in doing the concrete.

Q. The concrete was on the critical path, wasn't it?

A. Part of it.

Q. Well, you couldn't complete the building without the concrete being up, could you?

A. Yes.
Q. And the structural steel erection was late on the incinerator, too, wasn't it?
A. I'm not aware of that. If the concrete was—the work on the concrete was late, certainly, structural steel was late.

*   *   *

Q. Almost all the treatment structure was delayed on the concrete work well over a year, wasn't it?
A. Yes, to a degree.
Q. And did [the electrical subcontractor] have things to do in the treatment structures?
A. Yes, they were working the treatment structures. They have to do their electrical, most of their electrical work in the tunnels.
Q. So that meant that . . . [the electrical subcontractor's] work was pushed substantially downstream?
A. Correct.
Q. By 1975 [the concrete subcontractor] had delayed the project for a year by themselves, hadn't they?
A. Something like that. . . .

The next issue to be addressed in this area of inquiry was the failure of the contractor's expert to determine when the contractor would have completed its work absent the owner delays to the project, as detailed by the *Canon Construction Corp.* decision.[17]
The witness's response to this area of inquiry was the following:

Q. There were a number of equipment delivery delays on this project, weren't there?
A. Yes.
Q. And there were a number of equipment delivery delays which in no stretch of the imagination can be described as the responsibility of the owner?
A. Correct, to a degree.
Q. Now, if we take away . . . the delays which you are asserting with respect to the instrumentation and the Pratt valves, we would still be left with those other equipment delivery delays, wouldn't we?
A. I have made no determination on that.
Q. Do you have any reason to believe that absent the delay or problem with the instrumentation and the problem with the Pratt valves that the problems of the tar in the lines would also not have occurred?
A. I can't say.
Q. When do you think the contractor would have completed this project if it had not been for the instrumentation and the Pratt valves?

---

[17] ASBCA No. 16,142, 72-1 BCA ¶ 9404 (1972).

A. Well, my estimate at that time was that the time extension granted, although it was not sufficient, we would have fallen pretty close to completion.

Q. You mean after the treatment structures are over a year late on the concrete that you still would have completed the whole project just about on time?

A. Well, I'm not saying on time. I'm saying: with a certain delay. But I have made no determination on that point, you know, how much of that delay, how much late it would have been.

Q. Looking at your chart here, from what I can understand of it . . . you are indicating that the owner, with the exception of the strike and weather delay, is responsible for the failure to complete the project on the scheduled time.

A. Uh-huh.

Q. Now, if you plugged in the other delays to show these other concurrent delays, such as [concrete] and [electrical] and . . . [equipment delivery] and the tar delay and the bus duct delay and substation delays, we would have an entirely different-looking chart, wouldn't we?

A. I would think so.

In this portion of the examination, the contractor's expert was to be deposed upon the issue of misrepresentations during claim presentations by the contractor that the owner had been given the benefit of all contractor delays in calculating the request for additional time and money. The contractor's expert disclosed that the manner in which the contractor gave the owner credit for contractor delays was to leave the delays totally off the contractor's critical path impact charts:

Q. In your analysis that you presented to the owner you supposedly gave the owner credit for all concurrent delays by the contractor.

A. Yes.

Q. And that analysis should have included any concurrent delays by [the electrical subcontractor]?

A. (Witness nods.)

*   *   *

Q. Did you reflect anything on these charts about delays by subcontractors?

A. No, not any.

Q. Why didn't you put subcontractor delays on those charts?

A. I wasn't aware—I didn't have any information on them.

Q. You know the concrete wasn't performed on time?

A. Yeah. But I mean, still, you know, it was put in very broad terms, very broad presentation.

Q. Why didn't you include anything for subcontractors' delays?

A. I didn't think there was any time in the frame set up by the company, you know, to put this record together, to put anything like that into it.

Q. Because it was a rush job?

A. Sure, it was a rush job.

* * *

Q. So, you left off the barminutors, the concrete delay on the treatment structures and the Incinerator Building, the bus duct. You left off . . . other things on this chart of yours, didn't you?

A. Yes, because they were all concurrent.

Q. They were all concurrent? Didn't you tell the agency that you were giving the agency credit for all concurrent delays in this analysis?

A. Yes, we did. There was no reason for those delays to be shown here.

Q. Well, why not, because they affected the project, didn't they?

A. They were negated by the longest delay.

Q. You mean when the concrete was delayed in the treatment structure and in the Incinerator Building and you did not have any concrete up to hang the Pratt valves from, there wasn't a delay?

A. Pratt valves don't go on the concrete.

Q. Where do they go?

A. On the piping.

Q. Does the piping attach to anything?

A. The question—I don't know.

Q. Does the piping attach to anything . . . ?

A. Sure. Piping is attached to the hangers.

Q. And the hangers are attached to what?

A. To the concrete.

Q. Thank you.

With respect to the contractor's concept that a delay occurring late in the project could supervene all prior delays to the critical path, the contractor's expert was queried about the circumstances when the contractor had allowed tar to get into the process lines for the entire plant. In this case, the contractor took nine months at the tail end of the project to clean the process lines. The contractor's expert acknowledged that the tar delay was one of the last delays impacting the project before it was turned over to the owner, but indicated that he had not made a determination as to its effect on the project completion.

When questioned about whether the claim presentation he had prepared on behalf of the contractor presented a fair assessment of the owner's responsibility for delays to the project, the expert's response was "I don't know."

Subsequent to the deposition of the contractor's in-house expert, the owner moved for summary judgment based upon the lack of foundation for any delay claim by the contractor. New counsel for the contractor filed pleadings advising that all prior deposition testimony and affidavits should be disregarded. A settlement was reached on terms agreeable to the owner within a short period of time thereafter.

§ 14.4   Humana Litigation

The Humana litigation concerned construction in the late 1970s and early 1980s of the 480-bed Audobon Hospital, the Humana, Inc., flagship facility, in Louisville. This dispute, like the Cedars litigation, had its genesis in difficulties encountered by the contractor and its subcontractors concerning plans for and changes to the project.

In this case the plans for the project had not been coordinated by the designer. Three sets of revisions to the plans were required within the first year of construction. During construction, major changes were ordered; holds were placed on major areas of construction; errors in the plans required constant requests for information and modifications in the design (for example, to drop ceilings and widen chases); and the foundation work performed by a prior contractor was misaligned a full six feet west of the proper location, delaying the entire project and requiring major modifications.

Also like the Cedars litigation, there were additional questions related to the timing of the completion, the certificates of need, and the owner's willingness to grant time extensions. As in the Cedars matter, the owner did not grant or consider contractor entitlement to time extensions for major delays during performance. Appropriate notices of the problems experienced by the contractor were provided during performance.

Due to major cost overruns encountered by the mechanical subcontractor on the project, the general contractor and owner agreed to advance funds to allow the mechanical contractor to continue in operation. It was also agreed that the contractor, at the close of construction, would make a detailed submission of its claims and the claims of its subcontractors; that the owner would have a period of time to review and audit the claim; and that thereafter, by a certain time, the owner would make a settlement offer and enter into negotiations with binding arbitration if the parties were unable to resolve the dispute.

The contractor proceeded to make a detailed submission of its claim, along with CPM scheduling data on project delays. The owner audited the claim costing and documentation.

When the time came for the owner to make its offer and enter into negotiations, the owner filed a legal action seeking the return of its advance to the mechanical subcontractor and seeking to repudiate the dispute resolution agreement between the parties, asserting duress.

Thereafter, litigation proceeded. Having done extensive preparation work (to establish and document durations of activities delayed by changes, defective specifications, and so on), the contractor had a solid framework to proceed with discovery and to seek admissions. The strategy adopted was to notice the deposition of the owner's key project representative,[18] an actual employee of the owner, and to seek confirmation from this representative of the contractor's entitlement to additional time and money, as well as confirmation of the key facts stated in the claim submission.

In the actual examination of the owner's representative, the witness admitted that the owner never acted on the contractor's time requests, but sought to avoid answering questions concerning entitlement by stating that he was not an "architect or engineer" and was not competent to express certain opinions within the context of various clauses. In addition, the witness asserted that the extensive modifications required when the various trades could not install the work in the allowed space were the contractor's coordination responsibility. Even though the plans provided clear design information that was not to be modified without permission, the witness asserted that the plans were diagrammatic.[19]

---

[18] The owner's representative was the key decision-maker at the site, with the architect/engineer in a subordinate role.

[19] This is, of course, directly contrary to legal authority in the field:

> In asserting that the drawings were diagrammatic, the Government contends, in effect, that this was a performance contract, with the Government merely specifying the desired end product and the contractor assuming the responsibility for achieving the desired result by his own methods. This is by no means true. Any drawing which limits a construction contractor's method of installation or requires that an item meet a fixed dimensional point is not, in that respect, a performance agreement, and cannot be made more so by describing it as diagrammatic.

* * *

> As a practical matter, construction drawings, particularly mechanical drawings of the type involved here, are a conglomerate of intertwined design requirements, which must be followed to achieve the design intent, and performance requirements, where routings and spatial adjustments are left for the contractor's adaptation to field conditions. In the case of a pipe or duct, the contractor cannot change the source of the service or the delivery point, but must adjust the intermediate pathways to avoid interference with other elements of the contract work. In this connection, it was pointed out in the testimony that the electrical drawings were more diagrammatic than the plumbing drawings and that the plumbing drawings were more diagrammatic then the ductwork drawings.
>
> In this area, the prime contractor has the responsibility, and the subcontractor the responsibility in its facets of the work, to coordinate installation as to time

Typical testimony included the following exchange:

Q. And would you agree that if the contractor here installed what was contractually specified that the contractor would have violated the contractual ceiling height specified and have ended up with only a five foot high ceiling inside the room?

A. I think the contractor would have violated the contract had he not called it to our attention. He is contractually required to call conflicts to our attention, and we work to straighten them out. The drawings say that they are diagrammatic. If there is a space problem, the contractor is to surface that problem.

Q. Well, he did, didn't he?

A. In that area, yes.

Q. And was the contractor required to make a different installation than that shown on the contract plans?

A. There was modifications, yes. Here again that is not uncommon because often changes are made when shop drawings are prepared. It is rare that the shop drawings follow the documents exactly.

What made the examination of the witness worthwhile was the fact that the claim submission spelled out on the CPM schedule the specific dates and activities affected by the mislocated foundations, three sets of plan revisions, suspensions, 700 changes and other delays (all of which were the owner's responsibility). Thus, questions were posed as to:

1. Whether the witness had reviewed the individual section of the claim.

2. Whether various changes and events had occurred on the dates stated in the claim.

3. Whether the information set out in the claim about specific dependent relationships of follow-on activities affected by the delays was accurate (for example, stud tracking could not be laid until floors on which the tracking would rest were poured).

4. If the witness believed that any of the facts stated in individual sections were incorrect, questions about the specific incorrect facts and the specific factual evidence that disproved the hard data in the contractor claim were posed.

---

and space to ensure that avoidable conflicts are avoided, and to maintain work progress as rapidly and effectively as possible.

The contractor, on the other hand, has the right to assume that the work can be installed reasonably in the area and in the relationship to other work reflected in the drawings.

J.W. Bateson Co., VACAB No. 1148, 79-1 BCA ¶ 13,573, at 66,495, 66,496 (1978).

In essence, the approach with the owner's representative was that he should "put up, or shut up." Either he had to acknowledge that the facts as stated in the claim were right or state exactly where the facts were wrong and describe the specific bases for his belief that the contractor records, pour records, daily logs, and photos were wrong.

During the examination the witness was unable to provide any substantial bases for denying the facts as stated in the claim. The witness still denied any right of the contractor to time extensions, but also confirmed his lack of understanding of basic CPM principles to assess entitlement to time extensions:

Q. Did you ever review PC's [proposed changes] to determine whether any of the work in the PC was critical as you understood that term or as you understand that term as it relates to [the contractor's] schedule?

A. There were some of the PC's that were on the critical path, yes, sir.

* * *

Q. But you made no evaluation of whether the time requested by that PC would affect that activity on the critical path?

A. That's correct.

Q. Again, was anybody superior to you making that type of analysis to your knowledge . . . ?

A. Not to my knowledge.

Q. You did understand, though, that delay to work on the critical path could have an adverse effect on completion?

A. No, sir, I wasn't.

* * *

Q. Isn't it your understanding that a delay to a critical activity can have an adverse effect on the overall completion of the project?

A. No, sir, I don't believe that it does.

Since this was the only witness for the owner who was in a position to affirm or deny the key contractor factual allegations, this deposition placed the owner in a difficult position. The owner, with the denial of knowledge by its representative, had no one with the capacity to dispute hard facts established by contractor records and witnesses.

However, one additional development occurred during the deposition examination of the key on-site owner representative that caused serious problems for the owner's litigation posture. Specifically, a memo was discovered during document discovery (at another location in the same facility), which was occurring at the same time as the deposition. This memo was authored by the owner representative during the course of construction and transmitted to the individuals at Humana in charge of construction operations. The memo classified the plans a "screwed up mess" created by the architect and totally impeached two days of testimony in which the witness had denied the inadequacy of the plans and their effects on the project. The memo stated:

[The contractor] is making every effort possible to top out the structure by mid to late August.

* * *

[T]he mechanical contractor on the job is in the process of roughing in mechanical and plumbing piping on all levels from the second basement up through and including the fourth floor level. They are experiencing numerous problems in installing their phase of the work due to numerous errors in [the architect's] plumbing and mechanical drawings. Ductwork, shop drawings, and shop fabrication of ductwork is being held up in its entirety on the second and third floor due to lack of coordination by [the architect]. There are several areas under the ductwork where there is little more than six foot of head room from the bottom of the duct to the floor slab.

* * *

[W]e are experiencing an unbelievable amount of problems in this phase of the project due to [the architect's] failure to produce a workable set of contract documents particularly mechanical and plumbing. As I have mentioned above, we are totally held up on the preparation of shop fabrication and the preparation of shop drawings for the ductwork on the second and third floor. This is also likely to be a problem on the floors above this area, however, we have not had the time to thoroughly check out other areas of the building.

At the present time, the following areas are on hold pending receipt of working documents . . . and mechanical and electrical drawings from [the architect].

1. Ground Floor East Section-Lobby Area: Contractor needs mechanical and electrical revised drawings of this area (Humana revised the main lobby area and relocated the Gift Shop to the Medical Office Building).

2. Radiology Area: This area is being held up pending receipt of revised architectural drawings increasing the wall thicknesses to compensate for the horizontal electrical raceway for the X-ray equipment. (This is a result of failure to coordinate the G.E. X-ray drawings with the architectural drawings).

3. Entire second and third floor air distribution system is held up due to errors in the . . . mechanical drawings. There are areas on these floors where there will be approximately six foot of head room from the bottom of the ducts to the floors. To rectify this problem it will require extensive ductwork redesign . . . and will result in additional cost to Humana.

4. For several months now there has been a pending change in Medical Records. This area is being held up pending receipt of revised architectural, mechanical, and electrical drawings. At the present time part of

the electrical conduit is roughed in from the original contract documents, part of the conduit is roughed in from the revised March 15
contract documents and as I understand it will be revised again with
the drawings that are now in progress.

[I]t is not the intent of this memo to holler "wolf-wolf," but we have very
serious problems on this job that could result in serious time delays and
expense to Humana. Several months ago I advised . . . of the problems
that we were experiencing with [the architect's] drawings and I recommended to him that [the architect] be forced to place personnel on this
project to resolve the numerous amount of conflicts and discrepancies on
their documents. It was also my recommendation . . . that [the architect]
provide this service at no additional cost to Humana in view of the fact
that they would be here to straighten out problems which they have created. I again recommend and strongly urge you to take whatever action is
necessary to see that [the architect] places a qualified person or persons on
this project to assist in straightening out their screwed up mess.

The question of how to best use the exhibit arose. The approach taken
was to ask lead-in questions about whether the witness had ever held certain opinions contained in the memorandum, then to provide the witness
with the memo for identification, then to query the witness as to whether
the memo was factually accurate, and then to give the witness the opportunity to correct his testimony. Of course, if the witness denied the accuracy
of the memo or portions of the document, the memo could be reviewed line
by line with the witness. The examination confirmed the accuracy of and
the facts as stated in the memorandum. Initially, the memorandum, dated
July 19, 1978, was marked for identification as Exhibit 20. Typical testimony included:

Q.   . . . have you had sufficient time to look at Exhibit 20?
A.   I believe I have, yes sir.

* * *

Q.   Was this memo accurate at the time you wrote it?
A.   To the best of my knowledge, yes.

* * *

Q.   Well, is there anything in this memo that is factually inaccurate?
A.   I would have to say that based on the information given to me at the time
     I wrote this, I would have to say that this information is correct.

* * *

Q.   Let's walk through it and see what you think you don't agree with.

* * *

"[W]e are experiencing an unbelievable amount of problems in this
phase of the project due to [the architect's] failure to produce a workable set of contract documents particularly mechanical and plumbing."

A. Based on information I had, that is correct.

Q. Do you believe that statement is factually accurate today, that [the architect] failed to produce a workable set of contract documents particularly mechanical and plumbing?

A. I am not an architect nor an engineer. I can't comment. I may have personal opinions, but not professional opinions.

Q. What is your personal opinion?

A. My personal opinion?

Q. Yes sir?

A. There were errors and problems in the documents.

Subsequent to the disclosure of the memorandum detailed above and the completion of the deposition, the parties negotiated a resolution of the dispute on terms acceptable to the contractor and its subcontractors.

§ 14.5   Edwards Air Force Base Test Support Facility

A $70 million construction program in the late 1980s for a new test support facility at Edwards Air Force Base provides a further example of actions violating basic scheduling provisions that can prove costly to an owner.

This project, which was managed for the Air Force by the Corps of Engineers, involved construction of a variety of new facilities for a major Air Force testing system. The facilities to be constructed included a hangar, multi-purpose building, engine run-up dock, and an entry building, plus associated sitework for electrical and mechanical services.

The contract specified $12,574 a day in liquidated damages and included stringent scheduling provisions requiring that a detailed CPM schedule be prepared and that the owner, on a weekly basis, include in the CPM schedule the time extensions due the contractor so that the contractor would have a properly adjusted schedule at all times. However, the bidders were not advised of certain key facts in this procurement. Specifically, because of critical Air Force need dates, the plans had not received the normal review and correction cycle. In addition, key Air Force and Corps of Engineers documents revealed that the Air Force need dates dictated there would be no time extensions (of any significance) on the project.

As a result, from the inception of the project the contractor and the various trade subcontractors were allowed no time extensions in spite of numerous and extensive compensable events. For example, the contractor encountered extensive errors due to conflicts in or lack of coordination of design between electrical installations and other trades, including conflicts encountered in the installation of manholes; internal discrepancies within electrical specifications and plans related to generators; errors in electrical specifications requiring out-of-sequence installation of fuse cut-outs; omission of critical details from design plans; conflicts caused by existing reinforced critical ductbanks, abandoned utility lines, and grade beams with new mechanical, electrical, and structural installations).

From the first day on the project the schedule was out of date. Like the *Fortec Constructors v. United States*[20] decision, the Edwards project had no properly up-to-date CPM schedule, because the owner would never grant any time extensions. The message was "work faster and get it done by the original completion date."

Within the context of this project, which was completed essentially on time but at great cost, the initial step undertaken in the claim investigation and preparation stage was to review the Corps and Air Force files on the project pursuant to a Freedom of Information Act request. The review revealed government knowledge of the serious problems with the plans and the fact that the schedule for the design and construction work had been extremely compressed to satisfy the need dates of the Air Force.

The strategy adopted thereafter in the claim submittal to the owner was to request rescission and restitution (as well as alternative theories of cardinal change, breach of contract, and equitable adjustment) on the bases that there had been knowing misrepresentations and nondisclosures of facts critical to the contractor in bidding the project. The contractor would not have bid the project had it been advised of the intent by the owner to accelerate performance from day one of the work (ignoring the clauses entitling the contractor to additional time) when the plans were seriously deficient and there had been no adequate survey of the site.

In this presentation, there was no necessity to provide any sort of adjusted schedule because the contractor had been accelerated from the project inception and the government had totally ignored the requirement that time extensions be included in the schedule and provided to the contractor on a weekly basis.

In this case, the parties negotiated a settlement within months of submission of the detailed claim presentation that included Air Force and corps documents relevant to the withholding of critical information at the time of project bidding.

§ 14.6   Integrity and Credibility in Dispute Resolution

The issues of integrity and credibility are central to the construction process and the resolution of disputes between all of the parties to the process,

---

[20] 8 Cl. Ct. 490 (1985).

whether one is the owner, contractor, construction manager, design professional, or consultant.

Both individuals and organizations have nothing more important to sell to the people and organizations with which they deal than their integrity. They may be able to get away with a lie or a misrepresentation once within the context of a construction project, trial, or business relationship, but if their conduct continues it is inevitable that the parties with whom they deal will discover how they operate. Their credibility with other parties will be nonexistent and they will be unable to receive a fair evaluation of their requests for action.

The consequences of failure to act in an appropriate and truthful manner are almost always disastrous. In addition, if companies or individuals engage in conduct that is outside the norms of society and involve others in their conduct, they provide other individuals with the opportunity to extort things from them with their knowledge of the guilty secrets.

This final section is intended to provide some idea of the kinds of conduct that can spell disaster. Due to the nature of this subject the examination will be circumspect. It will look to six examples of the kind of conduct that can prove harmful. Each example concerns a large institutional or commercial development project from within the past 25 years:

The first example concerns a contractor's request for additional compensation arising out of a major trade installation. The claim rested on excellent grounds. It concerned the relationship of this trade contractor's installation with the structural aspects of the project. The design errors were so great in this instance that the public authority considered condemning the facility during construction. The claim was a good one, and the trade contractor should have received a good recovery. However, this was not to be the case. During discovery, the defendant located internal contractor documents that revealed a practice of providing the owner with estimates of labor, material, and other such costs with the contract stipulated mark-up (for general and administrative expense and profit), while at the same time maintaining internal estimates that indicated mark-ups many times that called out in the contract. With the contract requirement clear about the limitation of the mark-up, the owner was in a position to threaten actions for misrepresentation or worse. The result of discovery of this practice was an end of any ability to obtain an affirmative recovery.

This loss of ability to recover occurred in spite of the fact that the trade contractor had lost a significant amount of money on the project because of the very serious structural design errors. This first example tells us that, although it is quite proper in an estimating and negotiating context to have a disagreement over the estimate (of the number of hours or other direct or impact costs for a change) and quite proper to include sufficient hours with a safety margin to accomplish the work, it is not proper to misrepresent your estimated costs.

The second example also concerns the performance of a major trade contractor. In this example, though, the concern relates to the manner in which the prime contractor handled the change order requests of the trade contractor. As in the first example, there was a contract-stipulated mark-up to be applied to direct costs. On this project, the trade contractor was submitting its requests in a proper and appropriate fashion. However, what it discovered, through inadvertence by the prime contractor, was that the prime contractor was retyping the trade contractor's estimates and reworking the dollar amount to increase it by a set percentage and then adding its markup on top of the retyped and recalculated trade contractor change proposal. In this circumstance, the trade contractor communicated its knowledge to the owner, and the practice of the prime contractor ended thereafter with appropriate consequences.

The third example concerns a trade contractor claim being submitted to a prime contractor as a part of a consolidated claim agreement in an overall request to the owner. The trade contractor claim submission, provided on the stationery of its counsel, indicated that it had been prepared in accordance with standard industry calculations of lost efficiency. However, the claimed amount appeared to represent aggressive pricing, considering the size of the contract.

The prime contractor and its representatives, as a part of the due diligence detailed in **Chapter 12**, posed certain elemental questions to the trade contractor about the amount of its original bid for labor; the amount it adjusted its labor estimate for change orders; and the amount it actually spent on the project for labor. Similar questions were raised about other direct or indirect cost calculations.

The responses were most interesting because the trade contractor revealed that the amount of its claim for labor was more than it had even spent for all labor on the project without giving the owner the benefit of any credit for the original bid. After asking further whether the trade contractor's claim had been sent via United States mail (to heighten awareness of potential mail fraud), it was suggested that a re-evaluation of its position was in order.

The fourth example concerns another trade contractor presentation that the subcontractor requested be included in a major consolidated claim presentation. In this case the mechanical trade contractor provided an extensive presentation with detailed charts and graphics and a narrative report. The major complaints in the claim were late owner approvals and heating, ventilating, and air-conditioning (HVAC) design problems.

Again, due diligence by the general contractor revealed serious flaws in the presentation. In response to the late approvals, the question only had to be asked, "So What?" To state it another way, the subcontractor was asked how the late owner approvals affected its ability to perform in a timely and economical manner. It was revealed that, while the late approvals were an irritant, they did not directly affect the field operations, which had been delayed by other causes. The complaints about the HVAC ductwork problems were well merited, but they had nothing to do with the great majority of the costs claimed by the mechanical trade contractor in its labor codes for mechanical equipment and piping (as contrasted with ductwork). Once again, the trade contractor was told as a part of the due diligence process to go back to the drawing board and to either come up with a real justification for the mechanical costs claimed or not claim these costs.

The fifth example concerns the necessity for a party to deal with its blemishes in a forthright, up-front manner in its presentation. In this manner, a significant error was present in the contractor's bid and was discovered within a short period after the bid opening by the contractor. The contractor met with the major trade contractors and all agreed to assume a portion of the error and that the job should be taken. Thereafter, significant buy-outs on material and equipment purchases ameliorated the effect of the error.

During performance of the project, very serious changes were encountered, as well as major changed conditions and structural design errors. The general contractor and its subcontractors pursued recovery on a modified total costs basis, but neglected to address or reveal the bid error in their presentation to the party charged with the responsibility for deciding the dispute. In presentations before the decision-maker, the contractor's bid error was revealed by the defendant after the close of the presentation by the claimant. The failure of the contractor to deal with its warts in its affirmative presentation affected the results achieved.

The last example concerns the relationship of general contractor with the trade contractors in performing a project on a cost-plus-fee basis. The general contractor was charged with supervising the efforts of numerous trade contractors and directly contracting with them. In one case, a trade contractor had its installation on the project literally destroyed over two seasons by the failure of the general contractor to protect the work as clearly spelled out in the specifications.

The cost of the trade contractor installation was increased by more than 100 percent. Recovery was sought with a detailed presentation of the specific activities and sequencing affected by the installation destruction and comeback operations. The pricing for the trade contractor claim, given the facts on the project, was for total cost recovery.

The presentation in this case for the total cost recovery was a little different than the normal case. The normal total cost approach is to take actual costs marked up for overhead and profit and then subtract current contract price from that total. However, in this case the amount in the subcontract did not represent the actual amount of the price agreed upon for the subcontract work. At the time that the trade contractor was bidding the project in question it was also bidding a second project to the same prime contractor. During the bidding and negotiation processes for the two projects, the trade contractor was told to submit a combined price on both projects. The trade contractor spelled out within the combined price the amount for each project. Subsequently, after it had been told it was receiving both projects the trade contractor was also told that it should transfer funds from the second contract to the project in question, thereby making the amount of the project in question higher than it otherwise would have been. When the trade contractor objected to the procedure it was told that the transfer had been made for the prime contractor's internal bookkeeping purposes.

When the trade contractor made its detailed total cost presentation it computed its claim for recovery starting with what the contract price should have been. The claim was transmitted to the prime contractor, the owner, and the architect/engineer with a brief footnote explaining the reasons why normal total cost computation methods were not used to price the claim. Within weeks of the claim submission, the prime contractor had arranged for a settlement of the case at a meeting without counsel present. At that meeting the prime contractor presented the trade contractor with the monetary settlement and also presented a settlement agreement for execution that stated the footnote explaining the pricing method in the trade contractor claim was inaccurate.

What these examples demonstrate is the importance of integrity and credibility in the claim process. No matter how strong one's legal and factual positions, failure to act in a truthful, forthright fashion (even regarding seemingly inconsequential matters) can have a disastrous impact on one's ability to achieve a desirable result. Consequently, it is crucial to bear in mind throughout any involvement with construction claims and disputes that the best approach is an honest approach.

APPENDIXES

A. AIA Document A201-1987, Paragraph 3.10—Contractor's Construction Schedules

B. 1988 State of California Department of Transportation Scheduling Specifications

C. 1985 Corps of Engineers Edwards Air Force Base Test Support Facility Construction Specification, Section 17—Contractor Project Management System

D. Veterans Administration Master Specification, Section 01311—Network Analysis System

E. United States Postal Service Specification, Section 01030—Scheduling and Progress

F. Model Scheduling Specification

G. Excerpt from Veterans Administration VACPM Handbook Part VI—Contract Changes and Time Extensions

AIA DOCUMENT A201-1987, PARAGRAPH 3.10— CONTRACTOR'S CONSTRUCTION SCHEDULES

3.10   Contractor's Construction Schedules*

3.10.1   The Contractor, promptly after being awarded the Contract, shall prepare and submit for the Owner's and Architect's information a Contractor's construction schedule for the Work. The schedule shall not exceed time limits current under the Contract Documents, shall be revised at appropriate intervals as required by the conditions of the Work and Project, shall be related to the entire Project to the extent required by the Contract Documents, and shall provide for expeditious and practicable execution of the Work.

3.10.2   The Contractor shall prepare and keep current, for the Architect's approval, a schedule of submittals which is coordinated with the Contractor's construction schedule and allows the Architect reasonable time to review submittals.

3.10.3   The Contractor shall conform to the most recent schedules.

---

*Subparagraph 3.10 from AIA Document A201, 1987 edition, reproduced with the permission of The American Institute of Architects under license number 91007. No further reproduction permitted.

1988 STATE OF CALIFORNIA DEPARTMENT OF TRANSPORTATION SCHEDULING SPECIFICATIONS

8-1.04   Progress Schedule—When required by the special provisions, the Contractor shall submit to the Engineer a practicable progress schedule within 20 working days of approval of the contract, and within 10 working days of the Engineer's written request at any other time.

The Contractor may furnish a form for the Contractor's use. If the Engineer furnishes a form, he will also furnish to the Contractor, on request, on or before the last day of each month a copy of the form showing the status of work actually completed during the preceding estimate period.

The schedule shall show the order in which the Contractor proposes to carry out the work, the dates on which he will start the several salient features of the work (including procurement of materials, plant, and equipment), and the contemplated dates for completing the said salient features.

The progress schedules submitted shall be consistent in all respects with the time and order of work requirements of the contract.

Subsequent to the time that submittal of a progress schedule is required in accordance with these specifications, no progress payments will be made for any work until a satisfactory schedule has been submitted to the Engineer.

* * *

10-1.06 Progress Schedule—Progress schedules will be required for this contract and shall conform to the provisions in Section 8-1.04, "Progress Schedule," of the Standard Specifications.

* * *

1985 CORPS OF ENGINEERS EDWARDS AIR FORCE BASE TEST SUPPORT FACILITY CONSTRUCTION SPECIFICATION, SECTION 17—CONTRACTOR PROJECT MANAGEMENT SYSTEM

17. CONTRACTOR PROJECT MANAGEMENT SYSTEM:

(a). *General:*

(1) The Contractor is required by this contract to provide, operate and maintain a Contractor Project Management System to assure adequate planning and execution of the work, to assist the Contracting Officer in appraising the reasonableness of the schedule, to evaluate progress of the work, to make progress payments, and to make decisions relative to time and/or cost adjustments which may result from changes in the work.

(2) The management system is to be based on a computerized Network Analysis System (Critical Path Method) operated by on-site personnel at terminals located in the Contractor's on-site office. On-site management shall be capable in using the system to address all project activities and resources on a real time interactive basis and be capable of rapidly evaluating alternative scenarios which will optimize project management. Evidence of technical expertise of on-site personnel with the proposed computerized Network Analysis System shall be submitted for Contracting Officer's approval prior to any on-site work.

(3) The Contractor Project Management System is to be staffed and prepared pursuant to Contract Clause, "SCHEDULES FOR

CONSTRUCTION CONTRACTOR", and Contract Clause, "SUPERIN-TENDENCE BY CONTRACTOR." In preparing this system the Contractor assumes responsibility for conformance with contract requirements, planning, sequencing of work, and determining the construction means and methods.

(4)   A computer terminal, Display and Printer compatible with the computerized Network Analysis System (hardware and software) selected by the Contractor shall be provided and maintained in the Corps of Enginers field office within thirty (30) days of the notice to proceed. This system will be for the sole use by the Contracting Officer in the review and evaluation of the proposed network diagrams, mathematical analysis and any subsequent change order proposals. All Contractor Project Management submittals shall be provided in paper copy. This equipment will remain the property of the Contractor and removed upon completion of the project.

(b).   Basic System Requirements:

(1)   The computerized Network Analysis System (NAS) must be capable of providing the following minimum on-site services: network analysis by IJ or precedence notation, progress and cost reports, network comparisons, super and sub-networks, resource reporting, report writer allowing flexible formatting and summarization, and graphical output using a dot matrix printer. In preparing the NAS, the Contractor shall insure that it represents an accurate and efficient plan for accomplishing the work.

(2)   The Contractor's project management system must be capable of at least weekly update and production of physical update reports, percent complete reports, and cost reports for payment purposes. Management effort required will include capability to analyze factors delaying progress and altering logic and durations on an interactive up-to-date basis to maintain an active weekly management schedule.

(3)   Access to the system for input and output must be by remote terminals located at the construction site. The Contractor shall provide a suitable area and furniture to support system installation including all equipment, paper, and computer time, and further specific requirements of the Contractor's chosen system.

(c).   Detailed System Requirements:

(1)   The system shall consist of diagrams and accompanying mathematical analysis. Flexibility of formatting and summarization of reports will be provided by selecting and prioritizing from the following menu of information: identifying activity number (Precedence System) or numbers (I, J), duration in work days, activity description, code relating to

party responsible to perform work, cost, manpower, estimate or labor hours, list of major items of construction equipment usage anticipated, cost item or pay item activity is associated with, milestones, identification of subnet when applicable, early start date, late start date, early finish date, late finish date, anticipated start date, and a list of all activities that precede or follow each activity. In calculating activity durations, Saturdays, Sundays, holidays, and normal inclement weather shall be considered.

(2) Windowing (chronologically selected portions of the network) specified for reports or diagrams must be possible. A network information report, listing the information contained in the reference menu and logic diagram, will be provided for the initially approved network as well as each update which incorporated a logic change.

(3) In addition to construction activities including checkout and testing, the schedule shall include activities for submittal of materials, samples, shop drawings, operation and maintenance manuals, master equipment lists, spare parts lists, and other related documents. Also included shall be activities for the procurement of all major materials and equipment, including fabrication and delivery, installation and testing. Of particular interest shall be those material and equipment procurement items that are expected to be critical to the progress of actual construction. Activities of the Government indicating reviews and approvals of materials, equipment, testing, and other actions that affect the progress shall be shown.

(4) The Contractor shall incorporate as a minimum any and all milestones and contract required events which are listed below and/or specified elsewhere within this specification. These and any other milestone events as identified by the Contractor as may be required by the Contracting Officer, shall be designated as milestone activities and shall consist of at least five percent (5%) of the network activities.

PHASE I

A. SITEWORK
1. Underground utilities, drainage and sewers, demolition, & underground utilities, roads, testing
2. Offsite utilities
3. Underground electrical
4. Cathodic protection
5. Testing and corrections

B. MULTI-PURPOSE BUILDING
1. Steel shop drawing submittals
2. Steel Fabrication
3. Steel delivery

    4. Steel erection
    5. Installation of equipment
    6. Installation of mechanical systems
    7. Installation of electrical systems
    8. Installation of ductwork and piping systems
    9. Installation of halon and sprinkler systems
    10. Testing and corrections

C. HANGAR
    1. Procurement, fabrication and delivery of 5 ton crane
    2. Erection of 5 ton crane
    3. Procurement, fabrication and delivery of hangar doors
    4. Erection of hangar doors
    5. Steel shop drawing submittals
    6. Steel delivery
    7. Steel erection
    8. Installation of mechanical systems
    9. Installation of electrical systems
    10. Installation of ductwork and piping
    11. Testing and corrections

PHASE II (Option)

A. BUILDING 205
    1. Procurement of mechanical and electrical equipment
    2. Demolition work
    3. Installation of mechanical and electrical systems
    4. Testing and corrections

B. ENTRY BUILDING
    1. Procurement and mechanical and electrical systems
    2. Excavation and utility work
    3. Installation of mechanical and electrical systems
    4. Testing and corrections

C. SITEWORK
    1. Above ground electrical work
    2. Installation of above ground utilities
    3. Installation of lighting and security systems
    4. Testing and corrections

D. ER DOCK
    1. Procurement of sound suppressor
    2. Procurement of exhaust ejector
    3. Procurement of 3 ton crane
    4. Installation of 3 ton crane

    5. Procurement of hangar doors
    6. Installation of hangar doors
    7. Procurement of mechanical and electrical systems
    8. Installation of mechanical and electrical systems
    9. Installation of exhaust ejector
  10. Steel shop drawings submittals
  11. Steel delivery
  12. Steel erection
  13. Testing and corrections

E. BUILDINGS 181, 182, and 204
    1. Procurement and equipment and materials
    2. Demolition work
    3. Correction work
    4. Testing and correction

F. HAZARDOUS STORAGE
    1. Procurement of pumps, tanks, and foundation
    2. Correction work
    3. Testing and Correction

    (5) Logic Diagrams:

       (a) Logic diagrams shall show the order and interdependence of activities and the sequence in which the work is to be accomplished as planned by the Contractor.

       (b) Detailed networks need not be time scaled, but drafted to have a continuous flow from left to right, showing how the start of a given activity is dependent on the completion of preceding activities, and how its completion restricts the start of the following activities.

       (c) A logic diagram of the complete project shall be submitted with the initial NAS, showing each activity identifying numbers, duration, description, with the critical path easily identified for Phase I and Phase II, for each item of work. Update diagrams will be provided as required by logic changes but not more frequently than the monthly update.

       (d) Activities for separate buildings and/or features shall be identified and grouped on the network and the interdependence of these groups shall be shown.

    (6) Each activity, except Government activities and nonpaid activities such as the preparation of submittals and master equipment lists, shall be assigned a corresponding monetary value. The value shall be based upon a cost estimate made for each activity and shall represent all the elements of cost, i.e., labor, equipment, materials, overhead, and

profit, and shall be based on the cost of the items from the bid item which are included in the activity. Upon approval of the schedule, activity values shall be frozen and no changes in the value of any activity shall be permitted without formal approval from the Contracting Officer. When requested, the cost estimate for each activity shall be submitted to the Contracting Officer. The estimate shall be itemized as required by the Contracting Officer. Unless otherwise directed, the breakdown shall be in sufficient detail to permit an analysis of all material, labor, equipment, subcontract, and overhead cost, as well as profit. Any amount claimed for subcontracts shall be supported by a similar price breakdown. These activity values shall be the basis for payments to the Contractor. The sum of all activity values shall equal the contract amount.

(7)   In addition to the detailed schedule, a summary schedule shall be developed by the Contractor. The summary schedule shall consist of a minimum of thirty (30) activities and be updated monthly.

(d).   Submission and approval of the system shall be as follows:

(1)   The Contractor shall submit for review and approval a description of the type and capabilities of the computerized network system proposed to be used. Submission shall within three (3) calendar days of the notice to proceed.

(2)   A detailed network defining the Contractor's planned operations during the first sixty (60) calendar days of the contract shall be submitted within fifteen (15) days of the notice to proceed. The first sixty (60) days of the preliminary schedule is a fragmentary network (subnetwork) of the total contract schedule and shall conform in all respects with the details and requirements for diagrams and mathematical analysis as specified. The Contractor's general approach for the remainder of the project shall be shown. At midmonth the Contractor shall submit a updated network of actual progress on this network for partial payment. This report shall contain costs of activities completed or partially completed with a tabulation of total earning.

(3)   The complete network system consisting of the detailed network mathematical analysis (including on-site manpower loading schedule and equipment schedule) and network diagrams shall be submitted for approval within thirty (30) calendar days after receipt of notice to proceed.

(4)   The Contractor shall participate in a review and evaluation of the proposed network diagrams and mathematical analysis by the Contracting Officer. Any revisions necessary as a result of this review shall be resubmitted for approval of the Contracting Officer within three (3) calendar days after the conference. The approved schedule shall be

used by the Contractor for planning, organizing and directing the work, reporting progress, and requesting payment for work accomplished.

(e).   Network Modifications:

(1)   In those cases where the contract performance is delayed due to causes beyond the control of the contractor, and a time extension may be allowable under one or more of the Clauses entitled "CHANGES", "DIFFERING SITE CONDITIONS", "DEFAULT (Fixed-Price Construction)", "SUSPENSION OF WORK" or other applicable causes, as a condition precedent to granting a time extension, the contractor shall submit a time proposal in such for as to identify the specific subnet diagram and activities affected.

(2)   Change order proposals shall include description or listing of all proposed changes to the network, by activity, and demonstrate the effect on the contract required completion date. A complete list of activities changed and a subnet of activities affected by the change shall be submitted.

(3)   Float or slack is defined as the amount of time between the early start date and the late start date, or the early finish date and the late finish date, of any of the activities in the NAS schedule. Float or slack is not time for the exclusive use or benefit of either the Government or the Contractor. Extensions of time for performance may be granted to the extent that equitable time adjustment for the activities affected exceed the total float or where otherwise justified, effect on the contract completion can be shown. The contract completion date is fixed, and will be amended only by modifications which include time and are signed by the Contracting Officer.

(4)   Rapid resolution of change orders and the granting of other time extensions where authorized by the Contracting Officer is a critical part of the overall management system. Implementation of all justified activity and logic changes shall be made and reflected in the next weekly update after approval of the contracting Officer.

(5)   If, in the opinion of the Contracting Officer, the current schedule no longer accurately reflects the Contractor's real plan for accomplishing the work, or no longer reflects a viable way of finishing the work on schedule, the Contractor shall be directed to revise the schedule and submit it for approval within seven (7) calendar days of direction.

(f).   Reports:

(1)   After the network approval, the Contractor shall review and evaluate the actual progress with the Contracting Officer's representative on a weekly basis, and submit any updated weekly reports three (3) workdays after the meeting.

(2) Three (3) weekly reports, selected from specific items of the menu will be required, for a specified time window of the project (such as the next two weeks). These reports must be flexible in format, allowing generation of reports relating specifically to critical work areas, or areas of particular interest. The Government will identify the subject of the requested reports for the following week at a weekly review meeting. All activities of the Government that affect progress will be coded to allow a separate report.

(3) Monthly update reports will be submitted at midmonth showing current status and actual start and finish dates of project activities, and will be capable of comparing the current status with the approved base schedule. Each monthly update report shall be stored on the Contractor's computer until the final pay estimate is processed. The content of the monthly update shall be flexible to show items listed in the menu. The midmonth report shall be used for partial payments.

(4) A meeting shall be held three (3) workdays before the delivery of the midmonth report to discuss all input data. If the Contractor desires to make changes in his method of operation and scheduling, he shall clearly present the proposed changes.

(5) A narrative report shall be submitted with the midmonth report indicating current and anticipated problems, delaying factors, and conditions that are, impacting the Contractor's work effort. An analysis showing the reasons for the delay/gain and their impact upon the current schedule shall be included. When it is apparent that scheduled milestone and completion dates will not be met, the Contractor shall proposed specific methods he intends to implement to bring the project back on schedule at no cost to the Government. Such measures may include but are not limited to:

(a) Increasing construction manpower in such quantities and crafts as will substantially eliminate the backlog of work effort.

(b) Increasing the number of working hours per shift; shifts per workday; workdays per week; the amount of construction equipment; or any combination thereof.

(c) Rescheduling of activities to achieve maximum practical concurrency of work efforts.

(6) The Contractor shall implement such procedures as may be necessary for the active participation by his subcontractors in preparing and updating the schedule. Subcontractor shall be provided with schedules which identify the interfaces of their work with the work of others. As a minimum, the Contractor shall provide bar graphs to each major subcontractor showing activity times with plots on an Early Start

basis. Copies of these schedules shall also be available to the Contracting Officer. The relationship between subcontractor and interdependency of work shall be managed by the Contractor. When these interdependencies are violated or impaired, the Contractor shall identify the problem, resolve it, and provide the information to the Contracting officer as part of the monthly report.

VETERANS ADMINISTRATION MASTER SPECIFICATION, SECTION 01311—NETWORK ANALYSIS SYSTEM

Veterans Administration
Washington, D.C. 20420

H-08-a
VA Master Specification
Section 01311
March 15, 1988

* * *

Section 01311
Network Analysis System

* * *

Part 1—General

1.1　Description

　　A. The Contractor shall develop a Network Analysis System (NAS) plan and schedule demonstrating fulfillment of the contract requirements, shall keep the network up to date in accordance with the requirements of this section and shall utilize the plan for scheduling, coordinating and monitoring work under this contract (including all activities of subcontractors, equipment vendors and suppliers). Conventional Critical Path Method (CPM) (I-J) technique will be utilized to satisfy both time and cost applications.

　　B. Use the principles and definitions of the terms in the Associated General Contractors of America (AGC) publication, "The Use of CPM in Construction, A Manual for General Contractors and The Construction Industry," Copyright 1976, except the provisions specified in this section shall govern.

1.2 Contractor's Representative

A. The Contractor shall designate an authorized representative in the firm who will be responsible for the preparation of the network diagram, review and report progress of the project with and to the Contracting Officer's representative.

B. The Contractor's representative shall have direct project control and complete authority to act on behalf of the Contractor in fulfilling the requirements of this specification section and such authority shall not be interrupted throughout the duration of the project.

> SPEC WRITER NOTE: In paragraphs 1.3,A; 1.3,B, and 1.3,C; (i) applies to competitively bid projects and (ii) applies to 8(a) projects. Edit as required.

1.3 CONTRACTOR'S CONSULTANT

A. To assist in the preparation of the project plan, arrow diagram, and tape, the Contractor shall engage an independent CPM consultant who is skilled in the time and cost application of activity on arrow (I-J) network techniques for construction projects, the cost of which is included in the //(i) Contractor's bid. //(ii) original contract price.// This consultant shall not have any financial or business ties to the Contractor, and shall not be an affiliate or subsidiary company of the Contractor, and shall not be employed by an affiliate or subsidiary company of the Contractor.

B. //(i) Prior to engaging a consultant, and within 10 calendar days after award of the contract, //(ii) With the initial cost proposal,// the Contractor shall submit to the Contracting Officer:

1. The name and address of the proposed consultant.

2. Sufficient information to show that the proposed consultant has the qualifications to meet the requirements specified in the preceding paragraph.

3. A list of prior construction projects, along with selected activity on arrow (I-J) network samples on current projects which the proposed consultant has performed. These network samples must show complete project planning for a project of similar size and scope as covered under this contract.

C. The Contracting Officer has the right to approve or disapprove employment of the proposed consultant, and will notify the

Contractor of the VA decision within seven calendar days from receipt of information. In case of disapproval, the Contractor shall resubmit another consultant within 10 calendar days for renewed consideration. The Contractor must have their CPM Consultant approved prior to//(i) submitting any diagram.//(ii) completion of contract negoiations.//

1.4 COMPUTER PRODUCED SCHEDULES

A. The Veterans Administration (VA) will provide to the Contractor monthly computer processing of all computer-produced time/cost schedules and reports as a result of the monthly project updates. This computer service will include up to five copies of any five reports currently available on the VACPM computer program. The VA will only provide computer processing and associated reports for the monthly project updates.

B. The VA will produce the five requested reports from the approved, cost loaded, interim arrow diagram or the complete project arrow diagram. The requested reports will be produced upon receipt of the completed Look-Ahead Report. The VA assumes responsibility for the correctness and timeliness of computer-produced reports. The Contractor is responsible for the accurate and timely submittal of the updated Look-Ahead Report and all CPM data necessary to produce the computer reports and payment request that is specified.

C. The Contractor shall report errors in computer-produced reports to the Contracting Officer's representative within seven calendar days from Contractor's receipt of reports. The Contracting Officer will reprocess the computer-produced reports to correct update errors only if the errors substantially affect the payment and schedule for the project.

1.5 INTERIM ARROW DIAGRAM SUBMITTAL

A. Within 21 calendar days after receipt of Notice to Proceed, the Contractor shall submit for the Contracting Officer's review, five blue line copies of an Interim Arrow Diagram on sheets of 28 inch by 42 inch paper, a 5-1/4 diskette(s), and five copies of a computer-produced I-J schedule. The I-J computer-produced schedule shall meet all contractual requirements such as contract duration, phases and phasing restraints. The Interim Arrow Diagram shall cover the following project phases and activities:

1. Procurement—Submittals, approvals, fabrication and delivery of all key and long lead time procurement activities.

SPEC WRITER NOTE: Use paragraph 2 when the project is not phased and delete paragraph 2'. When project is phased delete paragraph 2 and use paragraph 2'.

2. The activities to be accomplished during the first 120 work days of the project.

//2.' The activities to be accomplished during the first 120 work days of the project and shall include the following phases or subphases.

   a.
   b.   SPEC WRITER NOTE: FOR PHASED
               PROJECTS ONLY TO BE FILLED IN BY
               SPEC WRITER IN CONJUNCTION WITH
   c.   VA PERSONNEL (08D3) PRIOR TO FINAL
   d.   DRAFT OF THE PROJECT MANUAL.
   e.   //

3. Summary activities which are necessary (not included under the paragraph above) to properly show:

   a. The approach to scheduling the remaining work areas or phases of the project. The work for each phase or area must be represented by at least one, (summary) activity so that the work cumulatively shows the entire project schedule.

   b. Approximate cost and duration for each summary activity which is the Contractor's best estimate for all the work represented.

   c. Realistic delivery dates for all procurement activities required and specified.

4. In addition to the Interim Arrow Diagram, the Contractor shall submit five copies of a computer-produced I-J schedule showing project duration; phase completion dates; all dummies; and other data, and activity cost. Each activity on the computer-produced schedule shall contain as a minimum, but not limited to, I-J nodes, duration, trade to code area to code, description, budget amount, early start date, early finish date, late start date, late finish date and total float. The Contractor shall submit a 5-$\frac{1}{4}$ diskette(s) for the Interim Diagram submission, as specified under Article ARROW DIAGRAM REQUIREMENTS, paragraph DISKETTE REQUIREMENTS AND CPM ACTIVITY RECORD SPECIFICATIONS.

B. The Interim Diagram shall describe the activities to be accomplished and their interdependencies subject to all requirements specified, where appropriate. All work activities, other than procurement activities, shall be cost loaded as specified and is the basis for partial payment during the beginning months of the contract, while the complete working arrow diagram is being developed and approved. Interim diagram shall not be used for time extension analysis. All CPM data supporting any time extension request, in accordance with Article ADJUSTMENT OF CONTRACT COMPLETION, will be derived from the approved final arrow diagram.

C. Within 21 calendar days of receipt by the Contracting Officer of the Interim Arrow Diagram, the Contracting Officer shall notify the Contractor concerning approval or disapproval of the Interim Arrow Diagram. In the event of disapproval, the Contractor shall resubmit, within 14 calendar days, five blue line copies of the revised arrow diagram, five copies of the revised computer produced I-J schedule and a revised 5-1/4 diskette in accordance with any agreements reached as a result of the Contracting Officer's review.

1.6 THE COMPLETE PROJECT ARROW DIAGRAM SUBMITTAL

A. Within 90 calendar days after receipt of Notice to Proceed, the Contractor shall submit for the Contracting Officer's review five blue line copies of the complete arrow diagram on sheets of 28 inch by 42 inch paper and 5-1/4 diskette(s) as specified. The submittal shall also include five copies of a computer-produced I-J schedule showing project duration; phase completion dates; all dummies; and other data, including activity cost. Each activity on the computer-produced schedule shall contain as a minimum, but not limited to, I-J nodes, duration, trade code, area code, description, budget amount, early start date, early finish date, late start date, late finish date and total float. The complete working arrow diagram shall reflect the Contractor's approach to scheduling the complete project, taking into account the accuracy of the logic and the experience gained from the interim diagram. The final diagram in its original form shall contain no contract changes or delays which may have been incurred during the interim diagram period. These changes/delays shall be entered at the first update after the final diagram has been approved. The Contractor should provide their request/time extension analysis for contract time as a result of these contract changes/delays after this update and in accordance with Article, ADJUSTMENT OF CONTRACT COMPLETION.

B. Within 30 calendar days after receipt of the complete project arrow diagram, the Contracting Officer or his representative, will do one or both of the following:

1. Notify the Contractor concerning his actions, opinions, and objections.

2. A meeting with the Contractor at or near the job site for joint review, correction or adjustment of the proposed plan will be scheduled if required. Within 14 calendar days after the joint review, the Contractor shall revise and shall submit five blue line copies of the revised arrow diagram, five copies of the revised computer-produced (I-J) schedule and a revised 5-$\frac{1}{4}$ diskette(s) to the Contracting Officer. The re-submission will be reviewed by the Contracting Officer and, if found to be as previously agreed upon, will be approved.

C. The VA will process and return approved arrow diagram and computer reports as specified to the Contractor. The approved arrow diagram and the computer-produced schedule(s) generated therefrom shall constitute the project work schedule until subsequently revised in accordance with requirements of this section.

D. The Complete Project Arrow Diagram will contain, including dummies, no less than _____ activities and no more than _____ activities.

1.7 ACTIVITY COST DATA

A. The Contractor shall cost load all work activities except procurement activities. The cumulative amount of all cost loaded work activities (including alternates) shall equal the total contract price. Prorate overhead, profit and general conditions on all activities for the entire project length. The VA will generate from this information cash flow curves indicating graphically the total percentage of activity dollar value scheduled to be in place on early finish, late finish, and 50 percent float dates. These cash flow curves will be used by the Contracting Officer to assist him in determining approval or disapproval of the cost loading. In the event of disapproval, the Contractor shall revise and resubmit in accordance with Articles, INTERIM ARROW DIAGRAM SUBMITTAL and THE COMPLETE ARROW DIAGRAM SUBMITTAL.

B. The Contractor shall cost load activities for test, balance and adjust various systems in accordance with the provisions in the General Conditions, Article, PAYMENT UNDER

FIXED-PRICE CONSTRUCTION CONTRACTS (VA SUP-PLEMENTAL CONDITIONS).

C. In accordance with Article PERFORMANCE OF WORK BY THE CONTRACTOR (VAAR 852.236) in the Section, GENERAL CONDITIONS, the Contractor shall submit, simultaneously with the cost per activity of the construction schedule required by this Section, a responsibility code for all activities (referred to as "branches" in the GENERAL CONDITIONS) of the network for which the Contractor's forces will perform the work.

//D. The Contractor shall cost load activities for ASBESTOS ABATEMENT. The sum of asbestos abatement activity costs shall equal the value of the asbestos bid item in the Contractors' bid.//

//E. The Contractor shall cost load activities for all BID ALTERNATES. The sum of the cost loading for each bid alternate's activities shall equal the value of the alternate in the Contractors' bid.//

1.8   ARROW DIAGRAM REQUIREMENTS

A. Show on the arrow diagram the sequence and interdependence of activities required for complete performance of all items of work. In preparing the arrow diagram, the Contractor shall:

1. Exercise sufficient care to produce a clear, legible and accurate diagram including all copies refer to the drawing, CPM-1 (Sample CPM Network). Group activities related to specific physical areas of the project, on the diagram, for ease of understanding and simplification. Provide a key plan on each diagram sheet showing the project area associated with the activities shown on that sheet.

2. Show the following on each work activity:

a. I and J, (beginning and ending event number respectively).

b. Concise description of the work represented by the activity. (29 characters or less including spaces).

c. Performance responsibility or trade code (five characters or less): GEN, MECH, ELEC, CARP, PLAST, or other acceptable abbreviations.

d. Duration (in work days).

e. Cost (in accordance with Article, ACTIVITY COST DATA of this section and less than $9,999,999 per activity).

f. Work location or area code (five characters or less), descriptive of the area involved.

g. Manpower required (average number of men per day).

h. CPM legend format shown on the drawing, CPM-1 (Sample CPM Network) is mandatory and shall be followed in preparing interim and final arrow diagrams.

3. Show activities as:

a. Contractor's time required for submittal of shop drawings, templates, fabrication, delivery and similar pre-construction work.

b. Contracting Officer's and Architect-Engineer's review and approval of shop drawings, equipment schedules, samples, template, or similar items.

c. Interruption of VA Medical Center utilities, delivery of Government furnished equipment, project phasing and any other specification requirements.

d. Test, balance and adjust various systems and pieces of equipment.

> SPEC WRITER NOTE: Use the following on multiple phased project only.

e. VA inspection and acceptance activity with a minimum duration of five work days at the end of each phase and immediately preceding any VA move activity required by the contract phasing for that phase. Schedule these activities so that only one phase is scheduled for completion within the same 30 consecutive calendar day period (except for those phases immediately preceding the final acceptance). Maintain this scheduling condition throughout the length of the contract unless waived by the Contracting Officers representative in writing.

> SPEC WRITER NOTE: Use the following on projects that require a separate bid item for asbestos abatement.

f. Asbestos abatement activities shall have a trade code designation of ASB.

> SPEC WRITER NOTE: Use the following on projects that have bid alternates.

g. Bid alternates shall be shown and identified separately from the work activities on the arrow diagram for the base bid Contract work. The activities for each bid alternate shall have trade Codes corresponding to the appropriate bid alternate e.g., (Alt1, Alt2, and other alternates).

4. Show not only the activities for actual construction work for each trade category of the project, but also include trade dummies to indicate the movement of trades from one area, floor, or building, to another area, floor, or building, for at least five trades who are performing major work under this contract.

5. Break up the work into activities of a duration no longer than 20 work days each, except as to non-construction activities i.e., (procurement of materials, delivery of equipment, concrete and asphalt curing) and any other activities for which the Contracting Officer may approve the showing of a longer duration. The duration for VA approval of any required submittal, shop drawing, or other submittals shall not be less than 20 work days. The construction time as determined by the CPM schedule from early start to late finish for any subphase, phase or the entire project shall not exceed the contract time(s) specified or shown.

6. Describe work activities clearly, so the work is readily identifiable for assessment of completion. Activities labeled "start," "continue," or "completion," are not specific and will not be allowed. Lead and lag time activities will not be acceptable.

7. Uniquely number each activity with event numbers ranging from 1 to 99998 only. The diagram should be generally numbered in sequence; left to right; top to bottom, and omitting numbers ending in 3, 6, and 9 with J node always being greater than I node.

B. Submit the following arrow diagram supporting data in addition to the arrow diagram, I-J schedule and 5-1/4 diskette(s). Failure of the Contractor to include this data will delay the review of the submittal until the Contracting Officer is in receipt of the missing data:

1. The proposed number of working days per week.

2. The holidays to be observed during the life of the contract (by day, month, and year).

3. The planned number of shifts per day.

4. The number of hours per shift.

5. The major construction equipment to be used on the site.

C. To the extent that the arrow diagram or any revised arrow diagram shows anything not jointly agreed upon, it shall not be deemed to have been approved by the Contracting Officer. Failure to include any element of work required for the performance of this contract shall not excuse the Contractor from completing all work required within any applicable completion date of each phase regardless of the Contracting Officer's approval of the arrow diagram.

D. Diskette Requirements and CPM Activity Record Specifications: Submit to the VA a 5-1/4 diskette(s) containing one file of the data required to produce an I-J computer-produced schedule, reflecting all the activities of the interim arrow diagram or complete project arrow diagram being submitted. Produce the file in the format specified and shown.

E. Diskette Format:
Only the following industry standard 5-1/4 diskettes, formatted using the MS-DOS operating system, are acceptable; in order of preference:

Double sided, high density, 96 TPI, 1.2 megabytes
Double sided, dual density, 48 TPI, 360K bytes
Double sided, 9-sectors per track, 40 tracks, 360K bytes
Double sided, 8-sectors per track, 40 tracks, 320K bytes
Single sided, 9-sectors per track, 40 tracks, 180K bytes
Single sided, 8-sectors per track, 40 tracks, 160K bytes

F. Exterior Label Information:
Provide the following information on an external label attached to the diskette(s):

1. VA project number and project location

2. Name and telephone number of a point of contact, preferably the person who created the diskette.

3. Version number of the MS-DOS operating system used to create the diskette.

G. File Requirements:

1. Use the MS-DOS COPY command to create the file.

2. Use "VACPM.DAT" as the destination filename.

3. Use the /A qualifier with the source filename to cause the file to be treated as an ASCII text file.

4. Write all 80-byte, fixed length, records to one file. Records can be written to the file in any sequence as they will eventually be sorted for VA CPM processing.

H. Data Record Specifications:

Enter each activity as either a Work Activty or a Dummy Activity, but not both (see Record Type "1" specifications). If the Work Activity has any Manpower greater than zero, generate a Record Type "4" record. If the Work Activity has Cost greater than zero, generate a Record Type "5" record. The total number of Work and Dummy activities (Record Type "1") will not exceed 32,000 activities.

1. Work Activity Record:

Pos.	Field Name	Data Requirements
1–5	Blank	Fill with spaces
6	Contract Code	Alpha character if multiple contract; else a space
7–11	I Node	Numeric, right justify, left zero fill; cannot = 00000 or 99999
12–16	J Node	Numeric, right justify, left zero fill; cannot = 00000 or 99999
17–21	Blank	Fill with spaces
22–24	Duration	Numeric, right justify, left zero fill
25–29	Trade or Responsibility	Alpha-numeric, left justify, right space fill
30–34	Area	Alpha-numeric, left justify, right space fill
35–37	Blank	Fill with spaces
38–72	Description	Alpha-numeric, left justify, right space fill
73–79	Blank	Fill with spaces
80	Record Type Code	Insert character "1"

2. Activity Manpower Record (if Manpower > 0):

Pos.	Field Name	Data Requirements
1-6	Blank	Fill with spaces
7–11	I Node	Numeric, right justify, left zero fill
12–16	J Node	Numeric, right justify, left zero fill
17–76	Blank	Fill with spaces
77–79	Manpower	Numeric, right justify, left zero fill
80	Record Type Code	Insert character "4"

3. Actvity Cost Record (if Cost > 0):

Pos.	Field Name	Data Requirements
1–6	Blank	Fill with spaces
7–11	I Node	Numeric, right justify, left zero fill
12–16	J Node	Numeric, right justify, left zero fill
17–18	Blank	Fill with spaces
19–28	Cost Amount	Numeric [9(8)V99], right justify (allowing positions 27 and 28 for cents), left zero fill dollars and zero fill cents if not available.
29–79	Blank	Fill with spaces
80	Record Type Code	Insert character "5"

4. Restraint or Dummy Activity (not a Work Activity):

Pos.	Field Name	Data Requirements
1–5	Blank	Fill with spaces
6	Contract Code	Alpha character if multiple contract; else a space
7–11	I Node	Numeric, right justify, left zero fill; cannot = 00000 or 99999
12–16	J Node	Numeric, right justify, left zero fill; cannot = 00000 or 99999
17–37	Blank	Fill with spaces
38	Restraint or Dummy Indicater	Insert character "<" (less than sign)
39–79	Blank	Fill with spaces
80	Record Type Code	Insert character "1"

1.9 PAYMENT TO THE CONTRACTOR

A. The monthly submission of the Veterans Administration "Look-Ahead Report" showing updated activities and cost data in accordance with the provisions of the following Payment and Progress Reporting is the basis upon which progress payments will be made pursuant to Article, PAYMENT UNDER FIXED-PRICE CONSTRUCTION CONTRACTS (VAAR 852.236-83) of Section GENERAL CONDITIONS. The Contractor is entitled to progress payment upon approval of estimates as determined from the currently approved updated computer-produced calendar-dated schedule unless, in special situation, the Contracting Officer permits an exception to this requirement.

B. When the Contractor fails or refuses to furnish the information and CPM Data, which, in the sole judgment of the Contracting Officer, is necessary for processing the computer-produced calendar-dated schedules, the Contractor shall not be deemed to have provided an estimate upon which progress payment may be made.

1.10 PAYMENT AND PROGRESS REPORTING

A. Monthly job site progress meetings shall be held on dates mutually agreed to by the Contracting Officer (or Contracting Officer's representative) and the Contractor. Contractor and the CPM consultant will be required to attend all monthly progress meetings. Presence of Subcontractors during progress meeting is optional unless required by the Contracting Officer (or Contracting Officer's representative). The Contractor shall complete their copy of the "look-ahead report" and all other data required by this section shall be accurately filled in and completed prior to the monthly progress meeting. The Contractor shall provide this information to the Contracting Officer or the VA representative in completed form three work days in advance of the progress meeting. Job progress will be reviewed to verify:

1. Actual finish dates for completed activities.

2. Remaining duration, required to complete each activity started, or scheduled to start, but not completed.

3. Logic, time and cost data for change orders, and supplemental agreements that are to be incorporated into the arrow diagram and computer-produced schedules. Changes in activity sequence and durations which have been made pursuant to the provisions of following Article, ADJUSTMENT OF CONTRACT COMPLETION.

4. Percentage for completed and partially completed activities.

5. Logic and duration revisions required by this section of the specifications.

B. The Contractor shall submit a narrative report as a part of his monthly review and update, in a form agreed upon by the Contractor and the Contracting Officer. The narrative report shall include a description of problem areas; current and anticipated delaying factors and their estimated impact on performance of other activities and completion dates; and an explanation of corrective action taken or proposed. This report is in addition to the daily reports pursuant to the provisions of

Article, DAILY REPORT OF WORKER AND MATERIAL in the GENERAL CONDITIONS.

C. After completion of the joint review and the Contracting Officer's Approval of all entries, the VA will generate an updated computer-produced calendar-dated schedule and supply the Contractor with reports in accordance with the Article, COMPUTER PRODUCED SCHEDULES, specified.

D. After each monthly update, the Contractor shall submit to the Contracting Officer three blue line copies of a revised complete arrow diagram showing all completed and partially completed activities, contract changes and logic changes made on the subject update. Monthly updates using the interim arrow diagram are exempted from this requirement.

1.11 RESPONSIBILITY FOR COMPLETION

A. Whenever it becomes apparent from the current monthly progress review meeting or the monthly computer-produced calendar-dated schedule that phasing or contract completion dates will not be met, the Contractor shall execute some or all of the following remedial actions:

1. Increase construction manpower in such quantities and crafts as necessary to eliminate the backlog of work.

2. Increase the number of working hours per shift, shifts per working day, working days per week, the amount of construction equipment, or any combination of the foregoing to eliminate the backlog of work.

3. Reschedule the work in conformance with the specification requirements.

B. Prior to proceeding with any of the above actions, the Contractor shall notify and obtain approval from the Contracting Officer for the proposed schedule changes. If such actions are approved, the CPM revisions shall be incorporated by the Contractor into the arrow diagram before the next update, at no additional cost to the Government.

1.12 CHANGES TO ARROW DIAGRAM AND SCHEDULE

A. Within 30 calendar days after receipt of any computer-produced schedule, the Contractor will submit a revised arrow diagram and a (I-J) list of any activity changes for any of the following reasons:

1. Delay in completion of any activity or group of activities, indicate an extension of the project completion by 20 working days or 10 percent of the remaining project duration,

whichever is less. Such delays which may be involved with contract changes, strikes, unusual weather, and other delays will not relieve the Contractor from the requirements specified unless the conditions are shown on the CPM as the direct cause for delaying the project beyond the acceptable limits.

2. Delays in submittals, or deliveries, or work stoppage are encountered which make replanning or rescheduling of the work necessary.

3. The schedule does not represent the actual prosecution and progress of the project.

4. Activity costs are revised as the result of contract modifications.

B. CPM revisions made under this paragraph which affect the previously approved computer-produced schedules for Government furnished equipment, vacating of areas by the VA Medical Center, contract phase(s) and sub phase(s), utilities furnished by the Government to the Contractor, or any other previously contracted item, must be furnished in writing to the Contracting Officer for approval.

C. Contracting Officer's approval for the revised arrow diagram and all relevant data is contingent upon compliance with all other paragraphs of this section and any other previous agreements by the Contracting Officer or the VA representative.

D. The cost of revisions to the arrow diagram resulting from contract changes will be included in the proposal for changes in work as specified in Article, CHANGES of the GENERAL CONDITIONS, and will be based on the complexity of the revision or contract change, man hours expended in analyzing the change, and the total cost of the change.

E. The cost of revisions to the arrow diagram not resulting from contract changes is the responsibility of the Contractor.

1.13   ADJUSTMENT OF CONTRACT COMPLETION

A. The contract completion time will be adjusted only for causes specified in this contract. Request for an extension of the contract completion date by the Contractor shall be supported with a justification, CPM data and supporting evidence as the Contracting Officer may deem necessary for determination as to whether or not the Contractor is entitled to an extension of time under the provisions of the contract. Submission of proof based on revised activity logic durations and costs is obligatory to any approvals. The schedule must clearly display that the schedule has used, in full, all the float time available for the work involved in this request. The Contracting Officer's determination as to the total number of days of contract extension will be based upon the current computer-produced calendar-dated schedule for the time period in question and all other relevaent information. Actual delays in activities which, according to the computer-produced calendar-dated schedule, do not affect the extended and predicted contract completion dates shown by the critical path in the network, will not be the basis for a change to the contract completion date. The Contracting Officer will within a reasonable time after receipt of such justification and supporting evidence, review the facts and advise the Contractor in writing of the Contracting Officer's decision.

B. The Contractor shall submit each request for a change in the contract completion date to the Contracting Officer in accordance with provisions specified under Article, CHANGES, in the Section, GENERAL CONDITIONS. The Contractor shall include, as a part of each change order proposal, a sketch showing all CPM logic revisions, duration changes, and cost changes, for work in question and its relationship to other activities on the approved arrow diagram.

END

UNITED STATES POSTAL SERVICE SPECIFICATION, SECTION 01030— SCHEDULING AND PROGRESS

1.04 *Contractor-Prepared Network Analysis System:* The progress chart to be prepared by the contractor pursuant to Clause 11-23, *Construction Progress Chart,* of the general contract clauses shall consist of a network analysis system as described hereinafter. In preparing this system, the scheduling of construction is the responsibility of the contractor. The requirement for the system is included to assure adequate planning and execution of the work and to assist the contracting officer in appraising the reasonableness of the proposed schedule and evaluating progress of the work. The system shall consist of diagrams and accompanying mathematical analyses.

A. Diagrams shall show the order and interdependence of activities and the sequence in which the work is to be accomplished as planned by the contractor. The basic concept of a network analysis diagram will be followed to show how the start of a given activity is dependent on the completion of preceding activities and its completion restricts the start of the following activities. In all cases, the project completion date (calendar date) shall be shown on the diagrams as the latest completion date of all activities.

B. The detailed network activities shall include, in addition to construction activities, the submittal and approval of samples of materials and shop drawings, the procurement of critical materials and equipment, and fabrication of special materials and equipment and their installation and testing. All activities of the Postal Service that affect progress and contract required dates for completion of all or parts of the work will be shown.

The activities which comprise the following separate buildings and features shall be separately identifiable by coding or use of subnetworks or both.

Building or Feature	Minimum Number of Activities
Process Mail Building	250
Vehicle Maintenance	40
Site Work	70
Mechanization	50

C. The selection and number of activities shall be subject to the contracting officer's approval. Detailed networks shall be drafted to show a continuous flow from left to right with no arrows from right to left. The following information shall be shown on the diagram for each activity, preceding the following event numbers: description of the activity, cost, activity duration, and manpower requirements in man-days.

D. Summary Bar Chart: A summary bar chart, provided on a 30″x42″ sheet, shall consist of a minimum of thirty activities and shall be based on and supported by detailed diagrams. The summary bar chart shall be time-scaled, using units of approximately one-half inch equals one week or other suitable scale approved by the contracting officer. Weekends and holidays shall be indicated.

E. The mathematical analysis of the network diagram shall include a tabulation of each activity. The following information will be furnished as a minimum for each activity:

1. Preceding and following event numbers;

2. Activity description;

3. Estimated duration of activities in calendar days;

4. Earliest finish date (by calendar date);

5. Actual start date (by calendar date);

6. Actual finish date (by calendar date);

7. Latest start date (by calendar date);

8. Latest finish date (by calendar date);

9. Slack or float;

10. Monetary value of activity with a labor and material cost breakdown;

11. Percentage of activity completed;

12. Contractor's earnings based on portion of activity completed; and

13. Manpower requirements in man-days.

F. The program or means used in making the mathematical computation shall be capable of compiling the total value of completed and partially completed activities and subtotals from separate buildings or features listed in paragraph 1.04B of this section.

G. The analysis shall list the activities in sorts or groups as follows:

1. By the preceding event number, from lowest to highest, then in the order of the following event number;

2. By the amount of slack, then in order of preceding event number;

3. By responsibility in order of earliest allowance start date; and

4. In order of latest allowable start dates, then in order of preceding event numbers, then in order of succeeding even numbers.

H. Submission and approval of the system shall be as follows:

1. A preliminary network defining the contractor's planned operations during the first 90 calendar days after receipt of notice to proceed will be submitted at the preconstruction conference after receipt of notice to proceed.

2. The complete network analysis consisting of the detailed network mathematical analysis, schedule of anticipated earnings as of the last day of each month, and network diagrams shall be submitted within 60 calendar days after receipt of notice to proceed.

I. The contractor shall participate in a review and evaluation of the proposed network diagrams and analysis by the contracting officer. Any revisions necessary as a result of this review shall be resubmitted for approval of the contracting officer within 10 calendar days after the conference. The approved schedule shall then be the schedule to be used by the contractor for planning, organizing and directing the work, reporting progress, and requesting payment for work accomplished. Thereafter, if the contractor desires to make changes in his method of operating and scheduling, the contractor shall notify the contracting officer in writing stating the reasons for the change. If the contracting officer considers these changes to be of a major nature, the contracting officer may require the contractor to revise and submit for approval, without additional cost to the Postal Service, all of the affected portion of the detailed diagrams and mathematical analysis to show the effect on the entire project. A change may be considered of a major nature if the time estimated to be required or actually used for an activity or the logic of sequence of activities is varied from the original plan to a degree that there is a reasonable doubt as to the effect on the contract completion date or dates. Changes that affect activities with adequate slack time shall be considered as minor changes, except that an accumulation of minor changes may be considered a major change when their cumulative effect might affect the contract completion date.

J.   The contractor shall submit at monthly intervals a report of the actual construction progress by updating the mathematical analysis. Entering of updating information into the mathematical analysis will be subject to approval of the contracting officer.

K.   The report shall show the activities or portion of activities completed during the reporting period and their total value as basis for the contractor's periodic request for payment. Payment made pursuant to the general contract clause, *Payments,* will be based on the total value of such activities or partially completed after verification by the contracting officer. The report will state the percentage of the work actually completed and scheduled as of the report date and the progress along the critical path in terms of days ahead or behind the allowable dates. If the project is behind schedule, progress along other paths with negative slack shall also be reported. The contractor shall also submit a narrative report with the updated analysis which shall include, but not be limited to, a description of the problem areas, current and anticipated delaying factors and their impact, and an explanation of corrective actions taken or proposed.

L.   Sheet size of diagrams shall be 30"x42". Each updated copy shall show a date of the latest revision.

M.   Initial submittal and complete revisions shall be submitted in three copies.

N.   Periodic reports shall be submitted in two copies.

O.   Network analysis system revisions occurring as a result of modifications or changes in the work will be in accordance with the provisions of Clause OB-246, *Network Analysis Systems Update (Construction)*.

P. Float or slack is defined as the amount of time between the early start date and the late start date of any of the activities in the network analysis system schedule. Float or slack time is not time for the exclusive use of or benefit of either the Postal Service or the contractor. Extensions of time for performance required under the general contract clauses entitled, *Changes, Differing Site Conditions, Termination for Default—Damages for Contractor Delay—Time Extensions, or Suspension of Work* will be granted only to the extent that equitable time adjustments for the activity or activities affected exceed the total float or slack along the channels involved at the time notice to proceed was issued for the change.

Q. The contractor will be paid for preparation, revision, and update of the network analysis system in accordance with the price schedule in Section A, Items and Prices, and payment schedule in Section F, Payment and Funding of the Contract.

APPENDIX F

MODEL SCHEDULING SPECIFICATION

As a guide to the type of information that should be included in a construction scheduling specification, the following is presented for review, discussion, and future consideration. This model specification is based on a situation in which a single general contractor is responsible for project completion and is contractually required to prepare a CPM schedule that meets the owner's approval.

GENERAL

1. Pursuant to Articles _____ of the General Provisions, the general contractor shall prepare and maintain a detailed progress schedule as described below. This schedule shall be the contractor's working schedule and shall be used to plan, organize, and execute the work, record and report actual performance and progress, and show how the general contractor plans to complete all remaining work as of the end of each progress report period. The schedule shall be in the form of an activity on arrow (I-J format) oriented network diagram (Critical Path Method) and the principles and definition of the terms used herein shall be as set forth in the Associated General Contractors of America (AGC) publication *The Use of CPM in Construction,* copyright 1976. In the event of discrepancies, this section shall govern the development and utilization of the CPM schedule.

2. A pre-bid conference shall be held at a time, date, and place to be determined later, to review with prospective bidders, how this section shall be implemented and to answer any questions regarding the scheduling and reporting requirements and the degree of participation, cooperation, and compliance that shall be required of the successful contractor.

Initial Timetable

Upon receipt of notice to proceed, the general contractor shall promptly prepare a Detailed Project Schedule in the form of a network diagram and shall submit the same for approval by the owner within thirty (30) calendar days after notice to proceed. Limited technical assistance is available to the general contractor upon written request and prior to any formal review and/or finalization of the initial schedule. Pre-submittal reviews are also available to facilitate coordination of the contractor's schedule with other preceding, parallel, and succeeding contracts.

Network Details

1. The Detailed Project Schedule for this contract shall be constructed to show the order in which the general contractor proposes to carry out the work, and to indicate the restrictions of access and availability of work areas and the availability and use of manpower, materials and equipment. The contractor shall utilize the Detailed Project Schedule in planning, scheduling, coordinating, and performing the work under this contract (including all activities of subcontractors, equipment vendors, and suppliers). The following criteria shall form the basis for assembly of the logic:

   a. What activity *must* be completed before a subsequent activity can be started?

   b. What activities *can* be done concurrently?

   c. What activity *must* be started immediately following a completed activity?

   d. What *major* economic facility or manpower restrictions are required for sequencing these activities?

2. The Detailed Project Schedule shall provide sufficient detail and clarity of form and technique so that the contractor can plan, schedule, monitor, control, and report on the progress of his work. In addition, it shall provide the owner with a tool to monitor and follow the progress for all phases of the work. The Detailed Project Schedule shall comply with the various limits imposed by the scope of work and by any contractually specified intermediate milestone and completion dates included in the contract. The degree of detail shall be to the satisfaction of the owner, but the following factors shall have a bearing on the required depth of activity detail:

   a. The physical and structural breakdown of the project;

   b. The contract milestones and completion dates;

   c. The type of work to be performed and the labor trades involved;

   d. All purchase, manufacture, and delivery activities for all major materials and equipment;

e. Deliveries of owner-furnished equipment and/or materials;

f. Preparation, submittal, and approval of shop and/or working drawings and material samples;

g. Approvals required by regulatory agencies or other third parties;

h. Plans for all subcontract work;

i. Assignment of responsibility for performing specific activities;

j. Access to and availability of work areas;

k. Identification of interfaces and dependencies with preceding, concurrent, and follow-on contractors;

l. Actual tests, submission of test reports, and approval of test results;

m. Planning for phased or total takeover by owner;

n. Identification of any manpower, material or equipment restrictions.

3. The activities included in the Detailed Project Schedule shall be analyzed in detail to determine activity time durations in units of project working days. Durations shall be based on the labor (crafts), equipment, and materials required to perform each activity on a normal work-day basis. Activity durations over 15 working days shall be kept to a minimum except in the case of nonconstruction activities such as procurement of materials, delivery of equipment, and concrete curing. All durations shall be the result of definitive manpower and resource planning by the contractor to perform the work in consideration of contractually defined on-site work conditions. The manpower to be assigned, by craft definition, shall be shown on each construction activity of the network. No more than five (5) crafts may be assigned to a specific activity. If more crafts are required, then the activity in question must be broken down into additional activities.

4. The contractor may use manpower or equipment restraints, separately noted, to optimize and level manpower and equipment requirements. The individual activities involved may be sequenced within the limits of the available total float. However, when this leveling technique is used in establishing the initial schedule, it shall be reflected in the logic with restraints identified as "restraint—for manpower or equipment leveling purposes only." Critical or near-critical paths resulting from the use of manpower restraints shall be kept to a minimum. Near-critical paths shall be defined as those

paths having 14 days or less of total float at the time of initial submission.

5. A unique event numbering system shall be required to code or identify activities by bid items, work items, areas, procurement, etc. No two activities shall have the same two event numbers for identification.

6. The estimated cost to perform each work activity shall be noted graphically on each activity included in the network. The sum of the costs assigned to all activities shall equal the contract value. No activity costs shall be assigned to manufacture or delivery activities.

7. The networks shall be prepared on (F) size sheets and shall have a title block in the lower right-hand corner. Exceptions to the size of the network sheets and the use of computer graphics to generate the networks shall be subject to the approval of the owner.

8. The networks shall clearly indicate all contract milestones and completion dates. All networks shall be drafted to show a continuous flow of information from left to right with no arrows from right to left. The primary path(s) of criticality shall be clearly and graphically identified on the network(s). Each network drawing shall have a standard grid coordinate system with alfa designations on the Y axis (top to bottom) and numerical designations on the X axis (left to right) for quick activity reference and for following the planned sequence when using multi-sheet networks. Logic ties which cannot be graphically demonstrated as continuous restraints between different segments of the network shall be identified as remote dummies, and shall be referenced as "to/or from event number _____, page number _____," followed by appropriate alpha, numeric grid references, or equivalent designation. See Attachment A for examples of how to present remote dummies.

9. As part of each update submission, the status of work in progress shall also be similarly identified and the reported percent complete graphically indicated on each activity remaining in progress as of the last report period.

Use of Computers

1. The mathematical analysis of the Detailed Project Schedule shall be made by computer and a tabulation for each activity shall include as a minimum the following:

   a. Preceding (i) and following (j) event numbers;

   b. Activity description;

c. Activity code(s);

d. Schedule and actual/remaining durations for each activity;

e. Earliest start date (by calendar date);

f. Earliest finish date (by calendar date);

g. Actual start date (by calendar date);

h. Actual finish date (by calendar date);

i. Latest start date (by calendar date);

j. Latest finish date (by calendar date);

k. Float in work days;

l. Monetary value of each activity;

m. Percentage of activity completed;

n. Contractor's earnings based on the reported portion of activity completed.

The computer programs used in making the mathematical computation shall be capable of compiling the total value of completed and partially completed activities. The program shall also be capable of accepting revised completion dates as modified by approved time adjustments and recomputation of all activity dates and float accordingly.

2. The following computer outputs shall be required as part of the initial schedule submission and each update thereafter:

a. Activity sort by preceding event number from lowest to highest and then in the order of the following event number;

b. Activity sort by the amount of total float, then in order of preceding event number;

c. Activity sort by early start for the next sixty (60) calendar days, then in order of preceding event number;

d. Activity sort by late finish for the next sixty (60) calendar days, then in order of preceding event number;

e. Activity sort(s) by organizational responsibility.

Outputs (a) and (b) above shall show all activities, including restraints for the duration of the project.

Master Summary Schedule

The contractor shall also prepare and submit a time-scaled Master Summary Schedule on a single sheet that shows the total project in approximately 50 to 100 activities. This schedule will accurately summarize the computerized Detailed Project Schedule and shall have common events for correlating the two levels of schedule indenture. Emphasis shall be placed on major milestones and key dependencies among the various parties involved. The Master Summary Schedule shall be updated monthly.

Cash Flow Projection

Using the cost assigned to each activity of the Detailed Project Schedule, the contractor shall develop a cash flow analysis illustrated by a computer listing and a graphic display, both of which shall depict the estimated cash drawdown in the aggregate, by month, over the life of the project. The cash flow projection shall be updated each month to show actual cash drawdown and a forecast of remaining payments to be made over the remaining life of the project.

Manpower Requirements Forecast

The contractor shall prepare a manpower analysis in the form of a series of graphic displays depicting manpower by principal trades in the aggregate, and in accordance with the Detailed Project Schedule. The graphs shall display the number of man-days of effort, for each month, over the life of the project. This submission may be computerized or manually prepared, but shall be correlated with the manpower assigned to each activity of the Detailed Project Schedule. The Manpower Requirements Forecast shall be updated monthly and shall include the manpower actually used by trade as of the current report period and the manpower required to complete all remaining contract work.

Submittals

1. The Detailed Project Schedule (logic diagrams and computer tabulations), the Master Summary Schedule, the Cash Flow Projection, and the Manpower Requirements Forecast shall be submitted to the owner for approval within thirty (30) calendar days after notice to proceed in the following quantities:
   a. Detailed and Summary Schedules (reproducible and 5 sets of prints);
   b. Computer tabulations (5 copies 8 1/2"x11" in size);
   c. Manpower Requirements Forecast (5 copies 8 1/2"x11" in size);
   d. Cash Flow Projections (5 copies 8 1/2"x11" in size).

2. In addition to the above, the contractor shall provide a copy of its computer file in the form of a hard or floppy disk. The disk shall include the information contained in the schedule submittal. If additional submittals are necessary, a disk for each submittal shall be provided by the contractor.

Approval Process

1. The owner shall approve or disapprove, in writing, the contractor's submission within fifteen (15) calendar days after receipt of all required information.

2. If the contractor fails to submit the initial Detailed Project Schedule, Master Summary Schedule, Manpower Requirements Forecast, Cash Flow Projection, or the computer disk within the time prescribed, or revisions thereof within the requested time, the owner may withhold approval of progress payment estimates until such time as the contractor submits the required information.

3. At the request of the owner or its authorized representative, the contractor shall be required to participate in any meetings necessary to reach a mutual agreement and approval of the initial Detailed Project Schedule, Master Summary Schedule, Manpower Requirements Forecast, Cash Flow Projections, or the computer disk.

4. If any of the required submissions are returned to the contractor for corrections or revisions, they shall be resubmitted along with a new computer disk for approval within ten (10) calendar days after the return mailing date. Resubmittals shall be in the same quantities as noted above. Review and response by the owner shall be given within ten (10) calendar days after receipt of each new submission.

Updatings

1. The initial updating shall take place during the first week after the approval of the contractor's schedule. Subsequent updates shall be scheduled at the beginning of each month thereafter for the duration of the contract. The Detailed Project Schedule and computer tabulations shall be reviewed jointly at a meeting with the owner's authorized representative for the purpose of verifying:

    a. Actual start dates;

    b. Actual completion dates;

    c. Cost value of work reported in place;

d. Activity percent completion;

e. Revised logic (as-built and projected) and changes in activity durations, cost, and manpower assigned;

f. Influence of change orders;

g. Revisions due to unauthorized modifications;

h. Incorporation of approved time extensions. The owner shall inform the contractor of the date, time, and place of each updating.

2. The contractor shall come to the updating meetings with the above data prepared in advance for each meeting to provide, as of the end of the updating period, a complete and accurate report of current procurement and construction progress and a depiction of how the contractor plans to continue the work of this project to meet all contract completion dates. All network changes and status data agreed to during each update shall be considered as acceptable by both parties unless written notice of any exceptions is given by an objecting party within ten (10) calendar days after receipt of the contractor's update submission. For major network changes that cannot be agreed to during an updating meeting, the contractor shall submit, in writing, such revisions for the owner's approval prior to inserting such changes into the network. Submissions may be in the form of marked-up networks, fragnets, or schedule abstracts, provided they are submitted with a letter of transmittal. The submission and approval procedures for this information shall follow the same timetable described for *Change Orders, Delays, and Time Extensions* noted below.

3. As part of the monthly updating process, the contractor shall prepare a Narrative Progress Report describing the physical progress during the report period, plans for continuing the work during the forthcoming report period, actions planned to correct any negative float predictions, and an explanation of potential delays and/or problems and their estimated impact on performance and the overall project completion date. In addition, alternatives for possible schedule recovery to mitigate any potential delay and/or cost increases should be included for consideration by the owner.

4. Five copies each of the Narrative Progress Report, the updated Detailed Project Schedule (networks, and computer computations), the Summary Master Schedule, the Cash Flow Projection, the Manpower Requirements Forecast, and an updated computer disk shall be submitted to the owner within five (5) calendar days after each updating meeting.

5. If the contractor fails to timely submit any of the update deliverables, the owner may withhold approval of progress payment estimates until such time as the contractor submits the required update reports.

Change Orders, Delays, and Time Extensions

1. When change orders or delays are experienced by the contractor and the contractor requests an extension of time, the contractor shall submit to the owner a written Time Impact Analysis illustrating the influence of each change or delay on the current contract schedule completion date. Each Time Impact Analysis shall include a fragnet demonstrating how the contractor proposes to incorporate the change order or delay into the Detailed Project Schedule. A fragnet is defined as a sequence of new activities and/or activity revisions that are proposed to be added to the existing schedule to demonstrate the influence of delay and the method for incorporating delays and impacts into the schedule as they are encountered.

2. Each analysis shall demonstrate the estimated time impact based on the events of delay, the date the change was given to the contractor, the status of construction at that point in time, and the event time computation of all activities effected by the change or delay. The event times used in the analysis shall be those included in the latest update of the Detailed Project Schedule or as adjusted for the events of delay.

3. Time extensions will be granted only to the extent that equitable time adjustments for the activity or activities affected exceed the total or remaining float along the path of activities at the time of actual delay or at the time notice to proceed was issued for a change. Each Time Impact Analysis shall be submitted in triplicate and within fifteen (15) calendar days after a delay occurs or notice of direction for proceeding with a change order is given to the contractor. In cases where the contractor does not submit a Time Impact Analysis for a specific change order or delay within the specified period of time, it shall be deemed to have irrevocably waived its rights to any additional time and cost.

4. Approval or rejection of each Time Impact Analysis by the owner shall be made within fifteen (15) calendar days after receipt of each Time Impact Analysis, unless subsequent meetings and negotiations are necessary. Upon approval, a copy of a Time Impact Analysis signed by the owner or its authorized representative shall be returned to the contractor for incorporation into the schedule.

5. Upon mutual agreement by both parties, fragnets illustrating the influence of change orders and delays shall be incorporated into the Detailed Project Schedule during the first update after agreement is reached.

6. In the event the contractor does not agree with the decision of the owner regarding the impact of a change or delay, it shall be resolved in accordance with the disputes clause of the contract.

APPENDIX G

EXCERPT FROM VETERANS ADMINISTRATION VACPM HANDBOOK PART VI—CONTRACT CHANGES AND TIME EXTENSIONS

CPM procedures for entering Supplemental Agreements, Change Orders and Time Extensions are basically the same. Likewise, the CPM analysis of their impact on the project schedule is similar. Such procedures are easily followed for relatively simple problems and can be easily accomplished in the field. If the contract changes are complex or involve extensive CPM analysis, it is advisable to request assistance from the VACPM staff.

1. *Entering and Developing CPM Input for Contract Changes*—Supplemental Agreement CPM information is obtained from the contractor's proposal for the changed work. Change Order data is normally developed by the resident engineer in conjunction with the contractor. Time Extension data is included in the contractor's request for time justification. However, all three must follow the same basic guidelines for preparation.

   a. The scope of changed or affected work is reviewed to determine where and how the CPM revisions should be incorporated.

   b. The activity revisions and additions are sketched on the current network. There are two basic types of logic entries:

      (1) The simultaneous work activity is associated with changed work that will be performed by additional work forces. It is shown as being parallel work with one or more existing activities on the network.

         Example:

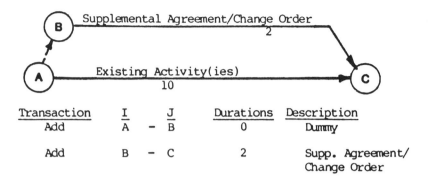

Transaction	I	J	Durations	Description
Add	A – B		0	Dummy
Add	B – C		2	Supp. Agreement/ Change Order

(2) The sequential work activity is associated with changed work that will be performed by existing work forces. It is shown as sequential work that is inserted in series with an existing chain of work activities.

Example:

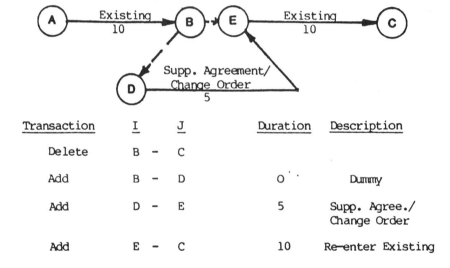

Transaction	I	J	Duration	Description
Delete	B – C			
Add	B – D		0	Dummy
Add	D – E		5	Supp. Agree./ Change Order
Add	E – C		10	Re-enter Existing

c. The logic revisions should include separate activities for each involved trade and must be associated with existing activities on the network. If it occurs in more than one work area, separate activities will be required for each involved area.

d. The technique used to display the changed work should be in keeping with the data format capabilities of the VACPM System. Numbering trades, areas, and descriptions must be compatible with the data sorting requirements of the specific project.

e. In addition to those activities required to describe the delay, network revisions may also be necessary. These changes include all the modifications and adjustments to the schedule for directly and indirectly related work as a result of the delay or change in work.

2. *CPM Time Analysis on Contract Changes*—The affect that changes or delays have on a CPM schedule is determined by a comparison of the schedules before and after the delaying activities are incorporated into the CPM Network. If such a comparison indicates that the predicted completion date will be affected, the contractor may or may not be entitled to additional contract time. Normally, the contractor is entitled to additional contract time only if the scheduled completion is delayed beyond the extended contract completion date.

    a. *Computer Analysis*—The VACPM staff and/or CPM consultant must make the schedule analysis which requires the use of the computer. The computer is used when the time analysis is complex or when there are numerous change activities which must be considered. This type of analysis is the only feasible method which can be used to accurately determine cumulative and concurrent delays on a schedule.

    b. *Manual Analysis*—The contractor and resident engineer can normally make this analysis. The following procedures are followed to make a manual time analysis: (See Examples 1h and 1i . . . [on the following pages], which show the appropriate calculations:

        (1) The changed work or delay is reviewed and the activities are drawn on the network or scratch sheets similar to the samples. The portion of the network under analysis should start with the existing activity immediately prior to the delay activity(s) and finish with the existing activity immediately following the delayed work.

        (2) Using the CPM schedules with an as-of-date immediately before the time the problem was encountered:

            (a) The float for the existing activities is marked on the sketch.

            (b) The predicted and extended contract completion dates are compared and the number of workdays ahead or behind are determined.

        (3) Two manual "forward pass" calculations are made and compared to see if project duration has changed.

            (a) The first manual pass is made on the existing activity network without any consideration for the changed work or delay activities.

SAME WORK FORCE—SEQUENTIAL LOGIC

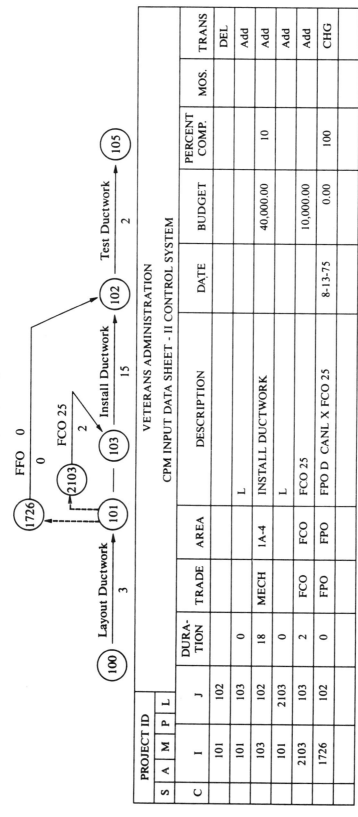

VETERANS ADMINISTRATION

CPM INPUT DATA SHEET - II CONTROL SYSTEM

| PROJECT ID | | | | | | | | | | | |
| S | A | M | P | L | | | | | | | |

C	I	J	DURA-TION	TRADE	AREA		DESCRIPTION	DATE	BUDGET	PERCENT COMP.	MOS.	TRANS
	101	102										DEL
	101	103	0			L						Add
	103	102	18	MECH	1A-4		INSTALL DUCTWORK		40,000.00	10		Add
	101	2103	0			L						Add
	2103	103	2	FCO	FCO		FCO 25		10,000.00			Add
	1726	102	0	FPO	FPO		FPO D CANL X FCO 25	8-13-75	0.00	100		CHG

TIME EXTENSION ANALYSIS

ACTIVITY 101 – 102 = 10 DAYS FLOAT (AS OF 26 JUL '75)

1. MANUAL FORWARD PASS W/O CHANGE ORDER = 20 + 10 = 30
2.   "   WITH FCO-25 = 22   (30 – 22 = 8) = NO TIME
3. ACTIVITY FLOAT (FCO-25) = 30 – 22 = 8
4. TOTAL CONTRACT FLOAT (FCO-25) = 8 – 2 = 10

PREDICTED CONTRACT COMPL. = 9- 7-78
EXTENDED CONTRACT COMPL. = 9-11-78
WORK DAYS AHEAD =   +2

NO CONTRACT TIME

EXAMPLE F 1h-1

ADDITIONAL WORK FORCE—PARALLEL LOGIC

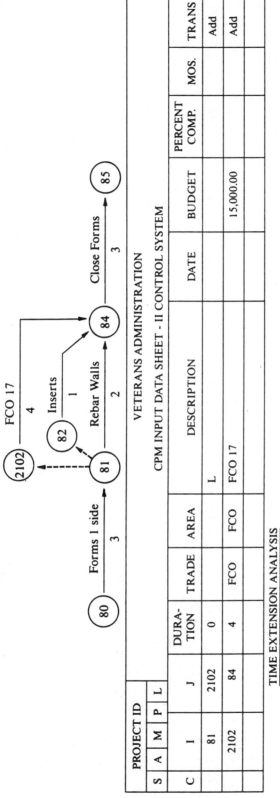

VETERANS ADMINISTRATION

CPM INPUT DATA SHEET - II CONTROL SYSTEM

PROJECT ID						DURA-TION	TRADE	AREA	DESCRIPTION	DATE	BUDGET	PERCENT COMP.	MOS.	TRANS
S	A	M	P	L										
C	I			J					L					Add
	81			2102		0								
	2102			84		4	FCO	FCO	FCO 17		15,000.00			Add

PREDICTED CONTRACT COMPL. = 9- 7-78
EXTENDED CONTRACT COMPL. = 9-11-78
WORK DAYS AHEAD = +2

TIME EXTENSION ANALYSIS

ACTIVITY 81 – 84 = 1 DAY FLOAT (AS OF 10 MAY '76)

1. MANUAL FORWARD PASS W/O CHANGE ORDER = 8 + 1 = 9
2. " " " WITH FCO-17 = 10
3. ACTIVITY FLOAT (FCO-17) = 9 – 10 = –1
4. TOTAL CONTRACT FLOAT (FCO-17) = –1 + 2 = +1 = NO TIME

NO CONTRACT TIME

EXAMPLE 1h-2

ADDITIONAL WORK FORCE—PARALLEL LOGIC

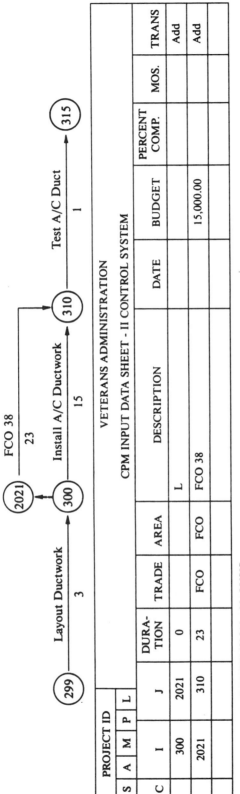

Network diagram:

299 → Layout Ductwork (3) → 300 → Install A/C Ductwork (15) → 310 → Test A/C Duct (1) → 315

300 → 2021 (FCO 38, 23)

2021 → 310

VETERANS ADMINISTRATION

CPM INPUT DATA SHEET - II CONTROL SYSTEM

PROJECT ID

S	A	M	P	L	C	I	J	DURA-TION	TRADE	AREA	DESCRIPTION	DATE	BUDGET	PERCENT COMP.	MOS.	TRANS
						300	2021	0			L					Add
						2021	310	23	FCO	FCO	FCO 38		15,000.00			Add

TIME EXTENSION ANALYSIS

ACTIVITY 300 − 310 = 2 DAYS FLOAT (AS OF 21 JUL '76)

1. MANUAL FORWARD PASS W/O CHANGE ORDER = 19 + 2 = 21
2. " " " WITH FCO-38 = 27
3. ACTIVITY FLOAT (FCO-38) = 21 − 27 = −6 = 6 WORK DAYS

PREDICTED CONTRACT COMPL. = 30 JAN 78
EXTENDED CONTRACT COMPL. = 26 JAN 78

WORK DAYS BEHIND = −2

6 WORK DAYS CONTRACT TIME = 8 CALENDAR DAYS TIME EXTENSION

EXAMPLE 1h-3

482

ADDITONAL WORK FORCE—PARALLEL LOGIC

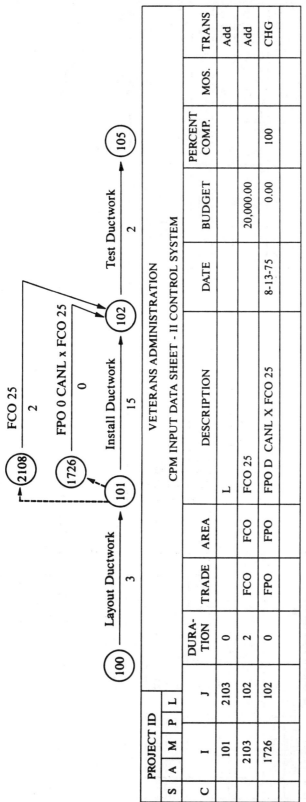

VETERANS ADMINISTRATION

CPM INPUT DATA SHEET - II CONTROL SYSTEM

PROJECT ID		
S	A M P L	

C	I	J	DURA-TION	TRADE	AREA	DESCRIPTION	DATE	BUDGET	PERCENT COMP.	MOS.	TRANS
	101	2103	0			L					Add
	2103	102	2	FCO	FCO	FCO 25		20,000.00			Add
	1726	102	0	FPO	FPO	FPO D CANL X FCO 25	8-13-75	0.00	100		CHG

FCO TIME EXTENSION ANALYSIS

ACTIVITY 101 – 102 = 10 DAYS FLOAT (AS OF JULY 26 '75)

1. MANUAL FORWARD PASS W/O CHANGE ORDER = 20 + 10 = 30
2. "   "   "   WITH FCO-25   = 7   (30 – 7 = 23) = NO TIME
3. TOTAL ACTIVITY FLOAT (FCO-25) = 25 – 2 = 23 DAYS
4. TOTAL CONTRACT FLOAT (FCO-25) = 23 + 2 = 25 DAYS

PREDICTED CONTRACT COMPL. = 9- 7-78
EXTENDED CONTRACT COMPL. = 9-11-78

WORK DAYS AHEAD   =   +2

NO CONTRACT TIME

EXAMPLE 1h-4

483

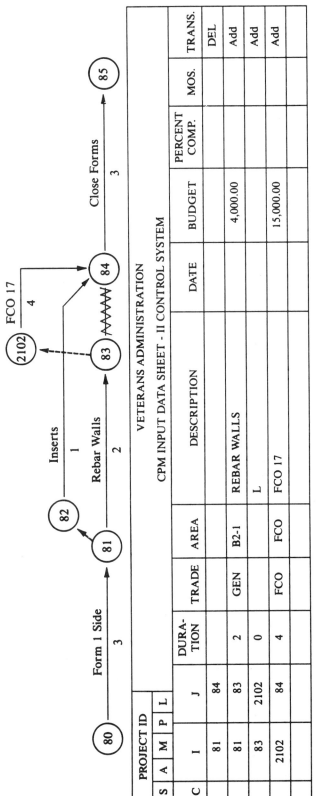

SAME WORK FORCE—SEQUENTIAL LOGIC

VETERANS ADMINISTRATION

CPM INPUT DATA SHEET - II CONTROL SYSTEM

PROJECT ID													
S	A	M	P	L									
C	I			J	DURA-TION	TRADE	AREA	DESCRIPTION	DATE	BUDGET	PERCENT COMP.	MOS.	TRANS.
	81			84									DEL
	81			83	2	GEN	B2-1	REBAR WALLS		4,000.00			Add
	83			2102	0			L					Add
	2102			84	4	FCO	FCO	FCO 17		15,000.00			Add

PREDICTED COMPLETION DATE = 9- 7-78
EXTENDED COMPLETION DATE = 9-11-78

WORK DAYS AHEAD = +2

TIME EXTENSION ANALYSIS

ACTIVITY 81 – 84 = 1 DAY FLOAT (AS OF 10 MAY '76)

1. MANUAL FORWARD PASS W/O CHANGE ORDER = 8 + 1 = 9
2. " " " WITH FCO-17 = 12
3. ACTIVITY FLOAT (FCO-17) = 9 – 12 = –3
4. TOTAL CONTRACT FLOAT (FCO-17) = –3 + 2 = –1 = 1 WORK DAY

1 WORK DAY CONTRACT TIME = 1 CALENDAR DAY TIME EXTENSION

EXAMPLE 1h-5

484

(b) The second manual pass is made on the same network except the changed work and delay activities are also included in the calculations.

(c) Once the number of activity days lost has been determined, it is subtracted from the existing float. This comparison will indicate if all the available float has been used and the workday impact on the predicted completion date.

(d) If the predicted completion date was delayed, it is compared to the extended contract completion date. This difference is the workday delay to the contract which is converted to a calendar day justification for additional contract time.

3. *CPM Analysis for Time Extensions*—Delays to the project because of strikes, weather and other acts of God are the only scheduling problems that require an "after-the-fact" CPM analysis. The CPM information required for in-progress delays of this type cannot be estimated and is a totally unknown condition. Once work on the project resumes, the CPM analysis can be made to determine the delay impact to the schedule. The CPM procedure for developing and making a time extension analysis is the same as for any other type of delay.

4. *Concurrent and Cumulative Delays*—If there are relatively few delays or contract changes incurred in any one CPM updating period, a manual analysis, as previously described, is used to determine total impact on the project schedule. However, all the CPM information for the alleged delays must be analyzed at one time rather than making separate calculations for each change. This analysis may be similar to that shown . . . [in examples 1h-6 and 1h-7].

Concurrent/Cumulative Affect Analysis can best be done only after *all* the contractor's proposal/requests for any one reporting period have been prepared. In addition the alleged delays from previous reporting periods must also be resolved to avoid conflicting or erroneous analysis for the delays in question. Because of the above, concurrent and cumulative delays are usually made on a reporting period by reporting period basis only after all the proposals are received for the elapsed time frame in question.

The procedures and calculations are exactly the same for both the manual and the computer analysis. The computer is only used when the required analysis is too complex to do manually.

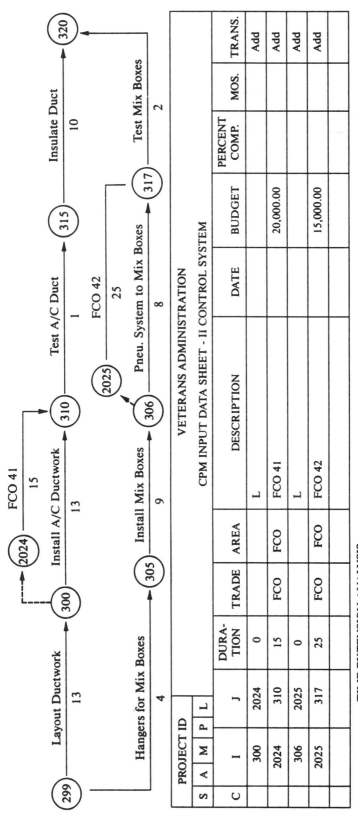

CONCURRENT DELAY

VETERANS ADMINISTRATION

CPM INPUT DATA SHEET - II CONTROL SYSTEM

PROJECT ID							DURA-TION	TRADE	AREA	DESCRIPTION	DATE	BUDGET	PERCENT COMP.	MOS.	TRANS.
S	A	M	P	L											
C					I	J									
					300	2024	0			L					Add
					2024	310	15	FCO	FCO	FCO 41		20,000.00			Add
					306	2025	0			L					Add
					2025	317	25	FCO	FCO	FCO 42		15,000.00			Add

PREDICTED COMPLETION DATE = 3 FEB 78
EXTENDED CONTRACT COMPL. = 14 FEB 78
WORK DAYS AHEAD = +8

<u>TIME EXTENSION ANALYSIS</u>

ACTIVITY 300 – 310 = 0 FLOAT (AS OF 10 APR '76)

1. MANUAL FORWARD PASS W/O CHANGES = 37 + 8 = 45
2.   "   "   "   WITH FCO-41 ONLY = 39   (45 – 39 = +6) = NO TIME
3.   "   "   "   FCO-42 ONLY = 40   (45 – 40 = +5) = NO TIME
4.   "   "   "   FCO-41 & 42 = 40   (45 – 40 = +5) = NO TIME

<u>NO CONTRACT TIME</u>
EXAMPLE 1h-6

486

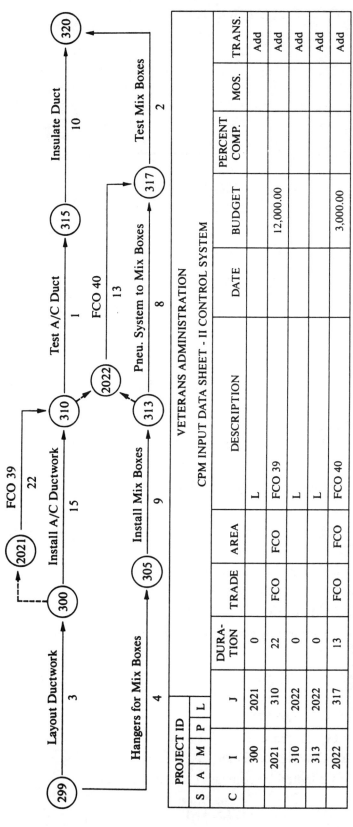

CUMULATIVE EFFECT

Layout Ductwork — 3

FCO 39 — 22

Install A/C Ductwork — 15

Test A/C Duct — 1

FCO 40 — 13

Insulate Duct — 10

Hangers for Mix Boxes — 4

Install Mix Boxes — 9

Pneu. System to Mix Boxes — 8

Test Mix Boxes — 2

Nodes: 299, 300, 2021, 310, 2022, 315, 317, 320, 305, 313

VETERANS ADMINISTRATION

CPM INPUT DATA SHEET - II CONTROL SYSTEM

PROJECT ID							DURA-TION	TRADE	AREA	DESCRIPTION	DATE	BUDGET	PERCENT COMP.	MOS.	TRANS.
S	A	M	P	L											
C					I	J									
					300	2021	0			L					Add
					2021	310	22	FCO	FCO	FCO 39		12,000.00			Add
					310	2022	0			L					Add
					313	2022	0			L					Add
					2022	317	13	FCO	FCO	FCO 40		3,000.00			Add

PREDICTED COMPLETION DATE = 3 FEB 78
EXTENDED CONTRACT COMPL. = 14 FEB 78
WORK DAYS AHEAD = +8

TIME EXTENSION ANALYSIS

ACTIVITY 300 – 310 = 0 FLOAT (AS OF 10 APR '76)

1. MANUAL FORWARD PASS W/O CHANGE ORDERS = 29 + 8 = 37
2. " " " WITH FCO-39 ONLY = 36
3. " " " FCO-40 ONLY = 33
4. " " " FCO-39 & 40 = 40

(37 – 36 = +1) = NO TIME
(37 – 33 = +4) = NO TIME
(37 – 40 = –3) = 3 WORK DAYS (CUMULATIVE)

3 WORK DAYS CONTRACT TIME = 5 CALENDAR DAYS TIME EXTENSION

EXAMPLE 1h-7

TIME EXTENTION ANALYSIS

PROBLEM:

A change order or a supplemental agreement was issued on 11/22/83 with fourteen (14) work days activity duration. Analyze the time impact and the appropriate time extensions to the contract based upon the following examples:

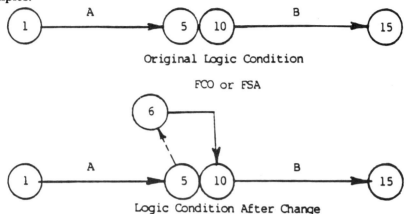

EXAMPLE 1:

Project status as of 10/31/83 from voucher (project update just before contract change):

—Contract Completion Date: 12/15/83

—Extended Contract Completion Date: 12/15/83

—Predicted Contract Completion Date: 12/15/83

Float on activity (1-5) affected by contract change (TF + 7).

EXAMPLE 2:

Project status as of 10/31/83 from voucher (project update just before contract change):

—Contract Completion Date: 12/15/83

—Extended Contract Completion Date: 12/27/83

—Predicted Contract Completion Date: 12/15/83

Float on activity (1-5) affected by contract change (TF + 7).

EXAMPLE 3:

Project status as of 10/31/83 from voucher (project update just before contract change):

—Contract Completion Date: 12/15/83

—Extended Contract Completion Date: 12/27/83

—Predicted Contract Completion Date: 12/27/83

Float on activity (1-5) affected by contract change (TF + 14).

EXAMPLE 1i-1

EXAMPLE 4:

Project status as of 10/31/83 from voucher (project update just before contract change):

—Contract Completion Date: 12/15/83

—Extended Contract Completion Date: 12/15/83

—Predicted Contract Completion Date: 12/12/83

Float on activity (1-5) affected by contract change (TF + 7).

EXAMPLE 5:

Project status as of 10/31/83 from voucher (project update just before contract change):

—Contract Completion Date: 12/15/83

—Extended Contract Completion Date: 12/15/83

—Predicted Contract Completion Date: 12/22/83

Float on activity (1-5) affected by contract change (TF + 9).

SOLUTION PROCEDURE (To be used with regular float reports only)

STEP A—Find the activity float in work days

1. The activity float in work days can always be found from the computer produced I-J listing or total float (TFL) reports.

STEP B—Find the number of work days impact the change affected the predicted completion date.

1. Number of work days impact to predicted completion date = activity float in work days (–) minus duration in work days for the contract change activity. NOTE: If you end up with a positive number or zero, there wasn't any impact to the predicted completion date, therefore, no time extension is due.

STEP C—Calculate the new predicted completion date with change. New predicted completion date with change = predicted completion date as of 10/31/83 (+) plus number of work days impact caused by the change (+) plus weekends and/or holidays.

STEP D—Find the extended contract completion date and predicted completion date from the payment voucher.

STEP E—Determine the time extension in work days.

1. If the predicted completion date from payment voucher as of 10/31/83 is before or the same as extended contract completion date then the time extension in work days = new predicted completion date with change (–) minus extended contract completion date (–) minus weekends and/or holidays (If a negative or zero number, no time extension is warranted.)

EXAMPLE 1i-2

2. If the predicted completion date from payment voucher as of 10/31/83 is after the extended contract completion date, then the time extension in work days = new predicted completion date with change (−) minus predicted completion date as of 10/31/83 (−) minus weekends and/or holidays (If negative or zero number, no time extension warranted.)

STEP F—Calculate the new extended contract completion date.

1. New extended contract completion date = extended contract completion date as of 10/31/83 (+) plus number of work days time extension warranted (+) weekends and/or holidays.

STEP G—Determine the time extension in calendar days.

1. Time extension in calendar days = new extended contract completion date (−) minus the extended contract completion date as of 10/31/83.

NOTE: The above solution procedures is good for the analysis of a single contract change only. Multiple changes during the same period would most probably require a computer analysis to determine if there were concurrently delaying changes issued during the same period.

EXAMPLE 1i-3

Example No.	Step-A Activity Float	Activity Duration for Contract Change	Step-B Change Impact	Step-C PC with Change	Step-D ECCD and PC as of 10/31/83	Step-E Time Extension	Step-F New Extended Contract Completion Date	Step-G Time Extension in Calendar Days
1	+7	14	7 − 14 = −7	12/15/83 + 7 work days or 12 calendar days (7 work days + Christmas Holiday + 2 Saturdays + 2 Sundays) = 12/27/83	ECCD: 12/15/83 PCD: 12/15/83	12/27/83 − 12/15/83 = 7 work days (Time Extension Warranted)	12/15/83 + 7 work days or 12 calendar days = 12/27/83	12/27/83 − 12/15/83 = 12 calendar days
2	+7	14	7 − 14 = −7	12/15/83 + 7 work or 12 calendar days = 12/27/83	ECCD: 12/27/83 PCD: 12/15/83	12/27/83 − 12/27/83 = 0 work days (No Time Extension Warranted)	12/27/83 + 0 work days or 0 calendar days = 12/27/83	12/27/83 − 12/27/83 = 0 calendar days
3	+14	14	14 − 14 = 0	12/27/83 + 0 work days or 0 calendar days = 12/27/83	ECCD: 12/27/83 PCD: 12/27/83	12/27/83 − 12/27/83 = 0 work days (No Time Extension Warranted)	12/27/83 + 0 work days or 0 calendar days = 12/27/83	12/27/83 − 12/27/83 = 0 calendar days
4	+7	14	7 − 14 = −7	12/12/83 + 7 work days or 9 calendar days = 12/17/83	ECCD: 12/15/83 PCD: 12/12/83	12/21/83 − 12/15/83 = 4 work days (No Time Extension Warranted)	12/15/83 + 4 work days or 6 calendar days = 12/21/83	12/21/83 − 12/15/83 = 6 calendar days
5	+9	14	9 − 14 = −5	12/22/83 + 5 work days or 8 calendar days (5 work days, 1 Saturday, 1 Sunday, 1 Christmas & Christmas Holiday) = 12/30/83	ECCD: 12/15/83 PCD: 12/22/83	12/30/83 − 12/22/83 = 5 work days (Time Extension Warranted)	12/15/83 + 5 work days or 7 calendar days = 12/22/83	12/22/83 − 12/15/83 = 7 calendar days

EXAMPLE 1i-4

1983 CALENDAR

S	M	T	W	T	F	S
		OCT				1
2	3	4	5	6	7	8
9	10	11	12	13	14	15
16	17	18	19	20	21	22
23	24	25	26	27	28	29
30	31					

S	M	T	W	T	F	S
		NOV				
		1	2	3	4	5
6	7	8	9	10	11	12
13	14	15	16	17	18	20
21	22	23	24	25	26	27
28	29	30				

S	M	T	W	T	F	S
		DEC				
				1	2	3
4	5	6	7	8	9	10
11	12	13	14	15	16	17
18	19	20	21	22	23	24
25	26 H	27	28	29	30	31

Year	1983
Month / Condition	December

Condition 1

‖ ‖ ‖ ‖ ‖ ‖ ‖ ‖ 12:15:83
|←— X′ —→|
■ ■ ■ ■ ■ ■ ■ 12:15:83
|←— X —→|
■ ■ ■ ■ ■ ■ ■ ■ 12:27:83

Condition 2

‖ ‖ ‖ ‖ ‖ ‖ ‖ ‖ ‖ ‖ ‖ ‖ ‖ ‖ ‖ ‖ ‖ ‖ 12:27:83
■ ■ ■ ■ ■ ■ ■ 12:15:83
■ ■ ■ ■ ■ ■ ■ ■ 12:27:83

Condition 3

‖ ‖ ‖ ‖ ‖ ‖ ‖ ‖ ‖ ‖ ‖ ‖ ‖ ‖ ‖ ‖ ‖ ‖ 12:27:83
■ ■ ■ ■ ■ ■ ■ ■ ■ 12:27:83
■ ■ ■ ■ ■ ■ ■ ■ 12:27:83

Condition 4

‖ ‖ ‖ ‖ ‖ ‖ ‖ ‖ 12:15:83
|← X′ →|
■ ■ ■ ■ ■ 12:12:83
|←— X —→|
■ ■ ■ ■ ■ ■ 12:21:83

Condition 5

‖ ‖ ‖ ‖ ‖ ‖ ‖ ‖ 12:15:83
|←X′→|
■ ■ ■ ■ ■ ■ ■ ■ ■ 12:22:83
|←— X —→|
■ ■ ■ ■ ■ ■ ■ ■ ■ ■ 12:30:83

Notes

‖ ‖ ‖ ‖ ‖ Extended Contract Completion Date (E.C.C.)
■ ■ ■ ■ ■ ■ Predicted Completion Date (P.C.) without Change
■ ■ ■ ■ Predicted Completion Date (P.C.) with Change
H Christmas Holiday December 26, 1983
X Time Extension Warranted in Work Days
X′ Time Extension Warranted in Calendar Days

EXAMPLE 1i-5

TABLE OF CASES

Case	Book §
Abbett Elec. Corp. v. United States, 142 Ct. Cl. 609 (1958)	§ 10.15
Able Elec. v. Vancanti Randazzo Constr. Co., 212 Neb. 619, 324 N.W.2d 667 (1982)	§§ 1.11, 3.6, 5.3, 5.9
Acme Process Equip. Co. v. United States, 177 Ct. Cl. 324 (1965)	§ 11.7
Active Fire Sprinkler Corp., GSBCA No. 5461, 85-1 B.C.A. (CCH) ¶ 17,868 (1984)	§ 9.18
Aerojet Gen. Corp., ASBCA No. 17,171, 74-2 B.C.A. (CCH) ¶ 10,863 (1974)	§ 10.14
Aerospace Corp. v. United States, 579 F.2d 586 (Ct. Cl. 1978)	§ 10.16
Aetna Casualty & Ins. Co. v. Board of Trustees, 223 Cal. App. 2d 337, 35 Cal. Rptr. 765 (1963)	§ 11.5
Aetna Casualty & Sur. Co. v. Butte-Meade Sanitary Water Dist., 500 F. Supp. 193 (D.S.D. 1980)	§ 11.10
Air-A-Plane Corp., ASBCA No. 3842, 60-1 B.C.A. (CCH) ¶ 2547 (1960)	§ 10.6
Al Johnson Constr. Co. v. United States, 854 F.2d 467 (Fed. Cir. 1988)	§§ 9.1, 9.13
Allied Contractors, Inc., IBCA No. 265, 1962 B.C.A. (CCH) ¶ 3501 (1962)	§ 7.4
Allied Materials & Equip. Co., ASBCA No. 17,318, 75-1 B.C.A. (CCH) ¶ 11,150 (1975)	§ 10.16
Allied Repair Serv., Inc., IBCA No. 1381-6-80, 83-1 B.C.A. (CCH) ¶ 16,204 (1982)	§ 10.4
Alpine Indus., Inc. v. Gohl, 30 Wash. App. 750, 637 P.2d 998 (1981)	§ 11.12
Ambrose v. Biggs, 156 Ill. App. 3d 515, 509 N.E.2d 614 (1987)	§ 11.13
American Bridge Co. v. State, 245 A.D. 535, 283 N.Y.S. 577 (1935)	§ 7.25
American Mach. & Foundry Co., ASBCA No. 10,173, 67-2 B.C.A. (CCH) ¶ 6540 (1967)	§ 5.6
American Pipe & Steel Corp., ASBCA No. 7899, 1964 B.C.A. (CCH) ¶ 4058 (1964)	§ 10.14
A&P Bakery & Supply Co. v. Hawateh, 388 So. 2d 1071 (Fla. Dist. Ct. App. 1980)	§ 11.12
Ardelt-Horn Constr. Co., ASBCA No. 14,550, 73-1 B.C.A. (CCH) ¶ 9901 (1973), aff'd, 207 Ct. Cl. 995 (1975)	§ 12.4
Argo Technology, Inc., ASBCA No. 30,522, 88-1 B.C.A. (CCH) ¶ 20,381 (1987)	§ 6.1

Case	*Book §*
Art Metal U.S.A., Inc., GSBCA No. 5898 (5245)-REIN, 83-2 B.C.A. (CCH) ¶ 16,881 (1983)	§ 10.4
Assurance Co. v. United States, 813 F.2d 1202 (Fed. Cir. 1987)	§ 10.6
Ashton Co., VACAB No. 1195, 76-2 B.C.A. (CCH) ¶ 11,933 (1976)	§ 7.31
Attlin Constr., Inc. v. Muncie Community Schools, 413 N.E.2d 281 (Ind. Ct. App. 1980)	§ 9.13
Austin v. Parker, 672 F.2d 508 (5th Cir. 1982)	§ 11.16
Automation Fabricators & Eng'g Co., PSBCA No. 2701, 90-3 B.C.A. (CCH) ¶ 22,943 (1990)	§ 10.17
Babylon Assocs. v. County of Suffolk, 475 N.Y.S.2d 869, 101 A.D.2d 207 (1984)	§ 11.4
Bagwell Coatings, Inc. v. Middle South Energy, Inc., 797 F.2d 1298 (5th Cir. 1986)	§ 5.10
Ballenger Corp., DOTBCA Nos. 74-32, 74-32A, 74-32H, 84-1 B.C.A. (CCH) ¶ 16,973 (1983)	§§ 1.16, 3.30, 5.16, 9.14
Barnet Bremer, ASBCA No. 6194, 1962 B.C.A. (CCH) ¶ 3381 (1962)	§ 10.8
Barton & Sons, Co., ASBCA Nos. 9477, 9764, 65-2 B.C.A. (CCH) ¶ 4874 (1965)	§ 5.24
Basic Constr. Co., ASBCA No. 22,931, 79-2 B.C.A. (CCH) ¶ 13,947 (1979)	§ 10.10
Bates Lumber Co., AGBCA Nos. 81-242-1, 84-210-1, 88-2 B.C.A. (CCH) ¶ 20,707 (1988)	§ 5.4
Bechtel Nat'l, Inc., NASABCA No. 1186-7, 90-1 B.C.A. (CCH) ¶ 22,549 (1990)	§ 6.1
Bell v. United States, 404 F.2d 975 (Ct. Cl. 1968)	§ 10.17
Berger v. McBride & Sons Builders, 447 S.W.2d 18 (Mo. Ct. App. 1967)	§ 11.4
Bethlehem Steel Corp. v. City of Chicago, 350 F.2d 649 (7th Cir. 1965)	§ 11.4
Better Food Mkts. v. American Dist. Tel. Co., 40 Cal. 179, 253 P.2d 10 (1953)	§ 11.3
Big Chief Drilling Co. v. United States, 15 Cl. Ct. 295 (1985)	§§ 12.4, 12.13
Bird v. American Sur. Co., 175 Cal. 625, 166 P. 1009 (1917)	§ 11.13
B.J. Harland Elec. Co. v. Granger Bros., Inc., 24 Mass. App. Ct. 506, 510 N.E.2d 765 (1987)	§ 5.4
Blackhawk Heating & Plumbing Co., GSBCA No. 2432, 75-1 B.C.A. (CCH) ¶ 11,261, *on reconsideration,* 76-1 B.C.A. (CCH) ¶ 11,649 (1975)	§§ 1.16, 9.15, 9.18, 14.3
Blake Constr. Co. v. C.J. Coakley, 431 A.2d 569 (D.C. App. 1981)	§§ 1.16, 5.3
Blinderman Constr. Co. v. United States, 695 F.2d 552 (Fed. Cir. 1982)	§§ 7.17, 9.18, 11.9

Case	*Book §*
Bonacorso Constr. Corp., GSBCA No. 2813, 70-1 B.C.A. (CCH) ¶ 8093 (1970)	§ 6.1
Boston Edison Co. v. Department of Utils., 393 Mass. 244, 471 N.E.2d 54 (1984)	§ 9.13
Boyajian v. United States, 191 Ct. Cl. 233, 423 F.2d 1231 (1970)	§ 10.5
Brady & Co. v. Board of Educ., 222 A.D. 504, 226 N.Y.S. 707 (1928)	§ 7.25
Brecher v. Laikin, 430 F. Supp. 103 (S.D.N.Y. 1977)	§ 11.5
Broadway Maint. Corp. v. Rutgers, 90 N.J. 253, 447 A.2d 906 (1982)	§§ 1.16, 5.11
Broome Constr., Inc. v. United States, 492 F.2d 829 (Ct. Cl. 1974)	§ 7.5
Bruce Anderson, Co., ASBCA No. 35,791, 89-2 B.C.A. (CCH) ¶ 21,871 (1989)	§ 10.14
Bruce Constr. Co. v. United States, 324 F.2d 516 (Ct. Cl. 1963)	§ 10.4
Bryant & Bryant, ASBCA No. 27,910, 88-3 B.C.A. (CCH) ¶ 20,923 (1988)	§ 5.4
Buckley & Co. v. State, 140 N.J. Super. 289, 356 A.2d 56 (Law. Div. 1975)	§§ 7.20, 7.22, 7.31, 11.6, 11.8, 12.4
Burgess Constr. Co. v. Morrin & Son Co., 526 F.2d 108 (10th Cir. 1975)	§ 5.3
Burrough Corp. v. United States, 634 F.2d 516 (Ct. Cl. 1981)	§ 5.24
Calumet Constr. Corp. v. Metropolitan Sanitary Dist., 533 N.E.2d 453 (Ill. App. 1988)	§ 11.8
Canon Constr. Corp., ASBCA No. 16,142, 72-1 B.C.A. (CCH) ¶ 9404 (1972)	§§ 5.24, 9.6, 9.15, 9.19, 9.22, 10.13, 14.3
Canon Constr. Corp., ASBCA No. 15,208, 71-1 B.C.A. (CCH) ¶ 8780 (1971)	§ 10.4
Capital Elec. Co., GSBCA No. 5316, 83-2 B.C.A. (CCH) ¶ 16,548 (1983), *rev'd on other grounds,* Capital Elec. Co. v. United States, 729 F.2d 743 (Fed. Cir. 1984)	§§ 10.13, 10.15
Carlon Davis Constr., Inc., ASBCA No. 32,578, 88-2 B.C.A. (CCH) ¶ 20,575 (1988)	§ 5.4
Carvel Walker, ENGBCA No. 3744, 78-1 B.C.A. (CCH) ¶ 13,005 (1977)	§ 10.14
Cates v. Morgan Portable Bldg. Corp., 591 F.2d 17 (7th Cir. 1979)	§ 11.12
Celesco Indus., Inc., ASBCA No. 21,928, 81-2 B.C.A. (CCH) ¶ 15,260 (1981)	§ 9.13
Certain-Teed Prods. Corp. v. Goslee Roofing & Sheetmetal, Inc., 26 Md. App. 452, 339 A.2d 302 (1975)	§ 11.14
C.H. Leavell & Co. v. United States, 530 F.2d 878 (Ct. Cl. 1976)	§ 7.18

Case	Book §
Chaney & James Constr. Co., FAACAP No. 67-18, 66-2 B.C.A. (CCH) ¶ 6066 (1967)	§§ 1.16, 4.2, 13.4
Chaney & James Constr. Co. v. United States, 421 F.2d 728 (Ct. Cl. 1970)	§ 7.16
Chantilly Constr. Corp., ASBCA No. 24,138, 81-1 B.C.A. (CCH) ¶ 14,863 (1980)	§ 10.13
Charles I. Cunningham, IBCA No. 242, 60-2 B.C.A. (CCH) ¶ 2816 (1970)	§ 7.4
Cieszko Constr. Co., ASBCA No. 34,199, 88-1 B.C.A. (CCH) ¶ 20,223 (1987), *on reconsideration,* 88-2 B.C.A. (CCH) ¶ 20,653 (1988)	§ 10.13
Cimarron Constr. Co. & Williams Bros. Co., ENGBCA No. 2862, 69-2 B.C.A. (CCH) ¶ 8003 (1969)	§ 5.14
Citizens Nat'l Bank of Orlando v. Vitt, 367 F.2d 541 (5th Cir. 1966)	§ 5.4
Clarke-Baridon, Inc. v. Merritt-Chapman & Scott Corp., 311 F.2d 389 (4th Cir. 1962)	§ 10.15
Claude C. Wood Co., AGBCA No. 83-106-3, 83-1 B.C.A. (CCH) ¶ 16,543 (1983)	§ 10.5
Clermont v. Secured Inv. Co., 25 Cal. App. 3d 766, 102 Cal. Rptr. 340 (1970)	§ 11.5
Cline Constr. Co., ASBCA No. 28,600, 84-3 B.C.A. (CCH) ¶ 17,594 (1984)	§ 9.18
C.N. Flagg & Co., ASBCA Nos. 26,444, 26,655, 84-1 B.C.A. (CCH) ¶ 17,120 (1983)	§§ 5.10, 9.26
Coatesville Contractors & Eng'rs., Inc. v. Borough of Ridley Park, 509 Pa. 553, 506 A.2d 862 (1986)	§§ 5.4, 5.10, 7.27
Coleman Eng'g Co. v. North Am. Aviation, 65 Cal. 2d 396, 420 P.2d 713, 55 Cal. Rptr. 1 (1966)	§ 7.19
Coley Properties Corp., PSBCA No. 291, 75-2 B.C.A. (CCH) ¶ 11,514 (1975)	§ 7.13
Commerce Int'l Co. v. United States, 167 Ct. Cl. 529, 338 F.2d 81 (1964)	§ 9.18
Commercial Contractors, Inc., ASBCA Nos. 30,675, 31,782, 88-3 B.C.A. (CCH) ¶ 20,877 (1988)	§ 5.4
Concrete Materials, Inc. v. Smith & Plaster Co., 127 Ga. 813, 195 S.E.2d 219 (1973)	§ 11.8
Consolidated Molded Prods., Inc., ASBCA No. 21,068, 76-2 B.C.A. (CCH) ¶ 12,177 (1976)	§ 7.6
Construction Diversification, Inc., *In re,* 36 Bankr. 434 (E.D. Mich. 1983)	§§ 11.6, 11.7
Constructors-Pamco, ENGBCA No. 3468, 76-2 B.C.A. (CCH) ¶ 11,950 (1976)	§§ 7.9, 7.31
Continental Consol. Corp., ENGBCA Nos. 2743, 2766, 67-2 B.C.A. (CCH) ¶ 6624 (1967), 68-1 B.C.A. (CCH) ¶ 7003 (1968)	§§ 2.4, 5.6, 7.31, 9.3
Continental Consol. Corp. v. United States, 200 Ct. Cl. 737 (1972)	§ 5.6
Continental Ill. Nat'l Bank v. United States, 121 Ct. Cl. 203 (1952)	§ 11.10

Case	*Book §*
Contracting & Material Co. v. City of Chicago, 20 Ill. App. 3d 684, 314 N.E.2d 598 (1974), *rev'd,* 64 Ill. 2d 21, 349 N.E.2d 389 (1976)	§§ 5.6, 7.31
Control Sys., Inc. v. Arundel Corp., 814 F.2d 193 (5th Cir. 1987)	§ 11.10
Corinno Civetta Constr. v. City of New York, 67 N.Y.2d 297, 493 N.E.2d 905, 502 N.Y.S.2d 681 (1986)	§§ 7.22, 7.23, 7.25
Crain v. Sumida, 59 Cal. App. 590, 211 P. 479 (1922)	§ 11.13
Crawford Painting & Drywall Co. v. J.W. Bateson Co., 857 F.2d 981 (5th Cir. 1988)	§ 7.27
Creative Elec., Inc., ASBCA No. 26,368, 83-1 B.C.A. (CCH) ¶ 16,363 (1983)	§ 10.17
Cunningham Bros. v. City of Waterloo, 254 Iowa 659, 117 N.W.2d 16 (1962)	§ 7.24
C.W. Schmid v. United States, 173 Ct. Cl. 302 (1965)	§ 5.24
D'Angello v. State, 46 A.D.2d 983, 362 N.Y.S.2d 233, *aff'd,* 39 N.Y.2d 781, 350 N.E.2d 615, 385 N.Y.S.2d 284 (1976)	§ 5.24
Dawson Constr. Co., GSBCA No. 3998, 75-2 B.C.A. (CCH) ¶ 11,563 (1975)	§§ 1.16, 9.16, 9.20
Dean W. Knight & Sons, Inc. v. First W. Bank, 84 Cal. App. 3d 560, 148 Cal. Rptr. 767 (1978)	§ 11.14
Della Ratta, Inc. v. American Better Community Developers, Inc., 38 Md. 119, 380 A.2d 627 (1977)	§ 5.4
Delta Equip. & Constr. Co. v. United States, 113 F. Supp. 459 (Ct. Cl. 1953)	§ 7.18
DeMatteo Constr. Co., PSBCA No. 187, 76-1 B.C.A. (CCH) ¶ 11,845 (1976)	§ 7.18
Department of Trans. v. Arapaho Constr., Inc., 180 Ga. App. 341, 349 S.E.2d 196 (1986), *aff'd,* 257 Ga. 269, 357 S.E.2d 593 (1987)	§ 5.5
District Concrete Co. v. Bernstein Concrete, 418 A.2d 1030 (D.C. 1980)	§§ 5.17, 9.22
Dravo Corp., ENGBCA No. 3915, 79-1 B.C.A. (CCH) ¶ 13,603 (1978)	§ 10.14
Dravo Corp. v. United States, 594 F.2d 842 (Ct. Cl. 1979)	§ 10.17
Drew Brown, Ltd. v. Joseph Rugo, Inc., 436 F.2d 632 (1st. Cir. 1971)	§ 5.3
Ealahan Elec. Co., DOTBCA No. 1959, 90-3 B.C.A. (CCH) ¶ 23,177 (1990)	§§ 9.16, 9.17, 9.24
E.C. Ernst, Inc. v. Manhattan Constr. Co., 387 F. Supp. 1001 (S.D. Ala. 1974), *aff'd in part, rev'd in part,* 551 F.2d 1026 (5th Cir. 1977)	§§ 5.3, 5.16, 5.19, 11.6, 11.7, 11.8
Edwin J. Dobson, Jr., Inc. v. State, 218 N.J. Super. Ct. 123, 526 A.2d 1150 (App. Div. 1987)	§§ 7.26, 7.27
Eichleay Corp., ASBCA No. 5183, 60-2 B.C.A. (CCH) ¶ 2688 (1960), *aff'd,* 61-1 B.C.A. (CCH) ¶ 2894 (1961)	§ 10.13

Case	*Book §*
Electronic & Missile Facilities, Inc., GSBCA No. 2787, 71-1 B.C.A. (CCH) ¶ 8785 (1971)	§ 9.21
Elrich Constr. Co., ASBCA No. 29,547, 87-1 B.C.A. (CCH) ¶ 19,600 (1987)	§ 9.23
Elte, Inc. v. S.S. Mullen, Inc., 469 F.2d 1127 (9th Cir. 1972)	§ 7.31
Emlyn T. Linkous, GSBCA No. 3832, 74-1 B.C.A. (CCH) ¶ 10,473 (1974)	§ 12.4
Ensign-Bickford Co., ASBCA No. 6214, 60-2 B.C.A. (CCH) ¶ 2817 (1960)	§ 10.4
Equitable Lumber Corp. v. IPA Land Dev. Corp., 38 N.Y.2d 516, 344 N.E.2d 391, 381 N.Y.S.2d 459 (1976)	§ 11.4
Essential Constr. Co. & Himount Constructors, Ltd., A Joint Venture, ASBCA No. 18,706, 83-2 B.C.A. (CCH) ¶ 16,906 (1983)	§§ 9.18, 9.25
Excavation-Constr., Inc., ENGBCA No. 3837, 86-1 B.C.A. (CCH) ¶ 18,638 (1985)	§ 10.13
Excavation Constr., Inc., ENGBCA No. 3858, 82-1 B.C.A. (CCH) ¶ 15,770 (1982)	§ 5.10
Fairbanks Builders, Inc. v. Morton DeLima, Inc., 483 P.2d 194 (Alaska 1971)	§ 7.19
F.D. Borkholder Co. v. Sandock, 274 Ind. 612, 413 N.E.2d 567 (1980)	§ 11.19
F.D. Rich Co. v. Wilmington Hous. Auth., 392 F.2d 841 (3d Cir. 1968)	§ 7.25
Federal Contracting, Inc., ASBCA No. 28,957, 84-2 B.C.A. (CCH) ¶ 17,482 (1984)	§ 10.14
Fields Eng'g & Equip. v. Cargill, Inc., 651 F.2d 589 (8th Cir. 1981)	§ 11.12
Fischbach & Moore Int'l Corp., ASBCA No. 18,146, 77-1 B.C.A. (CCH) ¶ 12,300 (1976)	§§ 1.16, 9.19
Fletcher & Sons, Inc., VACAB No. 2502, 88-2 B.C.A. (CCH) ¶ 20,677 (1988)	§§ 1.16, 9.15, 9.24
Folk Constr. Co. v. United States, 2 Cl. Ct. 681 (1983)	§ 10.10
Forsberg & Gregory, Inc., ASBCA No. 17,163, 76-2 B.C.A. (CCH) ¶ 12,037 (1976)	§ 1.16
Fortec Constructors v. United States, 8 Cl. Ct. 490 (1985), *aff'd,* 804 F.2d 141 (Fed. Cir. 1986)	§§ 1.16, 3.30, 4.2, 4.6, 4.10, 4.11, 5.6, 5.15, 9.3, 9.14, 9.15, 9.30, 13.4, 14.3, 14.5
Framlau Corp. v. United States, 568 F.2d 687 (Ct. Cl. 1977)	§ 10.17
Franklin L. Haney v. United States, 230 Ct. Cl. 148, 676 F.2d 584 (1982)	§ 9.26
Fred A. Arnold, Inc., ASBCA Nos. 27,151, 27,156, 27,170, 27,186, 27,191, 27,200, 84-3 B.C.A. (CCH) ¶ 17,517 (1984)	§ 9.15

Case	*Book §*
Fred A. Arnold, Inc., ASBCA No. 18,915, 75-2 B.C.A. (CCH) ¶ 11,496 (1975)	§ 7.13
Freeman-Darling, Inc., GSBCA No. 7112, 89-2 B.C.A. (CCH) ¶ 21,882 (1989)	§§ 9.13, 9.18
Fruehauf Corp., PSBCA No. 478, 74-1 B.C.A. (CCH) ¶ 10,399 (1974)	§ 11.15
Fruin-Colnon Int'l, S.A. v. Concreto, S.A., 231 F. Supp. 14 (D.C.Z. 1964)	§ 11.7
Fuller Co. v. United States, 69 F. Supp. 409, 108 Ct. Cl. 70 (1947)	§§ 5.17, 9.22
Fullerton Constr. Co., ASBCA No. 12,275, 69-2 B.C.A. (CCH) ¶ 7876 (1969)	§§ 4.5, 5.15, 9.23
Gaasland Co. v. Hyak Lumber & Millwork, Inc., 42 Wash. 2d 705, 257 P.2d 784 (1953)	§ 11.12
Gardner Displays Co. v. United States, 346 F.2d 585 (Ct. Cl. 1965)	§ 5.24
Gary Constr. Co., ASBCA No. 19,306, 77-1 B.C.A. (CCH) ¶ 12,461 (1977)	§ 11.10
G. Bliudzius Contractors, Inc., ASBCA No. 37,707, 90-2 B.C.A. (CCH) ¶ 22,835 (1990)	§§ 4.5, 9.23
General Builders Supply Co. v. United States, 409 F.2d 246, 187 Ct. Cl. 477 (1969)	§ 10.14
General Ins. Co. of Am. v. Commerce Hyatt House, 5 Cal. App. 3d 460, 85 Cal. Rptr. 317 (1970)	§ 11.7
General Ry. Signal Co., ENGBCA Nos. 4250, 4299, 4312, 4366, 4386, 4398, 4399, 4402, 4404, 4409, 4468, 85-2 B.C.A. (CCH) ¶ 17,959 (1985)	§ 5.11
George A. Fuller Co. v. United States, 69 F. Supp. 409 (Ct. Cl. 1947)	§ 5.3
George Hyman Constr. Co. v. Washington Metro. Area Transit Auth., 816 F.2d 753 (D.C. Cir. 1987)	§ 10.13
Georgia Power Co. v. Georgia Pub. Serv. Comm'n, 196 Ga. App. 572, 396 S.E.2d 562 (1990)	§ 9.13
Gibbs Shipyard, Inc., ASBCA No. 9809, 67-2 B.C.A. (CCH) ¶ 6499 (1967)	§ 7.31
Glasgow, Inc. v. Department of Transp., 108 Pa. Cmmw. 48, 529 A.2d 576 (1987)	§ 10.5
Glassman Constr. Co. v. Maryland City Plaza, Inc., 371 Supp. 1154 (D. Md. 1974), *aff'd,* 530 F.2d 968 (4th Cir. 1975)	§§ 5.4, 11.7, 12.4
G.M. Shupe, Inc. v. United States, 5 Cl. Ct. 662 (1984)	§§ 9.15, 12.4
Goudreau Corp., DOTBCA No. 1895, 88-1 B.C.A. (CCH) ¶ 20,479 (1988)	§ 5.10
Grant Constr. Co. v. Burns, 92 Idaho 408, 443 P.2d 1005 (1968)	§ 7.24
Gravitt v. General Elec. Co., 680 F. Supp. 1162 (S.D. Ohio 1988)	§ 10.2
Green Builders, Inc., ASBCA No. 35,518, 88-2 B.C.A. (CCH) ¶ 20,734 (1988)	§ 9.22

Case	*Book §*
Grenite-Groves v. Washington Metro. Area Transit Auth., 845 F.2d 330 (D.C. Cir. 1988)	§ 10.17
Grow Constr. Co. v. State, 56 A.D.2d 95, 391 N.Y.S.2d 726 (1977)	§§ 5.24, 9.22
G&S Constr., Inc., ASBCA No. 28,677, 86-1 B.C.A. (CCH) ¶ 18,740 (1986)	§§ 9.22, 9.26
G&T Dev. Co., DOTCAB No. 75-4, 77-1 B.C.A. (CCH) ¶ 12,494 (1977)	§ 10.16
Gulf Contracting, Inc., ASBCA Nos. 30,195, 32,839, 33,867, 89-2 B.C.A. (CCH) ¶ 21,812, *aff'd on recon.,* 90-1 B.C.A. (CCH) ¶ 22,393 (1989)	§§ 1.16, 9.15, 9.17, 13.1, 14.3
Gunther & Shirley Co., ENGBCA No. 3691, 78-2 B.C.A. (CCH) ¶ 13,454 (1978)	§ 10.14
Haas & Haynie Corp., GSBCA Nos. 5530, 6224, 6638, 6919, 6920, 84-2 B.C.A. (CCH) ¶ 17,446 (1984)	§§ 5.3, 5.23
Hall Constr. Co. v. United States, 177 Ct. Cl. 870, 379 F.2d 559 (1966)	§§ 1.12, 5.11
Haney v. United States, 230 Ct. Cl. 148, 676 F.2d 584 (1982)	§§ 9.1, 9.17, 9.19, 9.30
Hardeman-Monier-Hutcherson, ASBCA No. 11,785, 67-1 B.C.A. (CCH) ¶ 6210 (1967)	§ 10.8
Hardeman-Monier-Hutcherson, ASBCA No. 10,444, 67-1 B.C.A. (CCH) ¶ 6158 (1967)	§ 9.15
Hardie-Tynes Mfg. Co., ASBCA No. 20,582, 76-2 B.C.A. (CCH) ¶ 11,972 (1976)	§ 7.18
Harold Benson, AGBCA No. 384, 77-1 B.C.A. (CCH) ¶ 12,490 (1977)	§ 10.6
Harper v. Goodin, 400 N.E.2d 1129 (Ind. Ct. App. 1980)	§ 11.19
Havens Steel Co. v. Randolph Eng'g Co., 613 F. Supp. 514 (W.D. Mo. 1985), *aff'd,* 813 F.2d 186 (8th Cir. 1987)	§ 5.4
Hayes Int'l Corp., ASBCA No. 9750, 65-1 B.C.A. (CCH) ¶ 4767 (1965)	§ 10.4
Helene Curtis v. United States, 160 Ct. Cl. 437, 312 F.2d 774 (1963)	§§ 5.4, 5.9
Hemenway Co. v. Bartex, Inc. of Tex., 373 So. 2d 1356 (La. Ct. App.), *cert. denied,* 376 So. 2d 1272 (La. 1979)	§ 11.14
Hensel Phelps Constr. Co., ASBCA No. 35,767, 88-2 B.C.A. (CCH) ¶ 20,701 (1988)	§ 5.9
Hensel Phelps Constr. Co., ENGBCA No. 3368, 74-2 B.C.A. (CCH) ¶ 10,728 (1974)	§ 7.13
Hensler v. City of Los Angeles, 124 Cal. App. 2d 71, 268 P.2d 12 (1954)	§ 7.18
Hewitt Contracting Co., ENGBCA Nos. 4596, 4597, 83-2 B.C.A. (CCH) ¶ 16,816 (1983)	§ 10.5
H.H.O. Co. v. United States, 12 Cl. Ct. 147 (1987)	§ 12.4

Case   *Book §*

H.I. Homa Co., ENGBCA No. PCC-41, 82-1 B.C.A.
   (CCH) ¶ 15,651 (1982)   §§ 4.3, 4.10, 5.15
Hoak Constr. Co., IBCA No. 353, 65-1 B.C.A. (CCH)
   ¶ 4665 (1965)   § 7.16
Hoel-Steffen Constr. Co. v. United States, 231 Ct. Cl.
   128, 684 F.2d 843 (1982)   § 5.5
Hoel-Steffen Constr. Co. v. United States, 197 Ct. Cl.
   561, 456 F.2d 760 (1972)   §§ 12.4, 12.13
Hoffman v. United States, 166 Ct. Cl. 39, 340 F.2d 645
   (1964)   §§ 1.12, 5.11
Housing Auth. v. J.T. Hubbell, 325 S.W.2d 880 (Tex.
   Civ. App. 1959)   §§ 5.5, 7.26
Houston v. R.F. Ball Constr. Co., 570 S.W.2d 75 (Tex.
   Civ. App. 1978)   §§ 5.4, 7.22, 7.24, 7.27
H&S Corp., ASBCA No. 29,688, 89-3 B.C.A. (CCH)
   ¶ 22,209 (1989)   §§ 9.18, 9.25
Hull-Hazard, Inc., ASBCA No. 34,645, 90-3 B.C.A.
   (CCH) ¶ 23,173 (1990)   § 9.15
Hungerford Constr. Co. v. Florida Citrus Exposition,
   Inc., 410 F.2d 1229 (5th Cir. 1969)   § 11.10
H.W. Detwiler Co., ASBCA No. 35,327, 89-2 B.C.A.
   (CCH) ¶ 21,612 (1989)   §§ 2.3, 6.1, 9.1, 9.13

Illinois Structural Steel Corp. v. Pathman Constr. Co.,
   23 Ill. App. 3d 1, 318 N.E.2d 232 (1974)   §§ 3.6, 5.17
Indiana & Mich. Elec. Co. v. Terre Haute Indus., Inc.,
   507 N.E.2d 588 (Ind. App. 1987)   §§ 9.2, 9.13, 9.14
Industrial Constructors Corp., AGBCA No. 84-248-1,
   90-2 B.C.A. (CCH) ¶ 22,767 (1990)   §§ 9.13, 9.18
Ingalls Shipbuilding Div., Litton Sys., Inc., ASBCA No.
   17,579, 78-1 B.C.A. (CCH) ¶ 13,038 (1978)   § 10.17
International Equip. Servs., Inc., ASBCA Nos. 21,104,
   23,170, 83-2 B.C.A. (CCH) ¶ 16,675 (1983)   § 10.6
Intertherm, Inc. v. Structural Sys., Inc., 504 S.W.2d 64
   (Mo. 1974)   § 11.7
Itek Corp., ASBCA No. 13,528, 71-1 B.C.A. (CCH)
   ¶ 8906 (1971)   § 10.14

Jack Picoult Constr. v. United States, 207 Ct. Cl. 1052
   (1975)   § 10.11
J'Aire Corp. v. Gregory, 24 Cal. 3d 799, 598 P.2d 60,
   157 Cal. Rptr. 407 (1979)   § 11.12
J.A. Jones Constr. Co., ENGBCA Nos. 3035, 3222, 72-1
   B.C.A. (CCH) ¶ 9261 (1972)   § 9.3
Jan R. Smith, Contractor, FAACAP No. 66-21, 65-2
   B.C.A. (CCH) ¶ 5306 (1966)   § 9.21
J&A Pollin Constr. Co., GSBCA No. 2780, 70-2 B.C.A.
   (CCH) ¶ 8562 (1970)   § 11.10
J.A. Tobin Constr. Co. v. Holtzman, 207 Kan. 525, 485
   P.2d 1276 (1971)   § 11.13

Case	*Book §*
J. Clutter Custom Digging v. English, 393 N.E.2d 230 (Ind. App. 1979)	§ 11.12
J.C. Hester Co., IBCA No. 1114-7-76, 77-1 B.C.A. (CCH) ¶ 12,292 (1977)	§ 7.9
J.D. Hedin Constr. Co. v. United States, 171 Ct. Cl. 86, 347 F.2d 235 (1965)	§§ 10.5, 10.13
J.G. Watts Constr. Co. v. United States, 174 Ct. Cl. 1 (1966)	§ 10.6
J.M.T. Machine Co., ASBCA No. 23,928, 85-1 B.C.A. (CCH) ¶ 17,820 (1984)	§ 6.1
John E. Faucett, AGBCA No. 396, 76-2 B.C.A. (CCH) ¶ 11,946 (1976)	§ 7.5
John E. Green Plumbing & Heating v. Turner Constr. Co., 742 F.2d 965 (6th Cir. 1984)	§§ 7.22, 7.31
John Murphy Constr. Co., AGBCA No. 418, 79-1 B.C.A. (CCH) ¶ 13,836 (1979)	§§ 9.18, 9.19
Joseph E. Bennett, GSBCA No. 2362, 72-1 B.C.A. (CCH) ¶ 9364 (1972)	§§ 5.24, 9.16
J&T Constr. Co., DOTBCA No. 73-4, 75-2 B.C.A. (CCH) ¶ 11,398 (1975)	§ 10.14
J.W. Bateson Co., VABCA No. 1148, 79-1 B.C.A. (CCH) ¶ 13,573 (1978)	§§ 12.12, 14.2, 14.4
J.W. Bateson Co., VABCA No. 1042, 73-2 B.C.A. (CCH) ¶ 10,340 (1973)	§ 10.5
Keco Indus., Inc., ASBCA Nos. 15,184, 15,547, 72-2 B.C.A. (CCH) ¶ 9576 (1972)	§ 10.8
Kehm Corp. v. United States, 119 Ct. Cl. 454, 93 F. Supp. 620 (1950)	§ 5.4
Kemmons-Wilson, Inc. (Florida) & South Patton, Inc., A Joint Venture, ASBCA No. 16,167, 72-2 B.C.A. (CCH) ¶ 9689 (1972)	§ 5.24
Kenworthy v. State, 236 Cal. App. 2d 378, 46 Cal. Rptr. 396 (1965)	§ 7.9
Kobashigawa Shokai, ASBCA No. 13,741, 69-2 B.C.A. (CCH) ¶ 7973 (1969)	§ 7.4
Kroeger v. Franchise Equities, Inc., 190 Neb. 731, 212 N.W.2d 348 (1973)	§§ 3.6, 5.17, 5.19
Laburnum Constr. Corp. v. United States, 325 F.2d 451, 163 Ct. Cl. 339 (1963)	§ 10.8
LaDuke Constr. & Krumdieck, Inc., AGBCA No. 83-177-1, 90-1 B.C.A. (CCH) ¶ 22,302 (1989)	§ 9.26
Lanco-Indus. Painting Corp., ASBCA No. 14,647, 73-2 B.C.A. (CCH) ¶ 10,073 (1973)	§ 10.14
Larsen v. Walton Plywood Co., 65 Wash. 2d 1, 390 P.2d 677 (1964)	§ 11.12
Layne-Minn., Inc. v. Singer Co., 574 F.2d 429 (8th Cir. 1978)	§ 10.9
Lecher Constr. Co., Comp. Gen. B-224,357, 86-2 Comptroller General's Procurement Decisions (C.P.D.) ¶ 369 (1986)	§ 10.14

Case	Book §
LeFebvre v. Callaghan, 33 Ariz. 197, 263 P. 589 (1929)	§ 7.3
Lester N. Johnson Co. v. City of Spokane, 92 Wash. 2d 1005, 588 P.2d 1214 (1979)	§ 5.24
Lewis v. Mobil Oil Corp., 438 F.2d 500 (8th Cir. 1971)	§ 11.12
Lewis-Nicholson, Inc. v. United States, 550 F.2d 26 (Ct. Cl. 1977)	§ 7.13
Lichter v. Mellon-Stuart Co., 193 F. Supp. 216 (W.D. Pa. 1961), *aff'd,* 305 F.2d 216 (3d Cir. 1962)	§§ 5.4, 7.22, 7.31
L.L. Hall Constr. Co. v. United States, 177 Ct. Cl. 870, 379 F.2d 559 (1966)	§§ 5.3, 10.10
Lofstrand Co., ASBCA No. 4336, 58-2 B.C.A. (CCH) ¶ 1962 (1958)	§ 10.4
Loggin Constr. Co. v. Stephen F. Austin Univ. Bd. of Regents, 543 S.W.2d 682 (Tex. Civ. App. 1976)	§ 11.4
Louis M. McMaster, Inc., AGBCA No. 80-159-4, 86-3 B.C.A. (CCH) ¶ 19,067 (1986)	§ 12.6
Lucariells v. Clayton D. Masonry Contracting, Inc., 115 A.D.2d 319, 495 N.Y.S.2d 873 (1985)	§ 11.19
Luria Bros. v. United States, 369 F.2d 701, 177 Ct. Cl. 676 (1966)	§§ 5.17, 9.22
Malley-Duff & Assoc. v. Crown Life Ins. Co., 734 F.2d 133 (3rd Cir. 1984)	§ 11.12
Mann Constr. Co., EBCA No. 362-6-86, 88-3 B.C.A. (CCH) ¶ 21,014 (1988)	§ 5.10
Maplewood Farm Co. v. City of Seattle, 88 Wash. 634, 153 P. 1061 (1915)	§ 7.3
Marathon Battery Co., ASBCA No. 9464, 1964 B.C.A. (CCH) ¶ 4337 (1969)	§ 11.5
Mars & Assocs. v. Facilities Dev. Corp., 124 A.D.2d 291, 508 N.Y.S.2d 87 (1986)	§ 11.8
Marshall v. Charles F. Schultz, Inc., 438 So. 2d 533 (Fla. Dist. Ct. App. 1983)	§ 11.12
Maryland Sanitary Mfg. Co. v. United States, 119 Ct. Cl. 100 (1951)	§ 10.15
Maurice L. Bein, Inc. v. Housing Auth., 157 Cal. App. 2d 670, 321 P.2d 753 (1958)	§ 5.24
McCarty Corp. v. Pullman-Kellogg, 571 F. Supp. 1341 (M.D. La. 1983), *modified,* 751 F.2d 750 (5th Cir. 1985)	§§ 3.6, 5.3, 5.4, 5.17
McDevitt & Street Co. v. Marriott, 911 F.2d 723 (4th Cir. 1990)	§ 9.13
McNamara Constr. of Manitoba, Ltd. v. United States, 509 F.2d 1166 (Ct. Cl. 1975)	§ 7.2
M.D. Funk, ASBCA No. 20,287, 76-2 B.C.A. (CCH) ¶ 12,120 (1976)	§ 7.18
Mendoyoma v. County of Mendocino, 8 Cal. App. 3d 873, 87 Cal. Rptr. 740 (1970)	§ 11.11
Merritt-Chapman & Scott Corp. v. United States, 429 F.2d 431, 192 Ct. Cl. 848 (1970)	§ 7.9
Metropolitan Paving Co. v. United States, 163 Ct. Cl. 420, 325 F.2d 241 (1963)	§ 5.24

Case	*Book §*
Meva Corp. v. United States, 206 Ct. Cl. 203, 511 F.2d 548 (1975)	§§ 10.5, 10.17, 12.6
Midwest Concrete Prods. Co. v. LaSalle Nat'l Bank, 94 Ill. App. 3d 394, 418 N.E.2d 988 (1981)	§ 11.14
Mid-West Constr. Co. v. United States, 461 F.2d 794, 198 Ct. Cl. 572 (1972)	§ 10.10
Mingis Constructors, Inc. v. United States, 10 Cl. Ct. 173, *aff'd,* 812 F.2d 1387 (Fed. Cir. 1987)	§ 12.4
Minmar Builders, Inc., ASBCA No. 3430, 72-2 B.C.A. (CCH) ¶ 9599 (1972)	§ 2.3
Monsen Eng'g Co. v. Tami-Githens, Inc., 219 N.J. Super. 241, 530 A.2d 313 (1983)	§ 11.3
Montgomery Constr. Corp., ASBCA No. 5000, 59-1 B.C.A. (CCH) ¶ 2211 (1959)	§ 7.5
Montgomery-Macri Co. & Western Line Constr. Co., IBCA Nos. 59, 72, 1963 B.C.A. (CCH) ¶ 3819 (1963)	§§ 9.10, 9.15
Montgomery-Ross-Fisher, Inc., PSBCA Nos. 1033, 1096, 84-2 B.C.A. (CCH) ¶ 17,492 (1984)	§ 9.22
Moorehead Constr. Co. v. City of Grand Forks, 508 F.2d 1008 (8th Cir. 1975)	§ 10.5
Morris v. Mosby, 227 Va. 517, 317 S.E.2d 493 (1984)	§ 10.17
M.S.I. Corp., GSBCA No. 2429, 68-2 B.C.A. (CCH) ¶ 7377 (1968)	§§ 5.6, 7.31, 9.10, 9.15
Multivision Northwest, Inc. v. Jerrold Elecs. Corp., 356 F. Supp. 207 (N.D. Ga. 1972)	§ 11.12
Myers-Laine Corp., ASBCA No. 18,234, 74-1 B.C.A. (CCH) ¶ 10,467 (1974)	§§ 7.9, 9.18
Natco, Inc. v. Williams Bros. Eng'g Co., 489 F.2d 639 (5th Cir. 1974)	§ 11.12
National Dairy Corp. v. Jumper, 241 Miss. 339, 130 So. 2d 922 (1961)	§ 11.13
Natkin & Co. v. George A. Fuller Co., 347 F. Supp. 17 (W.D. Mo. 1972)	§§ 3.6, 5.16, 5.19, 5.23
Nello L. Teer Co., ENGBCA No. 4376, 86-3 B.C.A. (CCH) ¶ 19,326 (1986)	§§ 1.16, 4.2
New Pueblo Constr., Inc. v. State, 144 Ariz. 95, 696 P.2d 185 (1985)	§ 7.3
Newbert v. Foxworthy, 71 Ill. App. 3d 438, 389 N.E.2d 898 (1979)	§ 11.18
Newell v. Mosley, 469 S.W.2d 481 (Tex. Civ. App. 1971)	§ 5.9
Nichols Dynamics, Inc., ASBCA No. 17,949, 75-2 B.C.A. (CCH) ¶ 11,556 (1975)	§§ 7.11, 7.13, 7.19
Nolan Bros. v. United States, 437 F.2d 1371, 194 Ct. Cl. 1 (1971)	§ 10.10
Nomelli Constr. Co. v. Department of Water Resources, 19 Cal. App. 3d 240, 96 Cal. Rptr. 682 (1971)	§ 11.6
Norair Eng'g Corp. v. United States, 229 Ct. Cl. 160, 66 F.2d 546 (1981)	§ 5.6

Case	*Book §*
Norman Co. v. County of Nassau, 27 A.D.2d 936, 478 N.Y.S.2d 719 (1967)	§ 5.11
North Slope Technical, Ltd. v. United States, 14 Cl. Ct. 242 (1988)	§ 10.4
Northeast Clackamas Elec. v. Continental Casualty Co., 221 F.2d 329 (9th Cir. 1955)	§ 7.8
N.P.D. Contractors Inc., ASBCA No. 14,798, 71-1 B.C.A. (CCH) ¶ 8862 (1971)	§ 10.16
Ogburn & Assocs., Inc., GSBCA No. 4700, 77-1 B.C.A. (CCH) ¶ 12,473 (1977)	§ 7.13
Oliver B. Cannon & Son v. Dorr-Oliver, Inc., 394 A.2d 1160 (Del. Super. Ct. 1978)	§ 11.12
Oliver-Elec. Mfg. Co. v. I.O. Teigen Constr. Co., 177 F. Supp. 572 (D. Minn. 1959)	§ 7.4
Orion Elecs. Corp., ASBCA No. 18,010, 75-1 B.C.A. (CCH) ¶ 11,006 (1974)	§ 7.9
Owen L. Schwamm Constr. Co., ASBCA No. 22,407, 79-2 B.C.A. (CCH) ¶ 13,919 (1979)	§ 9.22
Paccon, Inc., ASBCA No. 7890, 65-2 B.C.A. (CCH) ¶ 4996 (1965)	§ 10.9
Paccon, Inc. v. United States, 185 Ct. Cl. 24, 399 F.2d 162 (1968)	§ 5.11
Pace Corp. v. Jackson, 284 S.W.2d 340 (Tex. 1964)	§ 11.12
Pan Arctic Corp., ASBCA No. 20,133, 77-1 B.C.A. (CCH) ¶ 12,514 (1977)	§ 7.13
Pat Wegren, IBCA No. 1612-8-82, 85-2 B.C.A. (CCH) ¶ 18,103 (1985)	§ 12.4
Pathman Constr. Co., ASBCA No. 23,392, 85-2 B.C.A. (CCH) ¶ 18,096 (1985)	§§ 1.16, 4.2, 5.10, 9.17
Pathman Constr. Co., ASBCA No. 14,285, 71-1 B.C.A. (CCH) ¶ 8905 (1971)	§ 7.31
Patt H. Dell, GSBCA No. 2811, 70-1 B.C.A. (CCH) ¶ 8152 (1970)	§ 7.5
Peter Kiewit Sons' Co. v. Iowa S. Utils. Co., 355 F. Supp. 376 (S.D. Iowa 1973)	§§ 3.6, 5.3, 7.27, 12.12
Peter Kiewit Sons' Co. v. United States, 151 F. Supp. 726, 138 Ct. Cl. 668 (1957)	§ 1.11
Petrofsky v. United States, 222 Ct. Cl. 450, 616 F.2d 494, *cert. denied,* 450 U.S. 968 (1980)	§ 5.4
Phoenix Contractors, Inc. v. General Motors Corp., 135 Mich. App. 787, 355 N.W.2d 673 (1984)	§ 7.23
Pierce Assocs., Inc., GSBCA No. 4163, 77-2 B.C.A. (CCH) ¶ 12,746 (1977), *on reconsideration,* 78-1 B.C.A. (CCH) ¶ 13,078, *aff'd and remanded,* 617 F.2d 223 (Ct. Cl. 1980)	§§ 1.12, 1.13, 1.14, 5.3, 5.11
Piracci Constr. Co., GSBCA No. 3477, 74-1 B.C.A. (CCH) ¶ 10,647 (1974)	§ 7.12

Case	*Book §*
Piracci Corp., GSBCA No. 6007, 82-2 B.C.A. (CCH) ¶ 16,047 (1982)	§ 10.15
Planetronics, Inc., ASBCA Nos. 7202, 7535, 1962 B.C.A. (CCH) ¶ 3356 (1962)	§ 10.6
Plant Planners, Inc. v. Pollock, 91 A.D.2d 1017, 457 N.Y.S.2d 890 (1980), *aff'd,* 60 N.Y.2d 779, 457 N.E.2d 781, 469 N.Y.S.2d 675 (1983)	§ 11.18
Poultry Health Serv. of Ga., Inc. v. Moxley, 538 F. Supp. 276 (S.D. Ga. 1982)	§ 11.12
Power City & Equip., Inc., IBCA No. 490-4-65, 68-2 B.C.A. (CCH) ¶ 7126 (1968)	§ 7.13
Prather v. Latshaw, 188 Ind. 204, 122 N.E. 721 (1919)	§ 7.3
Preston-Brady Co., VABCA Nos. 1892, 1991, 2555, 87-1 B.C.A. (CCH) ¶ 19,649 (1987)	§ 9.14
Priebe & Sons, Inc. v. United States, 322 U.S. 407 (1947)	§§ 11.3, 11.4, 11.5
Progressive Builders, Inc. v. District of Columbia, 258 F.2d 431 (D.C. Cir. 1958), *cert. denied,* 358 U.S. 881 (1958)	§ 12.4
Psaty & Furman v. Housing Auth., 76 R.I. 87, 68 A.2d 32 (1949)	§ 5.2
PT&L Constr. Co. v. Department of Transp., 108 N.J. 539, 531 A.2d 1330 (1987)	§ 12.12
Quaker Empire Constr. Co. v. D.A. Collins Constr. Co., 88 A.D.2d 1043, 452 N.Y.S.2d 692 (1982)	§ 5.4
R.A. Weaver & Assocs., Inc. v. Haas & Haynie Corp., 663 F.2d 168 (D.C. Cir. 1980)	§ 5.4
Ray Martin Co., VACAB No. 333, slip op. (Nov. 3, 1961)	§ 11.10
Raytheon Serv. Co., GSBCA No. 5695, 81-1 B.C.A. (CCH) ¶ 15,002 (1981)	§ 5.5
R.C. Hedreen Co., ASBCA No. 20,004, 76-2 B.C.A. (CCH) ¶ 12,202 (1976)	§ 10.14
Reeder v. Old Oak Town Center, 124 Ill. App. 3d 1045, 464 N.E.2d 113 (1984)	§ 11.12
Reliance Enters., ASBCA No. 20,808, 76-1 B.C.A. (CCH) ¶ 11,831 (1976)	§ 7.13
Richardson Elec. Co. v. Peter Francese & Son, Inc., 21 Mass. App. Ct. 47, 484 N.E.2d 108 (1985)	§§ 5.5, 5.9
Road-Roc Inc., AGBCA No. 263, 73-1 B.C.A. (CCH) ¶ 9,938 (1973)	§ 10.5
Roanoke Hospital Ass'n v. Doyle & Russell, Inc., 215 Va. 796, 214 S.E.2d 155 (1975)	§§ 11.2, 11.14, 11.16
Robert J. DiDomenico, GSBCA No. 5539, 82-2 B.C.A. (CCH) ¶ 16,093 (1982)	§ 10.17
Robert McMullan & Son, Inc., ASBCA No. 19,023, 76-1 B.C.A. (CCH) ¶ 11,728 (1976)	§ 9.23
Robglo, Inc., VABCA Nos. 2879, 2884, 1990 VABCA LEXIS 27 (Pubcon Library, VABCA file) (Oct. 30, 1990)	§§ 9.16, 9.22

Case	Book §
Robinson v. United States, 261 U.S. 486, 32 S. Ct. 420 (1923)	§ 11.7
Rottau Elec. Co., ASBCA No. 20,283, 76-2 B.C.A. (CCH) ¶ 12,001 (1976)	§ 7.18
Royal Painting Co., ASBCA No. 20,034, 75-1 B.C.A. (CCH) ¶ 11,311 (1975)	§ 7.18
R.S. Noonan, Inc. v. Morrison-Knudsen Co., 522 F. Supp. 1186 (E.D. La. 1981)	§§ 5.4, 7.27
S.A. Healy Co. v. United States, 576 F.2d 299 (Ct. Cl. 1978)	§ 5.5
St. Joseph Hosp. v. Corbetta Constr. Co., 21 Ill. App. 3d 925, 316 N.E.2d 57 (1974)	§ 11.17
San Ore-Gardner v. Missouri Pac. R.R., 496 F. Supp. 1337 (E.D. Ark. 1980)	§§ 11.6, 11.8
Santa Fe Engineers, Inc. v. United States, 801 F.2d 379 (Fed. Cir. 1986)	§ 10.13
Santa Fe, Inc., VABCA No. 2168, 87-3 B.C.A. (CCH) ¶ 20,104 (1987)	§§ 1.16, 2.6, 4.5, 4.10, 5.15, 9.15, 9.23, 13.4, 14.3
Santa Fe, Inc., VABCA Nos. 1943, 1944, 1945, 1946, 84-2 B.C.A. (CCH) ¶ 17,341 (1984)	§§ 9.15, 9.18, 9.21, 11.9
Savoy Constr. Co. v. United States, 2 Fed. Procurement Dec. (F.P.D.) ¶ 210 (Fed. Cir. 1984)	§ 10.13
Schuster Eng'g, Inc., ASBCA Nos. 28,760, 29,306, 30,683, 87-3 B.C.A. (CCH) ¶ 20,105 (1987)	§§ 9.23, 10.5, 10.6, 10.13, 12.6
Seattle v. Dyad Constr., Inc., 17 Wash. App. 501, 565 P.2d 423 (1977)	§§ 7.11, 7.13, 7.19
S&E Contractors, Inc., ASBCA No. 97-12-72, 74-2 B.C.A. (CCH) ¶ 10,876 (1974)	§ 7.9
Shank-Artukovich v. United States, 13 Cl. Ct. 346 (1987)	§ 10.4
Shea-S&M Ball v. Massman-Kiewit-Early, 606 F.2d 1245 (D.C. Cir. 1979)	§ 1.12
Shintech, Inc. v. Group Constructors, Inc., 688 S.W.2d 144 (Tex. Ct. App. 1985)	§§ 1.11, 5.4, 5.9, 5.10, 11.6
Shirley Contracting Corp., ASBCA No. 29,848, 87-2 B.C.A. (CCH) ¶ 19,759 (1987)	§ 10.13
Siefford v. Housing Authority, 192 Neb. 643, 223 N.W.2d 816 (1974)	§ 7.31
Sierra Blanca, Inc., ASBCA Nos. 32,161, 33,333, 33,336, 33,337, 33,555, 90-2 B.C.A. (CCH) ¶ 22,846 (1990)	§§ 9.18, 9.22
Singer Co. v. United States, 568 F.2d 695 (Ct. Cl. 1977)	§ 10.16
Singleton Sheet Metal Works, Inc., ASBCA No. 12,402, 69-1 B.C.A. (CCH) ¶ 7444 (1968)	§ 9.23
S. Leo Harmonay, Inc. v. Binks Mfg. Co., 597 F. Supp. 1014 (S.D.N.Y. 1984), *aff'd,* 762 F.2d 990 (2d Cir. 1985)	§§ 1.11, 5.4

Case	*Book §*
S.L. Rowland Constr. Co. v. Beall Pipe & Tank Corp., 14 Wash. App. 297, 540 P.2d 912 (1975)	§ 11.4
Smith v. Johnston, 591 P.2d 1260 (Okla. 1979)	§ 11.19
Smith & Pittman Constr. Co., AGBCA No. 76-131, 77-1 B.C.A. (CCH) ¶ 12,381 (1977)	§§ 12.4, 12.13
S.N. Nielsen Co. v. United States, 141 Ct. Cl. 793 (1958)	§ 10.4
Sommerville v. Delbsa, 133 W. Va. 435, 56 S.E.2d 756 (1949)	§ 11.13
Southern Fireproofing Co. v. R.F. Ball Constr. Co., 334 F.2d 122 (8th Cir. 1964)	§ 3.6
Southwest Eng'g Co. v. United States, 341 F.2d 998 (8th Cir.), *cert. denied,* 382 U.S. 819 (1965)	§§ 11.3, 11.4, 11.6
Sovereign Constr., Ltd., ASBCA No. 17,793, 75-1 B.C.A. (CCH) ¶ 11,251 (1975)	§ 10.8
Spearin v. United States, 248 U.S. 132 (1918)	§ 5.9
Spec, Inc., ASBCA No. 29,790, 88-2 B.C.A. (CCH) ¶ 20,756 (1988)	§ 5.5
Specialty Assembling & Packing Co. v. United States, 174 Ct. Cl. 153, 355 F.2d 554 (1966)	§§ 5.10, 10.6
Stagg Constr. Co., GSBCA No. 2664, 69-2 B.C.A. (CCH) ¶ 7914 (1969), *aff'd on rehearing,* 70-1 B.C.A. (CCH) ¶ 8241 (1970)	§ 5.24
Standard Coil Prods., Inc., ASBCA No. 4878, 59-1 B.C.A. (CCH) ¶ 2105 (1959)	§ 11.5
State v. Illinois Commerce Comm., 202 Ill. App. 3d 917, 561 N.E.2d 711 (1990)	§ 9.13
State v. Parson Constr., 93 Idaho 118, 456 P.2d 762 (1969)	§ 11.6
Stephenson Assocs., Inc., GSBCA Nos. 6573, 6815, 86-3 B.C.A. (CCH) ¶ 19,071 (1986)	§ 5.11
Steve Beylund, AGBCA No. 87-215-3, 87-3 B.C.A. (CCH) ¶ 19,975 (1987)	§§ 10.5, 12.6
Subcontractor Trade Ass'n., Inc. v. Carroll, 92 Misc. 2d 917, 401 N.Y.S.2d 962 (1978)	§ 11.16
Sun Ship Bldg. & Drydock v. United States Lines, Inc., 439 F. Supp. 671 (E.D. Pa. 1977)	§ 5.24
S.W. Electronics & Mfg. Corp. v. United States, 228 Ct. Cl. 333, 655 F.2d 1078 (1981)	§§ 6.1, 10.6
Sydney Constr. Co., ASBCA No. 21,377, 77-2 B.C.A. (CCH) ¶ 12,719 (1977)	§§ 5.24, 7.9, 9.22, 9.26
T.C. Bateson Constr. Co., ASBCA No. 6028, 1963 B.C.A. (CCH) ¶ 3692 (1963)	§ 10.11
T.D.S., Inc. v. Shelby Mut. Ins. Co., 760 F.2d 1520 (11th Cir. 1985)	§ 11.11
Teledyne McCormick-Selph v. United States, 588 F.2d 808 (Ct. Cl. 1978)	§ 10.1
Timber Investors, Inc. v. United States, 218 Ct. Cl. 408, 587 F.2d 472 (1978)	§ 10.5
Titan Mountain States Constr. Corp., ASBCA Nos. 22,617, 22,930, 23,095, 23,188, 85-1 B.C.A. (CCH) ¶ 17,931 (1985)	§§ 9.14, 9.15

Case	*Book §*
Titan Pac. Constr. Corp., ASBCA Nos. 24,148, 24,616, 26,692, 87-1 B.C.A. (CCH) ¶ 19,626 (1987), *summary judgment granted,* 17 Cl. Ct. 630 (1989), *aff'd,* 899 F.2d 1227 (Fed. Cir. 1990)	§§ 5.9, 9.16, 9.17, 9.18, 13.1
Tombigbee Constr. v. United States, 420 F.2d 1037 (Ct. Cl. 1970)	§ 7.3
Tribble & Stevens Co. v. Consolidated Serv., Inc., 744 S.W.2d 945 (Tex. Ct. App. 1987)	§ 5.4
Tri-State Constr. Co., IBCA No. 63, 57-1 B.C.A. (CCH) ¶ 1184 (1957)	§ 7.4
Turner Constr. Co., ASBCA Nos. 25,447, 29,472, 29,591, 29,592, 29,593, 29,830, 29,851, 29,852, 90-2 B.C.A. (CCH) ¶ 22,649 (1990)	§§ 1.14, 9.17
Turzillo Contracting Co. v. Messer & Sons, Inc., 234 Ohio App. 2d 179, 261 N.E.2d 675 (1969)	§ 11.6
Tutor-Saliba-Parini, PSBCA No. 1201, 87-2 B.C.A. (CCH) ¶ 19,775 (1987)	§§ 10.6, 10.10
Umpqua Marine Ways, Inc., ASBCA Nos. 27,790, 29,532, 89-3 B.C.A. (CCH) ¶ 22,099 (1987)	§§ 9.1, 9.13
United States v. Callahan-Walker Constr. Co., 317 U.S. 56 (1942)	§§ 10.4, 10.14
United States v. F.D. Rich Co., 439 F.2d 895 (8th Cir. 1971)	§§ 3.6, 5.17
United States v. John Kerns Constr., 140 F.2d 792 (8th Cir. 1944)	§ 12.4
United States v. Spearin, 248 U.S. 132 (1918)	§§ 1.11, 5.9
United States v. United Eng'g-Contracting Co., 234 U.S. 236, 34 S. Ct. 843 (1914)	§ 11.17
United States *ex rel.* Control Sys., Inc., v. Arundel Corp., 814 F.2d 193 (5th Cir. 1987)	§ 11.10
United States *ex rel.* Gray-Bar Elec. Co. v. J.H. Copeland & Sons, 568 F.2d 1159 (5th Cir. 1978)	§§ 5.17, 9.22
United States *ex rel.* Heller Elec. Co. v. William F. Klingensmith, Inc., 670 F.2d 1227 (1982)	§§ 3.6 5.3, 9.22
United States Indus., Inc. v. Blake Constr. Co., 671 F.2d 539 (D.C. Cir. 1982)	§§ 10.5, 10.15
United States Steel Corp. v. Construction Aggregates Corp., 559 F. Supp. 414 (E.D. Mich. 1983)	§ 10.5
United States Steel Corp. v. Missouri Pac. R.R., 668 F.2d 435 (8th Cir. 1982)	§§ 5.4, 5.10, 7.22, 7.27
United Telecommunications, Inc. v. American Television & Communications Corp., 536 F.2d 1310 (19th Cir. 1976)	§ 11.14
Urban Plumbing & Heating Co., IBCA No. 43, 56-2 B.C.A. (CCH) ¶ 1102 (1956)	§ 11.10
Utley-James, Inc., GSBCA No. 5370, 85-1 B.C.A. (CCH) ¶ 17,816 (1984), *aff'd,* Utley-James, Inc. v. United States, 14 Cl. Ct. 804 (1988)	§§ 1.16, 5.9, 9.2, 9.18, 9.20, 11.9, 14.2

Case	*Book §*
V.C. Edwards Contracting Co. v. Port of Tacoma, 83 Wash. 2d 7, 514 P.2d 1381 (1973)	§§ 7.9, 7.13
VEC, Inc., ASBCA No. 35,988, 90-3 B.C.A. (CCH) ¶ 23,204 (1990)	§§ 9.22, 9.26
Virginia Elecs. Co., ASBCA No. 18,778, 77-1 B.C.A. (CCH) ¶ 12,393 (1977)	§ 7.9
Volpe-Head (A Joint Venture), ENGBCA No. 4726, 89-3 B.C.A. (CCH) ¶ 22,105 (1989)	§ 9.26
Waldinger v. Ashbrook-Simon-Hartley, Inc., 564 F. Supp. 970 (C.D. Ill. 1983)	§ 11.17
Walter Kidelie Contractors, Inc. v. State, 37 Conn. Super. Ct. 50, 434 A.2d 962 (1981)	§ 1.16
Walter Toebe & Co. v. Dept. of State Highways, 144 Mich. Ct. App. 21, 373 N.W.2d 233 (1985)	§ 9.13
Walter Toebe & Co. v. Yeager Bridge & Culvert Co., 150 Mich. Ct. App. 386, 389 N.W.2d 99 (1986)	§§ 1.16, 9.13
Warren Painting Co., ASBCA No. 18,456, 74-2 B.C.A. (CCH) ¶ 10,834 (1974)	§ 10.5
Warrior Constructors, Inc., ENGBCA No. 3134, 71-1 B.C.A. (CCH) ¶ 8915 (1971)	§ 7.9
Warwick Constr., Inc., GSBCA Nos. 5070, 5387, 5388, 5457, 5543, 82-2 B.C.A. (CCH) ¶ 16,091 (1982)	§ 11.9
Washington & Old Dominion R.R. v. Westinghouse Co., 120 Va. 633, 91 S.E. 646 (1917)	§ 11.16
Weaver-Bailey Contractors, Inc. v. United States, 19 Cl. Ct. 474, *recon. den.,* 20 Cl. Ct. 158 (1990)	§§ 1.16, 4.8, 9.2, 9.16, 9.18, 13.1
Webber Constructors, IBCA No. 721-6-68, 69-2 B.C.A. (CCH) ¶ 7895 (1969)	§ 10.5
Wells Bros. Co. v. United States, 254 U.S. 83 (1920)	§ 7.22
Wells & Newton Co. v. Craig, 232 N.Y. 125, 133 N.E. 419 (1921)	§ 7.25
Western Engrs. v. State Road Comm., 437 P.2d 216 (Utah 1968)	§ 7.24
W.F. Magann Corp. v. Diamond Mfg. Co., 580 F. Supp. 1299 (D.S.C. 1984), *aff'd in part, rev'd in part,* 775 F.2d 1202 (4th Cir. 1985)	§§ 5.9, 5.22
White & Steinmeyer v. King County, 57 Wash. App. 170, 787 P.2d 58 (1990)	§ 9.13
William F. Klingensmith, Inc. v. United States, 731 F.2d 805 (Fed. Cir. 1984)	§ 7.17
William P. Bergan, Inc., IBCA No. 1130-11-76, 79-1 B.C.A. (CCH) ¶ 13,671 (1979)	§ 10.6
William Passalacqua Builders, Inc., GSBCA No. 4205, 77-1 B.C.A. (CCH) ¶ 12,406 (1977)	§ 7.17
Williams Enters., Inc. v. Strait Mfg. & Welding, Inc., 728 F. Supp. 12 (D.D.C. 1990)	§§ 1.16, 5.17, 9.1, 9.15, 9.16, 9.18, 9.20

Case   *Book §*

Wilner Constr. Co., ASBCA No. 26,621, 84-2 B.C.A.
    (CCH) ¶ 17,411 (1984)   § 9.13
WRB Corp. v. United States, 183 Ct. Cl. 409 (1968)   §§ 6.1, 10.5, 12.6
Wunderlich Contracting Co. v. United States, 173 Ct.
    Cl. 180, 351 F.2d 956 (1965)   §§ 9.18, 10.5, 11.9

X.L.O. Concrete Corp. v. John T. Brady & Co., 104
    A.D.2d 181, 482 N.Y.S.2d 476, *aff'd,* 66 N.Y.2d
    970, 489 N.E.2d 768, 498 N.Y.S.2d 799 (1984)   § 11.8

Zinger Constr. Co., ASBCA No. 23,853, 84-1 B.C.A.
    (CCH) ¶ 16,993 (1983)   § 10.15

INDEX

ABANDONMENT
Owner's damages for delay § 11.1
Time-related clauses and claims
§ 7.25
ABANDONMENT, PROJECT OR
SCHEDULE
See RIGHTS AND OBLIGATIONS
IN SCHEDULING
ACCELERATION
See also TIME-RELATED CLAUSES
AND CLAIMS
Critical Path Method (CPM)
techniques applied to contract
claims § 9.7
ACTIVE INTERFERENCE
Time-related clauses and claims
§ 7.27
ACTIVITIES, NUMBER OF
Legal aspects of schedule
specifications § 4.4
ACTIVITY FLOAT SPLITTING
Scheduling methods §§ 2.8, 2.9
ACTIVITY-IN-PROGRESS
REPORT
Project schedule, developing and
maintaining § 3.24
ACTIVITY LISTS
Project schedule, developing and
maintaining §§ 3.9, 3.24
ACTS OF GOD
Critical Path Method (CPM)
techniques applied to contract
claims § 9.6
Investigation, preparation,
presentation, and defense of claims
§ 12.6
Project record-keeping § 6.5
Project schedule, developing and
maintaining §§ 3.27, 3.29
Schedule claims, expert's role in
preparation and defense § 13.4
Time-related clauses and claims
§§ 7.3, 7.5

ACTUAL COSTS
Contractor's damages for delay,
disruption, and loss of efficiency
§ 10.4
Investigation, preparation,
presentation, and defense of claims
§ 12.10
Scheduling methods § 2.2
ACTUAL DAMAGES
Owner's damages for delay
§§ 9.3–9.18
AIA DOCUMENT A201
Legal aspects of schedule
specifications § 4.10
Project schedule, legal significance
§ 1.5
Time-related clauses and claims § 7.7
ALTERNATIVE DISPUTE
RESOLUTION (ADR)
Investigation, preparation,
presentation, and defense of claims
§ 12.24
AMERICAN INSTITUTE OF
ARCHITECTS (AIA)
See also AIA DOCUMENT A201
Case histories § 14.2
Legal aspects of schedule
specifications § 4.10
Owner's damages for delay § 11.2
Time-related clauses and claims
§§ 7.5, 7.7, 7.16
APPORTIONMENT
Owner's damages for delay § 11.8
ARCHITECTS AND ENGINEERS
Case histories § 14.2
Investigation, preparation,
presentation, and defense of claims
§ 12.10
Legal aspects of schedule
specifications § 4.4
Owner's damages for delay § 11.1
Project schedule, developing and
maintaining §§ 3.9, 3.10, 3.37

513

ARCHITECTS AND ENGINEERS
(Continued)
Project schedule, legal significance
§ 1.5
Rights and obligations in scheduling
§§ 5.5, 5.8
Scheduling methods §§ 2.1, 2.3
Time-related clauses and claims § 7.7
AS-BUILT, AS-PLANNED, AND
AS-ADJUSTED SCHEDULES
Schedule claims, expert's role in
preparation and defense §§ 13.4,
13.5
ASSOCIATED GENERAL
CONTRACTORS (AGC)
Contractor's damages for delay,
disruption, and loss of efficiency
§ 10.10
ATTORNEYS AND ATTORNEYS'
FEES
Owner's damages for delay § 11.17
Project schedule, developing and
maintaining § 3.37
Project schedule, legal significance
§ 1.3
AUDITS
Investigation, preparation,
presentation, and defense of claims
§§ 12.20, 12.23

BAD FAITH
Time-related clauses and claims
§ 7.26
BAR CHARTS
See also SCHEDULING METHODS
Project schedule, developing and
maintaining §§ 3.1, 3.3
BIDS
Contractor's damages for delay,
disruption, and loss of efficiency
§ 10.5
Project record-keeping § 6.1
Project schedule, developing and
maintaining § 3.38
Project schedule, legal significance
§§ 1.2, 1.4
Rights and obligations in scheduling
§ 5.14
Time-related clauses and claims
§ 7.4
BREACH OF CONTRACT
Project record-keeping § 6.1

BREACH OF CONTRACT *(Continued)*
Rights and obligations in scheduling
§§ 5.3, 5.5, 5.17
Time-related clauses and claims
§§ 7.14–7.16

CALENDAR, PROJECT
Project schedule, developing and
maintaining § 3.13
CASE HISTORIES
Cedars-Sinai litigation § 14.2
Durham Wastewater Treatment Plant
litigation § 14.3
Edwards Air Force Base Test Support
Facility § 14.5
Humana litigation § 14.4
Integrity and credibility in dispute
resolution § 14.6
Purpose § 14.1
CEDARS-SINAI LITIGATION
Case histories § 14.2
CHANGE ORDERS
Critical Path Method (CPM)
techniques applied to contract
claims § 9.11
Investigation, preparation,
presentation, and defense of claims
§ 12.13
Project record-keeping § 6.10
Project schedule, developing and
maintaining §§ 3.33, 3.34, 3.37, 3.38
Schedule claims, expert's role in
preparation and defense
§§ 13.2–13.5
Time impact analysis procedures
§§ 8.2, 8.4, 8.6, 8.7
CHARTS
See PROGRESS CHARTS AND
REPORTS
CLAIMS
See also COUNTERCLAIMS;
INVESTIGATION,
PREPARATION,
PRESENTATION, AND
DEFENSE OF CLAIMS;
SCHEDULE CLAIMS, EXPERT'S
ROLE IN PREPARATION AND
DEFENSE; TIME-RELATED
CLAUSES AND CLAIMS
Contractor's damages for delay,
disruption, and loss of efficiency
§ 10.16

CLAIMS *(Continued)*
  Project record-keeping § 6.1
  Project schedule, legal significance
    §§ 1.2, 1.5
COMPENSABLE DELAYS
  See TIME-RELATED CLAUSES
    AND CLAIMS
COMPUTERS
  See also FLOAT IDENTIFICATION
    AND COMPUTATION;
    MICROCOMPUTERS; OUTPUT;
    PROJECT SCHEDULE,
    DEVELOPING AND
    MAINTAINING; TAKEOFF
    DATA
  Investigation, preparation,
    presentation, and defense of claims
    § 12.6
  Legal aspects of schedule
    specifications § 4.11
  Project record-keeping § 6.16
  Project schedule, legal significance
    § 1.2
  Rights and obligations in scheduling
    §§ 5.6, 5.16
  Scheduling methods §§ 2.3–2.6
CONDITIONAL DATES
  See TARGET AND CONDITIONAL
    DATES
CONSTRUCTION CONTRACTS
  Investigation, preparation,
    presentation, and defense of claims
    § 12.12
  Legal aspects of schedule
    specifications §§ 4.1, 4.2, 4.6,
    4.9–4.11
  Owner's damages for delay § 11.1
  Project schedule, legal significance
    §§ 1.1, 1.5, 1.15, 1.16
  Rights and obligations in scheduling
    §§ 5.1–5.24
  Schedule claims, expert's role in
    preparation and defense
    §§ 13.1–13.5
  Time-related clauses and claims § 7.2
CONSTRUCTION MANAGER (CM)
  Case histories § 14.2
  Project record-keeping § 6.8
  Project schedule, developing and
    maintaining § 3.4
  Project schedule, legal significance
    § 1.8

CONSTRUCTION MANAGER
  PROCUREMENT
  Project schedule, legal significance
    § 1.13
CONSULTANTS
  See SCHEDULING
    CONSULTANTS
CONTRACT DISPUTES ACT OF
  1978 (CDA)
  Contractor's damages for delay,
    disruption, and loss of efficiency
    § 10.17
CONTRACTORS
  See also GENERAL
    CONTRACTORS; MULTIPLE
    PRIME CONTRACTORS; PRIME
    CONTRACTORS;
    SUBCONTRACTORS; TRADE
    CONTRACTORS
  Case histories §§ 14.1–14.6
  Critical Path Method (CPM)
    techniques applied to contract
    claims § 9.11
  Investigation, preparation,
    presentation, and defense of claims
    §§ 12.4–12.9, 12.11–12.25
  Legal aspects of schedule
    specifications §§ 4.2, 4.11
  Owner's damages for delay § 11.1
  Project record-keeping §§ 6.1,
    6.6–6.16
  Project schedule, developing and
    maintaining §§ 3.5, 3.6, 3.25–3.27,
    3.32, 3.37, 3.38
  Project schedule, legal significance
    § 1.2
  Scheduling methods §§ 2.1, 2.4
  Time impact analysis procedures
    §§ 8.1, 8.5–8.7
  Time-related clauses and claims
    § 7.16
CONTRACTOR'S DAMAGES FOR
  DELAY, DISRUPTION, AND LOSS
  OF EFFICIENCY
  Generally § 10.1
  Claim preparation cost § 10.16
  Credibility § 10.2
  Disruption versus delay costs § 10.3
  Equipment costs § 10.10
  Extended home office overhead
    § 10.13
  Extended jobsite expense § 10.12

CONTRACTOR'S DAMAGES FOR
DELAY, DISRUPTION, AND LOSS
OF EFFICIENCY *(Continued)*
Extended supervision § 10.11
Forward pricing § 10.7
Interest § 10.17
Jury verdict method § 10.6
Labor costs § 10.8
Loss of efficiency § 10.15
Material escalation § 10.9
Profit § 10.14
Reasonable and actual costs § 10.4
Total cost method § 10.5
CONTRACTS
See BREACH OF CONTRACTS;
CONSTRUCTION CONTRACTS
CONVENTIONAL CONSTRUCTION
PROCUREMENT
Project schedule, legal significance
§ 1.11
CORPS OF ENGINEERS BOARD OF
CONTRACT APPEALS
Scheduling methods § 2.4
CORPS OF ENGINEERS (CORPS)
Case histories § 14.5
Contractor's damages for delay,
disruption, and loss of efficiency
§ 10.10
Critical Path Method (CPM)
techniques applied to contract
claims §§ 9.3, 9.4, 9.27
Investigation, preparation,
presentation, and defense of claims
§ 12.6
Legal aspects of schedule
specifications § 4.10
Rights and obligations in scheduling
§ 5.6
CORRESPONDENCE
Investigation, preparation,
presentation, and defense of claims
§ 12.20
Project record-keeping § 6.12
Time impact analysis procedures
§ 8.4
COST ESTIMATES
Project schedule, developing and
maintaining § 3.29
Scheduling methods § 2.2
COST LOADING
Legal aspects of schedule
specifications § 4.7

COST RECORDS
Project record-keeping § 6.14
COSTS
See also ACTUAL COSTS;
CUMULATIVE COSTS;
EQUIPMENT COSTS; LABOR
COSTS; REASONABLE COSTS
Contractor's damages for delay,
disruption, and loss of efficiency
§§ 10.3–10.5, 10.8, 10.10, 10.16
Investigation, preparation,
presentation, and defense of claims
§§ 12.10, 12.15
Legal aspects of schedule
specifications §§ 4.7, 4.11
Project record-keeping §§ 6.1, 6.5,
6.10, 6.14
Project schedule, developing and
maintaining §§ 3.12, 3.30, 3.33,
3.35, 3.37
Project schedule, legal significance
§§ 1.2, 1.6, 1.11
Rights and obligations in scheduling
§§ 5.3, 5.9, 5.11, 5.13, 5.23
Schedule claims, expert's role in
preparation and defense
§§ 13.2–13.5
Scheduling methods §§ 2.2, 2.3
Time impact analysis procedures
§§ 8.1, 8.4, 8.6, 8.7
Time-related clauses and claims
§§ 7.8, 7.18
COUNTERCLAIMS
Investigation, preparation,
presentation, and defense of claims
§ 12.25
CREDIBILITY
Contractor's damages for delay,
disruption, and loss of efficiency
§ 10.2
CRITICAL PATH METHOD (CPM)
See also SCHEDULING METHODS
Case histories §§ 14.1, 14.2
Legal aspects of schedule
specifications §§ 4.2–4.4, 4.9–4.11
Owner's damages for delay § 11.9
Project schedule, developing and
maintaining §§ 3.3, 3.14, 3.22, 3.33
Project schedule, legal significance
§§ 1.2, 1.16
Rights and obligations in scheduling
§§ 5.6, 5.9, 5.16, 5.17, 5.23

CRITICAL PATH METHOD (CPM)
(Continued)
Schedule claims, expert's role in
preparation and defense §§ 13.1,
13.4
Time impact analysis procedures
§§ 8.1–8.3, 8.5, 8.7
CRITICAL PATH METHOD (CPM)
TECHNIQUES APPLIED TO
CONTRACT CLAIMS
Courts' and boards' acceptance of
CPM techniques
–Generally § 9.1
–CPM issues addressed § 9.2
Courts' and boards' recognition of
CPM's dynamic nature
–Generally § 9.3
–Major public owners' recognition of
CPM's dynamic nature § 9.4
CPM technique used for time-related
claims through 1970s
–Generally § 9.5
–Acceleration claim analyses § 9.7
–Delay claims § 9.6
CPM concerns from 1970s' issues
–Generally § 9.8
–Credit determination for innovative
sequence changes and when to
measure delay § 9.10
–Float time and its availability § 9.9
–Time due contractor for change
orders after completion date § 9.11
CPM developments and issues since
1974
–Generally § 9.12
–Acceptance of buy-back time and
sequence changes § 9.20
–*But for* test for extended duration
claims § 9.19
–Cause and effect relationship, need
to establish § 9.14
–Concurrent delay, issues involving
§ 9.18
–CPM acknowledged as preferred
method for proving delays § 9.13
–Demise of *impacted as planned*
proof § 9.17
–Denial of automatic time extensions
for changes after completion date
§ 9.21
–Fragnets, windows, and time impact
analyses § 9.27

CRITICAL PATH METHOD (CPM)
TECHNIQUES APPLIED TO
CONTRACT CLAIMS *(Continued)*
–Limiting recoverable time in CPM
claims presentations § 9.24
–Need to delineate plan for
performance in initial CPM
schedule § 9.26
–Potential abuses in microcomputer
programs § 9.28
–Presumptions from CPM approvals
and time modifications § 9.23
–Recognition of float as expiring
resource available to all parties § 9.16
–Requirement for contemporaneous
baseline in measuring quantum of
delay § 9.15
–Risk taking to negate effects of
delays to critical path § 9.25
–Safeguards for establishing delay
quantum baselines § 9.30
–Specification of time impact
analysis § 9.29
–Using CPM to establish early
completion claims § 9.22
CUMULATIVE COSTS
Scheduling methods § 2.2

DAILY AND WEEKLY REPORTS
Project record-keeping § 6.4
DAMAGES
See also ACTUAL DAMAGES;
CONTRACTOR'S DAMAGES
FOR DELAY, DISRUPTION,
AND LOSS OF EFFICIENCY;
EXEMPLARY DAMAGES;
LIQUIDATED DAMAGES; NO
DAMAGE FOR DELAY
CLAUSES; OWNER'S DAMAGES
FOR DELAY; SPECIAL
DAMAGES
Project record-keeping § 6.1
Project schedule, developing and
maintaining §§ 3.34, 3.37
Project schedule, legal significance
§§ 1.11, 1.14
Rights and obligations in scheduling
§§ 5.4–5.6, 5.10, 5.11, 5.16, 5.17,
5.21, 5.23, 5.24
Schedule claims, expert's role in
preparation and defense §§ 13.1–13.5
Time-related clauses and claims § 7.9

DATA-GATHERING PHASE
  See INVESTIGATION AND
    DATA-GATHERING
    PHASE
DATA SOURCES
  Investigation, preparation,
    presentation, and defense of
    claims §§ 12.6, 12.15
DEFAULT DATE
  Case histories § 14.2
DEFENSE OF CLAIMS
  See INVESTIGATION,
    PREPARATION,
    PRESENTATION, AND
    DEFENSE OF CLAIMS
DELAYS
  See also EXCUSABLE DELAYS; NO
    DAMAGE FOR DELAY
    CLAUSES; OWNER'S DAMAGES
    FOR DELAY; PURE DELAYS;
    TIME-RELATED CLAUSES AND
    CLAIMS
  Contractor's damages for delay,
    disruption, and loss of efficiency
    § 10.3
  Critical Path Method (CPM)
    techniques applied to contract
    claims §§ 9.6, 9.10, 9.13, 9.15,
    9.18, 9.25, 9.30
  Legal aspects of schedule
    specifications §§ 4.1, 4.2, 4.9,
    4.10
  Project record-keeping §§ 6.1, 6.4,
    6.5, 6.11
  Project schedule, developing and
    maintaining §§ 3.7, 3.26, 3.33,
    3.37, 3.38
  Project schedule, legal significance
    §§ 1.4, 1.11, 1.14, 1.16
  Rights and obligations in scheduling
    §§ 5.3–5.6, 5.11, 5.14, 5.17,
    5.22–5.24
  Schedule claims, expert's role in
    preparation and defense
    §§ 13.1–13.5
  Scheduling methods §§ 2.4, 2.8
  Time impact analysis procedures
    §§ 8.1–8.6
  Time-related clauses and claims
    §§ 7.1–7.9, 7.14–7.27
DELIVERIES
  Project record-keeping § 6.8

DESIGN-BUILD TECHNIQUE
  Project schedule, legal significance
    § 1.15
DIAGRAM TYPES
  Legal aspects of schedule
    specifications § 4.3
DIARY
  See JOB DIARY
DISRUPTION
  See also TIME-RELATED CLAUSES
    AND CLAIMS
  Contractor's damages for delay, dis-
    ruption, and loss of efficiency § 10.3
DOCUMENTATION
  See also PROJECT SCHEDULE,
    DEVELOPING AND
    MAINTAINING
  Investigation, preparation,
    presentation, and defense of claims
    § 12.16
  Time impact analysis procedures § 8.7
DRAWINGS
  See SHOP DRAWINGS
DURHAM WASTEWATER
    TREATMENT PLANT
    LITIGATION
  Case histories § 14.3

EARLY-START SORT
  Project schedule, developing and
    maintaining § 3.24
ECONOMICS
  Project schedule, legal significance
    § 1.2
EDWARDS AIR FORCE BASE TEST
    SUPPORT FACILITY
  Case histories § 14.5
EFFICIENCY
  See also LOSS OF EFFICIENCY
  Project schedule, legal significance
    § 1.2
ENGINEERS
  See ARCHITECTS AND
    ENGINEERS
EQUIPMENT COSTS
  Contractor's damages for delay,
    disruption, and loss of efficiency
    § 10.10
EQUITABLE ADJUSTMENT
  Contractor's damages for delay,
    disruption, and loss of efficiency
    §§ 10.4, 10.16

ERRORS AND OMISSIONS
ANALYSES
Investigation, preparation,
presentation, and defense of claims
§ 12.20
Project record-keeping § 6.15
ESTIMATES
See COST ESTIMATES
EVALUATION PHASE
See FACT-FINDING AND
EVALUATION PHASE
EVIDENCE
Legal aspects of schedule
specifications § 4.2
Project record-keeping §§ 6.1, 6.7
Project schedule, developing and
maintaining § 3.34
Project schedule, legal significance § 1.16
Scheduling methods § 2.3
EXCAVATION
Case histories § 14.2
Critical Path Method (CPM)
techniques applied to contract
claims § 9.28
Rights and obligations in scheduling
§ 5.9
Scheduling methods § 2.6
EXCUSABLE DELAYS
Time-related clauses and claims § 7.1
EXEMPLARY DAMAGES
Owner's damages for delay § 11.19
EXHIBITS
Investigation, preparation,
presentation, and defense of claims
§§ 12.16, 12.20
EXPERT'S ROLES
See SCHEDULE CLAIMS,
EXPERT'S ROLE IN
PREPARATION AND DEFENSE
EXPRESS OBLIGATIONS
Rights and obligations in scheduling
§ 5.7
EXTENSIONS
See TIME EXTENSIONS
EXTRA WORK
Legal aspects of schedule
specifications § 4.2

FACT-FINDING AND EVALUATION
PHASE
Schedule claims, expert's role in
preparation and defense § 13.4

FAMILIARIZATION PHASE
Schedule claims, expert's role in
preparation and defense § 13.2
FAST-TRACK CONSTRUCTION
See PHASED OR FAST-TRACK
CONSTRUCTION
FEASIBILITY OF SCHEDULE
Legal aspects of schedule
specifications § 4.2
FEDERAL ACQUISITION
REGULATIONS (FAR)
Contractor's damages for delay,
disruption, and loss of efficiency
§§ 10.10, 10.16, 10.17
FEDERAL INSURANCE
CONTRIBUTIONS ACT (FICA)
Contractor's damages for delay,
disruption, and loss of efficiency
§ 10.8
FINANCING
Owner's damages for delay § 11.14
FLOAT IDENTIFICATION AND
COMPUTATION
See PROJECT SCHEDULE,
DEVELOPING AND
MAINTAINING
FLOAT USE AND REPORTING
Critical Path Method (CPM)
techniques applied to contract
claims §§ 9.9, 9.16
Legal aspects of schedule
specifications § 4.8
Time impact analysis procedures § 8.2
FORWARD PRICING
Contractor's damages for delay,
disruption, and loss of efficiency
§ 10.7
FRAGNETS
Critical Path Method (CPM)
techniques applied to contract
claims § 9.27
Time impact analysis procedures § 8.1
FRAUD
Contractor's damages for delay,
disruption, and loss of efficiency
§ 10.2
Owner's damages for delay § 11.19
Time-related clauses and claims
§ 7.26
FREE FLOAT
Project schedule, developing and
maintaining § 3.16

FRINGE BENEFITS
 Contractor's damages for delay,
  disruption, and loss of efficiency
  § 10.8
FUNDAMENTALS
 Scheduling methods §§ 2.2, 2.5, 2.8

GENERAL AND ACCOUNTING
  EXPENSE (G & A)
 Investigation, preparation,
  presentation, and defense of claims
  §§ 12.11, 12.15
 Project schedule, legal significance
  § 1.6
GENERAL CONTRACTORS
 Project schedule, developing and
  maintaining § 3.5
 Project schedule, legal significance
  §§ 1.6, 1.11, 1.13
 Time impact analysis procedures
  § 8.5
GENERAL SERVICES
  ADMINISTRATION (GSA)
 Contractor's damages for delay,
  disruption, and loss of efficiency
  §§ 10.4, 10.17
 Rights and obligations in scheduling
  § 5.9
GOOD FAITH
 Legal aspects of schedule
  specifications § 4.8
GRAPHICS
 Project schedule, developing and
  maintaining § 3.24
GUARANTEED MAXIMUM PRICE
  (GMP)
 Project schedule, developing and
  maintaining § 3.4

HINDRANCE
 See INTERFERENCE
HINDSIGHT PRICING
 Contractor's damages for delay,
  disruption, and loss of efficiency
  §§ 10.6, 10.7
HOME OFFICE OVERHEAD
 Contractor's damages for delay,
  disruption, and loss of efficiency
  § 10.13
HUMANA LITIGATION
 Case histories § 14.4

IMPLIED OBLIGATIONS
 See RIGHTS AND OBLIGATIONS
  IN SCHEDULING
INDEPENDENT FLOAT
 Project schedule, developing and
  maintaining § 3.17
INJUNCTIONS
 Rights and obligations in scheduling
  § 5.5
INSPECTIONS
 Project record-keeping § 6.8
 Project schedule, legal significance
  § 1.5
INTEGRITY AND CREDIBILITY IN
  DISPUTE RESOLUTION
 Case histories § 14.6
INTEREST
 Contractor's damages for delay,
  disruption, and loss of efficiency
  § 10.17
 Owner's damages for delay § 11.18
INTERFERENCE
 See also ACTIVE INTERFERENCE
 Time-related clauses and claims
  §§ 7.19, 7.27
INTERROGATORIES
 Case histories § 14.2
INVESTIGATION AND
  DATA-GATHERING PHASE
 Schedule claims, expert's role in
  preparation and defense § 13.3
INVESTIGATION, PREPARATION,
  PRESENTATION AND DEFENSE
  OF CLAIMS
 Claim defense
 –Generally § 12.21
 –Actions upon receipt of claim
  § 12.22
 –Alternatives to confrontation and
  litigation § 12.24
 –Assertion of defenses § 12.26
 –Audits § 12.23
 –Choice of forum and value of going
  first § 12.27
 –Counterclaims § 12.25
 –Defensive measures § 12.28
 Claim investigation
 –Generally § 12.5
 –Bases of claims § 12.11
 –Change orders § 12.13
 –Claim preparation § 12.14

INVESTIGATION, PREPARATION,
PRESENTATION AND DEFENSE
OF CLAIMS *(Continued)*
–Claims costing § 12.10
–Contract provisions § 12.12
–Costing and documentary data
    sources § 12.15
–Data sources § 12.6
–Final claim compilation § 12.17
–Physical characteristics § 12.7
–Planned versus actual performance
    § 12.9
–Scheduling documentation and
    non-network exhibits § 12.16
–Sequence of work § 12.8
Claim monitoring, warning signs
–Generally § 12.1
–Dollars § 12.2
–Duration § 12.4
–Sequence § 12.3
Claim presentation
–Generally § 12.18
–Structure of narrative § 12.19
–Supporting exhibits § 12.20

JOB-COORDINATION MEETINGS
Rights and obligations in scheduling
    § 5.21
JOB DIARY
Project record-keeping § 6.7
JOB-MEETING MINUTES
Project record-keeping § 6.2
JOBSITE
Contractor's damages for delay,
    disruption, and loss of efficiency
    § 10.12
Investigation, preparation,
    presentation, and defense of claims
    §§ 12.6, 12.10
Project schedule, developing and
    maintaining §§ 3.9, 3.19
Project schedule, legal significance
    §§ 1.6, 1.8, 1.11
Schedule claims, expert's role in
    preparation and defense § 13.2
Time-related clauses and claims
    § 7.13
JURY VERDICT METHOD
Contractor's damages for delay,
    disruption, and loss of efficiency
    § 10.6

LABOR AND MATERIALS
Contractor's damages for delay,
    disruption, and loss of efficiency
    §§ 10.8–10.10
Investigation, preparation,
    presentation, and defense of claims
    §§ 12.10, 12.14, 12.24
Legal aspects of schedule
    specifications § 4.3
Project record-keeping § 6.11
Project schedule, developing and
    maintaining §§ 3.5, 3.10, 3.12,
    3.28, 3.30, 3.35, 3.37
Project schedule, legal significance
    § 1.8
Rights and obligations in scheduling
    §§ 5.4, 5.10, 5.17
Schedule claims, expert's role in
    preparation and defense
    §§ 13.3–13.5
Scheduling methods § 2.2
Time-related clauses and claims
    §§ 7.4, 7.6
LABOR BURDEN
Contractor's damages for delay,
    disruption, and loss of efficiency
    § 10.8
LABOR COSTS
Contractor's damages for delay,
    disruption, and loss of efficiency
    § 10.8
LATE-START SORT
Project schedule, developing and
    maintaining § 3.24
LEAD AND LAG TIME
Project schedule, developing and
    maintaining § 3.18
Scheduling methods § 2.8
LEGAL ASPECTS OF SCHEDULE
SPECIFICATIONS
Generally § 4.1
Approval § 4.5
Cost loading § 4.7
Feasibility of schedule § 4.2
Float use and reporting § 4.8
Number of activities § 4.4
Poor schedule specifications, factors
    contributing to § 4.11
Schedule specification examples § 4.10
Time extensions and major revisions
    § 4.9

LEGAL ASPECTS OF SCHEDULE
SPECIFICATIONS *(Continued)*
Type of diagram § 4.3
Updating § 4.6
LEGAL EVIDENCE
See SCHEDULE ANALYSIS AS
LEGAL EVIDENCE
LEGAL SIGNIFICANCE
See PROJECT SCHEDULE, LEGAL
SIGNIFICANCE
LIABILITY
Contractor's damages for delay,
disruption, and loss of efficiency
§ 10.2
Owner's damages for delay § 11.3
Project schedule, developing and
maintaining § 3.3
Project schedule, legal significance
§§ 1.6, 1.14
Rights and obligations in scheduling
§§ 5.7, 5.10, 5.11, 5.22
LIQUIDATED DAMAGES
Owner's damages for delay
§§ 9.3–9.10
Rights and obligations in scheduling
§§ 5.6, 5.11
Time-related clauses and claims
§§ 7.17, 7.31
LITIGATION
Case histories §§ 14.2–14.4
Investigation, preparation,
presentation, and defense of claims
§ 12.24
LOG/AN NETWORKS
Case histories § 14.2
LOGIC CONNECTORS
Scheduling methods § 2.8
LOSS OF EFFICIENCY
Contractor's damages for delay,
disruption, and loss of efficiency
§ 10.15
LOSS OF USE
Owner's damages for delay § 11.13

MAINTENANCE
Legal aspects of schedule
specifications § 4.11
Owner's damages for delay § 11.15
Project record-keeping § 6.10
Project schedule, developing and
maintaining § 3.7
Scheduling methods § 2.4

MANAGEMENT REPORTING AND
DOCUMENTATION
See PROJECT SCHEDULE,
DEVELOPING AND
MAINTAINING
MANAGERS
See CONSTRUCTION
MANAGERS
MANPOWER
Contractor's damages for delay,
disruption, and loss of efficiency
§ 10.3
Legal aspects of schedule
specifications § 4.11
Project schedule, developing and
maintaining §§ 3.6, 3.28, 3.37
Schedule claims, expert's role in
preparation and defense
§§ 13.3–13.5
Scheduling methods §§ 2.2, 2.3
MASTER SUMMARY CONTROL
SCHEDULE
Project schedule, developing and
maintaining §§ 3.4, 3.36
MATERIAL ESCALATION
Contractor's damages for delay,
disruption, and loss of efficiency
§ 10.9
MATERIALS
See LABOR AND MATERIALS
MEASURED MILE TECHNIQUE
Contractor's damages for delay,
disruption, and loss of efficiency
§ 10.15
MEMORANDA
Project record-keeping § 6.13
MICROCOMPUTERS
Critical Path Method (CPM)
techniques applied to contract
claims § 9.28
Project schedule, developing and
maintaining § 3.20
MODELS
Schedule claims, expert's role in
preparation and defense
§ 13.5
Time impact analysis procedures
§ 8.5
MULTIPLE PRIME CONTRACTOR
PROCUREMENT
Project schedule, legal significance
§ 1.12

MULTIPLE PRIME CONTRACTORS
Project schedule, developing and
maintaining §§ 3.7, 3.18, 3.31,
3.35
Project schedule, legal significance
§ 1.3
Time impact analysis procedures
§ 8.3

NARRATIVE, STRUCTURE OF
Investigation, preparation,
presentation, and defense of claims
§ 12.19
NEGATIVE FLOAT
Project schedule, developing and
maintaining § 3.15
NETWORK TECHNIQUES
Case histories § 14.2
Investigation, preparation,
presentation, and defense of claims
§ 12.16
Legal aspects of schedule
specifications §§ 4.2–4.4, 4.6,
4.9–4.11
Project schedule, developing and
maintaining §§ 3.1, 3.5, 3.11–3.14,
3.22, 3.27, 3.30, 3.38
Project schedule, legal significance
§§ 1.2, 1.16
Scheduling methods §§ 2.5, 2.6, 2.7
Time impact analysis procedures
§ 8.1
NO DAMAGE FOR DELAY CLAUSES
See also TIME-RELATED CLAUSES
AND CLAIMS
Project schedule, developing and
maintaining § 3.37
Project schedule, legal significance
§ 1.6
Rights and obligations in scheduling
§§ 5.6, 5.11
Schedule claims, expert's role in
preparation and defense § 13.3

OPERATION EXPENSES
Owner's damages for delay § 11.15
OUTPUT
Project schedule, developing and
maintaining § 3.24
OVERHEAD
See also HOME OFFICE
OVERHEAD

OVERHEAD *(Continued)*
Investigation, preparation,
presentation, and defense of claims
§§ 12.6, 12.10
Project schedule, developing and
maintaining § 3.35
Project schedule, legal significance
§ 1.6
Rights and obligations in scheduling
§ 5.10
OVERRUNS
Project schedule, legal significance
§ 1.2
OWNERS
Critical Path Method (CPM)
techniques applied to contract
claims § 9.4
Investigation, preparation,
presentation, and defense of claims
§ 12.1
Legal aspects of schedule
specifications §§ 4.4, 4.7, 4.10,
4.11
Project record-keeping §§ 6.1,
6.5–6.16
Project schedule, developing and
maintaining §§ 3.4, 3.5, 3.7, 3.10,
3.25–3.27, 3.32, 3.37, 3.38
Project schedule, legal significance
§ 1.4
Time impact analysis procedures
§§ 8.1, 8.3, 8.7
Time-related clauses and claims
§§ 7.3, 7.8, 7.14, 7.18, 7.30
OWNER'S DAMAGES FOR DELAY
Generally § 11.1
Actual damages for delay
–Generally § 11.11
–Attorneys' fees § 11.17
–Extended maintenance and
operation expenses § 11.15
–Increased financing § 11.13
–Interest § 11.18
–Loss of profits § 11.12
–Special damages § 11.16
Exemplary damages § 11.19
Liquidated versus actual damages
–Generally § 11.2
–Apportionment of liquidated
damages § 11.8
–Concurrent delay as bar § 11.7
–Concurrent delay § 11.6

OWNER'S DAMAGES FOR DELAY
(Continued)
–Critical Path Method (CPM) use
§ 11.9
–Lack of actual damages § 11.3
–Prohibition against penalty § 11.5
–Substantial completion and
beneficial occupancy § 11.10
Scope of recoverable damages § 11.2
OWNER'S ROLE IN SCHEDULING
See RIGHTS AND OBLIGATIONS
IN SCHEDULING

PAYMENTS
See also PROGRESS PAYMENT
SCHEDULE REPORTS
Legal aspects of schedule
specifications § 4.7
Project record-keeping §§ 6.7, 6.14
Project schedule, developing and
maintaining §§ 3.3, 3.35, 3.37
Project schedule, legal significance
§ 1.6
Time impact analysis procedures § 8.4
PAY-WHEN-PAID CLAUSES
Project schedule, legal significance
§ 1.6
PERFORMANCE
Critical Path Method (CPM)
techniques applied to contract
claims § 9.26
Investigation, preparation,
presentation, and defense of claims
§§ 12.9, 12.19
Legal aspects of schedule
specifications §§ 4.1, 4.6
Owner's damages for delay § 11.1
Project record-keeping §§ 6.1, 6.3,
6.5, 6.10
Project schedule, developing and
maintaining §§ 3.18, 3.31, 3.34
Project schedule, legal significance
§§ 1.1–1.9, 1.11, 1.14–1.16
Rights and obligations in scheduling
§§ 5.3–5.5, 5.9, 5.11, 5.13, 5.17
Schedule claims, expert's role in
preparation and defense § 13.2
Scheduling methods §§ 2.3, 2.4
Time impact analysis procedures
§ 8.4
Time-related clauses and claims
§§ 7.19, 7.21, 7.31

PHASED OR FAST-TRACK
CONSTRUCTION
Project schedule, legal significance
§ 1.14
Rights and obligations in scheduling
§ 5.11
PHOTOGRAPHS
Investigation, preparation,
presentation, and defense of claims
§ 12.20
Project record-keeping § 6.6
Schedule claims, expert's role in
preparation and defense § 13.3
PHYSICAL CHARACTERISTICS
Investigation, preparation,
presentation, and defense of claims
§ 12.7
PLANNING
See also PROJECT SCHEDULE,
DEVELOPING AND
MAINTAINING
Scheduling methods §§ 2.4, 2.6
PLANS AND SPECIFICATIONS
Case histories § 14.2
Project record-keeping §§ 6.7,
6.11
Project schedule, developing and
maintaining §§ 3.37, 3.38
Rights and obligations in scheduling
§§ 5.4–5.10
Schedule claims, expert's role in
preparation and defense
§ 13.2
PRECEDENCE DIAGRAMMING
METHOD (PCM)
See SCHEDULING METHODS
PREPARATION OR PRESENTATION
OF CLAIMS
See INVESTIGATION,
PREPARATION,
PRESENTATION, AND
DEFENSE OF CLAIMS
PRESENTATION PHASE
Schedule claims, expert's role in
preparation and defense § 13.5
PRICE
See also FORWARD PRICING
Investigation, preparation,
presentation, and defense of claims
§ 12.20
Project schedule, legal significance
§§ 1.1, 1.13

PRIME CONTRACTORS
  See also MULTIPLE PRIME
    CONTRACTORS; RIGHTS AND
    OBLIGATIONS IN
    SCHEDULING
  Legal aspects of schedule
    specifications § 4.11
  Project schedule, developing and
    maintaining § 3.2
  Time-related clauses and claims
    § 7.31
PRIVITY
  Project schedule, legal significance
    § 1.5
PROCUREMENT
  See CONSTRUCTION MANAGER
    PROCUREMENT;
    CONVENTIONAL
    CONSTRUCTION
    PROCUREMENT; MULTIPLE
    PRIME CONTRACTOR
    PROCUREMENT
PROCUREMENT RECORDS
  Project record-keeping § 6.8
PROFITS
  Contractor's damages for delay,
    disruption, and loss of efficiency
    § 10.14
  Investigation, preparation,
    presentation, and defense of claims
    § 12.10
  Owner's damages for delay § 11.12
PROGRESS CHARTS AND
  REPORTS
  Project record-keeping § 6.3
PROGRESS PAYMENT SCHEDULE
  REPORTS
  Project schedule, developing and
    maintaining § 3.36
PROJECT MANAGEMENT ROLES
  See SCHEDULING AND PROJECT
    MANAGEMENT ROLES
PROJECT RECORD-KEEPING
  Change orders § 6.10
  Computer use for job record-keeping
    § 6.16
  Correspondence § 6.12
  Cost records § 6.14
  Daily and weekly reports § 6.4
  Errors and omissions analyses
    § 6.15
  Good records, need for § 6.1

PROJECT RECORD-KEEPING
  (Continued)
  Investigation, preparation,
    presentation, and defense of claims
    § 12.14
  Job diary § 6.7
  Job-meeting minutes § 6.2
  Memoranda § 6.13
  Photographs § 6.6
  Procurement records § 6.8
  Progress charts and reports § 6.3
  Schedule claims, expert's role in
    preparation and defense §§ 13.2,
    13.3
  Shop drawings § 6.11
  Test reports and test records § 6.9
  Time impact analysis procedures
    § 8.4
  Weather § 6.5
PROJECT SCHEDULE,
  DEVELOPING AND
  MAINTAINING
  Generally § 3.1
  Choice of right scheduling method
    § 3.2
  Computerization of project schedule
  –Generally § 3.19
  –Computer outputs § 3.24
  –Getting started § 3.21
  –Guidelines for data takeoff § 3.23
  –Inputting network information
    § 3.22
  –Major projects, popular systems
    used § 3.20
  –Schedule reviews § 3.26
  –Schedule submittals and approval
    § 3.25
  Float identification and computation
  –Generally § 3.14
  –Float allocation possibilities § 3.18
  –Free float § 3.16
  –Independent float § 3.17
  –Total float § 3.15
  General contractors' roles of § 3.5
  Management reporting and
    documentation
  –Generally § 3.32
  –Cash flow forecasting and progress
    payment records § 3.35
  –Good project record needs § 3.34
  –Problem-identification philosophy
    § 3.33

PROJECT SCHEDULE,
DEVELOPING AND
MAINTAINING *(Continued)*
–Summary networks use § 3.36
Planning phase
–Generally § 3.8
–Activity list preparation § 3.9
–Level of detail § 3.10
Project schedule updating
–Generally § 3.28
–Joint update meetings § 3.31
–Need for updating § 3.29
–Update preparation § 3.30
Schedule preparation responsibility
§ 3.4
Schedule review and approval
procedures § 3.27
Schedule specifications, development
of § 3.3
Schedule systems
–Generally § 3.37
–Schedule implementation guidelines
§ 3.38
Scheduling phase
–Generally § 3.11
–Activity durations § 3.12
–Computation of event times § 3.13
Subcontractors' roles § 3.6
Successful scheduling requirements
§ 3.7
PROJECT SCHEDULE, LEGAL
SIGNIFICANCE
Project players and their objectives
–Generally § 1.3
–Architects and engineers § 1.5
–Construction managers § 1.8
–General contractors § 1.6
–Owners § 1.4
–Scheduling consultants § 1.9
–Subcontractors and suppliers § 1.7
Risks in scheduling and project
structure alternatives
–Generally § 1.10
–Construction manager procurement
§ 1.13
–Conventional construction
procurement § 1.11
–Design-build technique § 1.15
–Multiple prime contractor
procurement § 1.12
–Phased or fast-track construction
§ 1.14

PROJECT SCHEDULE, LEGAL
SIGNIFICANCE *(Continued)*
Schedule analysis as legal evidence
§ 1.16
Scheduling and project management
roles § 1.2
Time importance in construction
contracts § 1.1
PROJECT-STATUSING FORM
Project schedule, developing and
maintaining § 3.24
PROMPT PAYMENT ACT
Contractor's damages for delay,
disruption, and loss of efficiency
§ 10.17
PUNITIVE DAMAGES
See EXEMPLARY DAMAGES
PURCHASE ORDERS
Project record-keeping § 6.8
PURE DELAYS
Contractor's damages for delay,
disruption, and loss of efficiency
§ 10.3

REASONABLE COSTS
Contractor's damages for delay,
disruption, and loss of efficiency
§ 10.4
RECORD-KEEPING
See PROJECT RECORD-KEEPING
RECOVERY
Owner's damages for delay § 11.2
Time-related clauses and claims
§ 7.16
REPORTING
See FLOAT USE AND REPORTING
REQUESTS FOR INFORMATION
(RFIs)
Investigation, preparation,
presentation, and defense of claims
§ 12.6
Project record-keeping §§ 6.1, 6.15
Schedule claims, expert's role in
preparation and defense §§ 13.3,
13.5
RESPONSIBILITY-AND-FUNCTION
SORTS
Project schedule, developing and
maintaining § 3.24
RESTATEMENT (SECOND) OF
CONTRACTS
Owner's damages for delay § 11.12

REVISIONS, MAJOR
Legal aspects of schedule
specifications § 4.9
RIGHTS AND OBLIGATIONS IN
SCHEDULING
Generally § 5.1
Express obligations § 5.7
Implied obligations
–Generally § 5.2
–Duty to cooperate § 5.5
–Duty to grant reasonable time
extensions § 5.6
–Duty to not delay, hinder, or
interfere § 5.4
–Duty to schedule and coordinate
§ 5.3
Owner's role in scheduling
–Generally § 5.8
–Multiprime contracting § 5.11
–Owner-issued schedule § 5.9
–Progress schedule execution § 5.10
Prime contractor's role in scheduling
–Generally § 5.12
–Bid-process review of scheduling
§ 5.13
–Coordinating subcontractors § 5.17
–Initial approved project schedule
§ 5.15
–Preliminary progress schedule § 5.14
–Project schedule updating § 5.16
Project or schedule abandonment due
inadequate scheduling
–Generally § 5.22
–Schedule abandonment effects
§ 5.23
Recognition of contractor's right to
finish early and to manage
schedule § 5.24
Subcontractor's role in scheduling
–Generally § 5.18
–Job-coordination meetings § 5.21
–Project schedule updating § 5.20
–Subcontractor rights in prime
contractor-issued schedule § 5.19
RIPPLE EFFECT
Time-related clauses and claims
§ 7.12
RISKS IN SCHEDULING AND
PROJECT STRUCTURE
ALTERNATIVES
See PROJECT SCHEDULE, LEGAL
SIGNIFICANCE

SAFETY
Project schedule, developing and
maintaining §§ 3.9, 3.12
Project schedule, legal significance
§ 1.11
SCHEDULE ANALYSIS AS LEGAL
EVIDENCE
Project schedule, legal significance
§ 1.16
SCHEDULE CLAIMS, EXPERT'S
ROLE IN PREPARATION AND
DEFENSE
Generally § 13.1
Fact-finding and evaluation phase
§ 13.4
Familiarization phase § 13.2
Investigation and data-gathering
phase § 13.3
Presentation phase § 13.5
SCHEDULE SPECIFICATIONS
See LEGAL ASPECTS OF
SCHEDULE SPECIFICATIONS
SCHEDULING AND PROJECT
MANAGEMENT ROLES
Case histories § 14.2
Investigation, preparation,
presentation, and defense of claims
§§ 12.16, 12.20
Project schedule, legal significance
§ 1.2
SCHEDULING CONSULTANTS
Project schedule, legal significance
§ 1.9
SCHEDULING METHODS
See also PROJECT SCHEDULE,
DEVELOPING AND
MAINTAINING; RIGHTS AND
OBLIGATIONS IN
SCHEDULING
Bar charts
–Generally § 2.1
–Fundamentals § 2.2
–Limitations § 2.3
Critical Path Method (CPM)
–Generally § 2.4
–Fundamentals § 2.5
–Pitfalls in CPM scheduling § 2.6
Precedence Diagramming Method
(PDM)
–Generally § 2.7
–Fundamentals § 2.8
–PDM pitfalls § 2.9

SCOPE OF THE WORK
   Project schedule, developing and
      maintaining §§ 3.5, 3.12
   Project schedule, legal significance
      § 1.1
SEQUENCE OF WORK
   Investigation, preparation,
      presentation, and defense of claims
      §§ 12.3, 12.8
SHOP DRAWINGS
   Investigation, preparation,
      presentation, and defense of claims
      § 12.15
   Legal aspects of schedule
      specifications § 4.11
   Project record-keeping § 6.11
   Project schedule, developing and
      maintaining §§ 3.3, 3.10, 3.37
   Project schedule, legal significance
      § 1.4
SPECIAL DAMAGES
   Owner's damages for delay § 11.16
SPECIFICATIONS
   See PLANS AND SPECIFICATIONS
SPOT-CHECK ACTIVITY
   Project schedule, developing and
      maintaining § 3.27
STRIKES
   Project schedule, developing and
      maintaining § 3.29
   Schedule claims, expert's role in
      preparation and defense § 13.4
   Time-related clauses and claims
      § 7.4
SUBCONTRACTORS
   See also RIGHTS AND
      OBLIGATIONS IN
      SCHEDULING
   Legal aspects of schedule
      specifications § 4.11
   Project schedule, developing and
      maintaining § 3.6
   Project schedule, legal significance
      § 1.7
   Time-related clauses and claims
      §§ 7.6, 7.27
SUBNETWORKS
   Project schedule, developing and
      maintaining § 3.10
SUBSTANTIAL COMPLETION
   Owner's damages for delay § 11.10

SUPERIOR KNOWLEDGE
   Rights and obligations in scheduling
      § 5.9
SUPERVISION, EXTENDED
   Contractor's damages for delay,
      disruption, and loss of efficiency
      § 10.11
SUPPLIERS
   Legal aspects of schedule
      specifications § 4.11
   Project schedule, developing and
      maintaining §§ 3.6, 3.7, 3.12,
      3.27
   Project schedule, legal significance
      § 1.7
SURVEYS
   Time-related clauses and claims
      § 7.13
SUSPENSION OF WORK
   See TIME-RELATED CLAUSES
      AND CLAIMS

TAKEOFF DATA
   Project schedule, developing and
      maintaining § 3.23
TARGET AND CONDITIONAL
   DATES
   Project schedule, developing and
      maintaining § 3.18
TECHNOLOGY
   See also COMPUTERS
   Project schedule, legal significance
      § 1.2
TEST REPORTS AND TEST
   RECORDS
   Project record-keeping § 6.9
THIRD PARTIES
   Project record-keeping § 6.1
TIME
   Critical Path Method (CPM)
      techniques applied to contract
      claims §§ 9.5–9.11, 9.20–9.24,
      9.27–9.29
   Project record-keeping §§ 6.10,
      6.11
   Project schedule, developing and
      maintaining §§ 3.4, 3.5, 3.11,
      3.12, 3.28, 3.30, 3.33, 3.34
   Project schedule, legal significance
      § 1.1
   Scheduling methods § 2.1

TIME EXTENSIONS
  Critical Path Method (CPM)
    techniques applied to contract
    claims §§ 9.18, 9.21
  Investigation, preparation,
    presentation, and defense of claims
    § 12.6
  Legal aspects of schedule
    specifications §§ 4.9, 4.10
  Rights and obligations in scheduling
    § 5.6
  Schedule claims, expert's role in
    preparation and defense
    §§ 13.2–13.4
TIME IMPACT ANALYSIS
PROCEDURES
  Concurrent delays § 8.3
  Critical Path Method (CPM)
    techniques applied to contract
    claims § 9.27
  Float § 8.2
  Recognition and incorporation of
    delays § 8.1
  Schedule claims, expert's role in
    preparation and defense § 13.4
  Time impact analyses advantages
    § 8.6
  Time impact analyses preparation
    § 8.4
  Time impact analysis model § 8.5
  Time impacts, guidelines for
    negotiating § 8.7
TIME-RELATED CLAUSES AND
CLAIMS
  Acceleration
  –Generally § 7.28
  –Actual acceleration § 7.29
  –Constructive acceleration § 7.30
  –Examples § 7.31
  Compensable delays
  –Generally § 7.8
  –Examples § 7.9
  Contract provisions pertaining to
    delay § 7.2
  Disruption
  –Generally § 7.10
  –Assumptions concerning disruption
    § 7.11
  –Examples § 7.13
  –Ripple effect § 7.12
  Disruption versus delay

TIME-RELATED CLAUSES AND
CLAIMS *(Continued)*
  –Generally § 7.19
  –Impact of disruption; pure delay
    versus disruption § 7.20
  Excusable delay examples
  –Generally § 7.3
  –Causes, other § 7.7
  –Materials, inability to obtain
    § 7.6
  –Strikes and labor unrest § 7.4
  –Weather, severe § 7.5
  Excusable delays, generally § 7.1
  No damage for delay provisions
  –Generally § 7.21
  –Interpretation § 7.22
  No damages clauses exceptions
  –Generally § 7.23
  –Delays amounting to abandonment
    § 7.25
  –Delays caused by active interference
    § 7.27
  –Delays caused by bad faith or fraud
    § 7.26
  –Delays not within parties'
    contemplation § 7.24
  Suspension of work
  –Generally § 7.14
  –Concurrent delay § 7.17
  –Examples § 7.18
  –Provisions § 7.15
  –Recovery by contractor § 7.16
TOTAL COST METHOD
  Contractor's damages for delay,
    disruption, and loss of efficiency
    § 10.5
TOTAL FLOAT
  Project schedule, developing and
    maintaining § 3.15
TOTAL-FLOAT SORT
  Project schedule, developing and
    maintaining § 3.24
TOTAL PROJECT ACCELERATION
  Case histories § 14.2
TRADE CONTRACTORS
  Project record-keeping §§ 6.11,
    6.14
  Project schedule, developing and
    maintaining § 3.4
  Project schedule, legal significance
    §§ 1.3, 1.8, 1.12

UNIONS
  Project schedule, developing and
    maintaining § 3.12
UPDATING
  See also PROJECT SCHEDULE,
    DEVELOPING AND
    MAINTAINING
  Legal aspects of schedule
    specifications § 4.6
  Rights and obligations in scheduling
    § 5.16
UTILITIES
  Project schedule, developing and
    maintaining § 3.9
  Rights and obligations in scheduling
    § 5.5

VETERANS ADMINISTRATION (VA)
  Critical Path Method (CPM)
    techniques applied to contract
    claims § 9.27
  Legal aspects of schedule
    specifications § 4.10

VIDEOTAPES
  Project record-keeping § 6.6

WARRANTIES
  Project schedule, developing and
    maintaining § 3.37
  Rights and obligations in scheduling
    §§ 5.2, 5.4, 5.9, 5.19
  Time-related clauses and claims § 7.8
WEATHER
  See ACTS OF GOD
WEEKLY REPORTS
  See DAILY AND WEEKLY
    REPORTS
WINDOWS
  Critical Path Method (CPM)
    techniques applied to contract
    claims § 9.27
WITNESSES
  Project record-keeping § 6.9
WORK
  See EXTRA WORK; SUSPENSION
    OF WORK